The Religious Question in Modern China

The Religious Question
in Modern China

VINCENT GOOSSAERT *and*
DAVID A. PALMER

The University of Chicago Press
Chicago & London

VINCENT GOOSSAERT is deputy director of the Groupe Sociétés, Religions, Laïcités at the Centre national de la recherche scientifique, Paris, and professor at the Chinese University of Hong Kong. He is the author of three books, most recently *The Taoists of Peking, 1800–1949: A Social History of Urban Clerics* (2007).

DAVID A. PALMER is assistant professor in the Department of Sociology and fellow of the Centre for Anthropological Research at the University of Hong Kong. He is the author of two books, most recently *Qigong Fever: Body, Science, and Utopia in China* (2007).

The University of Chicago Press, Chicago 60637
The University of Chicago Press, Ltd., London
© 2011 by The University of Chicago
All rights reserved. Published 2011.
Printed in the United States of America

20 19 18 17 16 15 14 13 12 11   1 2 3 4 5

ISBN-13: 978-0-226-30416-8 (cloth)
ISBN-10: 0-226-30416-7 (cloth)

The University of Chicago Press gratefully acknowledges the generous support of the Chiang Ching-kuo Foundation toward the publication of this book.

Library of Congress Cataloging-in-Publication Data

Goossaert, Vincent.
    The religious question in modern China / Vincent Goosaert and David A. Palmer.
       p.   cm.
    Includes bibliographical references and index.
    ISBN-13: 978-0-226-30416-8 (hardcover : alk. paper)
    ISBN-10: 0-226-30416-7 (hardcover : alk. paper) 1. China—Religion. 2. Religion and politics—China. 3. Buddhism—China. 4. Christianity—China. I. Palmer, David A., 1969– II. Title.
    BL1803.G66 2011
    200.951'0904—dc22

                                                                                    2010025776

Contents

Acknowledgments

We owe a strong intellectual debt to Kristofer Schipper and Prasenjit Duara, whose insights have been an important source of inspiration for this work. Genial colleagues and friends have read and commented on our manuscript and helped us avoid mistakes and sweeping judgments: David Ownby, Paul Katz, Frédéric Keck, Sébastien Billioud, and Philip Clart. Students at the University of Geneva and the Chinese University of Hong Kong were treated to early drafts as we both taught courses based on this work; they have responded to it in many useful ways. Other colleagues have been extremely supportive in the fieldwork and documentation research that fed into various parts of the book, notably Fang Ling, Ji Zhe, Tam Wai-lun, Pan Junliang, Yau Chi-on, and Liu Xun.

This work is the fruit of several years of conversations between the two of us, electronically and on the sidelines of conferences on three continents; most of the writing took place in a studio in Paris and in a rooftop garden in Sai Kung, with editing done in a Mongolian yurt, at a cottage in Quebec, in various buses, planes, and airports, and on the slopes of Mount Carmel, Israel. We worked most intensely together when Vincent was visiting professor at the Institute of Chinese Studies (ICS) of the Chinese University of Hong Kong in spring 2007, where David was also posted as the Hong Kong representative of the Ecole française d'Extrême-Orient (EFEO); we are both extremely grateful to the ICS and its director, Jenny So, for its support, as well as to Franciscus Verellen, director of the EFEO. The Groupe Sociétés, Religions, Laïcités (GSRL, EPHE-Centre national de la recherche scientifique) and the Department of Sociology at the University of Hong Kong have provided each of us with a supportive working environment.

Since we began this project in 2003, the academic field of religion in modern and contemporary China has grown rapidly, marked by a series of international workshops and conferences on various related themes, at which we had the privilege of participating as paper presenters, discussants, or co-organizers. The opportunity to test some of our ideas at these conferences, the fresh data and perspectives we obtained, and the lively discussions and friendships developed with our leading colleagues in this field have all substantially enriched this work. We are especially grateful to the organizers of these conferences and workshops, as well as the host institutions and sponsors, including Wang Liuer and Bill Powell (China Academy of Social Sciences, 2003); Fan Lizhu (Fudan University, 2003), John Lagerwey (Institut européen en sciences des religions, Paris, 2003),[1] Ed Irons (Hong Kong Institute for Religion, Culture and Commerce, 2003), Gordon Melton (Institute for the Study of American Religion and Brigham Young University, 2004), Yoshiko Ashiwa and David Wank (Stanford University, 2004),[2] Gilles Guiheux and K. E. Kuah-Pearce (Hong Kong University and French Centre for Research on Contemporary China, 2005),[3] Adam Chau, Michael Puett, and Robert Weller (Harvard University, 2005), Paul Katz (Academia Sinica, 2005),[4] Mayfair Yang (University of California, Santa Barbara, 2005),[5] Koen Wellens (Oslo Coalition for Freedom of Religion or Belief, 2005), Liu Xun (Harvard University, 2006),[6] Fan Chun-wu and Wang Chien-ch'uan (Foguang University, 2007 and 2009),[7] Peter Ng (Chinese University of Hong Kong, 2007),[8] Glenn Shive (Hong Kong

1. Lagerwey, ed., *Religion et Politique en Asie.*
2. Ashiwa & Wank, eds., *Making Religion, Making the State.*
3. Guiheux & Kuah-Pearce, eds., *Social Movements in China and Hong Kong.*
4. Katz, "'It Is Difficult to Be Indifferent to One's Roots.'"
5. M. Yang, ed., *Chinese Religiosities.*
6. Palmer & Liu Xun, eds., *Daoism in the Twentieth Century.*
7. Billioud & Palmer, eds., "Religious Reconfigurations"; Wang Jianchuan & Palmer, eds., "Redemptive Societies and Religious Movements"; Ownby, ed., "Recent Chinese Scholarship on the History of 'Redemptive Societies.'"
8. Goossaert & Ownby, eds., "Mapping Charisma in Chinese Religion"; Goossaert & Palmer, eds., "Catégories et politiques du religieux en Chine"; Laliberté, ed., "A New Take on Secularization Theory."

America Center, 2007 and 2008),[9] Julia Huang (National Tsinghua University, 2008), Yang Fenggang and Lu Yunfeng (Beijing University, 2008),[10] and Thomas Jansen (Cambridge University, 2008, and University of Wales at Lampeter, 2009).

Much of David's work and field research was supported by a grant from the French Centre for Research on Contemporary China, with additional trips to Mainland China and Taiwan funded by the Antenne expérimentale de sciences humaines et sociales à Pékin and the Institute of History and Philology of the Academia Sinica. Vincent's most recent work on modern and contemporary Taoism was supported by the Taoists & Temples project funded by the Chiang Ching-kuo Foundation for International Scholarly Exchange and the ANR (Agence nationale de la recherche). We gratefully acknowledge all these grants.

Fanny Parent and Wu Zhengxuan heroically took on the task of translating the work into French and Chinese respectively, and Michele Wong provided invaluable assistance with the references and bibliography. Finally, our deeply felt appreciation to Leila and Isabelle, and to Jean, Danielle, Lou, and Solenne, for enduring our long hours at the computer, and our scholarly conversations at dinnertime!

We are grateful to the following publishers for their permission to reproduce text that originally appeared in their pages. A section in chapter 1 appeared in Vincent Goossaert, "Chinese Popular Religion," in *Encyclopedia of Religion, 15 Volume Set*, 2nd ed., ed. Lindsay Jones (Farmington Hills, MI: MacMillan, 2005), 3:1613–21. © 2005 Gale, a part of Cengage Learning, Inc. Reproduced by permission. www.cengage.com/permissions. A section in chapter 2 is based on Vincent Goossaert, "1898: The Beginning of the End for Chinese Religion?" *Journal of Asian Studies* 65, no. 2 (2006): 307–36. Reprinted by permission of the Association for Asian Studies. An earlier version of chapter 3 appeared in Vincent Goossaert, "Republican Church Engineering: The National Religious Associations in 1912 China," in *Chinese Religiosities: Afflictions of Modernity and State Formation*, ed. Mayfair Mei-hui Yang (Berkeley and Los Angeles: University of California Press, 2008), 209–32. Used by permission of University of California Press. Sections of chapter 10 are revised from David A. Palmer, "Religiosity and Social Movements in China: Divisions and Multiplications," in

9. Palmer, Shive, & Wickeri, eds., *Chinese Religious Life*.
10. Yang Fenggang & Lang, eds., *Social Scientific Studies of Religion in China*; Tamney & Yang Fenggang, eds., *Confucianism and Spiritual Traditions*.

Social Movements in China and Hong Kong: The Expansion of Protest Space, ed. Gilles Guiheux and K. E. Kuah-Pearce (Amsterdam: ICAS / Amsterdam University Press, 2009), 257–82. Used by permission of Amsterdam University Press. A section of chapter 12 reproduces parts of David A. Palmer, "Heretical Doctrines, Reactionary Secret Societies, Evil Cults: Labeling Heterodoxy in Twentieth-Century China," in *Chinese Religiosities: Afflictions of Modernity and State Formation*, ed. Mayfair Mei-hui Yang (Berkeley and Los Angeles: University of California Press, 2008), 113–34. Used by permission of University of California Press. Also used in this section is David A. Palmer, "China's Religious *Danwei*: Institutionalizing Religion in the People's Republic," *China Perspectives* 4 (2009): 17–31. Used by permission of the publisher.

Chapter 9 is based on research published by Fang Ling and Vincent Goossaert as "Les réformes funéraires et la politique religieuse de l'État chinois, 1900–2008," *Archives de Sciences Sociales des Religions* 144 (2008): 51–73.

Translations, Character Sets, and Abbreviations

We use hanyu pinyin for transliterations, except when the organization, individual, or author is already known by another spelling (for example, Chiang Kai-shek, KMT) or self-identifies in English publications using another transliteration (for example, Tzu Chi).

In footnote references for non-Chinese authors, we use surnames only. For most authors whose surname and given name are Chinese, both names are used, in the Chinese order (surname followed by given name). Authors with a Chinese surname and foreign given name are listed in the Western order (given name followed by surname).

Traditional Chinese characters are used, except in the bibliography, where simplified characters are used for works published in the mainland People's Republic of China.

Frequently used abbreviations:

CCP: Chinese Communist Party
KMT: Kuo-min tang; Nationalist Party
PRC: People's Republic of China

Introduction

Until little more than a decade ago, popular and scholarly discourse on China relegated religious practices to the domain of the quaint customs of a rapidly fading past and the lofty platitudes of ancient sages. Whether the subject was yearly offerings to the Kitchen God or the abstruse learning of Confucius, these traditions, if they could even be called religion, were never considered to have much bearing on the real life of Chinese society today. But since the end of the twentieth century, a clear shift in perception has been taking place. The Chinese world has not been immune from the global resurgence of religion and from the growing impact of religion on social and political life.

In 1970, one author wrote of "the astounding fact of our time: a nation state, with one fourth of the earth's population . . . with hardly a trace of religion as man has known it."[1] Today, we witness instead the multiplication of new and rebuilt temples in the countryside, forming what some scholars have called a second level of government in rural Mainland China; the sixty-fold increase in the number of Christians since 1949, the largest in all of Asia; the sudden eruption, seemingly out of nowhere, of millions of Falun-

1. Bush, *Religion in Communist China*, 9–10.

gong exercise practitioners in 1999, and their subsequent harsh repression; the religious dimensions of the Tibet and Xinjiang issues, and their impact on China's international relations; the emergence of Taiwan as a cauldron and exporter of global Buddhism and new religious movements. Yet these are but the most visible points of a rapidly shifting landscape, in which all forms of religion, be they traditional or modern, indigenous or foreign, ancient or recently invented, seem to be rapidly expanding and transforming themselves. Mainland China's Communist leadership has long abandoned the slogan of religion as the opiate of the people, has cast aside prophecies of its imminent extinction, and has resigned itself to a policy of "mutual accommodation" with religious communities, even seeking the positive contributions of religion for the execution of its social plans.

In recent years, with the reemergence of religious movements in the Chinese world and their impact on its domestic and international politics, there has been a great interest among scholars, intellectuals, the general public, and Chinese officials themselves in understanding what China's leaders have termed the "religious question" (*zongjiao wenti* 宗教問題).[2] We use the same term to qualify the uneasy and constantly evolving mutual adaptation of religion and the modern political and social framework of Chinese societies, beginning with the first attempts at religious reform in 1898. Indeed, religion now poses a question worldwide ever since the modernist teleology—which foresaw religion's gradual slide into social irrelevance alongside the triumph of science, reason, and economic progress— has been cast into doubt. But the question posed by religion in China is perhaps a more perplexing one than elsewhere, owing to the peculiar ways in which, until and into the twentieth century, the relationships between religion and other dimensions of social and political life have been configured. In most modern societies that have a dominant majority religion with clearly defined doctrines and institutions such as Christianity, Islam, or Buddhism, the religious question has been mostly about the adaptations and tensions between the dominant religion and the rest of society— including the state, minority religious communities, and social, political, and economic modernity. In China, on the other hand, where the religious, the political, and the social were not clearly distinguished before the twentieth century, no single religious institution or tradition has ever claimed the explicit and exclusive adherence of a majority of the population. And

---

2. For Chinese books that define and discuss the religious question on the mainland, see Zhongyang dangxiao, *Xian jieduan*; Wang Zuo'an, *Zhongguo de zongjiao wenti*; Chen Jinlong, *Zhongguo gongchandang*.

modernist attempts to impose such a differentiation have only added more layers and fault lines to the variegated outlook of the Chinese religious landscape. Maybe more than in most other places, Chinese modernist secularism has actually created "religion" as a foil and autonomous category.

Looking back at the span of the twentieth century, we can see the tremendous diversity of the religious productions of Chinese society during this period. Before the twentieth century, Chinese religion was also characterized by diversity, but one with an ordering center of gravity: the religio-political state. The end of the imperial regime and the 1919 anti-traditionalist May Fourth movement ejected this ordering center; the twentieth century was witness to a succession of substitutes, from the New Life movement to the Mao cult, which did not endure. The result is a de-centered religious universe, exploding centrifugally in all directions. Since traditional Chinese cosmology and society were religiously structured, the result is a de-centered society, a de-centered China: a Middle Kingdom that has lost its Middle. Thus the religious question: will there ever be, once again, a spiritual center of gravity for the Chinese world?

Our aim in this book is to provide a comprehensive overview of how this question arose and persistently resurfaced as one of the central issues in the history of modern China, from 1898 to 2008. In the summer of 1898, during the Hundred Days' reform 戊戌變法, the Guangxu emperor and the reformist leader Kang Youwei launched a radical program for the transformation of China's society and culture. At the core of these reforms, through the "convert temples to schools" movement, was an attack on the religious foundations of China's traditional social organization. This was the first of a wave of political and cultural reforms and revolutions that spanned most of the twentieth century, each of which involved the rejection of Chinese religion and the construction of a new spiritual civilization, through either secular substitutes to religion or modern reinventions of Chinese religious traditions. The goal of these projects of social, cultural, and political modernization was to overcome China's weaknesses in the face of foreign powers and establish its position as a strong and independent member of the world community of nations. With the Beijing Olympics of 2008, this goal was symbolically attained; and after the meltdown of Wall Street a few months later, when the world's leaders turned to China to prevent a global economic depression, it became a political reality. Meanwhile, over a century of campaigns and convulsions had not wiped religion out. Religion was booming, and a confident Chinese state was increasingly willing to compose with it—opening a new chapter in the history of religion in Chinese society.

We consider the evolution of Chinese religion not as an eternal, unitary whole but as several elements in constant interaction and mutual interdependence that were in a state of dynamic equilibrium by the Qing dynasty (1644–1911). From the late nineteenth century onward, the equilibrium of Chinese religion, and with it that of the Chinese society and state as a whole, was shattered; since then, no new equilibrium or stable recomposition of the religious landscape has been achieved. From the moment it appeared as a distinct category, religion in itself became a "question," an anomaly whose very definition and whose place in a new secular order have always been contested, and which, far from disappearing or confining itself to the Western church-style institutions established for it by the state, has consistently resurfaced in a bewildering variety of old and new forms.

HISTORIES

Much of China's current religious question is a direct outcome of processes set in motion at the end of the nineteenth and early twentieth centuries. What is often described as a revival of tradition in post-1978 Mainland China or elsewhere in the Chinese world is often, as we will try to show, a wave of reinventions and innovations that have been constantly evolving and adapting to modern contexts ever since the late nineteenth century, often blossoming during the 1920s and 1930s and again one or two generations later. We therefore feel that a historical perspective is essential to understanding the players and the issues at stake in the present religious situation. Furthermore, we feel that this historical perspective should be as broad as possible, weaving into a single narrative many different histories that each follow their own trajectory, but illuminate one another.

Until now, most academic treatments of religion in twentieth-century China have focused on a single religious tradition, such as Buddhism or Christianity, in the context of a single political entity, such as the late Qing imperium, the post-Mao People's Republic, or Taiwan. Besides separate confessional histories (of Buddhism, Taoism, Islam, Christianity), historiography has also been marked by disciplinary cleavages: political scientists have looked at the laws and ideologies of contemporary regimes and the political behavior of religious groups, while ethnographers and anthropologists have looked at the survival and adaptations of local temples and religious communities. Sinologists have searched in the field for living remnants of traditions described in textual sources, while sociologists have focused on contemporary forms of religious reinvention, often testing and modifying theories developed in a Western context. Disciplinary interests have reinforced strong distinctions between the traditional and the modern, which often do not do justice to a long century of continuous change. As, respectively, a historically minded anthropologist and an anthropologically minded historian, both of us are trained in the sinological tradition and employed by institutions affiliated with the discipline of sociology. We hope that we have been able to build on the contributions of the different disciplines while transcending their barriers.

In this book, we will also attempt to transcend the ruptures between pre- and post-1949, and between socialist and nonsocialist Chinese states; we then will go beyond a static view of Chinese religion that merely sees its "decline" in the Republican period and its "revival" in the post-Mao era. Rather, we look at the transformations of the religious landscape, not only under the impact of state policies, but also in its interactions with the overall social, cultural, and economic changes of the modern Chinese world; by so doing, we try to go beyond dominant paradigms of decline and revival, and of state repression and popular resistance.[3] We consider the "Chinese world" in broad terms, including all populations under Chinese cultural influence, whether through emigration (Chinese diasporas) or through incorporation into Chinese states (ethnic minorities)—leading us to consider and compare several polities, including the late Qing regime, the Republic of China, and the People's Republic of China; colonial and postcolonial entities ranging from Japanese-controlled Taiwan and Manchukuo to Hong Kong and Singapore; and minority Chinese communities from Malaysia to France and the United States. We also pay attention to China's gradual integration into the global religious sphere in the twentieth and twenty-first centuries, studying not only the import of foreign religions and discourses related to religion but also the export of Chinese religious movements and practices toward the non-Chinese world.

One effect of this historical treatment of the religious question is to return religion to the center of modern Chinese history. Many historians of modern China have tended to follow Communist and/or Nationalist historiography in considering the secularist narrative of China's modernization as a fact, whereas it now rather appears to be an ideological project.[4] Telling the history of this project, and following the many ways traditional cosmologies and practices have been transformed and recycled when rejected from the officially defined realm of religion, appear to us to be useful ways

3. On the dominant paradigms in the field, see Goossaert, "Jindai Zhongguo de guojia yu zongjiao."
4. The best surveys of modern Chinese history, even though they do not pay much attention to religion, include Zarrow, *China in War and Revolution*, and Gray, *Rebellions and Revolutions*.

of understanding present-day Chinese societies, not specialized topics better left to religious studies departments and publications.

INVENTING A RELIGIOUS FIELD

While leaving open the question of the ultimate definition of *religion*, we have chosen to take China's religious landscape as part of an evolving ecology of elements in constant interaction with one another, and in which a major change in one element, or the addition of a new element, may lead to a cascade of changes in the rest of the system. This "ecological" approach is based on an anthropological perspective of religion as a "total social phenomenon,"[5] which cannot be fully isolated as a distinct institution. This perspective has been confirmed by what has by now become a long and rich tradition of ethnographic studies of local religious practices in the Chinese world, inaugurated by J. J. de Groot in the late nineteenth century[6] and exemplified by both British and American studies in anthropology,[7] the French school of Taoist studies,[8] and a growing corpus of ethnographies and field reports produced in Taiwan and, increasingly, in Mainland China,[9] in addition to research in Chinese social history.

All these studies have demonstrated, not only that local religious practices and their social organization can be described and analyzed solely through their organic connection to local economic and political life, but that in traditional Chinese society, the latter find structure and expression through religious forms. What has been amply demonstrated for local society has also been attempted at the macrosocial level, beginning with Marcel Granet's early studies of the differential forms of religion among the royalty, aristocracy, and peasantry of ancient China, down to Max Weber and his project of identifying the connection between the religious

5. Mauss, *The Gift*.

6. De Groot, *The Religious System of China*.

7. Hsu, *Under the Ancestors' Shadow*; Freedman, *Chinese Lineage and Society*; Wolf, ed., *Religion and Ritual in Chinese Society*; Baker, *A Chinese Lineage Village*; Ahern, *Chinese Ritual and Politics*; Feuchtwang, *The Imperial Metaphor*; Feuchtwang and Wang, *Grassroots Charisma*; Watson & Watson, *Village Life in Hong Kong*; Sangren, *History and Magical Power*; Faure, *The Structure of Chinese Rural Society* and *Emperor and Ancestor*.

8. Schipper, *The Taoist Body* and *La religion de la Chine*; Lagerwey, *Taoist Ritual*; Dean, *Taoist Ritual and Popular Cults* and *Lord of the Three in One*.

9. Lin Meirong, ed., *Taiwan minjian xinyang*; for more recent studies on Taiwan see Lin Meirong, *Jisiquan*; Wang Zhiyu, *Simiao yu cunluo*; on the mainland, see Wang Ch'iu-kuei, ed., *Min-su ch'ü-i ts'ung-shu*; Lagerwey, ed., *Traditional Hakka Society Series*; Overmyer and Chao, eds., *Ethnography in China Today*.

dimension of Chinese social organization and the dynamics of its economic life—followed by Hill Gates, who has taken a Marxian-inspired approach to many of the same questions—and C. K. Yang's classic *Religion in Chinese Society*, which highlighted the simultaneous operation of "institutionalized" and "diffused" religion, the latter being present in all forms of social organization, as well as the religious element in both rebellions and political institutions.[10] Anthony Yu has given historical perspective to the latter aspect, tracing the religious dimensions of the Chinese state through the dynasties.[11] More recently, Li Xiangping 李向平 has, among other scholars in Mainland China, also tried to paint a detailed and comprehensive analysis of the structural dynamics of religion and politics in Chinese social history.[12] All these studies have taken a holistic approach to Chinese history and society, and attempted to sketch the dynamic relations between the structural components as well as describe the role of religious components within the structure.

To be sure, one may criticize these macrosocial portraits for reifying China. But they have the virtue of demonstrating that separating the religious from the secular in traditional society is impossible; that vastly different forms of religion may be found at different locations in the social structure; and that complex connections, interpenetrations, tensions, and negotiations occur between these different social locations and forms of religion, which are far more significant than, say, comparing the rise and decline in memberships among structurally analogous and institutionally autonomous congregations or sects.

On the other hand, the holistic approach lends itself best to the study of stable traditional societies; it cannot account for the massive changes and convulsions that have rocked, torn, and recomposed Chinese society since the nineteenth century. Various formulations of the secularization thesis may at first glance appear to be more suited to account for these changes, in which the more integrated traditional order has become increasingly inoperative and replaced by a new dynamic of modernization and science.[13] But one of the central theses of this book is that China's religious question poses

10. Granet, *La religion des chinois*; Weber, *The Religion of China*; Gates, *China's Motor*; Yang C. K., *Religion in Chinese Society*.

11. A. Yu, *State and Religion in China*.

12. Li Xiangping, *Zhongguo dangdai zongjiao* and *Xinyang, geming yu quanli zhixu*; see also Dai Liyong, *Xiandaixing yu Zhongguo zongjiao*, 360–541.

13. Kipnis, "The Flourishing of Religion in Post-Mao China"; Ji Zhe, "Secularization as Religious Restructuring"; Laliberté, "Introduction"; Szonyi, "Secularization Theories and the Study of Chinese Religions"; Dobbelaere, "China Challenges Secularization Theory."

itself precisely because the logic of secularization has been realized only incompletely, and has led to unexpected outcomes.[14] At the same time that the ideology and process of secularization were forcibly imposed over a period spanning a century,[15] the category of religion was simultaneously created and autonomous religious institutions were established;[16] Christianity imposed itself as a major institutional presence and normative model; the most successful ideology and political regime was the one with the highest level of political sacralization; and all the while, the traditional order was never fully eradicated, showed an exceptional resilience and adaptability, repeatedly reconstituted itself at the local and transnational levels, and spawned several waves of new religious movements, from the redemptive societies to Falungong. The result has been neither full secularization nor a return of the traditional order—but a complex ecology in which all these heterogeneous elements are in relation to and mutually influencing one another.

Our use of an ecological metaphor is the result of an inductive process in which, while bringing our data together, we concluded that the religious question needed to be apprehended in the macrosocial context of an open system in which all elements are in constant interaction with one another and with their broader social, political, and economic environment.[17] Elements of the system include the sum of individual needs, memories, and desires; the environmental, technological, and economic conditions of social life; the pool of cultural symbols, practices, and cosmological or ideological systems; the range of groups and modes of social organization; and the forms of violence and coercive social control. Under certain conditions, a dynamic equilibrium may arise between elements of the system, producing situations of relative stability, whereas in other circumstances, changes in some of the elements may lead to chain reactions, loss of equilibrium, and rapid phase changes.

The Chinese social ecology was transformed from the late nineteenth century onward by the injection of several new elements that typically are given the convenient label of *modernity* but actually constitute a wide range of distinct but mutually reinforcing phenomena and historical processes. A nonexhaustive list of these might include (1) normative ideologies and

14. M. Yang, introduction, *Chinese Religiosities*; Ashiwa & Wank, "Introductory Essay," *Making Religion, Making the State*.

15. Duara, *Rescuing History from the Nation*.

16. For comparative perspectives, see the conclusion to this volume; also Asad, *Genealogies of Religion*; Van der Veer & Hartmann, eds., *Nation and Religion*.

17. Ecological metaphors have been used in many ways by various social scientists; perhaps closer to our own usage is Bellah et al., *Habits of the Heart*, 289.

discourses of modernization, which promote a particular worldview and advocate a specific direction to social change; (2) state expansion, policies, campaigns, and revolutions, which attempt to implement such ideologies by political means; (3) rationalized and industrialized modes of mass economic production made possible by new technologies; (4) the transformed social relations that result from economic and demographic changes; (5) new styles of individual subjectivity that emerge under the reconfigured social, political, economic, and cultural order; (6) new styles of production and dissemination in art, literature, religion, and other cultural areas, which express these new subjectivities, worldviews, and technological possibilities. These processes are not coordinated with one another, nor do we support a simplistic "materialist" or "idealist" view that would privilege one type of change as a motor cause directly producing all the others. Rather, we might say that changes in each area are affected by changes in all the others and have a ripple effect on all of them. Mapping the evolution of the religious landscape in twentieth-century China, then, would involve tracking how this new set of elements has led to a redistribution and reordering of the preexisting elements, and the disappearance of old ones and the emergence of new ones. In defining the theme of this book, we thus use *religion* and *modernity* without reifying them, and merely as labels of convenience for broad and open-ended sets of phenomena in interaction with one another.

Within this context, one strategy might be to formulate an operational definition of *religion* that would allow us to precisely identify which elements in the system are religious and to chart their role in these changes. However, our goal here is not to draw an a-priori line between which of these elements, or what part of these elements, constitutes "religion" as distinct from other social institutions. Instead, we have purposely chosen to cast a wide net in deciding what types of phenomena should be included within the purview of our survey. The category of religion is a contested one, and the history of China's religious question is to a great extent the story of how this category has been imposed, rejected, appropriated, expanded, contracted, and assigned a place within ideological systems by different actors over the past century—the dramatic and often painful story of how a "religious field," in Bourdieu's terms, has been created and resisted by actors who have struggled to control, monopolize, co-opt, convert, or destroy the symbolic resources that it potentially contains.

Indeed for Bourdieu, a religious field comes into being when a class of specialists appears that attempts to centralize, systematize, and control a body of knowledge, simultaneously disqualifying the nonspecialists or laypeople and creating a field of power between those who hold religious authority and those who do not. When political or ecclesiastical elites elevate one religious system over another, the displaced beliefs and practices, associated with the vulgarity of the common people, become stigmatized as "magic," "sorcery," and "superstition."[18] While Bourdieu's model of a religious field is based on the Roman Catholic Church's institutional monopolization of religion in mediaeval Europe, the Chinese case presents a much more complicated picture. Before the nineteenth century, as described in chapter 1, religious knowledge and authority were differentially distributed, not only among several different institutions and categories of clerics, but also among the laypersons who controlled most temples, forming highly complex social fields that did not include an autonomous space designated as "religion." In the nineteenth and early twentieth centuries, a self-consciously "religious" field was opened in China, both by Christian missionaries and by secularizing political reformers and revolutionaries.[19] The project of the former, establishing the church in China as an exclusive religion, negated much of the religious culture of the Chinese people and relegated their practices to the status of superstitions. The latter, through their secularizing ideologies and state policies, sometimes in tandem with and sometimes in opposition to the Christian project, sought to define an autonomous field of religion, in order to precisely delimit its boundaries and restrict its influence within clearly defined areas of social activity. These areas largely corresponded to the religious field as occupied by the churches in the West, that is, private belief, morality, and philanthropy, but did not fit neatly with the social organization of Chinese culture.

This two-pronged Christian and secular attack on Chinese religion, which was relegated by both to the status of superstition, triggered three types of responses: to claim a position within the religious field and reinvent Chinese traditions as "religions" according to Christian norms; to claim positions in secular fields such as science, medicine, or philosophy, and reinvent Chinese traditions as forms of "culture" according to secular norms; or to undermine the boundaries between fields by claiming positions in several at once. Contemporary debates on whether Confucianism is a religion or not; on the boundaries between "religious" and "philosophical" Taoism; on whether or not Chinese medicine is scientific; on whether or not Chinese martial arts can qualify as Olympic sports; on whether "folk beliefs" are motley heaps of foolish superstitions, colorful traditional cus-

---

18. Bourdieu, "Genèse et structure du champ religieux," 304–5, 308–9.
19. DuBois, "Introduction: The Transformation of Religion."

toms, or highly organized religious systems—all simply reflect the many possible positions that can be claimed for these traditions inside or outside the religious field as constituted in the nineteenth and twentieth centuries. In other words, while we follow the vicissitudes of the "religious field" as a political project, we always place it in the much larger religious landscape that it attempts to shape.

For us to impose a narrow set of criteria to define *religion* would thus lead us to take sides in the debates we are retelling. The history of the category and institutions of religion in modern times must of necessity recount the history of the categories and institutions against which religion has been defined and confined, including science, superstition, and the state, and of how the boundaries between these categories have been drawn and contested. It needs to follow the diverging trajectories of cultural elements—from moral systems to healing traditions and forms of worship—as they end up on different sides of these shifting boundaries (or are split in two by them, or suddenly flip from one category to another). And it needs to describe how new forms of culture, such as political utopianism, fill the functional space previously occupied by cosmologies rejected as religion or superstition while consciously or unconsciously drawing on their symbolic resources. In other words, in our case a history of religion is also a history of secularism.[20]

For instance, campaigns against Taoist healing practices and self-cultivation in the temples, and their reinventions and reconfigurations, cannot be isolated from the evolution of secularized medicine, including the institutionalized forms of Chinese traditional medicine and the emergence of the *qigong* movement; similar changes have affected martial arts and the sport institutions. The rise of the redemptive societies during the Republican period is deeply connected to the way morality, civic education, and philanthropy were conceived and propagated during that period. This is not to say that medicine, sport, and civic education are religious; rather, the process by which these fields have been constituted by drawing boundaries between the scientific, the religious, and the superstitious, and the concurrent process by which "traffic" has continued across these boundaries even after they have been drawn, are essential to any analysis of China's religious field.

We take a historical approach and do not advocate a single explanatory framework; indeed, we accept the usefulness of many conceptual tools and do not aim, in this work, to engage in theoretical debates. However, we do

20. See Asad, *Formations of the Secular.*

feel the need to state our position concerning two models that have been gaining currency in recent discussions. First is the "religious markets" approach, which is increasingly being employed in academic discussions on the sociology and history of Chinese religion; it is often loosely used to describe any type of religious activity as occurring in a "market" of competing religious "firms." While such language has been elevated to the status of a new paradigm in the American sociology of religion,[21] it has found fertile soil in China, where a pervasive commercialization and fascination with social changes brought about by the market economy has contributed to a trend of applying economic concepts to the discourse on all dimensions of life. Since the market provides the greatest realm of freedom in socialist China, couching religion in the language of supply and demand is one strategy for legitimating it. And, to be sure, commercialization and commodification are obvious characteristics of much religious activity in China today, as indeed they have been since at least the Song dynasty.[22] Studies using the market theory have brought useful insights into the dynamics of Chinese salvationist movements,[23] temples,[24] and religious specialists.[25] But these studies have, for the most part, limited themselves to specific types of religious groups, for which the theory applies better than for other cases.[26] In this volume, we do not use market metaphors to describe any situation other than commercial markets for religious products and services, which are but one of the many configurations of social relations that exist in China's religious landscape. Markets for religious services and commodities are among the many elements of the landscape, and should be treated as such; but we do not use the language of markets to describe other phenomena, which do not operate following market relations.

Second is the "religious ecology" model, which has been proposed by some scholars in China. It takes a holistic view to describe all forms of religiosity within a community, from communal temples to the Three Teachings of Confucianism, Taoism, and Buddhism; Christianity; and Islam.[27] Such an approach is a significant advance, breaking out of the narrow defi-

---

21. Stark & Bainbridge, *The Future of Religion* and *A Theory of Religion*; Stark & Finke, *Acts of Faith*.

22. Szonyi, "Secularization Theories."

23. Lu Yunfeng, "Entrepreneurial Logics" and *The Transformation of Yiguan Dao*; Seiwert, *Popular Religious Movements*.

24. Lang, Chan, & Ragvald, "Temples."

25. Yang Der-Ruey, "The Changing Economy"; Goossaert, "Daoists in the Modern Chinese Self-Cultivation Market."

26. A more general application is Yang Fenggang, "The Red, Black, and Gray Markets."

27. Mou Zongjian, "Zongjiao wenhua shengtai"; Chen Xiaoyi, *Zhongguo shi zongjiao shengtai*.

nitions that have long constrained the discourse on religion in China, and looking at the interrelations between different forms of religious practice and social organization. Though we share the use of an ecological metaphor when we talk of a religious landscape, we do not speak of an autonomous religious ecosystem; rather, we see religious practices, networks, and institutions as part of a broader, open "social ecology" in which, as described above, religious elements are in perpetual relation with other elements, and in which the components and boundaries of the religious field are constantly contested. The ecology we speak of refers to dynamic processes of interactive change, adaptation, and innovation, and implies neither a nostalgia for a premodern state of religious equilibrium (and rejection of disturbing "alien" elements) nor a call to preserve China's religious landscape as it appeared at a particular moment in time. As China becomes a full player in an increasingly integrated global society, and even begins to have an influence on the global religious arena, its religious question will remain an open one.

STRUCTURE OF THE BOOK

We are fully aware that this book is an excessively ambitious project that covers more ground than we could possibly master. The collaboration of an anthropologist and a historian was most certainly fruitful in extending our gaze; nonetheless, even when combining our expertise, we know very little firsthand about many of the topics discussed here, and have relied greatly on the specialized contributions of our colleagues. Although we have not refrained from interpreting their writings in our own light, we have attempted to provide a large array of references in the footnotes, so as to allow readers to explore the issues in more detail. Some passages are based on our own new materials and field data, while others rely mostly on previously published research. At the same time, we take responsibility for the sometimes speculative and perhaps provocative narrative and interpretative framework, with the interconnections and parallels it creates.

We have avoided structuring our book according to confessional traditions (with separate chapters for Buddhism, Christianity, popular religion, and so on), or according to bounded historical periods and polities (the Republican period, the Mao era, and so on). Moreover, we have deliberately tried to underline parallels, continuities, and contrasts by linking materials from different polities and traditions in the same chapter, sometimes in unconventional ways. While the overall narrative is broadly chronological—beginning in the late Qing and ending in the early twenty-first century—

the thematic focus of each chapter leads us to move back or forward in time according to the needs of the argument, and the same movements and phenomena are sometimes discussed from different angles in several chapters. Readers are thus invited to make good use of the index to locate our treatment of a specific group, person, or phenomenon at unexpected locations in the text.

The book begins with an overview of the religious landscape at the turn of the twentieth century, introducing all the major actors (the Three Teachings, the forms of local communities, the imperial state as religious regulator) that will be embroiled in the religious question throughout the text. Chapter 2 traces the sea change in state policies toward religion from the last years of the Qing empire (1898–1911) to the advent of the Sino-Japanese War in 1937, with the first invention of "religion" and concomitant antisuperstition policies. Chapters 3 through 5 detail the impact of the new political situation on the religious field in the first half of the twentieth century. Chapter 3 describes the new model of a religion, accepted if not encouraged by the new Republican regime, inspired by a Christian-liberal conception of religion but adapted and reinvented by a vast array of Buddhist, Confucian, Muslim, and Taoist reformists who became the most prominent religious leaders of the period. Chapter 4 examines the institutions and practices that were excluded from this model and eventually recycled in either secular guises, such as healing and body practices, or new types of religious groups—the redemptive societies. Chapter 5 turns to those religious institutions and practices that were targeted for repression: "superstition" and traditional temple life, especially in the countryside, where the impact of repression varied greatly and generated different forms of resistance. Chapter 6 focuses on the emergence of the most important political actor of the twentieth century, the Chinese Communist Party, and traces the genesis and evolution of its religious policies from its creation in 1921 to the Cultural Revolution, having a profound impact on the organization of religion on the Chinese mainland. The regulation of religion by the state, whether colonial, nationalist, or socialist, has always gone hand in hand with a political civilizing project aiming to replace religion with a modern, if not revolutionary, system for creating a new nation of moral citizens; this phenomenon is discussed in chapter 7, which covers the entire span of the twentieth century.

The Mao cult was the apotheosis of political religiosity, which was accompanied by the apparent wiping out of all forms of religion on the mainland during the Cultural Revolution (1966–76). But this was not to be. The second part of the book examines the resilience, resurgence, and reconfigurations of religion, first at the margins of the Chinese world, and increasingly penetrating to the center of Chinese cultural, social, and political life by the early twenty-first century. The stage is set in chapter 8, in which we explore the history of religion in the various colonial and post-colonial regimes (Hong Kong, Taiwan, Singapore, Southeast Asia) from the early twentieth century through the 1970s, looking at the trajectories of the so-called margins (colonies and diasporic communities), which often provided leads to later developments within Mainland China. The remaining chapters deal with different levels of religiosity, from the most individualized to the most institutionalized, bringing the story down to the first decade of the twenty-first century while paying attention to continuities with earlier periods. Chapter 9 addresses religion at the family level, and looks at the evolution of family rituals—death rites in particular, from the funerary reforms of the Republican era onward. Chapter 10 examines communal religion around temples and traces the processes and significance of their reconstruction (in Mainland China) or expansion (in other parts of the Chinese world) beginning in the 1970s. Chapter 11 describes the development, during the same period, of movements based on an individualized spirituality, faith, or body cultivation, and their organizations and networks. These include the evolution in Taiwan and overseas of the redemptive societies that had appeared earlier in the century; the *qigong* movement and Falungong in the People's Republic of China and their international expansion and impact; the rise of new Buddhist movements (notably Foguangshan and Tzu Chi) in Taiwan; and the growth of evangelical Christianity and the house church movement on the mainland and among overseas Chinese. All these movements spread not only to the Chinese diaspora but even beyond the Chinese world, making China into an exporter of new religious movements. Chapter 12 looks at the political and ideological framework within which the various religious practices discussed in the previous chapters developed. It also explores how new orthodoxies (as providers of "social harmony" and as keepers of "cultural heritage") and heterodoxies ("evil cults") were defined by state agents, scholars, and religious leaders, at the sites of discursive production where the terms of the religious question and its answers were being constantly debated. Finally, the last chapter addresses what is certainly the most debated and studied aspect of the religious question, namely the connection between religious and ethnic identities and political allegiance: it compares the role played during and after the Cultural Revolution by four global religious communities—Islam, Tibetan Buddhism, Roman Catholicism, and Protestantism—at the articulation between ethnic and grassroots communities, the Chinese nation-state, and international relations. And we end the book with a brief comparison of the Chinese case with other nations such as Turkey, Russia, and India; sketch three scenarios for the future of religion in China, which all point to an increasing growth and complexity of the religious question; and, finally, unpack China's religious question into five layered and interconnected issues which, from 1898 until 2008, have added onto and reinforced one another. Now that China enjoys a growing influence in global society, the religious question is not China's alone but the world's.

PART I

Religions and Revolutions

ONE

The Late Qing Religious Landscape

The twentieth century was a time of uninterrupted, rapid, and often violent change for religion in China. By contrast, it is tempting to describe what preceded as stable tradition. It was not. Our purpose here, however, is not to describe the nineteenth-century history of Chinese religion but to provide a point of departure for the narrative that we chose to start in 1898. Therefore, in this chapter we will consider the Chinese religious landscape as a system in dynamic equilibrium, privileging structures over change. Like any system, it was an easy prey to unsustainable demands and to built-in contradictions and conflicts, and we will pay particular attention to those contradictions and conflicts as forerunners of the twentieth-century mutations. Here, as a way of introducing the basic categories and actors of Chinese religious life—cults, traditions, specialists—we will sketch the basic structural elements of Chinese religion as they stood in the nineteenth century—elements that we will follow in later chapters as they evolved along different trajectories in the twentieth century, following beaten tracks, crisscrossing, or breaking into new territory. In this general sketch of the religious landscape at the beginning of our historical survey, we proceed first from the basic structure of Chinese religious practice in late imperial times and the state's management of these practices, and then look at the causes of instability: challenges from inside and outside, and built-in tensions and dynamics of change.

CHINESE RELIGION AT ITS LATE QING STAGE

Western descriptions of Chinese religious life have long tended to emphasize its motley, disorganized nature. However, with better knowledge and a more neutral outlook, twenty-first-century social scientists can describe the varied field of China's religious practices, beliefs, and organizations as belonging to a coherent system (but a system with several hierarchies) that we choose to term "Chinese religion" (sometimes called "Chinese traditional religion").[1] This system integrated traditions of individual salvation, such as self-cultivation through meditation and body techniques, moral living, and spirit-possession techniques, including spirit writing; kinship-based rites, such as life-cycle rituals and ancestor worship; and communal religion, such as cults to local saints and deities—all of which were only partly framed within the three institutionalized teachings of Confucianism, Taoism, and Buddhism. Islam and Christianity were later arrivals; owing to their exclusive claims of truth, they did not become fully integrated into the system, even though they gradually became thoroughly sinicized and, in the period covered by this book, had a powerful impact on the changes to the religious landscape.

As Chinese religion does not have a single canon that could be a source of textual authority, there is no unified formal theology. All communities and religious specialists, however, share common cosmological notions, even though these notions are interpreted in many different ways. In its classical form, this cosmology, formed during late antiquity and the Han period (210 BCE–220 CE), dictates that the material and spiritual realms are not separate. The universe is an organic system, constantly evolving according to knowable rules, described through operative symbols (including *yin* 陰 and *yang* 陽, the five phases 五行, and the eight trigrams 八卦). All beings—humans, animals, and even plants—are in constant interaction (*ganying* 感應), even at long distances. Due to their different inherent qualities and histories, beings are more or less pure and endowed with spir-

---

1. Among various scholars who argue for the notion of "Chinese religion," see Feuchtwang, "A Chinese Religion Exists."

itual power (*ling* 靈), which can be understood as efficacy and charisma. All beings can purify themselves through morality and self-cultivation before and after death, and thereby ascend the ladders of the spiritual hierarchy and increase their *ling*. Dead humans become, according to the circumstances, ancestors, gods, or ghosts, and each of the three types has a particular kind of *ling*, and receives a particular kind of cult.[2] Humans who suffer unnatural death and do not receive postmortem sacrifices become ghosts (or demons) and are a major cause of unrest, hence a highly developed demonology. Miracles and the answering of prayers are manifestations of *ling*. Beyond these basic principles, the formulation of cosmological and theological thinking was entrusted to clerical specialists who were invited by cult communities to write texts (such as stele inscriptions, scriptures, hagiographies, and liturgical hymns) to legitimize their cults and practices and place them in a larger orthodox framework, usually but not exclusively defined in terms of one of the Three Teachings.

Communities and individuals by and large shared similar values within the framework of a common ethics, integrating elements of Confucian, Taoist, and Buddhist origin, that were expressed in morality books (*shanshu* 善書), the most widely read and revered normative texts in pre-1900 China.[3] While often overlooked by philosophers and highbrow intellectuals trying to define moral norms, they reflect common thinking and practice as articulated by local moral authorities and their audience. Morality books were both authoritative (their core sections were revealed by gods and saints) and inclusive, seeking consensus in that they articulated a vision much more encompassing than strict Confucian morality. They agreed that actions carry good or bad retribution (conceived as either automatic karmic accounting or, more often, a postmortem judicial process administered in courts of hell),[4] and this concept determines the fate of each human being after death. The theoretical elaborations on this principle provided by specialists were supplemented by an abundance of "popular theology," mostly in accord with clerical formulations, that expressed itself in vernacular genres such as the novel or the opera. Novels such as *Investiture of the Gods* (*Fengshen yanyi* 封神演義), *Journey to the West* (*Xiyouji* 西遊記), or *Outlaws of the Marsh* (*Shuihuzhuan* 水滸傳) played (and still

2. Wolf, "Gods, Ghosts, and Ancestors."

3. On morality books, see Yau Chi-on, *Shan yu ren tong*; Brokaw, *The Ledgers of Merit and Demerit*; Goossaert, *L'interdit du boeuf*, chap. 4.

4. On the crucial importance of religious beliefs and rituals in modern Chinese conceptions and practices of justice, see Katz, *Divine Justice*.

play) a major role in transmitting lore on gods, rituals, and retribution; however, their authors were sometimes accused by some officials of encouraging heterodox interpretations and inspiring rebellions.[5]

What we see at the level of ideas and values—common frameworks and varying interpretations—is also true at the level of the social organization of religious life. The Three Teachings were precisely defined, each with a distinctive clergy,[6] a canon of scriptures, a liturgy, and training centers— the monasteries (Buddhist *si* 寺 and *yuan* 院, Taoist *gong* 宮 and *guan* 觀) and academies (*shuyuan* 書院) where the canon was kept and the clergy was trained and ordained. The institutions defined by these four characteristics can be referred to as Buddhism, Taoism, and Confucianism *stricto sensu*. Within Chinese religion, the Three Teachings did not function as self-contained institutions that provided lay followers with an exclusive path to salvation, as in the nineteenth-century Western concept of religion; rather, their function was to transmit their tradition of practice and to serve the entire society, either through the teaching of individual spiritual techniques or through the provision of liturgical services to associations and communities. In late imperial times and well into the twentieth century, only clerics and a small number of devout laypersons (*jushi* 居士) would identify themselves as Buddhist or Taoist,[7] but most people at least occasionally engaged in rituals officiated by Buddhist or Taoist priests. A state doctrine of the coexistence of the Three Teachings reinforced the increasing overlap and mutual influences between them after centuries of interaction and universal acceptance among the populace, although functional differences remained, with Confucians monopolizing statecraft and playing a privileged role in kin-based worship; Taoist liturgy often structuring communal festivals; and Buddhist priests often being the preferred choice for conducting funerals.

The Three Teachings served the whole of Chinese religion, within which they were expected to coexist and even cooperate with one another, but without merging. This form of pluralism was thus not equivalent to syncretism, such as that practiced by many salvationist groups, in which there was a conscious attempt to integrate, synthesize, and supersede all existing teachings. The myriads of autonomous groups that formed the social basis of

---

5. Shahar, *Crazy Ji* and "Vernacular Fiction."

6. While the definitions of the Buddhist and Taoist clergy raise no major problem, the notion of Confucian clergy is more debated. We mean by *Confucian clergy* the whole gentry, since those who had passed the first degree of civil service examinations were qualified not only to teach the Confucian scriptures but also to perform rituals and sacrifices on family and communal occasions.

7. On engaged lay Buddhists in Qing times, see Goldfuss, *Vers un bouddhisme*, chap. 6.

Chinese religion—households, lineages,[8] territorial communities, professional guilds, devotional associations, political entities—each chose, from among the shared repertoire of beliefs and practices, those services offered by clerics of the Three Teachings that served their needs. Certain scholars have suggested that the Three Teachings correspond to an elite religion, in contrast to "popular religion."[9] However, the relationship between the Three Teachings and local cults hinged on socioeconomic, ideological, and theological considerations much more complex than an elite/popular dichotomy can suggest. Therefore, most communities were not Confucian, Buddhist, or Taoist: they are often placed under the label of *Chinese popular religion*, but this term does not necessarily imply a lower social class, lack of intellectual sophistication, or deviation from orthodoxy. On the other hand, while the Three Teachings had nationwide institutions, cult communities were fundamentally local in nature, and they have been therefore aptly described as "vernacular," "communal," or "local religion."[10]

Most religious communities were organized around temples. A temple belonged to either the clerical or, more often, the lay community that built it. It was the meeting place for a community constituted through its alliance with its saints: local heroes, healing gods and goddesses, or ancestors, who all embodied local identity and history. Only temples built by and for clerical communities—that is, Buddhist and Taoist monasteries and Confucian academies, all three being training institutions for literate specialists—could be said to be specifically affiliated with one of the Three Teachings. For all other temples, community leaders were chosen, usually every year, through a variety of methods, including bids (leaders were usually wealthy locals who paid dearly for the symbolic capital of religious leadership), rotation, heredity, and election by the god through divination or drawing by lots. These lay leaders presided over the rituals and managed temple assets, including landed property and natural resources (ponds, trees, mountain lands, wells), and enforced temple regulations. If they wanted and could afford it, they hired Buddhist or Taoist priests and spirit mediums to conduct rituals and, in a minority of cases, to reside in the temple.

The typology and relative importance of the social structures of Chinese religion varied in the different regions of the Chinese world, between rural

---

8. In line with sinological usage, we use the term *lineage* to denote both biological descent lines and master-disciple filiations that keep long recorded genealogies and worship their ancestors.

9. See two excellent state-of-the-field articles summarizing debates on Chinese popular religion: Teiser, "Popular Religion"; Clart, "The Concept of 'Popular Religion.'"

10. Von Glahn, *The Sinister Way*, introduction.

and urban areas, and between China proper and the diaspora. Some of these social structures were coterminous with local society (villages and lineages), and others, such as devotional associations and self-cultivation networks, were more purely religious. Thus, even though religious groups were often inseparable from secular social organization, the former did not merely reflect the latter, and religious communities had their own logic and agency. In the imperial order, many socioeconomic groups, such as lineages, guilds, or village communities and alliances, were officially sanctioned as cult communities. For instance, the important construction guilds were incorporated as associations devoted to the cult of their patron saint Lu Ban (魯班; the mythic creator of Chinese architectural techniques), and it is as such that they negotiated with the local officials, organized strikes, or regulated wages and prices.[11]

What best characterizes the social organization of Chinese communal religion is the fundamental autonomy of each community. While they could, and often did, negotiate alliances and build networks for both religious and secular purposes, be it staging festivals, maintaining order, building infrastructure, or arbitrating local conflicts, all temples and religious groups were independent, not subjected to any external authority, be it secular or spiritual. For instance, in many parts of China all village temples within a given area cooperated for both festivals (rotating between themselves the responsibilities and the hosting) and funding and controlling shared resources, such as a large irrigation system. During a festival, the leader of each village community arbitrated disputes and promulgated regulations (taking an oath to observe them) in front of the gods. Some scholars have described such networks of cult communities as a potential site for China's much-debated and elusive civil society.[12]

One highly operative distinction among Chinese religious groups is that between ascriptive communities, in which adhesion is compulsory for all households, and congregations characterized by free, individual participation. Three main types of ascriptive communities were common: territorial communities, lineages, and corporations. Territorial communities, such as villages and neighborhoods, united for the cult of either an impersonal earth god (*she* 社, *tudi gong* 土地公) or a local hero. Participation, primarily in the form of financial contributions toward temple upkeep and the

11. Moll-Murata, "Chinese Guilds."
12. Davis, *Society and the Supernatural*, 200–225; Katz, "Religion and the State in Post-War Taiwan," 398; Weller, *Alternate Civilities* and "Worship, Teachings, and State Power"; Schipper, "Structures liturgiques et société civile."

organization of the yearly festival, was compulsory for all residents of the territorial god's precinct (*jing* 境), well delineated from adjoining precincts by a procession in the course of the festival. Lineages (that is, groups tracing their descent from a common ancestor) were also found throughout China, but with diverse modes of organization. While each household (*jia* 家, defined by common residence) honored immediate forebears, families also allied on a large scale to write genealogies and to worship at the tombs of more distant ancestors and, in some cases, freestanding ancestor halls. Some parts of southern China were famous for their large-scale lineages commanding huge corporate resources, including land and schools.[13] Corporations included professional guilds and common-origin associations (*huiguan* 會館, *gongsuo* 公所), all of which were organized around cults to patron saints, either in the corporation's own temple or in a shrine within a large temple.[14]

The voluntary congregations were extremely varied. Buddhist and Taoist pious societies financed, within or without monasteries, activities such as rituals, the making of scriptures or icons, and mutual aid between members. They were often under clerical leadership. The incense associations (*xianghui* 香會) worshipped local saints and could be housed in temples. These devotional associations might organize rituals to celebrate the birthday of their saint or contribute to the upkeep of a temple by making specific offerings or by maintaining and cleaning shrines; the best-endowed ones built their own temples. Pilgrimage associations also developed on a large scale, as pilgrimages to holy mountains (such as Taishan 泰山, Wudangshan 武當山, and Miaofengshan 妙峰山 near Beijing) drew hundreds of thousands of pilgrims a year during the late Qing.[15] Amateur troupes for liturgical or paraliturgical music, dances, theater, and martial arts also performed during temple festivals, processions, or pilgrimages. Many congregations ran charitable programs, offering tea or food to pilgrims or beggars and providing medicine, clothes, or coffins to the needy. Groups focused on charity sometimes institutionalized themselves into philanthropic foundations (*shantang* 善堂), without abandoning their devotional activities.[16]

13. The literature on late imperial lineages is very large; for recent assessments, see Szonyi, *Practicing Kinship*; Faure, *Emperor and Ancestor*; Feng Erkang, *Shiba shiji yilai*.

14. Naquin, *Peking*, chaps. 14, 15, has a detailed description and analysis of these corporations in Qing Beijing.

15. Naquin & Yü, eds., *Pilgrims and Sacred Sites*.

16. Yau Chi-on, *Shan yu ren tong*; Shue, "The Quality of Mercy"; Handlin Smith, "Benevolent Societies."

Finally, many congregations were oriented toward individual salvation and spiritual practice. This category formed a continuum ranging from groups led by clergy and geared toward lectures and meditation practice, to spirit-writing (*fuji* 扶箕/乩, *fuluan* 扶鸞) cults formed of laypersons. In spirit writing typically, by holding a Y-shaped stick in a box of sand, one or two spirit mediums would transmit written messages from the gods to individual supplicants and to the congregation as a whole, the latter being then published in book form. Many such texts were morality books. These cults also engaged in charity, and their work largely overlapped with philanthropic foundations.[17]

Other groups were also geared toward revelation, the study of sacred texts, and meditation, but with a distinctive body of scriptures: the "precious scrolls" (*baojuan* 寶卷), a theology and cult of the Eternal Unborn Mother 無生老母, and an apocalyptic eschatology in three cosmic cycles, expecting the imminent end of the second (or third) cosmic cycle. The notion of the Eternal Unborn Mother as creator of humanity and savior of wayward humans before a final cataclysm is shared by most of these groups, even though they otherwise differed widely in their doctrine and practices, and had few or no texts in common with each other. The label *sectarian* is often used by scholars in discussions of these groups, more for convenience than accuracy,[18] designating a very diverse category of activist, nonclerical groups informed by the millenarian, salvationist theology of the *baojuan*; they ranged from stable devotional communities to distended networks of masters and disciples transmitting salvationist and healing lore. Some scholars, considering the distinctiveness of the theology and scriptures of this tradition, have considered it China's fourth religion.[19] On the other hand, fieldwork observation shows that most "sectarian" groups were not (and are not) marginal or exclusive communities. Rather, they were devotional associations whose leaders provided—to members and outsiders alike—services such as healing, teachings on morality, death rituals, and local leadership in village affairs. These social services were very similar

17. Clart, "The Ritual Context of Morality Books" and "Moral Mediums"; Lang & Ragvald, "Spirit-Writing."

18. Ownby, "Sect and Secularism"; see notably Overmyer, *Folk Buddhist Religion*; Seiwert, *Popular Religious Movements*.

19. Overmyer, *Precious Volumes*. Naquin, "The Transmission of White Lotus Sectarianism," has also called it the "White Lotus religion," a label strongly disputed by ter Haar, *The White Lotus Teachings*, who argues that White Lotus was a category invented by the Ming and Qing state, not used by the groups themselves, and creating a conceit of homogeneity among them.

to those offered by other groups of religious specialists.[20] Since the term *sectarian* is problematic, we will refrain from using it in this volume, preferring to use the term *salvationist*.[21] In the minority of cases when such groups coalesced into large-scale militant coordination and action to change society, we use the term *millenarian movements*. A wave of salvationist groups appeared and flourished in the Republican period; following Duara, we refer to the groups in this wave as redemptive societies[22] (see chapter 4).

THE LATE QING STATE AND RELIGION

The late Qing religious landscape was strongly, but by no means entirely, shaped by the imperial state. Seeing itself as mandated by Heaven to enforce the moral order of the cosmos, the imperial regime was based on religious underpinnings. The emperor, Son of Heaven (Tianzi 天子), had in theory absolute religious authority in both theological and institutional matters. While the throne often chose to leave religious groups to themselves in dealing with issues of doctrine, ritual, and organization, it maintained its privilege to intervene in such matters when it saw fit. The emperor decided on the basis of his own judgment what practices, beliefs, and institutions were orthodox (*zheng* 正), that is, moral, legal, and mandatory, and which ones were heterodox (*xie* 邪), that is, immoral, prohibited, and subject to repression.

The emperor was thus expected to regulate both the world through his ritual role, and the religious behavior of his subjects. This was a cosmic mission of some complexity. To apprehend the religious practices and policies of the imperial state, we must first consider the clear division between state and court (more precisely, the palaces and personnel managed by the Imperial Household Department [Neiwufu 內務府]). The court was the private realm of the emperor and his extended kin and personnel, where all sorts of religious practices thrived and whence patronage issued in all directions, following the personal beliefs of individual emperors and their kin, especially their mothers; the empress dowager Cixi, who controlled the court between 1861 and 1908, was especially famous for her generous patronage of Chinese Buddhism, Tibeto-Mongol Buddhism, Taoism,

---

20. DuBois, *The Sacred Village.*
21. See M. Cohen, "Souls and Salvation," for an earlier use of the term *salvific* in reference to this type of religious group.
22. Duara, *Sovereignty and Authenticity*, 89–129; Palmer, "Chinese Redemptive Societies."

and more.[23] These individual beliefs could find a proper expression in the court, though never in exclusive ways. Within the realm of the state, on the other hand, the Son of Heaven enjoyed much less leeway. The state's religious policies were constrained by the code of laws and the opinion of officialdom, which not infrequently disapproved of what was going on at court. The baseline of the late imperial state's religious policies was the implementation of a pluralist, but not tolerant, view of religion: pluralist because a fairly large array of different beliefs and practices were recognized as orthodox; but intolerant, because anything else, including anything new, was prohibited. State cults were at the center of orthodoxy, with the highest sacrifices—to Heaven, other cosmic deities, and imperial ancestors—performed according to Confucian liturgy by the emperor in person acting as priest; a second tier of sacrifices to Confucian saints (the highest of which were Confucius and Guandi 關帝) performed by high officials; and lesser sacrifices performed in each prefecture and county by state agents, that is, local officials (such as the county 縣 magistrates), throughout the country.[24]

Certain aspects of the state cult were off-limits to ordinary Chinese— beginning with the most sacred sacrifice to Heaven personally performed by the emperor at winter solstice. There were also times of coexistence and even cooperation between official rituals and popular celebrations. One fascinating instance is the cult of the City Gods (Chenghuang 城隍), of which there was at least one in each county. The City God was considered the equivalent of the local official in the other world, collecting taxes (in spirit money), administering divine justice, and upholding public morality—indeed, it was common among officials to believe that they would be nominated as a City God after their death. Thrice a year in every single county, the City God had to travel from his temple to an altar situated outside the city walls, where he would preside over a sacrifice to appease the suffering souls of victims of bad death, notably fallen soldiers. This was both an official ritual, presided over by local officials, and a wildly popular celebration, with the whole city taking part in the boisterous procession: playing music, putting on processional shows and skits, or dressing as penitents to atone for their sins.[25]

Besides the performance of state rituals, the political management of

23. Rawski, *The Last Emperors.*

24. One early twentieth-century foreign observer of Confucian state rituals who was particularly sympathetic was Shryock, *The Temples of Anking.*

25. Goossaert, "Managing Chinese Religious Pluralism."

the religious landscape by the late imperial state consisted in recognizing as well as attempting to control clerical communities (Confucian, Buddhist, Taoist) as well as a large number of cultic groups (lineages, corporations, temple cults to local saints), and banning others that were stigmatized as "improper cults" (*yinci* 淫祠) or "heretical teachings" (*xiejiao* 邪教; this term most often used to qualify salvationist groups). It is a widely shared opinion among scholars that late imperial state control over the three clerical traditions was a success story,[26] but with a hidden downside, like many success stories: very little control over other, more dynamic parts of the religious world (namely, the salvationist groups). Through the schools and public examination system, the state quite effectively controlled the Confucians. By contrast, the administrative apparatus for controlling Buddhists and Taoists (Senglusi 僧錄司 and Daolusi 道錄司, respectively) was ineffective, and state agents and clerics rarely saw each other, except for a thin clerical elite that cooperated with local officials.[27] Clerics almost never organized political challenges, and state agents in turn let them live alone, only rarely intervening, albeit with occasional brutality, to punish excesses when lay community leaders sued clerics for misconduct or when scandals became public. The late imperial state maintained, right until its demise in 1912, the old doctrine of the coexistence of the Three Teachings, but it increasingly attempted to relegate Buddhism and Taoism to separate, isolated realms of self-cultivation communities outside the public sphere.

The same laissez-faire approach applied to local communities. The religious policy of the late imperial state drew a line between voluntary congregations, which were outlawed in principle, and ascriptive communities, which respected the natural patriarchal structures of local society and were recognized as orthodox. Indeed, their rituals often included sacrifices (the most common sacrificial animal being the pig) following a Confucian liturgy comparable to that practiced by the state cults—the liturgical continuity from the emperor to the village was a major cause for the religious cohesion of the empire, which was brutally severed in the early twentieth century. Officially sanctioned ascriptive communities included descent groups for ancestor worship, of course, since this is what the imperial Confucian ideology promoted. But, just as important, they also included territorial temple cults. The orthodox nature of territorial cults was already

---

26. See for instance A. Yu, *State and Religion in China*. Most Chinese historians posit a decline of Taoism and Buddhism in late imperial times, in part due to strict state control (e.g. Qing Xitai, ed., *Zhongguo daojiao shi*, vol. 4).

27. Goossaert, "Counting the Monks" and "Taoism, 1644–1850."

spelled out in the basic law on religious heterodoxy in the Qing code 大清律例, namely the article "Jinzhi shiwu xieshu" (禁止師巫邪術, Ban on spirit mediums and heterodox practices).[28] In practice, however, most congregations were left to themselves and operated openly, since it proved impossible for the authorities to clearly separate the two kinds of groups.

The imperial state did try, however, to curtail the number and the size of temple cults, for a host of theological, economic, and sociopolitical reasons. The state recognized certain local cults by canonization, that is, integrating them into its own register of sacrifices (the *sidian* 祀典)—in practical terms, the list of cults in this register (providing titles of registered gods, the dates for the sacrifices, and the liturgy to be used) for each county or prefecture was found in the relevant section of the local gazetteer (地方志). The canonization process constituted an important channel for establishing symbolic relationships between the imperial state and local communities. It flourished during the 1860s, when many local gods were canonized for having sided with the state during the Taiping Rebellion.[29]

All other cults were deemed *yinsi* 淫祀, a complex notion meaning "immoral," "profligate," or "wanton," that is, causing financial and emotional excesses and eventually bearing no benediction 福 but only harm. In the late Qing discourse, *yinsi* was always understood as a deviant minority of cults, and did not concern nationwide cults to saints such as Guandi, Mazu 媽祖, Zhenwu 真武, Wenchang 文昌, and others, which were included in the official register of sacrifices. As a marker of illegitimate practice, the *yinsi* label always meant different things to different people, some interpreting it in a narrow sense, focusing on a few downright "immoral" cults such as the lascivious Wutong 五通,[30] which were traditional targets of Confucian fundamentalists (those literati and officials who rejected all ideas and practices that were not in the Classics, probably a minority in late Qing times, but a vocal one), others casting a much wider net. But in all cases, the label referred only to a portion of all the existing cults, those judged perverse and heterodox as opposed to acceptable cults to orthodox deities (*zhengshen* 正神).

Cults labeled as *yinsi* were forbidden but nonetheless remained extremely common; state toleration and accommodation was punctuated by occasional repression. Stories of officials destroying "immoral" temples were widely reported but represented the exception; arguably, these de-

---

28. The classic discussion of this legislation is De Groot, *Sectarianism and Religious Persecution*.

29. Sawada, "Seimotsu no shiten mondai."

30. Jiang Zhushan, "Tang Bin jinhui Wutong shen"; von Glahn, *The Sinister Way*, chaps. 6, 7.

structions were used as threat in a game of negotiation between local officials and local populations, and not systematically carried out.[31] Late imperial law also forbade women to visit temples,[32] which they nonetheless did
in great numbers. Nighttime celebrations and activities of spirit mediums
were also targeted by officials, with little success either. All these activities
were depicted in both state and elite writings as distasteful, ugly, immoral,
and sacrilegious (*xiedu* 褻瀆). Indeed, it was in the name of maintaining
the ritual purity of state-approved temples, rather than out of skepticism,
that state agents prohibited the presence of women, spirit mediums, and
"immoral theater plays."

Rather than ritual impropriety, however, the core of Qing legislation
and jurisprudence concerned the salvationist groups, stigmatized as
"heretical teachings" and seen by most of officialdom as a major threat, because of both real events—the history of rebellions associated with millenarian movements—and phantasmic representations of these groups bent
on tearing apart the social fabric and conventional morality.[33] Christians,
who were outlawed from 1725 until British guns forced a radical policy
change in 1842, had been categorized among the heretical sects. There
was less room for state accommodation and negotiation with salvationist
groups than with the world of local temple cults, which most of the time
managed to thrive under the magistrates' eyes even though they were technically illegal. Yet magistrates, hard pressed to manage, on their own and
with tiny operating budgets, counties populated by tens if not hundreds of
thousands of people, often looked the other way when salvationist groups
carried on their activities peacefully, as they usually did. Repression came
in cycles, provoked by orders from higher up the hierarchy, often because
of external pressures—such as a violent incident elsewhere in the country,
or an imperial order to get tough.

In its multifaceted aspects, then, the religious policies of the late imperial state were predicated on a utopian project to enforce, from the top
down, a moral order on the whole of society—a project that was severely
limited by lack of means of enforcement, and by lack of documentation (in
the absence of census procedures, as shown by local gazetteers, officials
only had consistent information about the largest urban temples and festivals, which were just a part of a much larger local religious scene). With
the exception of some activist officials who systematically intervened in

31. Goossaert, "The Destruction of Immoral Temples."
32. Zhou Yiqun, "The Hearth and the Temple"; Goossaert, "Irrepressible Female Piety."
33. Ter Haar, *The White Lotus Teachings*.

temple life, cults, and rituals in their jurisdiction, state agents mostly used the more gentle means of inciting and negotiating, and only occasionally adopted more intrusive methods.

A similar approach prevailed in the Qing dynasty's approach to the religious culture of the vast frontier areas of its empire, which were inhabited by non-Han peoples with different religious beliefs and practices. Manchuria, Mongolia, Xinjiang, and Tibet, which all had long and complex histories of relations with the Chinese heartland, alternating between tributary relations and mutual invasion and conquest, were, during the Qing, more fully integrated into an imperial system of governance. Under this system, a distinction was made between the domestic subjects of China proper and the vassals of the peripheral areas, which were governed by hereditary local lords appointed by the Qing state, often called *tusi* (土司), with a considerable degree of autonomy, and according to the customs and religious laws of the local elites. In the distant Uighur stronghold of Kashgar and the surrounding area of southern Xinjiang, for example, a local civil and religious bureaucracy, the *begs* and *akhunds*, administered the villages and towns according to Islamic law in the name of the Qing emperor.[34]

In the case of Tibet, the basic model was the same, with the Dalai Lama recognized by the Qing (and, on two occasions in the eighteenth century, directly installed by Qing troops following unrest and civil war in Tibet) as the spiritual and temporal head of the area, governing it according to the Tibetan theocratic political system. After defeating a Nepalese invasion in 1791, the Qing administration played a greater role in Tibetan political and religious affairs. Emperor Qianlong decreed a new method for selecting reincarnations of the Dalai Lama and Panchen Lama, the leading authorities in Tibetan Buddhism, by means of a lottery administered by the Chinese high commissioners in Lhasa, the Ambans. Although this method was only employed for the selection of two Dalai Lamas in the nineteenth century, all Dalai Lamas during this period were recognized after the fact by the Qing emperor.

The relationship between the Qing throne and Tibetan Buddhism was complicated by the fact that it was the religion not only of the Tibetans but also of the Mongols and Manchus (the ethnic group of the ruling dynasty). In order to reinforce its legitimacy among these peoples, the regime officially patronized and sponsored the leading clerics and rituals of this tradition. Thus the relationship between the emperor and the Dalai Lama was, on a political level, seen by the Qing as one between sovereign and

---

34. Dillon, *Xinjiang*, 18.

vassal, but on a religious level as one between patron and priest. Meanwhile, the Dalai Lamas recognized the emperor as the reincarnation of the bodhisattva Manjusri.

LATE QING ELITE CRITIQUES OF THE RELIGIOUS SYSTEM

The equilibrium of the religious system we have just described came under increasing strain during the nineteenth century. Aggression from religious elements external or marginal to the system—millenarian revolts, Christian proselytizing, the Taiping Rebellion, and Muslim rebellions—occurred with a growing frequency, just as China's elites, from the inside, were questioning the pluralism and subtle accommodations which had been woven between different strands of state, society, and religious traditions over the centuries. As they faced religious challenges to their ideal social moral order, late imperial Chinese elites did not turn secular. These elites, well into the first years of the twentieth century, thought according to the cosmological system proper to Chinese tradition, believed in a postmortem destiny, practiced death rituals and sacrifices to ancestors, and believed in divine retribution for one's actions. Officials and members of the gentry (紳士; those who had passed at least the first degree of the civil service examinations, the vast majority of which never reached the third degree that opened a career) may have understood these beliefs differently from other actors in Chinese society, but this did not necessarily preclude a sense of sharing the same religious world. The religious ideals, commitments, and practices of late imperial Chinese elites have often been neglected by a secular scholarship, but they are evidenced in the more personal writings of officials and gentry members, from the highest ranks of the imperial bureaucracy down to village laureates.[35]

Elite religiosity informed changes in religious policy as implemented by state agents. While considerations of maintaining social order often loomed large in the practice of official religious policy (especially in relation to salvationist groups), it would be very misleading to reduce the whole of the imperial state's policies to security concerns, as quite often decisions on recognizing or banning certain cults, specialists, or rituals hinged on purely moral-theological reasons. For instance, spirit mediums, lay female congregations, and all sorts of operatic rituals were banned not because they threatened the state but because they contravened the moral

35. See notably the remarkable study of the inner world of a poor Shanxi scholar in Harrison, *The Man Awakened from Dreams.*

and symbolic order of the cosmos as imagined by fundamentalist Confucians. One of the core missions of state agents, and one that some zealots took as their personal crusade, was to civilize (*jiaohua* 教化) the masses through moral education.[36]

Late Qing state agents and local elites partook in a project to implement a homogeneous, elite religious culture throughout China. Under pressure and incentive, many local religious communities and specialists adapted to this drive, but most aspects of such adaptation are better analyzed as accommodation and disguise than actual cultural homogenization. Local elites were, until the last years of the Qing, players on both sides, arbitrating between the logic and the interests of the two worlds[37] by transmitting state norms while also acting as leaders of local temples, even though they were, in a context of growing polarization and intolerance, ever more numerous in declining to assume this second role.

While many Chinese elites still engaged in some way with Chinese religion, an expanding polemical discourse on religious practice was being produced by members of the gentry. Much of this discourse had been around well before the nineteenth century. It can be found in sources ranging from essays, official decisions, and manuals to, increasingly from the 1870s onward, the press. In addition to criticism aimed at Christianity and, to a much lesser extent, Islam, as being in total contradiction with Chinese values and social ideals, these polemics touched on several themes. They continued the long tradition of attacks on millenarian movements, with added stridency as a result of the violent rebellions of the late Qing. They also criticized "immoral cults" (*yinsi*) and spirit mediums for offending the elite's disciplined, aesthetic approaches to the sacred.[38] Communal celebrations were also lambasted: opera, large processions, nightly activities, voluntary devotional associations such as pilgrimage associations and Buddhist pious societies, and in particular those in which women participated. Elite opposition to such forms of celebration was grounded in both concerns for social order—fear of trouble arising in mass celebrations, sometimes real, often phantasmic—and considerations of orthopraxy or "style" and theology.[39] Such discourses were based on the defense of canonical

36. Rowe, *Saving the World*, chap. 12.

37. Guo Qitao, *Exorcism and Money*; Watson, "Standardizing the Gods"; Duara, "Superscribing Symbols"; and the special issue of *Modern China* (33, no. 1 [2007]) devoted to that issue.

38. Sutton, "From Credulity to Scorn."

39. See notably the wealth of documents gathered in Wang Liqi, *Jinhui xiaoshuo xiqu shiliao*.

Confucian religious values and norms regarding who may offer sacrifices
to whom, and according to which ritual.

Another type of criticism was aimed at the participation of Buddhist and
Taoist clerics in social activities, notably the performance of rituals outside
monasteries, such as funerals and ceremonies during temple festivals, the
organization of lay pious societies, and fund-raising.[40] The elite's attitude
toward Buddhism and Taoism was complex. They sometimes treated both
as *yiduan* (異端), heterodoxies to be banned altogether. However, most
of the time members of the gentry considered, as did imperial orthodoxy,
that these two religions were legitimate as long as they were limited to the
individual quest for sanctity within the confines of proper places, that is,
monasteries or the private realm.

The historian William Rowe (discussing the eighteenth century, but his
analysis holds for the nineteenth century as well) has described such polemics as part of the "great religious war waged by devout *lixue* 理學 [neo-
confucianist] adherents against Buddhist and Taoist beliefs and practice"
and "the more persistent assault on popular culture."[41] The term *religious
war*, while controversial, is certainly thought-provoking. The antagonists
in this "war" are easy to identify: Confucian fundamentalists against local
society and its religious structures, that is, the local cults. Although the
tone of exchanges between them was often vitriolic, this was a conflict
that made few physical victims; it was mostly a war of words and political
decisions.

It should furthermore be stressed that even the most aggressive discourses were pronounced from within Chinese religion. In other words,
the elite discourse proposed to reform Chinese religion by returning it to
the purity of its origins as described in canonical scriptures, and stripping it
of all noncanonical later accretions: this was, strictly speaking, Confucian
fundamentalism—the rejection of all ideas and practices absent from the
Confucian canonical scriptures[42]—and not rejection of Chinese religion
as such.

Besides Confucian fundamentalism, there is a second notion, anticlericalism, that may help us understand the late Qing discourse on the gentry
side of the religious conflict. Anticlericalism is the rejection of institution-

---

40. Goossaert, "Starved of Resources."
41. Rowe, *Saving the World*, 436.
42. This fundamentalism overlaps very much with what historians of ideas have identified as late
imperial Confucian "purism" (see e.g. Chow Kai-wing, *The Rise of Confucian Ritualism*).

alized religion, especially monasteries and professional clerics living off liturgical services. It refers here mainly to the rejection of the Buddhist and Taoist clergies, while upholding Buddhism and Taoism as doctrinal systems or spiritual traditions. The anticlerical discourse described the moral and intellectual depravity of religious professionals and their bad influence on society at large. What we are talking about is outright hostility, mostly on the part of certain members of the gentry (by no means all of them) toward Buddhist and Taoist clerics as people with, in their view, questionable lifestyles and activities.

Anticlericalism was sometimes part of a fundamentalist discourse, since much of the outright rejection of Buddhism and Taoism by the most fundamentalist Confucians was based on anticlerical arguments rather than on a rejection of Laozi's or the Buddha's teachings. The anticlerical discourse also prefigured secularist religious modernity by condemning clerical institutions and rituals while valorizing individual spiritual practice such as meditation and studying scriptures. At least until 1898, most anticlerical discourses can be considered "faith-based anticlericalism," grounded in a rhetorical dichotomy between the noble Buddhist and Taoist ideals and their actual practice. This view was not restricted to the elite, since many lay salvationist groups also shared this attitude of respect for the Buddha and his teachings while despising the monks and nuns.[43]

In short, elite discourse on religion in late Qing China was characterized by aggressive reform plans and ferocious verbal attacks on temples, cults, rituals, and specialists. These boil down to three overlapping concerns: a struggle between gentry and clerics for the status of moral/religious authority; a cultural conflict between social classes (the gentry against the rest of the population) about religious and artistic styles; and an undercurrent of more abstract, theological anticlericalism (religion should not be a profession). Debates raged on who should run temples and local communities, and how, but none of these three concerns implied a radical questioning of the temple-based religious organization of Chinese local society, such as we will see from 1898 onward.

CHALLENGES TO THE ESTABLISHED ORDER

Some scholars have looked at Chinese religion as a field of resistance to state power.[44] For the most part, however, local cults did not develop an

43. Goossaert, ed., "Anticléricalisme en Chine."
44. Feuchtwang, "Religion as Resistance"; see also Weller, *Resistance, Chaos, and Control.*

ideology of opposition and resistance; the vast majority of communities aligned themselves with law and order. But since all social organizations in imperial China were centered on some type of cult, and since temple communities incarnated local identity and autonomy, it is only natural that resistance movements came to be religiously organized.

Yet the strongest challenge to the late imperial political and religious order was not the potential resistance of local religious communities; it was the large-scale dissent, which could become violent, of supralocal religious movements that spread throughout a whole region or even the country itself. In the nineteenth century, these included millenarian movements, the Taiping Heavenly Kingdom, Christianity, and the Boxers. These movements shook the Chinese heartland, while at the northwestern periphery (present-day Gansu, Shaanxi, and Inner Mongolia provinces) as well as in Yunnan, a string of insurgencies by the Chinese Muslims, the Hui, plagued the late Qing state through the 1860s and 1870s. The Hui rebellions usually occurred in the context of internal warfare between rival Sufi orders, in areas where they commanded huge material resources and very strong loyalties, and were met with brutal interventions by the state.[45] These rebellions cut off the supply lines of the Qing army in Xinjiang to the far west, and news of the massacres of the Hui caused fear among the Muslims of Xinjiang of all ethnic backgrounds. Added to festering discontent caused by high taxes and other reasons, these factors triggered a string of rebellions in 1864, which spread to all of Xinjiang. Islamic holy war became the unifying ideology of the scattered groups fighting the Qing infidels, who were driven out of southern Xinjiang (East Turkestan). Until 1877, the whole area was controlled by the commander Ya'qūb Beg (1820–1877), who attempted to rule by enforcing strict Islamic law. After the Qing recaptured the area, they abandoned their previous policy of indirect rule and incorporated Xinjiang as a province of China.[46]

In China proper, although the salvationist groups had undergone unprecedented development since the sixteenth century, it was only by the late eighteenth century that millenarian rebellions, often associated with Unborn Mother or related cults, became a major concern for the imperial state. It should be stressed that salvationist groups with millenarian teachings only rarely rebelled: major cases include the 1796–1804 so-called White Lotus rebellion in the unruly highlands of the Shaanxi-Hunan-Sichuan borders, the 1813 Eight Trigrams attempt at capturing the impe-

---

45. Lipman, *Familiar Strangers*.
46. Kim, *Holy War in China*.

rial city, and other smaller but still bloody local revolts.[47] The apocalyptic doctrines shared by many of the salvationist groups provided symbolic resources for legitimizing acts of rebellion, but these doctrines were usually kept in the background, and were only rarely activated by leaders acting out of a variety of motives.[48] Although millenarian rebellions challenged the existing imperial dynasty, they were an inevitable corollary to the politico-religious system, in which, according to the doctrine of dynastic legitimation prevailing since the Zhou (eleventh to third century BC), changes in dynasties are the result of the Mandate of Heaven being removed from a morally corrupt imperial family that drives the realm to chaos, and conferred on the new dynasty that brings back order and virtue. Under the influence of this idea, religious expectation of a change in cosmic cycles necessarily implied a new Mandate of Heaven and a change in dynasties; on the other hand, political opposition to an emperor could only be legitimized in apocalyptic terms, with the rebel leader claiming to fulfill millenarian expectations of a new Heavenly Mandate. The rebellions thus caused the political elite to see all salvationist groups worshipping the Unborn Mother, and many local cults by extension, as a threat to society.

The Taiping movement was in many ways comparable to those rebellions in its utopian millenarian inspiration, but its effects were much more profound: it caused what is probably the bloodiest civil war in the history of humanity, with an estimated 20 million to 50 million casualties. It is best explained as a collusion of the Chinese tradition of millenarian rebellion and Christian messianism. The leader, a modest scholar of the Hakka 客家 ethnic group, Hong Xiuquan 洪秀全 (1812–1864), was exposed in 1836 to Protestant tracts, which caused him to reinterpret earlier visions as a revelation of his being Christ's younger brother. In the first case of iconoclasm in modern China, Hong smashed the deity statues in local temples. In 1851, he organized disenfranchised Hakka laborers into a utopian society in the Guangxi highlands and, with the help of other visionaries who were acting as spirit mediums possessed by members of a wildly expanded holy family, directed the group as an army bent on toppling the Qing regime and establishing a utopian paradise on earth (destroying all temples on their way). While it failed to conquer Beijing, the Taiping Heavenly Kingdom held on to its capital in Nanjing from 1853 to 1864, causing untold destructions and provoking a radical recomposition of local society and state as the

---

47. Naquin, *Millenarian Rebellion* and *Shantung Rebellion*; Gaustad, "Prophets and Pretenders."
48. Ownby, "Imperial Fantasies."

latter responded to the lethal threat by militarizing society and devolving political and economic power to local elites that ran the loyalist militias.⁴⁹

While the Taiping were, in the end, thoroughly crushed, and completely disappeared as a religious movement, they can be said to represent the irruption of modernity into Chinese religious history, combining for the first time—and in a bloody blast—three elements that would, throughout the next century, never cease to interact with explosive consequences: apocalyptic revolution, Christian influence, and communist utopianism. The latter aspect could be seen in Taiping doctrines advocating the abolition of private land property, the equitable distribution of land and surplus produce, the equality (and segregation) of men and women and a ban on foot binding, the use of vernacular language and punctuation, and the hierarchical organization of society in nested units of twenty-five families fully integrating religious, civil, and military functions. Prefiguring many elements of Chinese modernism, socialism, and Maoism, these ideals would inspire future generations of Chinese revolutionaries, including Sun Yat-sen 孫中山 (1866–1925), while the CCP (Chinese Communist Party) would claim an explicit filiation to the movement.⁵⁰

Although less violent, the Christian challenge to late imperial Chinese society was certainly the most unsettling. First, it was intellectual: the articulated and forceful critique of Chinese religion by missionaries⁵¹ was a very strong factor behind changes of attitudes by part of the elite toward their own religious tradition. It was also social. Christian converts were actually not very numerous—maybe around 500,000 Roman Catholics and 40,000 Protestants by 1890—but they constituted a highly visible and active population. They were protected by foreign powers under the 1842 and 1858 "unequal treaties," and whereas Protestants were careful when taking advantage of such protection, the Catholics, under the consular protection of France, resorted systematically to diplomatic action whenever they felt wronged. The French legation, when informed of a complaint, intervened with the newly created Ministry of Foreign Affairs (Zongli yamen 總理衙門), which forced local magistrates to protect Christian interests. This led to numerous conversions of questionable motivation, even though some missionaries were careful to screen such self-interested postulants as well

49. The literature on the Taiping is very large; the most readable introduction is Spence, *God's Chinese Son*; see also Reilly, *The Taiping Heavenly Kingdom*.
50. P. Cohen, *History in Three Keys*, 292–93.
51. Reinders, *Borrowed Gods*.

as "rice Christians" interested in charity from the church. Such use and abuse of external force created widespread resentment and rejection of the missionaries' uncompromising stand, and even strong anti-Christian feelings among local gentry, who circulated vitriolic anti-Christian tracts.[52]

In such a context, the integration of Christian converts within Chinese society was at best uneasy. The 800-odd documented conflicts between local Christians and non-Christians (*jiao'an* 教案) were mostly about nonreligious issues, such as land rights or local taxes.[53] However, purely religious conflict was quite often behind such cases. In most Chinese villages, all the inhabitants were customarily mandated to pay a yearly contribution toward the territorial temple and its festivals (and in particular the opera performance). Christian converts were encouraged by missionaries to refuse to pay for such "pagan" activities, thus in effect seceding from the village community. This caused tension in countless villages, notably throughout northern China, thereby contributing to the Boxer uprising.[54]

The Righteous and Harmonious Militia (*yihetuan* 義和團), labeled *Boxers* by contemporary Western observers of the group's displays of Chinese boxing to attract recruits, was a type of self-defense village militia practicing martial arts along with possession cults that provided magical invulnerability. Whereas such groups normally limited their activities to the village level, a chain of events in the years 1899 and 1900 caused them to spread and unite throughout northern China (particularly in Shandong and Hebei provinces) and launch campaigns against Westerners and Christians, seen as the cause of all problems in a rapidly impoverishing and state-neglected countryside. They mobilized much of the unemployed population, obtained the support of a large part of the local elites, killed missionaries and Chinese Christians, and took control of the cities, including Beijing. The disastrous choice by the empress Cixi to officially side with them and declare war on Western powers on June 21, 1900, caused a brutal military retaliation by the allied forces.[55] The Boxer Rebellion can be seen as a revolt of local culture and religion against Western power and churches, hoping to compensate for its material weakness through recourse to magic.[56] In the end, the humiliating defeat, with its heavy human, political, and financial costs, convinced China's political elites that Chinese religion,

52. P. Cohen, *China and Christianity*.
53. Sweeten, *Christianity in Rural China*.
54. Litzinger, "Rural Religion and Village Organization"; Thompson, "Twilight of the Gods."
55. P. Cohen, *History in Three Keys*; Esherick, *The Origins of the Boxer Uprising*.
56. P. Cohen, "Boxers, Christians, and the Gods."

from which the Boxers had emerged, was a major hindrance and threat to China's survival in the modern world.

After each of these shocks, the dense fabric of Chinese religion seemed to weave itself back together—most remarkably after the destruction of the Taiping wars, which was followed by a wave of temple rebuilding at the end of the nineteenth century. Destructions had an impact, however, which was more than psychological: they upset the balance of power, as local elites, as a result of their role in the reconstruction process, gained a stronger hand over clerics and local congregations in controlling temples and other religious institutions. By the turn of the twentieth century, the diverse and delicately balanced religious system of the Middle Kingdom appeared, on the surface, to continue to live on through its million temples, its proliferation of devotional associations, and its myriad festivals, rituals, and priests of all stripes, in which, in some way or another, all people participated, from the emperor to the most lowly peasant. But the intensification of internal and external tensions would soon lead to the traumatic tearing apart of the religious fabric, beginning with the organic link between the elites and the people. Within the traditional worldview, elite polemics of Confucian fundamentalism and anticlericalism were aiming ever more stridently at the "hot and noisy" (*renao* 熱鬧) religion of the masses, while for modernizing intellectuals concerned with how China could respond and defend itself against the imperialist West and Japan, it was this same popular religious culture that needed to be stamped out if China was to stand strong. So, although the social ecology of Chinese religion was already evolving into new directions by the last years of the nineteenth century, it was the Western impact that caused its brutal destruction and reinvention.

TWO

Ideology, Religion, and the Construction of a Modern State, 1898–1937

Around the turn of the century, the Qing empire was a crumbling state, bankrupt, militarily humiliated by dangerous predators—Japan in 1895 and the Western powers in 1900—and in ideological crisis. Although the empire survived until 1911, attempts at radical departures and the invention of a modern state were made as early as 1898. The construction of a nation-state implied the destruction and reconstruction of the whole of society, including religion. Indeed, destroying the religion of the old regime and inventing a new place for religion in the nation-state were important components of all the modernizing projects that reshaped China as it moved from empire to Republic, warlordism, and nationalism.

We begin by looking at the first radical reforms in 1898 that, albeit short-lived, introduced and popularized the idea of nationalizing temples to build the infrastructures of a modern nation-state. We then explore the conceptual changes that made this reform possible by introducing the Western concepts of religion and superstition, and the policies that these concepts enabled. Finally, we see how these concepts and policies evolved through the warlord period, to be implemented nationwide by the Nationalist regime.

THE 1898 REFORMS AND THE BEGINNING OF TEMPLE DESTRUCTIONS

The first all-out assault on Chinese religion in the name of modernization was the confiscation of temples. During the 1890s, several voices among the leading intellectuals of the time were calling for radical actions toward temples, including seizing their property in order to finance the new schools, destroying their statues, and expelling their religious specialists, notably Buddhists, Taoists, and spirit mediums. The governor of Huguang (present-day Hubei and Hunan), Zhang Zhidong 張之洞 (1837–1909), has been seen by many as the father of the "build schools with temple property" (*miaochan xingxue* 廟產興學) movement,[1] mostly because of his very influential essay of April 1898, "Exhortation to learning" (*Quanxue pian* 勸學篇), which included a proposal to seize 70 percent of Buddhist and Taoist monasteries and their landed property in order to build schools.[2] What Zhang was after, then, was temple resources, not the religious institutions themselves.

Whereas seasoned officials like Zhang Zhidong represented a traditional attitude inspired by Confucian fundamentalism and anticlericalism, new political reformers envisioned a radical religious transformation as an important part of their overall project. For instance, a young and influential reformer, Zhang Taiyan 章太炎 (1869–1936), wrote in the spring of 1898 that "now is not the time for performing rituals and following the way of the gods anymore."[3] The reformist leader Kang Youwei's 康有為 (1858–1927) project was even more articulated and comprehensive: he wanted to destroy the temple cults and build something entirely new on their ruins. On July 10, 1898, Kang memorialized the throne, proposing that all academies and temples in China, with the exception of those included in registers of state sacrifices (*sidian*), be turned into schools. The Guangxu emperor was so pleased with the proposal that he promulgated an edict (*shangyu* 上諭) the same day, taking over Kang's phrasing. Sources such as essays, diaries, and press reports show that both reformers and the general public understood the July 10 edict as calling for the destruction,

1. Makita, "Seimotsu irai ni okeru byôsan kôgaku," 292–97.
2. In *Zhang Zhidong quanji*, 9739–40: *Quanxue pian*, chap. 3, "Shexue."
3. *Qiushu*, 99.

not of a few select temples, but of *all* temples bar the handful where state sacrifices were performed. Thus, although they seemed to stand on similar grounds—the use of temple property to finance a modern educational system—Zhang Zhidong and Kang Youwei in fact adopted very different positions: extracting money from the existing religious system, or destroying it altogether.

On three occasions in the following weeks, the editorial in the famous Shanghai daily *Shenbao* 申報 discussed the edict, not as a piece of legislation aimed at facilitating the ex-nihilo creation of a nationwide network of public schools, but as the declaration of a religious reform, that is, a change in religious policy that would rid China of temple cults and their specialists: Buddhists, Taoists, and spirit mediums. This it was, indeed, although both Chinese and Western historiography to date have usually neglected to appreciate the importance of the religious element in the so-called One Hundred Day (Wuxu 戊戌) reforms (June 11–September 21, 1898) and later modernist policies. This importance can be gauged both in the writings of some of the reformist leaders, and among the populations affected by the practical consequences.

This edict, which we see as the first turning point in the modern Chinese state's management of religion, was part of a larger movement that encompassed attempts at creating a modern, Western-inspired educational system and military and economic institutions, all designed to enhance China's strength and chances at survival in an imperialist context. Whereas issues of institutional reforms (schools and examinations, military and political institutions, economic and industrial development) were primary in the reform literature, recent research has shown that social and moral reform, including gender issues, was also part of the reformers' agenda.[4] The issues of temple seizure and religious policy pertained to both institutional change and social reform.

Kang's memorial[5] ends with an attack on immoral cults, *yinsi*. In each village, he writes, there are several temples that have landed property. These could be seized and made into schools where attendance would be compulsory for all village children. This idea clearly fits into his larger scheme to set up Confucianism (called by him Kongjiao 孔教, a new term)

---

4. The essays gathered in Karl & Zarrow, eds., *Rethinking the 1898 Reform Period*, attempt to show how the 1898 and subsequent late Qing reforms constituted a first attempt to systematically formulate a Chinese vision of modernity.

5. In *Wuxu bianfa wenxian ziliao xiri*, 770–73: *Qing chi gesheng gai shuyuan yinci wei xuetang zhe* 請飭各省改書院淫祠為學堂摺 (Memorial requesting [the emperor] to order that academies and improper temples be changed into schools throughout the country).

as the national religion (*guojiao* 國教) and to ban any other religious institution, although Kang did not elaborate much on this scheme during
the 1898 reform. He had already proposed in May 1895, in famous letters to the emperor, to transform into Confucian temples all improper
temples (*yinci*), and even proper temples to Confucian saints other than
Confucius.[6] Later, his famous "Memorial requesting that Confucius be
worshiped as [the founder] of the National religion, that a Ministry of religion and a Church be established, that years be counted from the birth of
Confucius, and that improper temples be suppressed"[7] (which was never
actually submitted to the throne) laid out a precise plan to eradicate Chinese religion and set up Confucianism as the exclusive national religion.
The text proposes creating a ministry for religion and compelling all Chinese to attend weekly Confucian masses in their local Confucian church,
where Confucian classics would be read by a Confucian pastor. It also includes fierce attacks on Chinese religion. A lax state, says Kang, has for
two millennia let people build temples to all sorts of immoral deities. Now,
"foreigners come in our temples, take photographs of the idols, show these
photographs to each other and laugh." Paganism, he goes on to argue, goes
as far as the worship of animals, and is a shame that debases China and
causes it to be ranked along with barbarian countries. Kang's project was
a wild hybridization of Confucian fundamentalism and Christianity under
the influence of, notably, the Scottish Baptist missionary Timothy Richard
(1845–1919)—indeed, a rumor that circulated after the publication of the
July 10 edict suggested that Kang had drugged the emperor and converted
him to Christianity.[8] That an edict protecting the missionaries was proclaimed the following day could only reinforce people's feelings that Christianity was out to eradicate Chinese religion. More generally, Kang exhibited a strong sensitivity to the Western perspective on Chinese religion,
and evinced what would be a major characteristic of Republican-period
writings on religion: a desire to remodel Chinese religion on a Christian-
based model of what a "religion" should be.

The radicalism of Kang's project for a new religion caused him to be
rather isolated. If he had few direct heirs, however, some of his ideas did
gain wider currency. Although most intellectuals did not adhere to his vision of a messianic Confucian religion, Kang was influential because he

---

6. *Kang Youwei quanji*, 2:97, 148.

7. In Huang Zhangjian, *Kang Youwei wuxu zhen zouyi*, 464–70: *Qing zun Kongsheng wei guojiao li
jiaobu jiaohui yi Kongzi jinian er fei yinci zhe* 請尊孔聖為國教立教部教會以孔子紀年而廢淫祠摺.

8. *Wuxu bianfa wenxian ziliao xiri*, 773.

was one of the first and most vocal proponents of a new way of thinking the religious question in China, a way that would after 1901 become the foundation of the antisuperstition movement. While rejecting Kang himself and his most extreme projects, the antisuperstition campaigners reverently quoted the July 10, 1898, memorial as the forerunner of their vision.

The Wuxu reforms themselves, including the edict on temple confiscation, were short-lived, and by October 1898 temple clerics and managers could sigh with relief as the confiscation was recalled.[9] It appears that only a few temples were effectively transformed into schools at that time. The relief itself, however, was only temporary, since as early as 1901, with the advent of the New Policies (Xinzheng 新政), and on a larger scale after 1904, a few local officials and a much larger number of reform activists began to act on the idea. They seized temple lands and infrastructures to build the new institutions that they were mandated to run: mostly schools in the beginning, and after 1908, self-administration bureaus (zizhiju 自治局), barracks and police stations, post offices, and other government buildings. Under pressure from these activists, who repeatedly published calls for the revival of the July 10, 1898, edict and praised local initiatives in this direction,[10] government approval finally came on January 10, 1904, when it published a comprehensive set of school regulations meant to overcome the confusion of previous ad-hoc decisions. These regulations endorsed the idea of using temple property and funds from religious associations to build schools.[11]

Large-scale temple confiscation thus began in 1901, and dramatically accelerated with the abolition of the traditional civil-service examinations in 1905. Those responsible for temple seizures and bans on festivals (notably in cities) were more often activists—graduates of modern schools

9. The September 26, 1898, edict says: "The temples [cimiao 祠廟] which are not in the sidian are to be maintained as before, and not be changed into schools, unless they are immoral cults (yinsi)": Guangxu chao donghua lu, 4203–4.

10. Four days after the September 14, 1901, edict mandating the construction of schools, a Shenbao editorial pointed out that the only way to finance the new schools was to use temples. This would have the most desirable effect of expelling all the "rascal Buddhists and Taoists." "Hui siguan yi chong xuetang jingfei yi 毀寺觀以充學堂經費議" (A proposal to destroy Buddhist and Taoist monasteries so as to finance schools), Shenbao, September 18, 1901. Many more such editorials would follow.

11. Zouding xuetang zhangcheng, "Gaodeng xiaoxuetang zhangcheng 高等小學堂章程" (Primary schools regulations), 1b (1: general rules, 4th item), "if there are funds collected among the public for useless endeavors such as temple festivals or opera, they may be used [for building schools]"; 19b (5: rules regarding school buildings, books, and other material resources, 10th item), "For the building of schools, one may borrow facilities such as guild halls [gongsuo] or monasteries [siguan]." Same rules in "Chudeng xiaoxuetang zhangcheng 初等小學堂章程," 2b (1: general rules, 5th item) and 24b (5: rules regarding school buildings, books, and other material resources, 11th item).

in China or abroad, who led educational associations and other grassroots reform movements—rather than local officials, who broadly backed activists but were more careful not to create troubles and, furthermore, were accustomed to the pre-1898 dominant pattern of accommodation with temples. For some of these educational activists, seizing temple property was simply a means of acquiring power and riches for their new institutions or for themselves, but many were indeed sensitive to the project of religious reform in itself.

Moreover, the social reform activists did not content themselves with preaching: the first years of the twentieth century were marked in several Chinese cities by forceful actions on the part of activists bent on reforming the use of public space, notably religious festivals and related folk art performances.[12] These actions often made use of newly established police forces. While some of these reformists' aims were not new, their strong impact certainly was.

The wave of confiscations prompted some Buddhist monasteries to seek affiliation with Japanese orders, and claim Japanese consular protection, as early as fall 1904, which in turn provoked outraged reactions against the monasteries.[13] More important, a large part of the rural violence after 1901 was linked to new administrative offices seizing village temples and to village communities fighting for their temple and their autonomy—the two being indissociable (see chapter 5). Temples were not the only local institutions to be taxed or seized, but they constituted a particularly sensitive target, and the attacks on them were often the most visible sign of the irruption of the expanding state in village life. Sweeping powers given from above to educational activists and other reformers brutally challenged the delicate balance of power that characterized the local management of common resources (temples, cultic associations, infrastructures such as bridges and dikes, charitable funds).

Some educational activists argued for a careful selection of temples to be singled out for transformation into schools; they were worried that the all-out seizure of temples would only serve to provoke violent reactions from temple communities against modern institutions and would thus in fact be detrimental to the cause of school building. One of them, the celebrated Zhang Jian 張謇 (1853–1926), complained that some activists were motivated less by educational zeal than by an urge to destroy "that re-

12. E.g., in Chengdu, see Wang Di, *Street Culture*.
13. Welch, *The Buddhist Revival in China*, 11–12, 165.

ligion" (*bijiao* 彼教).[14] Indeed, the seizure of local temples caused localized but violent armed conflicts, pitting the local elites in charge of political modernization against village communities and religious leaders. The best-known bouts of iconoclastic fury occurred later, during the revolutionary fervor of 1911 and 1927–28; but iconoclasm was already present during the early phases of the antisuperstition movement. In 1908, Hu Shi 胡適 (1891–1962; he was eighteen and not yet a renowned scholar) in a fiery editorial exhorted his readers to go into temples, smash statues, and expel or kill the clerics.[15]

Not all temple seizures were conflictual; in many, perhaps most, cases during the 1900s and 1910s, a negotiation allowed temple resources to be shared between school and cult, and some temple managers were voluntary participants in this process, thinking that village resources should be used for both cult and education. For instance, in 1904 in Chongqing (Sichuan Province), an alliance of temples negotiated an agreement with the educational activists whereby temples contributed 20 percent of their income to schools (a contribution later unilaterally doubled by the provincial governor).[16] In that area, about three-fourths of the new schools were set up in temples. It was probably the antisuperstition zeal and iconoclasm of some activists, as well as the intolerant reaction of some religious leaders, that ignited the worst outbreaks of violence; such attitudes were not the norm, but they were nonetheless very influential in shaping discourse and opinion.

In brief, from 1898 to 1911, and later during the whole course of the twentieth century, the confiscation and destruction[17] of temples were more than a side effect of social and political modernization. They were the effect of a religious policy, that is, a conscious, purposeful new relationship between the state and religious institutions, and this policy was initiated by the religious reform heralded in 1898. The slogan "Destroy temples to build schools" (*huimiao banxue* 毀廟辦學, often used in lieu of "Build

---

14. *Zhang Jizi jiulu*, "Jiaoyu lu 教育錄," 2.11a–12a.

15. Hu Shi, "Lun huichu shenfo 論毀除神佛," in *Hu Shi zaonian wencun*, 164–67. As he became a leading intellectual, Hu Shi later moved toward much more balanced views of traditional society and culture.

16. Liang Yong, "Qingmo 'miaochan xingxue.'"

17. We use *destruction* here although in most cases, temples were not razed to the ground but affected to other uses. We find the term useful, though, since many religious objects were destroyed in the process, and the eradication of religious life was often intended. Furthermore, many of the sources mentioned here use the word *hui* 毀, "destroy," to describe the taking over of temples for other purposes.

schools with temple property"), and the many texts that advocated it, laid
equal stress on both religious and educational reform.

THE BIRTH OF ANTISUPERSTITION

At the same time, and intimately connected with the advent of the temple
destruction movement, a discursive change took place that totally turned
the relationship between state and religion on its head. Shortly after 1898,
new words began to appear in the discourse on religion, usually introduced
in newspaper articles. Most important among these are *zongjiao* for "religion," *mixin* 迷信 for "superstition," and *shenquan* 神權 for "divine authority." All were adopted from Japanese neologisms crafted a few years before,
and were used to express Western notions that had not existed in the Chinese discourse until then.[18] These neologisms were part of a larger set of imported categories used to reclassify the whole of knowledge and social and
political practices, including such words as *science* or *philosophy*. *Zongjiao*
and *mixin* seem to have been made popular in 1901 by Liang Qichao 梁啟
超 (1873–1929), a disciple of Kang Youwei.[19] Religion was understood in
the Western postreformation sense of a system of doctrine organized as a
church separated from society; the word was first equated with Christianity, and debate began (and continues one century later) regarding what, in
the Chinese tradition, might be put under this category. As religion was
considered a strong, moralizing, and unifying force behind the Western
nation-states, it was, in this early period, generally received by Chinese intellectuals as something positive. "Science" often came to be the touchstone
in dividing between "religion" (compatible with science) and "superstition"
(unscientific), so that the three formed a triangle in modernist rhetoric.

   The question of vocabulary is far from innocent: the use of Western notions to describe religious practices or ideas that were heretofore discussed
with native terms expressed the authors' determination to distance themselves from Chinese religion. Many of the themes and rhetoric found in
pre-1898 texts, which we have labeled "Confucian fundamentalist" and/or
"anticlerical," continue to appear after that date, and indeed some are still
current today. But from 1898 onward, they are mixed in various degrees
with a new vocabulary to discuss the religious question, new genres to deal
with it, and new targets for the polemical discourse.

   These notions brought with them distinctions and fissures that had not

18. Chen Hsi-yuan, "'Zongjiao'"; Nedostup, "Religion, Superstition," 18–27.
19. Bastid-Bruguière, "Liang Qichao."

existed before: the great divide was now between acceptable *zongjiao* and the unacceptable *mixin*. This distinction is quite different from the traditional orthodox (*zheng*)/heterodox (*xie*) divide[20] in that many local cults and practices independent from national organizations and textual traditions, once regarded as orthodox, were now branded as superstitious. Notably, all temple cults, not being part of a "religion," were now categorized as superstition and therefore slated for transformation into schools.

Indeed, the most important effect of the adoption of the religion/superstition discourse was the birth of antisuperstition. It would be an anachronism to speak of antisuperstition before 1900, when the notions of "religion" and "superstition" first appeared in the Chinese discourse. But the term seems appropriate to label the new trends after 1901. *Antisuperstition* can be defined as the corpus of all discourses against religious practices using the word *mixin*, and the distinction *mixin*/*zongjiao*: it targets whatever is not grounded in and strictly limited to the spiritual and moral self-perfection delineated by the theological scriptures of a world religion (Confucianism, Christianity, Islam, Buddhism). Antisuperstition may overlap with some extreme forms of Confucian fundamentalism, but it is much broader than anticlericalism, because it aims at the very principle of the organization of local Chinese society as cult groups. It is quite different from—but often overlaps with—antireligion, the rejection of all kinds of self-consciously religious ideas and practices.

The rejection of religion as such did not appear until the 1920s. The antireligious, or atheist (*fei zongjiao* 非宗教), movement was formulated at that time under the direct influence of European Marxists and freethinkers and was primarily aimed at Christianity in its relationship with imperialism.[21] The first episode of this movement was the creation in 1922 of the Antireligious Alliance (非宗教大同盟), in reaction to a Christian meeting at Qinghua University in Beijing; another outburst of violence came in 1924, and again during the Northern Campaign of 1926–28. The most brilliant and famous advocate was Chen Duxiu 陳獨秀 (1879–1942), a professor at Beijing University but also a leading member of the Communist Party. But Chen's position was, until the Communist takeover, quite marginal among the Chinese intellectual and political elites. Most of these espoused antisuperstition as part of a *proreligious* discourse.

Indeed, in early twentieth-century China as in many other countries during the modern period, the debates and assaults on religion, more often

---

20. Duara, "Knowledge and Power," 76.
21. Bastid-Bruguière, "La campagne antireligieuse"; Yang Tianhong, *Jidujiao yu minguo zhishi fenzi*.

than not, did not pitch rational atheists against believers—rather, they opposed different religious visions.[22] Most reformers adhered to a secularist paradigm whereby individuals should be free to believe and practice, but social institutions created out of religious beliefs and practices could only exist in a separate realm of religion and not have a political role. Many leading intellectuals were active practitioners of spiritual traditions: some, like Zhang Taiyan and Liang Qichao, being part of a strong and influential movement of Buddhist intellectual revival;[23] others, like Sun Yat-sen and other future leaders of the Nationalist Party (國民黨, KMT), having converted to Christianity; others yet, like Kang Youwei, envisioning the invention of a state religion out of Confucian elements.[24] It was actually such spiritual traditions, rather than rationalism or atheism, that drove political leaders to reform the religious scene.

For this reason, while the reformers' discourse on superstition, religious reform, and temple seizures was self-serving and partly motivated by social and political projects, it would be a mistake not to consider that it was at the same time also a religious project aimed at improving China's spiritual condition. The new cause of separating "religion" from "superstition" beginning in the 1900s was part of a larger campaign to "reform the customs" (*fengsu gaige* 風俗改革), which overtook the traditional notion of *jiaohua*, "civilizing [the common people] through moral education," and was expressed in all styles of ideological literature or propaganda, notably public lectures, periodicals in vernacular language, pamphlets, and novels.[25] For instance, the novel *Saomi zhou* 掃迷帚 (The broom to sweep away superstitions), first serialized in 1905, appears to be the first comprehensive catalogue and attack on Chinese superstitions in the modern sense; it devotes much space to proving that there are no such things as gods, immortals, or buddhas and to lambasting temple festivals, while leaving Confucianism, Christianity, and Islam out of the discussion altogether.

The new, single category of superstition included more than the traditional targets of Confucian fundamentalism and anticlericalism: it also encompassed Confucian practices[26] such as geomancy (*fengshui* 風水,

---

22. Chang Hao, *Chinese Intellectuals in Crisis*.

23. Goldfuss, *Vers un bouddhisme*.

24. See also the case of Liang Shuming 梁漱溟 (1893–1988): Alitto, *The Last Confucian*.

25. On this literature, see Li Xiaoti, *Qingmo de xiaceng shehui qimeng yundong*, which touches on antisuperstition on pp. 36–37, 144. For a detailed study of the "reform the customs" campaigns, see Yan Changhong, *Zhongguo jindai shehui fengsu shi*.

26. We call these practices Confucian in the sense that they were routinely engaged in by self-identified Confucians and were grounded in Confucian classics.

that is, choosing the locations and arrangement of houses and graves in order to tap beneficial energies and avoid harmful ones), divination, and spirit writing, which before 1898 were sometimes criticized for their excesses but usually not on principle, and were in fact still largely practiced by members of the gentry in the 1900s. Cults dear to pre-1898 Confucian fundamentalists, such as those worshipping Wenchang or Guandi (who were actually more widely worshipped than Confucius), were suddenly rejected outright, along with any form of praying to icons or statues, "which are mere blocks of wood or mud." This, of course, eventually led during the 1910s to the questioning of all Confucian cults, including state religion and ancestor worship. For instance, leading members of the first Republican government in 1912 established a Society for Social Reform 社會改良會 that advocated fighting against funeral rites, adoptions, temple festivals, the worship of statues of any kind, and geomancy.[27]

Antisuperstition, then, was a frontal attack not only on local cults but, just as important, on the late imperial Confucian religion in all its devotional and liturgical aspects: its belief in ancestors, traditional cosmology, and the moral retribution of actions. Late imperial Confucianism ceased to be the religion of most of the governing elite, who turned, as we will see in the next two chapters, to other, new forms of religiosity.

In other words, the birth of the antisuperstition movement and the beginning of the destruction of temples may be best understood as a transition between two approaches: one that implied being part of Chinese religion and trying to improve it from the inside, as the anticlericals and fundamentalists did, and the other in which one viewed Chinese religion critically from the outside, without (or at least attempting not to use) its vocabulary or categories. Antisuperstition campaigners and others who tried to apprehend Chinese religion from the outside envisioned a radical destruction in a way no "insider" could. In the first case, that of "insiders," the model was antiquity and its scriptures (which describe a fully religious world); in the second, the paradigm was the continual progress of humanity from an ignorant stage characterized by fear of supernatural forces (*shenquan*) toward science and self-reliance, a vision often combined with a spiritual-ethical adhesion to Buddhism, Christianity, or reinvented Confucianism. In post-1898 texts, Chinese religion (but not religion in general) is constantly described as what prevents China from developing and enriching itself.

This vision "from the outside" that emerged around the turn of the century gained momentum and coalesced with a larger rejection of anything

27. Zheng Guo, "Jindai geming yundong," 54.

Chinese (clothes, food, even written characters) by some intellectuals when they invented Chinese nationalism. This phenomenon accompanied a growing estrangement from traditional religious culture among elites who were trained in Western-style schools, lived in cities, and were distending their links with their extended family. Thus, while other Asian nationalisms made great use of local religious traditions, the public face of Chinese nationalism was largely devoid of native, traditional religious elements.[28] The wholesale rejection of China's religious heritage was finally expressed during the 1919 May Fourth movement, which explicitly targeted Confucianism while identifying it with the whole of Chinese tradition, thereby creating the myth of a "Confucian China."[29] But while iconoclastic May Fourth leaders and, more generally, members of the larger and more loosely defined New Culture movement 新文化運動 of the 1910s and 1920s (of which the May Fourth movement was a political expression) took their models from the West, the neoconservatives[30] who opposed them rather turned to native ideologies and religiosities; all of them nonetheless agreed that late imperial ways of thinking and living religion were dead, and that something new needed to be devised.

How may one account for such a transition? Several factors were at work, but the immediate influence of Kang Youwei and Liang Qichao was probably rather limited. It was instead stimulated by the general sense of crisis shared by most intellectuals, which induced in many of them a deeply felt hatred of traditional Chinese society. The introduction of Western science and the consequent undermining of traditional knowledge played a role. The end of the civil service examinations and the decline in state rituals also contributed to the discarding of traditional cosmology. Also instrumental was the widespread influence of Christianity, even among nonconverts. This influence had many different effects. First, Christians, both foreigners and Chinese converts, set the example of temple destruction and iconoclasm,[31] such as the young Sun Yat-sen, who had begun

28. Cohen, "Being Chinese."

29. On the May Fourth movement, see notably Doleželová-Velingerová & Král, eds., *The Appropriation of Cultural Capital*; Chow Tse-tsung, *The May Fourth Movement*.

30. The term *neoconservatives* usually refers in the scholarly literature to public intellectuals linked to scholarship on "national essence" (*guocui* 國粹) who attempted to rephrase classical learning in modern terms. We use it here in a larger sense that also includes religious activists (on which see chapters 3 and 4) who recycled traditional texts and rites in new universalistic movements.

31. Gangs of Christian students toured and vandalized Guangzhou temples in 1911: Rhoads, *China's Republican Revolution*, 254–55.

his career by smashing a statue of Zhenwu (the protector god of the Ming dynasty) in his home village.[32] Others, while resisting Christian influence, agreed with the Christian missionaries that Chinese religion was mere idolatry. Seeing Christianity as the main spiritual threat to China, they tried to engage the missionaries in a debate on the religious situation in China, thereby adopting many of the Christian notions and categories, especially the religion-superstition dichotomy.

A very explicit cause for the adoption of the antisuperstition discourse in many post-1900 texts was the shock of the Boxer insurrection and its dreadful consequences for China, which pushed many into the camp of those willing to do away with village religion. Another, less explicit, motive was the religious organization of local society around temple cults, the "nexus of power," as Prasenjit Duara describes it:[33] temples were (and still are) places where symbolic power was vested in local leaders, where intra- and intervillage disputes were settled, and where local projects and resource management were negotiated. This organization was seen, not without reason, as the main obstacle to the building of a new, vertically integrated society, where the state is physically present in the villages and where all villagers obey the state alone—in other words, a nation-state. Local cults were the sites where the traditional and autonomous structures of local society were rooted, and which the modern state wished to destroy in order to take over their material and symbolic resources. Thus, antisuperstition deepened the split in Chinese society between local social organization and the national elite. The gentry, which had long served to bridge the two worlds, disappeared with the 1905 abolition of the civil service examinations, leaving elites and local cults in irreconcilable opposition.

THE NEW NATION-STATE AND ITS RELIGIOUS POLICIES, 1912–27

Changes in the state religious policies were ushered in by the intellectual redefinition of Chinese traditions as either religions or superstitions, and the antisuperstition campaigns, including the "destroy temples to build schools" movement. This context had already led to reinterpretations of state cults and practices during the New Policies period. While the Confucius cult was exalted to the highest rank in state sacrifices in 1906,

32. Poon Shuk Wah, *Negotiating Religion*, 1.
33. Duara, *Culture, Power, and the State*.

briefly elevating a nationalist-cultural symbol above imperial authority and power,[34] the process of canonization whereby local cults were integrated into state sacrifices was terminated in 1904, severing an important symbolic link between the state and the religious organization of local society.[35] This decision should be understood in a larger context in which the building of a constitutional state during the last decade of the empire that marginalized the state rituals, a progressive desacralization of conceptions of the state taking place since the nineteenth century; and a sharp decline of ritualistic studies among Confucians—furthered by thinkers such as Kang Youwei—made issues such as the canonization of local cults irrelevant to most central government officials.[36] This represents an important turn, since pre-1898 texts maintained that the imperial state was a religious institution, governing through cults and civilizing the realm through the gods (*yi shendao shejiao* 以神道設教).[37]

Proposals to revive the state Confucius cult were put forth during the first decade of the new Republican regime that became the official government with the last emperor's abdication on February 12, 1912, but these were rejected. For many intellectuals, notably but not only in the circle of Kang Youwei, China needed a national religion, *guojiao*, to bring it cohesiveness and unity of purpose, and this could only be Confucianism, which was, in their view, the natural religion of China.[38] The Confucian association (Kongjiaohui 孔教會) established in October 1912 campaigned for this project and managed to have it discussed by parliament, first in 1913 and again in 1916, but it was twice voted down, and the project was then buried forever.[39] Hostile parliamentarians considered that a national religion contradicted the constitutional freedom of religion, and that the Republican state should be both neutral and disengaged in matters of religion. Thus, the early Republic flirted with the idea of imitating the Japanese model of inventing a national cult (Shintô) alongside established religions, but decided against it.[40]

Confucianism consequently lost the status of official ideology that it

34. Kuo Ya-Pei, "Redeploying Confucius" and "The Emperor and the People."

35. Sawada Mizuho, "Seimotsu no shiten mondai."

36. Bastid-Bruguière, "Sacrifices d'Etat."

37. This phrase from the *Zhouyi* 周易 (*Book of Changes*), hexagram *guan* 觀, is the epitome of the religious doctrine of the imperial state. On the demise of institutionalized Confucianism in the realm of both education and ritual, see Gan Chunsong, *Zhiduhua rujia jiqi jieti*.

38. Liang Qichao, though, rejected this idea as early as 1902: Nedostup, "Religion, Superstition," 24–25.

39. Chen Hsi-yuan, "Confucianism Encounters Religion," chap. 4.

40. Hardacre, *Shintô and the State.*

had enjoyed for over two thousand years. Sacrifices to Confucius in schools were even abolished by the first Education Minister of the Republic, Cai Yuanpei 蔡元培 (1868–1940), in the name of the separation of state and religion. Ceremonies honoring the sage were later reintroduced in schools: sacrifices during the 1913–27 period, and then a modern civic rite with bowing but no sacrifice. That some antisuperstition campaigners and Republican politicians (beginning with the president Yuan Shikai) honored Confucius does not mean that they were "Confucians" in the same sense as late imperial Confucians were. Not only were ceremonies for honoring Confucius curtailed and limited to schools, but the other Confucian state cults (Wenchang, Guandi, and so on) were abolished altogether. The latter measure, most tellingly, was also espoused by those disciples of Kang Youwei who campaigned for a Confucian national religion during the 1910s.[41] Even those who tried to maintain a link between Confucianism and the state advocated something that was altogether different from late imperial Confucian religion.

Overall, the Republican period witnessed a clean sweep of all the ideas and practices of the Chinese imperial state's religious dimension. Except for the brief period in 1915–16 when Yuan Shikai planned to restore an imperial regime to his benefit, state sacrifices were totally abolished, and new Western-style state ceremonies, complete with a national flag and anthem, were invented.[42] One of the first acts of the new Republic was the inauguration of the Gregorian calendar beginning on January 1, 1912, simultaneously abolishing the traditional lunar-solar calendar. The rationale for this was not simply to imitate the modern states of the West but also and primarily to eliminate the numerous festivals and deity birthday rituals punctuating the traditional calendar with countless local and regional variations and cycles—all of which were occasions for "hot and noisy" crowds and unbridled "superstition"—and replace them with a new set of civic rituals.

The Republican regime's management of the religious scene was based on a thorough promulgation of the religion-superstition paradigm. The provisional constitution of the Republic of China, proclaimed on March 11, 1912, stipulated the "freedom of religious belief" (*xinjiao ziyou* 信教自由). This text did not guarantee protection against destructions and violence in temples, but elites saw no contradiction between protecting the freedom of religious belief on the one hand, and eradicating superstition and destroying temples on the other.

41. Chen Hsi-yuan, "Confucianism Encounters Religion," 226–28.
42. Harrison, *The Making of the Republican Citizen.*

The early Republican government elaborated a new official doctrine for religious policies, and religious affairs were entrusted to a bureau under the Ministry of Education. In June 1912 this bureau published a blueprint in which it declared its intention to reform (*gailiang* 改良) existing religions so that they might contribute to social progress.[43] This document's historical importance should not be overestimated, as it was published in a situation of political chaos in which leaders and ideas came and went in rapid succession. Yet it deserves attention inasmuch as it established quite clearly, and very early on, the modern Chinese state's fundamental positions in matters of religious policies, and these positions have more or less remained the same ever since: the state was ready to recognize "religions" as doctrinal, spiritual, and ethical systems with a social organization, but only if they got rid of "superstition," including most of their ritual. The document left open the list of such "religions," which were to be protected by the constitutional clause on religious freedom; but it did include Christianity, Islam, and Buddhism (if cleansed of its ritual practices), while it excluded Confucianism (the debate on this point would rage through the 1910s) as well as Taoism. Shortly afterward, however, Taoism, or rather a very purist, streamlined interpretation of Taoism, was included among the religions recognized by the Beiyang (1912–27), Nationalist, and Communist states. Thus, during the first months of the Republic, five religions — Roman Catholicism, Protestantism, Islam, Buddhism, and Taoism — came to acquire state recognition, a situation that would remain in place for the following century. National associations were set up for each of them in order to define and negotiate the scope of their autonomous organizations, a process described in the next chapter.

The criteria by which the modern Chinese state decided whether to include a religious tradition within its list of recognized religions have mostly remained hazy, with few explicit guidelines. Other countries, notably in Asia, have experienced comparable processes of selecting recognized religions, but they often had clearer and more precise criteria religions-to-be had to conform to.[44] The Chinese state's attitude has been quite pragmatic: a religion was recognized if it could prove it was "pure" (spiritual and ethical in nature) and well organized (hence the national associations) as well as useful (patriotic and contributing to social welfare and progress).

At the same time, any public ritual, devotional, or spiritual activity not

43. "Guanli zongjiao zhi yijian shu 管理宗教之意見書," *Shenbao*, June 22, 1912.

44. On the case of Indonesia, see Picard, "What's in a Name?" On Japan, see Garon, "State and Religion." See also DuBois, ed., *Casting Faiths*.

integrated into these religions was not covered by any official protection. Within the field of Chinese religion, this amounted to dramatically redefining and reducing the extent of legally and intellectually legitimate religious practices, notably by excluding local temple cults. The Beiyang government tried to bring control over this realm by legislating on temples. The 1913 provisional law followed by the 1915 law, amended in 1921, attempted to bring this embarrassing heritage of late imperial local autonomy into the fold of state management and condoned the nationalization of temples for educational and other purposes, but without planning it. The provisional law protected temples on the condition that they "belonged to a religion."[45] Those temples that were not nationalized were allowed to work according to "custom," but under the supervision of local officials who were now considered as representing the "public" (gong 公) that had built the temples in the first place. The ascriptive and associative communities that had actually built the temples were not recognized as legal entities. This amounted to a reinterpretation, in the state's favor, of the notion of "public." On the other hand, as it focused on national religions and local temples, the Beiyang-period government, in contrast to its Qing predecessor, lost interest in the salvationist groups and let them develop. Many ministers and generals of this period were members of those groups. Indeed, the 1910s and 1920s witnessed the birth of hundreds of new redemptive societies and a staggering rate of growth in their membership, as will be discussed in chapter 4.

Although these policies were enacted at the level of the central government, the country sled into disintegration and warlordism after the death of the autocratic president Yuan Shikai in 1916, and religious policy in practice depended very much on local authorities. The situation, therefore, varied to a huge extent between areas controlled by warlords who were often little interested in religious issues or merely favored the religion of their choice, and those where local leaders enforced antisuperstition policies, confiscating temples and radically remodeling the place of religion in public life. In the early phase, 1912–13, regional assemblies had passed legislation defining their own rules for deciding what constituted religion to be protected, and what was earmarked for destruction. Some regional governors set the example themselves by destroying the City God temples that had until a few months before been among the sacred sites under their protection.[46]

45. *Siyuan guanli zhanxing guize* 寺院管理暫行規則, June 20, 1913; *Guanli simiao tiaoli* 管理寺廟條例, October 29, 1915; *Xiuzheng* 修正 *Guanli simiao tiaoli*, May 20, 1921: see Qu Haiyuan, "Zhonghua minguo youguan zongjiao 'faling,'" 114–20.
46. Zheng Guo, "Jindai geming yundong," 54.

The struggles over what China's "national religion" (if any) should be and whether traditional forms of worship should be retained or discarded took place in the context of the modern imagination of China as a member of the family of nations, each of which should share a common language, culture, territory, economic life, and religion. Under Sun Yat-sen's formulation of the Chinese Republic being made up of five constituent nationalities 五族共和, the term *minzu* 民族—borrowed around 1903 from the Japanese *minzoku* rendering of the Western concept of people or nation— was used to designate the Han 漢, the Man 滿 (Manchus), the Meng 蒙 (Mongols), the Zang 藏 (Tibetans), and the Hui 回 (Muslims). Under this schema, the religious identity of the dominant Han remained open to debate, whereas for the four other *minzu*, it was naturalized as a function of their ethnic identity. At an ideological level, the policy aimed to unite the five constituent nationalities (particularly the four non-Manchu groups) as equals in the struggle for national dignity and independence, first from the foreign Qing dynasty, then against Japanese and Western imperialists; but on a practical level, in many ways it reformulated late-Qing approaches to managing the non-Chinese peoples living in the strategically important border territories—attempting to secure their loyalty by giving special regard to their own culture and customs, including religious practices. So, while religion became a passionate field of conflict among the Han, nobody questioned that Buddhism was and would remain the religion of the Tibetans and Mongols, and Islam the faith of large populations in the northwest—the latter so much so that, despite the great variety of languages, lifestyles, customs, and sects among these people, they were all grouped as a single nationality, the Hui, defined by their religion. Although Sun Yat-sen had proposed this formulation, its contents were contested, and it was far from universally accepted. For many Republican-era officials in Han-dominated areas, the Hui were not a nationality but merely "citizens with special customs" or "Han people who believe in the Hui religion" (*huijiao* 回教, as Islam was called in China before the 1950s). The new Hui associations, discussed in the next chapter, waged campaigns for their full recognition as a nationality, and their treatment and special political rights on a par with Tibetans and Mongols.[47] Thus, as the features of the nation-state came to be fixed and defined (five nationalities and five religions), the Hui became the only category for which there was an exact correspondence between a nationality and a religion, which could thus claim protection and special treatment as both—and their spokesmen were credited, as we

47. Ding Hong & Zhang Guojie, eds., *Bai nian Zhongguo musilin*, 53.

will see in the next chapter, for actively contributing to the Chinese nationalist cause.

For the entire twentieth century, including under the PRC, state management of Islam, Tibetan Buddhism, and indigenous ethnic minority religions would be subsumed under nationalities policy and dealt with in the context of broader ethnic and geopolitical issues.[48] This would have a profound impact on China's religious landscape, since there was an essential contradiction between religious and nationality policies: one the one hand, religious policy pursued an agenda of secularization in which religion, if it were retained at all, would be a matter of private choice and managed by specialized institutions cut off from communal cults. Nationalities policy, on the other hand, was based on the principle of the equality of nationalities and the protection of their autonomy and customs, of which religion was recognized as an essential component and marker of ethnic identity and identification. Under nationalities policy, members of an ethnic group were automatically ascribed to its religion and not considered to have any choice in the matter; minority ethnic religious leaders were to be accorded special regard, and their authority buttressed by the state; and communal cults and rituals that, under religious policy, would be banned or stigmatized in Han areas as "superstition" deserved protection and praise in minority areas as "ethnic customs." The result of the differential application of religious and nationalities policies would be the forced secularization of the Han people on the one hand, and the reinforced (and fixed) religious identity of minority ethnic groups on the other.

THE NATIONALIST MOMENT

The advent of the Nationalist regime in 1927, after the Northern Campaign that gave it control over most of the country, marked a new stage in the relationship between state and religion.[49] Even though the KMT had already been experimenting with radical antisuperstition policies in its base in Guangzhou during the 1920s,[50] the establishment of the Nationalist government in Nanjing was immediately followed by innovative religious policies. As Rebecca Nedostup has shown, after some KMT leaders had during the early 1920s dallied with the idea of radically opposing religion,

48. Gladney, *Muslim Chinese*, 81–87.
49. Most of the following is based on Nedostup, "Religion, Superstition." See also Mitani Takashi, "Nankin seiken."
50. Poon Shuk Wah, *Negotiating Religion*.

the leadership rallied behind the program of supporting, while controlling, the established religions along a corporatist model on the one hand, and launching an all-out attack on superstition on the other. Although, as we have seen, this was not new, the Nationalist leaders were more committed than anyone before them, and the party-state apparatus also gave them more opportunity at implementation.

The Nationalist approach to religion, as with much of society in general, was predicated on a set of utopian ideas: first, that society was knowable and changeable by science (in our case, social surveys and the emergent science of folklore studies), and second, that history was moving toward a new stage in which the harmful legacies of the past (especially ignorance and superstition) could be dealt a fatal and definitive blow.

The Nationalist regime established a new relationship with established religions through refounded national associations. "Progressive" leaders emerged who could enter into constructive negotiation with the government and, in exchange for political support and endorsement of the state's antisuperstitious policies, were rewarded with some autonomy. For instance, the Buddhist and Taoist associations were given a say in the administration of temples by the December 1929 temple management law (*Jiandu simiao tiaoli* 監督寺廟條例), and agreements were made with the Catholics and Protestants regarding church property and confessional education.

At the same time, a forceful program of eradication of superstition was launched on several fronts. First, legislation was passed to eradicate it in all its forms. Laws banned superstitious professions such as diviners and spirit mediums (September 1928), faith healing (April 1929), and the trade in superstitious items (offerings, spirit money, and so on, March 1930). Most famous was the November 1928 *Standards to determine the temples to be destroyed and those to be maintained* (*Shenci cunfei biaozhun* 神祠存廢標準). This lengthy text, which purports to be a scientific study of the forms of religious life, provides criteria and a list of examples for both categories, "to be preserved" and "to be destroyed." The authentic "religions" (particularly Buddhism and Taoism in their purist form) and temples dedicated to heroes of Chinese civilization, Confucius among them, were to be preserved; the rest had to be destroyed. This distinction turned out to be impossible to apply on the ground, especially in the case of Taoism, which was indissolubly associated with local cults. In many places, the *Standards* were understood as a call to intensify antisuperstition campaigns and nationalize temples, but were not applied strictly; but in a few cases, they were: in 1936, the Kunming municipal government seized sixty-one temples and produced a detailed justification based on the different articles in the *Standards*, explaining for each seized temple—including a good number of Buddhist and Taoist clerical institutions—why they were not "religious" enough.[51] Although we will discuss the effects of the anti-superstition campaigns on the ground in terms of destruction and resistance in chapter 5, we need to insist here how much the Nationalist laws completely reinvented the parameters for conceiving the relation between state agents and local religion.

Along with efforts at suppression, the party-state also embarked on efforts to explore the religious situation in order to better control and change it, as Nationalist officials were well aware that their imperial and Beiyang predecessors had to a large extent let temples and cult communities live in a separate realm mostly out of the reach of the state. Laws enacted in 1928 and 1936 mandated and planned for the first nationwide survey of temples; even if it was properly carried out only in a small number of places (the largest cities), this survey still provided unprecedented information to local officials on the numbers and resources of temples in their jurisdiction.[52]

This grand plan at control and suppression was largely a failure. While all state agents and party members agreed on the need to stamp out superstition in order to let China become a strong, rich, and modern country, they did not always agree on the procedures; and hot-headed party activists, who incited students to burn religious books and smash down statues—which often led to popular hostility or even antigovernment riots—were confronted by more pragmatic local officials. Lawsuits and local conflicts concerning destroyed or seized religious property clogged the courts and paralyzed official business. The utopian nature of the legal framework, which was utterly irrelevant to the reality of Chinese religion, became apparent whenever it was applied. But, as we will see, the policy was far from being without effect.

TIBET AND THE MUSLIM NORTHWEST

Following the collapse of the Qing empire, the new Chinese state retained little if any authority (which, by the late nineteenth century, had been largely symbolic) over the peripheral territories of the western frontier. These areas were not immune from modern state-building projects, but,

---

51. Xiao Jihong & Dong Yun, *Yunnan daojiao shi*, 135–59.
52. Goossaert, *The Taoists of Peking*, 65–73.

owing to their large Muslim and Tibetan Buddhist populations and powerful religious institutions, the dynamics of change were very different from
those of the Han areas.

In 1912–13, the Thirteenth Dalai Lama returned to Lhasa from exile in
India and his volunteer force drove all Chinese officials and troops out of
Tibet. In order to protect Tibet's independence from future military threats
from China and Nepal, as well as to strengthen his own autonomy from
the three powerful monastic Seats of the Lhasa area (Sera, Drepung, and
Ganden), the Dalai Lama decided to develop a modern army, as well as
to initiate other reforms to modernize Tibet. He chose one of his close
favorites, Tsarong Shape, to build the army and lead the reforms. Tsarong
and his fellow military officers, many of whom had been trained in British India, wore Western clothes and uniforms, openly admired Western
culture, were secular in orientation, and opposed the influence of religion
on government policy. However, their proposal to significantly expand the
size of the army, modernize government administration, and build an English school met with fierce resistance from the monastic establishment:
the cost of the new troops would need to be paid through higher taxes on
the vast estates of the monasteries, a secular army would undermine the
authority and influence of religion, and an English-educated elite would
cease to patronize the monasteries. The religious conservatives persuaded
the Dalai Lama to dismiss Tsarong and his commanders in 1924–25, killing
all the reforms and permanently weakening the army.

For the rest of the period until 1949, several other modest attempts at
reform, which would involve a partial secularization of aspects of government and the opening of another English school to train technicians to
operate wireless broadcasting equipment, were squashed by the Buddhist
institutions as well. The religious establishment was adamantly opposed
to any form of modernization. As a result, though Tibet was free from Chinese control during this period, its government did not build a modern
nation-state, having neither army nor personnel familiar with the outside
world and capable of conducting diplomacy in a foreign language. The path
chosen by Tibet was diametrically opposite that pursued by China's elites.
When the Chinese Red Army advanced into Tibet in 1950 (see chapter 6),
the government in Lhasa was not equipped to resist.[53]

In Xinjiang, the warlord Yang Zengxin 楊增新 (1864–1928) ruled from
1911 until his assassination in 1928, retaining most of the features of the
Qing imperial approach to administering the region, with designated lords

53. Goldstein, *A History of Modern Tibet*.

and elites managing their towns according to local practice and Islamic law. He also protected the interests of the established clergy by banning the opening of private mosques and the creation or introduction of new sects,[54] notably the reformist, anti-Sufi, Muslim Brotherhood–inspired movements that were being introduced from the Middle East and making inroads among the Hui in Gansu, as mentioned below. Yang's successor Jin Shuren 金樹仁 (1879–1941) was notoriously intolerant of Muslims, leading to increased ethnic tensions between Han and Uighurs, and several revolts and insurrections erupted. In southern Xinjiang, a Turkic-Islamic Republic of Eastern Turkestan was proclaimed in Khotan on November 12, 1933, with the aim of establishing an Islamic state governed in accordance with *shari'a* law. After less than three months, however, this republic was crushed by the army of the Hui Muslim warlord Ma Zhongying 馬仲英 (ca. 1910–1936?) of Gansu.[55]

Ma Zhongying was one of several Muslim warlords who attained fame during the Republican era. Three of them (known as the "three Ma" 三馬) controlled the Gansu, Ningxia, and Qinghai areas, which had large Muslim (as well as Tibetan and Mongol) populations, through much of this period. To reinforce their legitimacy among Muslims, they sponsored the rebuilding of major mosques and supported the reformist leaders of the Ikhwan movement or "New Teachings" directly inspired by the Muslim Brotherhood, in an alliance against the traditionalist Sufi orders that dominated local society. Under the three Ma warlords, Muslims acquired an unprecedented influence in the provincial administrations of the northwestern panhandle (east of Xinjiang and sandwiched between Tibet and Mongolia), with a large proportion of Muslims among clerks and officials. Most of these were affiliated with the Ikhwan movement, and pursued its goals of unifying Muslims under a single, modern sect.[56]

---

54. Ding Hong & Zhang Guojie, eds., *Bai nian Zhongguo musilin*, 203, 267.
55. Dillon, *Xinjiang*, 20–21; see also Forbes, *Warlords and Muslims*.
56. Ding Hong & Zhang Guojie, eds., *Bai nian Zhongguo musilin*, 87–88.

THREE

Model Religions for a Modern China
Christianity, Buddhism, and Religious Citizenship

Chapter 2 traced the evolution of policies toward religion of the successive imperial, early Republican, and Nationalist regimes. Politicians drafting and enacting policies were not alone on the scene; leading religious reformers also played a major role in reshaping the religious field and reinventing religion. This chapter covers the same period seen from the perspective of the latter as they attempted to create model religions that fit the new political and ideological context.

The new religious policies of the Chinese nation-state entailed relationships with religious traditions that comprised a complex mix of repression, ignorance, and cooperation. Many ideas and practices, labeled as superstition, were repressed, but others were appraised positively as fitting the needs and ideals of modern China. Indeed, the Republican state promoted and used certain religious ideas and practices to develop its notion of citizenship. These constituted a set of norms that sketched what a religion should be in order to adapt and thrive in the modern context.

This chapter will consider the normative models at work in the con-

struction of religious institutions by Christian, Buddhist, Taoist, Confucian, and Muslim leaders and reformers. Two models seem to have been
dominant, and were combined with traditional forms by the religious reformers: the legally incorporated, secular social association registered with
the nation-state; and forms of Christian church organization, more specifically those of liberal Protestant denominations that were themselves under
secularizing influences. Chinese Muslim leaders adopted parallel reforms
inspired by modernizing Islamic movements in the Middle East. Both the
Christian and the Muslim models were shaped by their emergence in the
context of secular nation-states—in which religion was, depending on
the polity, more or less separated from the state, and then provided with a
specialized space within the public sphere.[1] The 1905 law of separation between church and state in France, for instance, was the clearest exposition
of this principle. When we speak of a "Christian" model here, we mean,
more precisely, a "Christian-secular" model that, in the Western nations,
was the outcome of over a century of struggles and negotiations which had
led to a redefinition of church-state relations within the nation-state. In
this model, the Christian and the secular are two sides of the same coin: it
is "Christian" because it is based on the notion of a church separate from
and independent of other social institutions, and at the same time "secular"
because it involves the state and other social institutions asserting their independence vis-à-vis the church—a line of contention and accommodation
is traced between religion and nonreligion, then, that was inconceivable in
the imperial Chinese system. We will begin with the impact of Christians
in the making of the Republican polity and the Chinese formulations of
the Christian-secular model; we will then examine the parallel Buddhist,
Taoist, Muslim, and Confucian reforms.

A CHRISTIAN REPUBLIC?

The empire had repressed Christianity for a century (1724–1842) before
Western military power forced an uneasy recognition of the foreign religion. Officials of the late Qing were mostly eager to separate Western
technology, which they wanted, from ideology (religion), which they did
not. The traditional elites (the gentry) were chiefly hostile to Christianity,
which they equated with political and cultural alienation. In 1912, some
of them squarely thought that, along with a change of regime, official religion had switched from Confucianism to Christianity. They considered,

---

1. On Muslim models for secularism, see Luizard, *Laïcités autoritaires*.

with horror and disgust, that they now lived under a Christian Republic.[2] By contrast, the new elites, largely composed of civil and military officials trained in modern schools (some of them Christian-run), as well as merchants and urban professionals, all of whom had close relationships with Westerners, often considered the idea of a Christian Republic in more positive terms.

Whether hostile or not, the idea of the new regime as a Christian Republic was grounded in the facts: the first and ephemeral president, Sun Yat-sen, had been baptized in 1884 at age 18, after having been trained in Christian colleges in Hawai'i and Hong Kong.[3] In his own words, it was "mostly from the church that I learned the truth of revolution. The establishment of the Republic today is due, not to my efforts, but to the service of the church."[4] Sun, a Hakka who was inspired by the memory of the Taiping movement, was part of an influential network of Christians who contributed, politically or financially, to the Chinese Nationalist cause. His father-in-law, Charlie Soong 宋嘉樹 (1863–1918), was an American-educated Methodist missionary, publisher, and revolutionary financier; besides his daughter Song Qingling 宋慶齡 (1893–1981), who married Sun, his two other daughters married Chiang Kai-shek, himself baptized as a Methodist in 1929, and H. H. Kong 孔祥熙 (1881–1967), an immensely wealthy banker and premier of China from 1938 to 1939. Kong had been converted during his childhood by missionaries from Oberlin College in the United States, where he later studied before returning to China to contribute to mission work and eventually become director of the Young Men's Christian Association (YMCA).[5] These and other Christian nationalists considered that the decline and decay of China were due to idolatry, while the strength, prosperity, and higher civilization of America were due to the Christian religion. Christianity, for them, could bring dignity and equality to China. Like the May Fourth nationalists, it could be said that it was a love for China as a nation that led them to despise the culture and gods of the Chinese people—an attitude which could easily shift from the Christian faith of these early revolutionaries, to the secular radicalism of the later May Fourth intellectuals, and then to the anti-Christian Communism that would eventually prevail.

2. Chen Hsi-yuan, "Confucianism Encounters Religion," 110–16. Madancy, "Revolution, Religion and the Poppy," shows that a 1912–13 local revolt in Fujian against Republican government taxation and mismanagement was turned primarily against Christians (and not foreigners).

3. Bergère, *Sun Yat-sen*, 28–30.

4. Tseng, "Chinese Protestant Nationalism," 20.

5. On the YMCA, see Zuo Furong, *Shehui fuyin*.

Among the 274 members elected (indirectly, through colleges of local elites) to the first national parliament between December 1912 and January 1913, sixty were Christians. This proportion was totally out of measure when we consider that Christians accounted for less than 1 percent of the population. It was, of course, not as Christians that these MPs were elected, but because a large proportion of the new classes of urban elites and political activists that fully supported the Republican enterprise, notably professionals (doctors, lawyers, engineers, custom officers), were Christians.

One key vehicle for Christian influence over the new elites was higher education. Many professionals and urban elites had been trained in Western colleges in China or abroad. Among the universities and technical training institutes founded since the last years of the nineteenth century, a good half were church run, and some private universities were founded by Christian Chinese philanthropists; the only, but important, exception to Christian influence was military academies.[6] Moreover, the press, which was still partly supported by Western interests, although to a lesser extent than during the last decades of the Qing, played a major role in the diffusion of Christian ideals about the building of a new China.

Christian organizations had been key players in the diffusion of progressive social ideals, such as the anti-foot-binding movement, which began with a group of sixty Christian women in Xiamen in 1874. The movement was then taken up by the Women's Christian Temperance Movement, founded in 1883, which also opposed opium, cigarette smoking, alcohol use, prostitution, and the selling of daughters. In addition, these ideas were advocated by missionaries such as Timothy Richard, who considered that Christianity could lead to the equality of the sexes, and enthusiastically supported by Liang Qichao and Kang Youwei, who were avid readers of Richard's works and personally acquainted with him. The Young Women's Christian Association (YWCA), founded in the late nineteenth century, initially focused its energies on foot binding; later, its activities expanded to include supporting literacy classes and leadership training for working-class women, promoting physical education for women and girls, and developing the role of women in service to society as citizens of the nation.[7]

As a result of such progressive social engagement, fair numbers of non-Christian political activists were, until the 1920s, happy to support and

---

6. Ng Peter Tze-ming, *Jidu zongjiao yu Zhongguo daxue jiaoyu*; Bays & Widmer, eds., *China's Christian Colleges*.

7. Kwok Pui-lan, "Christian Women and Social Reform," in *Chinese Women and Christianity, 1860–1927*, 101–46.

work with the political and civic initiatives of Chinese Christians. Institutions such as the YMCA united Christian and non-Christian local leaders in projects to promote education and hygiene. Such non-Christian acceptance of Christian elites sprang from their sharing a political vision of a new, modern, democratic China that espoused both Western political ideals, most notably the U.S. model, and a readiness to stand up and criticize Western powers for any encroachment on Chinese sovereignty.[8] Far from being enslaved to missionary interests, then, elite Chinese Christians were ready to stand up to Western coreligionists when their nationalist feelings commanded it. At that point, and unlike in later periods, Christian politicians were not widely seen as traitors to the national cause.

The most important contribution of Christians to the political debate was the notion of religious citizenship.[9] Being a citizen of the Republic was very different from being a subject of the empire, and early Republican politicians lacked indigenous models of citizenship. Chinese Christians served as intermediaries in the transfer from the West of ideas and practices of a modern nation-state, such as civic rituals centered on the flag or the national anthem. Furthermore, Christians promoted the notion that a good believer, that is, a public-minded, thrifty, honest, sober, decent person, was de facto a good citizen. The involvement of many Chinese Christians in public life, civic projects, and campaigns against opium, foot binding, and other "social ills" convinced many urban Chinese of the practical benefits of religious citizenship, and they became sympathizers or even converted. Christian ideals would later be recycled, stripped of their confessional framework, into civic movements, notably the New Life movement in 1934.

If Christian ideas of religious citizenship did have a deep influence, the fears or hopes for a Christian Republic—depending on one's opinions— vanished by the mid-1920s. There were several reasons for this turn. One was that the presence of Christians among the new political elites was largely limited to the civilian apparatus (MPs and local officials) and did not extend much into the military, which rapidly became the real center of power. There were some exceptions, most famously the northern warlord Feng Yuxiang 馮玉祥 (1882–1946), notorious for baptizing his troops with a hose. However, the military establishment under the Beiyang regime by and large kept its distance from Christianity, and this remained, to some extent, the case under Nationalist rule. Even then, the generalissimo Chiang Kai-shek converted to Methodism and was publicly baptized in

8. Dunch, *Fuzhou Protestants*; see also Lian, "Western Protestant Missions."
9. Duara, "Religion and Citizenship."

1929, and seven of the ten cabinet ministers in the new Nanjing KMT government, established in 1929, were Christians.[10] Second, the association of Christians with imperialism was made ever more forcefully by critics after the May Fourth movement and during the 1920s, notably through the student and Marxist-led "antireligion" campaigns.[11] In this context, non-Christians became ever more suspicious of explicitly Christian projects for the Republic of China.

Meanwhile, however, despite declining official support, Chinese Christianity grew steadily during the whole Republican period, providing an expanding support base for its projects. Protestants, still only numbering about 180,000 in 1906, were nearly a million in 1949; Roman Catholics grew from over 500,000 to 3 million during the same period. The major part of this growth still largely occurred through missionary societies that were divided against each other, sometimes bitterly, preventing a truly integrated Christian organization to emerge, while each denomination was already organized on a China-wide basis. However, a movement did begin among foreign and Chinese missionaries to help Chinese churches become self-managing, self-supporting, and self-propagating—the "Three-Self" movement, which would later be co-opted by the CCP in the 1950s. Among the Protestants, the National Christian Conference met in 1922 to launch the Church of Christ in China, which counted a significant number of Chinese among its leaders. Many Protestant organizations joined the council, but not the Anglicans, Lutherans, and new indigenous Christian movements. The first plenary council of the Chinese Catholic Church convened in 1924 in Shanghai, prompted by the Vatican's taking direct control over various missionary societies. Not before the Communist period did national, nondenominational Catholic and Protestant associations form on the model already adopted in the Republican period by the Buddhist, Taoist, and Muslim associations, as we describe below.

At the same time, the Republican period witnessed the very strong growth of indigenous churches, mostly within the Protestant tradition, founded by Chinese Christians without the support of missionary societies. These groups were all launched by charismatic preachers, were strongly shaped by fundamentalist and Pentecostal ideas, and had a distant, and often altogether hostile, relationship with Western missionaries and their institutions. Among them, the largest groups were the True Jesus Church

10. "Christian Majority," *Time Magazine*, January 7, 1929; online at http://www.time.com/time/magazine/article/0,9171,929380,00.html?promoid=googlep (accessed January 26, 2008).
11. Bastid-Bruguière, "La campagne antireligieuse."

(Zhen Yesu hui 真耶穌會), founded in 1917;[12] the Little flock (Xiaoqun 小群) or Assembly Hall (Juhuichu 聚會處), established during the 1920s by Ni Tuosheng 倪柝聲 (1903–1972), known as Watchman Nee; and the autarkic communes of the Jesus Family (Yesu jiating 耶穌家庭).[13] These groups represented the most dynamic and deeply acculturated component of Chinese Christianity, but they were not at all politically oriented in the sense the YMCA and other groups led by elite Christians were. The new movements were all focused on spirituality, and were suspicious of the ideas of religious citizenship advocated by their more socially engaged coreligionists. Thus, the idea of a Christian Republic faded, for both political and religious reasons. But it did inspire leaders from other creeds.

THE CHRISTIAN-SECULAR NORMATIVE MODEL

More than the number of converts and the direct action of the Christian elite, the greatest impact of Christianity in Republican China was through its normative model, in its various Catholic and Protestant versions, of what a religion should be, which were adopted by the intelligentsia, the state, and even the leaders of other religions. We have already seen how Christian-based understandings of "religion" informed the Republican state's policies. Not only was Christianity the model for "religion," but throughout the twentieth century, Chinese political and intellectual leaders had been extremely sensitive to Western (almost always Christian-inspired) judgments and analyses regarding Chinese religion.[14] A particularly telling case of such sensitivity is Kang Youwei's utterance: "Foreigners come in our temples, take photographs of the idols, show these photographs to each other and laugh."[15] This sentence was later copied verbatim in the introduction of the most important and famous antisuperstition law of the Nationalist government, the 1928 "Standards to determine the temples to be destroyed and those to be maintained." Thus, the desire to conform to Western expectations regarding Chinese religious practices ran deep among both lay and religious leaders.

The Christian normative model operated on several levels. First, it forced individuals, especially laypersons, to rethink their religious engagement

---

12. Lian, "A Messianic Deliverance."

13. Bays, ed., "The Growth of Independent Christianity"; Lian, "The Search for Chinese Christianity."

14. On the missionary discourse about Chinese religion, see Reinders, *Borrowed Gods*.

15. This famous sentence was first published in a "fake" memorial (written by Kang but, contra Kang's later assertion, not sent to the emperor during the 1898 reforms): see chapter 2, note 7.

and how they should live, think, and act as Buddhists, Confucians, Taoists, or otherwise. Second, at the level of institutions, the most important vehicle for the adoption of the Christian-secular normative model was the national religious association. This particular form of organization, as it appeared in 1912 and developed throughout the rest of the century, indigenized Christian models of clerical training, community organization, confessional identification, and social engagement. In the Republican context in which a "religion," to be recognized by the state and protected by law, had to conform to the Christian-secular model, Chinese traditions, whether Confucian, Buddhist, or Taoist, had to reinvent and redefine themselves. They had to represent themselves as distinct religious institutions, independent and disconnected from the local cults of village society. They had to create national associations capable of representing them to the state. For the first time, Buddhism, Taoism, Confucianism, and Islam attempted to organize themselves into unified national, hierarchical institutions. Such a reinvention was no easy enterprise, not only because it generated internal conflicts and confusion, but even more so because traditionally these religions did not operate as centralized organizations. Instead, they operated as independent clerics in the service of local cults, temples, and mosques, to which they provided salvation techniques, rituals, and religious specialists trained to take over all sorts of clerical work (temple management, fundraising, writing history and other kinds of texts, and so on). And with the exception of Islam and some salvationist groups, they did not have a membership of declared adherents.

Being in a legal limbo, and fearing, with cause, for their temples and monasteries, Buddhists and Taoists alike were impelled to muster whatever kind of organized defense they could. Confucians and Muslims also had to redefine their place in the new political and social order. Thus, faced with both the fresh possibility and the urgent need to form associations to unite and act on the political scene, Confucians, Buddhists, Taoists, and Muslims reacted with energy as well as predictable confusion. Many of them had ideas about how to adapt their religion to the new context, and all proceeded to create their own national associations. Some of these were mostly engaged in apologetics, while others had more radical plans for a religious modernization. As early as the spring and summer of 1912, several Buddhist, Taoist, Muslim, and Confucian associations had been set up, and many similar associations continued to mushroom throughout the Republican period. Most had only an ephemeral existence, with tiny memberships and grand projects that were never translated into reality. Naturally, the competition between so many associations contradicted their common project of representing the whole of their religion. The only associations that managed to build a China-wide membership, obtain government recognition, and score some success in the legislative battles against radical projects such as temple confiscations were those presided over by prestigious leaders, usually charismatic clerics, and commanding widespread respect among lay sympathizers.

The various national religious associations formed in 1912 with both enthusiasm and a sense of panic failed to turn most of their projects into reality; their most notable achievement was official recognition by the state and the limited, but not negligible, amount of protection that this entailed. The grand plans to create hierarchical churches with countless bureaus for research, propaganda, education, and discipline as well as branches in every part of China and the world were never realized. The associations themselves seem to have been locked in the national political arena, focusing their efforts, up to the late 1920s, on lobbying the president of the Republic and the parliament to the exclusion of other possible fields of action. The Confucian Association is an extreme case, as it identified itself so much with its project of a national religion that it became a marginal group after this project was voted down by the parliament.

The real growth in relevance for the remaining national religious associations came only later, under the Nationalist regime, thanks to two factors: first, the official recognition of the Buddhist and Taoist associations' role in the management of temples and monasteries in the Temple Management Act (December 1929), and second, the creation in many counties of local branches of these associations. These local branches often managed to include the various orientations and factions among the local clergy and to work quite efficiently, avoiding the advocacy of any grand reform plan while striving more modestly to protect and help local temples and clerics through negotiation with local authorities.[16] Their mission was to advise and assist local officials in temple affairs (for example, replacing a departed or condemned cleric, advising local officials in case of lawsuits involving temple property) and in general manage routine religious affairs in a corporatist way, leaving officials to intervene only in criminal or high-profile cases. While the national associations originally aimed to adopt the Christian-secular model—eliminate superstition, ritual, and autonomous local communities—they ended up finding a new raison d'être by taking over the role played under the imperial regime by the clerical officials

16. Nedostup, "Religion, Superstition," chap. 2. On the situation in Beijing, see Goossaert, *The Taoists of Peking*, chap. 1.

(Daolusi and Senglusi). The association as an institutional form thus found a place in the religious landscape.

National religious associations were characterized by a marked continuity in ideology and leadership from 1912 to 1949, and by resemblance with one another. Beneath the surface of a tumultuous history—these associations, from 1912 onward, have often been used as vehicles for personal ambitions and competing ideas—they all share a common model that is a new phenomenon in the history of state-religion relationships in China, and that in and by itself has far-reaching implications: bureaucratic control of religion, assimilation of political ideology into the religious discourse, antiritual rhetoric, and attempts at national unification of each religion, contributing to the unification of China itself.

These associations' leaders envisioned on paper (we will never know how much they themselves believed in such projects) vast bureaucratic organizations. What paradigm was at work here? The reorganization of the bureaucratic state, with a staggering expansion of the number of state agents, ongoing since the last years of the Qing, certainly formed the background for this organizational culture. Indeed, the religious traditions were not the only quarter of society that engaged in such institution building.[17] The organization of Christian missionary societies (and possibly also Japanese Buddhist missionary societies) provided another source of inspiration. The most efficient aspects of the missions' organization, such as the confessional press, were adopted by all the national religious associations, and so appeared Buddhist, Muslim, and Confucian journals.[18] Another direct imitation was the missionary organization: Confucians were now seen preaching and dreamed of converting Europe and America, and Buddhists developed grand plans to reintroduce Buddhism to India.

Another feature shared by all the Republican-period national religious associations was their efforts toward redefining their relationship to the state. All of them insisted that the Republic proclaimed the separation of religion and state, yet all also claimed a special relationship for themselves. The various Buddhist and Taoist associations presented themselves as the natural ally and moral arm of the secular state; the Muslim Association for Progress aimed to contribute to the process of state building; and both the Taoist Association and the Confucian Association claimed the status of "national religion" through an ethical formulation of religious citizenship.

The religious associations also endorsed the religious reform goals of

---

17. On professions, see Xu Xiaoqun, *Chinese Professionals*.
18. Löwenthal, *The Religious Periodical Press*.

the state. For instance, liturgy and ritual services to the population are markedly absent from the texts the associations produced, and they gradually incorporated the antisuperstition discourse. Moreover, the rhetoric of unification pervaded the discourse of the various associations, which all insisted on the weakness of their current situation and the necessity of unity as the only way to revival. This is clearly related to the strong desire among the Republican political elites to unite the people behind a single, unitary national project and ideology. This vision rejected the traditional structure of Chinese society, in which the people belonged to multiple autonomous communities, each with their own cults and religious practices. From this perspective, the state and its nationalist project found natural allies in some religious leaders who also held the ambition to unite and standardize their religion through the suppression of the autonomy of local temples, communities, and traditions of practice. As a consequence, all the Republican associations envisioned the enforcement of internal discipline. This certainly reflects a frustration, that must have existed long before 1912, among religious leaders unable to control fellow clerics and practitioners, and seeing in the national religious association a means to gain at last the power to impose discipline.

The Republican-period associations thus developed a rhetoric of the unification of the religious community, but without a clear idea about how to proceed, because they lacked a clear definition of the laity. Most of the associations' charters refrained from positing a precise definition, even though they made great use of their politically connected lay supporters. As a matter of fact, the Buddhist and Taoist associations remained, by and large, clerical associations throughout the twentieth century. The very notion of a unified China-wide Buddhist or Taoist community indeed remained an elusive goal, and the institutional leaders can be excused for being at a loss of ideas about how to conjure that modern dream. Their subsequent failure can be contrasted with the situation of the Muslim community, which, through its associations, managed as early as the 1930s to mobilize, notably through its print media, large numbers of militants to stage protests against perceived insults or threats.[19]

The most visible manifestation of the Christian-liberal normative model of a good religion was social action in the field of education and charity. In terms of education, Christianity totally dominated the field: by 1914, there were 11,545 Christian-run elementary schools (8,034 Catholic and 3,511 Protestant), and 542 high schools and universities (all of them Protes-

19. Allès, "A propos de l'Islam."

tant); by contrast, Muslim schools were few, and Buddhist schools mostly were for training novices; there existed local community schools financed (rather than run) by temples or monasteries, but their numbers could not compare with Christian schools. Protestant universities trained the elite and recorded conversion rates ranging between 30 and 80 percent among their students, even though such rates tended to decline after the 1920s,[20] at the same time that the KMT government increased its control over the curriculum, management, and property of Christian schools and universities. Incidentally, it is in Christian universities, notably Yenching University in Beijing, that religious studies first developed in China, with many of the leading scholars, such as Chen Yuan 陳垣 (1880–1971) or Xu Dishan 許地山 (1893–1941), being converts; the leading folklorist Gu Jiegang 顧頡剛 (1893–1980), who although not a Christian was quite close to the KMT and influenced its views on religion,[21] was from the same milieu.

In this context, the importance of education in the charters of the Buddhist, Taoist, and Confucian associations becomes self-evident, even though it took a long time for them to realize their dreams of emulating Christian education: the first Buddhist university opened in Taiwan in 1989, in sharp contrast with Japan, where Buddhist universities have been flourishing for over a century. The main exception was the Muslims, among whom a movement to reform the traditional education of imams with modern schools began quite early, with new-style Islamic schools combining religious and secular subjects appearing from 1906.[22] Redemptive societies (discussed in the next chapter) were more successful, with movements such as the World Wide Ethical Society (Wanguo daodehui 萬國道德會) opening thousands of primary schools during the 1920s and 1930s.

In the realm of philanthropy and disaster relief, native responses to the Christian model were more impressive. The social engagement of Christians in famine relief—as early as the great North China famine of 1876–79, when missionaries such as Timothy Richard played a major role in relief operations—and public health, notably through the building of hospitals (over three hundred missionary facilities by 1937, some of which aggressively proselytized patients[23]), pushed many members of local elites to take part in charity as Buddhists or as Confucians, in both imitation and

20. Song Guangyu, "Ershi shiji Zhongguo yu shijie zongjiao," 6–9.
21. Nedostup, "Religion, Superstition," 171–74.
22. Ding Hong & Zhang Guojie, eds., *Bai nian Zhongguo musilin*, 20–23.
23. Song Guangyu, "Ershi shiji Zhongguo yu shijie zongjiao," 19–22.

contradistinction to Christian initiatives. Often such identities were far from exclusive; the famed Shanghai philanthropist Wang Yiting 王一亭 (1867–1938) was a self-professed lay Buddhist but also took an active part in redemptive societies and Christian and Confucian charities.[24] Wang, an entrepreneur and artist widely admired for his dedication and social engagement, is maybe typical of Republican-era engaged laypersons. While not associated with any traditional ascriptive community (lineage or territorial temples), he was a leading force of reformist groups, including the Buddhist associations, martial arts associations, and several spirit-writing groups, notably the Jishenghui 濟生會, created in 1916 in Shanghai.[25] The latter, while having a public face as "secular" charities, were actually, for the initiated members, devotional groups dedicated to the worship of Taoist and Buddhist saints and to saving the world. Wang's connections in these various milieus allowed him to raise considerable funds for famine and flood relief on several occasions. Such overlaps are typical of the milieu of lay activists to this day in Taiwan and Hong Kong. What characterizes the Republican-period religious philanthropy is the rise, on the basis of local charities (*shantang*) of the Qing period, of larger, pan-Chinese organizations.[26] The Red Cross was generally seen as a model of religious engagement, and was widely imitated within both Buddhism and redemptive societies: the Red Swastika (Hong wanzi hui 紅卍字會, discussed in the next chapter), for a while China's largest charity, was founded in 1922 by the Daoyuan.

Reformist Buddhism

Of all the Chinese religious traditions, Buddhism saw the most sustained engagement with the Christian normative model and its ideas of religious citizenship. This engagement was part of a large movement of revival and reform that had already begun during the last years of the Qing dynasty.[27] Historians and Buddhist leaders alike agree that the movement coalesced around the figure of Yang Wenhui 楊文會 (1837–1911), a former lower official stationed in the Chinese embassy in London for six years, who in 1866 embarked on a lifelong mission to reprint, disseminate, and teach the Buddhist scriptural legacy with a focus on speculative and philosophical

24. Katz, "It Is Difficult to Be Indifferent."
25. Wang Jianchuan, "Qingmo minchu Zhongguo de Jigong xinyang."
26. Song Guangyu, "Ershi shiji Zhongguo yu shijie zongjiao," 12–19.
27. Welch, *The Buddhist Revival in China.*

texts. The press he founded in Nanjing reprinted a large number of texts, some of which were not widely available or even almost lost. In the seminary he set up in 1908, he formed disciples, including clerics and laypersons, in his vision of a doctrinal, spiritual, text-based Buddhism, as opposed to the temple-based Buddhism of clerics providing ritual services.[28]

Whereas Yang was not anticlerical, and saw his contribution as distinct but not opposed to the clerical institution, some of his disciples were. The person who saw himself as the true heir to Yang's mission was Ouyang Jian 歐陽漸 (1870–1943). A true anticlerical who once forbade monks to attend his seminar, Ouyang dreamed of reinventing Buddhism as Buddhist studies (Foxue 佛學), the intellectual practice of laypersons versed in Buddhist philosophy. Respected as a scholar, Ouyang was too extreme in his views to have a large institutional role. Yet he established in March 1912 the Buddhist Association (Fojiaohui 佛教會), which was granted recognition by Sun Yat-sen's government, with the barely disguised aim of wrenching control of monastic property from clerics.[29] This prompted a reaction by the monastic establishment, which on April 1, 1912, established in Shanghai a broad-based national organization, the General Buddhist Association of China (Zhonghua fojiao zonghui 中華佛教總會), under the direction of the celebrated ascetic and abbot Bazhi 八指 (Jing'an 敬安, 1852–1912).[30] It was the latter association that became the official representative of Buddhism, but it was later disbanded in 1918, when its requests displeased the Republican government. Up to 1949, the same story of various Buddhist associations jostling for supremacy continued along the lines of a division between radical reformers and the monastic establishment.[31]

The most influential Buddhist reformist figure of the Republican period, the monk Taixu 太虛 (1890–1947), was also a student of Yang Wenhui's.[32] Taixu had begun a rather typical clerical career, ordained at age fourteen and trained in meditation with charismatic abbots. He became a self-described "revolutionary monk" around 1908 after reading works by Kang Youwei, Liang Qichao, and other political thinkers, and decided to save Chinese society through social reform and Buddhism. Taixu was en-

---

28. Goldfuss, *Vers un bouddhisme*; Zhang Hua, *Yang Wenhui*.

29. Charter and letter to President Sun Yat-sen in *Foxue congbao* 2 (1912).

30. The charter of the association was published in *Foxue congbao* 1 (1912), and *Zhonghua minguo shi dang'an ziliao huibian*, 705–14.

31. On the history of Buddhist associations, see Welch, *The Buddhist Revival in China*, 23–50; and Chen Bing & Deng Zimei, *Ershi shiji Zhongguo fojiao*, 29–74.

32. Pittman, *Toward a Modern Chinese Buddhism*.

gaged both in revolutionary activism in Shanghai, and in plans to radically reform the Buddhist clergy through a complete overhaul of clerical training and management of monastic property. In 1912, his rash attempt to revolutionize the traditional monasteries backfired, and he withdrew in a three-year meditational retreat, during which he read extensively.

When he came out of his isolation, Taixu remained an activist and political leader, but with more charisma and a solid text-based foundation on which to lay plans for religious reform. Until his death in 1947, Taixu established countless associations, institutes, and seminars; curried favor with Nationalist politicians; traveled all over China and the world; and published books and tracts laying out ambitious ideas for reform. His grandiose plans and his directorship of hundreds of paper associations earned him some derision, and he never became the recognized leader of a major faction of the Chinese Buddhist world. Among common Chinese and the ordinary clerics, his prestige did not match that of charismatic abbots and meditation masters, such as Chan masters Yuanying 圓瑛 (1878–1953) or Xuyun 虛雲 (1840?–1959), or the musician turned monk Hongyi 弘一 (1880–1942).[33] Taixu's influence was nonetheless widespread among lay intellectuals and kept growing after his death. By the early twenty-first century, he had become an icon to which all major Buddhist leaders trace their teachings and practices.

Taixu's vision for a reformed Buddhism and religious citizenship bore many parallels with liberal Protestant thinking, which is why he so fascinated Western Protestants in his lifetime and ever since. His vision of modern Buddhism was text-based, ethical, socially engaged, and "humanist." His most popular motto was to create a "humanistic Buddhism" (*renjian fojiao* 人間佛教), largely built as the antithesis of "funerary Buddhism," that is, Buddhism as a provider of liturgical services to the population. Taixu's focus on textual education, inherited from Yang Wenhui and shared with other lay intellectuals such as Ouyang Jian (Taixu also sometimes used the notion of "Buddhist studies" in place of "Buddhism"), was partly an answer to Christian criticism that Buddhists did not even know their canonical texts. This kind of development was not limited to China, as Christian perspectives stimulated a reorientation toward text-based religiosity throughout Asia.[34]

Another goal of Taixu-led Buddhist reformism was to build a global Buddhism in which the Chinese practice would merely be one ethnic or

33. On Hongyi, see Birnbaum, "The Deathbed Image."
34. See e.g. Lopez, *Curators of the Buddha*.

national branch. Taixu was an active promoter of links with Japanese, Tibetan, and South Asian Buddhists, not only to complete and enrich the scriptural legacy of Chinese Buddhism by gaining access to new texts, but also to strengthen the hand of Chinese Buddhists in their dealings with the Republican government. Similarly driven by a mixture of textual and political motivations, lay and clerical Buddhists alike during the 1920s and 1930s developed a very keen interest in esoteric Buddhism, particularly in its Tibetan form, inviting Tibetan masters to the Chinese cities to grant initiations and perform large-scale "nation-saving" rituals.[35] Although such unprecedented transcultural Buddhist encounters could be used to political ends (such as Nationalist attempts to recover sovereignty over Tibet), they were seen by most believers as enhancing their practice as part of a world religion on a par with Christianity and Islam. Self-avowed Buddhist members of the Nationalist government, such as Dai Jitao 戴季陶 (1891–1949), favored all these trends, including Buddhist reform, its globalization, and its use to political ends. So to a certain extent did the vibrant world of lay Buddhists in the largest cities that included many of the prominent artists of the time, such as the famed painter and cartoonist Feng Zikai 豐子愷 (1898–1975).[36]

The story of Buddhist reinvention does not stop at Taixu, for the more conservative monastic leaders opposed to his radicalism did not merely aim to stick with nineteenth-century practices. Far from it: they too adopted a Christian model. As early as 1912, the charter of the General Buddhist Association of China (Shanghai) emphasized the diffusion of Buddhism. It envisioned the founding of schools—thereby institutionalizing various local initiatives toward Buddhist schools since the early 1900s—but also confessional universities. It also planned for the establishment of a corps of missionaries who would be sent to work in the military, in prisons, in hospitals, and abroad; and presses and journals, research institutes, and various welfare programs.

At the same time, the association granted itself the authority to control the behavior of its members (in particular monks and nuns) and the power to prevent a master from taking a disciple who would not be fit for a clerical career. Historians of modern Chinese Buddhism have emphasized the revolutionary aspects of the associations set up by Taixu, Ouyang Jian, and other reformers who ambitioned to gain control of religious landholdings and other resources, which were traditionally managed in complete au-

---

35. Tuttle, *Tibetan Buddhists*; and Jagou, *Le 9e Panchen Lama*.
36. Tarocco, *The Cultural Practices*.

tonomy by each monastery or temple. Yet the innovations, notably those regarding the control over clerics and centralized discipline, brought up at least on paper by the more "conservative" and "consensual" General Buddhist Association of China (Shanghai) are quite remarkable. They suggest the extent to which, in the context of the Republican period, even conservative leaders envisioned a radical and far-reaching reinvention of the way their religion worked.

The implications of the Buddhist reforms came to the fore during the Sino-Japanese War in the 1930s and 1940s, when monks were faced with a conflict between Buddhist discipline, which preached nonviolence, and loyalty to the nation, which implied supporting or participating in armed resistance against Japan. Many young reformist monks consciously reinterpreted Buddhist teachings to justify "compassionate warfare," took part in the relief operations of "sangha [monastic community] rescue teams," or even, as in the case of the communist monk Juzan 巨贊 (1908–1984), organized monks into guerilla units which attacked Japanese troops. These experiences, by forcing many monks into direct social engagement, contributed to a greater acceptance of Taixu's reforms among Buddhists.[37]

Reinventing Taoism, Confucianism, and Islam

Buddhists led the way in adapting the Christian model and attempting to create an alternative model religion for Republican China. Buddhist reformism has been both more successful (in terms of numbers of participants and actual achievements) and more widely reported in scholarship than its Taoist or Confucian counterparts, but it should be considered as part of a larger phenomenon. The Christian-secular normative model transformed the whole religious field through state incentive, intellectual prestige, and institutional developments. We now turn to its effect on the other established traditions: Taoism, Confucianism, and Islam.

Taoism. The Taoists followed the Buddhist example in trying to build up an organization capable of acting on the political stage, and also in exhibiting their divisions, although along different lines. They mostly split between the two major clerical orders, the monastic Quanzhen 全真 order and the Zhengyi 正一 order of priests under the liturgical authority of the Zhang Heavenly Master 張天師. The first national organization, named Taoist Association (Daojiaohui 道教會), was formed in March 1912 at the initia-

---

37. Xue Yu, *Buddhism, War, and Nationalism.*

tive of Chen Mingbin 陳明霦 (1854–1936), the abbot of the Baiyunguan 白雲觀, a very prestigious Quanzhen monastery in Beijing.[38] It published a manifesto as well as an open letter to the parliament, and on April 8, 1912, it obtained government approval and recognition.[39] This association clearly aimed to entrust the future of Taoism to the small group of abbots at the major Quanzhen monasteries in northern China. The manifesto insisted on Taoism being the most ancient indigenous religion of China, and thus best placed to become the national religion, *guojiao*. On the other hand, and in order to conform to the new notion of "religion," it claimed to be universal and planned for branches to be set up in every country. It offered a political vision of Taoism as the moral and spiritual arm of the Chinese state, and criticized those who only saw Taoism as an individual pursuit of transcendence. According to the manifesto's authors, only by co-opting the indigenous Taoist religion could the Republic gain the support of the people and expect compliance with its laws. Laozi, they wrote, had already, over two thousand years earlier, set out a blueprint for democracy and freedom, nationalism and social progress. Practically, the association proposed to organize the study of inner alchemy (*neidan* 內丹) and Quanzhen discipline for clerics, and the management of charity and morality programs for the laity. Its organization, laid out in great detail on paper, was very hierarchical, with the Baiyunguan abbot as ex-officio president. Membership was open to clerics and "believers"; the association's charter made it an obligation for all members to congregate on Sundays for joining a Taoist service.[40]

This document is a surprising and sometimes uneasy mixture of three different concerns: the ambition of Quanzhen dignitaries to become effective leaders of Taoism as a whole, in which they saw themselves as the natural elite; a hurried reaction to pressing political needs (getting Taoism recognized and protected by the new regime, which, as we saw, was not self-evident at all); and an awkward attempt to recast Taoism as a church with a national hierarchy, Sunday services, an organized laity, and other Christian-style features. It is not clear to what extent this attempt to reinvent Taoism was just a ploy to help gain government recognition as a "religion" or whether the abbots really meant to introduce Sunday prayers and other features of a church organization. To be sure, Sunday prayers and hierarchical congregations were never implemented.

38. Qing Xitai, ed., *Zhongguo daojiao shi*, 4:291. On Chen Mingbin and the Baiyunguan, see Goossaert, *The Taoists of Peking*, 75, 175–77.

39. *Daojiaohui bugao*.

40. Ibid., "Daojiaohui dagang 道教會大綱," 10.

The actual working of the Taoist Association (Beijing) is not known, and it is likely that it went dormant until times of urgency, when it mobilized its political friends and networks of support. However, branches were created in various provinces, notably Sichuan, where they seem to have been active throughout the Republican period.[41] In a few places, such as Nanyang (southern Henan), Quanzhen leaders not only managed their local branch of the Taoist Association but worked actively to participate in local reforms, setting up schools, vocational training programs, and collective farms.[42] Nonetheless, the Beijing-based Taoist Association, dominated by Quanzhen leaders, did not meet with universal approval among Taoists, and immediately after its foundation a rival association, the General Taoist Association of the Republic of China (Zhonghua minguo daojiao zonghui 中華民國道教總會), was established in Shanghai by the Sixty-second Heavenly Master, Zhang Yuanxu 張元旭 (?–1924, Heavenly Master in 1904).[43] This association, however, failed to develop outside the Shanghai area.[44]

Whereas among the Buddhist, Confucian, and Muslim leaders there were earnest, zealous reformers who conducted real (albeit limited) experiments in changing their communities' practices and implementing a reinvention of religion, there was no such figure among the Taoist leadership, who remained clerics invested with traditional modes of authority. This was not due to a general backward-looking attitude among early twentieth-century Taoists, far from it; various Taoist masters emerged who engaged with the modern media in order to create new networks and institutions for the transmission of their practice.[45] For instance, Chen Yingning 陳櫻寧 (1880–1969),[46] a married doctor self-trained in Taoist spirituality, established seminaries and journals in Shanghai during the 1930s (on which, more in chapter 4). Although much less assertive and aggressive than Buddhist radical reformers like Taixu, Chen Yingning did share some ideas with the famed leader. Chen and Taixu both developed a vision of a scientific religion, rid of its liturgical tradition, concentrating on systematic self-cultivation made available to the masses through a unified curriculum. Chen drew up plans for a modern, nonsuperstitious, and nationalist Taoism, with a larger role for laypersons. But before the 1940s

41. Qing Xitai, ed., *Zhongguo daojiao shi*, 4:430–33.
42. Liu Xun, "Quanzhen Proliferates Learning."
43. On the Zhang Heavenly Master, see Goossaert, "Bureaucratic Charisma."
44. Chen Yaoting, "Shanghai daojiao shi," 428–34; Qing Xitai, ed., *Zhongguo daojiao shi*, 4:426–44.
45. Goossaert, *The Taoists of Peking*, chap. 7.
46. Liu Xun, *Daoist Modern*.

neither Chen nor the other new Taoist masters were interested in using the medium of the national association to further their project and vision. It is only after the end of World War II that Chen Yingning became really involved with the Taoist associations, and his ideas of a Taoist citizenship made large inroads. Thus, the Taoist trajectory in following the Christian model followed the Buddhist experience, but with more resistance, and much less zeal.

Confucianism. Reinventing Confucianism proved even more difficult than reinventing Buddhism and Taoism. In 1912, Confucianism had just lost its status as the official doctrine of the defunct imperial regime. Confucians did not necessarily reflect on this change with nostalgia, as it offered the possibility of renewal. Since the last decades of the imperial period, some reformers had been thinking that the strength and cohesiveness of Western countries were due to their (supposedly) having a single national religion. During the 1890s, Kang Youwei had formulated a project of a national religion based on a hybridization of Confucianism and Christianity. He envisioned the transformation of all Chinese temples into Confucius temples operating as the centers of parishes where the local population would gather every Sunday to hear Confucian pastors read Confucian scriptures and preach. Although Kang's extreme views and personality repelled most of his contemporaries, many of his ideas were widely shared by intellectual and political leaders. In particular, the movement to "protect Confucianism" (*baojiao* 保教) by adopting the enemy's own weapons in the face of Christian adversity met with a large success. Quite a few of Kang's contemporaries, including some of his declared opponents, developed projects similar to his, aimed at transforming Confucianism along the Christian model by adopting proselytizing, missionary activity, and social engagement.

As Chen Hsi-yuan has shown, this widespread but informal intellectual movement organized and institutionalized itself in 1912.[47] A number of self-declared Confucians, many of whom were direct or indirect disciples of Kang Youwei, established Confucian associations with the aim of having Confucianism declared as the national religion. The most influential of these associations, with over 130 local branches, was the Confucian Association (Kongjiaohui), established in October 1912 and presided by Chen Huanzhang 陳焕章 (1881–1933).

Like its Buddhist and Taoist counterparts, the Confucian Association's

---

47. Chen Hsi-yuan, "Confucianism Encounters Religion."

project failed, at least as far as its immediate explicit aims were concerned, since after several public debates in parliament, the proposal for instituting Confucianism as the national religion was voted down. Notwithstanding this failure, the Confucian Association deserves as much attention as the other national religious associations, with whom it shares some common features. Just like the Buddhist and Taoist associations, it developed a project of religious reform and reinvention. Chen Huanzhang and the other leaders of the Kongjiaohui set out to radically reinvent Confucianism, notably by making the cult of Confucius universal in every Chinese home and village (until 1911 it had been the privilege of the gentry) and, in the same movement, by totally suppressing the cult of all the other Confucian saints (such as Guandi, Wenchang, and so on). The association launched a confessional journal 孔教會雜誌 and institutionalized a Confucian proselytizing program (Chen himself preached on Sundays in New York's Chinatown when he was a student at Columbia in 1905–11). Through an audacious reading of the classics, Chen Huanzhang justified the seven-day week and Sunday worship, and strove to prove that Confucianism is a religion: like Christianity, it had ceremonial vestments, a canon, rules, a liturgy, a theology featuring a single god and the immortality of the soul, a doctrine on retribution, schools, temples, and holy sites.[48]

The failure of the Confucian religion project in Republican China was due more to the political context than to inherent defects; the promoters of Confucianism would find other outlets for the dissemination of their values and ideals. In the next chapter, we will discuss how in Mainland China much of the Confucian movement merged into the larger galaxy of redemptive societies. The recognition of Confucianism as a religion did meet with some success in the newly independent nations of Southeast Asia, notably Indonesia, and later Hong Kong, as described in chapters 8 and 12. And in chapter 7, we will consider how Confucianism became an element of inspiration for modern state-sponsored civilizing and social reform projects such as the New Life movement.

Muslim associations. In late imperial China, Islam had a rather particular place as an officially recognized religion (in spite of occasional bouts of intolerance by officials) but without any official organization of control. In 1912 the Chinese-speaking Muslims (Hui 回) established several associations, the largest and most influential of which was the Chinese Muslim Association for Progress (Zhongguo Huijiao jujinhui 中國回教俱進會),

---

48. Zufferey, "Chen Huanzhang."

established in Beijing in July 1912[49] by Muslim officials and reformist *ahong* (imams) employed in various Beijing mosques and exposed to the Middle East in their travels. The association's aims, as detailed in its charter, included the publication of journals and translations into Chinese of Muslim texts, the foundation of schools and vocational training programs, the completion of surveys on the social conditions of the Hui, and the promotion of frugality, hygiene, and nationalism. The case of the Muslim Association for Progress is in a way distinctive, as it combined the reinvention of religion with the inscription of the Hui into the ethnic category (*zu* 族), actively upholding, in the face of opposition,[50] Sun Yat-sen's idea of China being made up of five constituent nationalities. On the other hand, many of its aims and tools (for example journals, schools, research) bear comparison with those of the Buddhist, Taoist, and Confucian associations.

The nationalist commitment of the founders and later institutional leaders of the Muslim Association for Progress proved to be a strong influence over Chinese Islam. The most influential Muslim leader of the Republican period, Ma Wanfu 馬萬福 (1853–1934), studied in Arabia between 1888 and 1892, and on his return decided to introduce to China a text-based reformed Islam opposed to particularistic and localist Sufi affiliations. His disciples advocated uniting the divided Muslim Chinese community, and—after one of Ma's disciples, Hu Songshan 虎嵩山 (1880–1956), had felt humiliated as a Chinese during the Mecca pilgrimage—contributing thereby to the building of a strong Chinese state. Such goals were fully supported by Muslim militarists and officials who had joined the KMT government, such as Ma Fuxiang 馬福祥 (1876–1932),[51] one of three Muslim warlords of the northwest mentioned in chapter 2.

The introduction of reformist ideas—which coalesced into the Ikhwan movement, directly inspired by the Muslim Brotherhood and today dominant in institutional Chinese Islam—was intimately linked to nationalist ideas, and both concurred in the invention of a Muslim citizen. Although here the normative model was inspired not by Christianity but by developments in the Middle East (themselves originally triggered by Western colonial secular ideals), just as in the cases of Buddhism, Taoism, and Confucianism, we observe a situation where religious leaders combined religious reform and nationalist engagement with state building.

49. Zhang Juling, "Zhongguo huijiao jujinhui"; Aubin, "Islam on the Wings of Nationalism." On other Muslim associations, see Ding Hong & Zhang Guojie, eds., *Bai nian Zhongguo musilin*, 23–28.

50. Ding Hong & Zhang Guojie, eds., *Bai nian Zhongguo musilin*, 53.

51. Lipman, *Familiar Strangers*, chap. 5.

CONCLUSION

A leading intellectual, writing in the 1950s, saw the reform movements as the only living parts of Chinese religion.[52] This shows the extent to which reformists dominated the discourse on religion during that period. But close examination of the historical evidence shows that there was much resistance to these projects, which were not easily accepted by the grass roots, especially as far as their centralization and unification projects were concerned. Thus, the religious associations have, from 1912 to this day, faced many failures and difficulties, such as certain clerics refusing to join, heated debates about who is qualified to join, competition between rival associations, and of course tense negotiations between religious institutional leaders and local state agents. For instance, the married Taoists in Guangzhou (the huge majority of Taoists there, as in most places) during the 1930s offer a fascinating case of such bitter division: when the local government twice attempted to ban them as not religious but mere "superstitious" workers, the local Taoist association (managed by celibate, monastic Taoists) offered no support, and they had to create their own ad-hoc association to unite and petition the government, explaining that they were real Taoists.[53]

The adoption of the Christian-secular normative model was nonetheless very creative and, beyond the aping of Sunday prayers, managed to foster truly innovative ways of thinking through religions' place in a modern state. There was no Chinese equivalent of the religious nationalism that flourished in Japan, where some movements, among both established Buddhist orders and new religions, actively promoted the expansionist and militarist agenda of the imperial regime. However, some sections of the religious milieu did engage intimately with the nationalist project in China, not only for the sake of state recognition but out of the conviction that there was a religious aspect of Chinese modernity. Such reinvention of religion along the lines of nationalism, antisuperstition, and citizenship was a widespread phenomenon that could be seen through much of the religious landscape, from established institutions such as Christianity, Buddhism, Confucianism, Taoism, and Islam to the new religious groups and neotraditionalist movements discussed in the next chapter.

52. Chan Wing-Tsit, *Religious Trends*. Chan was to become a leading authority on Confucianism. In his book, however, he dismissed the Kongjiaohui movement and ignored Taoist modernism.
53. Lai Chi-tim, "Minguo shiqi Guangzhou shi 'Namo daoguan.'"

Cultural Revitalization

Redemptive Societies and Secularized Traditions

肆

The reinvention of Chinese tradition in response to modern ideologies and institutional forms was a process that spanned a wide range of practices and beliefs, all of which had to be positioned within the new religion-science-superstition triangle. In the previous chapter, we have seen how Buddhists, Taoists, Confucians, and Chinese Muslims attempted, with varying degrees of success, to recast their traditions as modern-style "religions." These groups, however, represented only the tip of the iceberg of Chinese culture. Many others also arose to actively engage with the challenges of modernity, but either did not accept, or could not fit into, the new category of religion. Instead, they proposed alternative forms of spiritual universalism or advocated the path of secularizing tradition. These projects found expression in a wave of salvationist congregations—the redemptive societies—and in movements to modernize Chinese body cultivation and healing traditions: meditation, martial arts, and medicine. We will be dealing in this chapter with a broad spectrum of movements, which often overlapped with one another: indeed, while each generated its own sets of texts and discourses, it was often the same people who circulated among them, forming a loosely bounded, neotraditionalist network of people who hoped to restore Chinese culture in the face of an onslaught of modern and foreign values. Although their responses to the category of religion varied greatly, most of them willingly appropriated the category of science—either trying to align themselves with its standards or claiming that Chinese tradition was already compatible with, or even superior to, Western science. In all cases, the goal was to resist radical modernizers' campaigns to cast all of Chinese tradition into the trash heap of superstition, and to reconstruct Chinese tradition in such a manner that it could find a respectable, and perhaps even leading, position in the emergence of a global modernity.

Almost all these movements emerged during the Beiyang regime, in the first fifteen years of the Chinese Republic—a brief period of intense cultural effervescence that, besides the well-known New Culture intellectual movement, witnessed a bewildering variety of creative attempts to reinvent Chinese tradition in response to modernity. This occurred against the backdrop of the brutality of World War I and the humiliating Treaty of Versailles,[1] which, for many, strongly dampened the attraction of the Western model of civilization. The ideological flux and the absence of a central state authority opened up a space of freedom, and a moral and spiritual vacuum, in which all manner of religious and cultural experiments could flourish. After the defeat of the northern warlords in 1927, however, the more assertive and centralizing KMT regime based in Nanjing played a more interventionist role in the evolution of the revivalist movements, banning the largest redemptive societies, while the martial arts and Chinese medicine were pressured to conform to KMT ideologies and projects of nation building. During the Sino-Japanese War from 1937 to 1945, and in the ensuing civil war from 1945 to 1949, a new wave of redemptive societies was the target of infiltration and cooptation policies by Japanese, KMT, and CCP alike. Once the People's Republic was established in 1949, however, the redemptive societies were ruthlessly exterminated, while secularized medicine, martial arts, and body cultivation techniques placed under the new category of qigong were fully integrated into the new state. These would flourish to an unprecedented degree, in a wave that reached its first climax during the Great Leap Forward (1958–60).

1. The treaty gave the German concessions and rights in China to another colonial power, Japan—not back to China, as the Chinese expected (as allies).

THE REDEMPTIVE SOCIETIES

In the confused political atmosphere of the early Republic, a wave of religious groups and spirit-writing societies which, under the Qing, would have been banned as "White Lotus" or "heterodox" sects emerged from obscurity or formed themselves anew, openly expanding and even dominating the religious landscape in some cities and regions. Shortly after the first generation of religious associations was born in 1912, several of these groups also founded national modern-style associations that registered with the state as religious, philanthropic, or public interest associations. Each featured a head office, a national organization with provincial and municipal branches, and a doctrine that attempted to modernize the traditional notion of the union of the Three Teachings with the aid of a more modern, academic language and by incorporating Christianity and Islam into the traditional Union of the Three Teachings. Each revered the founders of the Five Teachings (Laozi, Confucius, Buddha, Jesus, and Muhammad), and held rituals to avert the world apocalypse of the end of the Three Kalpas (三期末劫). The largest and most sophisticated of these associations, which registered with the government during the Beiyang regime, included the Teaching of the Abiding Principle (Zailijiao 在理教), incorporated in 1913 as the All-China Association for Promoting Abstention from Opium and Alcohol; followed by the Moral Studies Society (Daode xueshe 道德學社) in 1916, the Fellowship of Goodness (Tongshanshe 同善社) in 1917, the Wanguo daodehui (Worldwide Ethical Society) and the Daoyuan 道院 (School of the Tao) in 1921, and the Jiushi xinjiao 救世新教 (New Religion to Save the World) in 1925, among others.[2]

In spite of the size of their followings and the many remarks on their importance by contemporary observers of Chinese society and religion,[3] these associations were largely ignored by historians of modern China—until the late 1990s, when scholars rediscovered them and Prasenjit Duara coined the term *redemptive societies*[4] to draw attention to their common project of saving both individuals and the world as a whole. This new classification has proved more useful than categories such as heterodoxies or

2. Shao Yong, *Zhongguo huidaomen*, 165–94.
3. See e.g. Rawlinson, *Revolution and Religion*.
4. Duara, *Sovereignty and Authenticity*, 89–129; also Shao Yong, *Zhongguo huidaomen*; Tan Songlin, ed., *Zhongguo mimi shehui*, vol. 7.

sectarian teachings, which have obscured these groups' pivotal role in modern Chinese religious history.[5]

The redemptive societies often had their own scriptures, philosophical systems, liturgies (simplified from Confucian, Buddhist, and Taoist sources), congregational modes of participation, and hierarchical national organizations. As such, they actually conformed as much if not more to the model of the Christian church that had become the new paradigm of religion in China, than the Buddhist, Taoist, or Confucian institutions. It is not surprising, then, that several of them obtained the status of religious associations in the first years of the Republic, and were rarely targeted in the polemics against superstition before the Nanjing decade.

The variety of these groups was bewildering, and it is difficult to categorize them: they ranged from local spirit-writing cults presenting little difference from traditional temple cults to integrated nationwide organizations claiming to be full-fledged religions.[6] The general configuration in the early twentieth century was the result of several waves of groups appearing in rapid succession and combining, in a radically new sociopolitical context, several forms of religiosity that had until then remained relatively distinct: (1) modern Confucian associations, (2) literati spirit-writing groups, and (3) lay salvationist groups which practiced, in varying combinations, meditation and inner alchemy, sutra recitation, vegetarianism, and millenarian proselytism. These three strands were completely merged in several of the redemptive societies, which were able to attain a degree of centralization and rapid geographic spread perhaps never seen in earlier types of lay salvationist movements.

The role of the Confucian associations and of the old-style, Confucian-educated literati in this configuration was the result of the tectonic collapse of Confucianism and its Mandarinate—the gentry—with the end of the empire. We have seen in the previous chapter how, following the abolition of the state cults and of the traditional examination system, several associations were formed that advocated the designation of Confucianism as the state religion of the new Republic. With the failure of this campaign, the Confucian associations became religious or philosophical societies like any other, detached from official orthodoxy and obliged to compete in the religious milieu like any other group by providing a broader range of spiritual services, blurring the distinction between them and lay salvationist

---

5. Bosco, "Yiguan Dao"; Ownby, "Sect and Secularism"; Palmer, "Heretical Doctrines" and "Chinese Redemptive Societies."

6. Jordan & Overmyer, *The Flying Phoenix*, documents such a variety for post-1949 Taiwan.

groups—evolving in the process from a yearning for a national religion to a universalist ideal of a world religion. At the same time, the abrupt end of the imperial system and its Confucian ritual and culture had left about 5 million[7] traditionally educated literati (as per ca. 1900), who were of an earlier generation than the younger graduates of the modern-style and overseas schools, suddenly bereft of a ritual and organizational outlet for their values and identity. This role was largely taken over by the redemptive societies, which aimed to transmit the classical scriptural legacy and traditional morality, but within a social organization adapted to new, Western-inspired models of a "religion"—with a church hierarchy, Sunday prayers and choirs, missions, journals, and even baptism in some cases. One example was the Heart-Cleansing Society (Xixinshe 洗心社), which literally carried out Kang Youwei's project of a Confucian church in the cities and large towns of Shanxi, with the support of the provincial governor. The society met every Sunday in local Confucius temples or public halls. Sermons by local notables and occasionally Christians were assorted with the burning of incense before a tablet of Confucius and ceremonial bows by the audience.[8]

Groups such as the Wanguo daodehui and the Daode xueshe maintained a strong Confucian identity, to which they added, however, a universalist tendency, honoring the founders of all major religions and advocating the realization, on a global scale, of the "Great Commonwealth" (datong 大同) dreamed of in the Book of Rites and elaborated on in the utopian mode by Kang Youwei and others (see chapter 7). These groups hoped to represent religious modernity in its universal dimension in opposition to the local cults they sometimes condemned in print as "superstition," even though we are not aware of any case of their active participation in repression. Many articulated spirit writing with science, and indeed, some prominent antisuperstition campaigners were members. Kang Youwei himself, who had launched the modern antisuperstition movement in 1898, was president of the Wanguo daodehui in the last year of his life, from 1926 to 1927. This society was first established in Ji'nan (Shandong) by Jiang Shoufeng 江壽峰 (1875–1926), who had been deeply involved in the Kongjiaohui movement, sending frequent petitions to various government departments calling for the establishment of Confucianism as the national religion and for the compulsory teaching of the classics in all schools. He even advocated the reinstatement of the official imperial titles of the Heavenly Mas-

7. Johnson, "Communication, Class, and Consciousness," 58–59.
8. Rawlinson, Revolution and Religion, 39–40.

ter of the Taoist Zhengyi order. His support for other religions marginalized him among the hard-line Confucians, but he gained an audience after his son, Jiang Xizhang 江希張 (1907–?), was found to be a child prodigy, able to write commentaries on the classics before the age of ten. He also wrote a pacifist tract that drew on the scriptures of the five main religions and called for the establishment of the Wanguo daodehui,[9] which father and son began to organize in 1916. They sent commentaries to scholars and political and military notables of the Beiyang regime, earning the enthusiastic support of some, and registered with the national government in 1921. Jiang Shoufeng argued that without a strong moral foundation, the nation's politics, law, and education could not flourish; and that the success of British, French, and Japanese colonialism rested on their policy of destroying the morality of the peoples they conquered.[10]

The society, which worshiped the founders of the Five Teachings, was officially inaugurated on the birthday of Confucius at Tai'an, Shandong, on September 28, 1921; its honorary presidents included the politician Wang Shizhen 王士珍; the governor and military commander of Shanxi, Yan Xishan 閻錫山; and American missionary Gilbert Reid 李佳白,[11] while the boy head of the lineage of the descendants of Confucius, Kong Decheng 孔德成 (b. 1920, seventy-seventh-generation heir of Confucius), was appointed honorary chairman. Over the next few years, branches of the society were established in several large cities, especially in northern and northeastern China; Jiang Xizhang was invited on several lecture tours; and a magazine, the *Morality Daily* 道德日報, was launched.

The organization underwent a significant shift in the years 1926–28, after Jiang Shoufeng passed away in 1926 and Kang Youwei, ill and dying, withdrew from active participation; Jiang Xizhang moved abroad, first studying at the University of Paris, then promoting Confucianism in Europe and Indonesia. Manchurian capitalist and philanthropist Du Yannian 杜延年 (1878–1957) of Heilongjiang assumed the leadership of the society. He recruited the charismatic Manchurian healer and educational activist Wang Fengyi 王鳳儀 (1864–1937), a self-taught ox herder and laborer who, at the age of thirty, had begun to preach traditional morality and to heal based on a method derived from Chinese cosmology, the "theory of spiritual nature and bodily life" (*xingming xueshuo* 性命學說). He started a movement to educate rural girls, the Voluntary Schooling 義學 movement,

9. Lu Zhongwei, *Minguo huidaomen*, 131.
10. Xia Mingyu, "Minguo xinxing zongjiao jieshe," 8–13.
11. On Gilbert Reid, see Tsou Mingteh, "Christian Missionary as Confucian Intellectual."

which by 1925 had established 270 girls' schools in the three provinces of the northeast. After the merger with the Wanguo daodehui, each of these schools became a branch of the Worldwide Ethical Society. By 1933, the society had 500 branches, 400 girls' schools, and 200,000 students. By then most of its activities were located in Manchuria.[12]

A popular form of religiosity among late Qing literati was spirit writing, in which worshippers sought practical aid and advice from the gods through the planchette. It had long been practiced by lay Taoist adepts seeking advice from the Immortals on alchemical cultivation, and had become an ever more widespread activity among the gentry throughout the Qing dynasty. The gods' exhortations also elaborated on broader themes of traditional morality—spirit writing indeed became the main source for the genre of morality books—and by the end of the nineteenth century drew on increasingly eclectic cultural sources. It then became common for the founders of all five major religions—Laozi, Confucius, Buddha, Jesus, and Muhammad—and even Tolstoy or George Washington—to make revelations during séances, and for gods to order their followers to establish new, universalistic religions. One example was the Society for Awakening to Goodness (Wushanshe 悟善社), founded in Beijing in 1919, with branches in all major Chinese cities. Active in charity and spirit writing, the Wushanshe evolved into a more public, explicitly religious form when it renamed itself Jiushi xinjiao, "New Religion to Save the World," in 1924.[13] This was a conscious attempt to construct a full-fledged religion, all elements of which were composed through spirit writing: a clear, standardized organizational structure, laws, teachings, and scriptures. It counted many members of the Beiyang elites and warlords among its members and leaders, notably Wu Peifu 吳佩孚 (1874–1939) and Jiang Chaozong 江朝宗 (1863–1943), Beijing mayor and collaborator during the Japanese occupation who had been one of the most active patrons of the Baiyunguan, the major Taoist monastery in Beijing, during the 1910s and 1920s—this is being one of many cases of close connections between Taoist circles and redemptive societies. It was a highly apocalyptic movement. Beginning in August 1922, it massively distributed tracts predicting a series of apocalyptic calamities on September 25, 1923, which caused a panic in some quarters.[14]

Another type of redemptive society descended directly from the lay sal-

---

12. On Wang Fengyi, see Song Guangyu, "Wang Fengyi."

13. Sakai Tadao, "Minguo chuqi," 7, 10–22.

14. Rawlinson, *Revolution and Religion*, 68–82; see also Wang Jianchuan, "Shijie zongjiao datonghui."

vationist groups of the Qing. One example is the Zailijiao, also known as Li-men 理門 or Lijiao 理教, which probably originated from other salvation-ist movements in the North China Plain during the seventeenth century. It proselytized by running charities and campaigning for total abstinence from alcohol, tobacco, and opium, and offering cures for addicts. On this account, as early as the last decade of the nineteenth century it had se-cured the respect of officials who were themselves fighting against opium addiction. In 1891, Zailijiao lodges in Rehe (Jehol), together with other salvationist groups, led a popular uprising against the Qing authorities, in a context of popular Han discontent with the privileges of the Mongol land-holding nobility and Roman Catholic extraterritoriality. Although the up-rising was crushed, the tensions festered and merged with the Boxer move-ment at the turn of the century. Yet in Republican-period cities, Zailijiao openly operated large numbers of lodges and Zailijiao leaders took over some temples (probably those in disrepair and/or without any manager or local leader), where they taught. The society was massively present in Tianjin, where it had originated, and was well entrenched in all parts of northern and central China.[15]

The lodges were managed by resident elders (*dangjia* 當家), who formed a clergy of sorts. Indeed, they served a very similar role to that of temple clerics, counseling local residents on ethics, devotion, and practical mat-ters, and arbitrating conflicts between community members. They gave talks on Zailijiao doctrine and ethics, and organized regular worship as-semblies. These elders pursued a rather intense self-cultivation regimen, and some were considered saints.[16] According to extant photographs, they tried hard to look like Quanzhen Taoists, with long beards, blue gowns, and a gourd permanently in hand.[17]

The most influential and enduring matrix for redemptive societies was the Way of Anterior Heaven (Xiantiandao 先天道) congregations, which had existed since the early eighteenth century. This tradition combined lay Taoist practices of inner alchemy (a tradition of highly speculative medita-tion aiming at forging a transcendent self with one's innate resources) with the cult of the Unborn Mother, also known as Golden Mother of the Jasper Pond (Yaochi jinmu 瑤池金母). Its doctrines, which had their roots in

---

15. Naquin, *Peking*, 597, 665; DuBois, *The Sacred Village*, chap. 5.

16. Li Shiyu, "Tianjin Zailijiao"; see also Jiang Zhushan, "1930 niandai Tianjin Duliu zhen shang-ren de zongjiao," on a township near Tianjin where all merchants belonged to the Zailijiao.

17. Li Shiyu, "Tianjin Zailijiao," 179, 181.

older millenarian movements, included the unity of the Three Teachings; an elaborate genealogy of spiritual masters that linked Xiantiandao patriarchs, through a single line of descent, to ancient religious figures such as Bodhidharma, the Buddha, Confucius, Laozi, the Yellow Emperor 黃帝, Shennong, and Fu Xi (that latter three being Confucian archaic civilizational heroes); and a millenarian three-stage eschatology that predicted the imminent end of the second (or third) cosmic cycle or *kalpa*, to be followed by a new dispensation ushered in by Maitreya Buddha and his Dragon Flower Assembly 龍華會, where the elect will meet with him. Xiantiandao devotees adhered to Buddhist precepts and attempted as much as possible to follow the meritorious example of the idealized monk figure (often contrasted with the debauched image of real-life monks), in congregations that offered the possibility of progressing along a spiritual hierarchy of at least fifteen levels. The movement experienced great growth in the early nineteenth century, leading to its repression as the "Black Lotus sect" (Qinglianjiao 青蓮教) by the state, and several of its leaders being executed.

Bursts of evangelism were frequent within the Xiantiandao tradition. Active and entrepreneurial temples would send missionaries to other cities, where they would found affiliated halls linked in a loose network. The originators of such expansions were often considered the newest in the line of Patriarchs, and gave a new name to their teaching, with slight modifications to the scriptures and practices. The result of this pattern was that by the late nineteenth century, several overlapping networks of Xiantiandao-related congregations, some of which had networks of temples covering most Chinese cities, could be identified, each having a different name. These networks were loose: the temples were quite autonomous, and they would evolve in many directions during the twentieth century. While many, for example in Hong Kong, operated as local temples and increasingly asserted a Taoist identity, others modernized the expansionist, network-forming pattern, creating large-scale and better-integrated redemptive societies, such as, most notably, the Tongshanshe, which had a profound influence on other societies such as the Daoyuan, and Yiguandao 一貫道, a small Xiantiandao-related group before it expanded into the largest of the redemptive societies in the 1930s. Other Xiantiandao-related redemptive societies were the Guiyi daoyuan 皈依道院, the Guigendao 歸根道, and the Yixin tiandao longhua shengjiaohui 一心天道龍華聖教會. Several Xiantiandao halls federated and registered with the authorities in 1923 as the Association of the Sagely Way of China's Three Teachings (Zhongguo sanjiao shengdao zonghui 中國三教聖道總會). Groups such as the Tiande shengjiao and the Vietnamese Cao dai, discussed below, can also be linked to Xiantiandao antecedents.[18]

The Tongshanshe was one of the most widespread Xiantiandao-descended groups to appear during the Beiyang period. This society was founded at the beginning of the twentieth century by Peng Tairong 彭泰榮, styled Ruzun 彭汝尊 (1873–1950), in Sichuan as an outgrowth of Xiantiandao communities. It initially attracted a following among the gentry of central Sichuan, and was introduced to the Qing court in 1910. The Tongshanshe was officially established in Beijing in 1917, with the sponsorship of Premier Duan Qirui 段祺瑞 (1865–1936) and General Cao Kun 曹錕 (1862–1938, who became president of the Republic of China in 1923–24). The Ministry of the Interior sent a circular to all provincial, municipal, and county authorities ordering them to support and protect the establishment of Tongshanshe branches;[19] by the early 1920s, the society had a national organization and over 1 million members: a spectacular expansion.[20] In Sichuan, Hubei, Hunan, and Gansu, military leaders were appointed honorary presidents of the provincial Tongshanshe branches.

The society's activities included rituals, sitting meditation, and inner alchemy. Through the Xiantiandao tradition, the Tongshanshe developed for its adepts a method of self-cultivation directly inspired by orthodox Taoist *neidan*, and this method was widely disseminated.[21] In Beijing, the Tongshanshe ran a press, the Tianhuaguan 天華館, which published a series of self-cultivation books and morality books. The society also engaged in charitable works such as supporting funerals for common people, ran schools for traditional learning (*guoxue* 國學), and offered English and Esperanto classes.[22]

The Tongshanshe seems to have served as a model for the other largest redemptive society of the Beiyang period, the Daoyuan. This society had begun in 1916 in a Shandong town as an informal group of spirit-writing enthusiasts, mostly county military commanders and magistrates. A year later, the society moved to the provincial capital, Ji'nan, where many of its members had also joined the newly founded Tongshanshe; following

---

18. On Xiantiandao, see De Groot, *Sectarianism and Religious Persecution*, 1:176–96; Topley, "The Great Way of Former Heaven"; Yau, "Xianggang Xiantiandao."

19. Lu Zhongwei, *Minguo huidaomen*, 64. On the Tongshanshe, see Wang Jianchuan, "Tongshanshe zaoqi."

20. Sakai Tadao, "Minguo chuqi," 6.

21. Goossaert, "Daoists in the Modern Chinese Self-Cultivation Market."

22. Wang Jianchuan, "Tongshanshe zaoqi."

the latter society's organizational model and adopting its meditation technique, they formally established the Daoyuan in Ji'nan in 1921. The society then established itself in Beijing with the help of former premier Xiong Xiling 熊希齡 (1870–1937, premier 1913–14) and American missionary Gilbert Reid (who was also an honorary president of the Wanguo daodehui, as mentioned above).[23] It expanded nationally between 1922 and 1928, and established a nationwide charity organization, the Red Swastika Society 紅卍字會, modeled on the International Red Cross Society, which was presided by Xiong Xiling and which would become China's largest relief organization during the Sino-Japanese War. The Red Swastika ran disaster relief operations as well as schools and war hospitals, in which Chinese medicine as well as talismans and spirit-writing cures were provided.

The Daoyuan also set up a separate organizational structure managed by and for women, which oversaw their religious activity, schools, and child care, along with research, education, and mobilization around women's concerns.[24] These activities expressed a new discourse on women that, while affirming traditional virtues, valorized their role in public service.[25] Western missionaries were fascinated by this group, which counted prominent Christians among its members—such as Wang Zhengting 王正廷 (1882–1961), son of a Methodist minister and himself a lifelong Christian, ambassador to the United States, and Foreign Minister of the KMT government from 1928 to 1931—and accorded an equal place to Jesus and Christianity; when the missionaries visited, they received spirit-writing revelations from Jesus and earlier Jesuit missionaries.[26]

A Daoyuan relief mission was sent to Japan after an earthquake in 1923, leading to the founding of a branch there and deep ties with Japanese new religions, based on a strong resonance with similar universalist worldviews. The first president of the Daoyuan Japan branch was Deguchi Onisaburô 出口王仁三郎 (1871–1948), a cofounder of the Great Root Teachings (Ômoto 大本教); other Daoyuan members included Ueshiba Morihei 植芝盛平 (1883–1969), founder of the Aikidô martial arts school; Okada Mokichi 岡田茂吉 (1882–1955), founder in 1935 of the Church of World Messianity (Sekai Kyuseikô 世界救世教); Nakano Yonosuke 中野與之助

23. Lu Zhongwei, *Minguo huidaomen*, 109.

24. Duara, *Sovereignty and Authenticity*, 140. On the Daoyuan, see also DuBois, "The Salvation of Religion?" and three articles by Song Guangyu in *Song Guangyu zongjiao wenhua lunwenji*, 487–620.

25. Duara, *Sovereignty and Authenticity*, 155.

26. Young, "Sanctuary of the Tao."

(1887–1974), founder in 1949 of the Three and Five Teachings (Ananaikyô 三五教); Goi Masahisa 五井昌久 (1916–1980), founder of White Light (Byakko 白光; and the founders of offshoots of these groups.[27]

The development of redemptive societies was even more pronounced in Vietnam, where, due to a religious culture in basic continuity with China's, indigenous versions emerged, notably the Cao Dai movement, which became a permanent fixture in the religious landscape there. This group originated in the early 1920s when the supreme divinity, (Heavenly Emperor of the) Supreme Platform (Cao Dai 高臺),[28] revealed himself through spirit writing to Ngô Van Chiêu, a colonial employee posted near the Cambodian border. After several more revelations, the church was officially founded in 1926; within a few years, it had half a million followers, a figure that soon grew to several million, comprising over 10 percent of the population of South Vietnam. The society was resisted by the Buddhist and Catholic institutions and by the French authorities; during the Japanese occupation and the ensuing war of independence, it established its own army and directly governed a large part of the south. Suppressed from 1955 onward by successive governments of Vietnam, it was legalized in 1997 and is now the country's third-largest religion.

Accounts of Cao Dai usually stress the colonial context of its emergence, in which the clash between modern and traditional culture led to a spiritual crisis conducive to the appearance and rapid growth of a new religion in which traditional divinities are worshipped along with French figures such as Joan of Arc and Victor Hugo. What has not been remarked on is how the Cao Dai religion arose from a distinctly *Chinese* religious culture, producing a movement that clearly falls into the same category as the Chinese redemptive societies. Indeed, it appeared in a context of spirit-writing groups of scholars, intellectuals, and petty colonial officials at around the same time as most of its Chinese counterparts. Like many Chinese lay salvationist groups, these groups propagated the doctrine of the Unity of the Three Teachings and millenarian expectations of Maitreya's arrival and of the Dragon Flower Assembly to be ruled by him. Born out of this religious culture, the core Cao Dai doctrines are essentially the same as those in the Xiantiandao-influenced redemptive societies: worship of the Golden Mother of the Jasper Pond as the supreme female deity; the universalist

27. Ibid., 4–5.
28. Abbreviation of 高臺天皇大菩薩摩訶薩, translation: "Heavenly Emperor of the Supreme Platform [and] Great Bodhisattva Mahasattva."

syncretism of the Three (or Five) teachings; and the three-phase eschatology, with the first dispensation associated with Moses and Fu Xi, the second associated with Buddha, Confucius, Laozi, Jesus, and Muhammad, and the third to be ushered in by Maitreya. The main difference with the Chinese groups was the organizational style, which drew its inspiration from the Roman Catholic Church, with its own Holy See and cathedrals and an ecclesiastical hierarchy of bishops, cardinals, and a pope. Revelations were often composed in French, and the original spirit-writing group was influenced by spiritism—attempts to communicate with the souls of the dead—which was popular in France and much of the West in the late nineteenth and early twentieth centuries.[29]

Connections between Chinese spirit writing and contemporary Western forms of spirit communication were also made by adepts in China—a process that began when Chinese students in Japan and the United Kingdom became acquainted with the new academic field of "psychical research" on paranormal phenomena, and set up dozens of associations in Shanghai and other large cities for "spiritual studies" (lingxue 靈學, a term borrowed from the Japanese translation of spiritualism) and hypnotism, which provided a scientific discourse that could be applied to Chinese spirit writing. For example, the Shanghai Spiritualism Society 上海靈學會, which owed much of its fame to its being ridiculed by Liang Qichao and the famous writer Lu Xun 魯迅 (1881–1936) in their polemical writings, mostly practiced spirit writing, but in a more modern, "scientific" setting than most groups of the kind: it presented itself as an academic society with membership fees and journals; provided correspondence courses which were publicized in popular magazines; and experimented with spirit photography, in which, following the logic of the X-ray, photographs of invisible gods and souls were produced.

Several of the redemptive societies also adopted lingxue discourses and displayed spirit photographs of their divinities. Enthusiastic supporters of lingxue included Yan Fu 嚴復 (1854–1921), considered the great master of Western studies, who had translated the works of Thomas Huxley, Adam Smith, and Herbert Spencer; the educational reformer Cai Yuanpei, who as Education Minister advocated replacing religion with aesthetics, but also translated a Japanese book on strange phenomena; Tao Chengzhang 陶成章 (1878–1912), an early revolutionary leader, cofounder with Cai Yuanpei of the China Recovery League (Guangfuhui 光復會, 1904), and member of Sun Yat-sen's Chinese Revolutionary Alliance (Tongmenghui

29. Jammes, "Le caodaïsme"; Hoskins, "From Kuan Yin to Joan of Arc."

同盟會, 1905); and Li Yuanhong 黎元洪 (1864–1928), twice president of China in 1916–17 and 1922–23.[30]

THE KMT AND REDEMPTIVE SOCIETIES

The KMT government, established in Nanjing in 1927, was much less favorably disposed toward these groups than the Beiyang regime. The largest redemptive societies, notably the Wushanshe, Tongshanshe, and Daoyuan, tainted by their close ties with the leaders of the deposed warlord regime, were almost immediately banned as "superstitious organizations" (*mixin jiguan* 迷信機關),[31] accused of being tools of warlords and local gentry to increase their influence under the cover of religious and philanthropic activities,[32] and of spreading superstition and retarding progress.[33] Society leaders such as the Tongshanshe's Peng Ruzun were suspected of nurturing ambitions to crown themselves emperor and establish a new dynasty. The Daode xueshe was also banned in 1931.[34]

The effect of these bans was uneven. In most cases, they were not implemented, as the societies enjoyed the protection of regional and even national political and military leaders. The authorities gladly approved their charitable deeds. The Daoyuan continued to operate and even expand under the front of its charitable branch, the Red Swastika Society, which retained its legal status after a plea by Xiong Xiling.[35] The Tongshanshe took a low profile and is alleged to have begun actively planning a rebellion, holding a meeting of its leaders in Wuxi in 1929 to prepare for the advent of Maitreya (Peng Ruzun himself) as the new emperor and to make both religious and military preparations. These plots were foiled and some leaders arrested, but Peng Ruzun escaped to his home base in a rural Sichuan village. Attempts to ban Zailijiao by the KMT authorities in Shanghai and Jiangsu were countered with much lobbying with the provincial and central governments, leading to the registration in 1935 of the China National Lijiao Association (Zhonghua quanguo lijiaohui 中華全國理教會).[36]

And a new wave of groups such as Yiguandao and Tiande shengjiao 天德聖教 appeared and expanded in the 1930s. The latter group was founded

---

30. Huang Kewu, "Minguo chunian Shanghai de lingxue yanjiu."
31. Du Jingzhen, "Lüelun Daoyuan zaojin (1928) hou de dongxiang," 227.
32. Lin Benxuan, *Taiwan de zhengjiao chongtu*, 325.
33. Wang Jianchuan, "Tongshanshe zaoqi"; Nedostup, "Religion, Superstition," 90–102.
34. Sakai Tadao, "Minguo chuqi," 24.
35. Nedostup, "Religion, Superstition," 145–53.
36. Shao Yong, *Zhongguo huidaomen*, 285, 301.

by Xiao Changming 蕭昌明 (1895–1943), first as the Society for the Promotion of Religious Unity (Zongjiao datong zujinshe 宗教大同促進社) in Changsha in 1921; but it was as the Society for the Study of Religious Philosophy (Zongjiao zhexue yanjiushe 宗教哲學研究社), established in 1930 in Wuhan, that the group began its national expansion. It aimed to use a rational and "academic" approach to the religions of the world while promoting meditation classes and "spiritual healing" (*jingshen zhiliao* 精神治療), based on the emission of vital energy (*qi* 炁) to patients. Xiao's reputation seems to have spread among the elite of the KMT, key members of which facilitated the founding of chapters in most main Chinese cities. It was a religion that aspired to be modern: deity statues were replaced with a framed yellow cloth representing the invisible realm, contemplation of which was said to produce spirit communications. The distinctive features of religious practice included recitation and practice of the "twenty characters" (念甘字) revealed by Xiao Changming as representing the essential human virtues, and provision of spiritual healing to patients. The movement also established a charitable arm, the Red Heart Society 紅心字會, which established its headquarters in Xi'an in a large building put at its disposal by the Red Swastika Society.

Yiguandao was a salvationist movement practicing spirit writing that had branched off from the Xiantiandao tradition at the end of the nineteenth century; in 1917, its patriarch, Lu Zhongyi 路中一, declared that he was Maitreya. For several decades, the group remained relatively small and limited to Shandong. This changed after 1930, however, when Zhang Guangbi 張光璧 (1889–1947),[37] one of the group's leading evangelists, proclaimed himself Patriarch and launched a large-scale expansion campaign. He reorganized the movement, established its headquarters in Ji'nan, shifted the target of evangelization to the more mobile and affluent merchant class, and sent disciples to rapidly establish new halls all over China.[38]

In 1936, Zhang Guangbi and his associates were arrested by the Blue Shirts, a fascist movement within the KMT, on their way to Nanjing, and detained for almost a year.[39] Tiandejiao was banned by the KMT in 1937.

37. Known as Zhang Tianran 張天然 by Yiguandao followers.
38. For general treatments of Yiguandao, see Lu Yunfeng, *The Transformation of Yiguan Dao*; Lu Zhongwei, *Yiguandao neimu*; Fu Zhong, *Yiguandao fazhan shi*; Jordan, "The Recent History of the Celestial Way," 435–62; Lin Rongze, *Yiguandao lishi, dalu zhi bu*. The development of Yiguandao in Taiwan is discussed in chapter 11 of the present text. Other essential studies comparing Yiguandao among other salvationist movements are Jordan & Overmyer, *The Flying Phoenix*; and DuBois, *The Sacred Village*.
39. Lu Zhongwei, *Minguo huidaomen*, 255–56.

But the Japanese invasion made it impossible to enforce the suppression of this and other redemptive societies. The Nationalist regime began to gladly approve the charitable deeds of these groups; in fact, it began a policy to systematically reorganize, infiltrate, and control the redemptive societies as tools for anti-Japanese resistance. In Shandong, for instance, each branch of a redemptive society in a given area was to be renamed as the "XXX Society self-defense association against the enemy for XXX county, Shandong province"; accept instructions in anti-Japanese defense from government agents assigned to work with each group; and receive regular military training.[40] This policy was attempted on the Red Swastika Society and was quite thorough in case of the Zailijiao.[41] The Japanese and CCP also had explicit policies to infiltrate and mobilize redemptive societies for their wartime objectives: the Xiantiandao, for example, was infiltrated by both the Japanese and the CCP.[42] (The Japanese co-optation of these groups will be discussed in more detail in chapter 8.)

After the Japanese defeat in 1945, as the KMT tried to reestablish its control over the country and mobilize all social forces in its civil war against the CCP, it accepted the redemptive societies that had operated in the Japanese-controlled areas, notably the Red Swastika Society, Zailijiao, and Xiantiandao. A policy of purging them of collaborationist elements was often overridden by plans to immediately turn them into anti-CCP forces. In some areas, the networks of agents and the policy of co-optation toward the societies were redeployed to use the groups in anticommunist resistance in the civil war. On the other hand, new measures were taken to suppress the Tongshanshe,[43] which had organized and controlled many self-defense associations known as Big Knives societies (Dadaohui 大刀會), especially in Fujian, and was involved in several insurrections against the KMT.[44] On January 31, 1946, the KMT government also decreed the suppression of Yiguandao on the grounds of collaborating with the Japanese; its headquarters in Nanjing were expropriated by the police and handed over to the KMT-friendly Zailijiao Society.[45]

But, as in the case of the Daoyuan two decades earlier, Yiguandao mobilized its friends among the political elite to have the edict overturned, and to secure the legal registration of a charitable organization as a cover for

40. Ibid., 234–35.
41. Ibid., 213–16.
42. Shao Yong, *Zhongguo huidaomen*, 373–80.
43. Lu Zhongwei, *Minguo huidaomen*, 376–77.
44. Shao Yong, *Zhongguo huidaomen*, 393–400.
45. Lu Zhongwei, *Minguo huidaomen*, 215.

Yiguandao activities, the China Moral Philanthropy Society 中華道德慈
善會, in August 1947. The Tongshanshe was also able to register as a charitable organization, the Society for Blessings through Goodness (Zhongguo
Fushanshe 中國福善社), in the same year; from then on, it allied with the
KMT to fight the CCP.[46]

After the end of the second Sino-Japanese War, between 1945 and 1949
Yiguandao continued to experience spectacular growth, with a presence
in 81 percent of China's prefectures by the beginning of the 1950s.[47] The
size of the phenomenon can be judged by the fact that the first mass political campaign launched by the new CCP regime after 1949 was the movement to stamp out the "reactionary sects and secret societies" 反動會道
門 (discussed in chapter 6). According to police reports, in all of China's
counties a total of 13 million followers (2 percent of the nation's population) were counted and 820,000 leaders and activists were either arrested
or turned themselves in.[48] These figures can be compared with the 500,000
Buddhist monks, the 1 million Protestants, and the 3 million Catholics in
China at the time. Redemptive societies thus constituted, by far, the largest group of organized religious congregations in Republican China.[49] Lin
Rongze has estimated, based on an analysis of CCP campaign reports in
local gazetteers published in Mainland China since 1980, that membership
in popular salvationist groups (excluding gangs and militias) in the early
1950s amounted to over 18 million, most of whom were affiliated to one
of the redemptive societies listed above.[50] While these figures need to be
taken with caution, they do give some idea of the considerable size of the
phenomenon.[51] Although the CCP campaigns did successfully eradicate
most redemptive societies on the mainland, they expanded in the postwar
years in Taiwan. There, led by Yiguandao, they also grew into some of the
largest religious organizations on the island, and were a major matrix for
the emergence of several new religious movements, such as the True Buddha School, Haizidao, and the Mile dadao (see chapter 11). In overseas Chinese communities in Southeast Asia, redemptive societies (notably Dejiao,

46. Ibid., 378, 397.
47. Fu Zhong, *Yiguandao fazhan shi*, 47.
48. Shao Yong, *Zhongguo huidaomen*, 452–53.
49. Of course, the practitioners of Chinese communal religion were far more numerous, and included almost the entire Chinese population; but Chinese communal religion does not have voluntary
congregational membership in the way that Christian churches and redemptive societies do.
50. Lin Rongze, *Yiguandao lishi, dalu zhi bu*, 58–62.
51. The figures could be inflated by zealous local officials trying to meet or surpass the targets of
political campaigns; on the other hand, they could also be underreporting the possibly large numbers
of members who did not turn themselves in or otherwise avoided detection.

Zhenkongjiao, and Yiguandao) became one of the most important forms of religious, social, and philanthropic association, discussed in chapter 8.

SECULARIZING TRADITION

In spite of the great diversity of redemptive societies, one of their common characteristics was their attempt to synthesize Chinese spiritual tradition into a single whole, structured within a single organization in which deity worship, spirit writing, study of the classics, philanthropy, moral exhortation, and body cultivation could be practiced under the same roof. A parallel and contrasting trend was to isolate some of these elements of Chinese tradition, extract them from "religion" and "superstition," and integrate them into secular nation-building projects. This trend could notably be seen in traditional technologies involving the training, nurture, and care of the body and mind: meditation, martial arts, and medicine. Intellectually, such nationalist recycling of the traditions was often linked to the "national essence" (*guocui* 國粹) movement and its related scholarship. It carried even further the standardization of tradition and the use of modern forms of classroom instruction and print media that had also been attempted by the redemptive societies.

Chinese Medicine and the "National Essence"

Chinese medicine provides an excellent case of a new split in Chinese traditional culture, between elements that could be recast as "cultural treasures" compatible with science, and "superstitions" that were to be cleaned away. To be sure, Chinese medicine never existed as a unified system before the modern era; in the late imperial era, one can speak of a highly diverse and unregulated "market" for healing and health, in which temple cults, Buddhists and Taoists, diviners, spirit mediums, exorcists, charismatic healers, salvationist groups, and herbalists were leading providers of therapeutic services, while a small class of "literati doctors," who based their practice on classical texts, denigrated other therapists as practitioners of "evil arts."[52] The secularizing tendency of the latter group was reinforced and radicalized in the twentieth century, when even the classical medicine of the literati came under attack.

In the dying days of the Qing dynasty, early reformist intellectuals had begun to see medicine as a crucial domain in the modernization of the

---

52. Fang Ling, "Les médecins laïques contre l'exorcisme."

Chinese nation. Comparing the public health policies of the Western powers with the near-total neglect of medicine by the Qing state, and shocked
by China's military defeat at the hands of the Japanese, they concluded that
the nation's weakness could be attributed at least in part to the poor health
and weak bodies of the Chinese—a fact that could, according to the social
Darwinist paradigm that was becoming dominant among the intelligentsia, ultimately lead to the extinction of the Chinese race. Leading reformers such as Kang Youwei and Liang Qichao accordingly placed a great emphasis on the development of modern medical institutions in their visions
of a new state. Though their advocacy of Western medicine did not foresee
the elimination of Chinese medical traditions, by the time of the founding
of the Republic, the terms of the debate had already shifted: traditional
medicine was excluded from the new education system established in
1912; the Education Minister, Wang Daxie 汪大燮 (1860–1929), declared
in 1914 that he had decided to "abolish" Chinese medicine.[53] Intellectuals
of the May Fourth movement—authors such as Lu Xun, Ba Jin, and Lao
She all ridiculed Chinese doctors in their stories—forcefully argued this
point, associating Chinese medicine not only with national weakness but
with everything that was backward, despicable, and superstitious in their
culture.[54] Many of the intellectuals of this generation were indeed trained
in Western medicine, often in medical schools of the Christian missionary universities, such as the Peking Union Medical College (established
1906)—which, though their orientation became increasingly secularized
in the first half of the twentieth century, played a key role in the training of
a new, antitraditionalist elite.[55]

The polemics reached their peak in 1929, when the KMT government's
Ministries of Education and Health moved to formally outlaw traditional
medicine. These attempts led practitioners, who had never previously organized themselves nationally, to establish, in a manner analogous to the
religious associations described in chapter 3, countrywide associations
and institutions, which ran (at least on paper) local branches, academic
journals, and modern-style clinics and schools. Such initiatives had already
begun with the abortive Chinese Doctors' Committee to Petition for Saving
Medicine from Extinction in 1914;[56] but it was a new national federation

---

53. Ye Xiaoqing, "Regulating the Medical Profession"; Croizier, *Traditional Medicine*, 59–69. On
Chinese medicine in the Republican period, see also Lei, "When Chinese Medicine Encountered the
State."

54. Croizier, *Traditional Medicine*, 70–80.

55. Croizier, "Medicine and Modernization," 24.

56. Croizier, *Traditional Medicine*, 69.

established in Shanghai that succeeded in mobilizing nationalist sentiment in favor of the "national medicine," so that the government shelved its proposals. The movement led to the establishment of the Shanghai Academy of National Medicine in 1929, with Zhang Binglin as its honorary president, which celebrated National Medicine Day on March 17. It culminated in the founding of the Institute for National Medicine (Guoyiguan 國醫館) in March 1931, with its headquarters in Nanjing and affiliates in the major cities and even in Chinese communities overseas.[57]

Through these attempts at national organization, a new discourse emerged in defense of what became the new category of "Chinese" medicine (*zhongyi* 中醫) or even "national medicine" (*guoyi* 國醫): the Chinese medical tradition was reformulated as part of China's "national essence," a priceless gem that, along with calligraphy and art, should be proudly preserved by any self-respecting countryman. This discourse fit squarely within the new nationalism; it vaunted Chinese medicine as much for its Chinese quality as for its intrinsic therapeutic value—indeed, as noted by Ralph Croizier, rarely in imperial times had the elite guardians of Chinese tradition held in such high esteem what had always been "demeaned as a craft."[58] This project of a Chinese medicine, which could exist alongside with, and complementary to, Western medicine, upheld the theoretical principles of the medical tradition while condemning the actual practice of Chinese doctors, who were blamed for the disrepute of the Chinese medical tradition. National medicine was thus to be "scientized" (*kexuehua* 科學化), with the goal of eliminating mystical and superstitious accretions, reformulating or reinterpreting classical medical theory in a manner compatible with science, and conducting laboratory research on the Chinese materia medica.[59]

Proponents of national medicine had limited success in obtaining symbolic recognition for Chinese medicine from a KMT government previously bent on eliminating it altogether.[60] Only after the People's Republic was founded would the project attain its full realization, with the strong backing of the socialist state. This was in spite of the fact that the first Chinese Marxists, though not especially interested in medical issues, had been, as a logical consequence of their modernist orientation, opposed to

57. Ye Xiaoqing, "Regulating the Medical Profession," 200–201.
58. Croizier, *Traditional Medicine*, 82; Xu Xiaoqun, "'National Essence.'"
59. Croizier, *Traditional Medicine*, 98.
60. Ibid., 131–48.

the traditional healing traditions associated with the old society.[61] In 1929, the Party had even discussed a policy proposal to abolish the old medicine in order to develop modern medicine and hygiene.[62] But after the experience of the Soviets in Jiangxi and Shaanxi, the Long March, and the deepening of the Party's rural roots in the 1930s, the CCP's attitude began to change: far from the cities, the Red Army had to resort to traditional therapists for medical care. A conscious policy was formulated in Yan'an in the 1940s, to make use of local medical resources within a "scientific orientation." Mao called on modern-trained doctors to unite with traditional therapists, who were closer to the people, and to "help them to reform." Traditional doctors were thus no longer seen as enemies of progress. Essential in the field, where there were no modern medical institutions, they could be used and reformed along the lines of the scientific medicine that would gradually and naturally replace traditional healing. Local Party and army leaders were thus free to call on traditional doctors for the care of injured and ill soldiers and officials.[63]

In the early 1950s, the new Communist state was faced with a health policy dilemma: on the one hand, Western-style medical institutions were politically tainted by their association with imperialist bourgeois culture; on the other hand, the country, whose medical system was in a shambles after decades of civil war, was desperately in need of qualified medical personnel. The answer was to institutionalize traditional Chinese medicine, which had struggled for recognition under the previous Nationalist government.[64] Chinese medicine was organized as a scientific-style medical institution, and a standardized theoretical system was elaborated, compatible with Marxist philosophy and dialectical materialism. Traditional doctors, who had previously operated independently in exclusive lineages bound by strong master-disciple relationships, were integrated into specialized medical work units.[65] Under the Party's direction, the new China would save valuable Chinese traditions from "feudal" decadence, spur them to new heights of development, and contribute them to the health

61. For in-depth accounts of Chinese Communist policy toward Chinese medicine, see Agren, "Patterns"; Croizier, *Traditional Medicine*, "Traditional Medicine," and "Medicine and Modernization"; Taylor, "'Improving' Chinese Medicine."

62. Agren, "Patterns," 41.

63. On the use of Chinese medicine in CCP-controlled areas before 1949, see Taylor, *Chinese Medicine in Early Communist China*, chap. 1.

64. Ye Xiaoqing, "Regulating the Medical Profession."

65. On the institutionalization of Chinese medicine, see Croizier, *Traditional Medicine*.

and welfare of the people. Thus institutionalized and modernized, Chinese medicine could be marshaled to serve the health policy needs of the new state. Chinese medicine research societies were established to stimulate the sharing of knowledge and experience among traditional doctors, who were used to jealously guarding their secret formulas. Learned journals were launched, and in 1956, specialized colleges of Chinese medicine were founded in Beijing, Shanghai, Guangzhou, and Chengdu, as well as hundreds of lesser training schools, in order to rapidly increase the number of medical workers. Over one hundred specialized hospitals of Chinese medicine were built. Fifteen thousand "unified" clinics and hospitals were also constructed, integrating modern and traditional doctors under one roof.[66]

With the growing rift between Maoist China and the Soviet Union in the late 1950s, Chinese medicine further benefited from an increasing nationalism and appreciation of native civilization. The exaltation of the "cultural heritage of the motherland" was expressed not only in medicine but also in architecture, theatre, and painting. The "popular" roots of the traditional medicine were emphasized; links with feudalism and Confucianism were played down. The mass media frequently published reports of remarkable cures brought about by simple remedies.[67] The years 1955 to 1958 were thus marked by the large-scale organization of a vast institutional system of Chinese medicine, which was promoted as part of Mao's "popular democratic culture." Large quantities of secret and folk remedies were collected and published, in a movement aiming to promote the medical wisdom of the masses, and "popular experts" were invited into the hospitals and medical schools. Thanks to its identification with nonprofessional popular culture, Chinese medicine became central to the nation's health policy during the Great Leap Forward, Mao's attempt to quickly modernize China's economy.[68]

Martial Arts

Another form of traditional culture to be nationalized in the Republican period was the martial arts. Training in fighting skills had very long been common in the countryside and was even more prevalent in the late nine-

66. Ibid., 166. See also Taylor, "'Improving' Chinese Medicine," for a detailed study of Chinese medicine in the years 1949–53.
67. Agren, "Patterns," 42; Croizier, *Traditional Medicine*, 167–80 and "Traditional Medicine," 10–11.
68. Croizier, *Traditional Medicine*, 186–88.

teenth century, as villagers were compelled to organize militias to defend themselves against the rebels, bandits, and soldiers who advanced back and forth across an increasingly chaotic realm. In many parts of China, village temples each had a martial arts association for recruiting and training the local youth (a tradition continuing in Hong Kong and other parts of the Chinese world), and in Muslim villages, the mosque played the very same role. Chinese fighting skills, especially the more refined styles, were often steeped in religious mythology and cosmology, such as the Buddhist Shaolin tradition[69] or the Yang-style *taijiquan* 太極拳 developed by Yang Luchan 楊露禪 (1799–1872), and *baguazhang* 八卦掌 developed by Dong Haichuan 董海川 (1813–1882),[70] that came to be associated with Taoist saints and holy sites (even though not all practitioners accepted such an association); indeed there was a large overlap between Taoists and martial arts instructors, both inside and outside the regular Qing military. While there were martial artists in the nineteenth and twentieth centuries who did *not* emphasize Buddhist/Taoist connections or even rejected them, others did play them up. Yet other fighting techniques, which featured in the repertoire of the rural self-defense movements discussed in the next chapter, involved the use of spirit possession, talismans, and invulnerability rites. All were immensely popular, as testified for instance by the vogue of martial arts novels that has not abated ever since the early nineteenth century.

The learning and practice of martial arts was associated with the early stirrings of Chinese nationalism against both the Manchus and the foreigners, and was a defining aspect of the Boxer Rebellion of 1900. The humiliation suffered by China as a result of the rebellion was a significant factor in the subsequent abhorrence of its elite for "superstition," including anything associated with traditional fighting skills. The martial branch of the traditional examination system was abolished in 1901, leading to the elimination of traditional fighting skills from military training.[71] The new schools instead vigorously promoted training in Western sports and physical education as fundamental prerequisites for strengthening the bodies of the nation. It was not long, however, before Chinese martial arts regained a certain prestige as exemplifying the *Chinese* martial spirit against Manchus and foreigners who taunted China as the "sick man of Asia." But this revival led to the modernization and secularization of the tradition away

69. Shahar, *The Shaolin Monastery.*
70. Wile, *Lost T'ai-Chi Classics.*
71. Lin Boyuan, *Zhongguo wushu shi,* 412.

from temples and Buddhist/Taoist settings. Public urban associations of practitioners sprouted in most large cities, beginning with the Pure Martial Athletic Association (Jingwu tiyuhui 精武體育會), founded in Shanghai in 1910 after the famous fighter Huo Yuanjia 霍元甲 (1867–1910) and his disciples defeated several Russian, Japanese, and Western bullies.[72] Another major association, the Chinese Martial Artists' Society (Zhonghua wushihui 中華武士會), was established in Tianjin in 1912.[73] About 1918, Ma Liang 馬良, commander in a warlord army, developed "New Martial Arts," which were promoted in the army and in the schools by the Beiyang government as "national essence physical culture," said to enhance the traditional warrior spirit.[74]

The martial arts promoted by these organizations were packaged as scientific and modern: no longer the preserve of neighborhood ruffians and superstitious hillbillies, they were presented as a form of sport, of education for the mind and body, which could be practiced with dignity and pride, just like basketball and football, by the prep-school boys (and even girls) of the new urban elite. Advocates of martial arts petitioned to the Education Ministry to have them taught as a mandatory course in the schools; their proposal was passed at the first National Education Conference in Beijing in April 1915. Similar to the standardization and mass teaching of meditation techniques, such a project involved reformatting the fighting methods: "superstitious" relics and "supernaturalism" (guidao zhuyi 鬼道主義), such as "spirit fists" (shenquan 神拳) and "divine swords" (xianjian 仙劍), were expurgated from the repertoire; routines were standardized as sets of connected postures; forms were simplified to facilitate their teaching to the masses; secret teachings were published in easy-to-follow didactic manuals.[75]

Throughout the 1920s, the Pure Martial Association, among others, was able to stimulate a wave of martial arts popularity in the Chinese world, placing martial practices as "national essence" at the core of a new universalistic value system, the Great Pure Martial Spirit (Dajingwu zhuyi 大精武主義), which, claimed its advocates, combined Confucian self-control, Buddhist equality, and Christian brotherhood, bringing health, wisdom, and morality to its practitioners. As a Chinese-style equivalent of the YMCA, the association, which had branches in most cities and an important pres-

72. Morris, *Marrow of the Nation*, 186–88.
73. Lin Boyuan, *Zhongguo wushu shi*, 414.
74. Brownell, *Training the Body*, 52–53.
75. Morris, *Marrow of the Nation*, 188–92.

ence in the Chinese communities of Southeast Asia, offered classes and competitions in martial arts but also bicycle racing, table tennis, hiking, roller skating, Mandarin instruction, Beijing opera, and special classes for women and workers.[76] The growing popularity of martial arts was also stimulated by a new wave of knight-errant novels (*wuxia xiaoshuo* 武俠小説), notably the work of Xiang Kairan 向愷然 (1889–1957), who wrote several, notably the *Lives of chivalrous and altruistic heroes* (*Xiayi yingxiong zhuan* 俠義英雄傳), in which the warrior exemplified traditional honor and a physical virtuosity far outclassing the foreign scoundrels with their guns, as well as magical prowess that still was acceptable in the context of fiction.[77]

Political figures such as Sun Yat-sen and Christian warlord Feng Yuxiang were outspoken advocates of martial arts. This support was transformed into a state-sponsored project to nationalize the martial arts, now called National Arts (*guoshu* 國術), by the KMT regime in Nanjing. The project, spearheaded by Feng Yuxiang's deputy to Chiang Kai-shek, Zhang Zhijiang 張之江 (1882–1966, a Protestant Christian), together with other former warlords and military figures and with the support of Cai Yuanpei, led to a Central *Guoshu* Academy (*Zhongyang guoshuguan*) being established, first in a small Nanjing church, then in a larger facility.[78] The organization established hundreds of branches at the provincial, municipal, and county levels, holding the hope of uniting the myriads of schools, traditions, and training lineages into a single, national system. A standardized curriculum was offered at the Central Academy in Nanjing, with courses in the major forms of martial arts as well as in physiology and hygiene, KMT principles, history and geography, and Sun Yat-sen studies. Many famous national and local martial artists joined the system, which aimed to popularize *guoshu* by spreading it among all the people. Formal examinations were held in both martial and intellectual subjects, ascending from the local to the provincial and national levels, with the highest level of examinations overlapping with the (Western) sport-dominated National Games.[79]

For the proponents of *guoshu*, the degradation of Chinese martial arts in late imperial times and their necessary revitalization reflected the state of the Chinese nation as a whole. Riven by superstition and factionalism, which were the causes of the physical and military weakness of China, the martial arts needed to be fused into a single body, a unified system for a

76. Ibid., 189, 197.
77. Brownell, *Training the Body*, 52.
78. Morris, *Marrow of the Nation*, 205.
79. Morris, *Marrow of the Nation*, 211–13.

unified nation. In this system, occultism, mysticism, and magic were to be replaced by science—a science that would restore the original purity of the national essence, exemplifying the profound knowledge of physiology, mechanics, physics, and biology of China's native wisdom. Violent matches and duels, which led to injuries, death, and intense feuds between cliques of practitioners—traditional martial arts were, after all, designed for real combat—were to be turned into friendly "sport," and competitions into the performance of sets of forms.[80] Thus rationalized, scientized, and unified, martial arts could spearhead the realization of the Nationalist revolution. And for some of its leading proponents, beyond helping to save the nation, *guoshu*, as a "science in its own right" and as a "basic element of the new civilization,"[81] could be offered as a "gospel" (*fuyin* 福音): "Spreading Chinese *guoshu* to the entire world will mean glad tidings for humanity."[82]

The Nationalist project of the martial arts was continued by the PRC, in which, during the 1950s, it followed a trajectory of planned secularization, institutionalization, and mass development which paralleled that of Chinese medicine. Less than a year after the PRC was established, the state-sponsored All-China Sports Society held a conference on the martial arts and called for the reorganization, rationalization, and popular dissemination of martial arts training—expurgated of its "nonscientific" contents. Martial arts groups began to sprout in factories, schools, railroad construction teams, and government units. In 1953, after the State Sports Commission 國家體育委員會 was established to promote physical education among the masses and train Chinese athletes for international competitions, martial arts were featured at a major fair and competition on ethnic sports held in Tianjin. The dream of creating a standardized, nationalized, and scientific martial arts, which had been promoted by the KMT's *guoshuguan* with limited success, was now given full political support and unprecedented institutional resources. A national martial arts team was established, and kung fu masters, who had previously lived as marginals, social outcasts at the edges between underground gangs, temple fairs, and street-side healing, now found themselves promoted to high-status jobs as teachers in sports colleges, delegates at People's Congresses, and members of state-sponsored sports federations.

The sudden legitimation and promotion of martial arts opened a space for the reconstitution and spread of some traditional martial arts networks,

---

80. Brownell, *Training the Body*, 54.
81. Morris, *Marrow of the Nation*, 217.
82. Quoted in Morris, *Marrow of the Nation*, 220.

which had not yet eliminated magical techniques from their practices and engaged in social predation. Thus, in 1955 the authorities ordered a temporary halt to the development of martial arts activities: existing groups in state work units were to be rectified, no new ones were to be formed, the growth of rural groups and other popular martial arts associations was to be stopped, and all activities using martial arts to engage in criminal activities or expand "reactionary secret societies" (that is, redemptive societies and sworn brotherhoods) were to be banned. Many martial arts masters were persecuted during this campaign, but within a year the government instructed the State Sports Commission to research the "scientific" value of martial arts and use various means to promote them; martial arts were officially inscribed as a performance sport in the new regulations for national-level sports competitions; and a state-sponsored China Martial Arts Association was established. By 1957, national-level training workshops were held, simplified forms were created, and martial arts groups were once again encouraged to gather in work units, as a "national cultural heritage" 民族文化遺產 and as a mass sports activity. A standardized format for competitions was established; contests were held at the local, provincial, and national levels; and with a delegation to Burma in 1960, the practice of kung fu performances as a form of cultural diplomacy began. In 1961, martial arts were integrated into the physical education curriculum for primary and secondary schools.[83]

Quiet Sitting and *Qigong*

A similar bifurcation process was at work in the softer, more meditative forms of Chinese self-cultivation traditions, which were practiced in the medical and martial networks discussed above, and were also central to the spiritual disciplines of Taoism, Buddhism, and Confucianism. These practices were widely disseminated in a religious context by the redemptive societies; at the same time, new projects appeared which aimed to secularize them and to institutionalize them along modern lines.

The earliest and most influential secularizer of meditation was Jiang Weiqiao 蔣維喬 (1873–1958), who revolutionized its practice and dissemination by couching the techniques in self-consciously modern, scientific terms and concepts. Jiang, who had been sickly and weak from his childhood, learned about *qi* circulation techniques through medical classics, experiencing such good results that at the age of twenty-seven he left his

83. Lin Boyuan, *Zhongguo wushu shi*, 473–80.

wife and children to devote himself exclusively to a strict regimen of meditation practice. The popularity in China of recent Japanese books on self-cultivation practice led him to criticize Chinese masters who clung to secret transmission to a few selected disciples, and he resolved to stimulate a new spirit of public dissemination and investigation of meditation techniques.[84] He became a well-known author of three popular books on "quiet sitting" (*jingzuo* 静坐). In these books, he criticized the abstruse and esoteric style of the old medical and Taoist texts, and described the meditation techniques using clear language rooted in common sense and his personal experience. He expounded a mechanistic view of the body, and changed the ancient terminologies. For example, claiming that the old terms encouraged mystical thinking rather than practical efficacy, he used the term "center of gravity" (*zhongxin* 重心) as a substitute for the Taoist term of "elixir field" (*dantian* 丹田), in reference to a point below the navel considered the root of the body's *qi*. Jiang Weiqiao's reformulation of the techniques in modern terms paved the way for meditation practices to become accessible to anyone.[85]

Another influential modernizer of self-cultivation traditions was Chen Yingning, the son of a family of absentee landlords and literati in Anhui. Educated in the Confucian classics, his poor health had led him to abandon the prospect of a career in officialdom and instead devote himself to learning Chinese medicine and then Taoist self-cultivation techniques. His outlook was profoundly affected by the breakdown of the traditional order, leading him to despair, like so many Chinese intellectuals of his generation, at the weakness of the Chinese nation. Under his elder brother's patronage, he studied the new Western sciences (physics, chemistry, and biology) and, having moved to Shanghai, became active in the reformist Buddhist circles there. Ultimately, however, Chen rejected the metaphysical idealism of both Buddhism and the prevailing interpretations of Taoist inner alchemy, which accorded the highest value to the void (*xu* 虚). Instead, and backing his arguments with scientific proofs, he claimed that Taoism had, at its origins, placed the highest emphasis on the body, not as an illusion to be overcome, but as the necessary vehicle of purification and transformation. In a strong polemic against Buddhism and its corrupting influence on Taoism and Chinese civilization as a whole, he accused it of being the root cause of the weakening of the Chinese body and nation.

Going back to the purported origins of the Taoist tradition before the Warring States period (and thus before Confucianism and Buddhism), Chen

---

84. Liu Xun, "In Search of Immortality," 15.
85. On Jiang Weiqiao's contribution to the birth of modern *qigong*, see Kohn, "Quiet Sitting."

founded Immortalist Learning (*xianxue* 仙學), a Taoist philosophy rooted in meditation, which was purified of what he considered the obsolete and corrupt ritualism prevalent among the people, and which held the ambition of becoming a new branch of knowledge both compatible with, and superior to, Western science. In one of his works, for example, Chen drew a table of correspondences between Taoist ontological states and physical particles of increasing complexity (atoms, molecules, cells, and so on).[86] Adhering to the theory, already expounded by some Western historians of science, that Taoist experiments were among the forerunners of modern chemistry,[87] he attempted to revive the practice of external alchemy (*waidan* 外丹) as a form of laboratory science that could demonstrate that China did possess the secret of turning mercury into gold and attaining long life. Inspired by the reformist Buddhist movements, in the late 1930s he established a modern-style institute, the Xianxueyuan 仙學院, and published mass-circulation journals, notably the *Yangshan banyuekan* 揚善半月刊 (1933–38), which became a forum for a China-wide community of lay practitioners to discuss and share letters, poems, and questions and answers about their practice, written in a vernacular language easy to understand. These practitioners included many urban elites (merchants, officials) as well as schoolmasters, housewives, and students. The drive to openness and clarity, however, did not extend to foreigners: Chen Yingning was adamant about not transmitting alchemical secrets to non-Chinese. Indeed, properly retrieved and disseminated, the techniques held the hope of overpowering the "murderous fiends" and their "sharp war machines of science."[88]

Following these haphazard efforts during the Republican period, it was under CCP guidance that self-cultivation practices were systematically integrated into a single category, secularized, and institutionalized. The innovation occurred in the Huabei "liberated area" in the late 1940s, when CCP cadre Liu Guizhen 劉貴真, suffering from ulcers and insomnia, sought treatment from a traditional master who taught him a technique of breath training and standing meditation. Following his recovery, his superiors in the Party, seeking economical solutions to the lack of modern medical facilities, appointed Liu to head a clinical team charged with researching breath techniques. Based on his master's teachings and on clas-

---

86. Liu Xun, *Daoist Modern*, 108.

87. This thesis was notably developed by the influential chemist and historian of Chinese science Joseph Needham (1900–1995), and by one of the first Chinese historians of Taoism, himself from a Taoist family and trained in chemistry, Chen Guofu 陳國符 (b. 1915).

88. Liu Xun, "In Search of Immortality," 172. On Chen Yingning, see also Liu Xun, "Scientizing the Body for the Nation."

sical texts, Liu and his team devised two methods that they named *qigong* 氣功, defined as the art of mastering one's breath. This category came to encompass all traditional techniques for disciplining the mind, the breath, and the body, but purged of all religious elements, and in which traditional cosmology was interpreted as a form of primitive materialist dialectics.

Qigong was practiced and taught in modern medical settings as a discipline alongside pharmacology, acupuncture, and massage in the newly institutionalized Chinese medicine. Secret transmission from master to disciple was replaced by public training of patients by modern-style clinicians, in the framework of public health institutions. The traditional notion of the "master" with its charismatic connotations was replaced by the notion of the modern doctor, the *qigong* "medical worker" engaged in a scientific enterprise. The old salvationist networks and medical lineages were replaced by a community of *qigong* specialists who were trained in formal workshops, worked in official settings, met at conferences to exchange their experiences, conducted clinical research, published the results of their work, and held public training classes.

Benefiting from high-level government support, *qigong* quickly spread within medical institutions. The first wave of *qigong* peaked during the Great Leap Forward, along with Chinese medicine in general. Traditional popular masters were recruited by clinics as *qigong* therapists. Eighty-one-year-old Jiang Weiqiao was invited to give a workshop at the Beidaihe Sanatorium in 1957.[89] Chen Yingning was hired by the Zhejiang Provincial Workers' Sanatorium to teach still meditation (*jinggong* 靜功) at its newly established department of quiet sitting therapy and rehabilitation, located at scenic Mount Fengping. He gave lectures, directed practice sessions, and prepared pamphlets for publication.[90]

Seventy *qigong* units were founded by the end of the 1950s, including clinics and sanatoria. A national conference on the discipline was held in 1959, and a national training course was organized a year later. Books were published on the subject, and several research units began clinical and laboratory trials on the physiological effects of *qigong*. The specialized sanatoria and prestigious urban hospitals in which *qigong* was practiced during this period were places reserved for the Party elite. But with its roots in Chinese popular culture and also the fact that it had no links to the West, was easy and cheap to learn, brought health benefits without requir-

---

89. Ding Shu, *Yangmou*, chap. 16. Jiang reportedly committed suicide shortly after the workshop, upon learning that his son had been labeled a rightist.

90. Liu Xun, "In Search of Immortality," 75–76; Chen Yingning, *Daojiao yu yangsheng*, 371–83.

ing costly investments in technology, and involved the transformation of body and health through the pure training of the will, *qigong* fit well with the spirit of the Great Leap Forward (discussed in chapter 7).

CONCLUSION

The Republican period witnessed a bifurcation among two types of projects to revitalize a traditional culture that was being marginalized by the forces of modernization. Both types flourished in the Beiyang period. One, exemplified by the redemptive societies, was to incorporate the traditions into a new synthesis that would give modern and universal value to Chinese tradition. Although the societies all worshiped deities and most practiced spirit writing, they never really fit into the new category of religion. Some, such as the Wanguo daodehui, the Daoyuan, and Yiguandao, explicitly denied being religions, proposing a higher form of cultivation that transcended the religions of the past; whereas others, though claiming to be religions, by virtue of their Three-in-One, Five-in-One, or All-in-One syncretism were incompatible with confessional classifications based on Christianity, Islam, Buddhism, Taoism, and, perhaps, Confucianism. In terms of the number of adherents and elite participation, the social impact of the redemptive societies was clearly greater than the reformist movements within the established religions, making it legitimate to consider them the most significant religious phenomenon of the Republican era.

The other type of project was to isolate and secularize elements of tradition and incorporate them into the construction of a modern national identity. The KMT regime was clearly more amenable to the second track, since the redemptive societies were, in a sense, competing with its own attempt at a new national synthesis, the New Life movement (discussed in chapter 7). Either way, KMT attempts to suppress redemptive societies and nationalize traditions such as Chinese medicine, martial arts, or meditation were never fully realized, and it was only under the CCP that the two tendencies met with radically opposite destinies: ruthless repression of the first and strong state support and institutionalization for the second. And yet, as the *qigong* movement would show in the 1980s, one type of project always contained the potential of transmuting into the other, leading from secularism back to religiosity.

FIVE

Rural Resistance and Adaptation, 1898–1949

The developments we have seen so far—a new thinking about the relationships between state and religion, modernist reformist movements among religious leaders, and the rise of redemptive societies and secularized traditions—all began among urban elites. Although they eventually percolated into rural society, this was a long and convoluted process. In this chapter, we will analyze the effects of these developments on traditional local religion and rural society. In contrast to the story of intellectual emulation between political elites, religious leaders, and foreigners, we shall shift here to the more explicitly conflictual, and sometimes even violent, side of the story. Indeed, both rhetorical and crude physical violence were already prevalent during the late Qing at the early stages of redefining Chinese religion, when the destruction of temples was initiated. The development of both secular and reformist projects during the Republican period further heightened the level of violence.

During this period, state agents often acted predatorily toward religious institutions for a host of reasons. These included antireligious or (more often) antisuperstitious ideology; ambitions to seize the social, economic, and political resources possessed by religious institutions; and the felt need to destroy all sources of local power and cultural/political autonomy in towns and in the countryside. The reaction of religious communities can be understood as resistance in the largest sense, which encompasses rhetorical subversion, apparent compliance hiding defiance, legal action, and even acts of armed resistance. Here we will look at the specific points of contact between the modern nation-state and the traditional structures of local society. We will proceed by examining the forms and impact of repressive policies, and the range of resistance strategies deployed by the various religious groups targeted for repression, before moving to the even larger realm of adaptation and unintended consequences of the state's attempts at reconfiguring the religious field.

THE IMMEDIATE EFFECTS OF REPRESSION

The penetration of modern notions and policies of religion into rural China occurred in fits and starts, and was very uneven. Modernist visions of religion, as notably conveyed by the associations of the officially recognized religions, failed to reach into most rural areas—with the exception of Islam, whose reform movements, although not unopposed, were more rooted in the grass roots than their Buddhist or Taoist counterparts, and proved much better at mass mobilization. By the late 1940s—and even much later— most counties did not have a local branch of the Buddhist and Taoist associations. Similarly, the discourse of religion and superstition, though very early on adopted by urban intellectuals and politicians, hardly penetrated the population at large, including conservative rural elites. For instance, local gazetteers (difangzhi 地方志) of the 1910s and 1920s by and large maintained the late imperial categories to describe the religious situation on the field (official sacrifices, local cults, the Three Teachings) rather than, or on top of, the new categories of official religions versus superstitions.[1]

Rather than the spread of ideas, then, the major impact of modern change on local religion took the form of the state's repressive policies. By *repression*, we mean the whole range of violent action on society by state agents, supported by legislation, official propaganda, and official institutions (army, police, tribunals), including discrimination—communal forms of religion not being granted privileges, protection, and otherwise access to the official world the way reformist movements were—the banning of festivals, and the

---

1. On the evolving local politics of religion as reflected in local gazetteers, see Brook, "The Politics of Religion."

destruction of buildings and violence on persons. In contrast to the Maoist regime, the Republican period witnessed relatively little violence directed at religious specialists or leaders (even though some were forcibly expelled from temples,[2] threatened, or harassed by the Nationalist army), and most violence targeted temple buildings and statues. However, few studies so far have focused on the details and particulars of temple destruction and iconoclasm,[3] and reliable quantified data are very scarce, which makes it difficult to assess the geographic and time variations and the scope of the destructions.

Until 1927, and to a somewhat lesser but still important extent under KMT rule, the actual unfolding of modern religious policies was characterized by extreme geographic diversity. The New Policies regime of the dying empire and the early Republic gave meek approval to local initiatives in destroying superstition and implementing the "build schools with temple property" movement, which was essentially spontaneous and fueled by grassroots initiatives and local activism. There were activist officials, but generally it was activists who did not hold formal office, such as the leaders of local autonomy bureaus (*zizhiju*), education societies (*jiaoyuhui*), and the KMT, who, fighting for a cause and trying to build a power base, had more interest in violence and conflict with local institutions such as temples than local officials trying to preserve order. It was only from 1928 that the central government itself began to orchestrate antisuperstition and temple seizure campaigns, and this explains why they were carried out so differently from one place to another, according to the convictions of local officials and elite leaders. Indeed, collective religious life had been badly disrupted in some places as early as the 1910s, while in some others it remained strong through the 1930s.

Differences in local religious conditions also contributed to the varying effects of religious policies and repression, as religious communities were better organized to resist and adapt in some areas than elsewhere. In those areas where all cult communities were integrated into a tight-knit system (as in the Fujian plains), resistance was effective, as local leaders had a stake in maintaining the status quo; in other areas, notably in most of northern China, local religious systems were much more loosely organized, so state agents were more successful in driving wedges between leaders and commoners and between various religious communities.

Some examples can provide an idea of the different trajectories followed

2. As early as 1912, hundreds of Buddhist nuns were forcibly expelled from their temples in Guangzhou: Welch, *The Buddhist Revival in China*, 328.

3. Nedostup, "Religion, Superstition," chap. 4, is focused on Jiangsu Province.

by state-religion relationships in different locales. In Dingxian, a rural area in central Hebei Province well known through social surveys conducted during the late 1920s, an area comprising 62 villages could boast 432 active temples in 1900, and only 116 in 1915. Among the 300-plus missing temples, some had fallen into neglect and disuse, but most were forcibly destroyed or turned into schools and other public buildings. Most of these forcible conversions had occurred in 1914–15 under the leadership of a local reformer official, Sun Faxu 孫發緒, who was personally responsible for converting 245 temples.[4] In Changli County (northern Hebei) as of 1933, among 42 temple landed endowments, 17 had become the property of the village government, 17 had been turned over to schools, and 8 continued to be used by temples. In Liangxiang County, also in the North China Plain, temples were turned into schools continually from 1908 to 1923, and all temple lands were confiscated by the village assembly (*gonghui* 公會) in 1911.[5]

Gazetteers and other data from other parts of China provide similarly contrasted pictures of progressive confiscation: sometimes already mostly completed by the early 1910s, in other cases only getting into full swing by the 1930s. The situations varied greatly, ranging from temples totally ruined or taken over by schools and other administrations, or even private individuals who turned them into their personal residences, to those temples that shared their premises with schools or bureaus while maintaining some degree of religious activity. All in all, when compiling data[6] one has the impression that less than half the temples operating in 1900 continued to be religiously active by 1937.[7]

The localized nature of the antisuperstition and *miaochan xingxue* movements also explains the fact that the targets were not always the same. In the early phases, in the years following 1904, some activists were still driven by traditional anticlerical ideas and targeted chiefly Buddhist and Taoist establishments. But soon after, as Buddhism reinvented itself as a "religion" and organized itself politically, local temple cults became the main and least protected target. Some large Buddhist and Taoist monaster-

4. Li Jinghan, *Dingxian shehui gaikuang diaocha*, 422–23.

5. 1933 *Changli xianzhi*, 4:38–39; 1924 *Liangxiang xianzhi*, 2:35; more data in Duara, *Culture, Power, and the State*.

6. This comparison is rather tricky, because the local data are to some extent incommensurable and all have their specific flaws: notably, lists of temples in local gazetteers are very rarely comprehensive, so the percentage of temples seized or destroyed is never based on the total number of existing temples.

7. Even in a northern city (Xuanhua), in which the impact of antisuperstition campaigns and political activism was moderate, about 40 percent of temples had been stripped of any religious function by 1948: Grootaers, *The Sanctuaries in a North-China City*.

ies were seized, like the Longhuasi 龍華寺 in Shanghai occupied by the Republican army from 1912 onward, which provoked loud outcries from the clergy. But most large public monasteries continued to operate quite normally until 1949—there again, with dramatic regional differences between the flourishing monasteries of Jiangnan (the rich and densely populated region between Shanghai, Nanjing, and Hangzhou) and the miserable conditions in most of the north, west, and south.[8]

Attacks on lineage halls (devoted to ancestor worship) and their landed endowments were rather few during that period—lineage leaders often had better political connections than temple leaders, and lineage resources had always been in part devoted to education. This is very significant, because of all the religious institutions they were probably the largest landowners. The proportion of land owned by religious institutions varied within a broad range, but was highest in southeastern China, where lineages had huge endowments.[9] David Faure has argued that lineages—which were central to state building, relations between local society and the state, and economic development up to 1900—became irrelevant in Republican ideas of the state, being replaced by urban, merchant models. Yet lineages also adapted to the new language of nation and democracy, even in a few cases participating in campaigns against local cults and inventing "lineage socialism."[10]

For a very different reason, great pilgrimage centers, which relied mostly on individual donations and less on landed property (and were less linked to local territorial power), also fared relatively well. For instance, the great Miaofengshan pilgrimage near Beijing remained vibrant with its hundreds of processional groups until it was stopped by the Japanese invasion in 1937, to resume only in the late 1980s. By contrast, large urban temples at the center of local religious-political systems, like the Chenghuangmiao (City God temple)[11] or the Dongyuemiao 東嶽廟 (Temple of the Eastern Peak) that federated neighborhood temples and devotional associations, were systematically targeted from 1912 onward, and by 1949, few survived in working order. They were the nexus of the local power that the

8. Welch, *The Buddhist Revival in China*, 246–52.

9. In most counties, lands owned by religious institutions (temples, monasteries, associations, lineages, and such) accounted for less than 5 percent of total lands, but in some counties of southeastern China, the huge lineage corporate endowments could push the figure upwards of 50 percent. See Overmyer & Chao Shin-Yi, eds., *Ethnography in China Today*, 363, for a discussion of western and northern Fujian, where in 1950 "sacrificial fields" 祭田 (owned by religious institutions) amounted to 20 to 30 percent of land in the richer coastal areas, and 50 to 60 percent in poorer mountainous areas.

10. Faure, *Emperor and Ancestor*, chap. 22.

11. Poon Shuk Wah, "Religion, Modernity, and Urban Space."

nation-state aimed to destroy, hence the fury of iconoclasm against such temples particularly, but not uniquely, when the Nationalist army marched into central and northern China in 1927–28.

Besides destroying statues and seizing land, modern political leaders disrupted local religion by regulating or banning public rituals and festivals. Whereas imperial regulations on festivals had rarely managed to achieve their goal of "civilizing the people" (prohibiting female involvement,[12] banning spirit mediums and "licentious" performing arts), the Republican state encroached on festivals from other angles. Its attitude was sometimes downright predatory, as when political leaders endeavored to appropriate the economic and political resources of temple festivals by heavily taxing ritual performances, or by appropriating the public spaces of festivals for their own political mobilization.[13]

The success of state attempts to both downscale and redefine festivals—either as mere commercial fairs or as public rituals of the new nation-state, in which offerings to the gods were replaced by political rallies—differed according to the effective might of the local state. Although many festivals declined or even disappeared during the 1920s and 1930s in cities that maintained effective urban administrations through the chaos of the warlord period, in rural areas the impact was more limited. The imposition of the Gregorian calendar, first enacted in 1912 but vigorously pushed by the Nationalist regime, in which only a few traditional festivals (such as the Lunar New Year) were retained, was a mitigated success in the cities and a total failure in the countryside. It proved impossible to eliminate the habits associated with the old calendar, and modernizing activists found themselves engaging in what Nedostup has called a "ritual competition" between two "affective regimes" in a bid to wrest the hearts and minds of the people away from their customs and into the new organization of sacred time, punctuated by solemn ceremonies and military parades held on public holidays such as the Gregorian new year. Other formal commemorations, marked by congregational singing of the national anthem, bowing three times, and placing wreaths and flowers at a portrait, tomb, or monument, included ceremonies for remembrance of Sun Yat-sen, Confucius, revolutionary martyrs, and "national heroes" such as Yue Fei 岳飛[14] and

---

12. Goossaert, "Irrepressible Female Piety."

13. Flath, "Temple Fairs."

14. Yue Fei (1103–1142) was a loyal general of the Song regime who was killed by traitors who opposed his policy of all-out attack in the face of "barbarian" invasion. He later became a local god in some areas, but his association with Guandi (many Guandi temples were renamed Guan-Yue temples) as a national god of martial resistance (against the Japanese) is a Republican invention.

Guandi, and the National Grave-Sweeping Day, at which officials would pay their respects at the tombs of national ancestors and dynastic founders such as the Yellow Emperor, Han Wudi, and Ming Taizu.[15]

Authorities also shifted a few traditional festivals to a new solar date and tried to give them new meanings and rituals: New Year celebrations were moved to January 1, and the Dragon Boat Festival to May 5. In Guangzhou, the Double-Seven 七夕 Festival (traditionally on the seventh day of the seventh lunar month)—during which single girls prayed for good husbands, and which was condemned for the extravagant sums spent on fruit, flowers, cosmetics, and miniatures of the legendary lovers celebrated during the festival—was converted into an official ceremony to honor Leizu 嫘祖, the first wife of the Yellow Emperor, who was known for her silkworm raising. The goal was to end superstitious worship, promote public awareness of sericulture, and give job opportunities to women through a public exhibition on silk production held at the Guangzhou YMCA. Similarly, the Ghost Festival (Zhongyuan 中元, on the fifteenth day of the seventh lunar month), which was particularly appalling to reformers, was turned into a commemoration of national heroes killed by the Japanese. As shown by Poon Shuk Wah, these campaigns superscribed secular, nationalist symbols onto the festivals, but were only partly successful in eradicating the traditional meanings and practices.[16]

Beyond the physical destruction and forcible banning of festivals, the state managed to disrupt local religion by bankrupting it—a strategy that bears comparison with other processes through world history. Taxing superstition—such as levying a tax on all temple festivals and traditional-style burials, as well as on the sale of incense and spirit money—was an idea that had always been in the political discussion since the late nineteenth century. The tax was sometimes encouraged and sometimes opposed by the central government, was applied very differently from one locale to the next, and in some cases worked as a strong incentive against large festivals. An ambivalent strategy, it both aimed at reducing the "waste" of ritual consumption and created a source of income that the local authority did not want to see totally disappear. For that reason, such taxes were eventually banned by the central government during the 1930s, and continued to be levied by many provincial or local authorities.

Most important, seizing the landed endowments that supported the running of temples and the organization of festivals crippled the ability of

15. Nedostup, "Ritual Competition," 88, 106.
16. Poon Shuk Wah, "Refashioning Festivals."

local communities to maintain public religious life—a blow that came on top of the general impoverishment of rural society in most of Republican China. Not only were lands seized, but levies on temples (*miaojuan* 廟捐), imposed as early as 1901 in some areas, forced them to sell their assets. Temples that were allowed to maintain a cult but were deprived of their landed endowments often could not afford restoration work and soon crumbled down, as Chinese wood-based temple architecture necessitates costly restoration once each generation. Furthermore, such impoverished temples often had to sack their resident clerics (when they had one, usually a Buddhist or Taoist), consequently provoking a widespread redefinition of religious roles. It would seem that the number of Buddhist and Taoist clerical specialists active in the countryside was in decline throughout the Republican period, though not the number of other religious specialists who provided services to households, such as spirit mediums and diviners; some switched to other occupations (many Taoists becoming teachers, accountants, or artists), but many moved to the richer cities, where their ritual services were still in considerable demand.[17]

The general trend during this period, which continued under the following regime, seems to be one in which the grander celebrations became rare or ceased altogether. Small-scale festivals continued, being shorter in duration and costing less, with fewer religious specialists and shrinking liturgical and paraliturgical repertoires, and requiring less intervillage cooperation.[18] The spirit of local religious life was not necessarily lost, but many ritual practices did disappear then and forever.

Another overarching phenomenon was the creation of an urban-rural divide, which was destined to become a deep rift under the Communist regime. The city was invented by modernists of all stripes as the forefront of progress and enlightenment, and rural China became the symbol of superstition and backwardness.[19] At the same time, most cities had set up police forces between 1900 and the 1930s that were well equipped to enforce real programs of social reform and antisuperstition by monitoring all festivals and processions,[20] whereas most villages were still free, apart from occasional raids from officers based in the county town, to organize their festivals as they wished. Rural China thus became the conservatory of religious practices and observances.

17. Goossaert, *The Taoists of Peking*, 84–86; Welch, *Practice of Chinese Buddhism*, appendix 1; and Lai Chi-tim, "Minguo shiqi Guangzhou shi 'namo daoguan,'" all show that in big cities the clerical population remained stable through 1937.

18. S. Jones, *In Search of the Folk Daoists*.

19. Faure & Liu, eds., *Town and Country in China*.

20. Wang Di, *Street Culture*; Imahori Seiji, *Peipin shimin*, on Chengdu and Beijing respectively.

Besides, in large cities police forces and municipal authorities had the means to take over, with varying degrees of success, social functions previously held by local cult associations, such as neighborhood communities and *shuihui* 水會, which used to run community welfare, patrolling, firefighting, water supply, and similar services, thus leading to a decline of these communities and their festivals. On the other hand, in cities with more conservative elites such as Beijing, where urban planning (street enlarging and rebuilding of old neighborhoods) caused temple destructions but where there was little iconoclastic activism, temple festivals and traditional funerals were still common in the public space during the 1930s. This was in stark contrast with revolutionary hotbeds such as Guangzhou, where as early as the 1920s city officials razed not only temples but even guild halls, ancestor halls, and family graveyards. In 1923, the Guangzhou city government seized all temples and auctioned 570 of them out, allowing some local communities to buy them back while many others were bought by entrepreneurs who sold entrance tickets.[21] This led to violent conflict between the city government and merchant associations that endeavored to protect temples.

All in all, the impact of the state's repressive antisuperstition policies varied hugely in space and time but was, as a whole, destructive and disruptive. This did not, however, lead to a wholesale disappearance of traditional religious practices. In the countryside, it was warfare that had the most dramatic effect, making large-scale gatherings, and especially pilgrimages, extremely dangerous or outright impossible. Whereas most pilgrimages, either national or local, were still very lively in 1937, warfare dealt them a blow from which most did not recover until the 1980s. So, in spite of the self-congratulatory reports by missionary observers and Chinese intellectuals claiming that the gods were disappearing from sight, there is little hard evidence of communities *spontaneously* discarding their religious habits.[22] In cases where outright confrontation between hotheaded activists and religious leaders was avoided and negotiation was possible, temple communities offered room to schools and other state outfits but maintained their cults and rituals, even if downscaled. Most people failed to see the incompatibility between them posited by urban intellectuals, and indeed a fair number of temples were built during that period, by rich individuals or by associations. Similarly, many guilds converted into chambers of com-

---

21. Tsin, *Nation, Governance, and Modernity*; Poon Shuk Wah, *Negotiating Religion*.

22. Welch, *The Buddhist Revival in China*, chap. 8; Day, *Chinese Peasant Cults*; Yang C. K., *Religion in Chinese Society*, chap. 13.

merce and professional associations, but cults to patron saints continued, even if on a lesser scale, suggesting only partial internal secularization.[23]

RELIGION AS RESISTANCE

Faced with repression, religious specialists and communities resorted to a wide array of tactics of resistance. The most violent instances of resistance, such as armed rebellions, appear as cases of desperate last-ditch defense of local traditions crushed by a mighty state. The Republican period witnessed the large-scale development of self-defense groups, of a kind that was already widely present during the late imperial period, but which took on an ever more prominent role when the traditional religious structures of local society were under attack and much weakened. During the first half of the twentieth century, many if not most northern China villages had militia groups that usually practiced rites of healing, martial empowerment, and magical invincibility, often derived from millenarian or mainstream Buddhist and Taoist traditions. Often called Red Spears 紅槍會 or Big Knives 大刀會, they embodied the notion of village autonomy and self-protection against all outside predators, be they roving bandits, tax collectors and other state agents, or even rival village organizations—and could, in some cases, turn into predators toward other villagers.[24] For this reason, they rarely entered supralocal networks or hierarchical systems, even though, in some cases and in exceptional circumstances, such as the Boxers in 1899–1900, they might coalesce into large-scale movements.

These militias were ready to take up arms to resist state attempts at seizing village resources, notably communal temples. A well-publicized case occurred in northern Jiangsu in 1928 when newly installed KMT officials seized temple property. The Red Spears–organized riots resulted in the killing of local officials, and only armies sent by the central government were able to put down the insurrection.[25] Similar incidents had marked the advent of temple seizures since 1905 throughout rural China. Local communities, being heavily taxed and deprived of their communal resources (notably temples), expressed widespread resistance toward state building by acts such as destroying schools, railway tracks, or telephone lines.[26]

---

23. On guild cults during the Republican period, see Burgess, *The Guilds of Peking*.
24. Perry, *Rebels and Revolutionaries*.
25. Nedostup, "Religion, Superstition," 340–69.
26. Many examples in Prazniak, *Of Camel Kings*; Wang Shuhuai, "Qingmo Jiangsu difang zizhi fengchao."

Temple leaders and/or Buddhists and Taoists were quite often found at the head of such mass actions, in collaboration with the village militia.

Another strand of popular religious resistance was the millenarian-inspired movements, which occasionally led violent action against the Nationalist state, the Japanese occupation army, or the Communists, with some groups having a record of fighting all three in sequence. In many cases it is difficult to separate village militia from millenarian uprisings; and Nationalists, Japanese, and Communists failed to come up with a coherent stand on this issue. Nonetheless, millenarian uprisings tended to differ from self-defense militia in that they drew from ad-hoc communities drawn together under charismatic leaders with an eschatological message, rather than uniting a village against the outside world. In both cases, however, the insurgents shared a program of maintaining traditional morality in the face of a crumbling world order. Such religiously inspired revolts were all small scale and eventually put down by superior military might, but were nonetheless quite common through the 1940s and 1950s and sputtered on afterward.[27] Similarly, native resistance to the Japanese colonial state in Taiwan (1895–1945) was mostly rooted in networks of salvationist groups, as apparent in the Xilai'an incident of 1915.[28] As a result, state builders, be they Japanese, Nationalists, or Communists, tended to see village religious culture as naturally rebellious. They focused their attention on the political potential of local religious groups, overlooking the fact that these groups were fundamentally concerned with preserving traditional morality—respect for gods and elders, or maintaining established gender roles—and never developed a program for actually seizing power and changing society.

All these instances of armed resistance to protect village society and values can be understood as natural byproducts of the dramatic extension of the nation-state into rural areas that were heretofore largely self-governed, and as such they are part of a worldwide phenomenon. Historiography is divided on the interpretation of the role of religion in such resistance. While some see religion only as a superstructure, a readily available cultural idiom for expressing resistance, we would like to draw attention to how concerns for religious life were at the core of both the cause of resistance—people were appalled that they were deprived of their ability to perform communal rituals for their own welfare—and the networks of mobilization for resistance.

27. Ownby, "Imperial Fantasies."
28. Katz, *When Valleys Turned Blood Red.*

Revolutionaries (both Nationalist and Communist), fascinated by such resistance, tried to rationalize and channel it to their own ends, and theorized that there were secular groups, that is, the "secret societies" (*mimi jieshe/shehui* 秘密結社/社會), a term adopted around 1912 by secular intellectuals from the Japanese term (itself translated from English)[29] to denote all mutual-support groups based on ritual kinship and initiation (including the Elders' Societies [Gelaohui 哥老會], the Triads [Tiandi-hui 天地會], the Red Spears, and the like), which devoted themselves to protecting the peasants, and "superstitious" groups such as the redemptive societies. Such a categorization prevented the revolutionaries from understanding how and why religion made sense to all these groups and their violent opposition to secular state building. As early as the late Qing, revolutionaries like Sun Yat-sen had allied with the so-called secret societies, which had a much larger membership and social base than political parties.[30] The Communists followed the same path, alternating alliances with such groups in the framework of United Front policy when it fit their interests, and repression of the same groups in the Communist bases when they considered that their control over society was firm enough to dispense with such allies (see chapter 6).[31]

Violence was the most spectacular type of resistance, but it only occurred in a minority of cases. Where traditional elites (lower degree holders, traditionally educated merchants, schoolmasters, and professionals) continued to sit on temple committees—that is, those places where these elites still existed and had not gone over to Nationalist antisuperstition projects—violence was rejected. In the eyes of most local power holders, the Boxers were the very model of what should be avoided. These elites, when they could still play their traditional role of cultural intermediaries, advocated different strategies of engaging the state on its own terms. They sued the state for abusively confiscating property and unlawful destruction under the banner of the constitutional "freedom of belief" (as well as the few safeguards in the 1915 and 1929 temple management acts), and argued that there was a place for local religion in the new China. The petitions they sent up the ladders of the state and the trials they brought to court in great numbers as early as 1912 often failed—or favorable rulings from the courts

29. One of the first attested uses of the term is in a book first published in Chinese in 1912 by a Japanese scholar, based on British colonial publications: ter Haar, *Ritual and Mythology of the Chinese Triads*, 36–37.

30. Price, "Popular and Elite Heterodoxy"; ter Haar, *Ritual and Mythology of the Chinese Triads*, 25–27.

31. Perry, *Rebels and Revolutionaries*.

were outright ignored by local officials—but certainly embarrassed the state and forced officials to realize that there was a problem with its approach to enlightening the people about superstition. In her study of the Nanjing period, Rebecca Nedostup has shown that unremitting legal protests forced the KMT government to reconsider its temple confiscation policies.[32]

Thus, outright violence always failed, and legal recourse very rarely obtained immediate satisfaction. Among the theoreticians of violence and resistance, several anthropologists have drawn attention to the ways in which religious communities faced with oppression, rather than revolting or organizing a political opposition, resorted to less spectacular but more efficient passive resistance in maintaining narratives and discourses of local history and identity stubbornly different from those of the state;[33] this corresponds with now well-established studies worldwide of peasant modes of resistance (the "weapons of the weak").[34] Many scholars agree that resistance to state religious policies overlaps very much with the defense of local identities and memories threatened by homogenizing state projects. Some have emphasized the success of such resistance by stressing that by manipulating the apparent and implied meanings of their religious practices, local communities were often able to resist state attempts at ideological control.[35] For instance, when Nationalist leaders reformulated festivals as political gatherings, replacing offerings to the gods with bowing to the portrait of Sun Yat-sen and holding speeches, populations proved apt at playing with apparent and implied meanings. They concealed traditional religion under the guise of politically correct gatherings, with sacrifices to the gods performed right after the political speeches.[36]

RECONFIGURATION

The process of repression and resistance that engulfed the whole of the Chinese religious field was not a static fight between two monolithic entities—modernist state and traditionalist society. Although communal reli-

---

32. Nedostup, "Religion, Superstition," chap. 3.
33. Feuchtwang, "Religion as Resistance."
34. Scott, *Weapons of the Weak*.
35. Weller, "The Politics of Ritual Disguise," arguing about colonial Taiwan, and *Resistance, Chaos, and Control*. Scholars of late imperial history have also conducted analyses of similar "disguises," "superscription," and other forms of accommodation whereby local celebrations continued basically unchanged under the name of officially sponsored orthodox ritual reform; see notably Watson, "Standardizing the Gods"; Duara, "Superscribing Symbols"; Szonyi, "Making Claims about Standardization."
36. Poon Shuk Wah, "Refashioning Festivals."

gion and its temple cults, even if scaled down, survived in many cases, the space opened up by the diminishing number of temples and their clerical specialists, at least in rural areas, was filled not by secularist ideals and practice but rather by other religious traditions that proved better suited to the demands of Nationalist China. While Christian groups, notably nativist, evangelical movements, did make some inroads, these paled in quantitative comparison with the growth of other new forms of Chinese religion. The redemptive societies assumed many of the social roles and functions of the ruined temple communities. In some cases they took over the actual buildings of temple cults and restored them for their own activities.[37]

The speed and extent of the rural expansion of the redemptive societies, notably in northern China, is as major and striking a phenomenon as the repression caused by the antisuperstition policies. It would seem that by the 1930s and 1940s, in most northern Chinese villages (if the areas that have been studied are representative, but there is no reason why they should not be) a sizable minority of the population belonged to a redemptive society, and some villages had converted in their majority; naturally, the societies' village form could be quite different from their more intellectual, universalist urban form.[38] Whereas these societies had distinctly urban origins, some managed to take roots in rural China, and the war waged by the PRC against them during the 1950s largely took place in the countryside.

This expansion can be explained by a number of factors. The apocalyptic message of many of these societies (notably in the case of Yiguandao) readily made sense to populations brutally exploited by repressive regimes and falling prey to war, roving bandits, and natural disasters (repeated famines, notably in northern China, caused millions of deaths in the 1920s and 1930s), whose effects the state was not able to mitigate. But just as important, these societies and their preachers provided an alternative to communal religion. Their leaders were able to provide liturgical services vital to the sense of communal wellbeing, such as New Year celebrations and praying for peace, prosperity, and welfare during the coming year, as well as individual services, notably healing and funerals. On the other hand, these religious groups were affiliated with branches throughout the

---

37. Examples in Goossaert, *The Taoists of Peking*, chap. 7; and *Chongjian Jinling Yuxuguan jishi zhengxin lu*, which documents how the Shanghai-based Jishenghui restored a Taoist temple near Nanjing during the 1920s.

38. Li Shiyu, *Xiandai huabei mimi zongjiao*; DuBois, *The Sacred Village*; Gamble, *Ting Hsien*, 420–25.

country, and often had a discourse on nation and modernity. They did not depend on landed endowments, as they had very few or no salaried clerics, and their rituals were very cheap in comparison with Buddhist or Taoist services. In other words, they offered a form of organization better suited to the sociopolitical context.

In those places where territorial and kinship forms of communal religion had suffered badly, the redemptive societies were thus able to take over most of their functions, including running temples and organizing rituals. But these were not just interchangeable forms of the same religion. The redemptive societies' focus on morality, discipline, and self-cultivation—many of these groups campaigned against opium and alcohol[39] and advocated the more traditional vegetarian diet—provided them with a ready answer to the state's campaigns for modern, militarized, hygienic citizenship, which culminated with the 1934 New Life movement. Their discourse on morality attracted schoolmasters and other local moral authorities who were very often the backbone of such societies. In this sense, though they rarely had an antagonistic relationship with territorial cults or lineage organizations, the voluntary, associational redemptive societies exhibited a better capacity to develop, convince, and convert in a context where the dominant discourse was overwhelmingly disparaging to traditional communal religion as superstitious, unethical, and useless.

Another group that attempted to fill up the same cracks opened up by the nation-state in the religious fabric of rural China was the Communist Party. Founded as an urban intellectual circle in 1921, the CCP turned into a rural grassroots movement under Mao's leadership after the end of its alliance with the KMT in 1927. Despite the hugely different nature of their social projects—the self-defense groups and salvationist groups sought to preserve traditional morality and village autonomy, while the CCP sought to transform the old social order—the revolutionary vision was often expressed in traditional moral idioms condemning corruption and exploitation. Moreover, the two types of grassroots organizations engaged in a complicated relationship grounded in a common concern for protecting rural society and resisting the predations of modern, urban-based elites. The moral project of the CCP, and its alliances with and subsequent repression of the self-defense and redemptive societies, will be discussed in detail in chapters 6 and 8.

---

39. The Zailijiao campaigned against alcoholism and provided detoxication cures, and many groups fought opium addictions; in such a role, these groups were in direct competition with Christian movements.

SIX

The CCP and Religion, 1921–66

陸

Having sketched how the KMT regime failed in its project of eradicating "superstition" from rural China, we now turn to the attitudes of the its main contender, the CCP, toward religious practices and communities, from the Party's foundation in 1921 until the first years of the People's Republic, culminating in the Cultural Revolution in 1966. This survey shows how the contours of the CCP's religious policy were shaped not only by ideological dogma in partial continuity with Nationalist policies but also by the Party's practical experience in rural liberated areas, in the Long March, in the anti-Japanese United Front, and in the civil war against the KMT. These experiences had taught the CCP that religion was a long-term phenomenon that could not be forcefully wiped out; that it enjoyed a strong popular base that needed to be respected, especially in the minority areas; and that religious leaders could play a role in legitimizing the CCP's political program.

In the first decade after the PRC was established in 1949, the socialist state dealt with the many expressions of Chinese religion: circumscribing

communal cults by seizing what was left of their land base and eliminating their elite patrons; ruthlessly exterminating the redemptive societies
and anything associated with Confucianism; secularizing and nationalizing elements of traditional culture such as folk arts, storytelling, opera,
martial arts, Chinese medicine, and body cultivation traditions; and re-
organizing the institutions of Buddhism, Islam, Protestantism, Roman Catholicism, and Taoism along state corporatist lines. While the five official
religions followed parallel trajectories of integration into the new political
regime, which guaranteed a narrowly defined "freedom of religion," the
CCP's attitudes toward each varied by its ethnic and geopolitical importance, and its stance toward the CCP during the civil war: Buddhism and
Islam were given particular attention as the religions of borderland ethnic minorities and as diplomatic bridges to other postcolonial third-world
states; the umbilical cord of Chinese Christianity was forcefully cut off
from its anticommunist parent churches in the capitalist West; and Taoism, poorly organized (in a nation-building sense) and unconnected to
ethnic or geopolitical interests, was, comparatively speaking, ignored.
During the years of the Great Leap, from 1958 to 1960, ideological radicalism eliminated whatever autonomy had been retained by China's religious
communities while the secularized traditions such as *qigong*, or Chinese
medicine, with strong political support, enjoyed their first heyday. The
early sixties saw the return of a more moderate approach, but this tendency
was aborted by the Cultural Revolution, during which any special regard
for religion was discarded and the state's own institutions for dealing with
religions, from the United Front to the official associations, were abolished,
while all forms of religious activity were banned.

EARLY ATTITUDES AND POLICIES BEFORE THE LONG MARCH (1921–34)

The early leaders of the CCP basically shared the ideas of the New Culture movement, of which they were the more radical spokespersons. Taking their tune from Western enlightenment philosophers and modernist
thinkers, they saw the demise of traditional religion and superstition as
the key to the rebirth of the Chinese nation. In his essay "On smashing
idols" 偶像破壞論, for instance, Chen Duxiu, Marxist intellectual and
founding secretary-general of the CCP, had argued that all gods, Buddhas,
and immortals are false idols, and that religion would disappear with the
advance of technology. In 1921, he had written of the Fellowship of Goodness (Tongshanshe) that the working and student masses did not believe

in these heresies, which recalled the humiliation of the Boxers and the political oppression and social decadence of China.[1] Li Dazhao 李大釗 (1888–1927), cofounder of the CCP together with Chen Duxiu, stressed in his writings that gods were mere creations of humans, although he admitted that the teachings of the five major religions—which he listed as Judaism, Confucianism, Islam, Buddhism, and Christianity—had had a significant impact on the progress of humanity.[2] And Yun Daiying 惲代英 (1895–1931), a leading organizer of Communist Youth, claimed that although "there are many good people in the churches," religion was an obstacle to science while Christianity was a tool of imperialism. Indeed, it was CCP leaders who were among the chief activists of the Anti-Christian movement and the Antireligious Alliance of 1922 and 1924 (described in chapter 2).

At the same time, true to the Western enlightenment tradition, the early CCP leaders, like other modernist intellectuals, affirmed the individual's freedom of religion, his freedom to believe in the religion of his choice, and also his freedom *not* to believe in a religion. On this basis, the CCP did not hesitate to strike alliances with religious believers who shared its short-term objectives, such as those involved in the labor, student, and peasant movements. The CCP was willing to work with the often well-organized Christian social reform movements and student and labor unions,[3] along with the "superstitious" secret societies and militias, to organize labor strikes and peasant resistance.

Indeed, the latter groups, such as the Red Spears, Green Gang 青幫, and Elders' Society, were seen as potential allies in revolution. In spite of the CCP's critique of the backward nature of these types of association, superstition was not to be an obstacle for tactical alliances: Chen Duxiu wrote of the Red Spears that despite the superstitious coloration of peasant thinking, the barbarian and destructive nature of their struggle against the ruling classes should not be opposed.[4] Zhu De 朱德 (1886–1976), one of the Red Army's top generals, was also a member of the Elders' Society,[5] and Mao's thinking was not without a certain romanticism for the bandit heroes and wandering knights of the popular novel *Outlaws of the Marsh*, whose mythology was maintained in the sworn brotherhoods. In 1926, Mao

1. Nedostup, "Religion, Superstition," 97.
2. Chen Jinlong, *Zhongguo gongchandang*, 18.
3. Ibid., 3–4.
4. Li Shiwei, *Zhonggong yu Zhongguo minjian wenhua*, 198.
5. Schram, "Mao Tse-tung and Secret Societies," 6; Smedley, *The Great Road*, 88–89.

described the secret societies—of which he enumerated a list that made no distinction between sworn brotherhoods, armed militias, and redemptive societies (Triads, Elders' Society, Big Swords, Morality Society, Green Gang, and so on)—as mutual help associations of floating populations in their economic and political struggle.[6] The CCP's second enlarged congress (1926) specifically discussed the question of the Red Spears, and passed a resolution stating that "the Red Spears are one of the most important forces in the national revolutionary movement," proposing to give them the means to organize and unify themselves in a systematic fashion, and stressing that "we should not oppose the superstitious beliefs of the Red Spears. They are the basis on which the association organizes and fights. Although they are only relics of ideas which the peasants cannot abandon, we must ensure that these superstitious activities are beneficial for the revolution."[7]

As the CCP shifted its energies after 1927 to organizing the peasants in the rural areas, it became more aware of the depth of religious sentiment among farmers. Although the ultimate goal was to eliminate their superstition, Party leaders stressed the need to avoid needlessly alienating peasants by attacking their gods. In his *Report on the Peasant Movement in Hunan*, Mao enumerated "divine authority" 神權 as one of the "four thick ropes" binding the Chinese people under feudalism, together with political authority, lineage authority, and patriarchy. But divine authority and religious worldviews would naturally disappear as a result of political and economic struggle, so there was no need to attack them directly; this would distract the revolutionary struggle: "It is the peasants who made the idols, and when the time comes they will cast the idols aside with their own hands; there is no need for anyone else to do it for them prematurely."[8] Class analysis, he stressed, was more important: to struggle against the landlords in charge of the cults, more than against the cults themselves. From 1927, and in the Jiangxi Soviet and other Communist bases in the early 1930s, this was translated into a policy banning the forceful destruction of deity statues but calling for the confiscation of all "public" temples, lineage halls, and church property that was in practice managed by members of the local elites or foreign clergy, and either turning such temples and properties into peasant association offices, schools, and sources of income for peasant associations, or redistributing them to the landless.[9] According to one direc-

---

6. Schram, "Mao Tse-tung and Secret Societies," 4.
7. Quoted in Tai Hsüan-chih, *The Red Spears*, 106.
8. Mao Zedong, "Report on the Peasant Movement in Hunan," in *Selected Works*, 1:46.
9. Chen Jinlong, *Zhongguo gongchandang*, 2, 8, 20, 41.

tive, Protestant pastors, Catholic priests, Buddhist monks, Taoist priests, vegetarian ritualists (*zhaigong* 齋公), geomancers, and diviners were to be placed in the class of "religious specialists" (宗教職業者) and denied political rights such as membership in peasant associations or the vote.[10]

THE LONG MARCH AND THE RELIGIONS OF BORDERLAND ETHNIC GROUPS (1934–36)

The Long March began in 1934, when Chiang Kai-shek launched an all-out offensive against the Communist bases in China, and crushed the Jiangxi soviet. Traveling on foot through mountains, forests, and deserts, crossing through some of China's most remote districts, the Red Army, number-ing one hundred thousand when it left Jiangxi, marched across the south, into the western provinces of Yunnan and Sichuan, and then north into Gansu and Shaanxi. The areas it crossed were heavily populated by ethnic minorities, especially Tibetans in Kham and Amdo (northern Yunnan and Xikang, now west Sichuan), and Muslims in Gansu and Shaanxi. These populations were weary in general of armies marching in from outside, and in many cases were particularly suspicious of the Communists. The Red Army, which needed the locals to provide food and supplies, and aimed to draw the peasant populations into the revolutionary cause, had to be par-ticularly vigilant not to needlessly alienate Tibetans, Muslims, and moun-tain tribes, such as the Yi, by offending their religious sensibilities. Real-izing the strong social and political influence of Tibetan lamas and Muslim *ahongs*, these personages were often the first local dignitaries called on by Red Army representatives upon arriving in a new locality. In their bid to re-assure them and secure their cooperation, the representatives stressed reli-gious freedom and guaranteed that Tibetan monasteries and Hui mosques would be spared from land reform and redistribution campaigns. In the case of Muslims, Red Army soldiers were given strict rules concerning the respect of Islamic customs: no insulting Islam; no talking about pork or taking pork into Muslim homes; no using the dishes of Muslims without their full permission; no entering mosques; no touching the Qur'an; and a requirement to display a brotherly attitude toward Muslims.

The respectful attitude was found to be a successful policy: in most (though not all) of the areas it passed through, the Red Army was able to build good relations with the Yi, Tibetan, and Muslim populations, and sometimes friendships with local religious leaders who would later be-

10. Ibid., 45.

come willing collaborators of the CCP regime. The experience became the foundation of many subsequent CCP religious and ethnic policies—one that, in relation to ethnic minorities, compromised antireligious ideology to secure ethnic loyalty to the CCP, in a discourse of one liberated China of several nationalities. Thus, while the CCP called for the systematic confiscation of Han temples and denied political rights to their priests and "superstitious" specialists, the temples, monasteries, and mosques of the minorities were to be protected, and their leaders could be appointed to political positions.

THE YAN'AN PERIOD AND THE ANTI-JAPANESE UNITED FRONT

When the Red Army arrived in 1936 at the base area of Yan'an, in the barren loess plateau of northern Shaanxi not far from the Mongolian steppes, only four thousand of its soldiers remained. And yet it was from this rump that the CCP would rebuild, and from the Yan'an soviet that it would learn and perfect the techniques of peasant mobilization, which it would then apply, twelve years later, as it established its dominion over all of China. Yan'an became the new utopian frontier, attracting idealist youth, intellectuals, and professionals from China's cities, willing to sacrifice material comforts for the rustic life in cave dwellings and for building a new China.

The CCP controlled the border area between Shaanxi, Ningxia, and Gansu, a region with large populations of Muslims and Mongols. The Long March policy of respecting minority religions, particularly Islam and Tibeto-Mongol Buddhism, continued to be applied in the area—the land owned by mosques and Buddhist monasteries was to be protected in land reform campaigns—while the soviet authorities built a new mosque for the Muslim population at the CCP headquarters of Yan'an. This policy, however, was the result of Mao Zedong's formally recognizing, as early as 1936, the Hui as a *nationality* and, in consequence, entitled to autonomy and respect for their customs and religious beliefs. The policy explicitly rejected, as a form of "Han chauvinism," the notion that the Hui were merely Han who believed in Islam; stressed that Islam was not merely a religious belief but an inseparable aspect of the social life of the Hui; and that the "Hui question" 回回問題 could not be reduced to a "religious question."[11] The same logic operated in the case of the Mongols, although there was no policy of protection for the communal religious practices of the Han, for whom

11. Ding Hong & Zhang Guojie, eds., *Bai nian Zhongguo musilin*, 69, 72–73.

religion was not considered an inseparable aspect of social life or ethnic identity. Indeed, in Communist base areas without sizable ethnic minorities, such as the Shandong-Hebei border area, a contrary policy stipulated that the army should confiscate village temples for materials storage.[12]

Meanwhile, the Japanese invasion in 1937 forced the KMT regime to divert its energies from the civil war against the CCP, and popular opinion pushed it into establishing a second United Front (the first was in 1922–27) with the CCP against Japan. For the CCP, the United Front became a systematic strategy to build alliances with all non-Communist sectors of society, including religious groups, against the common enemy. In a speech on the New Democracy in 1940, Mao Zedong stated that "Communists may form an anti-imperialist and anti-feudal united front for political action with certain idealists and even with religious followers, but we can never approve of their idealism or religious doctrines."[13] Editorials echoing this line were published in the CCP-run *Xinhua Daily*; undercover operators embedded within religious organizations were to encourage certain religious groups, such as the YMCA, to become more effective tools of anti-Japanese resistance while at the same time coming under the influence of the Party. The *Xinhua Daily* also encouraged patriotic religionists to organize themselves into national salvationist associations that were being formed in KMT-controlled areas, such as the National Chinese Federation of Christians 中華基督徒全國聯合會 and the China Muslim Salvation Association 中國回民救國協會, both established in 1938, followed by similar groups of Buddhists and Catholics, and even an association of Tibetan monks from Gansu, Qinghai, and Sichuan, the Association for the Cultural Advancement of Tibetan People 藏民文化促進會. By 1943, these efforts were crowned by the establishment of the Chinese Federation of Religious Believers 中國宗教徒聯誼會 on the initiative of General Feng Yuxiang, Taixu, Roman Catholic bishop Yu Bin 于斌 (1901–1978), and other notable figures.[14] Such associations continued the trend, described earlier, of the formation of national religious associations throughout the Republican period; now the Japanese threat and the Communist support facilitated these efforts. These associations were established on the initiative of non-Communist religious believers and even KMT members, but under the framework of the United Front they received varying degrees of open encouragement and covert guidance from the CCP—in

---

12. Chen Jinlong, *Zhongguo gongchandang*, 75.
13. Quoted in MacInnis, ed., *Religious Policy*, 13.
14. Chen Jinlong, *Zhongguo gongchandang*, 104.

some ways prefiguring the official religious associations that would later be established in the PRC. Indeed, some of the activists of these anti-Japanese religious associations, such as Wu Yaozong 吳耀宗 (1893–1979) of the YMCA, would later play leading roles in the PRC religious associations.

The United Front also applied to the sworn brotherhoods and secret societies, which were now seen as neither irredeemable enemies nor revolutionary comrades. The CCP's strategy was to find common ground with them on tactical objectives, such as defense and lower taxation. Mao published an "Appeal from the Central Soviet Government" to the "Brothers of the Elders' Society," in which he warmly praised its anti-Qing tradition and called on them to join the anti-Japanese front.[15] CCP cadres did not hesitate to establish secret society shrines that were but fronts for Party cells, which could then infiltrate and control the group.[16] Friendly leaders of such groups were to be co-opted, while leaders who resisted were to be shot. But the ultimate goal was to render these groups useless by creating grassroots revolutionary associations that could better meet the needs of the people. Local mass mobilization systems would ultimately undermine the secret societies and make them superfluous.

Religious groups were also manipulated and infiltrated by the Japanese, who created Buddhist, Taoist, and Muslim associations in the occupied areas, not only to influence Chinese believers, but also as part of an international strategy to position Japan in Asia as a defender of Buddhist and Islamic values against the materialist West. Sworn brotherhoods and redemptive societies were also sites for a battle of influences between the CCP and the Japanese. In the Wuxi area (southern Jiangsu), for instance, the Xiantiandao (Way of Anterior Heaven) was infiltrated by both sides. But once the CCP had managed to spur several of its lodges into violent anti-Japanese action, the latter's praise for the "religious faith" of the believers turned into denunciation of the group as an "evil cult" deluding the masses.[17]

INTENSIFICATION OF CIVIL WAR AND ITS AFTERMATH IN THE PRC: CAMPAIGNS AGAINST COUNTERREVOLUTIONARIES AND CLASS ENEMIES (1945–57)

Following the Japanese surrender in 1945, the CCP and KMT turned against each other again, in an all-out civil war. This time, from its bases in

---

15. Schram, "Mao Tse-tung and Secret Societies," 11–13; Munro, ed., "Syncretic Sects," 99–101.

16. Chen Yung-fa, *Making Revolution*, 488–92.

17. Shao Yong, *Zhongguo huidaomen*, 378–79.

the hinterland, the Red Army was able to systematically expand the areas under its control, eventually leading to its conquest of all of China bar Taiwan. As revolutionary governments and land reform campaigns were established in different areas, the CCP's religious policies were also carried out—with, at least on paper, a higher degree of leniency than in the earlier soviets—in order to ensure the support of local populations. Thus, in confiscating land from churches, lineage halls, and temples, a small portion of land was to be left for their maintenance and for the subsistence of their religious personnel. Foreign missionaries who did not oppose the CCP were also to be allowed to operate freely. In practice, however, zealous Party activists and soldiers often violently destroyed temples, churches, and other public buildings—acts condemned by Deng Xiaoping in a 1948 circular for stirring up popular antagonism against the CCP.[18] In dealing with religious groups that did not oppose land reform, other Party documents stated that the objective was to encourage their collaboration or allow them to take a neutral stance; in the meantime, Party operators were to nurture the loyalty of their lower-class believers in order to cut them off from their leaders. But religious groups that opposed the land reforms were to be attacked.[19] Again, however, Muslim mosques and Mongol monasteries, as well as their clergy—numerous where the CCP expanded its control in the northeast—were to be spared.

The civil war led to the breaking down of much of the United Front with religious communities, many of which split into pro- and anti-Communist factions. Fearing communist atheism and instrumentalized by the KMT, many religious groups became overtly involved in anti-Communist resistance. The Muslim KMT generals of the northwest urged the China Islamic Association to take a stronger stance against the CCP. The Vatican established diplomatic relations with the Nanjing government in 1946 and actively supported the KMT in the civil war, issuing a decree in 1949 banning all Catholics from reading any CCP publications, under threat of punishment or excommunication. As for Protestants, in the intensifying postwar cold war atmosphere, many of the US- and UK-based missionary societies and denominational headquarters actively supported the KMT against the Communist threat.

The redemptive societies also had a tendency to side with the KMT. As we have seen earlier, their leading supporters were often KMT and warlord-regime officials and generals, and their active core was typically

18. Chen Jinlong, *Zhongguo gongchandang*, 109–12, 114.
19. Ibid., 112.

remnants of the old Confucian literati. The groups had especially flourished in the Japanese-controlled areas and, especially in Manchuria, had been used by the Manchukuo regime as providers of social services. All these factors made them natural enemies of the CCP. As the Communist victory became imminent, apocalyptic rumors spread and contributed to the growth of the redemptive societies, especially Yiguandao, which had established branches, many with large memberships, in almost all cities and countries of China (see chapter 4). At the same time, as KMT authority collapsed and the CCP took over, popular anti-Communist revolts erupted in many regions, which, similar to past rebellions in Chinese history, built religious networks, drew inspiration from apocalyptic visions, and aimed to install a new emperor. Yiguandao branches and other redemptive societies were accused of stirring up these armed uprisings and organizing underground anti-Communist resistance in the newly liberated zones—a depiction that was almost a mirror image of the CCP underground itself. Since the redemptive societies were the largest and best-organized popular organizations—contrary to other anti-Communist forces, they had a strong popular base—the Red Army's policy was, unless they were caught in active opposition, to begin by leaving them alone in order to avoid stirring popular antagonism. Then it would concentrate on stabilizing its control by clearing out bandits, carrying out land reform, and enrolling the people in mass organizations. Only after Communist control was firmly secured did the new regime move to eliminate the redemptive societies.[20]

Thus, on January 4, 1949—ten months before the People's Republic was established—the People's Government of North China banned all manner of "sects and secret societies," using two categories crafted by CCP ideologues during the Yan'an period, the secret societies (*huimen* 會門) and the sects (*daomen* 道門). It emphasized that these organizations were not only "feudal" 封建 (meaning the psychological manipulation and economic exploitation of the masses by landlords and religious institutions) and superstitious, but also "instruments of the counter-revolutionaries" and "enemy spies" who "propagate rumors," "agitate popular sentiment," "organize armed revolts," and "disturb social order." The leaders of these organizations were summoned to turn themselves in to the authorities and to repent if they wanted to avoid a harsh punishment. Meanwhile, the ordinary followers, who had been "fooled" by the reactionary societies, were ordered to withdraw from these associations and to cease any activity if they wanted to avoid being prosecuted, and were promised a reward if they

20. Tan Songlin & Peng Bangfu, "Dangdai huidaomen," 9.

provided information on these associations and their acts of "sabotage."[21] Other regional governments did the same later in 1949. Official discourse crystallized: the groups in question became "reactionary secret societies" (*fandong huidaomen* 反動會道門), a category that fused the two earlier categories of *huimen* and *daomen*.

Consequently, when the People's Republic was founded in October 1949, the CCP authorities were already, especially in Manchuria, deeply engaged in a campaign to destroy the redemptive societies—a campaign that now was going to be implemented throughout China. The *huidaomen* were to be ruthlessly exterminated in the national campaign against counterrevolutionary activities launched at the end of 1950, which called for the death sentence or life imprisonment for those who used "feudal secret societies" (*fengjian huidaomen*, a synonym for "reactionary secret societies") to engage in such pursuits. Official circulars stressed the difference in nature between the *huidaomen* and "religion" (Buddhism, Islam, Catholicism, Protestantism, and Taoism), which was to be protected under the principle of religious freedom, as well as ordinary superstition, which was not to be automatically confused with organized counterrevolutionary activity. Thus, some groups were classified as "superstitious" (and treated more leniently) in some counties and "counterrevolutionary" in others.[22] The campaign against the *huidaomen* reached its climax in 1953 and 1954, during which, according to police reports, 13 million followers cut their ties with the groups and 820,000 leaders turned themselves in or were arrested.[23] It is not known how many of the latter were executed.

By far the largest of these societies, and hence the principal target of the campaign, was Yiguandao, which thus found itself at the center of the struggle against reactionary forces. All forms of propaganda were deployed against it, from editorials and speeches by Mao published in the *People's Daily* and the rest of the press, to posters, comics, exhibits, denunciation assemblies, and even theatrical performances. The name Yiguandao became a synonym for the counterrevolutionary sect and even a favored insult used by children in schoolyards.[24] One wonders to what extent *Yiguandao*, like *White Lotus* centuries earlier, became a stigmatizing label used to demonize any suspect individual or group during the revolutionary fervor, even those with no real link to Yiguandao. Indeed, according to one Taoist monk, the

21. Shao Yong, *Zhongguo huidaomen*, 405–6.
22. Tan Songlin & Peng Bangfu, "Dangdai huidaomen," 55.
23. Shao Yong, *Zhongguo huidaomen*, 452, 455.
24. Ibid., 465; DuBois, *The Sacred Village*, 148.

anti-Yiguandao campaign was a pretext for arresting most of Chengdu's Taoists in the early 1950s, thereby circumventing the religious-freedom principle that was supposed to protect Taoism as an official religion. Newspapers at the time claimed that 30 percent of Sichuan's population were members of Yiguandao: a fantastic figure that enabled one to see the Yiguandao danger everywhere.[25]

This campaign occurred in a context in which, although the KMT had been defeated and the CCP had established itself as China's sole political authority on the mainland, the civil war was not completely over: pockets of armed resistance remained, took religious and apocalyptic overtones, and were often associated with redemptive societies such as Yiguandao or the Tongshanshe.[26] The campaign against the *huidaomen* and Yiguandao appears to have been largely successful. In the region of Hebei studied by Thomas DuBois, Yiguandao was already little more than a memory by the end of the 1950s.[27] Nonetheless, well into the 1960s, the police continued to arrest purported "emperors" claiming the Mandate of Heaven, and to repress *huidaomen* groups.

Meanwhile, the land reform campaigns, which were among the first acts of the new regime—and had already been completed in many of the "old" liberated zones—aimed to radically transform the society by creating a new social structure based on class categories. Land and property were distributed from landlords to landless peasants, who were given the highest status—something unimaginable for them in the past, which turned them into a grateful and loyal base of CCP supporters. The land reform and the social reorganization necessarily had important consequences for the configuration of local religion, even where it was not directly attacked: the large estates that supported lineages were appropriated, and the lineage leaders, who were often members of the local elites ("landlords"), were executed or forced to become ordinary farmers. The same went for territorial temples, whose main financial sponsors were typically members of the local elites. At the same time, the new forms of rural social organization and land management—teams, brigades, cooperatives, and communes—were often organized around patrilineal kin groups, so that lineages continued to structure rural social relations in many places.[28] Although kinship

25. Deliusin, "The I-Kuan Tao Society," 232.

26. Tan Songlin & Peng Bangfu, "Dangdai huidaomen," 40–52.

27. DuBois, *The Sacred Village*, 148–51.

28. Potter & Potter, *China's Peasants*, 251–69; see also A. Chan et al., *Chen Village*; E. Friedman et al., *Chinese Village, Socialist State*.

groups were now completely stripped of ritual life and thus invisible to the outside, in the post-Mao period they would suddenly resurface and stimulate ritual revivals (as described in chapter 10).

And yet, while the general trend and political atmosphere of the first decade of the People's Republic made it increasingly difficult for temples to operate, and encouraged their confiscation or destruction by local activists and authorities, CCP policy was to focus on struggles against "landlords," "class enemies," and "counterrevolutionary elements"—who were often active in temple management—rather than on attacking temples themselves.[29] The press on occasion criticized fanatical activists who desecrated temples and ancestral halls, upsetting the people and thus causing them to support the landlords.[30] In parts of North China studied by Adam Chau, the social stability and economic recovery brought about by the new regime actually stimulated a new flourishing of communal religion and the reconstruction of temples destroyed by the Japanese or the civil war. The impetus for this endeavor was now coming more from the peasants than from the overthrown landlords and rich merchants, who had often been the traditional temple sponsors.[31] But in other areas, even where temples were not destroyed, the land reform and other campaigns severely disrupted the cycles of communal festivals until only domestic rites remained. Factories and workshops producing incense and paper items for burning in worship were converted to make other products, notably toilet paper. Campaigns were launched to secularize the main festivals such as Chinese New Year, abolishing worship, banning images of door gods and kitchen gods, and changing auspicious couplets into revolutionary slogans. For the National Grave-Sweeping Day, the cleaning of graves continued, but offerings and burning incense for the ancestors was discouraged. By 1966, the festival was renamed National Memorial Day, for commemorating revolutionary martyrs.[32] Data from rural Guangdong indicate that through the 1960s, there was no temple or lineage activity during the main festivals; however, domestic ancestor worship did continue, on a smaller scale and in a low-key fashion, turning the festivals into private family affairs.[33] And throughout the 1950s and early 1960s, crowds continued to flock to wher-

---

29. Gong Xuezeng, *Shehui zhuyi yu zongjiao*; Feuchtwang & Wang Mingming, *Grassroots Charisma*, 36–37.

30. Aijmer & Ho, *Cantonese Society*, 147.

31. Chau, "Popular Religion in Shaanbei," 41–42. A similar wave of temple construction in Lianjiang County, Fujian, in the early 1960s is cited by Perry, *Challenging the Mandate of Heaven*, 289.

32. Bush, *Religion in Communist China*, 404–12.

33. Parish & Whyte, *Village and Family*, 273–97.

ever sources of magical water 神水, or other substances with miraculous healing properties, were rumored to have been found.[34]

INSTITUTIONALIZING RELATIONS WITH THE FIVE RELIGIONS, 1949–57

The redemptive societies and temple cults discussed above—which together structured the religious life of the vast majority of Chinese—did not constitute "religion" in the eyes of the CCP. The former were part of the larger category of counterrevolutionary *huidaomen*, together with sworn brotherhoods, criminal gangs, and secret societies, and were to be thoroughly wiped out; the latter were "feudal superstitions" that, even when they were not directly attacked, enjoyed no protection or legitimacy under the new regime. Regarding "religion," however, the CCP, having already accumulated three decades of experience in dealings with religious groups, had developed a much more nuanced approach by the time the PRC was established on October 1, 1949, which it could now apply throughout the nation. The "religions" under consideration here were essentially the institutionalized clergies and their followers: monastic Buddhism of the Han, Tibeto-Mongol, and Thai (Theravada) varieties; the Islam of the *ahongs* and Sufi brotherhoods of the Hui and Turkic minorities; the Protestant congregations; and the Roman Catholic Church. Taoism, most of which was perceived as superstition, was almost forgotten; it was only the existence of the Quanzhen monastic clergy and the famous monasteries under its control, which were analogous to the situation of Buddhism, that permitted Taoism to be belatedly recognized as a religion. As for Confucianism, when it was not perceived as a purely secular humanist philosophy it was entirely subsumed under feudal and reactionary ideology, and had no place whatsoever under the new order.

A fundamental ideological opposition to religion, and the goal of its elimination, remained central to CCP doctrine. Practical experience, however, had shown that this goal could only be achieved in the very long term, and was secondary to the more immediate objectives of defeating the CCP's enemies, establishing CCP control, and rebuilding the socioeconomic structure. Indeed, though victorious, the CCP still considered itself at war—both literally, since the Korean War pitted China against the United States as early as 1950–53; and virtually, since the cold war era was in full swing, placing it firmly at odds with America and its allies, such as

34. S. Smith, "Local Cadres Confront the Supernatural."

the KMT regime in Taiwan, which still hoped to annihilate the Communist regime and reestablish its rule over China. Thus, in many ways, the CCP maintained many of the attitudes and strategies developed during the wars against Japan and the KMT. This involved, on the one hand, eliminating all anti-Communist elements in society while, through the United Front, building alliances with sympathetic non-Communist forces. In the case of religion, the strategy was to reinforce friendly elements within each religious community (these sympathetic individuals were collectively referred to as the "religious sector" 宗教界) so that, with CCP guidance, they could then lead an internal struggle to purge uncooperative religious leaders and networks. This involved avoiding frontal attacks on people's beliefs, displaying overt respect for religion, and nurturing friendly clerics within each community. The latter were appointed to political positions in bodies such as the People's Congress or the People's Consultative Conference at the local, provincial, or national level. Such appointments gave the leading clerics a higher social status than they could have ever hoped for in the previous political regime, and integrated them into the socialist political culture.

At the same time, such individuals, with the guidance of CCP leaders (notably Zhou Enlai), took the initiative to establish "patriotic" religious associations loyal to the CCP. A single association came into being for each of the five recognized religions, representing believers of all subtraditions and nationalities. The plethora of Republican-era associations were abolished—though some, such as the Buddhist Association of the Republic of China, had followed the KMT to Taiwan. However, the new generation of groups achieved, with PRC support and purges of uncooperative elements, the Republican-era dream of creating single representative institutions for each religion: the China Islamic Association and the China Buddhist Association, both founded in May 1953; the (Protestant) Three-Self (for "self-governing, self-financing, and self-expanding") Patriotic Movement in July 1954; the China Taoist Association in April 1957; and the Chinese Catholic Patriotic Association in June 1957. The order in which these associations were established reflected the quality of the relationship between their leaders and the United Front: relatively unproblematic for the Buddhists and Muslims, virtually nonexistent for the Taoists, and extremely tense for the Catholics. These associations, though nominally independent of the government, were in fact under the authority of the Religious Affairs Bureau 宗教事務局 (RAB) of the State Council, established in 1954.

The mission of the RAB was to "implement the policy of religious freedom": although on the one hand it carried out policies and regulations that placed strict restrictions on the organization of religious activities, on the other hand, to a certain degree, it protected the interests of religious communities—and the "freedom of belief" of their members—within a larger political system that, overall, had no commitment to religion and whose leaders, ideologically, were more inclined to abolish religion altogether. In practice, one of the main functions of the RAB was to conduct frequent political indoctrination sessions for religious leaders and communities through lectures and study groups.[35] Similarly, the religious leaders who operated within this system acted as spokesmen for the government vis-à-vis their followers, but at the same time they tried to defend the interests of their communities within the system itself.

A state corporatist system of religious management thus came into being, with two principal components: the United Front Department 統戰部 (a department of the CCP) developed relationships with religious leaders as individuals, while the RAB—an agency of the State Council at the national level, and of provincial and local governments at lower levels—dealt with the official religious associations as institutions. The United Front Department and the RAB thus worked together on religious issues, especially when choosing slates of candidates at the "elections" of leaders of the official associations. Often, especially at the local level, it was the same cadres who ran the United Front and Religious Affairs offices. A parallel system of agencies was the Nationalities Commission, in charge of ethnic affairs; though separate from Religious Affairs at the national level, at lower levels and especially in the minority autonomous regions, the Nationalities Commission was usually combined with Religious Affairs.

Wherever it went, the CCP had to deal with different sets of religious issues. There was the religious arm of Western imperialism in the form of Christianity, which now had deep roots in Chinese soil. There was the religious identity of the minority peoples, especially Tibetans, Muslims, and Mongols, which had to be placated to secure their allegiance. And there were the deep-seated beliefs and practices of the peasants at the grass roots, which had to be transformed without alienating the people. Furthermore, there were the religious sensibilities—especially Buddhist and Muslim—of the People's Republic's erstwhile third world allies in the postcolonial struggle against imperialism—sensibilities that would be cultivated by using Chinese Buddhist and Muslim delegations, and exchanges of Buddhist relics, as conduits for international diplomacy. By the mid-1950s, the CCP's view of religion came to be summarized under the notion of the

35. Bush, *Religion in Communist China*, 31–32.

"five characteristics" of religion: its long-term nature 長期性, its mass nature 群眾性, its ethnic nature 民族性, its international nature 國際性, and its complex nature 複雜性. Each religion was seen as having its own peculiar problem to solve: imperialism in the case of Catholicism and Protestantism, feudalism in the case of Buddhism and Taoism, and feudalism compounded by minority ethnic issues in the cases of Islam and Tibetan Buddhism. How the CCP handled what it called the religious question would thus be a fundamental factor in determining its success or failure in acquiring popular and international legitimacy.

Tibetan Buddhism

The first major religious issue to be tackled concerned the question of Tibet. Within a year of the founding of the PRC, the new regime set out to establish its sovereignty over central and western Tibet, which had been free of any form of Chinese control since 1913 (the eastern Tibetan areas of Kham and Amdo, which were not under the authority of the Tibetan government in Lhasa and had historically strong ties to the neighboring Han-populated areas, were already incorporated into the provinces of Yunnan, Sichuan, Gansu, and Qinghai). The CCP's approach, building on the experience described above, aimed to induce the voluntary submission of the Tibetans by guaranteeing to respect their religious freedom, protect their religious institutions, and even leave intact Tibet's theocratic political system, in which the Dalai Lama was both the supreme spiritual and political leader. This approach convinced a part of the Tibetan clerical elites: on October 1, 1949, dignitaries acting for the eleven-year-old Panchen Lama, Choekyi Gyaltsen (1938–1989), who had just been enthroned in June with the blessings of the KMT, sent a telegram to Mao Zedong and Zhu De, congratulating the founding of the People's Republic and hoping for the "early liberation" of Tibet. Meanwhile, a senior lama, Sherab Gyatso (喜饒嘉措, 1884–1968), was appointed vice-chairman of the People's Government of Qinghai Province.[36] But by sending Red Army troops to the Tibetan border and crushing armed resistance there, the new regime made it clear that it was capable and willing to conquer Tibet militarily.

At the same time, the American government, seeing Tibet as a potential cold war front, informally encouraged the fifteen-year-old Fourteenth Dalai Lama, Tenzin Gyatso (b. 1935), to seek exile and lead an anti-

36. He Guanghu, ed., *Zongjiao yu dangdai Zhongguo shehui*, 42; Goldstein, *A History of Modern Tibet*, 683–85, 523–24, 640.

Communist resistance (but without recognizing Tibetan independence, since this would offend the KMT regime in Taiwan).[37] But when formal appeals for help sent to the United States, western Europe, and the UN went unanswered, the Dalai Lama saw that he had no choice but to negotiate with the PRC and send a delegation to Beijing. In May 1951 his representatives signed the "Agreement of the Central People's Government and the Local Government of Tibet on Measures for the Peaceful Liberation of Tibet." This document, known as the "Seventeen-Point Agreement," recognized Chinese sovereignty over Tibet and committed the Tibetan government to help the People's Liberation Army—the PLA, as the Red Army had been formally named after the Sino-Japanese War—enter Tibet and integrate its troops into the Chinese army. At the same time, it guaranteed that the Tibetan political structure and the status of the Dalai Lama would remain intact, along with Tibetan religious customs and monasteries. The document was signed by the Dalai Lama's representatives without his knowledge, and he was urged by the Americans to repudiate it and flee to India or Ceylon. But after consulting his State Oracle, and worried for the safety of his people should he go in exile, he chose to return to Lhasa and abide by the agreement. Meanwhile, the Panchen Lama, who had been kept in protective custody in Qinghai by the Communist authorities, returned to Lhasa, declaring his support for the new regime.

For most of the 1950s, although the PLA was present in Tibet, little effort was made to change that country's religious, political, or economic system. The estates through which the monasteries and noble families controlled most of the land were left alone, and religious life continued as before. Moreover, the Dalai Lama continued as head of the Tibetan government. He was also appointed to political offices within the PRC, as honorary chairman of the China Buddhist Association and as vice-chairman of the Standing Committee of the National People's Congress.[38] The Panchen Lama was appointed to this latter body as well, and in 1954 became a deputy chairman of the Chinese People's Political Consultative Conference.

Islam

The case of Islam was handled following essentially the same principles as those used in dealing with Tibetan Buddhism, within the context of minor-

---

37. Knaus, "Official Policies and Covert Programs," 69; Goldstein, "Introduction" and "The United States, Tibet, and the Cold War."
38. Goldstein, "Introduction."

ity nationality policy. Since Hui Muslims had been active within China's nationalist movement early on, and strong ties had been developed with Muslim communities in the northwest during the Yan'an period, the organizing in 1953 of the China Islamic Association was a relatively smooth affair. Until 1958, no attempts were made to radically change the institutional structure of Muslim communities: mosques, Sufi brotherhoods, and Muslim cemeteries retained large properties and estates, which were exempt from land reforms and taxes; and imams retained significant social influence. In Kashgar, where the Muslim clergy had an extremely powerful position, the religious courts were abolished in 1950, but they continued to operate unofficially.[39] Unlike the Protestants, who were forced to merge their denominations, policy toward Muslim sects was "to each its own teachings, for each its own business, with mutual respect." The three major Islamic festivals were respected as public holidays in Muslim areas; meat and foodstuffs were to be provided at a discount and free of tax on such days. In 1956, the term *Yisilan jiao* 伊斯蘭教 was officially adopted by the State Council as the Chinese term for *Islam*, banning the traditional label of *huijiao* 回教. A year later, the government felt that since the Uighurs, Mongols, Tibetans, and Zhuang minorities all had or were preparing to establish their own autonomous regions, the Hui, if they were to be treated equally in the "great family of the motherland," should have their own autonomous region as well. However, since the Hui were dispersed throughout China, there was no obvious location for a Hui region. Finally, the Ningxia Hui Autonomous Region was established by separating from Gansu Province the area with the highest concentration of Hui people.[40]

With Xinjiang and Ningxia, China now had two autonomous regions with Muslim majorities, a fact that became an important component of the PRC's diplomacy with other third world countries, in addition to delegations of pilgrims to Mecca and visits with religious and political leaders from Muslim countries. This is not to say, however, that all Muslims easily accepted the new regime. Riots and revolts were reported in several parts of western China, especially Gansu and Ningxia, often during the land reform campaigns. A Kazakh rebellion raged around the borders of Xinjiang, Qinghai, and Gansu in 1950–51, stoked by fears of the CCP eradicating religion, until its leader was executed.[41]

39. Dillon, *Xinjiang*, 29.
40. Ding Hong & Zhang Guojie, eds., *Bai nian Zhongguo musilin*, 138–44.
41. Bush, *Religion in Communist China*, 269–70; Ding Hong & Zhang Guojie, eds., *Bai nian Zhongguo musilin*, 406–8.

Christianity

The other main religious issue was that of the Christians, both Catholic and Protestant. Here the new regime had to deal with a religion whose number of followers was relatively low (in the range of 1 million Protestants and 3 million Catholics in 1949), but which had strong institutions and deep ties with the Western capitalist and "imperialist" powers. The Protestant churches had generally supported the KMT during the civil war, while the Roman Catholic Church had taken a firmly anticommunist stance, threatening communist collaborators with excommunication. The CCP's strategy here was to respect the "religious freedom" of Chinese Christians while cutting them off from their foreign ties, by encouraging those individuals from the churches who already had close ties to the CCP through the United Front, and by aiding the organization of the "three-self" movement within the churches themselves, which, since the 1920s, aimed to make Chinese churches "self-propagating, self-governing, and self-financing" 自治、自養、自傳. At the same time, the general political atmosphere made it very dangerous for Christians to resist the movement and maintain ties with Western coreligionists.

The severing of foreign ties was especially traumatic for the Catholic Church. In July 1949, the Holy Office in Rome ordered all Catholics to boycott Communist influence; they were later forbidden from reading CCP publications, joining CCP-run schools, and joining the PLA. In late 1950, these orders were rejected by a group of Catholics in Guangyuan, Sichuan, who called for the "self-support and reform" of the Chinese Catholic Church, and demanded that the administration of the church be managed by Chinese clergy, not foreign missionaries. Other Catholics followed suit, and the Holy Office threatened their excommunication.

Starting in 1951, the PRC government began expelling foreign missionaries. More Catholics openly endorsed the autonomy movement, while others remained loyal to Rome, which condemned any move to autonomy. However, with CCP support, in 1953 the "autonomist" clergy met at a synod in Nanjing, in which they chose the name of Chinese Patriotic Movement. Some Catholic figures were appointed to political organizations such as the National People's Congress, although by doing so they risked excommunication by Rome. Pope Pius XII condemned the movement in encyclicals in 1952 and 1954, but in the 1955 campaign to suppress counterrevolutionaries, pro-Roman and uncooperative Catholic leaders were arrested. In June 1957, the pro-government Catholics established the Chinese Catholic Patriotic Association (CCPA), which was run by lay

Catholics rather than by clergy. Rome urged Catholics to resist this move to the point of martyrdom.

Among the Protestants, the Party's chief ally was Wu Yaozong, the publications secretary of the YMCA, who had been an active supporter of the United Front and was author of a "Christian manifesto" urging Chinese Christians to oppose imperialism and accept CCP leadership. The Korean War provided the pretext for severing links with foreign churches. From 1951 to 1954, the Chinese Protestant Anti-America, Aid Korea Three-Self Reform Movement (TSRM) became the instrument for mobilizing Protestant Christians around CCP leadership. In 1951, 151 Protestant leaders were summoned to Beijing, told to cut their foreign ties, and taught how to conduct accusation meetings against reactionaries and imperialist collaborators. The TSRM organized local committees to struggle against anti-Communist elements within the churches; by 1953, all foreign-founded Protestant churches had been brought under its control. In July 1954, a National Christian Conference was called, which renamed and institutionalized the TSRM as the Three-Self Patriotic Movement.[42] The indigenous churches were then targeted, and leaders who resisted, such as Wang Mingdao 王明道 (1900–1991), were arrested.

Han Buddhism and Taoism

In the eyes of the CCP, Han Buddhism and Taoism, together with Islam and Tibetan Buddhism, suffered from a strongly feudal structure—that is, clergy managed landholding estates and maintained paternalistic relationships with their followers which extended beyond the strictly religious domain—and were thus in need of reform. But although the minority ethnic dimension of Islam and Tibetan Buddhism gave them (temporary) respite from forced changes, Han Buddhism and Taoism bore the brunt of land reforms and antifeudal campaigns. Whereas these campaigns did not directly target Buddhism and Taoism per se, the result was the complete evisceration of both religions as social entities. A 1951 circular ordered the protection of the great monasteries at famous mountains and those temples containing historic relics, but all temples without resident clerics—which was the vast majority—were to be handed over to the government. In cities that had many temples, only a few large temples were to be maintained, with all monks and nuns residing there, so that they could "conduct Buddhist

42. See Wickeri, *Seeking the Common Ground*, for a study of the Three-Self Patriotic Movement and its relations with the United Front.

rites and feel that their religious freedom is being protected."[43] The land estates that were the main source of income for the large monasteries were expropriated and redistributed to landless peasants, while "superstitious" activities such as divination, fortune-telling, and holding exorcistic rites—an important source of income for monks—were banned both inside and outside temple precincts. Deprived of income from land and from ritual services—and with donations from wealthy devotees also drying up—clerics were at the same time required to engage in productive labor, either by doing farmwork or working in small factories or temple enterprises. The Buddhist and Taoist clergy, which had traditionally been organically linked to local communities by providing ritual services to their temples and to individuals, was now completely cut off and required to live according to monastic norms of communal self-sufficiency and spiritual study. The practice of monastic wandering, in which monks could freely move from one monastery to another, was also abolished, each monk being permanently attached to a single temple. Householding priests, who were the vast majority of the Taoist clergy, were granted no religious status whatsoever, and were stigmatized as promoters of feudal superstition. Taixu's dream was realized, although spiritual study now included political education as well: study sessions were organized to participate in political campaigns, to draw the lines between friends and enemies of the motherland, and to purge the religious ranks of imperialists, KMT spies, and *huidaomen* initiates. In the 1950s, the number of Buddhist monks fell from around 500,000 to over 100,000—a development hailed as proof of the success of religious freedom, as people previously forced to don the monastic robes, or who had become monks to escape poverty, were now "free" to return to secular life.

As early as the first People's Consultative Conference, held shortly before the inauguration of the PRC, Buddhist figures, such as Zhao Puchu 趙樸初 (1907–2000), a lay Buddhist who had been active in Buddhist, charitable, and political associations during the Republican period, had been invited as delegates, together with representatives from the Protestant, Catholic, and Muslim communities. As with those religions, Buddhist leaders were mobilized to support the Korean War effort; this then led to the establishment of the China Buddhist Association in May 1953, with broad representation from Buddhists of various nationalities: Tibetans (the Dalai Lama and the Panchen Lama), Mongols (Chagan gegen 查干葛根, 1887–1957), and Han (the widely admired, 113-year-old Chan monk Xuyun 虛雲, 1840?–1959) were appointed as honorary chairmen,

43. He Guanghu, ed., *Zongjiao yu dangdai Zhongguo shehui*, 43.

the monk Yuanying as chairman, and Zhao Puchu as secretary-general. The association gave itself the mission of promoting the cultural and religious education of monks, academic research and preservation of cultural relics, and helping the government eradicate exorcism, sorcery, and "other harmful superstitions."[44]

The Taoists were much slower in organizing themselves and acquiring recognition under the new regime: they were entirely absent from the early People's Consultative Conferences and People's Congresses, which did include representatives from the other religions, and they did not participate in the Korean War mobilization. It was only in 1956 that, for the first time, the abbot of the Taiqinggong 太清宮 monastery in Shenyang, Yue Chongdai 岳崇岱 (1888–1958), was invited to the People's Consultative Conference. In the same year, speeches by Mao Zedong and by the director of United Front mentioned Taoism for the first time among the religions to be dealt with. Shortly thereafter, the China Taoist Association was established in April 1957, with Yue Chongdai as chairman and Chen Yingning as secretary-general.[45]

THE GREAT LEAP FORWARD

With the anti-rightist campaign of 1958, followed by the Great Leap Forward of 1958–61, all the religious communities were subjected to a more extreme political radicalism.[46] In the countryside, with the establishment of the People's Communes, most temples that had survived the previous decade were now abandoned or desecrated. In 1957–59, political education meetings were held for the leaders and clergy of each religion in the Han areas, to deepen their struggle against imperialism and rightism, and to support the People's Communes. The new line was made explicit by Buddhist leader Sherab Gyatso, who, in a *People's Daily* editorial, called for a struggle against rightist elements within religious circles. Several religious leaders were purged as rightists, including Yue Chongdai, who, less than a year earlier, had spearheaded the establishment of the China Taoist Association. He was replaced by Chen Yingning as the acting chairman of the association.

In the fall of 1958, Protestant pastors of the Three-Self Patriotic Movement were summoned for six-month education sessions away from home,

44. Welch, *Buddhism under Mao*; Bush, *Religion in Communist China*, 303.
45. Li Yangzheng, *Dangdai Zhongguo daojiao*, chap. 3.
46. MacInnis, ed., *Religious Policy*.

where they were taught the class basis of their ministry. The two typical political orientations found among Protestants—the social reformism of liberal Christians and the apolitical stance of conservatives and fundamentalists—were attacked, and clergy were "educated" to adopt the "People's stance" of anti-imperialism and patriotism. They were given a choice: to voluntarily become factory workers or to be sent to labor camps as punishment. Most congregations were thus left without ministers, and church buildings emptied. Most churches combined with others and gave their buildings to the state. The number of churches in Shanghai fell from 200 to 8; in Beijing, from 66 to 4. The remaining churches came under the direct control of the Three-Self Patriotic Movement, in which all Protestant denominations were abolished.

During the anti-rightist campaign, the Patriotic Catholic Association consolidated its influence and took control of all the Catholic churches that were still open. The process began of establishing an all-Chinese clergy loyal to Beijing, after the foreign missionaries—who accounted for the vast majority of bishops in China—were expelled, and those Chinese clerics who remained loyal to Rome were purged or driven underground. In December 1957, a diocese in Sichuan held episcopal elections, followed by other Chinese dioceses; these bishops were consecrated in Hankou on April 13, 1958. The results were telegrammed to Rome, with a request for ratification. But Rome invalidated the election, ordered the candidates to withdraw from the consecration, and threatened their excommunication. In June 1958, a new papal encyclical denounced the CCPA as a Communist tool to destroy the Catholic faith and establish a schismatic church. But Rome's protests were in vain: by 1965, over fifty bishops had been consecrated without the approval of the Vatican. Other Catholics refused to follow the CCPA— forming an "underground" church that remained loyal to the pope.

During the Great Leap Forward, the policy of respecting the institutions of minority religions was abandoned: it was decided that they were the last remaining bastion of feudalism, so campaigns were launched to reform them, notably Tibetan Buddhism and Islam. In minority areas, all "feudal powers" and remaining political roles of religion, including the prisons and armed guards maintained by large monasteries and mosques, were eliminated; their landholdings and commercial enterprises were confiscated, except for a small remnant for subsistence. Obligatory financial contributions to temples and mosques, such as the Islamic *zakat*, were banned, as were forced religious vocations: one could join a religious order only voluntarily, at the age of maturity, and could leave as one wished; this heralded a sea change since, just as in Han Buddhism and Taoism, the clergy mostly recruited and trained children and teenagers. Clerical training schools were closed, monastic and mosque land estates were expropriated and redistributed; many mosques and temples were merged, drastically reducing the number of places of worship. In parts of Xinjiang and other Muslim areas, Islamic practices such as prayer, fasting, circumcision, and the remembrance of the dead were banned. A good proportion of clerics and monks were struggled against as reactionaries.[47] Finally, traditional monastery and mosque management systems as well as hierarchies between temples were abolished, to be replaced by "democratic temple management committees."

This process of reform had already begun in 1956 in Sichuan Province, triggering a chain reaction of events that would have devastating consequences, both for the institutions of Tibetan Buddhism and for the CCP's popular legitimacy in Tibetan areas. In Sichuan—which included parts of the eastern Tibetan regions of Kham and Amdo—and where the Seventeen-Point Agreement did not apply—provincial authorities decided in 1956 to implement land collectivization throughout the province, with no exception for Tibetan and other minority areas. This involved the confiscation of land from landlords and monasteries, as well as restrictions on religious activity and other unpopular actions.

These measures led to armed clashes between Tibetans and PLA troops. When PLA aircraft bombed two famous monasteries in Litang, popular resistance was galvanized and lasted for three years. Although the CIA organized over thirty airdrops of weapons and ammunition to the rebels, they were ultimately crushed by the Chinese forces.[48] At the same time, the insurrection spread to other parts of eastern Tibet and led to an increasingly tense and volatile atmosphere in Lhasa. When, on March 10, 1959, the Dalai Lama was invited to watch a theatre performance in the PLA camp, but without his escort of bodyguards, rumors spread that the Chinese intended to kidnap him. Thousands of Tibetans massed around his summer residence of Norbulinka, hoping to stop him from going; the PLA called in reinforcements, and riots turned into full-fledged battles. The Dalai Lama, his entourage, and other elites—altogether some eighty thousand people—fled to India, establishing a government-in-exile at Dharamsala, India.

From then on, the Seventeen-Point Agreement was rescinded by the CCP. Most of Tibet's major monastic leaders were arrested, the land estates were redistributed, and the traditional religio-political system was dismantled. Thousands of monks were sent home (mass monastic centers

47. Ding Hong & Zhang Guojie, eds., *Bai nian Zhongguo musilin*, 418–20.
48. Knaus, "Official Policies and Covert Programs," 69.

such as Drepung and Sera each had over ten thousand residents) and monasteries ceased to be centers of religious life. Private worship did continue in homes, however.[49]

TOWARD THE CULTURAL REVOLUTION

The period of the Great Leap Forward had thus led to most religious activity coming to an end. Although some temples and churches remained, as well as the official religious associations and a reduced clergy, these had become empty shells, arenas for political struggles like so many other sectors of Chinese society. This situation can be contrasted in the same period with the state-supported flourishing of the secularized traditions, such as popular arts, Chinese medicine, *qigong*, and martial arts (see chapter 4).

And yet, religious ideas had far from disappeared. Records uncovered in the Shanghai archives by S. A. Smith show that the famines caused by the Great Leap Forward (causing between 20 million and 40 million deaths) were being interpreted among the rural populace as divine retribution for failing to worship the gods and Buddhas in recent years, and there was widespread concern that, with temples destroyed and incense unavailable, nothing could be done to restore the cosmic balance. The millions who died of famine and had not had proper funerals were feared as ghosts who continued to haunt the living for years.[50] Prophecies circulated about an imminent return of Chiang Kai-shek, or of new wars and famines, and prescribed worship and incense burning to avert disaster. Other rumors claimed that Mao had authorized the building of temples, that he had joined Yiguandao, or even that he had sentenced to death officials preventing the people from burning incense.[51]

In 1960, at the sixth national meeting on religious work, attempts were made to correct the excesses of the Great Leap. But when in 1962 Mao called for class struggle to be expanded and deepened, this led to religious issues being seen as issues of class struggle and of class consciousness, undermining attempts to give any special consideration to religion. In 1963, this line was formally incorporated into the work of the Religious Affairs Bureau, leading to more political struggles. The Dalai Lama, who in spite of his exile had retained his political titles (the CCP claimed in its propaganda that he had been kidnapped to India), was stripped of them in 1964.

49. Goldstein, "Introduction" and "The United States, Tibet, and the Cold War."
50. Mueggler, "Spectral Chains," 64–65.
51. S. Smith, "Talking Toads and Chinless Ghosts."

The Panchen Lama, who had supported the CCP's religious work for over a decade, but in 1962 had presented to Zhou Enlai a petition lamenting the brutality of the treatment of the Tibetan people over the previous years, was equally accused and purged for treason.

In the Socialist Education Campaign of 1964, over a million cadres organized into thousands of work teams were sent to the villages to eradicate capitalistic practices as well as religion, superstition, and lavish life-cycle rituals (births, weddings, and funerals). By the 1966 Smash the Four Olds campaign, rural communal religion and its temples were almost completely obliterated for more than a decade—although deity statues and sacred objects were often buried or hidden by temple activists, ritual activity continued in secret, and rumors continued to circulate. Indeed, the fact that by the mid-1960s, over fifteen years after the People's Republic had been established, there was still enough ongoing religious activity to warrant more mass campaigns to smash it is a testimony to the resilience of popular religiosity. In the same year, with the Cultural Revolution, the United Front Department was branded a "revisionist organ," and all United Front, nationality, and Religious Affairs units were condemned and disbanded. Religious leaders were all condemned as ox demons and snake spirits. Even the handful of remaining officially registered temples, monasteries, mosques, and churches were forced to close during the Cultural Revolution. In the minority areas, even simple expressions of private religiosity were suppressed. It was during this period that Christians began to meet informally in their homes, in what was the beginning of the house church movement. During political campaigns, when work teams or Red Guards came to confiscate ancestral tablets from homes, many people hid them or copied complete records of the tablets onto sheets of red paper, which were later transcribed onto new tablets. Photographs of the deceased or red paper marked with innocent double-happiness characters could also be innocuously placed where the tablets had been. Local cadres, who were village natives, were often aware of and tolerated these dissimulations. Even bowing to Mao's portrait, which was often placed at the location of the ancestral tablets, could be done while muttering the family genealogy in a low voice.[52]

---

52. Thireau, "Recent Change in a Guangdong Village," quoted in Aijmer & Ho, *Cantonese Society*, 151–52. For a description of death rituals in rural Guangdong during the 1970s, see Parish & Whyte, *Village and Family*, 260–66.

SEVEN

Spiritual Civilization and Political Utopianism

If the Cultural Revolution produced the most thorough destruction of all forms of religious life in Chinese and, perhaps, human history, it was far from being a secularizing movement. Rather, it represented the apotheosis of a parallel trend of political sacralization, which had roots in imperial Chinese political and religious culture, as well as in the utopian and apocalyptic dimensions of modernist revolution.

The modern Chinese state, in its various incarnations, has always incorporated, in its identity, in its ideology, and its practices, many elements that bear functional and structural similarities to a religious institution— a pattern which climaxed with the CCP's revolutionary eschatology and with the Mao cult.[1] Although this tendency to sacralize the state and the nation as the embodiment of moral absolutes is akin to Western "civil

1. Duara, "Religion and Citizenship," 64.

religions"[2] and to Japanese imperial ideology (as seen in the next chapter in Manchukuo and Taiwan), the KMT and CCP filiation deserve separate treatment here. Thus, while the KMT and CCP policies toward Chinese religion can, on the one hand, be seen as consequences of a secularizing project, as we have seen so far, they also reflect a continued process, not only of the sacralization of the nation and of the state,[3] but also of a quasi-spiritual belief in the power of human will and morality to transform society. As carriers of this spiritual political project, the KMT and CCP regimes perhaps had more affinities than they were ever ready to admit with religious communities and beliefs against which they were, consciously or not, in direct competition.

The sacralization of the state and the moralization of governance—which we will call "political religiosity"—occurred through the convergence of traditional and modern influences. Imperial-era models of the throne, the state, and the state's agents as founts of cosmic legitimacy, as regulators of the ritual order of the world, and as exemplars of moral civilizing or transformation 教化, while often explicitly rejected by modern reformers, continued to be reproduced in practice—indeed, as Ci Jiwei has argued, destroying the visible memory of entrenched patterns of thought simply allowed them to live on, unconsciously, under a new garb.[4] This new vestment was the process of modern nation building, which required forging the "Chinese people" as a new community of citizens bound together by new rituals and moral norms. A modern civilizing project, carried out by a new intelligentsia that saw itself as being at the vanguard of national progress in the battle against the ignorance and superstition of the masses, was partly conflated with traditional notions of the literate elite as moral exemplars and educators of the "foolish" populace. It was not enough for the new elite to possess modern thinking and scientific knowledge: they had to be embodiments of a new ethic of service to the people, which drew as much on neo-Confucian notions of self-cultivation—a discipline of training the body and mind, and controlling desires through

---

2. The comparison is limited by the fact that "civil religion" as theorized in the West is intimately linked to democracy. Another perspective of comparison is offered by the "political religions" of European totalitarian regimes of the twentieth century.

3. For a critique of this notion of the sacralization of the state, see Nedostup, "Ritual Competition."

4. Ci Jiwei, *Dialectic of the Chinese Revolution*, chap. 3. The contemporary philosopher Li Zehou 李澤厚 (b. 1930) has made a similar point, arguing that over time a relatively stable "cultural-psychological formation" has emerged in Chinese society, a propensity toward particular forms of thought and attitudes that persists even when concrete forms differ (Woei Lien chong, "Mankind and Nature," 147).

examining one's thoughts and keeping records of one's progress, which itself drew on Taoist and Buddhist antecedents—as on revolutionary asceticism.[5]

As the twentieth century unfolded, political religiosity expressed itself at roughly four levels of intensity. The most basic level was through the creation of the civic rituals characteristic of any nation-state: a new calendar, national holidays, state funerals, monuments to national heroes and martyrs, and so on (as discussed in chapters 2 and 9).[6] Second was the active promotion, through organized campaigns, propaganda, and education, of new forms of civil morality, designed to forge Chinese into a unified and advanced people. This type of moralization was promoted by the KMT, notably through the New Life movement in the 1930s, and again in Taiwan in the Cultural Renaissance Movement 中華文化復興運動 of the 1970s. It can also be seen in the postindependence decades of the Singapore state, and in the postrevolutionary period by the CCP through its efforts to "raise the overall quality" 提高人口的整體素質 of the Chinese people beginning in the 1990s. Third and even more intense was revolutionary asceticism, which aimed to create a new race of humans who would sacrifice themselves for the cause of the Communist Party. It developed within the CCP in the first half of the twentieth century, was systematized into "thought reform" methods in the 1930s, was imposed on all intellectuals in the early years of the socialist regime, and was institutionalized throughout the country in the years leading to the Cultural Revolution. Finally was the cult of Mao, which intensified revolutionary asceticism and violence, but led to the breakdown of utopian solidarity and the dislocation of the crypto-religious synthesis of the Maoist state—state ritual, the Mao cult, self-cultivation, and state-sponsored moral education all following autonomous trajectories in the post-Mao era.

In this chapter, we will begin with a brief discussion of the themes of collective eschatology and individual moral asceticism, which recur throughout twentieth-century Chinese political history and resonate with both traditional religious lore and modern/revolutionary models. We will then go over key phases in the crystallization of political religiosity during the twentieth century: the elaboration of modern state rituals; the New Life movement, the Yan'an synthesis, the Great Leap, the Mao cult, and the Cultural Revolution. Finally, we will trace the postrevolutionary trajectories of the products of political religiosity.

5. Thornton, *Disciplining the State.*
6. On state rituals in the Mao era, see Hung Chang-tai, "Mao's Parades."

UTOPIAN HERITAGES

Demonology, Messianism, and Utopianism

In the early decades of the twentieth century, the old civilization had collapsed: chaos, disease, invasions, and civil wars plagued many parts of the country. These were apocalyptic times, in which even the most nostalgic and conservative were impotent to preserve an old order that was frittering away: it was only possible to imagine another world, a world of peace and prosperity, a mythic past or a mythic future. Here, revolutionary eschatology and communist ideals found resonance in traditional notions of demonology, messianism, and utopianism. In a suggestive article, Barend ter Haar has argued that what he calls the "demonological paradigm" of Chinese religion had a profound impact on modern Chinese politics, particularly in its revolutionary and utopian dimensions.[7] Demons—which symbolize the forces of chaos, destruction, and death, threatening the health, peace, and prosperity of the people—are pervasive in Chinese religion, whose ritualists, notably the Taoist priests, specialize in violent magical warfare to subjugate and expel them from the community, and reestablish the cosmic order of culture and civilization. A fundamental theme of Chinese religion is the exorcistic role of the priest in establishing order in the face of demonic disease and chaos. The emperor as Son of Heaven played such a role as the high priest of all under Heaven—and, in what ter Haar calls the "messianic" demonological paradigm, popular apocalypticism also imagined a savior figure who would play such a role in times of chaos. In this lore, apocalyptic disasters are caused by demons and lead to plagues, famine, and invasions. A savior youthful prince (who incarnates a new dynasty) will appear, supported by divine generals and armies; they will expel the demons, bring order to the world, and usher in the Great Peace 太平. Contrary to conventional demonology and exorcism, which are local in scope and occur on the level of the invisible and symbolic, in messianic lore the scale of demonic attacks is universal, and the exorcism is conducted by an actual ruler (or contender for the throne) against physical enemies.

The messianic paradigm, which goes back to the Taoist movements of the Han dynasty (second century BCE to second century CE), is found in countless permutations in millenarian movements and texts through the centuries, including the novels that have maintained their hold over popular imagination during the twentieth century (Mao himself was said to be,

---

7. Ter Haar, "China's Inner Demons."

like the Boxers before him, very fond of the exorcistic novel *Outlaws of the Marsh*). It is also fundamental to the mythology of the sworn brotherhoods of South China—notably the Triads[8]—and in the lore of the bandits, bullies, and social outcasts of the "rivers and lakes." The Taiping Rebellion (see chapter 1), which emerged in the Hakka areas of Guangdong and Guangxi, rife with the activity of sworn brotherhoods, was a historical instantiation of the demonological messianic paradigm—with Hong Xiuquan playing the role of messiah, and the Taiping armies physically slaughtering the enemy "demons" in a frenzied bloodbath, promising to build a utopian, proto-communist Great Peace on earth. For the following decades, stories of Taiping heroism circulated among the folk, propagating an egalitarian lore of a moral obligation to attack the rich and share with the poor, which was an early source of inspiration for future CCP generals such as Peng Dehuai 彭德懷 (1898–1974) and Zhu De.[9] Sun Yat-sen 孫中山 (1866–1925), who grew up in a Hakka village listening to such tales, built his first alliances with sworn brotherhoods (called secret societies by revolutionaries; see chapter 5), and tried to recast their anti-Manchu messianism into a modern ideology of nationalist revolution. And again, when the CCP—which saw the Taiping movement as its precursor in the history of Chinese revolution[10]—established its first large-scale rural base in the Jiangxi Soviet in the 1920s and early 1930s, it was with the bandits and sworn brotherhoods that Mao Zedong built the strongest local alliances against the established gentry and power holders.[11] The extensive contacts at the grass roots between peasants and CCP cadres—many of whom, especially at the local level, were peasants themselves—naturally led to mutual resonances between the peasant messianism and dreams of egalitarian fraternity, and the socialist utopian visions.[12]

Utopian ideas were not limited to popular messianism; elite utopianism was just as enthusiastic, if not more. The Confucian ideal of the Great Commonwealth (*datong* 大同) became a widely used concept and symbol in the last decade of the empire and the early years of the Republic. Described in the Liyun 禮運 section of the *Book of Rites* 禮記, the *datong* referred to an ancient communistic golden age, which was followed by a period of relative prosperity (*xiaokang* 小康) under the ancient monarchs, and con-

8. Ter Haar, *Ritual and Mythology of the Chinese Triads*.
9. Thaxton, "Mao Zedong, Red Misérables," 142–43.
10. On the CCP use of the Taiping, see Cohen, *History in Three Keys*, 292–93.
11. Polachek, "The Moral Economy of the Kiangsi Soviet."
12. Thaxton, *China Turned Rightside Up*; "Mao Zedong, Red Misérables."

trasted with the disorder of the times of Confucius. Kang Youwei inverted the order of the three periods, projecting the *datong* into a utopian future of a unified humanity, which he elaborated in his *Book of the Great Commonwealth* (*Datongshu* 大同書).[13] *Datong* ideals were often evoked by Sun Yat-sen and in KMT ideology, and were an important theme in the teachings of the redemptive societies. At Yan'an, Mao Zedong, speaking of the future under communism, referred in different speeches to both the five-stage Marxist scheme of history (primitive communism, slavery, feudalism, capitalism, and communism) and to the three-stage Chinese scheme culminating in the Great Commonwealth. Both visions perceived the final phase as characterized by harmony and peace. Mao predicted that after the war, there would be perpetual peace and the elimination of classes and of self-interest.[14]

Self-Cultivation and Discipline

Reformers and revolutionaries were acutely aware that the realization of their utopian visions would require the creation of a new kind of man.[15] A modern China required a new system of moral norms to order the relationships between citizens. Traditional morality, with its focus on filial piety (*xiao* 孝), was particularistic, rooted in filial obligations to kinship networks, which served as the model for personalistic loyalty to rulers (*zhong* 忠). Society was constituted of overlapping spheres of reciprocal ties. The new model of the nation required universalistic standards to harmonize relationships between individuals who had no particularistic ties or loyalties, who were equal citizens in a homogenous collective body. Sun Yat-sen had famously stated, "Foreign observers say that Chinese are like a sheet of loose sand. Why? Simply because our people have shown loyalty to family and clan but not to the nation."[16]

The first attempts to create a sense of national citizenship through self-cultivation occurred in the New Policies reforms of 1902–11, in which the old system of Confucian academies and imperial examination was abolished and replaced by a nationwide network of modern schools that taught Western subjects but emphasized moral cultivation 修身 and reading the

13. Kang Youwei, *Datongshu*. The *Datongshu* was written in stages between the 1880s and the early 1900s, but was only published in 1935.

14. Knight, "From Harmony to Struggle."

15. Cheng Yinghong, *Creating the "New Man."* For a comparison with Japan and Russia, see Hua Shiping, *Chinese Utopianism*.

16. Sun Yat-sen, *San Min Chu I*, 5.

classics 讀經 as essential to instilling a sense of Chinese national identity and patriotism. Also in this network, the newly elevated official cult of Confucius (discussed in chapter 2) was no longer reserved for the gentry elite, but turned the sage into a symbol of the nation, to be universally honored by all students—as mentioned by Kuo Ya-pei, "shifting the center of the imperial order from the sacred body of the emperor to a Confucian image of the nation."[17]

Yet, while the ideal of moral self-cultivation was carried over from the old academies to the new schools, and from the gentry service of imperial state to the universal service of the nation, revolutionaries still found a problem with the political elites' lack of moral discipline. In his later years, Sun Yat-sen compared the failure of the Chinese Revolution of 1911 to the success of the Bolshevik Revolution of 1917. He attributed the problem to moral cultivation: Chinese revolutionaries had not put their ideals into practice in their own lives, lacking the discipline and unity of the Bolsheviks. Sun and other revolutionaries thus advocated adopting the methods, organization, and training of the Russian Communists. They admired both the organizational efficiency of the Russians and their asceticism, which they associated with Chinese ideals of spiritual discipline—a discipline that, through the power of the human will itself, could have a transformative effect on society.

Several scholars have traced the historical roots of Chinese revolutionary voluntarism through the ancient idea of the unity of Heaven and man (that is, the emperor) 天人合一: by the embodiment of his moral will, the ruler brings order to the entire universe.[18] Buddhist, Taoist, and Confucian traditions of moral asceticism and self-cultivation further refined and developed these ideas over the centuries, culminating in the leading neo-Confucian philosopher Wang Yangming 王陽明 (1472–1528), who denied the distinction between the mind and the objective world and advocated, through self-cultivation, the total integration of knowledge, action, and subjectivity. These ideas had a profound influence in the subsequent centuries, including the intelligentsia and reformers of the late imperial and early Republican periods, and notably on Mao Zedong himself.[19]

Put into practice, this well-entrenched conviction of the transformative power of the moral will resulted in a combination of Leninist organization and neo-Confucian self-cultivation. As early as 1919, CCP founding mem-

17. Kuo Ya-pei, "Redeploying Confucius," 67, and "The Emperor and the People."
18. Woei Lien chong, "Mankind and Nature," 161.
19. Ibid., 140, 166. On Wang Yangming and Mao, see Wakeman, *History and Will*, chaps. 16, 17.

ber Li Dazhao had claimed that Marxism was too deterministic and needed to be supplemented by a greater stress on consciousness and human will.[20] Over time, the dimension of moral cultivation, with its profound resonances in Chinese tradition, became far more prevalent in the CCP than in the Soviet Communist Party, in which political study and self-criticism were limited to a Party elite and were never intended for the masses. By the 1930s, this was increasingly abandoned in the USSR in favor of propaganda, material incentives, administrative measures, individual competition, and omnipresent surveillance by secret police—whereas in the CCP, the trend was increasingly to spread ideals and techniques of moral cultivation to the entire population.[21]

THE NEW LIFE MOVEMENT

Before the CCP embarked on the largest-ever attempts at moral reform of the Chinese population, the KMT had already launched its own such attempt during the 1930s. The KMT project of civilizing the people was largely focused on public space and public behavior, rather than inner ideological purity. Public spaces had become important signifiers of the new social order ever since the earliest urban reforms of the 1901–11 period.[22] It was outside the private world of the household—in streets, in restaurants and teahouses, on the sidewalks, in buses, in public squares, in new schools and government buildings—that the collectivity of individuals had to learn to display themselves. The new civic morality thus placed a strong emphasis on the proper forms of embodiment in public spaces. This involved not only norms of behavior but also standards of hygiene, which were given an enormous significance. Condemning public spitting, defecating, and flatulence, Sun Yat-sen had claimed that "competent governance of the body's natural functions" was a "necessary condition for competent government." A strong and healthy body was considered a necessary condition for building a strong nation. Reformers recast a traditional concern with the body, health, ritualized behavior, government, and moral civilizing into modernizing discourses of state-sponsored campaigns for public hygiene and civic virtues.[23]

---

20. Li Dazhao, "Wode makesi zhuyi guan," *Xin Qingnian* 6, no. 6 (1919); quoted in Schram, "To Utopia and Back," 411.

21. Whyte, *Small Groups*, 26; Nivison, "Communist Ethics," 57. See also Li Zehou, *Makesi zhuyi*, 44, and Jin Guantao, "Dangdai Zhongguo makesi zhuyi de rujiahua," 152–83, discussed in Billioud, "Confucianism."

22. Wang Di, *Street Culture*.

23. Culp, "Rethinking governmentality."

Christian, Buddhist, and Confucian reformists, as described in chapter 3, and the redemptive societies, as described in chapter 4, all actively contributed to the discourse of public morality. But the state itself, recasting in new terms the old notion of *jiaohua*, gave itself an increasingly prominent role in the promotion of modern virtues, culminating in the New Life movement 新生活運動, launched by Chiang Kai-shek.

The campaign, which was a response to CCP methods of popular mobilization, started on March 11, 1934, with a rally of one hundred thousand people in the Public Athletic Ground of Nanchang, the capital of Jiangxi, after the KMT forces had crushed the Red Army and destroyed the Jiangxi Soviet the previous year. The goal was to launch a state-directed popular movement for a national renaissance, building on Confucian values to overcome the cultural backwardness of the people. It was hoped that such a movement, mobilizing the masses under the leadership of the state, would undermine CCP attempts to foment revolution at the grassroots level.[24]

Detailed in a pamphlet written by Chiang Kai-shek himself, the *Essential Significance of the New Life Movement* 新生活運動之要義,[25] the new code of behavior lamented the "filthiness," the "laziness," the "indolence," and the "barbarity" of the Chinese people. National regeneration was to begin from the simple and move to the complex, start with the self and spread to others. The first steps were to ensure proper manners of "clothing, eating, living, and walking." This discourse on public morality called on the people to brush their teeth, to stop growing long fingernails, to stop spitting, and to put an end to vulgarity. On the streets, they were taught to stop wandering and shuffling about aimlessly, to walk on the sidewalks and stop blocking the traffic, and even to keep to the left when walking. Opium smoking and gambling were to be eradicated, as were superstitious belief in ghosts and wasteful expenses on weddings and funerals. Instead, the watchwords were orderliness, cleanliness, simplicity, frugality, promptness, precision, harmony, and dignity—ideals encapsulated in the four traditional virtues of propriety, rectitude, honesty, and sensitivity to shame 禮儀廉恥—drawn from Confucian tradition but given a modern meaning within the framework of loyalty to the state. *Li* 禮 was the key virtue—this was no longer the traditional civility of Confucian rites, however, but the civic responsibility of the Republican subject, modeled on military discipline.[26] Indeed, for Chiang the goals of the campaign were militarization 軍事化,

24. Dirlik, "The ideological Foundations."
25. Chiang, "Xin shenghuo yundong."
26. Dirlik, "The ideological Foundations," 966.

productivization 生產化, and aestheticization 藝術化. At the same time, Madame Chiang compared it to the Christian program of concern for the poor, out of which would emerge a strong and united China.[27]

Chiang's call was met with an enthusiastic mobilization, which rapidly spread to all the cities. Boy scouts, police, voluntary labor corps, and other groups set out to sweep the streets, promote hygiene among city dwellers and the peasantry, and so on. All this was coordinated by New Life organizations established in the provincial capitals, which began by holding mass demonstrations and then encouraged and followed up with specific projects and groups.

The campaign leadership was highly integrated with the KMT and military organizations. Two factions had the most influence in the movement: in the first few years, the upper hand was held by the fascist Blue Shirts 藍衣社, who controlled much of the police, admired Lenin, Stalin, Mussolini, and Hitler, and advocated the need for a "central idol" for "strengthening the power of social organization, promoting the development of national culture, and unifying the trust of the mass spirit."[28] After 1936, it was Madame Chiang and the Christian-oriented elements of the KMT, linked to the YMCA, who dominated the movement, and in some areas, Western missionaries such as American George W. Shepherd (1895–1980) were put in charge.[29]

Despite the initial enthusiasm, however, China did not become a clean and orderly nation, and the Japanese invasion hampered the efforts. Since the campaign was blind to social structure, it did not address the crying poverty and social ills of China, nor did it challenge the rampant corruption within the KMT and its government. Many intellectuals became disillusioned, and were increasingly attracted to the more radical vision of a new life being promoted by the CCP from its new base in Yan'an.

REVOLUTIONARY MORALITY: THE YAN'AN SYNTHESIS

It was in the remote northern Shaanxi Communist base of Yan'an that from 1936 to 1948, building on its experiences in the Jiangxi Soviet, the Long March, and peasant organizing in rural Shaanxi and Gansu, the CCP established the model of popular mobilization and political control which,

27. Duara, "Religion and Citizenship," 52.
28. Blue Shirts document; quoted in Eastman, "Fascism in Kuomintang China," 6. See also Wakeman, "A Revisionist View."
29. Oldstone-Moore, "The New Life Movement."

after 1949, it would put into practice throughout China. This was a model that fully integrated Leninist principles of organization with moral self-cultivation and consciousness-raising among intellectuals and the masses. It bore certain continuities with the New Life movement, notably its faith in the state's power to radically transform the morality of its people through top-down campaigns and education;[30] but the methods and the focus were quite different, and its effect much deeper.

The militarized revolutionary morality had been developed since 1927, when the Fourth Red Army had tried to forge a volunteer army driven by ideology and belief in revolutionary ideals: the gap between officers and soldiers was reduced; soldiers were held to strict moral standards, and engaged in political study and propaganda among peasants.[31] And in 1929, the CCP had discussed adopting a set of requirements for member selection in which, besides the ideological standard of "no errors in political outlook," all the other criteria were moral: the candidate was to be loyal, demonstrate a spirit of sacrifice, not be motivated by the desire to enrich oneself, and not be an opium smoker or a gambler.[32]

Thought Reform of Intellectuals

These initial policies were elaborated into a highly systematic method of "thought reform" 思想改造 in Yan'an, in response to the challenge of integrating a growing stream of urban intellectuals who moved to the Communist base areas to offer their services to the revolutionary cause. These volunteers were typically of "bourgeois" or "feudal" class backgrounds. As allies in anti-Japanese and anti-Western struggle, they could be enlisted, but they had to be ideologically "reeducated" 再教育 if they were to be useful instruments of the Party. At the same time, given the decentralization of the base areas and the poor communication between them, it would be impossible to supervise so many new cadres through organizational means alone: the Communist needed to be able to scrutinize his own conscience, in the words of Liu Shaoqi 劉少奇 (1898–1969), to "watch himself when alone."[33]

The resulting system of moral asceticism aimed (in violation of Marxist orthodoxy) for the class consciousness of nonproletarians to be changed, through education alone, into a proletarian outlook—but also claimed that

30. R. Smith, "The Teachings of Ritual."
31. Whyte, *Small Groups*, 30.
32. Schram, "To Utopia and Back," 418.
33. Nivison, "Communist Ethics," 52.

even if the exploiting classes were eliminated, the lax and selfish view-point of the petit bourgeoisie was a pervasive force against which constant struggle was required, through persistent self-cultivation 鍛煉, self-criticism 自我批評, and criticism by others.

Liu Shaoqi and other CCP ideologues, in their writings of the 1930s and 1940s, used familiar proverbs and classic quotations to elaborate on this ethic of embodying the Marxist ideal in one's own life.[34] In his famous essay "On the self-cultivation of a Party member" (論共產黨員的修養, known in English under the title "How to be a good communist"),[35] which is riddled with quotes from Confucius's *Analects* 論語 and the *Great Learning* 大學 and from neo-Confucian philosophers (but makes no mention of filial piety or loyalty to the family and traditions), Liu Shaoqi argued that self-cultivation was necessary for keeping one's faults and ideals before one's consciousness. In order to attain freedom from the determining force of history or of a situation, the Communist needed to conduct a class struggle within his own mind, to cleanse out the remnants of ideology and the habits of the old society. In his struggle to acquire communist virtues, the Party member was to transcend the ego and become a selfless being: "He is able to have a great firmness and moral integrity which riches cannot corrupt, poverty cannot alter, and terror cannot suppress." Such a person was not afraid of criticism because he was his own critic, and not afraid to criticize others because he sought no flattery or recognition.[36]

Other texts exhorted Party members to practice what Weber would have called this-worldly asceticism: to live in the stream of society without being contaminated by it; to avoid being ensnared by the enticements of money, women, and honor, which would cause "eternal regret"; and to avoid attachment to the illusory sensory world. Just as in Buddhist and neo-Confucian practices of "watching oneself when alone" 慎獨—and inspired by stories of heroes of past dynasties—the Party member was to become aware of and eradicate every trace of selfishness in his mind; otherwise, it would gradually corrupt his mind and body, and lead him to lose sight of objective reality and of his true self. This attentiveness to the self was also expressed through meticulous attention to even the smallest details of life and conduct.[37]

---

34. Ibid., 54.

35. Liu Shaoqi, *How to Be a Good Communist.*

36. Liu Shaoqi, "How to Be a Good Communist"; quoted in Nivison, "Communist Ethics," 58.

37. Nivison, "Communist Ethics," 70–72; Meisner, "Utopian Goals and Ascetic Values"; Potter & Potter, *China's Peasants,* 283–95.

Three short speeches by Mao Zedong—"Serve the People,"[38] "In Memory of Norman Bethune,"[39] and "The Foolish Old Man Removed the Mountains"[40] (an old tale from the Taoist classic *Liezi*)—which by the 1960s and 1970s were studied and memorized by hundreds of millions of schoolchildren, peasants, workers, and cadres, came to encapsulate in the popular mind the essence of Maoism and communism: an ethic of selfless service to others (not to the particularistic circle of kin but to an abstracted People), of heroism and perseverance in the face of difficulty: "We must all learn the spirit of absolute selflessness. . . . A man's ability may be great or small, but if he has this spirit, he is already noble-minded and pure, a man of integrity and above vulgar interests."[41]

The objective was, in the words of Liu Shaoqi, to "reform mankind into the completely selfless citizenry of a Communist society."[42] Through a series of speeches and documents,[43] a method was devised to rapidly, intensively— and if necessary, forcibly—nurture, in the minds of Party members, indi- viduals, and eventually the entire population, the this-worldly asceticism of communist self-cultivation. A uniform culture could thus be created among the scattered, heterogeneous, and growing numbers of Party members; and through ideological conversion, all Chinese classes and masses (the ma- jority of whom were not proletarian by Marxist standards) could thus be transformed, with minimal violence, into a revolutionary proletariat.[44]

The first wave of thought reform occurred in 1939–40, when study and mutual criticism sessions were organized for four thousand cadres and students near Yan'an; in 1942, the model was further solidified in the larger-scale "rectification" or "correcting the mores" 整風 campaign throughout the CCP-controlled areas. All cadres and students, and some intellectuals—rarely peasants—were organized into "small groups" for the study of doctrinal texts and group criticism and struggle sessions.[45]

As the CCP took control of larger parts of Chinese territory, and finally all of China, thought reform was used to convert the large numbers of intel- lectuals and former KMT cadres, whose loyalty to the regime was suspect,

---

38. Mao Zedong, "Serve the People," in *Selected Works*, 3:177–78.
39. Mao Zedong, "In Memory of Norman Bethune," in *Selected Works*, 2:337.
40. Mao Zedong, "The Foolish Old Man Removed the Mountains," in *Selected Works*, 3:322.
41. Quoted in Madsen, "The Maoist Ethic," 153.
42. Quoted in Comptom, *Mao's China*, 146.
43. Mao Zedong, *On Practice*; Liu Shaoqi, "How to be a Good Communist"; Mao Zedong, *New Democracy*; Liu Shaoqi, *Lun dangnei douzheng*.
44. Walder, *Communist Neo-Traditionalism*, 126.
45. Selden, *The Yenan Way*.

but who were needed to staff the new regime's schools and bureaucracy. This was intensively implemented in six-month courses in "revolutionary colleges" from 1948 to 1952, considered a program for reforming China's intellectual elite, administrators, bureaucrats, professors, technicians, former KMT officials, recent university graduates, returnees from overseas, and CCP cadres who had committed "political errors."

The psychiatrist Robert J. Lifton, who in the 1950s interviewed several Chinese and foreigners who had fled to Hong Kong after undergoing thought reform in prisons and in revolutionary colleges, identified three common stages in the program described by his informants, which can be compared to rites of passage and to processes of religious conversion: an initial phase of togetherness and friendly bonding; a second phase of intense criticism and struggle, leading to the breakdown of self-identity; and a third phase of "rebirth," when the participant rebuilds his identity in complete submission to the Party.

In the first phase, which Lifton called the "Great Togetherness," the participant arrives at the revolutionary college to discover a warm, simple, and friendly atmosphere, with informal study and plenty of time to relax and get acquainted. In a free and enthusiastic atmosphere, the participants were encouraged to vent their pent-up hostility toward the defeated KMT regime, building camaraderie in the process. Then, through "thought mobilization" lectures and discussions, they learned to draw the line between themselves and the evil and corrupt old society; next they followed courses on Marxism and historical materialism, where they learned the vocabulary of "exploiting classes," "evil remnants," "ideological poisons," and so on, and acquired the desire to become a new man in the new society. In this phase, the participants developed a sense of unity and common purpose, full of excitement for building the new China. Such discussions and bonding were quite appealing for intellectuals who were critical of the old culture and disillusioned with the KMT and the failures of the previous decades' reforms. Torn and confused, they welcomed the clear rupture and the new, victorious order promised by the CCP.

In the second phase, however, which Lifton called "the Closing in of the Milieu," the discussions shifted from theory to personal and emotional analysis. Each individual was repeatedly required to write and submit "thought summaries." Group study turned to increasingly intensive criticism, self-criticism, and confessions. The group leader would support the emergence of radical activists among the group. The pressure would increase, as every word, thought, and idea was scrutinized and criticized as "individualism," "subjectivism," "objectivism," "sentimentalism," "deviationism," "dogmatism," "bureaucratism," "revisionism," "idealism," and countless other symptoms of petit-bourgeois ideological remnants, which the participants were to confess and extirpate through constant self-examination. "Backward elements" were singled out and became objects of relentless criticism, leading to mass "struggle" meetings where they were ritually denounced by faculty, cadres, and fellow students. Participants often fell ill with anxiety, fear, and psychosomatic symptoms, and were told by doctors that the cause was that "your thoughts are sick." Through written confessions, which circulated among faculty and students and were used to measure progress, the participants reviewed everything that had happened in their past life, and even the history of their family over several generations, pointing out the signs of their evil bourgeois class consciousness. Typically, in their anxiety, they vied with one another to write wildly exaggerated confessions, describing chance encounters, casual conversations, and romantic liaisons as plots to provide intelligence to imperialist spies. But conformity was also criticized as lacking in sincerity and as formalism. The only way to demonstrate genuine reform was through enthusiastic participation and eager criticism of others, and moralistic condemnation of their pride, conceit, rudeness, boastfulness, and other "bourgeois" sins. Redemptive revival meetings would be held, at which a student with an especially evil past made a public confession to an audience of hundreds, describing his past sins in engrossing detail, then expressing his relief at "washing away all of my sins" and his gratitude to the CCP for making him into a "new man."

In the third phase, which Lifton called "Submission/Rebirth," students took ten days to write a final thought summary/confession in the form of a biography going back two generations. The confession was submitted for intensive criticism by the group, and constantly revised until the final version was completed. It contained a detailed analysis of the student's class origin and a denunciation of his father—a key component, which sealed the student's rupture from the old world of filial piety, and his loyalty to the new cause of the Party.

The thought reform campaigns were partly successful. Some resisters felt suffocated and turned against the regime, fleeing to Hong Kong; another minority became zealous converts; and the majority were only partly convinced, but, primarily concerned with survival and adaptation to the new regime, they learned the new rules of the political game and the danger of insubordination—becoming outwardly docile, if only sporadically enthusiastic, followers of the regime.[46]

46. Lifton, *Thought Reform and the Psychology of Totalism* and "Thought Reform." See also Strauss, "Morality, Coercion, and State Building."

Throughout the 1950s to 1970s, the model of thought reform and small-group political study and mutual criticism was implemented, on a larger scale but with a much reduced level of intensity, throughout the state apparatus, including government units, schools, and factories. Consequently, in addition to Party members and cadres, most workers and urban residents were integrated into small groups. Research has shown that the model usually did not succeed in creating the desired "strict political atmosphere," and even led to antagonism on the shop floor toward political enthusiasts, who were bullied by rank-and-file workers—but it did succeed in enforcing a high level of outward political conformity through the mutual monitoring and criticism of group members, without requiring the heavy apparatus of spying and violent repression which had characterized the USSR under Stalin.[47]

Another form of ideological reform of intellectuals and nonproletarians was the campaigns to send the youth "up the mountains and down to the countryside" 上山下鄉, in order to be educated by the poor peasants. By living with the farmers and doing manual agricultural work with them, the bourgeois thoughts of the young students could be washed away, and they could be redeemed by merging into the mass of the peasant proletarians. The model for these campaigns had first been developed at Yan'an, and small-scale experiments took place in the 1950s. By the early 1960s, the movement grew until, at the height of the Cultural Revolution, Mao launched a mass campaign in 1968 to send all students to the countryside. The ideological project of moral transformation was combined with the practical need, at that time, to prevent the rising unemployment of urban youth and to channel the destructive energies of the Red Guards by sending them to work in the fields.[48]

Peasant Mobilization

The methods of thought reform just described were designed primarily for cadres, intellectuals, and urban residents. In the rural areas, other methods were employed to transform the consciousness of the peasantry, including forms of propaganda that drew on traditional arts and performances, and new collective rituals.

Many of these methods were systematized during the Yan'an period as the CCP, for reasons both practical and ideological, proceeded to strip

---

47. Whyte, *Small Groups*; Walder, *Communist Neo-Traditionalism*.
48. Bonnin, *Génération perdue*.

many elements of folk culture of their religious content and reinvent them as secularized instruments for the propagation of revolutionary culture. Thus, at the Yan'an Forum on Literature and Art, held in May 1942, Mao stressed the importance of art and literature in raising the consciousness of the peasantry. He called on artists and intellectuals, as part of the "down to the village" movement, to take their inspiration from folk art, and encouraged the use of traditional art forms for the delivery of propaganda messages.[49]

Shaanbei storytellers 說書, notably, were selected to become propagandists for the new regime, telling stories about a socialist future. These blind orator-musicians were in fact ritual specialists, highly solicited among the people for Prayer Storytelling 口願—a practice in which the storyteller visits the home of the client, invokes and worships the gods, and prays for the client's good fortune, before rewarding the assembled gods with a story. Storytellers were also called upon to diagnose illnesses, tell fortunes, and hold rites for children to protect them from disease. For the CCP, then, as these storytellers were poor, blind, and illiterate, they were unquestionably members of the popular underclass that was the basis of its support; on the other hand, their prayers and divination practices made them spreaders of superstitions. In 1945, a storytelling group was established under the Cultural Federation of the Shaanxi-Gansu-Ningxia Border region, which launched programs to retrain the storytellers in socialist ideals and revolutionary thought, within the framework of which they could compose new stories, often in collaboration with intellectuals. The newly minted storytellers were given stable jobs with the Cultural Bureau, organized in teams of four, and sent to the villages as propagandists, evangelists of the new communist gospel, spreading revolutionary education and transmitting messages from the CCP to remote hamlets—often following the same routes they had previously tracked in as ritual service providers. Some of the stories presented concepts of gender equality and political participation, such as criticizing the sale of daughters, while others directly attacked superstitious practices. Often, the storytellers were at the same time surreptitiously hired by communities to perform Prayer Storytelling and conduct healing rites—a practice that stopped in 1963, when the atmosphere became too tense. Opera troupes and *yangge* dance groups, which typically performed for the gods at temple festivals, were also trained to turn their repertoire into revolutionary propaganda.[50]

---

49. McDougall, *Mao Zedong's "Talks at the Yan'an Conference . . ."*
50. Holm, *Art and Ideology in Revolutionary China.*

Many ritual art forms were also enlisted in the service of socialist propaganda: folk paper cuttings, which had previously been used as talismans to paste on windows and in homes, now depicted revolutionary themes; *nianhua* 年畫, New Year prints that depicted the old auspicious symbols of long life, high social position, and wealth, were redesigned to portray colorful, optimistic images of soldiers, workers, militiamen, and CCP leaders, to be pasted all over the walls of homes. Even the posters of door gods, depicting fierce protective deities, now depicted PLA cavalrymen brandishing enormous sabers.[51] And in the ultimate symbolic superscription, portraits of Mao and other CCP leaders were pasted at the focal point of homes, on the spot above the family altar previously reserved for ancestral tablets.

Village Political Rituals

In addition to the methods of propaganda described above, through which the Party inscribed itself in the place of traditional incantations and talismans, a new set of rituals were designed to consolidate the new social/moral order in the villages, following, in a format adapted for the peasantry, many of the principles of the intellectuals' thought reforms. Richard Madsen, in his study of morality and politics in a Guangdong village during the Mao era, identified two types of political rituals: what he calls "rituals of struggle," which were designed to tear apart the old social fabric; and "ceremonies of innocence," which could unite people around the new symbols and ideals of the regime.[52]

The model of the rituals of struggle had been shaped in the early peasant mobilizing at the Jiangxi Soviet, where peasants were encouraged to "speak bitterness" 訴苦, pouring out their sufferings in life, which activists then led them to connect to class analysis and criticism of landlords—creating class solidarity among exploited peasants while instigating a new social cleavage between them and the landlords, with whom they typically had strong traditional kinship and ritual ties. The new divisions, and the inversion of power relations, were cemented at "struggle meetings," where local elites and landlords were the subject of mass criticism, accusations, and even violent beatings.[53] The targets were forced to confess, but the con-

51. Wu Ka-ming, "The Return of the Folk," 167–211; Aijmer, "Political Ritual," 224; Landsberger, "Mao as the Kitchen God," 197. See also Flath, *The Cult of Happiness*.
52. Madsen, *Morality and Power*, 21–24.
53. Whyte, *Small Groups*, 31, 138.

fessions were never accepted as sincere, and attacked as further proof of the fundamentally rotten nature of their authors. They were then paraded in the streets and publicly humiliated, wearing paper hats and placards labeling them as traitors or class enemies. Ter Haar has compared these processions to rituals of the City God temples, where trials were held and processions conducted, at which the populace could heap verbal abuse at criminals, and where it was customary for people to join the processions dressed up as criminals, as a form of penance to redeem one's sins.[54] Less severe were the "denunciation sessions" where the individual was publicly criticized and humiliated for his moral lapses, but where his public confessions were accepted and he was reintegrated into the masses.[55]

These rituals of struggle were based on a rigid use of doctrinal language, in which discursive orthodoxy was used as a weapon to separate those who conformed to dogma from those who did not. On the other hand, the "ceremonies of innocence," led by "Mao Zedong Thought Counselors,"[56] used songs and drama to focus less on points of doctrine and more on the celebration of Mao and revolutionary heroes as powerful symbols of hope and victory, which could arouse common emotional feelings. Interpreted vaguely, often in terms of folk morality without a single discursive explanation, and allowing for a multiplicity of possible meanings, these ceremonies could integrate villagers around a shared sense of purpose. According to Madsen, the combination of the rituals of struggle and the ceremonies of innocence eventually led to a new, ambiguous moral synthesis of traditional village morality and the universal revolutionary morality promoted by the CCP—which became the subject of much popular nostalgia in the 1980s and 1990s—but one that was short-lived, as the full implications of the Mao cult were played out in the Cultural Revolution.[57]

MENTAL ENERGY AND THE ATOMIC BOMB: FROM THE GREAT LEAP TO THE CULTURAL REVOLUTION

Contrary to the Marxism of the USSR, the CCP did not believe that economic development and establishing the "socialist relations of produc-

54. Ter Haar, "China's Inner Demons," 82–83. On the contemporary persistence of traditional Chinese judicial rituals, including public atonement of sins and penance, see Katz, *Divine Justice*, chaps. 7–8.

55. Madsen, *Morality and Power*, 80–81.

56. Ibid., 130–50.

57. Ibid., 68–101; see also Zuo Jiping, "Political Religion."

tion" would automatically usher in communism. Voluntarism and internalized values were fundamental, and were indeed the prerequisites for longer-term technical and economic transformation. Slogans and speeches by Mao Zedong and Liu Shaoqi during the Great Leap Forward explicitly described how changes in the consciousness of the masses could lead to massive increases in productive forces, also noting that, in direct contradiction to Marxist orthodoxy, "men are not the slaves of objective reality," that "the subjective creates the objective."[58] This led to the belief that through willpower alone, changes could be achieved beyond what was objectively possible, such as ten- and twentyfold increases in grain production, and so on.

This development occurred in the context of the growing Sino-Soviet rift, during which the PRC sought to establish its independence from the USSR. Materially, this was symbolized by the construction of China's own atomic bomb in 1964—an achievement that, it was fantasized, could be paralleled by releasing the subjective energies of the people like a nuclear bomb.[59] Mao became fond of applying concepts of atomic physics to politics. The key to creating massive explosions of energy through human willpower lay in the law of contradictions: just as basic particles can always be split into smaller ones, releasing huge amounts of nuclear energy, the contradictions and struggles between the people could be sharpened to release massive explosions of energy. Mao developed a friendship with Japanese Einsteinian and Marxist physicist Sakata Shoîchi 坂田昌一 (1911–1970), inviting him to visit China several times between 1956 and 1964. An article by Sakata was published in Hongqi 紅旗, the theoretical journal of the CCP—the first time a physics article was published in this journal—and amply commented on; Party groups were ordered to study it.[60]

The theory of atomic fission was invoked to justify the launching of the Cultural Revolution in the absence of any objective basis for class struggle, the classes of the old society having already been destroyed. The night before the Cultural Revolution was launched, Mao met in person with delegates of a physics conference on Sakata's model of atomic division.[61] Even as late as 1973, Mao surprised the visiting Nobel Prize–winning Chinese-American physicist Yang Zhenning 杨振宁 (Chen-Ning Franklin Yang,

58. Schram, "To Utopia and Back," 422.
59. E. Friedman, "Einstein and Mao," 57.
60. Hongqi, no. 6 (1965); referenced in E. Friedman, "Einstein and Mao," 64.
61. Friedman, "Einstein and Mao," 54, 60–61, 64, 66.

b. 1922), demonstrating that he kept abreast of recent developments in elementary particle and high-energy physics.

By the time of the Cultural Revolution, the idea of eternal change and impermanence in particle physics led Mao to say that Marxism could and would change, that communism would not last forever, that there would be contradictions in communism, and that it would be surpassed by something else. On the one hand, Mao was thus merely carrying to its logical conclusion the Marxist notion of the dialectical laws of history, and the Party's victory coming from following those objective historical laws. On the other hand, some have argued that Mao's cosmology was essentially neo-Confucian: cosmology and ethics are indistinguishable; human action should follow the pattern of the universe; the universe is constant impermanence and oscillations between the polar opposites of yin-yang, high-low, light-dark, and so on. But Mao replaced the Confucian idea of harmony with the idea that the cosmos is governed by conflict and struggle; therefore, human action should be conflict and struggle, through which it finds its highest expression.[62]

The Mao Cult

The culmination of political religiosity occurred with the Mao cult, which was manufactured and promoted from 1959 onward by the People's Liberation Army under Lin Biao 林彪 (1907–1971) as a means to reinforce Mao's charismatic authority at a time when, following the disaster of the Great Leap, his own influence within the CCP was declining. The cult had two sides: on the one hand, the deification of the person of Mao and the sanctification of revolutionary heroes such as Lei Feng 雷鋒 (1940–1962)[63] and others; on the other hand, the demonization of any individual suspected of lacking in loyalty to Mao.

The model of Mao and of the revolutionary heroes—exemplified by the image of Mao's fifteen-kilometer swim in the Yangtze in 1966, at the age of seventy-three—aimed not only to demonstrate how willpower alone could overcome the obstacles of the material world, but also how Mao himself was endowed with unique and extraordinary powers. In propaganda posters, he was depicted as the Great Teacher (to humbly learn from), the Great

---

62. Woei Lien chong, "Mankind and Nature," 168.

63. A PLA soldier, Lei Feng died of injuries sustained in an accident in 1962; but the "Study Lei Feng" campaign, launched in 1963, held him up as a model of self-sacrifice.

Leader and Great Helmsman (to loyally follow), the Supreme Commander (to submissively obey), and a benevolent father figure (to be revered with filial piety). In one poster entitled "The growth of all things depends on the sun," he was portrayed standing in a cotton field, surrounded by peasants, radiating life as if he were the sun.[64]

The "Little Red Book" of the *Quotations of Chairman Mao*, first published in 1964 for mass study within the People's Liberation Army, then disseminated in hundreds of millions of copies to the entire population, became a magical scripture whose mere handling could trigger miracles. It was said to have "'supplied the breath of life' to soldiers gasping in the thin air of the Tibetan plateau; enabled workers to raise the sinking city of Shanghai three-quarters of an inch; inspired a million people to subdue a tidal wave in 1969, inaccurate meteorologists to forecast weather correctly, a group of housewives to re-invent shoe-polish, surgeons to sew back severed fingers and remove a ninety-nine pound tumor as big as a football."[65] When Mao shared a basket of mangoes, offered him by a visiting Pakistani delegation, to a group of workers in 1968, they were treated as holy relics: preserved in formaldehyde, replicated in wax, and reproduced as images on millions of posters, quilts, and teapots.[66]

Mao's portrait—which was treated with special care as a sacred object— became ubiquitous in public spaces and homes, on trucks, boats, and locomotives, and even in the fields, on placards carried by villagers and planted in the soil or in heaps of grain.[67] Overall, 2.2 billion portraits and as many Mao badges were produced during the Cultural Revolution (an average of 3 per person in China), and 40 billion volumes of Mao's works were printed (15 sets per person).[68]

Daily rituals to Mao were promoted in the homes: "asking for instructions in the morning, thanking Mao for his kindness at noon, and reporting back at night." Loyal revolutionaries were to bow three times each morning to the portrait or bust of the Great Helmsman, sing the national anthem, read passages from the Little Red Book, and announce what efforts they would make that day for the revolution. The ritual could also involve dancing a "loyalty dance" derived from a Xinjiang folk dance and singing the song "Beloved Chairman Mao." The nighttime rite involved reporting on

64. Landsberger, "Mao as the Kitchen God," 206.
65. Bloodworth, *The Messiah and the Mandarins* (New York: Atheneum, 1982), 258; quoted in Landsberger, "Mao as the Kitchen God," 204.
66. Dutton, "Mango Mao"; Chau, "Mao's Traveling Mangos."
67. Aijmer, "Political Ritual," 221.
68. Barmé, *Shades of Mao*, 8, 40.

the actions of the day and on one's plans for the next.[69] Weddings were also conducted by saying vows before the bust of Mao.[70]

At the same time, class enemies were struggled against with increased virulence, drawing on the imagery of Chinese demonology—they were labeled as "ox demons and snake spirits" 牛鬼蛇神, "ghosts" 魔鬼, "monsters" 魔怪, and "vampires" 吸血鬼 that could be repelled thanks to the "demon-exposing mirror" 照妖镜 of Mao Zedong thought. In the most extreme instances of violence, ritual cannibalism occurred in parts of Guangxi. Class enemies were killed and disemboweled in a fashion similar to the gory torture scenes depicted in traditional images of Buddhist hells in City God temples, and their hearts, livers, and other parts were consumed in communal banquets, physically enacting rites portrayed, if not carried out, in popular lore and literature.[71]

The Mao cult began to be dismantled after the fall of Lin Biao in 1971, but propaganda in the same style continued even after the end of the Cultural Revolution. It is difficult to assess to what extent the cult was sincerely followed by the masses, but it would appear that popular reaction to the cult was ambivalent, with a few activists leading the way and the majority simply following along as a pragmatic adaptation to the new reality. One explanation given is that since ancestor worship, communal worship, and tradition in general had been destroyed and banned, the Mao cult acted as the only available substitute—an effect which was perhaps consciously intended, since its rituals and symbols often occupied the same spaces as traditional worship.[72] And for many peasants, Mao was indeed seen as the savior figure in the demonological messianic imagery described earlier: in North China, for instance, he was often described as a turtle spirit, whose power came from his possession of secret mantras and esoteric books, and who scared away all the evil spirits.[73] Another explanation is that it was simply too dangerous to be suspected of not engaging in the cult, and indeed, zealous enthusiasm was often the only way to demonstrate sincerity and avoid being struggled against. In this context, Mao portraits, rituals,

69. Landsberger, "Mao as the Kitchen God"; see also his Web site at www.iisg.nl~landsberger/index/html (accessed January 10, 2005).

70. On the Mao cult and the Cultural Revolution, see James Myers, "Religious Aspects of the Cult of Mao"; Landsberger, *Chinese Propaganda Posters*; Hiniker, *Revolutionary Ideology*; Pye, *The Mandarin and the Cadre* and *The Spirit of Chinese Politics*; D. Munro, *The Concept of Man in Contemporary China*; Baum & Teiwes, *Ssu-Ch'ing*; Urban, ed., *The Miracles of Chairman Mao*.

71. Sutton, "Consuming Counterrevolution."

72. Aijmer, "Political Ritual," 227; M. Yang, *Gifts, Favors, and Banquets*, chap. 7.

73. Dorfman, "The Spirits of Reform," 269.

and paraphernalia did play a talismanic role, since they offered real protection against attack in an atmosphere of increasing anxiety and fear of political criticism, which could arise at any time and from anywhere owing to constantly changing political campaigns.

With the Cultural Revolution, however, as rival and warring factions of Red Guards and revolutionary committees appeared and fought each other—some heeding Mao's initial call for youthful rebellion and chaos, others defending their positions and accomplishments, and others trying to restore order—any sense of moral consensus collapsed. As the battling groups evoked Mao with growing stridency and self-righteousness to defend what increasingly boiled down to self-preservation, the Mao cult lost all its efficacy to offer protection or communal unity amid endless rituals of struggle.[74]

For the zealous activists, often students, young intellectuals, and members of previously marginalized social classes who believed in the Communist cause, the path of revolutionary self-cultivation, asceticism, and sacrifice was one they initially followed with devotion and steadfastness. But in contrast to religious regimens of spiritual cultivation, the anticipated rewards of the ascetic path were not spiritual but this-worldly: symbolic recognition and praise by the Party, and advancement in a political career. Since the number of opportunities in the political hierarchy was limited, most were bound to be disappointed and disillusioned, and to cloak resentment and competition for honor and positions in terms of ideological attacks against rivals. Those who did succeed, inevitably targeted by ever-shifting and unpredictable campaigns, lost any sense of idealism and became utilitarian opportunists concerned only with self-survival.

The Post-Mao Breakdown

It was in such a context that by the early 1970s, the utopian ideals of communism imploded into the institutionalized corruption of what Andrew Walder has called "communist neo-traditionalism."[75] The socialist system was a "virtuocracy" in which students were assessed not only on academic merits but also on ideological "performance" (biaoxian 表現)—their emulation of models of selfless socialist heroism—which was monitored and then factored into rewards and college admission.[76] At work, the same principle

74. Madsen, *Morality and Power*, 153–98.
75. Walder, *Communist Neo-Traditionalism.*
76. Shirk, *Competitive Comrades.*

applied, with rewards and incentives awarded according to one's degree of ideological commitment. Although ideological ties were intended to create a new type of egalitarian social bond, the result was a hierarchy based on a system of rewards (pay, benefits, promotions, punishments, and so on) that were unequally distributed, based on a subjective evaluation of ideological level. In practical terms, ideological "performance" could not be objectively measured and was typically equated with loyalty to leaders. Whereas the majority of workers chose passive-defensive orientations, resenting and even bullying activists, a minority would enthusiastically volunteer for extra work and spearhead political campaigns, often confusing a sincere idealism with personal ambition. Virtuocracy became an ideologically legitimated favoritism for those who demonstrated loyalty, which in turn developed into personal ties and led to particularistic ties of patronage.[77]

As utilitarianism, patronage, corruption, and market relations based on self-interest came to dominate growing portions of the social fabric in the late Mao and post-Mao periods, the Maoist synthesis of utopianism, messianism, demonology, self-cultivation, and collective ritual collapsed — creating what many in China called a spiritual void 精神空虚 and a crisis of faith 信仰危急, a fertile soil for the religious revivals of the post-Mao era (discussed in chapters 10 and 11). But the pieces did not all disappear — some elements continued to evolve in post-Mao society, but in a scattered and unpredictable fashion.

The Mao cult, for example, though officially terminated in 1979 with bans on the sale of most memorabilia, and new regulations restricting the public display of portraits of Party leaders, continued to live on in the popular imagination. By the early 1980s, popular demand remained high, and following increasing complaints that posters and books could no longer be found, a new policy was issued in 1983 calling for the massive production and sale of portraits of Mao Zedong, Liu Shaoqi, Zhu De, Deng Xiaoping, and Chen Yun during the Spring Festival period each year.[78] Mao's popularity grew in tandem with the rising popular anger over corruption; as a symbol of utopian ideals and youthful rebellion, his portrait was brought to Tian'anmen Square by student protesters in the spring of 1989. The adoption of Mao by protesters was not unanimous, however: protesters from Hunan spattered his giant portrait on Tian'anmen Gate with paint. A violent storm broke out soon afterward; rumors spread that it was the spirit of Mao showing his anger. This was but one of the many urban legends

---

77. Walder, *Communist Neo-Traditionalism*, 123–61; Lü Xiaobu, *Cadres and Corruption*.
78. Barmé, *Shades of Mao*, 7–8.

and miraculous tales about Mao that were spreading at the time. The use of hanging Mao portraits as talismans by truck and taxi drivers was first reported in 1991 and soon became ubiquitous. Shrines to Mao, either independent structures or located in other temples, appeared in a few places. The Sanyuansi 三元寺 temple in a Hunan village, for example, contained statues of Mao Zedong, Zhou Enlai, and Zhu De, among other deities, and was reported to attract tens of thousands of incense-burning worshippers daily. It was closed in May 1995 for encouraging superstition,[79] but more shrines remained active, with some having spirit mediums talking with Mao's voice. And in one part of rural Guangdong, Maoists became ritualists: troupes of old women dressed in Red Guard uniforms and styling themselves "Mao Zedong thought propaganda teams" 毛澤東思想宣傳隊 were observed in 2007 performing revolutionary songs at temple festivals.[80]

Mao was popular among people who felt frustrated politically and were angry at the increasing corruption, nursed a nostalgia for a simpler past, and even longed for a new sage-king or hero. After resisting the trend, the state tried to capitalize on and even encourage the posthumous Mao cult, especially after the crackdown on the Tian'anmen uprising of 1989 and with the approaching centennial of Mao's birth in 1993. Tens of millions of copies of Mao portraits and of his *Selected Works* were once again printed. Revolutionary songs were reproduced in karaoke and pop form. Several historical movies and television miniseries on Mao were produced and aired in 1993. Mao biographies became a new genre of pulp literature, with seven best-selling books on his life totaling print runs of 3.67 million copies by June 1991. There were so many other works of questionable quality that new regulations in 1993 stipulated that political biographies had to be "accurate, serious, and healthy." Similarly, his sayings and image had become so commonplace in commercial marketing that a new advertising law banned their use in 1994.[81]

By the late 1990s and early 2000s, remembrances of Mao and of revolutionary history were again being promoted by the CCP, in a bid to shore up its legitimacy and inculcate patriotic values. "Red tourism" to revolutionary sites, including Shaoshan 韶山, Mao's birthplace in Hunan, became a mass enterprise—and a highly lucrative one, as state-owned enterprises were encouraged to book "red" itineraries for their staff on reward

79. Ibid., 23.
80. Liu Yongsi, "Duoyuan yiti."
81. Barmé, *Shades of Mao*, 29, 30.

junkets. Meanwhile, among the new class of successful urban entrepreneurs and cosmopolitan cultural creators—many of whom were former Red Guards—the image of Mao as a subversive pop-culture icon gained increasing currency. Through its multifaceted permutations, the posthumous Mao cult was a popular phenomenon, never fully reintegrated into state propaganda, ultimately helping to domesticate the godlike tyrant and savior, turning him into a cheap charm and a kitschy cultural commodity.[82] Now he was worth only a few fleeting mentions in the new history curriculum adopted by the Shanghai educational authorities in 2006,[83] and was completely absent from the pharaonic rituals of the opening ceremony of the 2008 Beijing Olympics.

As for the discourse of self-cultivation, it eventually found new outlets through the growth of Christianity, Buddhism, and, by the early 2000s, popular Confucian movements (described in chapter 12). But its first and most widespread post-Mao incarnation, in the 1980s and 90s, was through the *qigong* movement. Though in appearance a phenomenon quite different from the moral self-cultivation and revolutionary asceticism of the Mao era—most significantly, it resurrected traditional body-centered cosmologies and practices focused on harmony rather than struggle—it was very much a product of the revolutionary period and carried over some of its patterns. As mentioned in chapter 4, *qigong* had first been institutionalized in the 1950s, and had seen its first heyday during the Great Leap. In the 1980s, atomic scientists and nuclear physicists—whose theories had reinforced Mao's fantasies about the infinite transformative power of the human will and the "bomb" of human energy that could be released by fissioning social relations—were the most enthusiastic promoters of state support for a revolutionary *qigong* science of mind over matter, reviving utopian dreams in the form of a future paranormal wonderland.[84] As discussed in chapter 11, by the mid- to late 1990s, *qigong* served as a conduit, through Falungong, for a new fusion of self-cultivation, demonology, mass ritual display, and messianism—with master Li Hongzhi often depicted in poses reminiscent of Mao, and his teachings evoking nostalgia for the revolutionary morality of bygone times.[85]

82. Hubbert, "(Re)Collecting Mao."
83. Joseph Kahn, "Where's Mao? Chinese Revise History Books," *New York Times*, September 1, 2006.
84. Palmer, *Qigong Fever*.
85. Penny, "The Body of Master Li."

THE STATE RENEWS ITS CIVILIZING MISSION

The project of state-sponsored moral transformation—*jiaohua*—of the people was not abandoned during the post-Mao era, and saw many new developments. These built on the symbolic and institutional legacy of the revolutionary era but were far less ambitious and, indeed, bore resemblances to the New Life movement and similar campaigns launched by other Chinese polities in the postwar period, all focused on civic morality rather than ascetic revolution. In Taiwan, as an answer to the Cultural Revolution, the Cultural Renaissance Movement had been launched in November 1966. The campaign aimed to improve educational standards and promote family education, with an emphasis on the Confucian virtues (including filial duty and fraternal love); to publish Chinese classic literary works and disseminate Chinese culture in Taiwan and abroad; to encourage good customs and morals; to guide national modernization based on the Confucian principles of the New Life movement; to build new cultural facilities, preserve historical relics, and promote cultural tourism; and to promote Chinese culture abroad through overseas Chinese groups and foreign scholars and intellectuals.[86] These aims were reflected in civic education in Taiwanese schools, which criticized religion in general and narrow visions of kinship and Confucian rituals in particular, and articulated morality and nationalism by focusing on the individual's moral duty and sacrifice for the nation.[87]

In Singapore in the decades following independence in 1965, the state conducted campaigns against spitting and littering, and promoted courtesy and water conservation among its many projects of social engineering. But here too the school was a key locus of the state's moral education mission. In 1982, a compulsory Religious Knowledge curriculum was introduced in the schools, with parents (not their children, to prevent them from choosing a different religion from their parents) given a choice between Buddhist Studies, Confucian Ethics, Bible Studies, Islamic Studies, Hindu Studies, and World Religions. This was the first time religion was taught at public schools in a Chinese context. Although the Confucian Ethics program was enthusiastically promoted by the Chinese Chamber of Commerce and the Clan Associations, it was met with resistance and distrust by Western-educated and Christian Chinese. The Religious Knowledge curriculum was downgraded in 1990 after government reports concluded that

---

86. Katz, "Religion and the State in Post-War Taiwan," 402–6.
87. Stafford, "Good Sons"; Meyer, "Teaching Morality in Taiwan Schools."

it was reinforcing religious identities and therefore risked creating social tensions. It was replaced with a new campaign to promote "Shared Values," actively promoted abroad as "Asian Values," which were focused on respect for authority and community by contrast to so-called Western values.[88]

It should be emphasized that Singapore's official promotion of Confucianism has nothing to do with the Confucian religious movement that had influenced overseas Chinese elites (including those in Singapore) since 1900. Like the KMT use of Confucianism from the 1950s to the 1980s as a resource for official morality, it was cut from its background in religious practice, and was therefore but a marginal aspect of lived Confucianism within society.[89] A telling sign is that the curriculum in Confucian ethics was partly designed by North American–based scholars such as Tu Wei-ming.[90]

Many of the features of the Taiwanese and Singaporean projects were included in several waves of PRC policy. Even though, by contrast to Taiwan and Singapore, religion cannot be taught in PRC schools (with the exception of basic information on religion in other countries in geography courses), civic education there evolved in rather similar directions.[91] In the 1980s and 1990s, campaigns to promote "constructing spiritual civilization" 精神文明建設 aimed to recast revolutionary ideology and morality into new models of civic virtue compatible with economic modernization, which could fill the post-Mao moral vacuum and prevent the spread of corruption. These campaigns included recycling classic propaganda tools such as promoting classes in Marxism and political ideology, and studying Lei Feng and other heroes of service to society—methods now greeted with skepticism and derision by most people—but they also involved a broader and widely accepted normative discourse on raising *suzhi* 素質, the civility or "quality" of the people.

The notion of *suzhi* referred to the moral and cultural attributes of a modern, civilized individual, and took as its model the clean and orderly civic behavior of modern Westerners and East Asians (Hong Kong and Singapore residents as well as Koreans and Japanese), in contradistinction to

88. Dirlik, "Confucius in the Borderlands"; Kuah-Pearce, *State, Society and Religious Engineering*, 189–214; C. Tan, "From Moral Values to Citizenship Education."

89. Jochim, "Carrying Confucianism."

90. Tu Wei-ming, *Confucian Ethics Today*.

91. Tyl, "The Formation of New Citizens"; Hirotaka Nanbu, "Religion in Chinese Education." Tyl, "The Formation of New Citizens," and Stafford, "Good Sons," note that in both the PRC and Taiwan, textbooks and public discourse have been evolving since the 1990s toward individual moral values (character building) and away from sacrifice for the nation.

the coarse appearance and unruly behavior of poorly educated peasants and working classes who, in the elite imaginary, spit, litter, never queue up, never obey regulations, care only for themselves, and have no consciousness of the public good. *Suzhi* symbolized a habitus embodied in personal hygiene and deportment; a set of conscious moral attitudes characteristic of a modern, broad-minded, and responsible citizen concerned for the common welfare; and the professional competencies of an individual working within the complex technical and managerial systems of a modern society. This habitus was represented by the Eight Honors and Eight Shames 八榮八恥—standards of behavior that from the early twenty-first century were taught in schools and integrated in propaganda campaigns.[92] Education was the key to enhancing the quality and "cultural level" 文化水平 of the people, and morality was seen as a necessary result of *suzhi* and education: it was to be expected that crimes would be committed by people of low "quality," but when educated people committed acts of immorality, it was positively shocking.[93] "Raising the moral quality of the population" thus intended to address a set of clearly identified moral problems: the cult of money 拜金主義, hedonism 享樂主義, extreme individualism 極端個人主義, putting private interests above the public good 見利忘義, the inability to discern between good and evil 善惡, and so on.[94]

The source of morality and virtue was no longer the proletarian class consciousness of the revolutionary period but the advanced cultural consciousness of the new urban elites. The CCP adjusted itself to the new paradigm with Jiang Zemin's doctrine of the Three Represents 三個代表, adopted into the official ideology in 2002,[95] in which the CCP shed its identity as the Party of the proletariat in favor of representing the "advanced productive forces," the "advanced culture," and the "overwhelming majority of the people of China." In practical terms, the CCP began to redefine itself as a party of the economic and cultural elite, who could define the interests and set the moral standards for the "overwhelming majority" of the people. This was most evident in the countryside, where local Party leaders were no longer chosen and promoted on the basis of proletarian

---

92. Billioud, "Confucianism."

93. On *suzhi* discourse, see Anagnost, *National Past-Times* and "The Corporeal Politics of Quality"; Bakken, *The Exemplary Society*; S. Friedman, "Embodying Civility"; Xie Sizhong, *Guomin suzhi yousi lu*; Kipnis, *Producing Guanxi*, chap. 9; Flower, "Portraits of Belief"; Murphy, "Turning Peasants into Modern Chinese Citizens"; Cao Nanlai, "Raising the Quality of Belief"; Brownell, "Beijing's Olympic Education."

94. Billioud, "Confucianism."

95. Jiang Zemin, *Lun "sange daibiao."*

class background but expected to acquire higher education and *suzhi*, become exemplars for the masses, and reward "civilized households" with gold stars and plates to hang on their entrance gates, in recognition of their respect for the law and birth-control policies, their sense of duty, their family unity, their children's upbringing, their new (nonfeudal) lifestyle, their hygiene, and their wealth.[96]

Again the CCP and the state were defining themselves as civilizing agents, renewing the tradition of *jiaohua* already illustrated by the late imperial state, the New Life movement, and more recent moves in Taiwan and Singapore. In seeking a spiritual source for this moral civilizing, in building coherence into the Party's ideological shifts, and in establishing new foundations for its legitimacy after the June 4, 1989, crushing of the Tian'anmen student movement, nationalism became an increasingly explicit reference for Party leaders, ideologues, and scholars—a trend that opened and expanded the space for the development and reinvention of Chinese tradition.[97] Coherence was found by portraying the Party as the incarnation of the national spirit that unfolded through the brilliance of ancient Chinese civilization, through the anti-imperialist struggles of the Chinese people in the nineteenth and early twentieth centuries, through the establishment of the new China in the Mao period, through the rising prosperity of the Deng era, and through the emergence of China as a global power in the twenty-first century.[98]

The *national spirit* 民族精神 was defined in official readers on ideology as the "synthesis of the nation's thought consciousness, value orientation, moral norms, qualities of character, and cultural tradition. It is the soul of the nation, which can unite the hearts of the people, stir up their spirits, and give it a strong life-force and cohesion." Its ancient spirit found modern expression in the "Long March spirit," the "Yan'an spirit," the "Daqing spirit,"[99] the "Lei Feng spirit," and so on, and more recently in the "spirit of rescue" following the Sichuan earthquake of May 18, 2008[100]—each being cases in which the Chinese people displayed selfless acts of collective solidarity.

Uneven, at times incoherent, and often contested within the Party itself, the ideological synthesis of Chinese socialism and traditional culture began

96. Thøgersen, "Parasites or Civilisers," 218.
97. Meissner, "Réflexions sur la quête."
98. Béja, "Nationalisme."
99. Daqing 大慶 is a district in Manchuria centered on a petrochemical complex that, during the 1960s, Mao proclaimed as the model of industrial development.
100. *Lilun redian mianduimian 2008*.

with dispersed and hesitant efforts in the 1990s, such as the dissemination of a new version of the children's *Three-character classic* 三字經, which taught a Marxist view of history as well as Confucian ethics;[101] the promotion of *qigong* by several leaders and ministries;[102] and the encouragement of national studies (*guoxue* 國學). By the early 2000s, however, it became an increasingly sophisticated and integrated effort.[103] Hu Jintao's promotion of a "harmonious society," as well as the decision to enhance China's "soft power" as part of its geopolitical strategy, provided an even wider conceptual space and a political opening for deeper connections between the official ideology and traditional culture, including its more religious aspects. One of his speeches on "harmonious society," for instance, quoted Confucius, Mencius, and the above-mentioned passage from the *Book of Rites* on the Great Commonwealth, as well as Kang Youwei, in addition to Fourier, the early European socialists, and the Communist Manifesto.[104] These connections paved the way for both top-down attempts to instrumentalize traditional symbols and values, and bottom-up diversions of openings in the official discourse to legitimize traditional activities and religious practices, as described in chapters 10 and 11.

101. Huai Bing, "La Chine en quête d'une nouvelle morale."
102. Palmer, *Qigong Fever*.
103. Béja, "The Rise of National-Confucianism?"; Yang Yehua, *Shehui zhuyi sixiang daode*.
104. Speech delivered on February 19, 2005; discussed in Billioud, "Confucianism." Available online at www.china.com.cn/chinese/news/899546.htm (accessed January 9, 2010).

PART II

Multiple Religious Modernities
Into the Twenty-First Century

EIGHT

Alternative Trajectories for Religion in the Chinese World

❧ 捌 ❧

From the nineteenth century onward, the whole of the Chinese world shared the experiences of going through the early stages of modernity; being exposed to Western ideas of democracy,[1] science, and progress; and taking part, whether in China proper or overseas, willingly or reluctantly, in reformist or revolutionary movements. But not all Chinese people were engulfed in the mainland's trajectory through a first, largely failed, modernist secular utopia under the KMT, followed by the bloody war against Japan and a new modernist utopia under the Communist Party. Many Chinese lived and still live in other polities, which organized the relationships between state, society, and religion quite differently: first under colonialist regimes (either Japanese or Western) and then under new states, either purely or largely Chinese, such as Singapore or the Republic of China in

---

1. For a case of Western (in this case, Dutch) nonrecognition and repression of Chinese practices of democracy among the autonomous Chinese republics in nineteenth-century Borneo, see Yuan Bingling, *Chinese Democracies*.

Taiwan; dominated by other ethnic groups, as in Southeast Asia (Thailand, Malaysia, Indonesia, the Philippines); or located in the West.

The religion of the Chinese people in these polities was rooted in the religious culture of the mainland whence the migrants had come, with selected elements carried on, left behind, or changed in the process of migration and acculturation. Such variety was accentuated as new conditions, colonial or postcolonial, informed developments specific to each place. In this chapter, we will consider the fate of Chinese religion in colonial and postcolonial polities outside Mainland China, from the early twentieth century until the late 1970s. Rather than seeing these developments as marginal or irrelevant to the grand narrative of the religio-political history of China, we consider them alternative trajectories that illustrate the very rich potential for different forms of religious modernity within Chinese society. This observation becomes even more relevant in the contemporary period of globalization, in which these trajectories intersect and as the models and practices of religion that developed at the periphery of the Chinese world penetrate back to the mainland.

WESTERN COLONIAL TRAJECTORIES

Chinese communities have existed outside Mainland China for centuries. Colonial situations, where a predominantly Chinese community was ruled by, and often expanded under, a non-Chinese empire, first appeared in the sixteenth century with the Portuguese settlements in Macau, Malacca, and the Moluccas, and the Spanish colony of the Philippines. These were followed by Dutch colonial expansion in present-day Indonesia; the British dominion, established from the late eighteenth century, over what is today Malaysia and its ports with large Chinese populations (notably the Straits Settlements: Penang, Malacca, and Singapore); and the establishment in the nineteenth century of French Indochina, which has a large Chinese population in the city of Saigon, and where the religious culture of the Vietnamese people followed much the same pattern as that of the Chinese. Such encounters between Chinese people and the colonial states occurred in multicultural—and thus multireligious—contexts, where the colonial authorities were simultaneously faced with Muslims, Hindus, Chinese religionists, and others, and strove to keep them separate. In the Philippines, mostly southern-Fujian migrants became a sizable minority among Pilipinos converted to Roman Catholicism and a few colonials;[2]

---

2. On the Chinese in colonial Philippines, see notably Wilson, *Ambition and Identity*.

with the American takeover in 1898, they became to a certain degree ostra-cized as "aliens." Unlike the situation in British and Dutch colonies and in Portuguese Macau, the majority of the Chinese migrants converted to the dominant religion, Catholicism (even though they often maintained Chi-nese religious practices). A different type of encounter took place in Hong Kong, which came under British rule in 1842, followed by the addition of the New Territories in 1899. In contrast to Singapore, Penang, Batavia, or Manila, Hong Kong society was more uniformly Cantonese-Chinese, with the quantitatively small addition of colonial officers, Western merchants, and the non-Chinese personnel they brought with them (mostly from the Indian subcontinent).

In all these situations, until independence or retrocession to Chinese sovereignty, the British, Dutch, French, Portuguese, Spanish, and Ameri-cans had to learn about Chinese religion and how to manage it. Such knowledge was also acquired in China proper by missionaries everywhere they went and by lay consular officials in the port concessions, where they shared judicial powers with Chinese state agents until the Japanese inva-sion in 1937. In the latter case, however, and by contrast to colonial situ-ations, the Western authorities tended to leave religious issues, with the exception of Christianity, to their native counterparts.

Even when they preferred not to interfere at all, the colonial authorities, confronted with Chinese social organization and religion, had to devise laws, regulations, and administrative procedures to deal with them—by codifying so-called customary practices just like the Chinese Republican government, crafting a civil law on the Western model, was also doing.[3] By the same token, they also created regimes of knowledge though field research, surveys, learned societies, reports, and scholarly publications.[4] Through this production of knowledge, they created categories of their own to order Chinese religion, in ways necessarily and vastly different from what the Qing empire did, but also different from the scientific categori-zations chosen by the Nationalist and later Communist regimes. British colonial authorities in Hong Kong and the Straits Settlements required all associations to register, and they identified secret societies, which they

3. P. Huang, *Code, Custom, and Legal Practice*. For how the British colonial authorities dealt with Chinese rites of marriage, adoption, and oath taking, making all sorts of awkward compromises that half-recognized the legal validity of Chinese rites, see Freedman, "Colonial Law"; and Katz, *Divine Justice*, chap. 6.

4. Among many examples, we may mention here the Hong Kong and Malay branches of the Royal Asiatic Society and their journals, which published many (often very good) reports on Chinese reli-gion written by British colonial officers, as well as the *Bulletin de l'Ecole française d'Extrême-Orient*.

distinguished from common-origin associations (*huiguan*), temple associations, and lineages, among other types—all of which ran temples with the authorities' approval.[5]

The interests of the colonial authorities and the KMT sometimes converged, however. The supreme importance granted to social order and the prevention of riots and even secession led to a large part of colonial attention being paid to so-called secret societies, the sworn brotherhoods. British officials, in particular, inquired in great detail about the Triads throughout the nineteenth and twentieth centuries, and banned them from 1890 onward.[6] The very categories crafted by British colonial authorities to think about these groups, beginning with the secret societies (even though there was often little secret about them), were later adopted by Japanese and then Chinese intellectuals (translating "secret societies" as *mimi sheshui*), who in turn used them to frame Nationalist and Communist policies and theory. Colonial authorities saw such groups as politically motivated and, with the exception of some officers who were themselves members of Masonic lodges, either downplayed or ignored their spiritual and religious dimensions as self-perfection brotherhoods. Later law enforcers in Republican and Communist China would do the same.

In contrast to intense interest in secret societies, the temples of territorial and common-origin associations (*huiguan*) were largely left alone by the colonial officials of all Western powers, who also took a laissez-faire approach toward festivals, even though Christian groups at home lobbied for a more interventionist (anti-idolatrous) policy. Authorities tried to register temples, if only because they controlled large amounts of land, which was at the same time being surveyed and registered; to this effect they created legal categories such as not-for-profit associations and charities. Temples that set themselves up as not-for-profit foundations running charities—hospitals and schools, in particular—received favorable treatment from the authorities. The colonial model of recognizing religious communities as not-for-profit foundations was a successful invention that was adopted in the later Chinese states, such as Taiwan.

Similarly, lineages and common-origin associations were also set up as trusts, and fully recognized by the colonial authorities who empowered them, first by devolving on them indirect rule and then, after colonial administration matured, by consulting informally with their leaders, or

5. Freedman, "Immigrants and Associations"; Topley, "The Emergence and Social Function of Chinese Religious Associations in Singapore."

6. DeBernardi, *Rites of Belonging*, chap. 3; ter Haar, *Ritual and Mythology of the Chinese Triads*.

even appointing them to administrative positions. The colonial authorities found it natural to consider the leaders of such groups as native community leaders.[7]

This policy tended to strengthen certain types of lay religious leadership. As in India, where the British also took over the role of the local kingdoms as patrons of temples, they fully entrusted the management of Chinese religious institutions to a small elite of upper-class merchants and professionals who worked very closely with the colonial regime, to the detriment of religious specialists and other local community leaders. As Joseph Bosco has argued, the British officials in Hong Kong strengthened the hand of the small group of the wealthiest merchants as leaders of local religion, which resulted in stifling creativity and diversity in temple life. After the KMT on the mainland passed laws to register temples and closely monitor their property and management from 1928 onward, Hong Kong's Chinese elite pressured the British authorities to do the same. New laws were thus passed in the colony, strengthening the procedures for the registration and financial monitoring of temples, and centralizing the management of most under a Chinese Temples Committee 華人廟宇委員會 in the hands of elite merchants, who were in fact uninterested in temples. The committee eliminated the competition between temples, which typically spurred lavish expansions and renovations; instead, it closed down certain temples considered too commercial and not "religious" enough, and siphoned the others' income into the secular Tung Hua 東華 Hospital charity.[8] Thus, even though Hong Kong experienced neither temple destruction nor antisuperstition campaigns, the ritual life of temples stagnated or declined—festivals and processions became smaller in scale and no longer involved the whole community—and temple reconstructions since that time have been comparatively modest.[9]

Through Hong Kong's Chinese Temples Committee, the colony's Chinese elite thus instrumentalized temples to generate income for modern-style social services. A comparable approach was adopted by the Thai government and also by the Chinese elite of Penang, Malaysia, which, starting in 1974, adopted a strategy of coordinating the celebration of the Ghost Festival, which it hoped to reorient from a ritual for placating ghosts into

7. On Hong Kong lineages, see Faure, *The Structure of Chinese Rural Society*.

8. Faure, *Emperor and Ancestor*, 335–36, shows that the Tung Hua Hospital, created in 1870, was a hybrid English-Chinese institution that served as a model for many other elite institutions in the Chinese world which also attempted to control religious and charitable activities.

9. Bosco, "Tianhou gong zhi chongjian yu huoli"; Lang & Ragvald, *The Rise of a Refugee God*, 45–49.

a campaign to raise funds for the poor and needy. Although they disparaged the superstitious content of the rites, the local leaders, in the context of Malaysian identity politics, did not stifle popular customs in the same way as their Hong Kong counterparts. Campaigning at the many neighborhood banquets held during the festival, they were able over the years to raise large sums to build Chinese-medium primary and secondary schools, charitable hospitals, and community centers.[10]

These cases reveal the common ground between overseas Chinese elites on the one hand and the mainland's modern intellectual elites and political regimes on the other, as both were opposed to "superstitious" temple life and wanted to redirect temple resources to welfare. The similarities were only partial, though. The link between religious institutions and local elites that was being severed in Mainland China, largely because new elites of political activists replaced the disappearing gentry, was, by contrast, strengthened in the colonies, where throughout the twentieth century the ties between conservative elite businessmen and temples were never cut, although they evolved with colonial practices.

Another major bifurcation between the mainland and the overseas trajectories concerned the connection between religion and nationalism. Whereas the KMT brand of nationalism by and large excluded religion, that which developed among the overseas Chinese, while influenced by KMT discourse (it was, after all, the overseas merchants who bankrolled Sun Yat-sen and his revolution), also found a place for religion. The Chinese not living on the mainland nonetheless supported the rise of China as a fully sovereign nation (many of them returned to help build the country in 1949), yet their nationalism was and still is distinctive, as it integrated pride in the spiritual and linguistic dimensions of the Chinese state of being. These two dimensions were intertwined and found expression through religious Confucian associations or redemptive societies like Yiguandao or Dejiao 德教, which ran Chinese-language schools in overseas communities, linking ethnic, linguistic, and religious identity.

Indeed, confronted directly with the powerful Muslim, Buddhist, or Christian majorities of the societies they were living in, for whom religious affiliation was central to ethnic identity, overseas Chinese included their own religious practice in their self-definition, and were expected to do so by the non-Chinese around them. That is not to say they supported all aspects of Chinese religion. Their community leaders were as antisuperstitious as politicians on the mainland; they vehemently opposed spirit me-

10. DeBernardi, *Rites of Belonging*, chap. 7.

diums and "popular" rituals, and tried to foster modern religiosities compatible with science. Even so, they openly expressed their own religiosity much more consistently than mainland politicians, notably through the vehicle of Confucian associations and redemptive societies.

The religious Confucian vision for a spiritual renewal and unification of the Chinese race and nation, coupled with social reform as developed by Kang Youwei and his disciples, was much more influential among the diaspora than inside China. Many Chinese elites in Malaysia, Indonesia, and other colonies established Confucian associations as early as 1900 (such as the Zhonghua huiguan 中華會館 in Batavia, now Jakarta), even though they never spread far beyond the merchant elites.[11] Some of these have survived to this day, especially in Indonesia, where they still operate as churches with Sunday prayers. Local Chinese leaders have been trying to have Confucianism protected as an officially recognized religion by the Indonesian state, meeting with an ambiguous response; Confucian weddings were recognized as legal under Indonesian law in 2000.[12]

It is to Hong Kong that Chen Huanzhang retreated after the failure of his project for a national Confucian religion during the 1910s, and since the 1970s his Confucian Association has engaged in a campaign to have Confucianism recognized by the Hong Kong authorities as the territory's sixth major religion (on top of the five recognized by the PRC: Buddhism, Roman Catholicism, Islam, Protestantism, and Taoism). The campaign has met with some success, notably after the 1997 retrocession: many interreligious meetings and official functions now include a Confucian representative. All these practical and political as well as social experiments in Confucian modern religiosity preceded and informed a revival of positive interest in religious Confucianism in the PRC since the late 1990s.

Like that of Confucianism, but on a larger scale, the development of redemptive societies among overseas Chinese is linked to their manner of framing modernity, nationalism, and Chinese ethnic identity in ways that resonated with the migrants' experience. The two overlap, moreover, since many late imperial Confucian practices were carried over by redemptive societies. These groups found particularly fertile ground for expansion among migrant communities in which different linguistic groups coexisted (the major ones throughout the overseas communities being the Canton-

11. Ibid., chap. 1; Coppel, "The Origins of Confucianism"; Duara, "Religion and Citizenship"; Suryadinata, "Confucianism."

12. H. Yang, "The History and Legal Position of Confucianism"; Ablahin, "A Sixth Religion?" Confucianism had already been briefly officially recognized in 1965–66.

ese, Hakka, Hainan, Chaozhou, Hokkien [southern Fujian], and Wenzhou, which often remained separate and only communicated through religious institutions) and where lineage and territorial structures were poorly or not at all reconstructed as a result of migrant dislocation. Redemptive societies thus provided not only meaning and identification but also services such as death rituals and community festivals that on the mainland were usually provided by ascriptive communities.

Colonial regimes developed an attitude toward the redemptive societies that was markedly different from the Nationalist and Communist ones, because they did not inherit the tradition of imperial bans on "heterodox sects"; they saw them as no more superstitious than temple cults or Buddhists and Taoists, and indeed sometimes categorized them as such. For instance, the temples affiliated to the Xiantiandao 先天道, a salvationist movement widespread throughout Southeast Asia, play a leading role in the Hong Kong Taoist Association and operate totally freely there, whereas the same congregations were banned as "reactionary sects and secret societies" (反動會道門) in the People's Republic. This is not the case of colonial regimes only; for example, the religious organization of the Chinese community in Thailand is dominated by powerful charitable foundations—the most important of which is the Po Tek Hsiang T'ung 報德善堂, based in Bangkok—belonging to a redemptive society, the Virtuous Teachings (Dejiao).[13] This movement was founded in 1939 in the Chaozhou area (north of Guangdong Province), when a group of friends set up an offering table to perform spirit-writing divination. They obtained a revelation from the Taoist deities Yang Junsong 楊筠松 and Liu Chunfang 柳春芳 that the final catastrophe was near, and the deities advised them to establish a charitable association to preach virtues, provide medical services to the sick, and carry out philanthropy.[14] A number of Dejiao associations were thereafter established in the Chaozhou and Shantou areas, but it was after World War II, when spirit-writing revelations ordered two of the leaders to establish Dejiao in Hong Kong and Southeast Asia, that the cult rapidly spread to Thailand, Malaysia, Singapore, Hong Kong, and San Francisco, while the Communist takeover on the mainland ended the cult's activities at its place of birth.

Following a logic similar to the division-of-incense (*fenxiang* 分香) system of temple branching, Dejiao was organized into several networks of

---

13. Formoso, "Chinese Temples and Philanthropic Associations in Thailand" and "Marchands et philanthropes."

14. Tan Chee-beng, *The Development and Distribution of Dejiao Associations*, 15.

temples affiliated to older, ancestral branches. Over time, variations developed in the practices of the different branches, notably over the use of spirit writing; some branches abandoned the practice. Otherwise, Dejiao temples retained the standard Five-in-One cult of honoring all five religions, a basic congregational ritual, and a strong emphasis on charitable works. Dejiao associations would become leading Chinese social organizations in Southeast Asia, especially among the Chaozhou people, whose business leaders were typically strong financial backers and directors of the temples.

Another redemptive society strongly associated with the Chinese diaspora in Southeast Asia is the Teachings of True Emptiness (Zhenkongjiao 真空教). This movement, established in Anhui in the 1860s and inspired by the Patriarch Luo 羅祖 salvationist tradition, proscribed gambling, opium, idols, and fengshui, and involved practicing sitting meditation, healing, and scripture recitation. The group expanded to Fujian in the late nineteenth century, from whence it spread to other parts of South China and by 1929 to Hong Kong, Singapore, the Philippines, and Malaysia.[15] In these colonial diasporic communities Zhenkongjiao came to play a similar function as Dejiao.

JAPANESE COLONIAL TRAJECTORIES

Up to 1945 and the final destruction of the Japanese empire, Japanese colonialism in Taiwan and Manchuria, and in the Chinese heartland itself from the late 1930s, affected larger populations of Chinese people than its Western counterparts. It also proposed an alternative set of ideas and practices aiming to invent a Chinese political and religious modernity. The engagement of Japanese colonial scholars and officials with Chinese religion was more intense than that of Western colonial authorities; their production of knowledge about Chinese religions was massive, and still influences contemporary scholarship to a great extent.[16] Japanese scholars elaborated ideological rationales for using the Chinese religious spirit in the building of the Asian co-prosperity sphere. They opposed the Christian idea that China had no religion, and considered that redemptive societies such as the Daoyuan represented a constructive, modern formulation of the Chinese religious spirit.[17]

15. Shao Yong, *Zhongguo huidaomen*, 157; Noguchi Tetsurou, "Dongnanya."
16. DuBois, "Local Religion and the Imperial Imaginary."
17. Duara, *Sovereignty and Authenticity*, 112.

Even before it began to act as a colonial power with Chinese subjects, Japan had been, like the Western powers, a source of inspiration for Chinese reformers in search of religious policies. Under Western pressure, Japan had adopted religious freedom in its 1889 constitution, and thus devised a system that distinguished between a national cult (state Shintô), the participation in which was compulsory for all Japanese subjects, and "religions," a matter of individual belief and practice. The latter included Shintô sects and other "new religions," Buddhism, and Christianity—which was reluctantly recognized by the state after centuries of bans and repression—and were free to organize within parameters of state control that grew ever more constraining through the 1900–1945 period as Japan militarized and engaged in war.[18] These religions were encouraged to modernize by adopting a nationalist and rational discourse, as most of them did.

The first Japanese colonial experiment was Taiwan, which was ceded to Japan by the Qing empire in 1895 and remained under direct colonial rule for exactly fifty years.[19] Many of the approaches to managing native religion devised in Taiwan were later applied in other parts of the Japanese empire, notably Korea after 1905. The colonial management of Chinese religion in Taiwan followed a course that can be divided into three stages.[20] From 1895 to 1915, not unlike the Western colonial practices, a laissez-faire approach was followed, centered on monitoring potentially dangerous groups. The massive surveys and field reports by anthropologists and police officials (the two groups overlapping in some cases) expressed a vision of Chinese religion embroiled in superstition and stuck at an earlier stage of development than the more "rational" Japanese religions (whether Buddhism or Shintô); yet they often also argued that overall, Chinese religion played a positive role in maintaining local order and instilling some morality among a population reputed to be feuding and unruly.[21] While their vision of popular practices as being superstitious shared some ground with that of the modernizing Chinese officials and ideologues, the Japanese colonial authorities never considered creating a new society without religion, but rather attempted to reform and uplift the existing religious configuration of society. That the grassroots structure of territorial temples was not attacked in the name of building schools or fighting superstition as it was on the main-

18. Hardacre, *Shintô and the State*; Garon, "State and Religion."

19. On religion in Japanese-controlled Taiwan, see Wang Jianchuan & Li Shiwei, *Taiwan de zongjiao yu wenhua*; Jiang Canteng, *Riju shiqi Taiwan fojiao*.

20. Ts'ai Chin-t'ang, *Nihon teikoku-shugika Taiwan*.

21. Tsu, "Between Superstition and Morality."

land explains why Taiwan has preserved many aspects of Chinese ritual culture that have disappeared in most of the rest of the Chinese world.

In 1915, a revolt organized around a messianic spirit-writing cult, called the Xilai'an 西來庵 incident for the name of that cult's core shrine,[22] forced the Japanese to rethink their approach and exercise much more control over Taiwanese temples and religious communities. They introduced stricter temple registration and police monitoring, but also embarked on religious engineering, actively suppressing certain types of temples, communities, and specialists—notably spirit mediums—[23] considered undesirable, and by contrast actively supporting those deemed compatible with the society they aimed to build. Japanese religions were introduced, notably with the active proselytism of Japanese Buddhist sects, but with little success; however, under the umbrella of these sects, and also in contact with mainland coreligionists, some Taiwanese Buddhist leaders engaged in a reformist movement to establish full-fledged monastic institutions and distance themselves from local cults.[24]

The beginning of the war in 1937 ushered in the third stage of managing native religion, characterized by much more violent repression. Fighting against the Chinese on the mainland, the Japanese were suspicious of Taiwanese loyalties, and strove to assimilate them completely as Japanese subjects. The "transformation into imperial subjects" (*kôminka* 皇民化) policy involved schooling in Japanese but also had religious aspects, with large numbers of temples forcibly turned into Shintô shrines, much property appropriated, and large numbers of objects—icons, texts, and liturgical items—destroyed in the process. Many temples and communities formed again after 1945, but the religious landscape had changed, opening up spaces for creating new religious institutions and practices.[25]

More complex was the case of Manchukuo, the state set up in 1931 in Manchuria under Japanese tutelage and military control. Unlike Taiwan, Manchukuo was not a colony but a nominally independent state, which the Japanese conceived as a real-scale experiment in inventing a modern nation committed to ethnic and religious pluralism.[26] Manchukuo authorities attempted to rally to their support for the same five recognized religions

22. Katz, *When Valleys Turned Blood Red.*
23. Japanese hostility to spirit mediums was not as unqualified as the KMT's, since some Japanese intellectuals saw spirit mediumism (or "shamanism") as the original pan-Asian religion that later evolved into Shintô.
24. C. Jones, *Buddhism in Taiwan.*
25. C. Jones, "Religion in Taiwan."
26. Duara, *Sovereignty and Authenticity.*

as the KMT, but there were major differences in their approach. Whereas KMT religious policies were influenced by Christian normative models, and its leadership at times openly favored Christianity, the Manchukuo leaders and their Japanese advisors considered Christians representatives of a foreign religion that had nothing to do with building a modern Asia. On the other hand, they found much to praise among some redemptive societies that provided an Asian equivalent of the Christian ideals of good, faithful, devoted citizens, and a basis for the religious aspect of national identity.

The regime thus actively courted and favored some salvationist movements and redemptive societies, both Japanese ones trying to develop abroad, such as Ômoto 大本, and Chinese ones, such as Zailijiao or the Daoyuan, even though they were not fully and formally allied with the state.[27] As a consequence, after the Japanese surrendered and Manchukuo collapsed in 1945, these groups were ferociously repressed as traitors and collaborators by both the KMT and the Communist regimes.

The case of the Japanese occupation of Mainland China is quite different. The territories of the Republic of China occupied between 1937 and 1945 were nominally ruled by puppet states that mostly maintained the legislation (religious and otherwise) of the Republic and had little attention to spare for religious issues anyway. The Japanese and their Chinese allies tried to make sure that Buddhist and Taoist leaders collaborated with pro-Japanese religious organizations such as the Buddhist Common Purpose Society 佛教同願會.[28] More actively and creatively, they called on all Muslims and Tibeto-Mongol Buddhists to unite under their banner so as to create a religiously as well as politically unified Asia, or to support a proposed Japanese puppet Muslim state in northwestern China.[29] As in Manchukuo, redemptive societies and their charitable affiliates expanded rapidly under the conditions of civil war and Japanese occupation. The Red Swastika Society became the largest philanthropic association in these areas, was the main provider of relief during the Nanjing massacre, and ended up as the best-established welfare organization in Shanghai after the Japanese surrender, from 1945 to 1949.[30]

The Japanese and Western colonial experiments, which left a strong mark on postcolonial regimes, were not anomalies. They shared with Na-

27. Ibid., chap. 3.

28. Xue Yu, *Buddhism, War and Nationalism*, 160–68.

29. Meng Guoxiang, "Riben liyong zongjiao"; Narangoa, "Japanese Imperialism and Mongolian Buddhism"; Esenbel, "Japan's Global Claim"; Ding Hong & Zhang Guojie, eds., *Bai nian Zhongguo musilin*, 92–95.

30. Duara, *Sovereignty and Authenticity*, 90.

tionalist and Communist approaches a modernist, secular discourse of separation between state and religion, and a civilizing project that entailed, to varying degrees, a fight against superstition which was accompanied by unprecedented efforts at registration, control, and institutionalization; village religion was the object of much surveying-cum-reform. But these common ideas led to colonial authorities and local Chinese elites pushing developments in different directions. Some supported institutional reformist Buddhism; others tolerated and even supported redemptive societies; still others favored Confucian churches, or elite-run charities, or Christianity — all the above being to some extent hostile toward local cults, but without destroying them to the extent the Nationalists and Communists did.

NEW CHINESE STATES

Taiwan

The answers brought by colonial regimes to the question of reconciling Chinese religion and Western-style modernity left a legacy, both in social practice and in law codes, in the states that took over these regimes. The first and still the most important of these states is the Republic of China (ROC) in Taiwan. The ROC is, of course, considered the one legitimate Chinese state by the KMT, which governed it until 2000 and since 2008; in contrast, people sympathetic to the Taiwanese independence movement regard it as just another colonial state. For our discussion, it will suffice to consider it a new Chinese state that inherited from both the Republican experience on the mainland and the Japanese colonial legacy in Taiwan.

The KMT regime established its control over Taiwan in 1945 with brutality before the major part of the army, as well as political, economic, cultural, and religious elites, moved there in the wake of the final defeat at the hands of the People's Liberation Army in 1949. The island population was henceforth divided between Mandarin-speaking Mainlanders holding all the positions of power, and the mostly Hokkien- and Hakka-speaking natives. Martial law and one-party rule continued until Chiang Kai-shek's death in 1975 and a decade beyond; under Chiang's son's rule, the regime began to liberalize, an evolution that matured under his successor's presidency with the lifting of martial law in 1986 and a swift opening up of society to multiparty democracy (leading to the end of KMT rule from 2000 to 2008), social liberalism, and vibrant religious pluralism.

During the years of martial law, religion was one aspect of the contrast and tension between the ruling mainland-born elites and the native populations. The elites had brought with them the KMT tradition of hostility toward all religions save the highly secularized, modernist churches such as Christianity (especially Protestantism) and reformist Buddhism. The Chiang dynasty upheld its Protestant faith, and its successor, President Lee Teng-hui, who brought democracy to the island, was himself a firm believer. In this context, the state's religious policy both continued that of the mainland KMT regime and paralleled that of its socialist enemy: to unite religious leaders under KMT leadership against communism, and to control religious communities through state-sponsored corporatist associations. In the mid-1950s, the KMT government in Taiwan attempted to organize the island's religious communities into a representative corporate body, the Chinese Federation of Religious Believers 中國宗教徒聯誼會 (first established on the mainland as part of the anti-Japanese war effort in 1943), which would act as an intermediary between the state and religious communities. Catholics, Protestants, Buddhists, and Muslims were represented in the association, but there were no Taoists.

The other main religious association was the Buddhist Association of the Republic of China (BAROC), reestablished in Taiwan in 1952 by leading Mainlander monks who had taken refuge on the island, leaving native Buddhists in subordinate positions. This association was dominated by conservative monks, marginalizing the reformist disciples of Taixu, who in the latter half of the twentieth century would transform Taiwan's religious landscape (see chapter 11). BAROC maintained close ties with the KMT—though not without tension on some issues such as the return of temples occupied by government offices—and was monitored by the Bureau for Social Affairs 社會司 and the Bureau for Civil Affairs 民政司 of the Ministry of the Interior. As the only legal Buddhist organization in Taiwan, all monks, monasteries, and Buddhist groups were required to become members; it monopolized the ordination of monks and nuns.[31]

There was also a Taoist association, the Taiwan Provincial Taoist Association 臺灣省道教會, established in 1951, followed by the Taoist Association of the Republic of China 中華民國道教會, established in 1966. They were led by the Sixty-third Heavenly Master, Zhang Enpu 張恩薄 (1904–1969), and the maverick Li Yujie 李玉階 (1901–1994), once a KMT politician, entrepreneur, and redemptive society organizer—both had come to Taiwan in 1949.[32]

31. On BAROC, see C. Jones, *Buddhism in Taiwan*; Laliberté, *The Politics of Buddhist Organizations*.

32. On Li Yujie, see Palmer, "Tao and Nation"; and on the Heavenly Master, see Welch, "The Chang T'ien Shih."

By contrast to the PRC, Catholics and Protestants were not forced into a single nationwide association. Thus, the only other legal religious associations in the 1950s were the Zailijiao redemptive society, registered as the China Lijiao General Association 中華理教總會 in 1949, and the Imperial Teachings of the Yellow Emperor (Xuanyuan huangjiao 軒轅皇教), which registered with the Minister of the Interior in 1956. The latter was a redemptive society created by Mainlanders close to the regime; it combined nationalist hero worship with social and moral values similar to those of the regime's 1930s New Life campaigns.[33]

Many of the larger redemptive societies also gained a foothold in Taiwan with the migration of mainland refugees. The KMT had banned many of these groups in the 1930s, then tried to co-opt them during the Sino-Japanese and civil wars; now in Taiwan, martial law policy banned Yiguandao, which was accused of collaboration with the Japanese and/or the CCP, first in 1950 as "superstition" and a danger to public order, then as a "heterodox doctrine" (*xiejiao*) in 1953.[34] Although repression was not extremely harsh, especially compared with the situation in the People's Republic, Yiguandao came to be seen as marginal and suspect in the eyes of most Taiwanese, although it grew rapidly as an underground organization (with its temples legally registered as Taoist, Buddhist, or Yellow Emperor).

The religious life of the Hokkien-speaking population mostly revolved around devotional associations as well as the complex alliances of temple cults and festivals that had developed on the island since the seventeenth century. The regime saw these cults and festivals as a realm of unassimilated Hokkien culture not fully controlled by the state and potentially hostile to it; hence government efforts until the end of the 1970s aimed to prevent the formation of pan-Taiwanese cults, pilgrimages, and networks. Yet the realm of local religion did not develop as an arena of active resistance to the regime; cult communities, in the face of official scorn and hostility, maintained a strict adherence to law and order and refrained from intervening in politics.[35] As Murray Rubinstein has noted, the only religious group that developed an articulate and vocal force of political contestation was the Presbyterian Church.[36]

The ROC in Taiwan kept the religious legislation that had been passed on the mainland between 1928 and 1937, but it was applied much less

---

33. Jochim, "Flowers, Fruit and Incense."
34. Lin Guoping, *Dangdai Taiwan zongjiao*, 137.
35. Weller, "Worship, Teachings, and State Power."
36. Rubinstein, "Christianity and Democratization."

strictly than during the heady revolutionary period, and was progressively amended with more liberal laws. Communal cults were still regulated by the 1928 and 1929 laws on temples, to which was added the 1948 Ban on Undesirable Popular Customs 查禁民間不良習俗, which outlawed building shrines for "evil cults" (*xiejiao* 邪教), swindling the people through the worship of "lascivious gods" 淫神, conducting spirit writing, and holding large-scale festivals and processions, as well as foot binding, girl slavery, and infanticide. This edict was invoked to ban Yiguandao as an evil cult in 1953, a ban reiterated throughout the martial law period.[37] Temples were required to register (though many did not), and laws detailed how the management committee should be composed; they also had to submit financial reports. A directive of the Ministry of the Interior in 1958 required temples to affiliate with either the BAROC or the Taoist Association, a requirement followed by some and strongly opposed by other temples.[38] All in all, however, temples were much more independent than in the PRC or even Hong Kong. Besides older territorial temples, in following with social changes, all sorts of entrepreneurial and salvationist temples were established as well (discussed in chapters 10 and 11).

Many unrecognized redemptive societies and spirit-writing groups registered as charitable or scholarly organizations, or as Taoist—or sometimes Buddhist or Xuanyuan huangjiao—temples affiliated with the official associations of these legal religions. When, in the mid-1960s, the Minister of the Interior considered designating the Cihuitang 慈惠堂, a large network of spirit-writing temples, as an evil cult, the Sixty-third Heavenly Master, in order to protect them from repression, repeatedly stressed that they were a branch of Taoism.[39] The official Taoist Association of the Republic of China became an umbrella organization providing legal protection to redemptive societies and temples. Included among its leading members, in addition to Zhengyi Taoist priests such as Zhang Enpu, were leaders of Tiandejiao, Zailijiao, Xuanyuan huangjiao, and Yiguandao, which was listed as a vegetarian teaching 齋教.[40] During the martial law period, a few other groups did manage to obtain official recognition as religious organizations, albeit after undergoing a period of surveillance for suspected pro-Communist sympathies:[41]

37. Laliberté, *The Politics of Buddhist Organizations*, 34–41, 45–64; Lin Guoping, *Dangdai Taiwan zongjiao*, 133–34; He Fengjiao, ed., *Taiwan sheng jingwu* (see pp. 1–4 for the text of this edict); Lin Benxuan, *Taiwan de zhengjiao chongtu*.

38. Lin Guoping, *Dangdai Taiwan zongjiao*, 136.

39. Wang Jianchuan, "Cihuitang yu Zhang Tianshi," 264–66.

40. Part of this document is reproduced in Liu Wenxing, *Li Yujie xiansheng nianpu*, 41.

41. He Fengjiao, ed., *Taiwan sheng jingwu*.

the Bahá'í faith, known as Datongjiao 大同教, which had begun activities in Taiwan in 1954 when some of its members moved to the island after leaving Shanghai, was registered in 1970; the Japanese new religious group Tenrikyo 天理教 was registered one year later, as well as the Korean-based Unification Church (which was subsequently banned from 1975 to 1990).[42]

The main thrust of the KMT government's religious policy during the period of martial law was its efforts to streamline "excessive and wasteful" festivals; the rhetoric of adopting a civic, rational attitude of cutting down on useless, wasteful celebrations (including marriages, funerals, and temple festivals) was continued from the campaigns of the 1920s and 1930s. All officials and village heads were enjoined to make sure traditional festivals were downscaled to last only one day.[43] The major achievement of the government was to break down the networks of the seventh-month Ghost Festival celebrations, in which local communities traditionally invited each other's participation over a monthlong cycle; when the celebration was limited to the fifteenth day, each community had to celebrate it independently.

The government established the national Council on Cultural Affairs in the late 1970s with the implicit goal of having it replaced temples as centers of local cultural life. However, the opposite was happening in several counties, with temples becoming more active in sponsoring cultural events, chess tournaments, and community classes; moreover, they became more professional and efficient in the delivery of charitable services and disaster relief. As relations between temples and local officials grew ever warmer, temples became completely embedded in local social and political once again and received considerable donations, which they put into foundations operating a vast array of social and cultural programs.

Singapore

Another Chinese state appeared in 1965 when Singapore seceded from the Federation of Malaysia and became an independent republic, dominated both demographically (77 percent) and politically by ethnic Chinese. The case of Singapore is specific, as the city-state also had Christians as well as very sizable Muslim and Hindu communities; it strove to make any kind of religious tension impossible by closely monitoring public expression of religious belief and identity.[44] The state registered all religious groups and

---

42. Huang Lixing, *Zongjiao jianjie*.
43. Feuchtwang, "City Temples."
44. Sinha, "Theorising 'Talk' about 'Religious Pluralism'"; Clammer, "Religious Pluralism."

allocated them land to build places of worship as it saw fit. This monitoring was part of a larger program of strict social control and, indeed, social engineering that extended to language (with Mandarin being imposed at the expense of other Chinese languages), residence, marriage, childbearing (including eugenics), and all other aspects of personal life, organized from above in a way not seen anywhere in the Chinese world outside the PRC.

Although the Singapore state managed religion with a rather heavy hand—as it did most sectors of society—unlike the KMT and CCP regimes, this was not done out of a desire to secularize society. Rather, similar to Hong Kong (and Macau) as a former British colony, the practice was for the government to outsource social services to religious groups, especially Christian churches. State schools were nonreligious, but about one-quarter of the 340 primary and secondary institutions were state-funded religious schools. Virtually all the latter were Christian, with the exception of three Buddhist schools, seven schools run by the Hokkien and Teochiu *huiguan*, and one school run by the Red Swastika Society. A deliberate policy to phase out Chinese-medium schools—which, though they taught Confucian values, were also conduits for Marxist influences from the mainland— in favor of English-medium schools led to a rise in the influence of Christian educational institutions.[45]

In contrast to the PRC policies, Singaporeans were free to practice ancestor worship, local cults, and salvationist traditions so long as they complied with the demands of state monitoring and ideology. This compliance entailed a specific regime of knowledge: Singapore was unique in the Chinese world in compiling official statistics on religious membership.[46] Accordingly, "Taoism" and "Ancestor Worship" were recognized registration items, suggesting a categorization and thus political management of local cults different from the PRC and, to a lesser degree, Taiwan. By contrast, Malaysia counted ethnic Chinese as "Buddhists," "Christians," or "others."

Chinese Minorities

In states with non-Chinese majorities, ethnic Chinese often faced oppressive nationalisms, as in Thailand during the 1950s and 1960s, Malaysia after 1969, or Indonesia between 1965 and 1999, where all aspects of Chinese selfhood, including religious ones, were criticized or banned. In such

---

45. Charbonnier, "World Religions," 216–17.

46. Taiwan has no official census data on religion, but has reasonably reliable social surveys with information on religious belief and affiliation.

situations, ethnic and religious identities were rigidified. Moreover, leaders of ethnic Chinese communities often reacted to this oppression by engineering an ethnic, cultural, and religious revival. Those communities in the West were not oppressed, but they too had to adapt. In predominantly Muslim or Christian countries, the Chinese often found themselves and their temples identified as Buddhist, whereas in the PRC or Taiwan, the tendency was to categorize temples to local gods as Taoist. In any case, Chinese residing in countries whose majority was Muslim (Indonesia and Malaysia), Christian (the Philippines, Europe, and North America), or Buddhist (Thailand and Cambodia) found that, in sharp contrast to the situation in the PRC or Taiwan, having a religious identity was positively seen and even expected.[47]

In some cases, in order to assimilate, minority Chinese have tended to convert to the dominant religion. The most remarkable case is the Philippines, where the large ethnic Chinese population (mostly of Hokkien origin) is predominantly Catholic while maintaining several active temples and festivals. Another case is the French overseas territory of Reunion Island in the Indian Ocean, where the Chinese are reputedly 95-percent Catholic, and French Polynesia, where they are mostly Protestant.[48] But resistance to conversion has been more common. Christian education played a role in converting Chinese elites in places such as colonial Singapore and Hong Kong. But overall, conversion rates remained rather low, at less than 15 percent in Hong Kong and Singapore;[49] even in North America, the proportion of Chinese Christians remained at one-third. Chinese converts to Islam were few anywhere.

Rather, the Chinese in minority contexts have tended to find compromises that allowed them to accept mainstream practices and discourses while maintaining their own ritual life, notably death rituals and ancestor worship.[50] For instance, ethnic Chinese in Thailand participated to a great extent in Thai Buddhism, but kept certain rites and festivals of their own.[51] All in all, Chinese religion in Southeast Asia and in the West remained largely below the radar of the state bureaucracies, as its practitioners did not engage in proselytizing, and when required to register, its communities usually did so as cultural and charitable associations.

47. For an overview of Chinese religion in Malaysia, see Soo Khin Wah, "Malaixiya huaren zongjiao."

48. Fer, "The Growth of Pentacostalism in French Polynesia."

49. On Chinese Christians in Indonesia, see Wijaya, "Family and Religion."

50. Chung & Wegers, eds., *Chinese American Death Rituals*.

51. Formoso, *Identités en regard*.

POLITICAL ALTERNATIVES

The many varied experiences of Western and Japanese colonies, of the new Chinese states such as Taiwan and Singapore, and of the diasporic communities were all unique and in a way marginal. Taken together, however, they played a crucial role in the modern history of Chinese religion. First, they served as a conservatory of practices and institutions that had become illegal or simply impossible in Communist China during the second half of the twentieth century. Already, migrants to Hong Kong in the 1930s brought with them cults and ritual practices banned by the KMT regime in Guangzhou;[52] on a much larger scale, religious leaders including Western missionaries, Taoist and Buddhist clerics, Confucian intellectuals, and redemptive society patriarchs flocked to Hong Kong and Taiwan in 1949, and either settled there, founding new communities, or moved on to other countries, not least in North America.

Second, many ritual practices, though often decried by the modernist reformists who dominated among political leaders everywhere, were not banned as severely as in the PRC, and were maintained in those polities. The recent use of temple festivals in the self-advertisement of Taiwan (and to a lesser extent Hong Kong) as a home of authentic traditional Chinese culture—a rather stunning change of discourse from the 1960s—is a testimony to this fact. Tradition, formerly represented as backward, is now being reinvented as authentic, in part for tourism. Here again, Taiwan and Hong Kong have shown the way to the PRC.[53]

With the gradual relaxing of restrictions in the post-Mao PRC from the 1980s onward, reverse flows of money, specialists, and ritual knowledge penetrated the mainland, with overseas Chinese building temples and sponsoring festivals in their native coastal provinces. This was not an entirely new phenomenon, as already during the nineteenth century, temple building in coastal provinces routinely implied fund-raising in Manila, Penang, and other such places. But now the peripheral states would export back to the PRC not only money for cults but also cults themselves. The cult of Wong Tai Sin 黃大仙, for instance, which had originated in Guangzhou around 1900 and flourished in Hong Kong after 1930, was actively spread in China after 1990 by Hong Kong believers and local governments seeking

---

52. Lai Chi-tim, *Guangdong difang daojiao*, describes in detail the migration of Guangdong Taoists to Hong Kong under political repression.

53. This phenomenon is of course not limited to the Chinese world: see e.g. the case of Korea in Kendall, "The Cultural Politics of 'Superstition.'"

tourist dollars; and with the cult came Hong Kong entrepreneurial models of temple management and liturgy, adapted to the PRC conditions.[54]

At the same time, the alternative Chinese states were not just passive conservatories; they were active laboratories. The path followed by the various colonial regimes and postcolonial states outside the PRC illustrates the many possibilities inherent in some general ideas—"popular" religion is superstitious; modern, rational, socially engaged religions should take its place—that more or less all governments accepted, but applied in different ways.

None of the alternative regimes protected Chinese religion per se; all saw these belief systems as so much backward superstition (and potential for popular mobilization) to be suppressed or reformed, and controlled. They all limited or even repressed large temple festivals and processions that police everywhere find abhorrent. Restrictions on the use of public space, so crucial for the working of Chinese religion, were put in place everywhere, as we see with the difficult negotiations that Chinese community leaders in Southeast Asia or the West have to go through to organize New Year parades or other processions. Such effects of modernity and its increasing policing of public life applied in all countries regardless of their official religious policy. Still, compared with what happened on the mainland during the Cultural Revolution, all these constraints on temple cults and festivals were rather benign, with the exception of the Japanization (Kôminka) policies in Taiwan, which were also very destructive. But nowhere were constraints without effect: temples were closed or declined in Hong Kong; the Ghost Festival was reduced to a minimum in Taiwan; spirit mediums were banned (more or less actively, and never very effectively) everywhere.[55]

While they repressed certain practices and ushered in religious changes from the top down, the alternative regimes also enfranchised various religious groups. In Taiwan, salvationist groups that were illegal under Qing rule were recognized by the Japanese as a full-fledged religion they called vegetarian teachings (*zhaijiao* 齋教), an honorable term still in use that has done much to elevate the standing of this tradition;[56] salvationist groups and redemptive societies such as the Xiantiandao and Dejiao enjoyed a similar fate in Southeast Asia. The alternative regimes, notably in Singa-

54. Lang, Chan, & Ragvald, "Temples"; see also Dean, "Daoists and Transnational Chinese Society."

55. See e.g. a discussion of the laws banning "Thai and Chinese" spirit mediums in Thailand since 1891 in E. White, "Fraudulent and Dangerous."

56. Wang Jianchuan, "Lüelun rizhi shiqi zhaijiao."

pore and Hong Kong, were also keen to devolve welfare services to favored (especially Christian) religious groups.[57]

Like the KMT and the CCP, then, all the alternative regimes had an activist religious policy, attempting to institutionalize, reform, and reorient religious traditions and engaging, to varying degrees, in religious engineering. All these brands of religious engineering, whether in Singapore, Taiwan, or Hong Kong, combined colonial practice with Nationalist ideals. By the beginning of the twenty-first century, such models would become less marginal in the Chinese world, as they gained increasing attention from the Beijing regime in its search for a new way to accommodate religion within its evolving project of a spiritual civilization.

57. Kuah-Pearce, *State, Society and Religious Engineering.*

NINE

Filial Piety, the Family, and Death

Family practices and values can be considered the sanctuary of traditional religion, especially in times of repression and change.[1] If colonizers, Nationalists, and Communists were more or less successful in controlling or even monopolizing public forms of religion, they had much more difficulty in changing commonly held values, notions of morality and divine retribution, ideas about life after death, and domestic rites. This was not through lack of effort: as we have seen in chapter 7, Chinese political regimes actively and systematically attempted to promote entirely new systems of moral values. In some aspects, the state's new moral codes directly contradicted late imperial moral discourse, and it is these aspects that provide the most insights on how authorities and the population at large have each exercised agency and inventiveness in negotiating and redefining norms and practices.

1. C. K. Yang, *Religion in Chinese Society*, has, through its widely influential concept of "diffused religion," proposed the classical formulation of this thesis.

The evolution of the value system and morality concepts of the Chinese is certainly one of the most intractable problems raised by the study of social, political, and religious modernization. Superficial analyses tend to go to one of two extremes: either a vision of the Chinese abandoning "traditional" values first for Maoism and then for Western-style amoral individualism and consumerism; or equally opinionated visions of timeless Confucian and/or "Asian" values—focused on family, community, and ancestors—supposedly inherited from ancient Confucianism and advocated in the 1990s by leaders such as Singapore's Lee Kuan Yew 李光耀 (b. 1923). The reality is a more complicated picture of moral values and practices adapting to the conflicting reformulations of norms developed by the various authorities, including the state, school systems, religious institutions, and traditional and new elites, as well as to changing configurations of economic and social structures.

In this chapter, we will attempt to trace the evolution through the twentieth century of Chinese family values as expressed in practices of filial piety (*xiao* 孝), including, notably, death rituals. Indeed, *xiao* is perhaps the single most important concept in traditional Chinese culture, encapsulating in a single continuum the moral structure of families in this world and relations with the dead in the next. The most ancient form of Chinese religion for which a detailed record is available is the ancestor cult of the Shang royalty (ca. 1751–1111 BC); the reverence for parents both living and dead was the root of the ethical system elaborated by Confucius and extended to all other social relationships; its ritual formulation in the *Scripture on filial piety* 孝經 was one of the most widely circulated texts in imperial China and a canon of state orthodoxy. As noted by Hugh Baker, it is the one common element found in all Chinese religious and cultural traditions and unanimously practiced by all Chinese,[2] as shown by the placement of the shrine to ancestors in the central hall of all traditional Chinese homes. The customary practice of a son's filial piety included treating his living parents with reverence through obedience and care, especially in their old age; holding proper death rites when they died; respecting their body through a proper burial in a geomantically appropriate site; and nourishing their soul through appropriate daily worship and offerings. Once married, a woman assisted her husband in accomplishing the duties of filial piety to her in-laws, rather than to her own parents. Her most important filial duty was to give birth to a boy, who could continue the paternal line and the worship of the ancestors—otherwise, the forebears would become tormented orphan ghosts.

2. Baker, *Chinese Family and Kinship*.

REPUBLICAN FUNERAL REFORMS

The radical intellectuals of the New Culture movement of the 1910s and 1920s launched a critique of traditional filial piety and its rituals, defined as the essence of Confucianism, itself identified as the prime enemy of modern China. They advocated the adoption of the nuclear family (*xiao jiating* 小家庭), composed of the husband, the wife, and their children, living separately from their parents[3] and making possible, at least in theory, the equal status of men and women. This entailed changes in wedding rituals, as marriage was no longer seen as an alliance of families made sacred and unbreakable through the joint worship of Heaven, but rather as secular contracts between two individuals. Consequent campaigns against child marriage were eventually given the weight of law with the 1931 Civil Code, which evacuated ancestors and ritual from the legal world and supported individuals against families.[4] Funerals, which involved complex rituals and numerous religious specialists (Confucian officiants [*lisheng* 禮生] and/or diviners taking care of the corpse; Buddhists and/or Taoists taking care of the soul),[5] proved to be an even more hotly contested arena. The Confucian "four rites" 四禮 (coming-of-age capping; wedding; death ritual; ancestor worship) were at the core of the civilizing mission of the Qing state; marriage and funeral reforms were now at the core of the Republican civilizing project.

Most famously, Nationalist scholar Hu Shi, when he lost his mother in 1919, announced publicly that he would not organize a traditional funeral for her, but would devote himself to mourning her in his heart. This famous gesture soon became the symbol of modern Chinese funeral reforms (*binzang gaige* 殯葬改革),[6] which indeed constituted one of the most salient aspects of the modern state's intervention in private religious practices so as to redirect filial piety from the limited circle of kin to the larger nation. The religious policies of the early Republican period already supported reform within religious traditions that would dispense with liturgical services and redirect the concern for one's immediate kin toward the welfare of the national community. Notably, Taixu and his reformist Buddhism actively fought "funerary Buddhism." At the same time, the state

3. Glosser, *Chinese Visions of Family and State*. This ideal slowly reached the countryside: Ikels, ed., *Filial Piety*, is a series of studies of how ideals and practices of filial piety are affected in contemporary China, especially the countryside, by the fact that parents and children now tend to live separately.

4. P. Huang, *Code, Custom, and Legal Practice*.

5. On classical death rituals, see Watson & Rawski, eds., *Death Ritual*.

6. Liang Jinghe, "Wusi shiqi."

stopped upholding in law and in practice the official Confucian family rituals, actively introducing Western rites, such as black armbands in place of traditional mourning clothes, military music at funerals, and funerary wreaths. These elements were introduced as early as 1916 in state funeral ceremonies (*guozang* 國葬), themselves part of the new civic rituals.[7] A strong sign of the Westernization of mourning rites was the interdiction, in public funerals, of prostration (*koutou* 扣頭), which was replaced with mere bowing.[8]

It was only after the Nationalist takeover that the state truly attempted to reform China's family rituals. Besides the ban on "superstitious specialists" (1928) and "superstitious items" (1930; see chapter 2) which directly affected death rituals, KMT activists and officials often tried to ban funeral processions as well as wedding and funeral banquets in the name of the fight against the wasting of resources. The state was at the same time actively promoting new forms of weddings and funerals, promulgated in 1928, made compulsory for soldiers and civil servants,[9] and actively put forward to the population in a campaign that reached its peak during the New Life movement. The new rituals were modern, hygienic, and restrained, dispensing with processions, meat offerings, tablets (central to ancestor worship, and replaced with photographs), banquets, Buddhist and Taoist salvation rituals, and most other aspects of death rituals. The new death rituals were exemplified in the solemn and austere state ceremonies for heroes and dignitaries, with participants listening to speeches and bowing to the photograph of the deceased. Reflecting a secular worldview, these practices made no reference to a soul needing assistance on its way to the afterlife or needing to be placated in order to prevent its return as a malevolent ghost; what was to be commemorated was simply the memory of the deceased's contributions to society in this world. Eulogies—a custom adopted from the West—shifted the focus away from corpse, to the narrative of the life of the departed.[10]

A 1928 law banning private burial and creating public cemeteries where all tombs were to be similar underscored the egalitarian purpose of the Nationalist funeral reform.[11] Private tombs and lineage cemeteries were to be moved, and some were destroyed by secular activists. The idea was

---

7. Yan Changhong, "Minguo shiqi," 171.
8. On the Western critique of Chinese prostration, see Reinders, *Borrowed Gods*, chap. 8.
9. Nedostup, "Religion, Superstition," 547–48.
10. Whyte, "Death in the People's Republic," 309.
11. Nedostup, "Religion, Superstition," 551–57; Yan Changhong, "Minguo shiqi," 176–77.

to wrest people, in death as well as in life, from their socioreligious or kin communities and to integrate them into the vast, undifferentiated body of the nation. In practice, however, and owing to lack of funds, very few public cemeteries were built outside the largest cities before 1949, and most people continued to be buried in private tombs.[12] In the Republican period, the new "modern" rituals were adopted by few people besides urban intellectuals and civil servants, even though many sorts of hybrid rituals appeared, incorporating Western rites (armbands, military music, speeches) with the traditional Confucian and Buddhist/Taoist ones.

COMMUNIST FUNERAL REFORMS

The Communist regime placed itself in direct continuation of its Nationalist predecessor as far as family ritual reform was concerned, but proved, in this regard as in many others, more efficient at implementation. Marriage and funeral reform, as carried out in the liberated areas during the war and nationwide after 1949, focused on the extreme simplification of ceremonies, the elimination of "superstitious" practices (in reference to souls and fate), and the taking over of the ceremonies and their cost by state outfits (the work unit [*danwei* 單位]), to the detriment of families.[13] The central ritual was the memorial service (*zhuidao hui* 追悼會), presided over by the deceased's hierarchical superior and performed in a public space (workplace, crematorium) as opposed to home, during or shortly after the burial or cremation. In contrast to the traditional death and mourning rites, which could last several days, the typical Communist memorial ceremony lasted less than one hour.[14]

The memorial service was a ritual invented during the early Republican period for state heroes and dignitaries, and which the Communist regime extended to most workers.[15] The Party death liturgy also dictated the conduct of the bereaved kin, who could not wail, wear traditional mourning clothes, present offerings, or exchange gifts and money with other mourners offering their condolences. It thus had the effect of preventing death ritual from creating or reinforcing social bonds with the bereaved family.

12. A good case study of the local politics and results of the Republican campaigns to reform marriage and death rituals (as well as related issues of foot binding and clothing styles) is S. Friedman, "Civilizing the Masses."

13. Whyte, "Death in the People's Republic."

14. See Jankowiak, *Sex, Death, and Hierarchy*, 266–68, for an ethnographic description of such a service.

15. Yan Changhong, "Minguo shiqi," 173.

Moreover, as it dictated that burial or cremation should take place within one or two days after death, traditional condolence visits and the hosting of visitors with banquets were made impossible. Unable to act as hosts, families lost to the state a major source of honor, self-respect, and status building.[16] Besides the state monopolization of social bonds arising from the ritual, funeral reforms had other objectives, similar to those of other Communist countries: fighting against kin groups and lineages; against religious specialists, displaced by the cadres as ritual organizers; against conspicuous consumption and large, costly banquets; and against social status and hierarchies built around rituals.

These various objectives had also been present in Nationalist reforms. Both KMT and CCP proponents of funeral reforms considered, not without reason, that "traditional" rituals reinforced social status and inequalities; they envisioned rituals and modes of disposal that would be the same for all citizens. This ideal, however, was not translated into practice. New hierarchies were substituted for the "feudal" ones. Specifically, funeral reforms were used during the Mao era to build up the new social classes, as they deprived class enemies, during the most violent political campaigns, of proper burial or cremation and of a memorial service. Less spectacularly, work-unit regulations detailed differences in the ceremonies according to the worker's rank and status. Higher-ranked work units organized larger-scale memorial ceremonies than smaller, local state-owned enterprises.

In practice, ceremonies were usually organized by the workers' union. By the 1980s, many urban employees ended up dependent not on state *danwei* but on private companies, which applied funeral rules less strictly, if at all. The number of Chinese people subjected to state funeral ritual procedures thus sharply declined after the 1970s, but these procedures remained hugely influential as a normative model.

One major aspect of the Communist funeral reform that set it apart from its Nationalist predecessor was the introduction of compulsory cremation. Cremation was supposed to save arable land and benefit public hygiene, and also bring a final blow to *fengshui* and the cult to the dead. Some Nationalist leaders had mooted the scientific, hygienic idea of imposing cremation during the New Life movement, but without success. Now the project was endorsed as a national goal in a political document signed by all major Communist leaders on April 27, 1956. The new funeral policy, including compulsory cremation, was implemented throughout

16. Chau, *Miraculous Response*, 125–37.

the cities and countryside during the Great Leap Forward. It was followed by a relatively laissez-faire period during 1961–64, when processions and public burials were again observed, only to be mercilessly reimposed after 1964. During the Cultural Revolution, not only was cremation imposed wherever feasible, but class enemies were mass cremated without the possibility of their kin's recovering the ashes. Moreover, large numbers of tombs and urns were desecrated, sometimes by cadres and Red Guards forcing people to destroy their own kin's tombs, causing untold suffering for people who considered themselves responsible for their parents' torments in the afterworld.

The Communist leaders set the example through their own cremation. Zhou Enlai, who died on January 8, 1976, had requested cremation, and his ashes were scattered over the country. A few months later, though, Mao, in a very different fashion, was embalmed and enshrined in a mausoleum built in the middle of Tian'anmen Square.[17] Subsequent dignitaries were cremated, but their ashes were enshrined in the Babaoshan 八寶山 columbarium in Beijing's western suburbs.

Like the Nationalist policy on cemeteries, though, the central government's goal of universal cremation was hampered by slow progress in implementation, as rural counties were slow to build crematoriums, and the majority of the population did not have access to one before the 1980s. Nor were the Communist memorial services common in the countryside, except in highly organized communes and state farms, and at the funerals of local cadres. Data from Guangdong indicate that for most people, simplified versions of traditional funerals were the norm. In some areas, Taoist priests could still be hired until the mid-1960s; after they were banned from practicing, older family members would take over some of the ritual roles. Similarly, when fengshui masters could not be consulted secretly, family members chose the gravesites themselves, drawing on their general geomantic knowledge. Political campaigns targeted "superstitious practitioners" as exploiting classes, and the material necessities of family rituals, such as incense, were hard to come by, sometimes replaced by mosquito coils or cigarettes. Those restrictions aside, families were left to their own devices to organize funerals, which became simplified versions of the traditional rites, with little interference from local cadres.[18]

The more relaxed atmosphere of the post-Mao era made possible the revival of traditional burials and rituals. As early as 1978, processions and

17. Wagner, "Reading the Chairman Mao Memorial Hall"; Wakeman, "Revolutionary Rites."
18. Parish & Whyte, *Village and Family*, 260–72.

proper burials, including the interment of remains desecrated during the Cultural Revolution turmoil, were seen again. In some areas, cremation rates dropped dramatically: from 43 to 4 percent in the city of Shantou (Guangdong Province), for example. Old people often refused to go to urban hospitals out of fear that they would be cremated there, whereas death in a rural area guaranteed burial.[19] The de-collectivization of land allowed rural families to bury their dead on their own plots, and the new valorization of competitive displays of wealth encouraged tendencies toward ostentatious traditional funerals.[20]

From the central state's perspective, these developments only demonstrated the need for a more thorough implementation of funeral reform. A regulation issued by the State Council on February 8, 1985, planned the progressive extension of compulsory cremation in all densely populated areas and allowed, for the other areas, burial only in nonarable land. The prohibition of "superstitious" practices such as burning spirit money was reinstated.[21] At the same time, propaganda units such as the Association for Wedding and Funeral Rites (Hongbaishi lishihui 紅白事理事會), devoted to the advancement of wedding and funeral reform, were established in the countryside during the 1990s, with their major objective defined in terms of cremation rates. In 2005, this rate was officially given as approximately 50 percent overall, with nearly 100-percent compliance in the largest cities, and about 30-percent compliance in the countryside.[22]

Ethnic minorities were officially exempted from this policy, even in urban areas, and thus the Chinese Muslims could perform Muslim burials.[23] This, however, did not stop central and local officials from attempting to reform minorities' funeral practices routinely described as archaic, with the case of Tibetan sky burial being the most popularized example. Implementation in Han areas was just as ambiguous. Tombs were tolerated (without formal authorization, but sometimes against a bribe) in most rural areas and were often clearly visible on hillsides around built-up areas. Local campaigns of destruction of unauthorized tombs were quite frequent since the 1980s, though, when zealous or concerned officials decided to strike.[24] Such officials invoked the regulations that only permitted burial in

19. Aijmer & Ho, *Cantonese Society*, 186n9, 174.
20. Whyte, "Death in the People's Republic," 300–301.
21. *Guowuyuan guanyu binzang guanli de zhanxing guiding* 國務院關于殯葬管理的暫行規定. Detailed yearly updates on regulations are provided in *Zhongguo binzang nianjian*.
22. Fang & Goossaert, "Les réformes funéraires," 61.
23. On Hui burials, see Allès, *Musulmans de Chine*, 200–208.
24. M. Yang, "Spatial Struggles," 729–34, documents destructions in Wenzhou in 2000.

public cemeteries[25] but also had hygienic and aesthetic motivations, as they considered that scattered tombs disfigured the landscape. Families caught up in such campaigns attempted to conceal existing tombs, if there was still time. Officials also banned the sale of coffins—a measure known to provoke the suicide of old people just before the ban was to go into effect.

Despite such cases of zealous enforcement by some local officials, the funeral-reform situation was still characterized by the strong dichotomy between city and countryside that also applied to temple cults and festivals. Rural areas were widely represented as the realm of tradition where, in contrast to cities, "traditional" death rituals were now once again performed,[26] encompassing Buddhist/Taoist salvation rites, banquets, processions, offerings, and geomantically chosen tombs.[27] Some lineage cemeteries were also reconstituted, in contradiction with the regulations.

The domestic cult of ancestors was revived in the rural areas, after having been carried out in a low-key fashion or discontinued during the Maoist period. By the late 1990s, almost every rural house in the Pearl River Delta had its own ancestral shrine.[28] In the cities, however, this was far from being the case. Although domestic ancestral shrines remained relatively common in Taiwan and Hong Kong (kept in almost two-thirds of households in the Kwun Tong District in 1981),[29] they were practically nonexistent in Mainland Chinese cities.

Indeed, in urban areas the continuation or revival of "traditional" rituals was far more difficult not only in the PRC but also in Taiwan and Hong Kong, even though the latter two polities had not undergone forceful funeral reform. In Hong Kong, regulations and lack of space made it almost impossible for families to hold funerals at home; virtually all were conducted in a handful of multistory commercial funeral parlors, which could simultaneously handle arrangements for several families in different funeral rooms. In contrast to traditional funerals, in which the family or a representative would mobilize dozens of kin and neighbors to organize the complex logistics of a series of rites and hosting occasions lasting several days, the commercial parlors offered one-stop standardized packages

---

25. David, "The Evacuation of Village Funerary Sites."

26. Oxfeld, "When You Drink Water, Think of Its Source." For ethnographic descriptions of funerals in post-Mao rural China, see Kipnis, *Producing Guanxi*, 96–103; Jankowiak, *Sex, Death, and Hierarchy*, 268–89; Liu Xin, *In One's Own Shadow*, 151–56; Chau, *Miraculous Response*, 124–37; Chen Gang, "Death Rituals."

27. Bruun, *Fengshui in China*.

28. Aijmer & Ho, *Cantonese Society*, 148–53.

29. John Myers, "Traditional Chinese Religious Practices," 279.

of all required objects and services, including the coffin, undertaking, offerings, ritual specialists, and so on. Two types of funerals were offered: "Chinese-style," chosen in 70 percent of funerals, with Taoist or (less often) Buddhist priests, and food and paper offerings; and for the remaining 30 percent of funerals, "Western-style," with Christian priests or church representatives.[30]

In Mainland Chinese cities, Buddhist and Taoist rituals were banned outside monasteries (although by the 1990s and 2000s, shortened Buddhist or Taoist funeral services could be held inside homes in some suburban areas);[31] funeral processions were out of the question; keeping the body at home after death was difficult; and cremation was nearly universal. Studies conducted on urban mainlanders in the 1970s and 1980s indicated that if the elderly still opposed cremation, the majority of urban residents accepted the prospect, if only because it was cheaper and more convenient.[32] At the memorial service at the crematorium, organized by the work unit or by the family, the Communist ritual was still observed, with increasing tolerance in most places for traditional elements such as wailing, offerings, and mourning clothes. Nonetheless families often organized a separate funeral banquet in a restaurant where the traditional exchange of gifts between kin, friends, and acquaintances could take place. Upon the death of a parent, individuals and families, particularly those of a more educated background, were often torn between a strongly held atheism and rejection of belief in the soul, feelings of guilt toward the parent and desire to provide them with a proper avenue to a happy afterlife, and confusion about the contradictory expectations of relatives, workmates, unit leaders, neighbors, and friends regarding the appropriate type of death ritual to give face to the dead and to the family—a confusion compounded by the lack of direct experience of traditional rites.[33]

If it succeeded in imposing cremation in cities, the PRC government seemed to have lost control over the treatment of ashes. Indeed, William Jankowiak's research on Hohhot in the 1980s concluded that while the younger generations had accepted the practice of cremation and rejected their elders' beliefs and practices pertaining to ancestor worship, he observed among them the beginnings of a new emphasis on the preservation

30. Chan Yuk Wah, "Packaging Tradition."

31. Yang Der-ruey, "The Changing Economy."

32. Whyte, "Death in the People's Republic," 303; Whyte & Parish, *Urban Life*, 313 (based on interviews with refugees from various cities in Hong Kong conducted in 1977–78); Jankowiak, *Sex, Death, and Hierarchy*, 264 (based on interviews in Hohhot, Inner Mongolia, in 1981–83).

33. Jankowiak, *Sex, Death, and Hierarchy*, 290–95.

of ashes.[34] Large columbaria were built on the mainland, even though they were not quite as popular as in Hong Kong.[35] Ritual practices in columbaria reproduced those traditionally observed for tombs, with family gatherings at Qingming 清明節, the traditional Grave-Sweeping Festival in the spring. Breaking with patrilineal tradition, women were more likely to worship their own parents rather than their husbands'.[36] Some families chose to keep the funerary urns at home and put them on the family altar, in the place formerly reserved for ancestral tablets, now mostly replaced by photographs—but this was an uncommon choice. It became much more frequent to pay for maintaining a lamp with the name and/or photograph of the deceased in a Taoist or Buddhist temple where rituals were regularly performed, a modern innovation that swept through the Chinese world in the 1980s. This option offered busy, secularized urbanites uncomfortable with the idea of regularly worshipping ancestors a relatively cheap method to "subcontract" the care of the dead, while temples enthusiastically promoted the practice as a major source of income.

By far the most popular choice in Mainland China was to bury the urn; the act of interment (*rutu* 入土) was still invested with huge significance. Small "tombs" for urns in public cemeteries were legally allowed[37]—regulations adopted by the State Council in 1997 let local authorities decide on the details. Rich families even buried the urn within a costly, traditional hardwood coffin. For many families, placing the urn in a columbarium was only a short-term expedient while waiting for a tomb in a public cemetery to be arranged. Such tombs were very expensive; some suburban townships ran highly profitable cemeteries which they advertised as geomantically excellent.

The high cost of tombs turned them into another kind of conspicuous consumption, but for family members this was justified, because a proper tomb was the only way to publicly restore face and honor to someone who had unduly suffered during the Cultural Revolution or later. Official propaganda exhorted people to "treat the living lavishly and the dead perfunctorily"

34. Ibid., 266.

35. Teather, "High-Rise Homes for the Ancestors."

36. Jankowiak, *Sex, Death, and Hierarchy*, 288–89, containing an ethnographic description of grave-sweeping rites near Hohhot in the 1980s.

37. In the Cantonese world and most of southeastern China, the universal practice of double burial (whereby coffins are opened after several years, and the bones are collected, cleaned, and reburied in an urn) may have facilitated the adoption of cremation. Ashes are considered the residual products of bones only, and thus ashes and bones are considered essentially equivalent. So the contemporary treatment of ashes follows the traditional treatment of bones during the second burial.

(*houyang bozang* 厚養薄葬), but many Chinese put the phrase on its head and considered that those who had been mistreated while alive must be treated lavishly now that they are dead (*houzang* 厚葬).

Paradoxically, then, by the 1990s on the mainland, the state imposed cremation, yet tolerated tombs for urns and the multiplication of cemeteries. Some ideologues, seeing the cemeteries for urns as hardly better than traditional tombs (in terms of both superstitious practice and land lost to more productive use), now launched campaigns in favor of the dispersal of ashes over the sea (*haizang* 海葬)—as was done for Deng Xiaoping in 1997. This procedure, however, was also quite costly. Beginning in the late 1990s, environmental discourse[38] became a major element in the always heated debates on funerals, and supported both dispersal at sea and memorial tree planting (*shuzang* 樹葬). In this lively discussion developing in the press and online, urban people were less critical of cremation than of the socially unjust options for disposing one's ashes. The central state may have won the moral battle on cremation thanks to scientific and environmental arguments, but it clearly lost in the case of ash burial and its significance for filial piety.

In this context of moral choices and economic constraints, funeral practices in the Mainland Chinese cities tended to converge with those in other Chinese polities. In Hong Kong, cremation was not compulsory but had been strongly promoted by the colonial administration since the 1960s; rigid zoning rules and the prohibitive cost of land and cemetery plots made traditional burial impossible for almost all but the indigenous inhabitants of the New Territories, who enjoyed special land-use rights. In Taiwan, cremation was gaining the upper hand, even though it was not compulsory there; remarkably, Taiwanese officials expressed their admiration of the Communist funerary policy, underscoring the deep continuity between the Nationalist and Communist reform projects. By the early twenty-first century, then, cremation rates were about 70 percent in Hong Kong and Singapore and 50 percent in Taiwan.[39]

The appropriation and diversion of funeral reforms by the people can be explained by the fact that they were not entirely convinced by these reforms' moral justifications and their subordination of filial piety to nationalism. Furthermore, one major objective of funeral reform since the

---

38. Weller, *Discovering Nature*.

39. Teather, "High-Rise Homes for the Ancestors"; Chan Yuk Wah, "Packaging Tradition." On Singapore, see Yeoh, "The Body after Death." On Taiwan, see Tremlett, "Death-Scapes"; Zheng Zhiming, "Sangzang wenhua."

early Republican period had been to "destroy superstitions," as explicitly stated in both the 1928 law and the 1985 regulation. Conditioning the success of funeral reform to that of the larger antisuperstition enterprise made it dependent on the success or failure of the latter. In Taiwan, antisuperstition policies were abandoned in the late 1980s, and they were increasingly marginalized on the mainland. This undermined the ideological coherence of the funeral reforms, as was flagrant in the case of local authorities who set up cemeteries and advertised their geomantic qualities at the same time that the central state was still committed to eradicating superstitious death rituals, the cult of dead, and tombs. Then in 2008, the Grave-Sweeping Festival was decreed a public holiday by the PRC government; in the words of one leader, it is a festival for the celebration of ancestors, and also a cultural and emotional link with overseas Chinese. This new decree, which also made the Dragon Boat Festival (Duanwu 端午節) and the Moon Festival (Zhongqiu 中秋節) into state holidays, was motivated by economic rationality—to spread the benefits and reduce the stress on the country's transport and tourist infrastructures during the weeklong Labor Day and National Day holidays. Paradoxically, it went against the intent of the policy aiming to restrain the cult of ancestors, and showed how economic rationalization and cultural revival could sometimes go hand in hand, resulting in a downgrading of the socialist celebrations of May first and October first.

CONCLUSION

The social valuation of filial piety as the first and foremost moral value was far from disappearing in the early twenty-first century, despite one century of state moral education geared against it; rather, it was taking on new forms of expression. Forced secularization could not do away with the problem of death, which remained an unavoidable moment for the persistent recourse to religious practices, specialists, and temples—though increasingly with the convenience of prepackaged commercial products for funeral services or for the worship of ancestors in temples. Indeed, if filial piety remained a strong value, it was far less centered on the care of the dead than it had been in the late imperial and early Republican periods. By the late 1990s, the idea of *xiao* was invoked in popular discourse about the relations among the living members of families, in which parents and grandparents had lost their traditional authority and, through the ownership of land and property, material control over their children. Now, in the absence or insufficiency of state pension plans, they often depended on their children for income and care in retirement.[40] From their marginalized position, they often found a new role in the care of their grandchildren.

In the cities of Mainland China, the family planning policy led to the birth of new generations of only children, while in other Chinese polities, the high cost of child rearing also led to a drastic reduction in family sizes. These children became the objects of the intense attentions and doting of two sets of grandparents, who often responded at their beck and call, acting as their "servants." The traditional logic of *xiao* was completely inverted: from the obedience of children to their ascendants and the emphasis on the proper ritual care of the dead, the culture was now focused on the loving nurturing of young children by their parents and grandparents — even in the case of deaths, it was now normal for parents to mourn at the passing of their children, breaking the traditional convention barring seniors from mourning their juniors. And although it had been through the proper reverence to the aged and to the dead that traditional morality found its primordial expression, it was now through the concern with the raising and educating of children — and even the fetal education 胎教 of the unborn — that secularized parents rediscovered a deep sense of moral responsibility, found a new interest in traditional virtues, and, increasingly, enrolled their children in moral education classes or courses for learning the Confucian classics.[41]

40. Ikels, ed., *Filial Piety.*
41. Billioud & Thoraval, "Jiaohua," 16–18.

TEN

Revivals of Communal Religion in the Later Twentieth Century

The mid-twentieth century was arguably the nadir of communal religion, especially as organized around temples, in the Chinese world. Where temples had not been destroyed by the Republican antisuperstition movements, decades of war and poverty had left much of China's religious patrimony in ruins. In Taiwan, after a period of Japanese restrictions on Chinese temples, the new KMT regime, though no longer as committed to the destruction of superstition as during its Nanjing phase, was still intent on curbing the influence of temple cults,[1] albeit with relatively little effect. In Mainland China after 1949, the new socialist regime, which was able to penetrate deep into every village, had the means to effectively carry out, for the same ideological and practical reasons, what had been the long-standing KMT policy of eradicating superstition, to which was now added the stigmatizing

---

1. We use the term *temple cults* as a convenient way of referring to local communal religion as taking place in and around temples, without implying any separation between it and other types of religious activities.

label of *feudalism*. In Southeast Asian countries such as Malaysia and Indonesia, the nationalist anti-Chinese policies of the newly independent states
forced Chinese cultural and religious life to adopt a low profile, whereas
the closing of the PRC to the outside world cut the ties between diasporic
cults and their places of origin on the mainland. Overall, then, the outlook
for temple-based communal religion by the 1960s was bleak: systematically
smashed and driven underground in Mainland China, it languidly survived
in Taiwan, Hong Kong, and the overseas communities, where it appeared as
the mark of a timeless folk tradition abandoned to the curiosity of anthropologists before its fated eclipse by the forces of modernization.

By the 1970s, however, and through to the early twenty-first century,
communal religion displayed a new vitality as temples and festivals rebuilt,
expanded, and multiplied in many parts of the Chinese world—a wave that
started in Taiwan and overseas, spread to the coastal provinces of the mainland, and soon reached the remote hinterland. Three interconnected factors
can help us to understand and trace this process: (1) the lessening of state
intervention and the relaxing of controls on communal religion, facilitating temples' participation in the reconfiguration of local sociopolitical relations; (2) the dynamics of globalization, which undermined nation-building
projects and allowed temples to become nodes along horizontal networks
linking local communities and identities to transnational flows of capital,
people, and memory; and (3) the growing prosperity of the Chinese world,
generating wealth that could be plowed into temples and festivals to an unprecedented degree. The end of the grand ideologies and the expansion of
a globalized market economy created a context that was more favorable to
the growth and adaptation of temple cults—while at the same time transforming their social foundations and imposing new material constraints
on temple building and activities. In this chapter, we will examine these
trends by first tracing the processes through which temples negotiated with
the state to expand the space within which they could become meaningful
social actors. We will then look at the role temples have played in the redefinition of local, national, and cultural identities. Finally, we will discuss
how the market economy has opened new opportunities for the flourishing of temple cults while profoundly modifying their social foundations
and restricting their scope for further expansion in metropolitan areas.

THE WAVE OF TEMPLE BUILDING

In Taiwan, under the mildly restrictive policies of the KMT before 1988,
it was typically sufficient for temples to practice what Robert Weller has

called the "politics of ritual disguise"[2] to provide a legitimate cover for their "wasteful" religious activities. Thus, organizers of a yearly festival in which worshippers competed to sacrifice the fattest pig joined forces with the local Farmers' Association to "promote agricultural productivity" by holding pig-raising contests—at which the fattest pigs were conveniently displayed in front of the temple.[3] Even during the period of martial law, then, communal religion survived; more temples were built and expanded in the more relaxed atmosphere of the 1980s, a trend that accelerated with the removal of most restrictions after 1986. Official statistics indicate that the number of registered Buddhist and Taoist temples in Taiwan (there is no category for popular religion)—which does not take into account the probably much larger number of *unregistered* temples—increased from 3,661 in 1930 to 5,531 in 1981, and again to 9,707 in 2001, an increase from one registered temple for every 3,300 inhabitants to one for every 2,309 during the final two decades of the twentieth century.[4] The prevalence of temples, from palatial sanctuaries to neighborhood shrines and street altars, was striking to any casual visitor, although not on a uniform scale. Village temples were still at the center of local life; larger cities were less dense in temples, while the most spectacular development took place on the urban margins, where new, monumental temples attracted devotees from the whole island. Most temples had been rebuilt, often on a grander scale and with increasingly baroque and gaudy ornamentation, while the scale of festivals and pilgrimages far surpassed anything previously reported.

But it was on the Chinese mainland in the post-Mao era, when virtually all its temples had been destroyed and official policy still banned most communal religion, that the resurgence of temple cults was most dramatic and unexpected (by both officials and scholars), the aggregated result of myriads of local struggles by individuals and communities who took advantage of the more open climate from the end of the 1970s. The extent of the temple revival on the mainland is hard to measure. Since there is no unified, self-conscious national community of temple cults or any criterion for membership based on belief, it is impossible to compile statistics of "numbers of believers" that could be compared with those of, say, Roman Catholics, Muslims, or Communist Party members. It is possible, however, to quantify, at least in some better-documented locales, the numbers of temples and the frequency of their ritual activities, which are the main

2. Weller, "The Politics of Ritual Disguise."
3. Ahern, "The Thai Ti Kong Festival."
4. Katz, "Religion and the State in Post-War Taiwan," 400.

occasions in which temples play a significant role in social organization, community gathering, cultural production, and circulation of resources. One quantitative indicator of popular participation in temple life is the percentage of households in a given village who have contributed money, labor, or materials to temple reconstruction projects.

No national statistics are available, but one government report counted over 10,000 temples in the Yulin area, northern Shaanxi Province,[5] for a population of 3.1 million in the mid-1990s—an average of one temple per 315 persons. In southeastern China, through a painstaking field survey of the Putian region of Fujian Province during the same period, Ken Dean and Zheng Zhenman identified some 1,639 temples in the 600 villages of the region: 2.7 temples per village of 1,200 inhabitants, on average—which amounts to one temple per 444 inhabitants. Furthermore, temple reconstruction ushered a renewal of community celebrations. In the area studied by Ken Dean, ritual events and festivals occurred within walking distance of the average village over 250 days per year.[6] All this took place in rural areas or small towns; in the major cities, no such large-scale rebuilding could take place. In Beijing, for instance, about 20 temples were open for worship by 2008 (many more were open as museums) out of some 1,500 a century ago.[7]

These figures are significant, because they can be compared with a China-wide estimation of one temple per 400 inhabitants in 1900.[8] To be sure, Fujian arguably had a higher than average temple density, while the number of temples was very low in other regions, where local state agents were much less amenable to temple reconstruction and a renewal of ritual activities. But the high number of temples in the impoverished, landlocked northern Shaanxi belies the assumption that communal religion flourished only in the more prosperous and liberal coastal areas.[9] Such figures can only give us a limited idea of the extent of temple religion, since they make no distinction between large monasteries and small shrines; nor do they give an indication of temple activity, as some may be dormant and others flourishing. The overall data nonetheless point to the exceptional resil-

5. Fan Guangchun, "Dangdai Shaandei miaohui kaocha yu toushi," *Yanan daxue xuebao (shehui)* 1 (1997), 97–100; quoted in Chau, "Popular Religion in Shaanbei," 44.

6. Dean, "Local Communal Religion," 341–42.

7. Naquin, *Peking*; Goossaert, *The Taoists of Peking*.

8. This is our estimation based on the best available surveys from the early twentieth century: Li Jinghan, *Dingxian shehui gaikuang diaocha*, 422–23; Grootaers, *The Sanctuaries in a North-China City*; Naquin, *Peking*, appendix 1.

9. See, e.g., Weller, *Alternate Civilities*, 85–86.

ience and dynamism of temple religion in some parts of Mainland China, where it would seem to have reached levels of activity comparable to those before the early twentieth-century antisuperstition campaigns.

In other parts of China, however, superficial observation indicated a much lower incidence of temple life: there were significant variations, not only between regions, but even from one village to another.[10] One cause of these differences was the changing attitudes of local authorities from place to place. Owing to the increasing decentralization since the 1990s, local authorities enjoyed more leeway to follow the inclinations of individual cadres in those aspects of policy with low political priority, such as the fight against superstition—when compared with the high-priority policies of economic growth, taxes, social order, or the one-child policy. Another explanation for variations between neighboring villages, according to field-work conducted by Thomas DuBois, was the differential preservation of religious resources. In some villages, the memory of rituals and local traditions was strong enough among a sufficient number of inhabitants to allow them to take the initiative to reestablish cults, while those conditions did not exist in other villages because of the untimely death of a few crucial religious leaders or specialists.[11]

In order to measure the role of temples and lineage halls in the provision of public services, in 2000 the political scientist Lily Lee Tsai conducted a survey of 316 villages, sampled from Shanxi, Hebei, Jiangxi, and Fujian—a combination including coastal and inland, northern and southern, and prosperous and poor provinces. Forty-six percent of the villages reported the existence of temple activities in 1949, indicating the level of local temple activity at the time the PRC was established. Eighteen percent of the villages had rebuilt or renovated temples since 1979, 14 percent had a temple manager (an indicator of an active and sustained temple organization), and among the villages reporting temple reconstruction projects, an average of 58 percent of households had participated.[12]

About one-third of the villages reported the existence of at least one ancestral hall building, although not all these were in use; 14 percent of the villages had ancestral halls containing spirit tablets, indicating the use of the building for worship. Ancestral hall reconstruction projects began in the early 1980s and showed a sharp increase in the late 1990s, so that by 2000, 19 percent of the villages reported the renovation or reconstruction

10. Feuchtwang, "Local Religion and Village Identity."
11. DuBois, *The Sacred Village*.
12. L. Tsai, *Accountability*, 124–25.

of at least one ancestral hall since 1979. In 73 percent of these villages, the majority of the relevant lineage members donated to the project, contributing an average of 17 percent of the village's annual per-capita income—a large amount, given that local tax burdens are not supposed to exceed 5 percent of per-capita income.[13]

The absence of temples did not mean the end of a village's religious life, however, even if it bespoke the lack of collective organization and/or specific local political constraints. In north-central Hebei Province, for example, the village religious tradition was often transmitted by amateur troupes of ritual specialists who organized the New Year and other yearly celebrations as well as death rituals; such troupes did not need or have temples, and indeed some stored their instruments, texts, and gods' paintings in the village committee offices.[14] Many of the salvationist groups worshipping the Unborn Mother operated in a very similar way. Other religious specialists, such as Taoist priests, diviners, and spirit mediums, worked from home altars, and could provide services and a sense of continuity with the local religious tradition without any formal organization.[15] Moreover, villages with a temple and/or a festival simply attracted people from neighboring villages lacking them, and so did the local pilgrimage centers that were revived. Many villages had one or several local activists (called *xiangtou* 香頭 in some parts of China), often elderly women, who rather frequently also operated as spirit mediums. They were the ones who would organize interested villagers for visiting temples elsewhere and would also organize private and communal rituals; these activities were invisible from outside the village but nonetheless very significant. Indeed, older women played an important role in the transmission and revival of communal religion: since they were politically marginal and tolerated as old, ignorant, and foolish, their "superstitious" activities were often ignored and tolerated during the Maoist and post-Mao period, even as male temple or lineage leaders met with resistance or, in the reform period, had to deal with complex restrictions and negotiations.[16]

Collective lineage activities also existed even in the absence of a functioning lineage hall. In Tsai's survey, 44 percent of villages reported "some form of collective lineage or kinship institution": collective worship at an-

13. Ibid., 156–57.

14. S. Jones, *Plucking the Winds.*

15. Chau, "Superstition Specialist Households?"

16. Kuah-Pearce, "The Worship of Qingshui Zushi"; Tan Chee-beng, "Chinese Religious Expressions"; Kang Xiaofei, "Rural Women."

cestors' graves (27 percent); lineage-organized weddings and funerals (21 percent); dispute mediation within the lineage (19 percent); the existence of a lineage or lineage head (17 percent); welfare assistance (17 percent); a genealogy organization (16 percent); an ancestral hall management organization (8 percent); and so on.[17]

Nonetheless, the long-term process of temple destruction and reconstruction affected the ritual life of the villages. The temple-based Buddhist and Taoist clergies had since the 1930s disappeared from large parts of the Mainland Chinese countryside, even though many officials, who considered them representatives of the orthodox, state-sanctioned traditions, now hoped to see them back and in control of local religion. By contrast, home-based specialists such as diviners and spirit mediums, and also vernacular priests of the local ritual traditions and amateur groups, had been able to lie low and stay below the radar of authorities, although in some cases the destruction of their ritual books, scores, instruments, and paintings during the Cultural Revolution was thorough enough to kill the tradition.

Even when the ritual tradition survived, liturgical impoverishment was the rule in most of China, continuing the Republican-period trend discussed in chapter 5. The lavish funerals (as performed for the richest families) or temple festivals lasting for three days, remembered from the early twentieth century, gradually disappeared in favor of two-day, then one-day versions. By the early twenty-first century, many ritualists (there are exceptions, especially in southern China) could only perform a two- to three-hour ceremony focused on music, dramatic elements, and the recitation of short hymns, with many rites of the former longer versions forgotten or drastically simplified.[18] For an outside observer born in a Protestant Christian or Islamic culture, this was still impressive liturgy, but a sense of loss permeates large tracts of contemporary Chinese communal religion. Where the extremely varied field of local ritual tradition is in decline, clerics from outside, sent by the Taoist and Buddhist associations to staff newly reopened or affiliated temples, are ready to replace these local traditions with their standard streamlined liturgy (see chapter 12). In many cases, official Buddhist leaders are actually happy to suppress "superstitious rites" (such as burning paper offerings, singing in local dialects, smashing hells open to liberate suffering souls); rituals performed in the larger monaster-

---

17. L. Tsai, *Accountability*, 154–55. M. Cohen, "Lineage Organization," also shows how contemporary lineages in North China operate without halls or common property.

18. S. Jones, *In Search of the Folk Daoists*; see also Overmyer, "Ritual Leaders in North China"; Zhao Xudong & Bell, "Miaohui."

ies are thus voluntarily streamlined when compared with earlier practice, a trend that had already begun during the Republican period and accelerated since the 1980s.[19]

Despite the liturgical impoverishment, rituals are still vibrant and very meaningful for local communities. All the ritual specialists promptly reappeared since the late 1970s and played a crucial role in the revival of ritual life, both in its communal forms (temple festivals, New Year celebrations, prayers for rain) and in its services to individuals and families (healing and death rituals). The situation was very uneven: in some places, a new generation of ritual specialists had been able to train with the older generation (who had practiced before 1949) during the crucial 1961–64 period of relative tolerance, and it was they who led the revival after 1978. In other cases, no one was trained between the 1950s or earlier and the 1980s, and the local ritual tradition was dying when folklorists and ethnographers took an interest from the 1980s onward; texts could be found, but no one knew how to perform them. The policy of granting a greater degree of freedom to minority nationalities favored an earlier and stronger revival of ritual life among those populations, especially in the southwest, even though in this case the nationality labels were frequently a convenient disguise for religious traditions that often continued the regionally differentiated customs and rituals of the rural Han people.[20]

A handful of temples of historical significance had been preserved from destruction during the Mao years by being handed over to the Bureau of Cultural Relics (wenwuju 文物局); during the reform years, some were turned into museums, while others, especially those located in famous scenic spots, were placed under the jurisdiction of local and provincial tourism bureaus. Transforming temples into museums became a way for the state to appropriate local culture while freezing it.[21] Numerous religious sites were added to the heritage lists, with various levels of protection (national, provincial, local); but most of the temples listed received no actual protection and funding, and some were actually destroyed.[22] None of these bureaucracies (Cultural Relics, Tourism) had the desire to return temples to their original purpose; although they might allow minimal worship in

19. Tan Hwee-San, "Saving the Soul in Red China."

20. See a critical discussion of current religious ethnography and issues of ethnic identity in Overmyer & Chao Shin-Yi, eds., *Ethnography in China Today*.

21. Dean, *Lord of the Three in One*, 270.

22. On the politics of heritage protection, see Fresnais, *La protection du patrimoine*.

the form of incense burning as ancillary to tourism, they would never re-vert them to self-management by local communities or allow large-scale rituals and the presence of religious specialists. In the prestigious ancient pilgrimage sites, temples could operate more independently, but they were included in larger parks (run by tourism companies on license by the authorities) that received most of the ticket sales. These companies re-invented and advertised "local culture" (in which religion was presented as a mere component) while keeping locals out of the decisions. They brought in cults and folklore that tourists expected to see while getting rid of actual local religious traditions, and constrained what temples could do in terms of rituals and celebrations; yet, as Kang Xiaofei and Donald Sutton show in the case of a UNESCO-listed pilgrimage site shared by Han and Tibetans, both clerics and local laypersons struggled to continue using the site as well as they could.[23]

Only the five religious associations officially sponsored by the state could "reclaim" the sites from other units, often through long and pro-tracted negotiations leading to, for example, the transfer of the Shanghai and Xi'an City God temples to their cities' respective Taoist associations during the 1990s and 2000s.[24] Indeed, it was the official Buddhist and Tao-ist associations that controlled the most famous temples and monaster-ies, staffing them with salaried monks who, until reforms of the *danwei* work-unit system during the 1990s forced them to become financially self-sufficient, had few ties to their surrounding communities.[25] Buddhists and Taoists were also dispatched or went by themselves to temples to live in, without much concern for the local religious traditions and culture.[26] Meanwhile, some local temples renamed themselves as Buddhist or Tao-ist monasteries in the hope of gaining official recognition, while resisting attempts by the Buddhist or Taoist association to send in their clerics. In general, there were complex and sometimes tense relationships between two factions: local groups, often led by elderly women and/or spirit me-diums, who provided most of the temples' funding and daily support; and Religious Affairs Bureau officials and young Buddhist and Taoist leaders, who provided legitimacy (see chapter 12).

23. Kang Xiaofei, "Two Temples" and "Rural Women"; Sutton & Kang Xiaofei, "Recasting Religion and Ethnicity."

24. Fan Guangchun, "Urban Daoism."

25. Goossaert and Fang Ling, "Temples and Daoists."

26. Fisher, "The Spiritual Land Rush."

PROCESSES OF TEMPLE RECONSTRUCTION

Temple reconstruction processes were very unequal between different places, and also between the different types of temples involved. Although these depended on how local religious systems (lineages, territorial communities, salvationist traditions) had weathered the Maoist years and were able to negotiate the reconstruction of their places of worship, priority was given to temples to local saints or ancestors' halls. Typically, the first sign of a temple's revival was an increase in the numbers of worshippers who, sensing the more open political atmosphere, began arriving to burn incense at the spot where the temple had previously stood—regardless of whether the original buildings were completely destroyed, dilapidated, or taken over for other purposes. Gradually, people would, in an unorganized fashion, clear the premises, install deity statues, and take on makeshift repairs. The turning point occurred, however, when one person took the initiative to launch a full-fledged rebuilding project—an undertaking requiring significant organizational capacity as well as the ability to mobilize networks of support among villagers, donors, and officials. Even though the traditional wooden architecture was commonly replaced with concrete, lowering the price of material, the costs of rebuilding a temple were usually very high; often they were covered by substantial donations from project leaders followed by years of patient fund-raising in the community. In addition, aged artisans still able to create statues, paintings, and other religious artwork had to be found, sometimes from far away, even though since the 1980s large statue factories had emerged to cope with the demand, and had changed the styles and tastes.

Each case of temple reconstruction was unique, as the individuals behind the rebuilding project had a range of backgrounds and motivations. Specific examples of these persons mentioned in the academic literature range from a devout farmer and old soldier to an unpopular local Party secretary seeking to regain his lost legitimacy.[27] A common case was individuals who had been stigmatized with a bad class background during the Mao years, and for whom temple building represented a way of reclaiming and reasserting their identity and dignity, and regaining social status.[28] For example, a temple manager one of us interviewed in Lianshan, northern Guangdong, was a retired primary school teacher whose landlord class background had caused him to be persecuted as a rightist; with no place

---

27. DuBois, *The Sacred Village*, 56; Jing Jun, *The Temple of Memories*, 89.
28. Aijmer & Ho, *Cantonese Society*, 207–9; Eng & Yi-Min Lin, "Religious Festivities," 1272.

to stay in the village, he had taken up residence in the ruins of the local temple. Feeling that the god had protected him during those terrible years, he had arisen to rebuild the temple in the 1990s. Other typical cases of temple reconstruction occurred after cadres who had desecrated a temple or divinity statue were struck by sudden death or strange illnesses, prompting villagers to speculate that the god was exacting revenge, or when someone dreamed that the village god resented not having a proper home.[29]

The group of people helping the initiator of the temple project would typically become the temple management board, on which the initiator may or may not have continued to play the dominant role. The people most commonly active on temple boards were senior male villagers interested in local customs and history, retired local government leaders, the village Party secretary and other Party members with good connections and organizational experience, and younger entrepreneurs who treated temple activity as spiritual, symbolic, and social capital. Their motivations ranged from devotion to public interest and village pride, to a sense of guilt among those who had played a role in the Mao-era temple destruction, to a desire to restore personal honor and status among those who had particularly suffered during the Cultural Revolution (in some cases because they had been religious specialists in the "old society"). The public face of temples was thus typically senior or rich men, even though the actual running of the place was often in the hands of elderly women.

Negotiations and tensions with state agents were an inescapable feature of temple life, and have been described in detail by several scholars. Emerging in several of these studies is a recurring picture of a constant "tug-of-war"[30] over the uses and appropriations of public spaces. For instance, in Fujian in the 1980s, hundreds of rebuilt temples were expropriated and converted into school dormitories, child-care centers, recreation centers, television-viewing centers, youth clubs, rest stops, and rain shelters, and festival funds were confiscated to build a reservoir. At the same time, the *Fujian Daily* denounced the conversion of primary schools, a noodle factory, food-processing plants, and cattle pens into temples—showing that the dynamic of temple revival and that of temple conversion were occurring in parallel, with buildings and spaces becoming the sites of an ongoing struggle between the state and local populations. In some cases this struggle took the form of demonstrations and riots led by spirit mediums and festival organizers against local Party offices, and in other cases it was

---

29. Feuchtwang & Wang Mingming, *Grassroots Charisma*, 63; Chau, *Miraculous Response*.
30. M. Yang, "Spatial Struggles."

expressed as a more subtle popular reappropriation, as when old ladies disrupted the school day by burning incense and worshipping in the midst of classroom activities.[31] Each temple festival necessitated negotiations, and repression could happen at any moment with the arrest of religious specialists and temple leaders.[32] Such situations were still commonplace in the mid-2000s, with local police curtailing certain parts of the processions. The destruction of unauthorized temples continued to take place sporadically into the 2000s, especially at times of more general religious tension at either the national or the regional level; shrines of lay salvationist groups were torn down when they became too large or too visible.

Temple reconstruction did not always occur in an atmosphere of conflict, however. In her studies of religion in Zhejiang Province, Mayfair Yang stresses the overlapping uses of the same spaces by the state and religious cults, citing, for example, the case of a lineage hall in rural Yongchang Township, which had been turned into an elementary school in the Republican era. In the early 1980s, faced with the imminent demolition of the building, still occupied by a school, to make way for road construction, lineage members organized themselves as an archaeological relic preservation team, and successfully petitioned higher levels of government to have the site protected as a cultural relic. Both the state and the lineage then simultaneously invested the building with competing meanings: at one time, ancestral portraits vied with political banners for the attention of the children attending school in the building. Later, the school moved out when the local government turned the structure into a museum dedicating the building as an example of ancient architecture, but *not* as a hall for ancestor worship—in which, nonetheless, lineage members continued to hold their annual sacrificial rites. In 1998, the museum's theme was extended to include a Base Area for National Defense Education; fees were charged for admission to exhibits on military history and displays of tanks, fighter planes, and warships placed on either side of the main altar for the ancestor tablets. Thus, while at one level the building appeared as the site of a "tug-of-war," at another level the competing uses encapsulated "the convenient conflation of honoring lineage ancestors with paying homage to patriotic heroes who resisted foreign invasions of national space." The

31. Anagnost, "The Politics of Ritual Displacement," 221, 241–45.
32. Dean, *Taoist Ritual and Popular Cults*, 104–17, and *Lord of the Three in One*, 269, on police interference in processions in Penglai Township, Fujian, in 1986 and 1987. The authorities were unable to halt the festivities, however, and triggered such strong popular resentment that they were hesitant to interfere again.

state-employed management committee of the museum was dominated by members of the lineage, who were proud to have received so much official recognition for their lineage hall, which was even designated as a provincial-level tourist attraction.[33] In many places, lineage activities continued in the guise of official local "old folks' associations" 老年人協會.[34]

In their study of a stretch of road in Sichuan along the route toward Tibet, the anthropologists John Flowers and Pamela Leonard explore the place of temples in local people's memories and moral worlds in the face of successive civilizing projects.[35] Rejecting the discourse on "everyday forms of resistance," they see a relationship of "mutual cooptation," which they contrast with cases of peasant riots and angry confrontations that were recurrent in the same region in the 1990s. They describe the reopening in 1992 of a temple to Chuanzhu 川主—the Lord of Rivers, who protects the community from flooding—whose statue was destroyed by township government officials a few days before the god's annual festival was to be celebrated. Just afterward, a flood swept through the area, destroying many houses, the main road, and the township high school, a disaster which was interpreted by the people as divine retribution for the desecration. The anger of the god focalized popular resentment against the corrupt local officials. Later, when the local leadership team was changed, new Party Secretary Gao supported the temple in order to restore the government's legitimacy. He had the government finance the temple's renovation, on the condition that it be promoted as a tourist attraction and be integrated into state bureaucratic structures by being designated as Buddhist, with nuns from the state-sponsored Buddhist association appointed to manage it (the temple leaders actually accommodated the nuns in a new side hall, thereby preserving the original cult to Chuanzhu). A few years later, Party Secretary Gao was recalled, and the local government once again attempted to restrict the temple's activities; Gao's name, however, was inscribed on a new stone tablet in front of the temple, to be forever associated with the upright virtues of the god Chuanzhu. Other scholars have likewise noted how the image of temple gods and temple managers as righteous servants of the people came to combine village history and tradition with the collective values of public duty previously inculcated by the CCP.[36]

In villages dominated by lineages, it was often lineage halls rather than

33. M. Yang, "Spatial Struggles," 737, 734–38.
34. Pan, "The Old Folks' Associations."
35. Flower & Leonard, "Defining Cultural Life"; Flower, "A Road is Made."
36. Feuchtwang & Wang Mingming, Grassroots Charisma, 77.

local gods' temples that became the major focus of tension and negotiation between local populations and state agents, as in the case of the Kong lineage of Dachuan village, Gansu, studied in detail by Jing Jun.[37] This village had doubly suffered during the Mao years, first on account of the "feudal" and "reactionary" background of its dominant lineage, which traced its descent from Confucius, and second since much of the village and most of its graves had been permanently flooded and forcibly resettled for the building of a reservoir. For the members of the Kong lineage, rebuilding their lineage hall and reviving its ancestral cult were ways of reclaiming their memory and rebuilding their shattered identity. Although the temple rebuilding project was initiated in the 1980s by an unpopular Party secretary hoping to regain legitimacy, he was driven out of office by younger Party members who were active in an unsuccessful campaign for compensation for the land lost to the reservoir. These younger members became, together with some old men who had received classical Confucian training in their youth, the core of the group of temple activists. In order to ensure legitimacy for the temple, the activists had its original purpose, as an ancestral temple restricted to Kong lineage members, joined with one as a hall to commemorate Confucius as a sage of the Chinese people, making it a public site for the promotion of Chinese culture and national pride. However, the installation of a statue crafted in the customary manner of local gods' statues caused most villagers to view Confucius like other gods, able to answer prayers and cure illnesses—making the Confucius temple one of the major centers of communal religion in the area. Here the temple was clearly a site for the expression of local tensions and political conflicts, but these were diffused by juxtaposing Kong lineage identity, the state's civilizing project, and local religious culture.

In lineage-dominated villages, local community leadership in matters of religion was naturally assumed by lineage elders; in multi-surname villages, however, the situation was much more open. In his study of the Black Dragon King temple in Yulin County, northern Shaanxi, Adam Chau depicts the emergence of a new type of local elite which drew its power from moral authority and access to tradition, in constant negotiation with two other types of local elite: business entrepreneurs and agents of the local state. His study focuses primarily on the latter two types, showing how temple boss Wang successfully ensured the legitimation and protection of the temple by having its old stone gate designated a cultural relic, by providing cash payments to police patrolling the huge annual temple festivals

37. Jing, *The Temple of Memories*.

and tax and income streams for the local commercial and electricity bureaus, and by spending temple revenues on environmental and educational
projects recognized and praised by the forestry and education bureaus. He
finally succeeded in having the temple officially registered as a Taoist place
of worship, with a ceremony scheduled to coincide with the high point of
the Dragon King's birthday festival, highlighted by the best opera performances in all of northern Shaanxi and the presence of thousands of local festivalgoers. The ceremony brought into one another's presence, with
mutual recognition and acknowledgment, the personal charisma of the
temple boss, the divine power of the god, the political authority of the state
representatives, and the communal energy of the crowds.[38] An originally
illegal temple and a once-unpopular local state leadership thus used each
other to obtain the legitimacy they respectively lacked: legal and political
for the temple, popular and divine for the local state agents.

   This case highlights what seemed to be the trend in many rural areas, in
both Mainland China and Taiwan: local political leadership and charisma
were being played out simultaneously in religious and "secular" terms.[39]
Local cults continued to be or once again became the focus of community
life and local politics. In Taiwan, temples became arenas for the accumulated symbolic and political resources of local elites, who had been cut off
from access to national power by the Japanese and then by the Mainlanders
of the KMT. Restricted to their local power bases, leaders in neighboring
localities thus competed to build the largest temple or host the most "hot
and noisy" festival; later, candidates for political office cultivated temple
communities as sources of potential grassroots support in elections. Even
national presidential candidates made campaign stops at major temples,
seeking the endorsements of temple leaders and even claiming the support of the gods themselves, allegedly made manifest through the casting
of divination blocks and other portents.[40]

   On the mainland, as had been the case for decades in Taiwan and Southeast Asia, some temples also began to expand their influence through the
provision of social and charitable services in rural areas, where often no
other actors or institutions had the will or ability to do so. The Dragon
King temple mentioned above, for example, used the surplus funds raised

---

38. Chau, "The Politics of Legitimation," 269. A similar encounter is described in Dean, *Lord of the Three in One*, 266.

39. Feuchtwang & Wang, *Grassroots Charisma*; on charisma in modern Chinese religion, see Goossaert & Ownby, eds., "Mapping Charisma."

40. Katz, "Religion and the State in Post-War Taiwan."

through incense donation boxes to launch a reforestation project that won international acclaim as the only nongovernmental arboretum in China, and it built a primary school that, with generous funding from the temple and excellent facilities, quickly became the best in the entire county.[41]

In her comparative study of villages in Jiangxi and Fujian, Lily Lee Tsai concludes that single-lineage villages which practice village-wide rituals or have an active temple association "provide broad community networks that village officials can draw on for public services." She notes that the committees formed to rebuild temples and lineage halls often evolved into "community councils" that organized religious, social, and philanthropic activities. Whereas villagers would not contribute to appeals for funds by village cadres, they "willingly and universally" contributed to public projects when solicited by temple boards. In one village, the temple committee's revenue was four times higher than that of the village government, and had taken over all the road-building projects in the community. Local cadres often sought the support of temple boards for their projects, and offloaded responsibility for social services to them, although they continued to take credit for those achievements when reporting to higher levels of the administration.[42] Thus, Ken Dean has claimed that communal religion became a "second tier of local government" in many parts of rural China.[43]

Indeed, in a context in which, throughout the 1980s and 1990s, the state increasingly disengaged itself from the village level, providing few resources to cash-strapped local governments and Party branches whose main function often came to be limited to the unpopular activities of tax collection and enforcing birth control and cremation policies, temples frequently emerged as alternative centers of resource collection and allocation, to which villagers willingly contributed funds, often spent by the temple board on local infrastructure such as the construction and repair of roads, bridges, schools, and even basketball courts.[44] Temples thereby recovered some of the social functions they had in late imperial times but, in contrast to the situation under the Qing, operated in close cooperation with a state that remained very present in the villages. With a fresh infusion of resources under the New Socialist Countryside program of the Hu

41. Chau, "The Politics of Legitimation," 258–59.
42. Tsai, "Cadres, Temple and Lineage Institutions," 9, 21–23.
43. Dean, "China's Second Government," "Local Communal Religion," "Ritual and Space."
44. M. Yang, "Putting Global Capitalism in Its Place," 486–89.

Jintao administration, however, it was possible that the state would reclaim some of the functions taken over by temples.

Although these examples show how temples could become the direct providers of public services offloaded by the state, other research has shown that temples could reinforce the accountability of village officials and their ability to provide public investments and services. A quantitative survey of 316 villages in North and South China, also led by Lily Lee Tsai, concluded that village-encompassing temples and lineages are informal institutions of accountability that, more than any other variable, ensure governmental performance and the provision of public services by village state agents. Compared with villages lacking temple groups, villages with temples had higher levels of government investment in public services, a higher probability of paved roads and paths, a higher percentage of class-rooms usable in rain, and a higher probability of running water. Using several statistical instruments to determine whether these higher levels of public services were caused by other factors or whether the temples were a consequence (and not a cause) of the better public services, Tsai concludes that "even when we control for level of economic development and in-dustrialization, variation in bureaucratic and democratic institutions, and differences in the demand for particular goods or the cost of particular goods due to the variation in location, geography, and size, village temple groups have a significant positive effect on village governmental provision of public goods." She reaches the same conclusion for village-wide lineage groups. Indeed, she even notes that the introduction in many regions of village-level democratic reforms since the late 1990s, in which village leaders could be elected in openly contested elections, was a less significant variable than the existence of an active temple or village-wide lineage in ensuring the village leaders' accountability and efficient provision of public goods.[45] In contrast, the relationship was less clear for villages with Catholic or Protestant churches, and notably negative for villages with multiple subvillage lineage groups.

Tsai defines temples, churches, and lineages as "solidary groups" in which members are "engaged in mutually oriented activities and share a set of ethical standards and moral obligations."[46] When solidary groups encompass all the members of the administrative village and embed local state officials as members, the village officials will be bound by the moral

45. L. Tsai, *Accountability*, 131, 130, 187–228.
46. Ibid., 2.

obligations of the solidary group, which can reward those who serve the group well with high moral standing, or punish corrupt officials by giving them a bad moral reputation. This constitutes a system of informal accountability, in a context where formal (democratic) systems of accountability are weak or nonexistent, and where higher levels of government are uninterested or unable to force accountability on village officials. Such village leaders have an added incentive to make an effort to provide public services, while leaders of the solidary group are willing to mobilize the villagers to cooperate with the officials, complying with regulations and voluntarily contributing funds for public projects. On the other hand, village officials who are not embedded in a solidary group have little incentive to perform, not being bound to a solidary group's mutual obligations and moral standards (and being provided with few incentives to perform by higher levels of government).

Temples and village-wide lineages are solidary groups that encompass all villagers and embed local officials within them, providing the common moral obligations and incentives to perform, cooperate, and comply. On the other hand, while the church in all-Christian villages is an encompassing solidary group, village officials (as atheist Party members) were banned from being embedded within them. While a church could, and often did, *bypass* the state by building schools or roads on its own, it could not provide a strong positive incentive for officials to provide higher levels of public services themselves. And villages with more than one active lineage group were worse off than those with no solidary groups at all: as members of only one of the lineages, village leaders had little motivation to provide villagewide services, and members of rival lineages had little motivation to comply with government projects designed to serve the entire village.

Many studies have stressed the support given to certain temples and lineage halls by local and regional governments in Mainland China, eager to promote tourism and to attract investment by overseas Chinese. Indeed, a good part of the rebuilding of Taoist and Buddhist monasteries was done with support, both financial and political, from overseas Chinese. Networks of Buddhist clerics and laypersons among the communities in Southeast Asia and the West lobbied the Chinese central and local governments to rebuild their "ancestral" monasteries, leveraging the willingness of overseas Chinese businessmen willing to invest in their home county.[47] Overseas Taoist networks were much less developed, but the Hong Kong Taoists

---

47. Ashiwa & Wank, "The Globalization of Chinese Buddhism."

played a similar role in lobbying for and financing temple reconstruction, primarily in the Guangdong area but also in other parts of China.

In her research on the role of Singaporeans in reviving religious activities in their ancestral villages in southeastern China, K. E. Kuah-Pearce has noted that while village cadres tended to support the revival of ancestor worship for sentimental reasons, officials at the county level also encouraged such activities for instrumental purposes, hoping that the ties thus created with Singaporeans would lead them to contribute funds to schools and hospitals and invest in infrastructures benefiting the entire county. Large-scale religious festivals for the Patriarch of the Clear Stream (Qing-shui zushi 清水祖師), who was worshipped by most Singaporeans on trips to their hometowns, and whose temples were renovated with local government support as designated tourist attractions, were staged with the active cooperation of the local authorities. They declared the festival a public holiday and had the schools closed; pupils performed dances and musicals and were provided with dress, drinks, and pocket money by the festival organizers.[48] The lucrative temple of the Patriarch of the Clear Stream was even the object of a struggle for control between local and provincial levels of government.[49] Instances of government-built temples were also increasingly common, as local authorities attempted to appropriate the popularity of religious activity and profit from its revenue streams by either building new temples or taking over existing ones.[50]

TEMPLE CULTS, NATIONALISM, AND IDENTITY

Since the late 1990s, some local officials actively supported the development of certain, but by no means all, local temple cults that they saw as embodying local identity and culture. The adoption by the Ministry of Culture of UNESCO's norms of "intangible cultural heritage" led, in some cases, to ritual traditions or cults being declared as intangible cultural heritage (see chapter 12). How the protection and management of such forms of "heritage" would lead to intervention by state cultural authorities remained to be seen. In the case of temples supported by local governments, the latter

48. Kuah-Pearce, *Rebuilding the Ancestral Village*, 167, 185–90, and "The Worship of Qingshui Zushi." On government sponsorship of festivals, see also Siu, "Recycling Ritual" and "Recycling Tradition."

49. Dean, *Taoist Ritual and Popular Cults*, 126.

50. See Lang, Chan & Lagvald, "Temples," for several examples of state-sponsored construction of Wong Tai Sin temples in Mainland China.

sometimes intervened with a heavy hand to impose a certain style in the building (such as palatial architecture, a uniform iconography, and so on) and in the celebrations. Some comments by local officials and scholars suggest that the state's growing tolerance for "popular faith" was linked to a nationalist project aiming specifically to curb the growing influence of Christianity in rural areas. This new approach, while less confrontational than the all-out destruction of the Mao period, was still strongly interventionist, was based on a vision of what is good and bad in local religion, and aimed to reshape popular practice according to official ideology.

In a small number of cases, governments sponsored temples for explicitly nationalist purposes. The cult of the Yellow Emperor, the mythical founder of the Chinese nation, was promoted as early as the 1900s by Chinese nationalists. From the early 1980s, it was conducted every spring during the Grave-Sweeping Festival at his tomb in Huangling County, Shaanxi Province, with significant support from the central government. Senior CCP leaders, beginning with Premier Zhao Ziyang 趙紫陽 (1919–2005) in 1983, visited the temple and even established a special foundation to raise funds in China and abroad for expanding the tomb and its attached temple. By the late 1990s, the cult began in the early morning with a closed-door ceremony reserved for senior national and provincial dignitaries and special overseas Chinese guests, while in the afternoon the temple gates were opened for a crowd of ten thousand local worshippers.[51]

The Taiwan issue loomed large at the ceremony, in which senior officials' elegies to the Yellow Emperor stressed the unification of China, which, following the retrocession of Hong Kong (1997) and Macau (1999), was destined to reach its consummation with the return of Taiwan to the motherland. At the same time, in an almost reverse scenario far from the parched loess hills of Shaanxi, on the small island of Jinmen (Quemoy) off the coast of Fujian but controlled by Taiwan, the KMT army had, since the 1950s, appropriated a local cult to the hungry ghost of a woman who had washed ashore and was said to have been raped and killed by Communist soldiers. Whereas locals worshipped her as a protective deity, military officers honored her as a patriotic heroine for her resistance to Communism.[52] But in the 1990s, the demilitarization of Jinmen, the opening of the island to tourism as well as to direct trade links to Mainland China just a stone's throw away, and the electoral defeat of the KMT government all contributed to blur the meanings of the cult, which acquired new significance as

51. Billeter, *L'empereur Jaune*.
52. Szonyi, *Cold War Island*, chap. 11.

a symbol of local authenticity for the boatloads of tourists who landed on the island each day.

The uses and dangers of the political appropriation of temples for nationalistic purposes were most evident in the case of the Mazu cult in Taiwan and its pilgrimages to its original temple in Meizhou, on the Fujian coast. Although Mazu is often seen as a symbol of an emerging Taiwanese identity, and Mazu worshippers were regarded as tending to support the pro-independence Democratic Progressive Party (DPP), the campaign by one temple to organize a direct pilgrimage to Meizhou in 2000, in contravention of Taiwanese policy, deeply embarrassed the newly elected DPP government. The move played into the hands of the CCP, which attempted to instrumentalize Mazu, billed in the Mainland Chinese press as the "Sea Goddess of Peace in the Taiwan Strait,"[53] to promote China's political reunification. Taiwanese temples made significant financial contributions and organized large-scale pilgrimages to the ancestral temple in Meizhou—activities legitimized by mainland state agencies' encouraging the organization of academic conferences on local gods to which local scholars, temple activists, and overseas donors were invited.[54] With its origin and the source of its spiritual power on the mainland, but with many of its worshippers being native Taiwanese, the Mazu cult undermined the nationalist projects of both the CCP and the Taiwanese separatists: "cross-strait Mazu pilgrimages are creating a regional ritual space and religious community of Chinese coastal peoples that do not conform to existing political borders."[55] Similarly, attempting to replicate the Mazu model and hoping to build ties with Hong Kong and Macau residents, the Shenzhen Cultural Bureau rebuilt the Mazu temple at Chiwan (just across the border from Hong Kong) in 1992 as an uneasy hybrid of secular museum and place of worship.[56]

Rather than a marker of ethnic or national divisions, then, Mazu appeared as a node linking and scrambling different polities and identities. The case of the Mazu cult in San Francisco illustrates how this logic operated in the vastly different social and religious context of the United States. Established in 1986 as a branch of the Chaotian gong 朝天宮, one of the principal Mazu temples in Taiwan, the goddess of the Ma-tsu Temple USA, as the shrine was called, was always addressed as "American Mazu" (*Meiguo*

53. *People's Daily Overseas Edition*, April 22, 1987; quoted in Liu Tik-sang, "Associating Local Traditions," 3.

54. Dean, *Taoist Ritual and Popular Cults*, 92.

55. Mayfair Yang, "Goddess across the Taiwan Strait," 216.

56. Liu Tik-sang, "Associating Local Traditions."

mazu), becoming a marker of Chinese-American identity. The procession, which would normally be held on her birthday, took place instead as part of the San Francisco Chinese New Year parade, during which non-Chinese were welcomed to carry flags, blow horns, hold incense sticks, and even perform as the two generals escorting the goddess. Religious meanings of the parade were downplayed so that the rites could serve to celebrate the larger civic and intercultural community relations. Rather than staking out her territory or asserting a local identity, as would occur during a traditional Chinese deity procession, American Mazu's participation in the Chinese New Year parade associated her with the celebration of successful Chinese integration into a multicultural society. The same tendency appeared in the designation of one of America's oldest Chinese temples, the Guandi temple in Mendocino, California, established in 1854, as a historic site and museum, celebrating the Chinese contribution to the city's multicultural heritage.[57]

The festival of the Nine Emperors 九皇[58] (known as the Vegetarian Festival) in Phuket, Thailand, is another instance of a Chinese cult becoming a link between ethnic groups. Although traditionally celebrated exclusively by the Chinese community of Phuket, the festival underwent an unprecedented growth in popularity since the 1980s, attracting growing numbers of ethnic Thais and Muslims among its participants and even its spirit mediums. The anthropologist Erik Cohen explains this trend by pointing to the greater confidence and openness of the Chinese community in contemporary Thailand, where there was a new prestige associated with things Chinese in general, while at the same time Chinese and Thai cultures were becoming further integrated, as exemplified by the popularity of the Guanyin cult among Thais.[59]

Yet in Penang, Malaysia, where the Nine Emperors Festival also grew to an enormous scale, the anthropologist Jean DeBernardi notes the opposite phenomenon: the festival was an occasion for the exclusive display of Chinese community power. "One young man," she reports, "proudly drew my attention to the fact that only Chinese were there."[60] This phenomenon can be attributed to the specific identity politics of Malaysia, where, reflecting

57. Jonathan Lee, "Contemporary Chinese American Religious Life."

58. The Nine Emperors are the stars of the Big Dipper (Ursa Major) who control human fate; their cult was once common throughout China, but on the mainland is now mostly confined to Taoist temples. On the Nine Emperors cult in Malaysia, see Tong Cheu Hok, *The Nine Emperor Gods* and "The Festival of the Nine Emperor Gods."

59. E. Cohen, *The Chinese Vegetarian Festival*; see also bin Ismail, "Two Faces of Buddhism."

60. DeBernardi, *Rites of Belonging*, 183.

the role of Islam as the essential marker of the Malay majority, each religion was understood as the exclusive identification of a single ethnic group. Among the Chinese, customs such as ancestor worship thus acquired a new meaning: in addition to nurturing a link with the individual's personal ancestors, the practice established and reinforced his identity as a member of the Chinese minority in a multiethnic, Islamic-majority state.[61]

Chinese temple cults, then, though solidly rooted in locality, extended outward in unexpected directions, multiplying links and ignoring ideological and political boundaries. While they played an important role in the negotiation of local and ethnic identities, the type of identity formation they facilitated did not neatly fit with the nation-building projects of states and political parties. The multiplication and expansion of temple cults could thus be said to contribute to the weaving of an open-ended, transnational Chinese web of horizontal rhizomatic networks, undermining the closed boundaries and vertical hierarchies of purported nation-states, which, as we have seen in chapter 2, were built *against* local society and its temples.

TEMPLES IN THE EXPANDING MARKET ECONOMY

The social context in which temple cults revived was completely different from that in which its traditional organizational forms had developed. In the land reform campaigns of the 1950s in Mainland China and in Taiwan, the land endowments that had previously sustained temple operations had been appropriated by the state and redistributed to the farmers, and the gentry society and traditional political economy through which temples had played their social role at the center of what Prasenjit Duara has called the "cultural nexus of power"[62] no longer existed. Long seen by both defenders and opponents as the last redoubt of "traditional society," from the 1970s onward temples actually mobilized people around new projects, on new socioeconomic foundations.

Temples now had to rely almost exclusively on donations, the sale of paraphernalia, and the provision of ritual services for income; they could survive only through the voluntary support of active worshippers. As it happened, rising incomes in many parts of the Chinese world led to significantly higher contributions of devotees to temples and festivals, whereas in Taiwan and even in parts of the mainland, individuals were able to endow their own private shrines. The average wealth of Taiwanese temples was

61. Clarke, "Ancestor Worship and Identity."
62. Duara, *Culture, Power, and the State.*

immeasurably greater than ever before.[63] Research by Song Guangyu has shown a direct correlation between peaks in economic growth in Taiwan in the 1970s and 1980s and, after a three-year lag, spurts of new temple construction, as funds contributed in times of prosperity materialized as finished temples a few years later.[64]

Fund-raising drives launched by temples and lineages for rituals and social projects were a regular feature of the social landscape in rural Mainland China as well as Taiwan. Ostentatiously excessive ritual consumption, in many ways comparable to the famed potlatch of the Kwakiutl Indians, has led Mayfair Yang to argue that "this ritual economy cannot be seen merely as the *result of* economic development, for ritual life has also *fuelled* economic growth (it often provides the organizational apparatus, site, and motivation for economic activity) and *constrained* and *channeled* it through the deployment of ritual consumption against capital accumulation."[65] In many places, temple reconstruction closely followed the revival of traditional market fairs (which used to be organized in front of temples). Indeed, ritual expenses helped to reconstitute and strengthen kinship and community ties, challenging the assumption that the penetration of capitalism would undermine kinship relations through the increasing mobility and commodification of labor. In the New Territories of Hong Kong, lineages, which often continued to own prime real estate, turned their assets into capital, which they invested in transnational business operations spurred by the migration of lineage members to Europe and North America and also by the revived ties between lineage branches on both sides of the Hong Kong-Shenzhen border. Ritual events were sponsored by the lineage members, most of whom were now dispersed in urban Hong Kong and around the world, and who regrouped every few years for the *jiao* festival at the ancestral village.[66]

And yet, such a "hybrid economy," in which capital flows were diverted by communal ritual and kinship, was perhaps more characteristic of certain parts of rural late-socialist China than the more "capitalist" economies of Taiwan, Hong Kong, and even large mainland cities such as Guangzhou. Other studies, indeed, point to temples becoming integrated into the capitalist mainstream, appealing increasingly to individuals rather than kin

63. Jordan, "Changes in Postwar Taiwan."
64. Song Guangyu, "Zongjiao yu lisu."
65. M. Yang, "Putting Global Capitalism in Its Place," 480.
66. S. Chan, "Selling the Ancestors' Land"; Watson, "Presidential Address."

groups or local communities, and in which temples and ritual specialists compete against each other like firms in a market.

Several scholars have noted that the ascriptive local communities were becoming weaker, while the most successful temples relied on open "belief spheres" (信仰圈, a concept developed by Taiwanese sociologists)[67] of individuals who voluntarily worship a deity without regard for territorial or community affiliations. Ease of transport lessened the temples' dependence on their immediate communities, allowing some to expand their catchment area—a phenomenon reinforced by the massive television coverage of festivals and pilgrimages. This trend was especially striking in Hong Kong, where the most popular temple was devoted to the "refugee god" Wong Tai Sin, who, like most urban Hong Kong residents, lacked deep local roots; located near a busy subway line, the temple attracted worshippers from the entire territory.[68] By contrast, with the transformation of villages into housing estates, ascriptive communal *jiao* celebrations became ever fewer.

A most extreme example of this individualism in worship was the cults of amoral ghosts that grew rapidly in Taiwan in the 1980s. For a few years, Taiwan's most popular temple was the shrine to the Eighteen Lords, at the grave of seventeen unidentified men whose corpses had floated ashore and a dog who had jumped into the grave to join its master. It was said to have been frequented especially by prostitutes, gangsters, gamblers, and people who hoped to get winning numbers in an illegal lottery. Not only did the gods of this shrine lack any ascriptive community, but they lacked even the pretense of morality, willing to entertain any request. Also in line with the increasing individualism, spirit-medium cults, based in private altars as a kind of private business, grew in popularity in the 1980s, providing utilitarian help to clients.[69] Such cults had been around for centuries, but their public presence, compared with other types of cults, increased to an important extent. Shrines often included up to fifty gods, covering every specialty from gynecology to success in exams, "like a shop that expands its selection of wares."[70] In the same vein, many gods who had previously specialized in a single type of problem—such as protection for fishermen

---

67. Lin Meirong, "You jisi quan dao xinyang quan"; Chapman, "The De-territorialization of Ritual Spheres." See also Zheng Zhiming, *Zongjiao zuzhi.*
68. Lang & Ragvald, *The Rise of a Refugee God.*
69. Chao Shin-yi, "A Danggi Temple in Taipei."
70. Weller, *Alternate Civilities*, 89–91, and "Matricidal Magistrates."

(Mazu) or curbing plagues (Wangye 王爺)—evolved into generalists who could cater to all needs.

An increasing proportion of temple and ritual activities thus operated according to the logic of a commercial marketplace. While markets for religious and ritual services had always existed in China,[71] their geographic fragmentation was giving way to greater integration, most notably in Taiwan and Hong Kong, with local and communal connections being weakened and temples competing for clients over larger geographic areas. In Mainland China, governments and entrepreneurs built or acquired temples as a form of business investment. In a study of eight Wong Tai Sin temples built in South China to emulate the success of the Hong Kong temple and attract its pilgrims, the most successful were those managed by private businessmen, who carefully studied the competition and marketing possibilities, and developed long-term business strategies.[72] Some temples in Hong Kong proudly displayed their ISO-9000 certificate for quality management, while Shanghai Buddhist monks enrolled in a special MBA program for temple business administration.

Certain types of religious specialists, who had traditionally offered their services in the form of commercial transactions with clients, adapted naturally to the capitalist environment. Throughout the Chinese world, and most remarkably on the mainland, the boom in house construction and grave restoration by farmers provided a flourishing business for *fengshui* masters.[73] In the cities, many of these masters established themselves as professional consultants with their own Web sites, serving a growing clientele of real estate developers and businessmen. Freelance Taoist priests in metropolitan centers such as Shanghai ran a highly lucrative business in ritual services, to the point where priests employed by the state-controlled Taoist temples overcame their disdain for the crass commercialism of their freelance counterparts and willingly rented temple premises to them— thus bringing the temples themselves back into the ritual economy.[74]

The combined result of market forces and the weakening of local ascriptive communities could be seen in the changes in festival rituals, which became ever more open to outside participation by both devotees and performers, and thus to evolving styles and tastes. For instance, the *jia-jiang* 家將 exorcistic dance troupes typically hired to join processions at

71. Chau, "Superstition Specialist Households?"
72. Lang, Chan & Lagvald, "Temples"; S. Chan & Lang, "Temple Construction."
73. Bruun, *Fengshui in China*, chaps. 4 and 5.
74. Yang Der-ruey, "The Changing Economy."

temple rituals in southern Taiwan exhibited an increasing prevalence of self-mortification rites after the 1970s. While the refined steps, make-up, and costumes of traditional *jiajiang* dances required years of disciplined training to master, bloody self-mortifying acts such as cheek piercing and beating one's back with a spiked iron ball, which required much bravado but little discipline or training, could draw larger crowds in the age of TV and action movies, and earned higher payment from temple managers. Where traditional troupes were typically attached to a single locality, leading to the development of distinct performance traditions associated with particular villages and lineages of masters, the newly multiplying troupes of self-mortifiers were not connected to a specific place, and their leaders acted as autonomous entrepreneurs, dealing with a wide range of temples and offering a more homogenized but highly dramatic repertoire of acts.[75] An extreme development of self-mortification as an effect of the same trends amplified by tourism occurred at the Chinese Nine Emperors vegetarian festival at Phuket, Thailand. There the number of spirit mediums increased exponentially, reaching the thousands, with growing numbers from the Thai and Muslim communities participating, while the feats of self-mortification became simply gruesome: the traditional iron spikes used to pierce both cheeks gave way to axes, potted plants, motorcycle parts, scissors, handsaws, fluorescent bulbs, diving equipment, cellular phones, and even entire bicycles.[76]

The professionalization and commercialization of festival performance troupes was widespread in the PRC as well. Farmers able to devote several months of the slack season to rehearsing as members of amateur troupes were fewer and fewer, even though some areas of Mainland China still managed to maintain New Year exorcistic Nuo 儺 rituals performed by the villagers themselves. Yet the amateur ideal lived on, even among urbanites such as the Beijing inhabitants who revived the Miaofengshan pilgrimage and its amateur performing troupes during the 1990s.[77] The increasing spectacularization of festivals was one way for temple religion to compete for the attention of modern individuals with weaker communal ties, for whom attending festivals (which, in Taiwan, were now often conveniently scheduled on weekends) was only one of a dazzling array of leisure and religious activities—even though going back once a year to the village to attend a festival was still commonplace.

75. Sutton, *Steps of Perfection*, 271–91.
76. Illustrations in E. Cohen, *The Chinese Vegetarian Festival*.
77. Fan Hua, "Miaofeng shan xingxiang zouhui"; Wu Xiaoqun, *Miaofengshan*, 229–85.

Indeed, if the studies show temples becoming dominant players at the core of local social, political, and even economic life in several rural villages and small towns of Mainland China, such a revival could not happen in most large cities, where most temples had been completely destroyed; the communities which might want to rebuild them no longer existed, because the people had been moved out and relocated; and policy still simply did not allow it. Official downtown Taoist and Buddhist temples staged festivals that were often well attended, but they could not organize any events outside their premises. Processions, for instance, were usually out of the question—with the exception of Quanzhou (southern Fujian), listed as a "historical city," and where a large proportion of the neighborhood temples were officially allowed to reopen and to organize processions.[78] Meanwhile, cities expanded by demolishing peripheral villages, razed (sometimes brutally) and rebuilt with rows of multistory housing blocks. In many PRC cities, these ex-villages attempted to keep their temple by rebuilding it on common land, and ex-farmers, now idle with their land turned to development but with compensation money, often turned to full-time temple management and devotional activities—especially in the case of older women, who formed sutra-recitation groups. Indeed, even though male leaders with social status (retired cadres, schoolteachers) often played prominent public roles in temple revivals, it was elderly women who did most of the temple running and festival organizing. However, these islands of local religious life around the cities were by no means safe, as increasing integration within the cities brought ever-more control of religious activities in public spaces.

Even in large metropolises outside the PRC, where the political restrictions did not exist, bureaucratic and economic factors severely limited the expansion or construction of new temples or the holding of communal festivals. In Hong Kong, the *jiao* festivals, still regularly organized by New Territories indigenous communities, ended wherever their villages were demolished for the construction of suburban towns. Zoning regulations in Malaysia made it next to impossible to construct religious buildings (with the exception of mosques) in the new housing estates resided in by a growing proportion of the urban Chinese population.[79] In Singapore between 1974 and 1987, 700 Chinese temples, 99 mosques, 27 Hindu temples, and 19 churches were acquired and demolished or converted to other purposes to make way for real estate development. At the same time, places of wor-

---

78. Abramson, "Places for the Gods"; Wang Mingming, "'Great Tradition.'"
79. DeBernardi, "Malaysian Chinese Religious Culture."

ship were considered necessary public amenities in the New Towns built in the suburbs, and a quota was established for their construction: one Chinese temple per 9,000 housing units, one church per 12,000 units, and one Hindu temple per 90,000 units. As a special privilege to the indigenous Malays, at least one mosque was to be built in each New Town, regardless of the number of units. In the case of Chinese temples and Christian churches, several groups would compete for government tenders for religious buildings, but they would often pool their resources to bid for one tender.

For Chinese temples, then, the trend was toward larger temple complexes, sometimes jointly managed by more than one association.[80] Elsewhere, with the interesting exception of Quanzhou or of some suburbs of Shanghai, in which new urban blueprints specifically called for the renovation or construction of new Christian churches and City God temples, planners and real estate developers throughout the Chinese world almost never reserved space for temples in urban development projects, preferring to bulldoze old shrines that stood in the way. Where land was theoretically available for purchase, the prohibitive cost of real estate made the building of new temples virtually impossible. Urban safety, noise, hygiene, and traffic regulations imposed strict restrictions on the temporary use of public space for communal rituals.[81] As spectacular and "hot and noisy" as some of the major urban temples and festivals may have been, their overall impact and influence on the broader metropolitan community and economy were very limited, with little space for further expansion.

---

80. Kuah-Pearce, *State, Society and Religious Engineering*, 169–70.
81. On the Singapore case, see Tong Chee Kiong, *Rationalizing Religion*, 251–56.

ELEVEN

The Evolution of Modern Religiosities

◄ 拾·壹 ►

Perhaps the most profound change that affected Chinese societies in the twentieth century has been urbanization: from an essentially rural, agrarian civilization at the turn of the nineteenth century, almost half the world's Chinese people lived in cities one century later. A constant flow of refugees from Mainland China, fleeing civil wars and the Communist regime, transformed Hong Kong from a marginal colonial outpost into one of the world's largest cities. The 1949 exodus of 1.3 million Mainlanders to Taiwan together with the fleeing KMT army, as well as the general trend of industrialization, turned Taipei from a provincial backwater into a major metropolis. During the Mao years, state-directed mass movements of populations from the large coastal cities to the hinterland, to build the "Third Line" of inland industrial belts and populate the frontier, as well as the household registration system (*hukou* 戶口), restricted the growth of the big cities while causing the appearance of new cities in the interior. In the Deng era, however, new waves of economic migrants flowed from the countryside to the urban centers on the mainland and overseas, depleting the villages, which were increasingly populated by elders and the babies entrusted to their care, while the cities became the home of a floating population of over 100 million.

In Mainland China, district after district and city block after city block, private real estate developers intensified and finished off during the 1990s and 2000s the demolition and rebuilding of entire cities, succeeding in eradicating local memories and communities (notably the neighborhoods and their cults) wherever previous generations of political activists and socialist urban planners had not yet turned their gaze, having perhaps a greater impact than explicit state restrictions on communal religion. But as mentioned in the previous chapter, even where such pressures were less intense, as in Taiwan, the ascriptive communities (notably incorporated neighborhoods) that traditionally supported communal religion had become rare in the cities by the mid-twentieth century; a new proliferation of storefront shrines and apartment temples supported individualistic client cults managed by religious entrepreneurs. While apartment temples did exist in Hong Kong, and presumably on the mainland as well, this phenomenon was invisible. Strict regulations made the storefront shrine impossible on the mainland, if we except the ubiquitous but inconspicuous shrines to Guandi 關帝 and the God of Wealth 財神 in restaurants, which were even the subject of an ill-fated eradication campaign in Beijing in 1995–96.[1]

In most Mainland Chinese cities, then, urban dwellers' only physical exposure to religion was the handful of officially designated monasteries, churches, and mosques. For the most part, the Buddhist and Taoist temples (very few local communal temples were allowed, except in some suburbs), functioned as tourist attractions, museums, and administrative offices of the official religious associations rather than as the centers of living communities. The yearly festivals they organized were often well attended, and suburban or rural lay devotional groups would visit once a year; but the entrance tickets charged by almost all such temples discouraged regular visits, even though some were free to registered lay devotees.

Until the Grave-Sweeping and Mid-Autumn Festivals were declared public holidays in 2008, as mentioned in chapter 9, the only traditional festival that had continuously enjoyed official status was the Lunar New Year, the sole date in the lunar calendar that had been maintained in the new, Gregorian calendar under the Republican and socialist regimes. It remained primarily a family affair, and was endowed with nationalist meaning, notably through the television extravaganza that became part of the

---

1. McCarthy, "Gods of Wealth, Temples of Prosperity," 50.

ritual; yet it was also the time of the year when many urbanites went to temples—and, when municipal authorities allowed it, set off firecrackers in the streets and parks.

The result of a century of mass internal migrations was that a growing proportion of Chinese lost any connection to the villages and, by extension, to the communal religious life which characterized local culture. Nothing in their formal education and little in the way of physical environment or family connections gave the new urban-born generations direct contact with any type of religion. By the early twenty-first century, for most Mainland Chinese youth in cities like Shanghai, Shenzhen, or Chengdu, descriptions of rituals and temple festivals sounded as exotic and foreign as ethnographic accounts of tribal life in New Guinea—unless they experienced repackaged versions for tourists on their May Day holidays, in which exoticized ethnic minority costumes and dances actually contributed to forgetting that similar customs had once been, and in some places still were, as prevalent in Han local culture.[2] As a result, by the 2000s the Mainland Chinese Buddhist and Taoist temples had begun the habit of entrusting young clerics with showing visitors how to light and burn incense, bow, step over gate thresholds, and so on, since knowledge about these most basic body acts, still ingrained among most rural and overseas Chinese, was lost among young urbanites. While Halloween parties were all the rage among students and skillfully promoted by trendy bars and restaurants, few youth were conscious that the Ghost Festival of the seventh lunar month had once been one of the most important events of any Chinese community's annual ritual calendar. Christmas was aggressively promoted by department stores and shopping malls, turning Santa Claus into a figure more familiar to children than any character in Chinese lore—and among teenagers and youth, the holiday rivaled in popularity with the Lunar New Year, precisely because it had no traditional significance: lacking the customs and family reunions of the Spring Festival—or of Christmas as practiced in Western societies—it was an entirely secularized celebration without community or prescribed forms.[3] Groups of friends would go for a night on the town—perhaps to listen to Christmas carols in overpacked churches, or to go dancing at nightclubs, or to invent playful new rituals, such as chasing and hitting each other with inflatable hammers and plastic baseball bats.

And yet it would be wrong to assume that religion had entirely disap-

2. Sutton & Kang Xiaofei, "Recasting Religion and Ethnicity."
3. Ji Zhe, "Non-Institutional Religious Re-Composition."

peared from the culture of urban Chinese. Outside the mainland, of course, although it was also common to live and work without coming into contact with religious sites and communities, religion remained visible in Chinese cities and neighborhoods, with more temples having survived, and more religious institutions operating openly. Even on the mainland, traditional concepts and cosmologies remained alive in people's minds, often transmitted by women within the family; religious stories and symbols were propagated, in a diffused fashion, through pop culture and the mass media; and practices involving the nurturing of the body and health, such as exercise regimens, traditional healing, diet, and vegetarianism, were usually rooted in traditional cosmologies and religious disciplines. These concepts and unorganized bits of knowledge would form the soil within which a great diversity of religious movements would flourish in the later decades of the twentieth century. Indeed, some of the better social surveys recently conducted in urban PRC show that religious culture and positive interest in things religious were much more prevalent than claims of religious affiliation would suggest. In a 2005 survey of various cities, formal religious affiliation was growing (5 percent, up from 2 percent in 1995) but still lower than in Taiwan, Hong Kong, or Singapore; and firm atheism and distrust toward things religious remained quite widespread (33 percent claimed to be atheist, and 26 percent thought that "religion is nothing other than cheating and nonsense"). Even so, most people engaged in incense burning for ancestors, Buddhas, or gods, and fate-manipulating techniques; 15 percent had deities' statues at home; and 77 percent believed in divine retribution.[4]

In this chapter, after briefly reviewing some of these elements of latent religious culture, we will then describe the main forms through which modern religiosity was outwardly expressed, notably body cultivation movements, Confucian revivalism, lay Buddhist movements, and evangelical Christianity. These movements were all born, and to a large extent remained, outside the orthodox religious institutions recognized by the socialist state on the mainland and by the KMT government on Taiwan until the lifting of martial law. And yet, by the end of the twentieth century, they were the most dynamic in the urban Chinese world. This chapter will continue by comparing the characteristics of these movements in terms of the central role they accorded to individual choice, their recasting of Chinese tradition in relation to Western modernity, and their affirmation of moral-

4. Yao Xinzhong & Badham, *Religious Experience*; Yao Xinzhong, "Religious Beliefs and Practice in Urban China."

ity within a market economy. Finally, we will compare the role these movements played in redefining identity and ethnicity in relation to the nation-state and globalization, and in the emergence of a modern public culture or "civil society" in Mainland China and Taiwan.

THE DIFFUSION OF RELIGIOUS CULTURE IN THE CITIES

Perhaps the most extreme case of a Chinese city lacking in religious culture was Shenzhen, the "special economic zone" created during the 1980s at the border with Hong Kong—a metropolis without a history, inhabited almost entirely by recently settled, young, single migrants from other parts of China, including cheap laborers, ambitious white-collar professionals, and visionary entrepreneurs. Field research by the sociologist of religion Fan Lizhu[5] has come to the surprising conclusion that within such a completely secular social environment, in which little overtly religious knowledge was available, people used an array of traditional concepts to navigate the uncertainties of life in the cutthroat capitalist environment of Shenzhen. Many of these were notions related to fate, such as predestination (*yuan-fen* 緣分), destiny (*mingyun* 命運), and retribution (*baoying* 報應), all of which explain the seeming randomness of specific events in life through reference to a broader, and ultimately metaphysical, cosmic order—even if informants were not always able to consciously elaborate the links between those concepts and religious notions of karma or of the heavenly will.

What appears from Fan's study, then, is that the lack of order or meaning, and the sheer luck which seems to be the deciding factor in the individual's success or failure, lead people to posit that there is a hidden order behind the apparent meaninglessness. Belying the notion that it is those who fail who tend to seek religious explanations and solace, it was often those who were successful—and acutely aware that their success was the result of fortuitous circumstances—who gave the most thought to the underlying significance of their good fortune, and in some cases gave an explicit form to their search. In the near total absence of religious institutions of any sort in Shenzhen, they engaged in body cultivation regimens such as *qigong*, established private shrines in their homes, or joined informal prayer or scripture-recitation groups—forms of religiosity that are discussed below. These seekers could find like-minded souls in small bookstores and vegetarian restaurants, run by Christians or Buddhists, which

5. Fan Lizhu, *Dangdai Zhongguoren zongjiao xinyang de bianqian*; Fan Lizhu, Whitehead, & Whitehead, "The Spiritual Search."

made literature available and held small discussion groups or *fangsheng* 放生 outings, that is, releasing captive animals to gain merit.

Indeed, even though the publication of religious literature was in theory strictly controlled in the PRC—Bibles and other scriptures could be sold only on the premises of officially designated places of worship—in practice, it was easier to find religious materials than the works of Marx and Mao. Bootlegged *fengshui* manuals, divinatory almanacs, and *qigong* handbooks were among the main offerings of street-side book vendors during the 1980s and 1990s. Hagiographies and novels on the miraculous feats of *qigong* masters were hot items, selling tens of millions of copies—*Zhuan Falun Part II* by Li Hongzhi was even listed on the best-seller list of the *Beijing Daily* in 1996.[6] Legal points of sale, from small kiosks to large bookstore chains, were invariably well stocked with Bible "stories" in various editions for children and adults, as well as Confucian, Taoist, and Buddhist classics translated into modern Chinese, not to mention the best-selling series of comic books on Laozi, Confucius, and all the great ancient philosophers and Chan masters.

The multistoried, consumer-oriented "book cities" that replaced the dusty Xinhua book depots by the mid-1990s—and that became popular sites for Sunday outings—provided a growing selection of academic works on the *Book of Changes* (*Yijing*) as well as all five of the officially recognized religious traditions (Buddhism, Catholicism, Islam, Protestantism, and Taoism), while works on Nostradamus, Atlantis, and the like—even, for a time, translations of L. Ron Hubbard's novels—were prominently featured on the central displays, alongside self-help literature (*Chicken Soup for the Soul*, *The Purpose-Driven Life*), New-Age titles, and motivational books and videos by management gurus. This type of quasi-religious literature, spanning the range from fringe science to creamy morality and positive-thinking spirituality, was one of the dominant offerings of the small airport bookshops frequented by the new business jet set, where picture books on Guanyin and on the history of Protestantism lay only a glance away from heavy manuals on business accounting and glossy architectural guides on property development—and, by the early 2000s, backpackers' guides to old towns, temples, and Tibetan Buddhist pilgrimage sites.

Among the popular, media-savvy authors who wrote best sellers introducing Chinese traditional spirituality to the public, probably none was as influential as Nan Huaijin 南怀瑾 (b. 1918). Trained in political economy in Mainland Chinese public universities during the war, but also in

---

6. Palmer, *Qigong Fever*, chap. 9.

Chan meditation with some of the leading Buddhist masters of the time, Nan moved to Taiwan with his family in 1949. He lived by writing popular works on Chan Buddhism and traditional culture, and rose in fame to become a highly respected figure in academic and political circles and among the general public. He used his fame to shape public debates, such as when he led a movement to reintroduce the Confucian classics in school training. Hailed as a master of Chinese studies (*guoxue dashi* 國學大師) throughout the Chinese world, he moved to Hong Kong in 1988 and eventually to his home province of Zhejiang on the mainland, whence he gave lectures, was involved in large business investment projects to develop China (he was even something of a management guru), and even acted as an unofficial diplomat between Taiwan and the PRC. His figure, although exceptional in the respect he commanded, was typical of the modern urban *maitre à penser*, blurring the lines between the academic, political, spiritual, and ideological repertoires.

The martial arts subculture became a major gateway into the religious universe of traditional China. The best-selling knight-errant novels by authors such as Louis Cha (pen name Jin Yong 金庸, b. 1924) of Hong Kong became standard reading fare for Chinese teenagers and adults in the 1980s and 1990s, while kung fu films, mass-produced both in Hong Kong and on the mainland, were one of the most popular forms of cinematographic fare.[7] Blockbusters such as *Shaolin Temple* triggered a craze for martial arts and contributed to the *qigong* boom. The kung fu genre strongly influenced the imperial-period soap operas that dominated prime-time television airwaves, starting with *Journey to the West* in the 1980s. All these novels, films, and TV shows were populated with Buddhist monks, Taoist magicians, and invincible heroes who could fly, disappear and reappear at will, read people's minds, and neutralize adversaries with their miraculous inner powers or secret magical potions. Indeed, for the younger generations, these stories were the main, if not the only, source of knowledge on Taoism and, perhaps to a lesser degree, on Buddhism as well; they inspired many vocations to enter the clergy. Children were also exposed to the Chinese pantheon and religious narratives through cartoons, again beginning with *Journey to the West*, in which the Earth God and the Jade Emperor were familiar characters. Also popular in the 1990s was a cartoon series featuring the mischievous child-god Nazha 哪吒 as its hero, not to mention the wave of Japanese cartoons and comics that also featured characters and narratives closely related to Chinese myths and legends.

7. Hamm, *Paper Swordsmen*.

Related to the martial arts lore, healing traditions also transmitted un-structured but deeply evocative bits of religious culture. The secularization and nationalist recycling of the medical and martial arts traditions by both the Nationalist and socialist governments (described in chapter 4) proved to have been incomplete; and although trained with manuals in which all "superstitious" elements had been removed, doctors of Chinese medicine and martial artists alike proved sensitive to discourses about supernatural powers, miracles, and spiritual techniques. Among the population at large, illness episodes frequently brought to the fore, even among secularized middle-class urbanites, themes of possession, exorcism, and magical heal-ing. In this context, the reappearance in Mainland China of spirit mediums giving meanings to illness episodes as well as cheap cures (beginning in the late 1980s, when medicine became increasingly privatized and expensive), working from inconspicuous suburban apartments, was a surprise only to the officials who occasionally found them out; in other parts of the Chinese world, the spirit mediums were more visible, and there were signs that their numbers had increased rather than decreased during the twentieth century.[8] It was common for urbanites to profess atheism and a rejection of superstition and yet consult a given spirit medium because he or she could offer effective cures.

Interest in understanding and controlling fate spurred a huge develop-ment of activities related to traditional divination and the *Book of Changes* (*Yijing*). Seminars, training courses, magazines, and societies devoted to these studies became a major business as well as a favored entry point for urban professionals into the world of traditional Chinese thought. While the real estate boom ushered the growth of a class of professional white-collar geomancers, first in Hong Kong during the 1960s and later through-out the Chinese world, from the mainland hinterland to Western China-towns, many urbanites developed an interest in *fengshui* as amateurs. Such people also studied fate-calculation techniques, especially the more intel-lectual and speculative techniques such as *liuren dunjia* 六壬遁甲, which became chic among investors who had to grapple with notions of luck and chance, not least when they played the stock markets—which became, together with the Macau casinos, the main outlet for the perennial passion for gambling. Easily packaged as scholarly endeavors, *Yijing* studies were an easy venue for recycling Chinese cosmology and fate-controlling tech-niques outside government interference.

Yet another venue for the diffusion of religious culture was the tourism

8. DeBernardi, *The Way That Lives in the Heart*.

industry. Religion had long been present in museums, in a form deemed safely abstracted and relegated to the past by cultural authorities, even though countless exhibitions on Tibetan culture since the late 1980s did play a role in the fad for Tibetan Buddhism among urbanites. But with the appearance of real holidays for urban workers during the 1990s, the local tourism industry brought an ever-increasing number of city dwellers to the famous pilgrimage mountains—such as, for instance, the Shaolin temple 少林寺, where a minority of devoted monks struggled to maintain Buddhism amid myriads of kung fu schools and theme parks—or to the exotic borderlands of Mongolia and Tibet, or the southern ethnic minority-populated areas.[9] Temples or festivals were invariably part of the package, changing local practices that reaffirmed local identities while adapting to tourist tastes[10] as well as the tourists' own perception of religion. There, urban executives rubbed shoulders with old ladies praying and prostrating themselves, and it became increasingly normal to burn some incense on such visits. While tourists were comforted in their view that the more "advanced" urban Han population had left traditional religion behind, they were also invited to rediscover something of the magic and mysterious in their lives.

Finally, starting in the mid-1990s, the Internet became a popular site for the dissemination of religious information, allowing seekers to even more easily circumvent official restrictions on the publication and distribution of printed literature. Thousands of Chinese-language sites on Christianity and Buddhism were available, dwarfing all other religious traditions, although Taoist temples in Hong Kong and Taiwan also established a presence in cyberspace, and individual seekers, mystics, seers, and *fengshui* consultants posted their experiences, formulas, and services.[11] Mainland Chinese cities were thus far from being spiritual and religious deserts. Through the mass media, publishing, and the Internet, it became relatively easy to obtain information produced inside or outside the mainland on a wide variety of traditions, not limited to the five official religions—including, besides Falungong until its banning in 1999, other groups banned on the mainland, such as Yiguandao, and new movements such as Scientology.

Indeed, it should be pointed out that the information on religion described above, while often subjected to some sort of censorship, was very

9. Kolås, *Tourism and Tibetan Culture*; Kang Xiaofei, "Two Temples."
10. Borchert, "Of Temples and Tourists," for a case study among the Yunnan Thai-speaking Buddhists.
11. Palmer, "Cyberspace."

often disseminated outside official or authorized channels for religious literature, which were severely restricted. Ironically, then, religious culture in urban China was to a great extent unregulated. As a result, it became during the 1990s quite similar to that of Taiwan, Hong Kong, and the rest of the Chinese world, where middle- and upper-class urbanites watched the same movies and read the same primers on traditional culture, *Yijing* studies, and self-improvement. Outside the mainland, in the absence of restrictions, religious organizations themselves could be much more active in producing and distributing their own literature—an activity that has traditionally been a privileged way to generate merit in Buddhism and local temples.

In Taiwan in particular, the morality book tradition was very much kept alive, especially by spirit-writing cults, which distributed thousands of titles—which, according to a major social survey, were actually read by a significant proportion (60 percent) of the population.[12] In spite of the intimate link between the discourse of the morality books and traditional cosmology, the collapse—at the official level—of the latter did not cause a fall into irrelevance of the former. Far from it, morality books continued to be revealed, commented on, printed, and distributed (usually for free) by the tens of millions of copies throughout the twentieth and twenty-first centuries, for distribution worldwide. Among the major producers were the redemptive societies, who inherited the role of moral authority and transmitter of the Confucian tradition, and most forcefully articulated morality as the vehicle to self-realization and salvation.[13]

Contrary to widespread opinion, though, morality books did not cling to "traditional values" as a lost paradise of moral virtue irrevocably lost to secular modernity. Contemporary descriptions of hells—a particularly graphic and didactic subgenre of morality books—include both age-old types of sinners (unfilial sons and daughters, butchers, gamblers, and so on) as well as contemporary ones, such as motorists who commit vehicular homicide.[14] Moreover, while prescribing respect for the gods, morality books have never put a strong moral onus on temple and festival attendance; they therefore adapt very well to a secular society in which religion and public life can be separated. Indeed, some argue that late imperial morality books already formulated a highly secularized vision of moral-

12. Ling Chi-Shiang, "Morality Books and the Moral Order."
13. Clart, "Moral Mediums."
14. Song Guangyu, "Cong *diyu youji*."

ity.[15] For instance, gender roles advocated in the morality books compiled since the 1970s are definitely more attuned to contemporary reality, where women work in offices and are potentially financially independent, than to the late imperial model of the house-cloistered, submissive housewife with bound feet.[16] But they have not thrown religiously based conceptions of gender roles through the window either, and have always emphasized the duty to one's kin, particularly filial piety, and proper recognition of one's place in the family and the duties this entails, in terms of mutual support and solidarity.

INDIVIDUAL MORAL PRACTICE: THE CASE OF VEGETARIANISM

Popular notions about morality and personal conduct, especially concerning the nurturing and disciplining of the body, were one domain through which urbanites could easily come into contact with religious culture. The case of food ethics, respect for animal life, and vegetarianism is particularly instructing in this regard. Moral norms defined as rules of purity (*zhaijie* 齋戒) had been shaped throughout imperial history by the contradictory needs to feed ancestors and gods with meat on the one hand, and on the other the widespread notion that taking (animal) life was sinful and that abstinence from meat could produce individual sanctity and purity. Solutions to this dilemma focused first on practicing periodic vegetarianism[17] (on certain dates, such as one's birthday, the eight Buddhist fasting days each month, or at least the first and fifteenth days of the month, as well as certain fasting days linked to specific cults); second, on taboos against eating certain meats (notably beef) considered especially sinful; and third, on avoiding killing animals oneself.[18] On the other hand, permanent vegetarianism (*changzhai* 長齋) was, in late imperial times and until the 1960s, a practice that tended to exclude one from many social networks, where banquets were prime occasions for creating social bonds, and tended to be practiced only by members of Xiantiandao-related groups and redemptive societies, such as the "vegetarian halls" of prewar Taiwan and Yiguandao.

15. Yu Yingshi, *Rujia lunli yu shangren jingshen.*
16. Clart, "Chinese Tradition and Taiwanese Modernity."
17. We include here under the general notion of vegetarianism both permanent abstention from meat and regular practice, whereby one is committed to abstain on fixed dates but not (necessarily) on other days.
18. Goossaert, *L'interdit du bœuf.*

Nineteenth-century Western/missionary polemics on Chinese religion often targeted conceptions of taking animal life as sinful;[19] this attitude was carried over by most of the twentieth-century Chinese intelligentsia, who advocated eating meat as a necessary way of both rejecting superstition and strengthening Chinese bodies.[20] Indeed, both Nationalist and Communist regimes vigorously supported the development of the meat industry, and in particular of the beef industry. While frugality was maintained as a moral value in civic education textbooks and other expressions of state-sanctioned morality, foodstuffs and animals were de-ethicized and medicalized. With the emergence of antisuperstition, vegetarian and purification practices (zhaijie) had been condemned by the state and intellectuals as irrational and backward.

Yet in spite of a century-long rejection by the state of moral diet in favor of a scientist nutritionist discourse, popular morality gradually reinvested vegetarian practices with considerable social and spiritual value. By the end of the twentieth century, changes in vegetarian practice could be observed at different levels. The most important, though the most difficult to apprehend, was a quantitative rise; this was much more apparent in Taiwan than in the rest of the Chinese world, where a similar phenomenon could be observed but on a much smaller scale. Relevant large-scale sociological studies are lacking, but the prevalent discourse of both vegetarians and nonvegetarians is that since the 1970s, vegetarianism has grown ever more visible in the public space. This visibility occurred in a context where meat had only recently become daily fare for the huge majority of the population.

The second change concerned the increasing social acceptance of vegetarian practice. Without having been really stigmatized, permanent vegetarianism had long been associated with socially marginalized religious groups such as Yiguandao. It was now much more easily and publicly assumed by adepts as an ethical lifestyle. Whereas in religious and traditionalist circles, vegetarianism had always been considered a praiseworthy ideal, the *passage à l'acte* was now proving much easier than before. For instance, vegetarian marriage banquets were becoming more common,[21] and in any case represented a real possibility for couples whose families did

---

19. Reinders, *Borrowed Gods*, chap. 10, "Blessed Are the Meat-Eaters."

20. There were some exceptions, though, such as Kang Youwei, who was envisioning universal vegetarianism as part of his political utopia.

21. This is linked to the invention of a Buddhist marriage ritual and discourse: Learman, "Modernity, Marriage, and Religion."

not belong to vegetarian groups. In other words, the social cost of being a permanent vegetarian had considerably decreased since the 1970s.

Concurrently, the social profile of vegetarians was changing. Vegetarianism was traditionally associated with women and older people; many women became vegetarian after the end of active life as a way of sanctifying themselves before death, and taking over a religious role in the family on behalf of relatives who were too immersed in professional life for this practice. As the composition of families changed, the ritual division of labor was also changing, and young people increasingly attempted to sanctify themselves, not entrusting this task to mothers and grandmothers who often did not live with them anymore. If, in fact and in the public eye, vegetarian practice remained a rather feminine type of spirituality and moral practice, its public endorsement by young, active men and women increasingly changed its social significance.

As a consequence, venues for vegetarian practice were also changing. It had always been common that within families, some women were periodic or permanent vegetarians, while cooking meat for their menfolk. But restaurants now reflected change in social practice.[22] Many quality restaurants added a vegetarian section to their menu, and the number of purely vegetarian restaurants increased, especially in the larger cities in the PRC, Taiwan, and Southeast Asia. In Taiwan, it was estimated that until the 1970s, over 90 percent of vegetarian restaurants were managed by Yiguandao adepts, and they were almost always small, cheap, inconspicuous places. Such restaurants were still numerous (maybe two-thirds of the total in Taiwan in 2005), but larger-scale, up-market, and explicitly Buddhist ventures were becoming more visible. In the PRC, the 1980s and 1990s saw the appearance of vegetarian restaurants sometimes linked to Buddhist or Taoist monasteries, catering to pilgrims, tourists, and devotees, but also of urban ventures that renewed the vibrant tradition of the lay engaged Buddhists of the Republican period, following the model of the Gongde lin 功德林 opened in 1922 in Shanghai by a lay Buddhist.[23] In Taiwan and the West, many vegetarian restaurants were opened by members of the charismatic Suma Ching Hai movement (see below) founded in Taiwan in the 1980s.

Indeed, vegetarianism was encouraged, much more actively than in late imperial times, by Buddhist leaders who attempted to construct a modern

22. Goossaert, "Les sens multiples du végétarisme."
23. For the lay vegetarian Buddhists of the Republican period, see Tarocco, *The Cultural Practices*, 31–39.

Buddhist identity and define specific practices for a Buddhist laity. Thus, the spectacular rise of vegetarianism among the Taiwanese middle classes since the 1970s can be linked to the rising profile of Buddhism as a self-assumed identity among the same classes. In Taiwan and Southeast Asia, the rise of vegetarianism was particularly linked with the success of the Tzu Chi Foundation.[24] In vegetarian redemptive societies such as Yiguandao, the peer pressure was such that almost all active members became permanent vegetarians. By contrast, vegetarianism was not imposed on Tzu Chi Foundation members outside the foundation's premises and communal activities. Nonetheless, a high proportion of its millions of members observed some form of periodic vegetarianism as one of their commitments to ethical living. In the PRC, the lay Buddhist communities (*jushilin* 居士林), even though they were not as large as the Tzu Chi Foundation or other Taiwanese new Buddhist groups, also adopted vegetarianism as a sign of their faith and morality.

Vegetarianism's closer identification with Buddhism raised the social prestige of vegetarian practice as a type of modern, socially engaged morality, at the same time that other types of moral practice of respect for life, such as releasing living animals and prohibiting certain meats, declined.[25] It also acquired a dimension of proselytism, with lay vegetarians attempting to convert their friends and kin, while Buddhist organizations exported vegetarianism to other Asian countries.

The rising prestige of vegetarianism as a moral practice was also linked to the globalization of vegetarianism. Reference to the Western vegetarian tradition in its historical depth and philosophical complexity, as well as to the recent flourishing of medical scientific publications advocating vegetarianism as natural and healthy, contributed to the legitimization of Chinese vegetarianism, and was prominent in the discourse of leaders and ordinary adepts; it was for instance adopted by the science-oriented Yan Xin *qigong* movement. The tendency was actually more prominent in the new Buddhist-oriented discourse than in that of the redemptive societies—Yiguandao discourse, for instance, remained closer to traditional morality books.[26]

For many Chinese adepts, vegetarianism was first a question of health—but health considered inseparable from morality. Religious motivations

---

24. C. Julia Huang, *Charisma and Compassion*, 170–71.

25. Goossaert, *L'interdit du bœuf*.

26. A Yiguandao authoritative book on the topic, *Chizhai de zhenyi*, clearly places scientific and health arguments in a position second to respect-for-life morality.

were often expressed only when asked for. For instance, the 2003 SARS epidemic boosted the advocacy and practice of vegetarianism: this came about as the epidemic spawned debates and questioning on the ethical relationship between health and the environment. On the other hand, the discourse on health (meat as toxic) cannot by itself explain the whole range of vegetarian practices, which largely continue to apply, both in individual practice and in restaurants, rules inherited from the older purity codes, including bans on the five pungent spices (*wuhun* 五葷 or *wuxin* 五辛: garlic, onions, and so on), alcohol, tobacco, eggs, and dairy products.

Contemporary justifications for these rules focused on self-control and body discipline as the precondition for a moral life—the *wuhun* and alcohol exciting desires and sexuality, and lowering the capacity for self-control—rather than medical health. A discourse distinguishing ethical/religious vegetarianism (including *wuhun* and alcohol) from medically supported abstention from meat was emerging, but it was certainly the former that represented *vegetarianism* for most people, adepts and nonadepts alike. Similarly, a sizable section of the vegetarian population criticized the "imitation meats" made of vegetarian ingredients but looking and tasting like meats, because these were seen as dishonest and morally ambiguous in contrast to sincere, simple vegetarian food.[27]

So, besides traditional forms of moral food practices (regular vegetarian observances on certain days, and the permanent vegetarianism of some of the redemptive societies), new forms appeared, such as chic, health-conscious vegetarianism (enhanced by the very high culinary standards of many vegetarian restaurants), often combined with concern for the environment and organic products, and termed "vegetarian food for prolonging life" (*yangsheng sushi* 養生素食). On the other hand, more ascetic forms were also in evidence, where diet was considered as one among several elements of a life of discipline and moral hygiene. This strongly ethical and, in some cases, "Protestant"-like inner-worldly ascetic approach to vegetarianism made it one of the strongest expressions of the contemporary reformulation of traditional morality in China. This ethical vegetarianism was advocated as a contribution not only to the motherland but to the whole universe: it was thus quite different from state formulations of ascetic devotion to the nation, and yet in some regards in continuity with it.

In some new urban settlements (such as Shenzhen discussed above), where traditional religious institutions were largely absent, vegetarian restaurants served as a meeting point for people in search of moral norms and

27. This debate was already lively in late imperial times: Kieschnick, "Buddhist Vegetarianism," 205.

ethical living.[28] Incidentally, these restaurants, along with temples, were the major places where morality books were distributed. The vegetarian business itself was described as a way of religious living (*xiudao* 修道), as it contributes to generating merit and advocating morality.

The numerous conversions to vegetarianism observed in the Chinese world since the 1970s thus illustrate the reinterpretation of traditional rules of ritual and moral purity by individuals in search of health, demonstrable ethical living, and this-worldly asceticism, through mixed references ranging from Buddhist and redemptive society merit generation to a global vegetarianism drawing on science and modernity.

EXPRESSIONS OF URBAN RELIGIOSITY

In the late twentieth century, the largest Chinese cities were thus characterized by weakened or nonexistent communal religious institutions, the proliferation in some areas (notably Taiwan) of individualistic cults, and religious knowledge widely but thinly diffused through modern media and practices of healing, morality, and disciplines of the body such as vegetarianism. In this context, it was possible for individuals to live their lives without ever actively thinking about religion or engaging in any form of religious practice, just as it was possible for seekers to follow their own pathways by seeking out and combining practices and experiences on their own. However, they were not completely left to their own devices: several movements, from *qigong* exercising to neotraditionalist piety, Buddhist charity, and cosmopolitan Christian spirituality, emerged as relatively structured outlets for people's religious and spiritual yearnings. They built on the common religious culture found in the media and echoed many of this culture's themes. Although these movements followed different trajectories, and enjoyed varying degrees of success in different political regimes, they can all be compared as religious productions of Chinese modernity, through which it was possible to cultivate one's personal identity as a modern individual by different forms of engagement with reinvented Chinese traditions and universal values.

Body Cultivation Movements

Body cultivation traditions were among the most resilient of the forms of religious culture to survive, and even to thrive, in the context of secular-

28. Fan Lizhu, Whitehead, & Whitehead, "The Spiritual Search," 57–59.

ized urban culture. On Mainland China, these took the form of the *qigong* movement, which represented, by far, the most prevalent expression of popular religiosity in the cities, from the late 1970s until the suppression of Falungong in 1999. The political aspects of *qigong* and the suppression of Falungong are discussed in chapter 12; we are interested for now in the *qigong* movement as an expression of urban religiosity. It is impossible to quantify the number of people who regularly practiced—many accounts claim 100 million practitioners—but we would estimate that about one-fifth of urban residents had some form of direct contact with *qigong* during that period.[29]

That *qigong* should have taken an increasingly "religious" turn during this period was not anticipated by the Party leaders, scientists, bureaucrats, and journalists who played an important role in promoting the movement. Indeed, the modern category of *qigong* had been created by health ministry officials in 1949, as part of a project of secularizing and institutionalizing Chinese medicine by extracting useful techniques from the "feudal superstitious" context in which they had traditionally been practiced (described in chapter 4). The *qigong* category was designed to incorporate all the useful traditional gymnastic, breathing, and mind control techniques, which could be utilized for medical therapy and for training healthy citizens. During the 1950s and 1960s, this modernized *qigong* had been taught and practiced in cadres' hospitals and sanatoriums in the big cities and at the coastal resort town of Beidaihe. Banned as a feudal superstition in 1964, the traditional body technologies continued to be practiced and taught underground during the Cultural Revolution.

By the mid-1970s, however, groups of cancer patients began to congregate in Beijing parks to learn *qigong* from the artist Guo Lin 郭林, who had cured herself of cancer through the breath and body techniques—inaugurating the use of public spaces for mass *qigong* practice, which spread to most urban parks by the early 1980s. This movement was spurred by the appearance of thousands of "*qigong* masters," who went public in the more open political climate. Each master taught his own standardized "method," or set of exercises—a *gongfa* 功法—which typically drew explicitly on Buddhist and Taoist cosmology and symbols to explain the technique in the instructional manuals. Informal groups of adepts formed around the masters, eventually becoming more structured national and international networks of trainers who led groups of practitioners at practice points throughout the country and abroad.

29. On the *qigong* movement, see Palmer, *Qigong Fever*.

While most methods involved standing and/or sitting meditation, several, such as the "Flying Crane" (Hexiangzhuang 鶴翔莊) and "Spontaneous Five-Animals Frolic" (Zifa wuqinxi donggong 自發五禽戲動功), were designed to trigger trance states called "spontaneous movements qigong," so that, in the 1980s, it became commonplace to see groups of qigong practitioners hugging trees, rolling on the ground, crying, burping, or making wild kung fu–style movements.[30] It was not rare for practitioners to begin chattering in incomprehensible "cosmic language" (yuzhou yu 宇宙語), a phenomenon akin to speaking in tongues.

One of the more salient qigong techniques was the external emission of qi by a master or trainer toward the body of a sick person. The fabled efficacy of this practice turned many masters into charismatic figures, who came to be seen as miracle doctors (shenyi 神醫) by the public. This perception was fanned by the media, which fueled a fascination with the paranormal through sensational reports on strange phenomena, such as children who had the ability to read with their ears, others who could move objects at a distance, UFOs, and the like. According to ancient texts, martial arts lore, and the miraculous feats attributed to contemporary grandmasters, the mysterious powers of qigong included the ability to control the winds and rains, to disappear and reappear at another spot, to predict the future, and to use qi to deflect incoming enemy missiles. These powers became a favorite subgenre in the booming pseudoscientific pulp literature on the unsolved riddles of the universe.

Many masters were invited to perform to packed auditoriums of government officials, while some were invited to perform their feats at the Chinese New Year television extravaganza. It was rumored that the most powerful masters, such as Zhang Baosheng 張寶勝 and Yan Xin 嚴新, were frequently summoned to Zhongnanhai to treat the ailing generation of CCP gerontocrats. Yan Xin and others acquired a following akin to that of a pop star—a phenomenon further amplified when they started giving "power-inducing scientific lectures" (daigong kexue shiyan baogaohui 帶功科學實驗報告會), in which they emitted their qi to audiences of up to twenty thousand (in the case of Yan Xin), filling sports stadiums in Guangzhou and Shanghai in 1990. Adepts came from all social classes, with large numbers of retired people and women represented.

Although initially focused on the body and healing, qigong practices and experiences drew practitioners ever deeper into the world of Chinese traditional mysteries. Qigong manuals and courses typically included references

---

30. Ots, "The Silenced Body—the Expressive Leib."

to, if not the direct study of, the *Book of Changes* and Taoist and Buddhist scriptures. Some methods, such as Zhonggong 中功, billed themselves as all-encompassing sciences or cultural systems, which could be applied not only for personal health and healing but also in the realms of scientific methodologies, social etiquette, organizational management, agricultural production, and space exploration.[31] Other methods insisted on the moral dimension of *qigong* practice, stressing that cultivation of the body should not be limited to the practice of outward techniques, but also must involve living a virtuous life at all moments. Here *qigong* became a basis for a moral critique of the prevailing atmosphere of materialism and corruption. Many methods displayed an implicit millenarian or utopian streak, holding the promise that *qigong* in general, or their method in particular, held the key to future bliss and prosperity, and vanquishing the moral decay of present-day society. Falungong, as one of the *qigong* methods, went farthest in this direction, elevating the practice and defense of the virtues of truthfulness, compassion, and tolerance into fundamental, transcendental principles.[32]

The banning of and crackdown on Falungong in July 1999—which will be further discussed in chapter 12—led to the disbanding of most *qigong* groups and the end of *qigong* as a mass movement. Although *qigong* could still be practiced in parks, only five simple and completely secularized forms vetted by the Sports Bureau were allowed. Body cultivation remained popular, but it was now more often practiced under other names than the now politically suspect *qigong*: in Chan summer camps offered by Buddhist monasteries and courses in nourishing life held by Taoist groups; in morning scripture-recitation and meditation sessions promoted by some Confucian movements;[33] and in the increasingly ubiquitous yoga studios and New Age therapies which became fashionable among upwardly mobile professionals seeking relaxation in the large urban centers, both in Mainland China and in Hong Kong and Taiwan.[34]

Meanwhile, beginning in the 1980s, the *qigong* movement had been exported outside the mainland and had become part of the local religious landscape in Taiwan, Hong Kong, Singapore, and overseas,[35] but it did not experience the same massive success as on the mainland. This was undoubtedly because body cultivation traditions were already well developed

31. Palmer, "Chinese Religious Innovation."
32. Ownby, *Falun Gong*.
33. Billioud & Thoraval, "Jiaohua," 15.
34. Chen Jialun, "Xin shidai yundong."
35. On Taiwan, see Zheng Zhiming, "Taiwan qigong tuanti"; on Singapore, see Lim Chee-Han, "Purging the Ghost of Descartes"; on the United States, see Komjathy, "Qigong in America."

and active in these areas. In Taiwan, for instance, and to a lesser degree in Hong Kong, a bewildering variety of Chan meditation and Taoist inner alchemical cultivation schools flourished among middle-class urbanites.[36] Urban meditation halls, offering training classes and retreats for professionals in refined downtown settings, provided a new type of sacred space, a refuge from the stresses of professional life in which individuals could nurture their bodies and plunge into other mental realms.

In 1979, a former KMT high official turned dissident newspaper publisher in Taiwan, Li Yujie, who had been a leading member of the Tiandejiao redemptive society, founded his own religion upon receiving a revelation from the Heavenly Lord (Tiandi). The group gave itself the dual mission of ending the cold war and averting the imminent world nuclear apocalypse, and of reuniting China and restoring Sun Yat-sen's Three Principles of the People. These goals were to be accomplished through congregational Confucian-style prayer, a modernized form of sitting meditation derived from Taoist alchemy, and a *qigong* method similar to the external *qi* therapy popular on the mainland. Like some of the mainland *qigong* associations, The Heavenly Lord Teachings (Tiandijiao 天帝教) claimed to be an all-encompassing system of scientific knowledge. In the first quarter century of its existence, the movement attracted two hundred thousand followers, largely professionals and intellectuals, and had established branches in Japan and California.[37]

The Numinous Possession (Lingji 靈乩) movement in Taiwan, like *qigong* on the mainland, democratized body cultivation techniques by making them easily accessible to all. Lingji drew on Taiwan's rich culture of spirit mediumism, but adepts, unlike traditional spirit mediums, acted not as instruments of gods operating to serve clients but were rather individuals on a pathway of spiritual fulfillment who entered trances for their personal benefit, during which they "communicated" with gods without losing themselves entirely to them.[38] Séances of informal groups took place anywhere, from temples to parks to ice cream parlors, undermining traditional configurations of sacred space. The basic practice of the Lingji, in which the adept begins in still meditation, then enters a state of spontaneous movements sometimes akin to Chinese opera or martial arts, was similar to phenomena common among *qigong* practitioners on the mainland, and was widespread among several new Taiwanese religious groups as well, rang-

---

36. Zheng Zhiming, *Dangdai xinxing zongjiao.*
37. Palmer, "Tao and Nation."
38. Marshall, "Moving the Spirit on Taiwan."

ing from the Imperial Teachings of Maitreya 彌勒皇教 to the apocalyptic Hai Tze Tao (Haizidao 亥子道). The first was founded in 1987 by Chen Jinlong 陳金龍, who claimed to be Maitreya after having practiced *qigong*; it conducted meditation and *qigong* classes and *qi*-healing sessions, and ran a meditation supplies and Buddhist amulet shop as well as a temple in Taipei. The Hai Tze Tao was founded in 1984 by Lin Xuanhe 林玄和, who broke off from Yiguandao. Lin combined spirit writing and *qi* healing with Yiguandao genealogy, and considered himself the Supreme Lawgiver of the Universe (Wushang fawang 無上法王).

Many of the groups mentioned above went global, with branches in all major Western and Asian countries. In the West, Chinese body cultivation traditions ranging from *taijiquan* to *qigong* and inner alchemy were, after an initial period of being promoted as "Chinese yoga" in the 1970s, usually disseminated under the label of Taoism. The Taoist Tai Chi Society, based near Toronto and founded in 1971 by immigrants from Hong Kong, opened a large network of Tai Chi centers and Taoist shrines in over twenty countries. The Thai Chinese Mantak Chia 謝明德 (b. 1944), together with American Michael Winn and other collaborators, wrote a set of popular *qigong* and *neidan* manuals and courses, with training centers in Europe, the United States, and Thailand.[39]

Perhaps the most globalized Chinese self-cultivation movement, and one that compares with Falungong or the True Buddha School (see below) in terms of its strong charismatic nature and focus on the method dispensed by the master, was the Supreme Master (abbreviated in English as Suma) Ching Hai 清海無上師 movement. Its founder, Ching Hai, was born in Vietnam in 1950 of ethnic Chinese descent and educated in both Catholicism and Buddhism. She studied and married in Europe before embarking on a spiritual journey in India and Nepal, to be initiated in yogic techniques based on meditating on cosmic light and sound—techniques that are also taught in various neo-Hindu movements in the West. She moved to Taiwan around 1984 and was ordained as a Buddhist nun. She initiated her own movement in 1986, teaching her meditation technique, called Guanyin famen 觀音法門, establishing meditation centers, and initiating disciples. Tensions with the monastic establishment rose, and beginning in 1990 Ching Hai quit the order, changing her monastic robes for self-designed flamboyant dresses and jewels, which she soon began to market as "celestial jewelry" (she also paints and engages in all sorts of fashion

---

39. Siegler, "Chinese Traditions," "Fluid yet Grounded in the Tao," "Daoism beyond Modernity"; Siegler & Palmer, *Dream Trippers*.

design and aesthetic pursuits). She moved to California in 1996, where she now manages a global movement (unofficially claiming as many as 2 million members, with a good number of nonethnic Chinese converts) and operates a TV channel and various media that vigorously promote vegetarianism, the Guanyin meditation technique, and the salvational power of the Supreme Master. While her teachings resemble New Age religiosity in their inclusion of all religions into a nature-oriented, individualistic, theistic discourse, her ethnic-Chinese followers in Taiwan and in the West seem to be mostly attracted by the charismatic powers of Ching Hai, and many have a salvationist vegetarian background that connect her to other Chinese self-cultivational movements.[40]

The Suma Ching Hai movement, along with Zhonggong and Falungong, were the most notable of what Patricia Thornton has called China's new "cybersects,"[41] groups banned in Mainland China that moved into cyberspace and "evolved into far-flung multinational conglomerates incorporating media enterprises, public relations firms, and commercial operations beneath a loose umbrella of shifting entrepreneurial, political, and spiritual interests."[42] Whereas Suma Ching Hai's virtual conglomerate focused on promoting vegetarianism and the sale of merchandise such as "Supreme Kitchen Fortune Cookies" and glossy pictorial books depicting the master and her ducks in a lush tropical park, Zhonggong and Falungong used cyberspace as a base for campaigns against the CCP (discussed in chapter 13).

Redemptive Societies and Confucian Movements

While the *qigong* movement evolved on the mainland, in Taiwan and the Southeast Asian communities it was the redemptive societies that seemed, at least until the 1990s, to represent the most widespread and fastest-growing type of "modern" religiosity. As inheritors of the reformist Confucian movements of the Republican period (see chapter 4), they were the principal vehicles for the transmission and popularization of Confucian-style ritual and texts—practices that later reappeared on the mainland in the 1990s, but independently of redemptive societies, to become a mass phenomenon in the early 2000s.

40. Ding Renjie, *Shehui fenhua*, 273–420, 525–40.
41. Thornton, "The New Cybersects."
42. Thornton, "Manufacturing Dissent," 182.

The largest redemptive society in post-1949 Taiwan was Yiguandao, which had been established there in the late 1940s in the wake of the KMT's flight to the island, just before it was banned and ruthlessly suppressed on the mainland. The postwar development of Yiguandao in Taiwan, where it had not been previously present, spreading from there to Southeast Asia, North America, and Europe, thus marked a significant rupture from its previous history on the mainland.[43] On the island, Yiguandao interacted with two types of related religious groups (integrating some of them, and spawning others) that had been present there since the Qing: the vegetarian halls 齋堂, which, to secure their legitimacy under the Japanese administration, had claimed a Buddhist affiliation; and the spirit-writing cults (phoenix halls 鸞堂), which claimed to transmit the true Confucian teachings through direct revelations by the gods. During the Japanese occupation of Taiwan, as part of a movement by teachers, entrepreneurs, and wealthy farmers to resist Japanization policies, an attempt had been made to unify the phoenix halls under a common liturgy and doctrine, called the Divine Teachings of the Confucian School (Ruzong shenjiao 儒宗神教). By 1978, some five hundred phoenix halls registered as an association titled the Republic of China Association of the Divine Teachings of the Confucian School 中華民國儒宗神教會. This was but one of several, often short-lived, attempts to federate phoenix halls into a single Confucian association; another was the China Confucian Society 中國儒教會, registered in 2000.[44]

Yiguandao actively proselytized among members and leaders of vegetarian halls and spirit-writing cults. Several of these groups' temples switched their affiliation to Yiguandao; others, while resisting this tendency, adopted elements of the Yiguandao pantheon, practices, and teachings.[45] Although banned in Taiwan by the KMT for its alleged ties with the Japanese and/or Communists, repression was mild enough that the movement was able to experience rapid and sustained growth. Even as it remained an underground network, with its temples registering under other names, according to some reports, 20 percent of the island's population had had some contact with Yiguandao. By the time it was legalized just after the lifting of martial law in 1987, the movement had become one of the largest or-

43. For a sketch of Yiguandao history in Taiwan, see Jordan, "The Recent History of the Celestial Way"; Lu Yunfeng, *The Transformation of Yiguan Dao*.

44. Clart, "Confucius and the Mediums," 21.

45. Clart, "The Phoenix and the Mother."

ganized religions in Taiwan, with the number of initiates reaching almost 1 million.[46] It also expanded among the Chinese communities of Malaysia, Thailand, Singapore, and elsewhere in Southeast Asia, where, along with other redemptive societies such as the Dejiao (discussed in chapter 8), it provided one of the main forms of social organization and cultural transmission for overseas Chinese communities.[47]

Yiguandao can be noted for how it integrated the many strands of the earlier salvationist groups, redemptive societies, and Confucian movements into a single system. It inherited the tradition of the vegetarian halls and was known for being behind the vast majority of the thousands of vegetarian restaurants that flourished on the island. It expanded the Eternal Unborn Mother cult, the three-stage eschatology, and the Three- (or Five-) in-One syncretism of earlier salvationist groups and redemptive societies. However, the importance of spirit writing was progressively reduced in the 1970s; this was replaced by the large-scale promotion of classes to study the Confucian classics and other Chinese scriptures. The teachers of these classes were Yiguandao "lecturers," who had to follow a four-year program of systematic training in the classics. Yiguandao thus made China's elite cultural tradition available to millions of upwardly mobile Taiwanese and overseas Chinese. Associated with Taiwan's new entrepreneurial class— Zhang Rongfa 張榮發 (b. 1927), the chairman of Asia's largest container shipping company, Evergreen (established in 1968), was a declared follower, and many company bosses established Yiguandao shrines in their factories—the movement promoted what was hailed as a "Confucian work ethic."[48] It had a certain influence on popular religious culture, with many splinter groups and new groups founded by ex-members offering endless variations on the basic Yiguandao structure, such as Hai Tze Dao mentioned above, and the Great Way of Maitreya (Mile dadao 彌勒大道).

Other Mainland Chinese redemptive societies, such as the Daoyuan/ Red Swastika Society, the Wanguo daodehui (Worldwide Ethical Society), the Zailijiao (Teaching of the Abiding Principle), and the Tiandejiao (Heavenly Virtues teachings), had also established themselves in Taiwan after the CCP takeover of the mainland. However, though some of them enjoyed a legal status denied to Yiguandao, most of them never penetrated deeply among the Taiwanese population, and stagnated. More significant were the new redemptive societies that were founded in Taiwan itself by former

46. Bosco, "Yiguan Dao," 424.
47. Soo Khin Wah, "A Study of the Yiguan Dao (Unity Sect)."
48. Song Guangyu, *Tiandao chuandeng*, 359–426.

mainland KMT officials, including the previously mentioned Tiandijiao. The Imperial Teachings of the Yellow Emperor (Xuanyuan huangjiao 軒轅 黃教), for instance, founded in 1952 by Wang Hansheng 王寒生 (1899– 1989), a former KMT leader in Changchun and member of the national legislature, aimed to restore the "national religion" of archaic (pre-Han) China, in which state and religion were a single entity. However, it was only able to legally register by abandoning such a political project and adopting a church-style congregational model, with the Confucian classics as its main scriptures. In practice, it became a federation of hundreds of communal temples registering under its banner. Although its membership expanded dramatically in the 1970s (from 10,000 to 100,000), most of the followers—as well as the temples affiliated with his organization—practiced a traditional style of popular religiosity, thwarting Wang Hansheng's attempts to eradicate "superstition" from his own national cult, which rapidly declined after his death in 1989.[49]

In Taiwan, Confucian ritual and scriptural study thus found expression through spirit-writing groups and redemptive societies, in which they were integrated in kaleidoscopic combinations with worship forms characteristic of temple religion, vegetarianism, body cultivation, Buddhism, and Taoism. This Confucian revival occurred in Taiwan from the 1950s to 1980s, at a time when, on the mainland, anything associated with Confucius was viciously attacked as the essence of reactionary feudalism. But in the post-Mao period, some scholars and officials proposed a positive reevaluation of Confucius. These discussions were largely confined to academics and reflected in some political speeches and state-sponsored rituals (at Confucius's ancestral hall at Qufu, for example), which will be discussed in chapter 12.

By the late 1990s and early 2000s, however—after the collapse of the *qigong* movement, which had been the main popular movement of cultural revitalization during the Deng era—the Confucian revival became a truly mass movement in Mainland China. This took a bewildering variety of forms, usually centered on the study of the Confucian classics and other ancient scriptures. Thousands of private academies of various forms sprouted across China, from university-affiliated institutes to charismatic networks of preachers, offering formal and informal courses in reading the classics, training programs for entrepreneurs seeking cultural capital and spiritual purpose, summer camps for youth, and children's moral education

---

49. Jochim, "Flowers, Fruit, and Incense"; Lin Guoping, *Dangdai Taiwan zongjiao*, 146–47; Wang Jianchuan & Li Shiwei, "Taiwan xuanyuanjiao."

classes.[50] While a few advocated a top-down imposition of Confucianism as a state religion, or as the PRC's civil religion, most were popular groups wary of state intervention; some of them even separated themselves from a "corrupt" mainstream society.[51]

Many of these initiatives drew inspiration from the Classics Recitation Movement 讀經運動, launched in Taiwan in 1994 by Wang Caigui 王財貴, a student of the Hong Kong–based philosopher Mou Zongsan 牟宗三 (1909–1995) and professor at the Taizhong Teachers' College in Taiwan, who urged the memorization of the classics by children as a way to develop their inner potential, nurture their virtues and social skills, and inculcate their love for Chinese culture. The movement quickly spread in schools, associations, temples, and redemptive societies (which had already been holding such classes for adults) in Taiwan and Hong Kong, and began to attract attention on the mainland. In 1997, Nan Huaijin, whose best-selling books had been the first point of contact with China's spiritual traditions for millions of Mainlanders in the post-Mao era, formally supported the movement through a foundation he had established in Hong Kong. Within the next decade, it was organizing programs at dozens of Chinese cities, reaching some 5 million to 6 million children.[52] Nan himself moved back to the mainland in 2004, where he established his own academy near Suzhou.

In contrast to Taiwan and the diasporic communities, where spirit-writing groups and redemptive societies had for decades been the main purveyors of popular Confucianism, the revival on the mainland typically took less explicitly religious forms, even if some intellectuals did renew the call for the establishment of Confucianism as the national religion (see chapter 12). Some academies held discreet rituals, and others republished the works of leading Republican-era redemptive society masters, such as Duan Zhengyuan 段正元 (1864–1940), founder of the Daode xueshe, and Wang Fengyi 王鳳儀 (1864–1937), a charismatic healer who had become a leader of the Wanguo daodehui in Manchuria. The latter's works were propagated by one of the largest Confucian-revivalist groups: the Yidan xuetang 一耽學堂, established in 2001 by Beijing University graduate Pang Fei 逄飛, which became a nationwide network of volunteers dedicated to the dissemination of a practical Confucian ethic in social relations. Yidan xuetang practice incorporated Confucian learning with body cultivation, with groups meeting in parks in the morning to do breathing

50. Billioud & Thoraval, "Jiaohua."
51. Billioud & Thoraval, "The Contemporary Revival of Confucianism."
52. Ji Zhe, "Educating through Music"; "Traditional Education."

exercises, and slow-rhythm recitation of the classics. In 2006, popular interest in Confucianism reached a new peak with the airing on China Central Television of a program on the *Analects*, read and commented by Yu Dan 于丹, a professor in media studies. Her commentaries, which gave easy-to-understand and practical interpretations of the Confucian teachings, were published in book form and were an instant best seller, with millions of copies sold.[53] In another striking example, an utopian ascetic community, the Lujiang Center for Cultural Education 盧江文化教育中心, founded by a Taiwanese Buddhist monk in rural Anhui, trained schoolteachers in Confucian morality with the slogan Harmonious Society Begins with Me, until it was closed by the government in 2009.[54] This was one case among many of Buddhists contributing to self-avowed Confucian movements.[55]

Lay Buddhist Movements

Besides redemptive society leaders, the Mainland Chinese refugees who settled in Taiwan in the wake of the KMT retreat also included Buddhist monks, who would play a significant role in the development of Buddhism on the island, where the presence of monastic Buddhism had been weakened by being cut off from the major training monasteries across the straits during the Japanese colonial period. Perhaps the weakness of Buddhist institutions provided favorable conditions for the development of reformist "humanistic Buddhism" there. Indeed, we may recall that Taixu's reforms had been largely rejected by the sangha (monastic community) in his day; under the socialist regime, political control over Buddhist orthodoxy stifled most innovation. In the post-Mao reform period on the mainland, the political orthodoxy of Buddhism did encourage, at least in theory, the religion's development along lines similar to those previously advocated by Taixu, but the institutional configuration was such that lay Buddhist movements were still constrained, and only small-scale modern movements opened to laity could be launched—such as the often-cited case of Bailin Temple 柏林寺 in Hebei, whose clerical leader, Jinghui 净慧 (b. 1933), advocated "living Chan" (*shenghuo chan* 生活禪) and held popular Chan-meditation summer camps for youth, many of them university students.[56]

53. Billioud & Thoraval, "Jiaohua."
54. Dutournier & Ji Zhe, "Social Experimentation."
55. Billioud & Thoraval, "The Contemporary Revival of Confucianism."
56. Ji Zhe, "Religion, Youth and Modernity"; Yang Fenggang & Wei Dedong, "The Bailin Buddhist Temple."

It was Taiwan, then, that became the world center of reformist Chinese Buddhism, which by the end of the 1990s had become the dominant form of institutionalized religion on the island.[57] Some of the groups within this movement adopted a radical stance of eschewing the monkhood altogether, such as the Modern Chan Society 現代禪 in Taiwan, which offered to lay Chan meditators an organized hierarchy in which they could become a form of lay clergy.[58] Other Chan groups were led by monks and combined monasticism with the active promotion of Chan Buddhist meditation, doctrines, and precepts among the general public through retreats, summer camps, research institutes, newspapers, TV stations, museums, and Web sites.[59] These developments stand in contrast to the late imperial and early twentieth-century practice, where only a few devoted laypersons would seriously engage in Chan meditation. The Chung Tai Chan Szu 中台禪寺, for example, beginning in the 1980s, established over sixty centers in Taiwan, Canada, and the United States. The Dharma Drum Mountain (Fagushan 法鼓山) Chan temple, built in 1989 by Sheng Yen 聖嚴 (1931–2009), who after long stays in Japan, America, and Europe promoted a cosmopolitan and modern form of Chan Buddhism, claimed 400,000 followers in Taiwan and 100,000 overseas by the early twenty-first century.[60]

The modern Chan movements' focus on individual meditation can be seen as a manifestation of the craze for self-cultivation within the intellectual framework of scriptural Buddhism, a framework that, thanks to the efforts of charismatic reformist and scholarly monks such as Yinshun 印順 (1906–2005) and laypersons such as Nan Huaijin, had risen in prestige since the 1960s and was widely recognized, in both academia and the general public, as one of the world's great intellectual traditions. Similarly, movements inspired from Tibetan Buddhism enjoyed a growing popularity among Han Chinese in Mainland China, Hong Kong, and Taiwan since the 1970s, renewing and expanding on the Sino-Tibetan cultural encounters of the Republican period. On the mainland, it was possible for intrepid seekers to find the "real thing" in Tibet itself, under Tibetan lamas. Tibetan monasteries, especially those located in the Sino-Tibetan border areas, such as the great monastic complex of Labrang in Gansu, reported growing numbers of Han Chinese joining the monastic orders, while thousands of laypeople, many of whom were Han, braved the impos-

---

57. Jiang Canteng, *Taiwan fojiao, Taiwan jindai fojiao.*
58. Ji Zhe, "The Establishment of a Lay Clergy."
59. Zheng Zhiming, *Taiwan dangdai xinxing fojiao.*
60. Hsiao & Schak, "Taiwan's Socially Engaged Buddhist Groups."

sible roads and harsh climate of the Golok grasslands to pitch camp at a complex near Serta in remote northwestern Sichuan, to study under the charismatic lama Khenpo Jikphun.[61] In cities such as Chengdu, Shanghai, and Shenzhen, wealthy businesspeople personally invited and hosted "living Buddhas" from Tibet.

But for even larger numbers, who had neither the stamina to make the trek to Tibet nor the wealth to maintain a relationship with a personal master, schools of Tantric practice provided a structured access to the famed spiritual mysteries of the Roof of the World. On the mainland, this access usually took the form of *qigong* organizations, such as the Tantric Qigong Association 藏密氣功專業委員會. Founded by Liu Shanglin 劉尚林, a CCP member who claimed to have been initiated by a reincarnate lama, the association was popular in the northeastern Manchurian provinces during the 1990s. In Taiwan, access came through explicitly religious groups, such as the Fu-chih Buddhist Academy 福智佛學院, founded by master Jih Chang 日常 (1929–2004) in 1987, and the True Buddha School 真佛宗, which was founded in 1969 through the revelation of a spirit medium of a Cihuitang spirit-writing temple to a member of the Presbyterian Church, Lu Shengyan 盧勝彥 (b. 1945). In the revelation, Lu Shengyan was ordered to accept instructions from Taoist masters, with whom he studied for a few years; eventually he turned increasingly to Tibetan Buddhism. The True Buddha School, which established its headquarters in Seattle, Washington, USA, in the early 1990s, offered practitioners a combination of body cultivation and meditation with congregational participation in Tantric rituals, as well as a relatively easy progression through a spiritual hierarchy. Mail-order initiations could be conferred through visualizations, by sending an application card and check to the head office in Seattle. In this fashion, the number of "members" increased from 40,000 in 1984 to 4 million in 1996.[62]

But it was the groups claiming an explicit affiliation to Taixu's "humanistic Buddhism" reforms that had the greatest impact. One of the earliest of these was Foguangshan 佛光山 (Buddha's Light Mountain), established in 1967 by Hsing Yun 星雲 (b. 1927), a student of Taixu's, who over the years built up a massive complex near Kaohsiung, including a monastery, a museum, a hotel, a library, study halls, offices, hospitals, and clinics, and a daily newspaper, the *Merit Times* 人間福報. Hsing Yun regularly traveled the world to spread his message at mass Dharma Assemblies featuring multimedia sound and light effects. With an international network of temples—including the Hsi Lai temple 西來寺, near Los Angeles, the largest Buddhist temple in the United States—and a claimed following of over 1 million in the early 2000s, Foguangshan established itself as the most influential comprehensive Buddhist institution in Taiwan. It put a strong emphasis on intellectual study, with a worldwide network of universities and an active program of research and publications.

Even more visible than Foguangshan from the second half of the 1990s was the Buddhist Compassion Relief Tzu Chi Foundation (Ciji gongdehui, 慈濟功德會), which, through its single-minded focus on volunteer charitable works, grew from an initial core of 293 followers in 1968 to reach over 5 million regular cash contributors in the mid-1990s, making the foundation into the largest NGO in Taiwan, with annual revenues of US$150 million and assets, in the form of hospitals and properties, valued as high as $9 billion.[63] The nun Cheng Yen 證嚴 (b. 1937), who founded the movement in 1966, was a disciple of the famous monk Yinshun, himself a student of Taixu's. She was reportedly stimulated to organize a small group of Buddhist laywomen to help the poor and sick after an encounter with Roman Catholic nuns, who asked her why Buddhists devoted all their energies to their otherworldly progress rather than helping those who suffer in this world. Her group of volunteers grew slowly, and she first gained renown throughout Taiwan when she succeeded against all odds to acquire government land and raise sufficient funds to build a modern hospital in the impoverished town of Hualien. Within ten years, from the late eighties to late nineties, the number of lay volunteer "commissioners," who wore distinctive navy-blue uniforms, grew from five hundred to fifteen thousand. They formed the center of wider networks of supporters who could be mobilized for disaster relief and related projects, whether in local communities or overseas, such as in North Korea, South Africa, or Iraq. The Tzu Chi Foundation caused a sensation after the great earthquake of September 21, 1999, in Taiwan, when its thousands of volunteers appeared within minutes of the quake, displaying a dedication, visibility, and logistical efficiency far greater than that of government rescue efforts.

The cumulative effect of these lay Buddhist movements in Taiwan was to turn Buddhism into the island's top religion in terms of declared adherents. Until the 1990s, though it was common for people to hire the services

---

63. On the Tzu Chi Foundation, see C. Julia Huang, *Charisma and Compassion*; C. Julia Huang & Weller, "Merit and Mothering."

of Buddhist monks for funerals and other rituals, it was rare to explicitly claim a Buddhist identity. But by the 1990s, surveys indicated that between 26 and 38 percent of Taiwanese claimed to be Buddhist, while 12 percent claimed to have taken part in a Tzu Chi Foundation activity.[64]

A similar trend could be observed in Singapore, where the number of Chinese claiming a Buddhist religious identity increased from 34.3 percent in 1980 to 53.6 percent in 2000, with most of the increase occurring in the 1990s.[65] In Hong Kong, where there were only two hundred Buddhist monks[66] and virtually no new vocations from within the territory during the mid-1990s, it was lay Buddhists who were increasingly active in the opening of schools, hospitals, and social services, especially after the 1997 handover to the PRC. The number of declared Buddhists likewise nearly doubled, from 6.6 to 11.6 percent of the population between 1988 and 1995, and surpassed the number of Christians (13 percent) in 1997.[67]

Urban Christianity

Although the number of Christians stagnated in Hong Kong and declined in Taiwan, where it accounted for 5 percent of the population in 1998,[68] in Singapore it grew at a rate comparable to that of Buddhism, from 10.9 to 16.5 percent between 1980 and 2000, although the growth slowed in the 1990s.[69] In North America, Christianity, after remaining virtually shut out of the Chinese community for a century, enjoyed an increase in conversions from the 1960s, typically of the evangelical variety, so that by the end of the 1990s it was the declared religion of one-third of Chinese Americans (compared with one-fifth who identified as Buddhists and half giving no religious identification).[70]

But it was in Mainland China that Christianity underwent the most astonishing growth. This phenomenon will be discussed in greater depth in chapter 13, but let us note here that although observers in the 1990s described this growth as occurring primarily among elder, poorly educated rural residents, it was clear by the late 1990s that Christianity also held a

64. Hsiao & Schak, "Les organisations bouddhistes," 47.
65. Pang, "Religious Composition of the Chinese in Singapore," 332.
66. Tsui, "Recent Developments in Buddhism in Hong Kong," 300.
67. Ng Peter Tze-ming, "The Changing Market Shares," 112–13.
68. Chiu Hei-yuan, *Taiwan shehui bianqian jiben diaocha: Disanqi disanci diaocha zhixing baogao*, cited in Madsen, *Democracy's Dharma*, 161 n. 1.
69. Tamney & Hassan, *Religious Switching*; Clammer, *The Sociology of Singapore Religion*.
70. Yang Fenggang, "Religious Diversity," 71.

strong appeal among educated urbanites and affluent entrepreneurs.[71] In the city of Wenzhou, one of China's richest coastal cities with a large number of Christians (estimated at around 10 percent of the population), a new breed of "boss Christians" appeared. These business owners, who were also zealous believers and leaders in congregations, preached a prosperity gospel and competed to build ever-larger and more dynamic churches. They consciously tried to refashion Chinese Christianity into a more modern and sophisticated lifestyle that could satisfy the aspirations of people living in a market-oriented culture.[72]

Receptivity to Christianity among urban youth is shown by one survey of college students at the elite Renmin University in Beijing, which concluded that although only 3.6 percent explicitly acknowledged belief in Christianity, 61.5 percent declared an "interest" in the religion, and over 70 percent considered that Christianity would "enrich social culture, help Chinese people to understand the West, and increase Sino-Western cultural exchange."[73] These findings were corroborated by another survey conducted in 1998 among Beijing high school students, college students, and working youth, among whom less that 8 percent agreed with statements about Christianity being a "foreign" religion harmful to Chinese tradition or to socialism, while there was nearly unanimously positive valuation of Christianity as a source of mutual love and support, of social stability in the West, and of a cultural spirit that should be absorbed to benefit Chinese development.[74]

While this passive receptivity was rarely translated into active commitment—perhaps more as a result of restrictions on Christian organizations, which limited people's direct exposure to Christian groups and teachings—Christian groups and networks did grow rapidly, and younger, well-educated believers accounted for an increasing proportion of new converts. The growth of Christianity in the cities was largely extra-institutional: while official churches were simply unable to respond to demand, McDonald's restaurants became as likely a place to conduct Bible study sessions as private apartments.[75]

71. Yang Fenggang, "Lost in the Market, Saved at McDonald's," 426–29; Gao Shining, *Dangdai Beijing de jidujiao.*

72. Chen Cunfu, *Zhuanxing qi de Zhongguo jidujiao;* Cao Nanlai, "Christian Entrepreneurs," "Raising the Quality of Belief."

73. Yang Huilin, "Some Characteristics of the Understanding of the Christian Faith."

74. Li Suju & Liu Qifei, *Qingnian yu "zongjiao re,"* 135–36.

75. Yang Fenggang, "Lost in the Market, Saved at McDonald's."

THE FEATURES OF CHINESE RELIGIOUS MODERNITY

The movements we have just described represent a great diversity of traditions and practices. It should be stressed, however, that although for the sake of convenience we have divided these movements into the four broad categories of body cultivation movements, redemptive societies and Confucian movements, lay Buddhist movements, and urban Christianity, there was much circulation of people, ideas, and practices between the categories, especially the first three. The discourses of cultural revitalization are an obvious common ground between the *qigong*, redemptive societies, and Confucian movements, while body cultivation practices were shared not only by *qigong* and Chan groups but also in several of the redemptive societies, and some experiences of Christian prayer are not so distant from those produced by Chinese body-centered spirituality—although this remains to be studied. Anecdotal evidence indicates that after the collapse of the *qigong* movement in the 1990s, many *qigong* practitioners turned to Christianity, Taoism, and Buddhism, especially of the Chan and Tibetan varieties, as well as new forms of self-cultivation, such as the yoga fever that emerged immediately afterward in the early 2000s. The category of *qigong* itself, though a creation of the political realities of socialist China, migrated to Taiwan, where it came to represent less of an autonomous movement but diffused into the religious milieu, and to the West, where it found a niche within the world of New Age spirituality and holistic therapy.

It is possible, therefore, to speak of a "modern" urban religious culture in the Chinese world, with structural characteristics that are shared by the different movements described, albeit with different degrees of emphasis in different groups and traditions, and in the specific contexts of different political regimes. In speaking of an urban Chinese "religious modernity," however, we should be careful not to assume a radical rupture with traditional types of religiosity. For instance, a defining characteristic of modern religiosity as defined by sociologists is the voluntary and personal nature of participation, where individuals worship out of their free choice, as opposed to kinship groups or ascriptive communities as collective units. In China, however, although traditional cults have usually been managed by corporate, kinship, or territorial communities, individual and voluntary worship, at temples or in groups freely chosen by the worshipper, has always been a fundamental form of religious practice. From the perspective of the individual worshipper, then, the transition from ritual participation in a communal territorial temple to a private entrepreneurial temple does not represent a radical rupture. Furthermore, lay Buddhist and salvationist groups have provided pathways for long-term personal spiritual commitments for centuries.

At a basic level, then, the emergence of religious modernity can be said to be characterized by a shift in the relative importance of preexisting forms of Chinese religiosity, from the ascriptive communal cults employing religious specialists to voluntary, congregational, and body-cultivational styles. The extent of this shift was to a great degree influenced by political and economic conditions. At one end of the spectrum, in Taiwan, one found the greatest degree of coexistence and circulation between the two types of religiosity (with local temples offering *qigong* courses, for instance), while at the other extreme, in the cities of Mainland China and North America, the near total absence of communal cults left the space wide open for modern forms of religiosity. Entities like Hong Kong and Singapore were situated somewhere in between.

Another point of continuity—which is also the defining "modern" characteristic of most of these movements—is their conscious identification with tradition, in relation to, though not necessarily in opposition to, a modern secularist culture in which religion is constantly obliged to justify itself, often resorting to modernist or scientific arguments. The traditions thus formulated can be considered "reinvented" in the sense that they create new compositions out of selected elements of tradition—elements often selected for their perceived compatibility with modern, secular values. At the same time, the "traditions" thus created defined themselves in relation to the West, constituting Chinese nationality and ethnicity within a cosmopolitan context. In all cases, the goal was to find an authentic Chinese essence or morality at the same time compatible with, or constituting an alternative form of, universalism. While the tension between the Chinese nature and universalism, and attempts to reconcile the two, was manifested in each movement, the emphasis on either side of the equation varied. In *qigong*, the redemptive societies, and the Confucian movements, the stress was clearly on Chinese tradition defining itself in relation to the West and asserting a new, Chinese-centered universalism that other nations could potentially adhere to. The conscious and explicit syncretism of some of these movements partook of a project of creating a unified Chinese tradition vis-à-vis the West.[76] The reformist Buddhist groups combined a doctrine and practice both solidly rooted in Chinese history and thought, and part of a sophisticated global community. At the other end of the spec-

---

76. For an early discussion of these issues, see Seiwert, "Religious Response to Modernization."

trum, Christianity, which offered the strongest symbolic connection to universal Western modernity, should not be seen as a rupture with Chinese tradition: the strong moral emphasis of the evangelical Protestantism most popular among Chinese was often explicitly perceived by believers as incarnating the essence of Chinese values of virtuous conduct, filial piety, and hard work.[77]

All the movements we have described here provided pathways for living and affirming Chinese identity and moral values in the chaotic and amoral environment of capitalism. Robert Weller has argued that as Chinese societies developed into full-fledged market economies, a "split" occurred between amoral cults, which accepted and reflected the cutthroat individualism of instrumentalized social relations—such as some of the temple cults mentioned at the end of chapter 10—and movements which, on the contrary, rejected capitalism's moral relativism and provided a strong ethical compass for their believers.[78] Most of the movements described in this chapter belong to the latter category. The *qigong* movement, however, represents a more complex case. In contrast to other polities, where a relatively higher degree of religious freedom allowed for a more strongly differentiated religious landscape, in Deng-era China *qigong* was the *only* legitimate label for most traditional magical and religious practices that did not fit within the narrow limits of acceptable practice for the five officially recognized religions. The *qigong* category thus brought together "masters" who operated according to a wide variety of modalities, from fortune-tellers and producers of *qi*-empowered talismans who provided healing services for a fee, to entrepreneurs such as Zhang Hongbao 張洪寶 and Ke Yunlu 柯云路, who saw business opportunities in the *qigong* publishing and training market, to charismatic figures such as Yan Xin, who played the role of saviors of humanity, and included a strong ethical dimension to *qigong* practice. As free-market reforms deepened the commercialization of social relations in the 1990s, and popular discontent with the amoral and corrupt behavior of businessmen grew, an earlier source of tension within the *qigong* movement—between those, such as Zhang Xiangyu 張香玉, whose practices closely reflected popular beliefs and expectations, and those, such as Zhang Honglin 張洪林, who advocated rational and "scientific" reforms of *qigong*—was overshadowed by another source of tension, between opportunistic masters such as Ji Yi 記一, who made a profitable business out of the *qigong* boom, and moral fundamentalists,

---

77. Yang Fenggang, "Chinese Conversion to Evangelical Christianity."
78. Weller, *Alternate Civilities*, chap. 5.

exemplified by Li Hongzhi, who ultimately rejected *qigong* and shifted the core emphasis from healing to salvation based on practicing and displaying moral principle: an orientation which, by expanding the focus from the body outward to the general moral climate, brought Falungong directly onto a terrain claimed by the CCP.[79]

MODERN RELIGIOUS MOVEMENTS IN THEIR POLITICAL CONTEXTS

The different orientations and trajectories of the movements described above reflect, in part, the dominant paradigm of identity and nationhood in each Chinese society. At the same time, they were significant components of the growing world of nongovernmental associations and contributed to the emergence of a "public sphere" of discourse and social engagement in the various Chinese polities. They can thus be considered major actors in Chinese "civil society"—but only if the notion of civil society is stripped of Western connotations of a social space entirely independent of, and defined in opposition to, the state. Indeed, the different religious and social orientations of these movements, combined with the ebb and flow of state expansion in the different Chinese polities, produced a great diversity of relationships between the state and modern religious movements, ranging from intimate interpenetration to radical opposition.

The *qigong* movement in Mainland China, for example, reflected the political and ideological dynamics of the People's Republic in its early and post-Mao phases. Created in the late 1940s by CCP cadres, *qigong* was a product of the CCP's pragmatic—and, later, nationalist—project of scientizing and institutionalizing Chinese medicine as an indigenous trove of popular knowledge, without the Western-trained doctors' suspect associations with foreign imperialists and missionary medical schools. Later, it was during the Cultural Revolution—even though *qigong* was banned—that the seeds were planted for *qigong* becoming a deinstitutionalized, popular mass movement; and in the post-Mao years, when Deng Xiaoping attempted to revive the CCP's flagging utopian drive through recourse to the wonders of scientific technology as the source of national salvation, *qigong* carried the dream to its extreme with its literal conflation of science and magic, where the laboratory became the scene of the *qigong* masters' consecration. For China's leading scientist, the nuclear bomb designer Qian Xuesen 錢學森 (b. 1911), who was the chief political proponent and ideologue of the *qigong*

---

79. Palmer, *Qigong Fever*.

movement, the "somatic science" based on *qigong* held the key to renewing Marxism and making China into a world leader in the paranormal "highest of high technologies." For these leaders, *qigong* was a natural extension of a revolutionary, sino-centered utopianism that would use Chinese tradition to transform the world where Maoism had failed.[80]

Qian and other senior political leaders had been attracted by the universal and democratic dimension of the mass dissemination of *qigong* practices, which fit well with revolutionary visions of popular knowledge and mass health; on that basis, they actively promoted the rationalization of *qigong* and its propagation. But they had not counted on how *qigong* experiences could stimulate and enhance the charisma of masters who ended up with large followings and significant organizations independent of the CCP. Repeated attempts to rationally manage the masters through bureaucratic procedures failed. By the early 1990s, many masters began to consolidate their networks by building large nationwide organizations while issues of the commercialization, traditional authenticity, and scientific validity became the subject of heated debates both in the press and within *qigong* circles. From the mid-1990s, political support for *qigong* had dissipated and the *qigong* movement fell into disarray, while Falungong was drawn into an increasingly antagonistic relationship with the state.

Starting in 1994, two years after he had gone public as a *qigong* master, Li Hongzhi introduced several new elements that transformed the nature of charismatic power in his movement. First, he dismissed *qi* experiences as something of a lower order, replacing *qi* with *gong* 功, understood as moral superiority, as the power to be pursued in Falungong practice. By emphasizing *gong*, Falungong thus set itself apart from the competition of myriads of groups all working with the same *qi*, and shifted the source of charisma from *qi* experiences to extraordinary moral purity and even militant defense of the Dharma. Morality, and disgust at the moral corruption of post-Mao society, was now the central issue, displacing the typical *qigong* concerns with science, paranormal abilities, and tradition. The evolution toward moral predication reinforced the tendency to political polarization. Falungong discourses of morality extended beyond body discipline to social criticism, social problems being perceived in China as the result of a moral decline in the people in general and in government leaders in particular.

Falungong grew rapidly, drawing millions of followers. After an initial period of positive coverage, it came under criticism in the Chinese media, to which followers responded by staging sit-ins and demonstrations around

80. Ibid., chap. 4.

newspaper and television offices. Ultimately, on April 25, 1999, ten thousand followers mobilized around the Zhongnanhai headquarters of the Chinese Communist Party—the largest popular protest in China since the 1989 Tian'anmen student movement. The CCP then outlawed Falungong and launched a ruthless repression campaign to exterminate it. Most other *qigong* groups were also disbanded, and although *qigong* could still be practiced in Chinese parks, only five standardized sets of exercises could be taught, by trainers certified by the State Sports Administration. Paradoxically, the Chinese state's repression of Falungong practitioners served as double confirmations of Falungong's moral claims: by enhancing the image of moral innocence and purity of the practitioners and, through narratives of resistance to torture, providing, for believers, confirmations of the extraordinary power of Falungong.[81]

Urban Christians in Mainland China, on the other hand, exemplified a cosmopolitan religious dimension to China's "opening up": as Yang Fenggang has aptly described, these Christians' proclivity for meeting at McDonald's reflects more than convenience and anonymity: "in a symbolic sense, adopting Christianity and eating at McDonald's make the Chinese feel they have gained an equal footing with the Americans and other Westerners as modern world citizens."[82] Some Christians also followed up on the Republican-era discourse of religious citizenship, explaining that as Christians, they were good citizens (honest, sober, law-abiding, and so on).[83] At the same time, Christians maintained an apolitical profile that belied CCP fears of them becoming a foreign-controlled "fifth column," as well as American evangelical fantasies of them turning China into a pro-Western power.[84]

There were some notable exceptions, however: several of the student leaders of the 1989 June Fourth movement, after fleeing to the West, converted to Christianity. Some of them produced a documentary video, widely disseminated in Christian circles in China, that inscribed the struggle for democracy in China within a narrative of China's redemption from over two thousand years of tyranny caused by the emperors or CCP leaders usurping the role of God.[85] And many of the new group of law-

---

81. Ownby, *Falun Gong*.
82. Yang Fenggang, "Lost in the Market, Saved at McDonald's," 438.
83. Huang Jianbo & Yang Fenggang, "The Cross Faces the Loudspeakers."
84. Aikman, *Jesus in Beijing*, is the best example of such fantasies.
85. Xie Wenjie & Yuan Zhiming, *China's Confession*.

yers on the mainland, who were willing to defend the rights of farmers, workers, and religious believers in the Chinese courts at great risk to their careers and lives, found courage and inspiration in their Christian faith. For these activists, religious faith translated into an active engagement to protect individual rights within the framework of what the Chinese state claimed to be an emerging rule of law. Although they did not oppose the Chinese government, they attempted to use the legal system to hold state agencies accountable for respecting the laws enacted by the state itself.[86] But for the vast majority of Mainland Chinese Christians, the politically suspect status of their religion made it virtually impossible to openly engage with issues of public life—while their own theological orientation led them away from this-worldly concerns.[87]

The Confucian revival on the mainland became a mass phenomenon in the early 2000s, at a time when the CCP itself, trying to reoccupy the moral field in response to the challenge posed by Falungong and the resurgence of religion, was increasingly viewing the Confucian heritage in a positive light. Similar to the *qigong* movement in the 1980s, the Confucian revival thus conjugated bottom-up popular initiatives with signals and encouragements from political leaders. It also occurred at a time when, as China became an increasingly influential player on the world stage, Chinese people could, with greater confidence than before, explore and assert the sources of their national identity.

In Taiwan, the new redemptive societies, such as the Yellow Emperor and Heavenly Lord teachings, had sacralized the traditionalist and restorationist orientations of the KMT, turning the Chinese nation itself into a virtual object of worship, in which the focus was to suture the torn body of the nation and to redeem China from Communist domination.[88] These movements paralleled the Cultural Renaissance Movement, which was the KMT's response to the CCP's Cultural Revolution. Such an orientation, combined with the personal political connections of the two groups' founders, Wang Hansheng and Li Yujie, helped them to secure legal recognition during the martial law period, while the largest redemptive society, Yiguandao, remained banned. Even Yiguandao evolved in a similar direc-

---

86. On Chinese Christian engagement with public issues on the Internet, see Wielander, "Protestant and Online."

87. For a discussion of the possibilities of religious (especially Christian) social engagement in China, see Xie Zhibin, *Religious Diversity and Public Religion.*

88. Another example is the Honghuayuan 弘化院, established by KMT politicians in 1969. See Lin Guoping, *Dangdai Taiwan zongjiao,* 142–45.

tion, spearheading the revival of Confucian study classes, an activity that could only be seen as legitimate in the context of the KMT's restorationist ideology.

Some studies have further noted how reformist religious movements in Taiwan reflected, sacralized, and popularized the ideals of the KMT's New Life movement. C. Julia Huang's study of the behavioral teachings of the Tzu Chi Foundation—whose "ten precepts," which include fastening one's seatbelts when driving, were reminiscent of New Life ideals of purifying society by brushing one's teeth[89]—is one example, while Tsai Yi-jia's study of the Taiwan Spirit Mediums' Association is even more telling. One of the latter group's leading activists, Deng Wenyi 鄧文儀, had been a member of the Blue Shirts (the KMT Nanjing-period fascist militia) and an author of New Life movement tracts. He attempted to revive the movement's ideals through a Moral Maintenance Movement in the city of Changhua. Meetings of the Spirit Mediums' Association—in which the spirits of figures like Sun Yat-sen, Chiang Kai-shek, and Mao Zedong revealed themselves and spoke with each other—aimed to heal the torn and divided memories of the Chinese nation and its myriad souls left orphaned and errant in the civil war.[90] Some temples even worshipped Chiang Kai-shek as a god.[91] These movements, particularly the new redemptive societies, reflected the concern with returning to and saving the lost motherland, characteristic of the KMT-dominated martial law period of Taiwan's history.

Taiwan's reformist lay Buddhist movements, which flourished after the lifting of martial law, expressed a different type of political and cultural orientation—one that reflected Taiwan's growing sense of identity and cosmopolitanism within a context of political democratization. Richard Madsen argues that they disproved commonly held ideas about Confucian-based "Asian values" being incompatible with democracy and leading to a future "clash of civilizations" between the authoritarian Confucian sphere and the West. Growing numbers of Taiwanese showed their adherence to "traditional" moral values through their involvement in the lay Buddhist and other religious movements, at the same time that they embraced democracy; for Madsen, the modernizing Buddhist and Taoist groups even "facilitated the democratic transition" and "made important contributions to Taiwan's civil society."[92] And yet this was a type of civil society that

89. C. Julia Huang, *Charisma and Compassion*, 196.

90. Tsai Yi-jia, "The Writing of History," 54–65; Paper, "Mediums and Modernity."

91. Lin Guoping, *Dangdai Taiwan zongjiao*, 142–43.

92. Madsen, *Democracy's Dharma*, 132; see also Kuo Cheng-Tian, *Religion and Democracy in Taiwan*.

did not define itself in opposition to the state or affirm its independence from the state. The reformist groups' autonomy came not through challenging the government, but from their religious concerns, which were independent of political demands. They emerged during the martial law period, and in their early years kept a low profile while cultivating good relations with government officials, even cooperating with state policies to use religious groups to provide charity. They were thus able to obtain land from the government for building temples and hospitals, providing a foundation for their subsequent growth. After the lifting of martial law, the groups continued to collaborate with the government in providing social services—but in contrast to American religious groups, which claim public funds to subsidize faith-based organizations and projects, the Taiwanese Buddhist groups offered their own funds and human resources to support government projects, such as rebuilding public schools after the earthquake of September 21, 1999. For Madsen, this type of collaboration, which reflected a Confucian approach that sees individual moral cultivation and service to the state as a single continuum, in contrast to Western liberal views of the tension between individual autonomy and state authority, provided stability and social harmony at a time of turbulent economic change and transition to democracy.

These Buddhist movements would seem to fit less easily with an attempt to show the links between modern religious movements and constructions of national/ethnic identity. The Tzu Chi Foundation, for instance, remained staunchly apolitical, although it certainly acted as a willing auxiliary to the Taiwanese state in providing social services.[93] Like the Mazu cult evoked in chapter 10, it would be impossible to categorize most Buddhist movements as either "pro-unification" or "pro-independence"—a fact which, perhaps, may be understood as revealing the ambiguous "postnational" condition of Taiwan: the Buddhist movements offered a modernized and universalistic rooting in tradition without forcing allegiance to a single national alternative. For Madsen, they constructed an "ecumenical nationalism," rooted in Taiwanese pride, while affirming a religious universalism that subordinated the interests of the nation to the good of the whole world. Counting among their followers a healthy mix of Mainlanders and native Taiwanese, they elaborated a gentle, compassionate, and cosmopolitan Taiwanese identity that contrasted with the confrontational stances of politicians.[94] Indeed, where the Taiwanese state and its leaders, unrecognized by the

93. Laliberté, "Tzu Chi and the Buddhist Revival in Taiwan."
94. Madsen, *Democracy's Dharma*, 137–39.

international community (and lacking political consensus to seek such recognition), could not fully incarnate "the moral aspirations that make its citizens into a national community," it was groups such as the lay Buddhist movements which acted as Taiwan's ambassadors abroad. Through their international philanthropy and gentle spirituality, they conveyed a compassionate, generous image of Taiwanese identity that had appeal on the global stage without provoking Beijing.[95]

Some groups, however, took a more radical stance. Beginning in the 1970s, the Presbyterian Church in Taiwan was one of the earliest promoters of Taiwanese independence.[96] The Wanfohui 萬佛會, a Buddhist group founded in 1980 by Shi Zongsheng 釋宗聖 (b. 1959), established its own pro-independence political party, the Truth Party 真理黨, which became known for its active participation in street protests and frequent clashes with police.[97]

In the United States, one study observed that Chinese Buddhist temples—the largest of which was Foguangshan's Hsi Lai Temple in Los Angeles—made a more conscious effort to reach out to the non-Chinese broader community than the Chinese Christian churches.[98] This reflected the Buddhists' marginal status as "exotic others" in the American landscape, which gave them the natural role of representing "Chinese" ethnicity in the topography of American multiculturalism, so that they would be actively sought out by local governments, political candidates, and other community groups—attention they welcomed, since they desired to come closer to the American mainstream. The Chinese-American Christian churches, on the other hand, provided an avenue for preserving traditional values while adopting the religion of the dominant culture.[99] In spite of their numerical dominance, however, as organizations they were not active in the Chinese community, and remained invisible to the mainstream: their narrow focus on evangelism led them to eschew associating with other community groups, whether Chinese or not, and to focus their outreach on proselytism among other Chinese as individuals. Generally, the

95. Ibid., 139–44; see also Weller, "Living at the Edge." For a collection of essays on religion and Taiwanese identity, see Katz & Rubinstein, eds., *Religion and the Formation of Taiwanese Identities*.

96. Rubinstein, "Christianity and Democratization."

97. Lin Guoping, *Dangdai Taiwan zongjiao*, 116–30.

98. C. Chen, "The Religious Varieties of Ethnic Presence." See also I. Lin, "Journey to the Far West"; Guest, "Liminal Youth among Fuzhou Chinese Undocumented Workers."

99. Ng Kwai Hang, "Seeking the Christian Tutelage"; Cao Nanlai, "The Church as Surrogate Family." On a similar process at work among the Chinese of French Polynesia, see Fer, "The Growth of Pentacostalism." On Chinese migrant workers converting to Christianity while in Israel, see Kalir, "Finding Jesus in the Holy Land."

Buddhist and other Chinese temples, such as those of Yiguandao,[100] were not as successful as the churches in socializing second-generation Chinese into the religion.[101] Chinese Christian youth, however, on going to college, would often join mainstream Bible study groups or "Asian" evangelical fellowships in which the specifically Chinese ethnic component was strongly diluted.[102] In the American case, therefore, we see how religion became an element in the dynamics of assimilation and ethnic identification of Chinese immigrants in the context of multiculturalism.

In places with smaller Chinese communities than Taiwan or the United States, the transnational nature of Chinese modern religiosities was even more exposed, with national issues being relegated to a very secondary role in favor of global networks based on common faith and interests.[103] In cities such as Paris, Chinese religious groups flourished beginning in the 1980s, with two main kinds dominating the scene: on the one hand the common-origin associations (*huiguan*), which typically built temples for Buddhas as well as gods from the home area, and on the other, branches of international organizations such as evangelical Christian churches, Foguangshan, the True Buddha School, or Supreme Master Ching Hai. Whereas the *huiguan* typically nurtured links with their place or origin in China, groups of the second type were often not branches of PRC- or Taiwan-based organizations but rather nodes of networks based in the United States—such as the Protestant Shengmingtang 生命堂, the True Buddha School, and so on. In these Chinese religious networks, Mandarin rather than English or Chinese regional languages was the medium of communication, but this communication was not centered on China.[104] Localities such as London, Cape Town, Auckland, and Sao Paulo were thus points on a truly global circuit of Chinese religious practices and organizations.

100. Clart, "Opening the Wilderness."
101. Yang Fenggang, "Religious Diversity."
102. Busto, "The Gospel according to the Model Minority?"; Jeung, "Creating an Asian American Christian Subculture."
103. C. Julia Huang, ed., "Wings of Belief."
104. Ji Zhe, "Une cartographie."

TWELVE

Official Discourses and Institutions
of Religion

拾·貳

In the previous two chapters, we saw how, from the later decades of the twentieth century, the Chinese world witnessed the flourishing and transformation of multiple forms of religiosity covering a vast range of practices, including family rites of passage, temple festivals, modern spiritual movements, and transnational networks. Many, if not most, of these developments occurred from the bottom up, outside the institutional sphere assigned to "religion" by the state. Nonetheless, although it was unable to fully control the bubbling forth of practices, beliefs, networks, and associations, the state remained a key player in shaping the religious field.

In the absence of a single, dominant religious institution, the state gave itself the central role of defining and protecting religious orthodoxy—fully so in Mainland China, and to varying degrees in other Chinese polities. In this chapter, as we follow the evolving state role in the contemporary religious field, we will map the discursive categories and institutional formations into which various types of religiosity have been assigned and redefined: "religion," of course, but also "superstition," "popular faith," "reactionary secret societies," "evil cults"—as well as secular categories such as science, sports, medicine, philanthropy, culture, heritage, or folk custom— each of which entails a different type of dynamic relationship with the state and its definitions of orthodoxy. The differential attribution of these categories to various traditions and communities determined their orthodox legitimacy and their legal status within each Chinese polity: the temples and rituals of Chinese communal religion, the Confucian associations, the institutions of Buddhism and Taoism, the Roman Catholic and Protestant churches, the redemptive societies and Chinese new religious movements, and the global religious organizations. We begin with the mainland, where the PRC authorities attempted to shift from ideological dogmatism to the political co-optation of religious leaders, the bureaucratic management of religious communities, and the harnessing of religious resources to the goals of economic development and social harmony; move on to Hong Kong and Macau, where the handover to the PRC led to subtle changes in the politico-religious equilibrium; next turn our sights to Singapore, where the social engineering of religion was most explicit and perhaps most successful; and finally focus on Taiwan, where the state shifted from a highly interventionist posture to one of almost complete laissez-faire.

THE PEOPLE'S REPUBLIC OF CHINA ON THE MAINLAND

The State-Led Institutionalization of Religion in the PRC

On the mainland, the overall orientation of the socialist state in its approach to religion gradually shifted away from the Cultural Revolution's destruction of all forms of religious culture, toward a more rationalizing and managerial approach to "meeting the religious needs of the population." Meanwhile, religious leaders continued to be co-opted, not only for the traditional objectives of the United Front, but also to contribute to state goals of economic development, to provide philanthropy and social services, and to build a "harmonious society." Discourse on religion evolved in a more positive direction, while basic definitions and categories (religion, superstition, evil cults, and so on) were increasingly debated and strained by a rapidly evolving social reality—but the fundamental ideological and institutional framework for religious issues remained the same as that which had been put into place in the mid-1950s.[1]

---

1. See, e.g., Leung, "Religious Freedom," "China's Religious Policy"; Lambert, "The Present Religious Policy"; P. Potter, "Belief in Control"; Kindopp & Hamrin, eds., *God and Caesar in China*.

In this chapter, we will examine how the state, from the late 1970s onward, attempted to shape religious orthodoxy and to draw clear demarcations between legitimate and illegitimate forms of religiosity, both through its structuring of public discourse on religion and through its attempts to institutionalize religious communities. On the one hand, the rejection of revolutionary iconoclasm and radicalism, and the policy of reform and opening up, led to a greater tolerance toward religion; and an increasingly prominent discourse on the positive contributions of religion to philanthropy and social morality even led to an exploration of ways of positively encouraging the development of religion. On the other hand, the Leninist model of state control of religious institutions was retained and even reinforced as the state expanded and modernized its bureaucracy. This tendency was spurred by fears of political challenges and separatism emanating from an exploding popular religiosity—as in the case of Falungong—and foreign links to religious communities, as in the case of Tibetans and Uighurs. The tension between these two tendencies could only be resolved by strengthening religious orthodoxy, at the level of both discourse and institutions, so that religion could both play its assigned role as an adjunct to social development while warding off political and separatist threats.

The post-Mao religious institutionalization, however, was not a primarily top-down enterprise as it had been in the 1950s; it was a project in which religious leaders, government officials, and scholars invested themselves, combining different discursive regimes and forming a hybrid religio-bureaucratic institution. At the same time, the narrowness of the legitimate category of religion—limited to the authorized forms of the five recognized religions—reinforced the deinstitutionalization of other forms of religiosity, which were forced to exist as dispersed networks or as underground organizations, and/or to seek institutionalization under other categories such as health, tourism or heritage, causing them to compose with the secular logics of those categories.

Here we focus on the religious institutions of the Han majority, with an emphasis on Buddhism and Taoism—for which the impact of institutionalization was the most profound, since they had no historical experience of national religious institutions, creating an unprecedented level of national integration of these two religions' clerical networks and liturgies. The cases of Christianity, Islam, and Tibetan Buddhism are discussed in the next chapter. Our discussion focuses here on what Benoît Vermander calls the state's "functionalization" of religion—how it creates what Yang Fenggang has called the "red market" of religion in China, in which "the red stain [of communist ideology] is reflected in the rhetoric of clergy, theological discourse, and practices of the sanctioned religious groups."[2] As with secular state building in China, the degree of institutionalization was stronger at the national level and was significantly weaker in more remote localities. The process did, nonetheless, profoundly shape the religious field.[3]

The Cultural Revolution had seen all the socialist religious institutions abolished, from the United Front Department to the Religious Affairs Bureau and the associations, as religion became a direct target to be eliminated. In the period of "reform and opening up," from 1979 onward, this system was reinstated, but in a radically different context. Even when the state stepped back to leave more space for religious activity, there were no strong indigenous religious institutions to occupy that space—in sharp contrast to the Roman Catholic and Orthodox churches, which quickly reinvested the religious field in postsocialist Eastern Europe and Russia. In the absence of a single, dominant religious institution, the Chinese state continued, by will and by default, to play the central role of defining and protecting religious orthodoxy. Historically, China's religious institutions had already been weak before 1949; the PRC regime had created new institutions in the 1950s, but they had been primarily political creations, and gutted by the Cultural Revolution. But it was these associations that were called on to organize China's resurgent religiosity, and which needed to be strengthened and further institutionalized.

The state-led institutionalization of Buddhism, Catholicism, Taoism, Islam, and Protestantism has created a relatively homogenous institutional structure for these five traditions, a hybrid of the secular socialist work unit (*danwei* 單位) and traditional forms of clerical organization, which became constitutive of the religious habitus of the leaders of these communities.[4] The *danwei* was the modular system of nested units to which, in socialist China, all units of production and administration were nationalized and organized, and to which all workers were assigned for life, provid-

---

2. Vermander, "Religious Revival and Exit from Religion"; Yang Fenggang, "The Red, Black, and Gray Markets," 97.

3. Institutionalization is understood here as formulated by Ji Zhe, taking inspiration from Giddens: "an 'institution' could be conceived of as the general manner of the reproduction of rules and resources. If an organization is reconfigured by the encompassing external institutional arrangement, so that its structure and its rules about the reproduction and distribution of resources tend to be identical with its institutional environment, then it can be seen as an 'institutionalized' organization." Ji Zhe, "Secularization as Religious Restructuring," 239–40, referring to Giddens, *Central Problems in Social Theory*. On religious institutionalization in the PRC, see also Li Xiangping, *Zhongguo dangdai zongjiao*, 50–55, 175–204, 277–95.

4. See Billioud and Thoraval, "Lijiao," for a discussion of the juxtaposition of the post-Mao socialist habitus and traditional Confucian ritual sacrality.

ing not only work but also residential, leisure, and welfare facilities. While officially registered religious communities, as associations, were not fully fledged *danwei*, they partook of the same institutional logic: bureaucratic positions (such as *huizhang*, "chairman," *bangongshi zhuren*, "general manager," and so on) took precedence over, or even fully replaced, ecclesiastic rank; the key hierarchical relationships were those between the association chairman (who was usually also the abbot or leading cleric of the main temple or church within a given jurisdiction) and the representatives of the CCP United Front branch and the Religious Affairs Bureau. These relationships played themselves out in the appointment of personnel to other positions and in the internal politics of resource allocation. Rewards for performance, in the form of increased resources and appointment to higher administrative rank or to prestigious political positions (People's Consultative Conferences), gave as much weight to political as to religious abilities. All these performances, positions, and resources were negotiated through the *guanxi* culture of relationship management, which pervades the religious institutions as much as any secular institution. As most *danwei* were, since the 1990s, encouraged and even required to become self-subsisting in the market economy, so did the religious communities, which were pressured to post positive economic performances by selling profit-making services and commodities.[5] However, while the *danwei* system was largely dismantled in the late 1990s, reducing if not eliminating most enterprises' requirement of political performance and leaving them free to live or die in the market, religious associations were among the categories of units along with schools, government administrations, the army, and strategic industries which remained under close political supervision.

Religious *danwei* were thus hybrids of religious culture with the institutional *habitus* of work units in the socialist market economy. This hybridization was not an easy process, and could be painful to religious practitioners seeking spiritual purity. Nor were the relations between the different components of the institutional structure always harmonious; indeed, conflicts were frequent, sometimes even violent, between clerics, official associations, and the Religious Affairs authorities, or between religious institutions and nonreligious units, as when tourism authorities fought over the use of scenic sites and their revenues.[6] But these conflicts, and the norms of playing them out and solving them, were themselves constitutive

5. Yang Der-ruey, "The Changing Economy"; Lang, Chan, & Ragvald, "Temples," 149–80.
6. See, e.g., the case of Nanputuo described in Wank, "Institutionalizing Modern 'Religion'"; Ashiwa & Wank, "The Politics of a Reviving Buddhist Temple."

of the institutional order. In order to understand this process of institutionalization, we need to consider the discursive networks in which the boundaries and forms of religion as a distinctive institution were defined, and the regulations that aimed to translate the discourse into reality. Then we need to consider the specific structure of the official bodies that created and reproduced these institutional forms. Although we discuss discourses and institutions separately for ease of presentation, we should bear in mind that the two were in fact mutually constitutive.

The Discursive Network on Religion

Each political system has its own regime of producing a discourse on legitimate forms of religion. This discourse not only assigns ideas, practices, and groups into a category of religion—with its distinct rights, restrictions, and position within the range of functionally differentiated social institutions in a given society—but also contributes to shaping the internal structure and norms of the religious groups themselves. Discourses on religion in the People's Republic of China should be seen in the context of the broader economy of discourse production and circulation between various official and unofficial actors, including Party leaders and organs, government departments, academic institutions, religious leaders and followers, and the media. We also need to bear in mind how, within this economy, a whole set of categories has evolved, often in opposition to one another, each of which has been used to label phenomena related to what, in anthropological terms, may broadly be considered as pertaining to the religious domain. These categories include religion (*zongjiao*), of course, but also superstition (*mixin*), reactionary secret society (*fandong huidaomen*), and evil cult (*xiejiao* 邪教); popular faith (*minjian xinyang* 民間信仰) as well as culture (*wenhua* 文化) and cultural relic (*wenwu* 文物), intangible cultural heritage (*fei wuzhi wenhua yichan* 非物質文化遺產), folk customs (*minsu* 民俗), exotic ethnic customs (*minzu fengqing* 民族風情), and anything that could be categorized as a tourist resource; as along with nourishing life, *qigong*, martial arts, Chinese medicine, sports, and science; and even philanthropy, national studies, and international exchange. Each of these categories was part of a distinct discursive network, entailing a different type of dynamic relationship with the state and its definitions of orthodoxy, and producing a different logic of organization and action, within the common structure of what some scholars have called the "post-Mao habitus."[7]

7. Billioud & Thoraval, "Lijiao."

In the case of "religion," the discursive network was composed of Party leaders giving speeches on religion; the United Front Department and the Religious Affairs Bureaus at the national, provincial, and local levels; several types of academic institution—notably the Institute of World Religions of the China Academy of Social Sciences[8] and departments of philosophy and religious studies at the main universities, some of which dominate academic discourse on a certain religion (such as Sichuan University's Institute for Taoism and Religious Culture);[9] and the leaders of the five religious associations, and of the official training institutes and seminaries of those religions. These different types of persons (officials, academics, religious leaders) had different perspectives but shared a globally reformist outlook that generally encouraged a secularized, ethical vision of religion; academics, no less than the religious leaders, were active in formulating their vision of how the religion they study should modernize.

Members of the discursive network on religion, as officials, scholars, or state-recognized religious leaders, were expected to speak within the framework of broader Party policy. As such, their pronouncements carried a certain degree of authority and contributed to official discourse on religion. On the other hand, each had his own interests, his allegiances, and his own integration into other discursive networks, so that there was a clear difference in the perspectives of the discursive actors. As Ryan Dunch has aptly formulated, a given policy pronouncement "functions as both code and cover: code for a set of officially sanctioned expectations, and cover for a broad range of intellectual and theological agendas invoking it as legitimation."[10] Party policy thus created a common discursive framework that was invested and reproduced by actors with different interests and loyalties. The primary allegiance of Religious Affairs officials was to the government—but within the government they often saw themselves (or were seen) as defenders of religious interests, or as promoters of a "proper" form of religion. Religious leaders toed the Party line in order to protect the interests of their communities, and also to reinforce their authority within the community. Scholars typically had a more liberal attitude than the government but also needed to establish and protect the legitimacy of their field of study; and they used academic norms of distance and objectivity to balance their sympathies with the religions they studied. The best-known case was the "cultural Christians," academics and intellectuals who did not

8. Zhuo Xinping, "Research on Religions."
9. Yang Fenggang, "Between Secularist Ideology and Desecularizing Reality."
10. Dunch, "Christianity and 'Adaptation to Socialism,'" 172.

explicitly profess belief in Christianity but took a Christian standpoint to engage in a critique of China's moral and social problems;[11] another example is a network of scholars claiming the label of *New Taoism* 新道家 who argued that Taoism should develop a new ideology for the twenty-first century based on environmentalism, gender equality, and traditional culture.[12] We may also cite the widespread influence among academics and intellectuals of reformist Buddhism through the writings and initiatives of clerics such as Hsing Yun or Jinghui.[13] It is in this context, of multiple allegiances and complex motives, that discourse on religion was generated, through various publications and journals, and through meetings and conferences that might include one or several categories of discursive actor.

The Evolving Discourse of Party Leaders

Speeches of CCP leaders, and a few related official documents, provided the overarching framework for the discursive network on religion. These documents and speeches, of course, took into account the other voices within the discursive network, and also reacted to the general evolution of the domestic and international political context. They provided the guidelines for drafting national regulations on religion, which were few in number; the bulk of the administrative texts that applied to religious institutions were actually enacted at the provincial or local level, with much more detail on procedures, and also with a high decree of discrepancy between different places—reflecting the even higher degree of discrepancy in the actual practices of local officials, who were quite open to reform and experimentation in some places and bent on tight control in others. Details of the rituals and practices (divination, healing rites, and so on) that were allowed or banned varied greatly from province to province.[14]

Every few years, speeches by the CCP's top leaders set the tone for the

11. Ibid.
12. Hu Fuchen, "21 shiji de xin daoxue wenhua zhanlue."
13. Yang Fenggang & Wei Dedong, "The Bailin Buddhist Temple"; Ji Zhe, "Religion, Youth and Modernity."
14. Ying Fuk-tsang (Xing Fuzeng), "Church-State Relations," "New Wine in Old Wineskins." See MacInnis, *Religion in China Today*, for a comprehensive compilation of translated official policy documents, speeches, and news reports from the 1980s. A complete collection of authoritative policy documents and speeches from 1979 to 1995 is published in Zhonggong zhongyang, *Xin shiqi zongjiao gongzuo wenxian*, also Guojia zongjiao shiwuju, *Quanguo zongjiao xingzheng fagui*. For a detailed, annotated directory of PRC regulations on religion from the national to local levels of government as of the early 2000s, see Chan Kim-kwong & Carlson, *Religious Freedom in China*. For translations of local regulations, see Madsen & Tong, eds., "Local Religious Policy."

discourse on religion. Each time, there were subtle adjustments in the discourse, in which the Marxist doctrine of the "disappearance of religion" was deferred to an ever more distant future, while the positive contributions of religion to society were given an ever-greater recognition. At the same time, the fundamental premise—of the CCP's ultimate authority over religion, and its duty to control and guide its development—always remained unchanged.

An important discursive change occurred when, in the early 1980s, scholars were permitted to debate and reinterpret Marx's comments on "religion as the opiate of the masses," claiming that this statement applied to the role of religion in nineteenth-century Germany and not to the essence of religion itself.[15] This opened the way for religion to be depicted as having positive as well as negative factors. The new thinking was reflected in a document issued by the CCP Central Committee on March 31, 1982, entitled "The basic viewpoint and policy on the religious question during our country's socialist period,"[16] often referred to as "Document 19," which was both a revision of the Party's basic viewpoint on religion and an outline of specific policies and regulations. The document stated that in socialist China, now that class exploitation had been successfully eradicated, "the class root of the existence of religion was virtually lost." But since people's consciousness lags behind changes in social structure, old ways of thinking would continue to persist, people would still need religion at times of disaster and misfortune, and religion would not disappear until the long stage of socialism was completed and communism was realized.[17]

Document 19 outlined the fundamental religious policy, which remained essentially unchanged thereafter. It stressed that religious freedom remained a long-term policy, that "the crux of the policy of freedom of religious belief was to make the question of religious belief a private matter, one of individual free choice for citizens"[18]—with the exception of Party members, who were required to be atheists. Loyal grassroots Party members in minority areas, however, were allowed to attend weddings, funerals, and rituals with a religious content; otherwise they would be cut-

15. Yang Fenggang, "Between Secularist Ideology and Desecularizing Reality," 23–25. For a translation of Chinese scholarship from the 1980s on religion, see Luo Zhufeng, ed., *Religion under Socialism in China*, esp. pp. 151–56, challenging the orthodox interpretation of religion as an "opiate." The role of Protestant intellectuals in the academic "opium wars" in which these reinterpretations were aired is analyzed in Dunch, "Christianity and 'Adaptation to Socialism,'" 165–68.

16. "Document 19" is translated in toto in MacInnis, *Religion in China Today*, 8–25.

17. "Document 19"; quoted in MacInnis, *Religion in China Today*, 10.

18. Ibid., 15.

ting themselves off from the masses.[19] The document also made it illegal to compel children under the age of eighteen to join a religion or a religious order, and banned the reinstatement of "feudal religious rights" (of master over disciples, of temple leaders over tenants, and so on), as well as the use of religion to undermine China's territorial integrity, the harmony between nationalities, or the socialist system. Religious sites were to be strictly regulated, and a clear separation was to be made between "normal" religious activities and illegal and superstitious activities. Religions were also expressly banned from "interfering" with education—a stipulation that arose in response to the growing number of religious schools, notably in minority Buddhist and Muslim areas, which enrolled underaged children and prepared them for clerical careers. Other cases had arisen where clerics preached religious teachings in public schools, or claimed that pupils of secular schools would go to hell.

Document 19 provided the ideological justification for the restoration of religious life following the Cultural Revolution, and for the protection of freedom of individual religious belief enshrined in the revised Constitution of 1982.[20] The official religious associations were reinstated, officially designated places of religious worship were reopened, and religious communities were allowed and even encouraged to engage in international exchanges with their coreligionists. But the policy drew a clear line between "normal" religious life, which was permitted, and other illegal activities. The 1982–84 crackdown on "spiritual pollution" targeted those activities: reactionary secret societies (*huidaomen*) and "spirit mediums and witches" (*shenhan wupo* 神漢巫婆) were to be prevented from returning to activity, while practitioners of superstitious professions such as divination, physiognomy, numerology, and *fengshui* were to be reeducated to find another profession to make a living; if they persisted, they were to be disbanded. The building of lineage halls and ancestral shrines was also banned, and those that had already been built were to be expropriated.[21]

Notwithstanding these campaigns, in the more open atmosphere of the 1980s, religious activities rapidly multiplied. The growing contacts with foreign religious networks began to worry CCP leaders. This concern became especially salient following the collapse of the USSR and the Tian'anmen

19. Chen Jinlong, *Zhongguo gongchandang*, 62.

20. "Article 36, Religious Policy"; translated in toto in MacInnis, *Religion in China Today*, 34–35.

21. Chen Jinlong, *Zhongguo gongchandang*, 271. On the crackdown on redemptive societies banned as reactionary secret societies, R. Munro, ed., *Syncretic Sects*; also Palmer, "Heretical Doctrines," 120–26. In spite of these policies in the 1980s, the reconstruction of ancestral halls has gone unabated, as described in chapter 10.

student movement of 1989, leading to a crackdown on underground Catholic and Protestant leaders in 1990–91.[22] At a National Religious Work Conference held in December 1990, CCP general secretary Jiang Zemin stressed the importance of the Party's religious work in order to ensure ethnic harmony and protect China's territorial integrity. He also emphasized its importance in the struggle against infiltration by foreign religious forces as well as against those, including Christians, who, through developing churches, were suspected of attempting, from the bottom up, to pressure the CCP to lead China on the road to democracy.[23] These points were laid out in a new policy document, "Document 6," issued by the CCP Central Committee and the State Council on February 5, 1991,[24] which called for a reinforcement of the institutional management of religion, and prompted provincial and municipal authorities in several jurisdictions to issue detailed regulations.

In the 1980s, the main culprits of religious infiltration and political interference were seen to be the Roman Catholic Church and Protestant missionary societies.[25] The possibility of establishing diplomatic relations with the Vatican carried the risk of the Holy See attempting to control Chinese Catholics.[26] Protestant missionizing was also seen as a threat, through its multipronged strategies of evangelism. Increasingly, the influence of the "Dalai Lama clique" based in India and widely supported in the West was blamed for stoking Tibetan separatism, and the possibility of Muslims in Central Asia promoting the idea of an independent "East Turkestan" among Uighurs of Xinjiang, especially after the collapse of the Soviet Union, was also feared (discussed in chapter 13).[27]

Jiang Zemin invited the leaders of the five religions to Zhongnanhai twice in 1991 and 1992 to discuss these issues and stress the importance of the "adaptation of religion to a socialist society" 宗教與社會主義社會相適應. At a meeting of the United Front in November 1993, Jiang explained that the concept of "adaptation to socialism" meant that religious believers were free to keep their theism and their religious faith, but politically they should love the motherland and defend the socialist system and the leadership of the CCP.[28] They were to change their teachings and

---

22. Asia Watch Committee, *Freedom of Religion in China*, 6–29.

23. Speeches reprinted in Zhonggong zhongyang, *Xin shiqi zongjiao gongzuo wenxian*, 189–204.

24. Reproduced in Asia Watch Committee, *Freedom of Religion in China*, 30–35.

25. "Document 19"; cited in MacInnis, *Religion in China Today*, 23.

26. Leung, *Sino-Vatican Relations*; Leung & Liu, *The Chinese Catholic Church*.

27. Chen Jinlong, *Zhongguo gongchandang*, 248–49.

28. Speech reprinted in Zhonggong zhongyang, *Xin shiqi zongjiao gongzuo wenxian*, 249–55.

institutions that were not compatible with socialism, and use the positive aspects of religious teachings, practices, and morality to serve socialism. For example, cultural relics could be used for cultural development and patriotic education. Religious teachings and concepts could be used for socialist development, such as the liberal "theological construction" advocated by Protestant bishop Ding Guangxun 丁光訓 (b. 1915),[29] the Catholic notion of "love the Nation and love the Faith," the Buddhist theory of "humanistic Buddhism" understood as using Buddhism to serve society,[30] and the Muslim idea that "patriotism is part of faith." Religious teachings on morality could be used to improve the moral standards of the people, and international religious exchanges could contribute to building friendships and unifying the motherland (Hong Kong, Macau, and Taiwan). The government would help the religious leaders to adapt to socialism by identifying the useful elements of their religious tradition, encouraging them to eliminate their unhealthy habits and teachings, encouraging them to participate in economic development, and giving them the role of bridge between the Party-state and the masses.[31]

By the early 2000s, the tenor of speeches on religion was becoming even more positive. On January 31, 2001, Li Ruihuan 李瑞環 (then a member of the Standing Committee of the Political Bureau of Fifteenth Central Committee of the Communist Party and chairman of the Ninth National Committee of the Chinese People's Political Consultative Conference [CPPCC]) gave a speech that for the first time discussed religion in a manner that legitimized CCP religious policy from the standpoint of traditional Chinese culture. Much of Chinese culture is related to religion, he said, noting that China is a culture of harmonious assimilation, which has always absorbed different cultures and religions: foreign religions were constantly absorbing nourishment from Chinese culture and becoming "sinified." In that sense, he stated, the CCP's policy of religious freedom was in tune with traditional Chinese culture.[32]

At the end of the same year, at a meeting on religious work, Jiang Zemin recognized the dual nature of religion, including both its negative and posi-

29. Wickeri, *Reconstructing Christianity in China*; Ying Fuk-tsang (Xing Fuzeng), "Jiang lunli daode de jidujiao," "Church-State Relations," 34–37; Dunch, "Christianity and 'Adaptation to Socialism,'" 171–75.

30. Ji Zhe, "Secularization as Religious Restructuring," 253–56.

31. For a discussion of the theory of "adaptation to socialism" by the Central Party School's leading theoretician on religion, see Gong Xuezeng, *Shehui zhuyi yu zongjiao*, 251–323.

32. Chen Jinlong, *Zhongguo gongchandang*, 274.

tive sides. The list of positive aspects was longer than in his 1993 speech: now, religion also provided philanthropy, ensured the emotional and psychological stability of the masses, and preserved social order and stability. He noted the deep historical roots of religion and its long-term existence and continued influence, and recognized that religion might continue to exist even after the disappearance of classes and states—admitting that the goal of religion's disappearance was even more distant than the realization of communism.[33] Following his speech, an editorial in the *People's Daily* on December 13, 2001, acknowledged that it was the CCP's duty to represent the "legitimate interests of the broad masses of religious believers," who were recognized as "a positive force in the construction of socialism with Chinese characteristics."[34] In a speech on December 18, 2007, at a high-level Party study meeting, Jiang Zemin's successor, Hu Jintao 胡錦濤, further reinforced the positive discourse on religion, stressing that the "basic line" of the CCP's religious work was to enable religious people to "play an active role in economic and social development"; to help them resolve their material difficulties and unite them in the goal of building a "moderately prosperous society" (*xiaokang shehui* 小康社會); and to strengthen the construction of the religious clergy, so that they would be well trained to have the political, academic, and moral foundations for releasing the positive effect of religion on society.[35]

This discourse seems to renew the normative model of a good religion that thrived during the Republican period (discussed in chapter 3), when officially recognized religions competed to offer social services, notably in the realms of education and health care. At the same time, many religious organizations outside Mainland China, eager to expand in the PRC, considered the talk on social harmony an invitation to do so; for instance, all larger temples and religious groups in Hong Kong publicized their sponsoring of local schools and other social services in the mainland countryside. On the ground, however, the obstacles to such active participation of religious institutions were many, most stringently for organizations from outside the mainland, but also for the many national and local officially registered Buddhist, Christian, Muslim, and Taoist charities. While these

33. Ying Fuk-tsang (Xing Fuzeng), "New Wine in Old Wineskins," 349. For a detailed discussion of the practical implications of Jiang's speech, see Ying Fuk-tsang, "Church-State Relations," 20–26.

34. Chen Jinlong, *Zhongguo gongchandang*, 254–58.

35. Xinhua, "Hu Jintao: Guanche dang de zongjiao gongzuo fangzhen, zuohao xin xingshi xia zongjiao gongzuo," http://news.xinhuanet.com/newscenter/2007-12/19/content_7281396.htm (accessed October 13, 2009).

charities were welcome, and sometimes directly called on to contribute money to various causes (disaster relief in particular), they were much less welcome to run large social service operations by themselves; for instance, they could sponsor schools, but not manage them directly.[36]

The System of Religious Management: United Front, Religious Affairs Bureau, Official Associations

It was through the institutional network on religion that the goals enumerated by Hu Jintao could be carried out. This network refers to the deeply imbricated system combining the Party, through the United Front; the state, through the Religious Affairs Bureau; the religious communities, through their official associations; and academia, through the Institute of World Religions of the China Academy of Social Sciences, as well as other religious research institutes. The post-Mao religious institution began to take shape as early as 1978, when, at the eleventh Party congress, the policy of religious freedom was restored, and the state was given the mandates of "strengthening the management" of religion and of actively guiding the adaptation of religion to socialism—while emphasizing that "feudal superstition" remained banned.[37] The United Front Department was restored in 1978; it proceeded to rehabilitate religious leaders (notably those who were famous and of high standing) who had been persecuted during the Cultural Revolution, and to take measures to return them to normal religious life: for those who had been defrocked, encourage them to rejoin the clergy; for those who had been expelled from religious sites, return them to their communities. Party leaders were encouraged to build good relations with religious leaders, owing to their strong influence over their believers. Officials were told to meet with them, pay special attention to them, look after their material problems, take them on trips to other parts of China, communicate important Party and policy documents to them, and make full use of them. As in the 1950s, religious leaders were appointed to political positions: by the early 2000s, 10,000 out of 300,000 registered clerics held positions in People's Congresses and in People's Political Consultative Conferences (PPCC) at various levels. In the National PPCC, a Religious Commission 宗教委員會 was established to collectively bring

---

36. Laliberté, "Harmonious Society," "Entre désécularisation et resacralisation."
37. "Fully Implement the Policy of Religious Freedom," in MacInnis, *Religion in China Today*, 26–32; Madsen, "Religion and Feudal Superstition."

suggestions and proposals to the National PPCC in the name of the religious sector.[38]

The Religious Affairs Bureau (RAB)[39] was also reestablished in 1979, and given the tasks of supervising the reestablishment and operations of the official religious associations, the registration and management of clergy, and the registration and management of places of religious worship. United Front departments and Religious Affairs bureaus and commissions were established at each level of government: national, provincial, municipal, and county. The United Front, as a branch of the CCP, was responsible for dealing with religious leaders as individuals, while the RAB, as a government unit, was responsible for dealing with the religious associations as corporate entities. RAB offices were responsible for administrative oversight of the official associations of the five recognized religions. The national RAB had a first division overseeing Buddhism and Taoism, a second division for Protestantism and Catholicism, and a third for Islam. (A fourth division, for "policy research," "popular faith," and "new religions," was established in 2005, as discussed below.)

In practice, at lower levels of government the same official was often in charge of the United Front, religious affairs, and minority nationalities affairs. This was not a centralized system, however: whereas lower-level Religious Affairs and United Front officials were supposed to follow the directives and policies of the central government, they were appointed by the provincial and local government and Party committee, to which they remained accountable, not to the central RAB and United Front. There were thus extreme variations in the application of religious policy at the local level. The same situation prevailed in the official religious associations, which were established at the provincial and local levels throughout the 1980s and 1990s: the leaders of these associations were "elected" by the members after extensive consultations with local United Front and RAB representatives, in order to ensure that the person elected would have religious legitimacy among the followers, while at the same time being politically acceptable to the government — the common understanding being that, if either of these conditions was not met, the work of the association would encounter serious difficulties, since it would lose the support of either the government or the religious community. Since local religious leaders owed their selection to these local bodies, their primary loyalty was to them and not to the national-level official asso-

---

38. Chen Jinlong, *Zhongguo gongchandang*, 304–17, 306.
39. It was renamed State Administration of Religious Affairs in 1998.

ciation. The RAB was responsible for managing the legal religious communities, while the Public Security Bureau (PSB) prosecuted religious activities deemed illegal. Since the RAB and PSB at a given jurisdiction level did not necessarily communicate with each other or have good relations, policy implementation was not always coherent. Religious policy did not necessarily apply to significant parts of the country and population, which were governed by the People's Liberation Army, the Production and Construction Corps in Xinjiang and other border areas, or the ministries of Petroleum, Forestry, and Railroads, which all had separate administrative systems.[40]

The national-level official religious associations were reestablished in 1980: the China Buddhist Association (CBA), the China Taoist Association (CTA), the China Islamic Association, and the Protestant and Catholic associations. In the latter cases, in order to compensate for the lack of legitimacy of the Mao-era Chinese Catholic Patriotic Association (CCPA) and the Protestant Three-Self Patriotic Movement (TSPM), the authorities established new Christian associations that could focus on internal theological, pastoral, and liturgical matters, while the patriotic associations continued to handle political relations with the government and CCP. These new bodies were, for the Catholics, the National Conference of Bishops 中國天主教主教團 (1980), which was led by clergy as opposed to the lay CCPA, and the National Administrative Commission of the Catholic Church in China 中國天主教教務委員會 (1980); and, for the Protestants, the China Christian Council 中國基督教協會, which had an overlapping membership with the TSPM.[41] These moves, and a generally more pragmatic posture, allowed the official churches to bring a greater proportion of the clergy and believers into their fold than had been the case in the 1950s, but they were still unable to fully establish their authority.[42] The YMCA and YWCA were also reestablished, in collaboration with the United Front, the Communist Youth League, and the All-China Women's Federation, to organize the youth activity of Christians and to build ties with Christian youth in Hong Kong, Macau, Taiwan, and overseas.[43] Following their establishment at the national level, provincial and local associations were created. For the Taoists, for instance, there were 83 local associations in the early 1990s, 133 by 1999, and over 200 by the early 2000s.[44]

40. Chan Kim-kwong & Carlson, *Religious Freedom in China*, 10–13.
41. Daiber, "Les associations des cinq religions officiellement reconnues."
42. Kindopp & Hamrin, eds., *God and Caesar in China*.
43. Chen Jinlong, *Zhongguo gongchandang*, 308.
44. Guowuyuan, *Zhongguo zongjiao tuanti ziliao*.

The Management of Religious Clergy

A key concern of the Religious Affairs authorities and of the official associations was the ordination, registration, and management of the five religions' clergy. To be permitted to work as religious professionals, clerics needed to be acknowledged by their local religious association, which then sent their file to the local RAB. In 1997 there were 200,000 Buddhist monastics, including almost 80,000 Han Mahayana clerics (about one-third female), 120,000 Tibetan monks and nuns and 1,700 reincarnate lamas, and 10,000 Theravada monks among the Dai and other minorities in Yunnan.[45] (These figures can be compared with those from the early 1950s: 240,000 Han; 400,000 Tibetan and 8,000 Theravada clerics.) The number of Taoist monastics was lower but growing, with 12,000 in the early 1990s and double that number a decade later.[46]

"Patriotic education" was implemented in all religious communities from 1994 onward. Here, the main issue was integrating traditional forms of training and ordination with modern, standardized procedures being promoted by the state, as well as the question of political loyalty. For the ordination of monks, regulations were promulgated by the CBA and CTA. The first cohort of 47 Buddhist monastics were ordained in 1980; in 1987, 1,008 monks were ordained at Jizushan in Yunnan; the rhythm of Buddhist ordinations accelerated during the early twenty-first century so that about half the clergy was ordained. For Quanzhen Taoists, *shoujie* ordination ceremonies were reinstated at Baiyunguan in Beijing for a first cohort of 75, and in 1995 at Qingchengshan, for 400 candidates; for them the number of ordinations was tiny in relation to the total monastic population.

The main issue for the state management of Taoist clergy concerned the nonmonastic (*huoju* 火居) Taoist priests, who operated as independent ritual specialists, had little clerical organization, and for the most part did not reside in temples. These priests were initially condemned as superstitious practitioners, but by the 1990s their legitimacy was gradually recognized. Then, following a procedure passed by the CTA in 1992—which allowed Zhengyi priests to register with local Taoist associations, provided that they only conduct rituals in designated places of worship[47]—local

45. On the Buddhism of the Dai in the contemporary period and its relations with the Chinese state, see Borchert, "Worry for the Dai Nation."

46. He Guanghu, ed., *Zongjiao yu dangdai Zhongguo shehui*, 147. On the institutional Taoist revival, see Lai Chi-tim, "Daoism in China Today."

47. Chen Qizhang, *Dalu zongjiao zhengce yu fagui*, 144–47, for the full text of the procedure.

authorities attempted to put into place procedures for their registration and management.[48] In October 1991, ordination rituals were held at Longhushan 龍虎山, the former headquarters of the Heavenly Masters, in Jiangxi. Since the Heavenly Master had fled to Taiwan in 1949 and a successor had never been recognized by the PRC, the ordinations were conducted by the CTA—a significant institutional innovation.[49] Thirty-six Zhengyi priests from Singapore and Taiwan were ordained; in 1995, the rites were repeated for 200 priests from Mainland China. But this figure was insignificant given that the total number of such priests was perhaps 1,000 times higher: in Hubei alone, the number of *huoju* priests was estimated at 30,000; and the number was rising to meet the demand for ritual services that accompanied the rise in economic prosperity.

In Gansu, the Zhengyi Taoists were organized into districts, with a leader appointed for each district to hold meetings and political study, with the purpose of eliminating their superstitions. In Zhejiang, Zhengyi priests were required to undergo training in Taoist orthodoxy and to obtain two official permits: a *daoshi* permit and a Taoist association membership card. This system aimed to reduce the incidence of superstition, spirit possession, and fortune-telling, and to unify the liturgy. The extent to which such training and political study was followed simply to go through the motions, or did result in any changes in practice, remains to be studied. The issuing of permits turned out to be a lucrative source of income for RAB offices, which in some districts freely did so for a high fee, while other government departments also got into the act, such as Culture offices issuing permits to them as "folk artists."[50]

The religious authorities were also concerned about the formal training of the clergy. Officials and scholars regularly lamented the poor quality (*suzhi* 素質) of clerics[51]—and stressed the need for raising up a new generation of well-trained religious leaders. That this should be properly done, under government supervision, was also important so that future generations of clergy would be loyal to the CCP's leadership and to the socialist system.[52] In 1991, the United Front and the central RAB issued a document detailing a policy to identify promising young clergy with good political at-

48. Lagerwey, "A Propos de la situation actuelle."
49. Dean, "Further Partings of the Way," 193–94.
50. He Guanghu, ed., *Zongjiao yu dangdai Zhongguo shehui*, 166, 211–12.
51. Cao Nanlai, "Raising the Quality of Belief."
52. Chen Jinlong, *Zhongguo gongchandang*, 309.

titudes and religious knowledge, and to nurture them so that within five to ten years they could become the next generation of religious leaders.

The chief instrument for this training was the official religious academies and seminaries. The year 1980 saw the reestablishment of the China Buddhist Academy, the China Islamic Academy 中國經修院, the Nanjing Theological Seminary, and the China Catholic Seminary 中國天主教神哲學院. After 1982, local academies were also created: 6 Buddhist, 5 Islamic, 5 Protestant, and 5 Catholic. In their first decade of operation, these academies produced 2,000 graduates.[53] Specialized Buddhist academies were set up for Han, Tibetan, and Pali (Theravada) Buddhism. The China Taoist Academy was finally established at Baiyunguan in 1990. By 1997, there were 74 official religious training institutes. These academies and seminaries were organized in standard academic style, with courses of study lasting two to four years, followed by examinations and the conferring of a diploma equivalent to an associate or professional degree along with a religious title. After graduation, the clerics returned to their religious units. The training, which included political studies, Marxism, and foreign languages, differed from traditional modes of transmission, especially for the Taoists;[54] it was often seen not as a true spiritual education but merely as a ticket to advancement in their official careers, giving clerics the academic and social background needed to successfully function within the system of relationship building and bureaucratic politics within which the religious associations are embedded.

If the first leaders after the reestablishment of the religious associations in 1978–80 often won huge respect for having survived the Cultural Revolution and invested all their energy in reviving their institutions, the next generation lacked such aura.[55] By the 2000s, many clerics were complaining that the top levels of the clergy were controlled by clerics with academic degrees (Ph.D. being preferred) who maintained good relationships with officials, spent a large part of their time in meetings and banquets, and were managers rather than religious persons, while spiritual training was disappearing. These bureaucratic leaders were in sharp contrast to charismatic types outside or on the margins of official institutions, even

53. Ibid., 310.
54. Yang Der-ruey, "Revolution of Temporality."
55. Wank, "Institutionalizing Modern 'Religion,'" contrasts the first post-1978 abbot of the main Buddhist monastery in Xiamen, whose funeral procession in 1995 was attended by tens of thousands of kneeling laypersons, with his bureaucratic successor, who did not elicit any comparable admiration.

though a few charismatic Buddhists and Taoists did get appointments in their associations.[56]

Managing Places of Religious Worship

Another task of the Religious Affairs authorities was to negotiate the "return" of religious sites to the official religious associations—especially famous monasteries, large churches, and temples in the cities and areas with high concentrations of believers and in ethnic minority areas.[57] Famous temples and churches of historic value were often restored at the government's expense, often more to impress foreign visitors (including official delegations from Buddhist and Muslim countries) than to accommodate local believers. The return of temples was a source of constant conflict, since most religious venues had been taken over by other units and departments during the Mao era, and the most important sites were often under the control of the tourism, cultural relics, or parks administrations, which were not willing to give them up. In 1983, a policy was enacted to open "key" national Buddhist and Taoist monasteries to the public as places of religious worship, and for them to be managed by monastics. This led to the paltry number of 142 Buddhist and 21 Taoist temples being opened up. Progress was so slow that in 1994 a new directive was issued by the United Front and the Religious Affairs Bureau, to rapidly resolve the many outstanding cases. By 1995, there were a total of 77,981 officially registered places of religious worship: 44 percent were mosques, 40 percent were churches (34 percent Protestant and 6 percent Catholic), 15 percent were Buddhist monasteries, and 2 percent were Taoist temples.[58] At the time of writing this book, over thirty years after the Cultural Revolution, negotiating the transfer of religious sites remains one of the major preoccupations of Religious Affairs officials and of the religious associations.

Officially designated places of worship were, according to Document 19,

56. On the training of Protestant clergy, see Vala, "Pathways to the Pulpit." On Catholics, see Leung, "Communist Party–Vatican Interplay." On Muslims, see Allès, "Muslim Religious Education in China."

57. See Goossaert & Fang Ling, "Temples and Daoists," for a more detailed study of the Taoist case.

58. The low proportions of Buddhist and Taoist temples reflect the fact that before 1949, and again today in many rural areas, most Chinese temples are built and managed by local laypeople and are unaffiliated with either Buddhism or Taoism, although they often hire Buddhist and/or Taoist priests to conduct rituals. As a result, they cannot be registered as official places of worship unless they manage to prove (or fabricate) a historical or doctrinal connection with either of the two religions. For an example, see Chau, *Miraculous Response*.

"under the administrative control of the Bureau of Religious Affairs, but the religions organizations themselves and professional religious themselves were responsible for their management."[59] In the case of Buddhist and Taoist temples, they were managed by their local Buddhist or Taoist association (which often had its offices within the premises of the major temples), following principles of "democratic management" (by resident clerics and not lay temple committees), under the supervision of the local RAB. Regulations for the management of temples stipulated the administrative structure and provided for the protection of historic relics. Religious life was to be "normalized" (*zhengchanghua* 正常化); "normal" religious life included scripture recitation in temples, rituals, and self-cultivation, whereas sorcery, exorcism, divination, spirit possession, spirit writing, and *fengshui*, as superstitions, were illegal. Since the latter activities were among the main traditional sources of revenue for temples, this forced them to seek alternative income streams, notably through tourism; however, market demand, and more relaxed controls by the late 1990s, meant that the "superstitious" activities became increasingly prevalent and visible in temples. Meanwhile, negotiating their autonomous space and control over resources with the local RAB and local Buddhist/Taoist association took much of the time of temple clerics.[60]

Temples that were major tourist attractions enjoyed high levels of revenue, leading to conflicts among religious associations and government agencies, all claiming a share of the pie. In some jurisdictions, for example, provincial Taoist associations levied a 5-percent fee on the revenues of all temples under their management. In some areas (as mentioned in chapter 10), RABs showed strong interest in profitable temples, and ignored others. In temples managed by clerics, corrupt relations of profit sharing between temple abbots and local authorities sparked frequent controversies. Often, the authorities simply outsourced the management of temples to private businesses, which invested in the construction and promotion, hired clerics to staff them, and reverted a part of the profits to the government.[61] The tourist and business potential of Buddhist sites led to a trend of local authorities and entrepreneurs building giant, open-air Buddhas in order to attract tourists and pilgrims—a phenomenon decried by Religious Affairs officials.

59. "Document 19"; quoted in MacInnis, *Religion in China Today*, 18.
60. Wank, "Institutionalizing Modern 'Religion.'"
61. He Guanghu, ed., *Zongjiao yu dangdai Zhongguo shehui*, 210; Lang, Chan, & Ragvald, "Temples"; Sutton & Kang Xiaofei, "Recasting Religion and Ethnicity."

Non-"Religious" Orthodoxies and Heterodoxies

The institutional framework for religious affairs, which has been described above, was based on a narrow definition of religion, which excluded much of China's religious culture. The very narrowness of the category of religion, restricted to official associations of the five recognized religions, and the political sensitivity and restrictions attached to the category, led to a rush on the part of other actors, both within and outside the state, to designate a wide range of practices under *nonreligious* labels, and thus to secure the legitimacy and legality of the practices—creating what Yang Fenggang has called the "gray market" of religion.[62] In so doing, however, they were subject to the norms associated with that nonreligious category, which were defined and debated within the discursive network surrounding that category.

A notable case was the body cultivation traditions, which had been institutionalized under the category of *qigong* in the 1950s, where they were integrated into the discursive network of medicine rather than religion (see chapter 4). The post-Mao era saw *qigong* spread from Chinese medicine into the discursive networks of sports, national defense, and science, where, far from the restrictions and sensitivities of the *religion* label, many forms of religiosity were able to find expression under a cloak of legitimacy. As described in chapter 11, for over a decade, from the late 1970s to the mid-1990s, while officially designated "religious" communities were banned from holding activities or publicly promoting their teachings outside the premises of designated places of worship, thousands of popular *qigong* groups could freely and publicly promote meditation, breathing, and gymnastic regimens that, in addition to the "triple discipline" of the body, breath, and mind of 1950s *qigong*, often included an assortment of magical practices: healing by "external *qi*," trance states, objects imbued with *qi* or "information" emitted by a master, glossolalia, or "cosmic language," and so on. The methods were often explicitly based on Buddhist and Taoist symbols and cosmology, and sometimes even involved deity worship.[63]

Millions of practitioners could congregate in urban parks and public spaces under the guise of "health" and "physical fitness," while laboratory research could be conducted on the techniques and their paranormal claims under the guise of "science," and the potential applications of paranormal powers for national defense could be investigated by the military.

---

62. Yang Fenggang, "The Red, Black, and Gray Markets."
63. Palmer, *Qigong Fever.*

A complex discursive network around *qigong* and "somatic science" thus emerged with the active support of the institutions and key leaders in the fields of sports, health, science, and defense.[64] Here we will look at the official institutional framework within which such activities took place.

The association of *qigong* with the discursive networks of science began in 1979, when, following the resumption of *qigong* therapeutic activities in clinics, speculation spread that there might be a connection between external *qi* therapy (when a master emits *qi* from a distance to his patient) and paranormal phenomena being reported in the newspapers at the time, such as children able to read Chinese characters with their ears. The idea was that external *qi* healing and ear reading were among a range of paranormal abilities which could be trained and developed through *qigong* practice. If true, it would constitute a scientific discovery of historic significance. This speculation caught the attention of the Party leadership; several members of the State Council, including Vice-Premier Fang Yi 方毅 (1916–1997), attended a meeting called by the State Administration for Chinese Medicine, at which reports were given on *qigong*, external *qi*, and paranormal abilities. This meeting, which brought together, under high political patronage, most of the main figures involved in *qigong* training, therapy, and research, gave birth to the "*qigong* sector" 氣功界—an officially recognized national network that included not only masters and practitioners but also scientists. *Qigong* was no longer seen as a mere branch of Chinese medicine, but was regarded as a scientific discipline in its own right, specialized in investigating the newly discovered material substance of external *qi*, which could be controlled and projected by the mind. The political leaders present praised and encouraged "*qigong* science," giving the green light to its development.

Qigong masters were federated in state-sponsored associations affiliated with state medical, scientific, and sports authorities. A space was thus opened within which traditional masters could practice their healing arts and create organized transmission networks under the guise of *qigong*. Millions of adepts congregated in parks and public spaces every morning to practice exercise routines disseminated by the networks. Throughout the 1980s, *qigong* became a legitimized outlet for the resurgence, reconfiguration, and "modernization" of popular beliefs and practices. The interplay and interpenetration of these popular networks and official institutions gave form to the "*qigong* sector."

Researchers from several universities gathered in Shanghai in January

64. Ibid.

1981 to share their findings on paranormal abilities, called extraordinary functions 特異功能. Research groups were formed in a number of scientific institutions. In 1982, a group of key universities, after conducting tests on a few individuals who had become media celebrities due to their extraordinary abilities, announced that that their powers "proved" to be real. Debate raged in the press, until the Propaganda Department of the Party Central Committee intervened in April 1982 to ban both promotion and criticism of the phenomena. The famous scientist Qian Xuesen 錢學森 (1911–2009), the architect of China's nuclear weapons program, then petitioned Premier Hu Yaobang 胡耀邦 (1915–1989) on behalf of extraordinary functions research, leading the Propaganda Department to change its line and authorize publication of data for scientific purposes. Extraordinary functions research was thus officially legitimized.

In early 1986, under the patronage of the National Association for Science and Technology, chaired by Qian Xuesen, the state-sponsored China Qigong Science Association was founded on a triumphant note, as Qian proclaimed a new scientific revolution. The new discipline of somatic science (*renti kexue* 人體科學), by integrating *qigong*, traditional medicine, and extraordinary functions with modern science and technology, was going to become a true Marxist science.[65]

The creation of the China Qigong Science Association was heralded as a turning point in the history of *qigong* and even of science, as *qigong* advocates cried: "*qigong* has left religion and folklore to enter the temple of Science!"[66] The National Science Commission officially recognized *qigong* as a scientific discipline. An interministerial Leaders' Working Group on Somatic Science, made up of representatives from the Ministry of National Security, the Central Party Committee Propaganda Department, the National Defense Commission for Science, Technology and Industry, and the National Association for Science and Technology, was formed to promote, coordinate, and supervise *qigong* and extraordinary-functions activities.

At the same time, by finding a home in the discursive regimes of medicine and science, *qigong* was required to submit to the normative standards and practices of those fields, thereby transforming and secularizing the practice. When the opposite occurred, *qigong* became the target of a polemical campaign launched by some scientists and journalists, who

---

65. See Lim Chee-Han, "Purging the Ghost of Descartes," for a study of the embodiment of Marxist faith through *qigong* practice. See Lü Xichen, "Yuanjidao," for a study of how *qigong* was applied for the reeducation of prisoners.

66. Zheng Guanglu, *Qijuan shenzhou*, 52.

declared it "pseudoscience," "superstition," and "evil cults" (*xiejiao*). The *xiejiao* label, previously used in the Ming and Qing dynasties, had resurfaced and entered Chinese media discourse in the mid-1990s, but this time to translate the term *cult* in Chinese press coverage of the tragedies of the Branch Davidians (USA, 1993), of the Order of the Solar Temple (Switzerland, Quebec, and France, 1994 and 1995), and of Aum Shinrikyo (Japan, 1995). In 1995, the State Council and the CCP Central Committee emitted a circular banning several groups designated as *xiejiao*, most of which had been denounced as heretical by the official Protestant associations: the Shouters (also known as the Assembly Hall), the All Ranges Church (*Quan fanwei jiaohui* 全範圍教會), the New Testament Church (*Xinyue jiaohui* 新約教會), the Oriental Lightning, the Assembly of Disciples (*Mentuhui* 門徒會), the Lord God Church (*Zhushenjiao* 主神教), and the Church of Spirits (*Linglinghui* 靈靈會),[67] as well as the Supreme Master Ching Hai movement and its method (*Guanyin famen*), then headquartered in Taiwan. In the same year, the Ministry of Public Security identified an additional seven groups as *xiejiao*: the Established King (*Beiliwang* 被立王), the Unification Church (*Tongyijiao* 統一教), the Three Kinds of Servants, the True Buddha School, the Children of God, the Dami Mission, and the World Elijah Evangelical Mission (the latter two being Korean churches).[68] The contemporary reappearance of the *xiejiao* label was thus associated with Christian and foreign groups and translated Western categories of the cult disseminated by the anticult movement, which, in North America, is dominated by Christian interests.[69]

The journalists and scientists who in 1995 were in a heated polemic against the "superstitious" and "pseudoscientific" deviations of the *qigong* movement noted the similarities between foreign *xiejiao* and some *qigong* organizations, and called for an immediate purge of such groups before they became Aum Shinrikyo–style cults and caused large-scale killings.[70] Following this polemic, the political support that had contributed so much to the spread of the *qigong* movement dissipated, and the state attempted to strengthen regulation of the thousands of *qigong* associations and networks. In 1998, several Buddhist magazines specifically attacked Falungong, which had become the most popular *qigong* form, as a *xiejiao* that

---

67. Dunn, "'Cult,' Church, and the CCP"; Kupfer, "Christian-Inspired Groups."
68. Internal documents listing and describing these groups are translated and reproduced in Center for Religious Freedom, *Report*, 11–30.
69. Chan Kim-kwong & Carlson, *Religious Freedom in China*, 15.
70. Palmer, *Qigong Fever*, 170–72.

drew lay Buddhists away from orthodoxy, and inscribed Falungong in a genealogy which linked it to Yiguandao and the White Lotus tradition.[71] Thus, through the combination of scientific polemics and Christian and Buddhist apologetics, a new Chinese discourse on "cults" emerged, which resuscitated the old imperial model of *xiejiao* as "White Lotus" heterodoxy and combined it with fears of the collective suicides and mass murders of Western and Japanese cults. Ironically, this reappearance of the *xiejiao* discourse in Mainland China occurred just after it had faded in Taiwan, with the end of martial law and the legalization of Yiguandao in 1987.

The Ministry of Public Security, which in 1997 had begun an investigation of Falungong as an "illegal religion" (*feifa zongjiao* 非法宗教),[72] launched a new investigation in 1998, this time designating it as a *xiejiao*.[73] Starting on July 22, 1999, when the CCP decreed the total suppression of Falungong, the *xiejiao* label, which had now become a mark of political demonization, was ubiquitous in the propaganda campaign that saturated the media for several months. Scholars and religious leaders were summoned to conferences in which the category of *xiejiao* was defined on the basis of Western cases, applied to Falungong, and distinguished from orthodox religion.[74] On October 30 of the same year, the state retroactively gave itself the legal instrument of repression when the highest legislative body passed a resolution banning *xiejiao* "which act under the cover of religion, *qigong*, or other illicit forms," and stipulated the punishment of those who "manipulate the members of *xiejiao* organizations to break the laws and decrees of the state, organize mass gatherings to disturb the social order and deceive the public, cause deaths, rape women, and swindle people of their goods and money, or commit other crimes of superstition or heresy."[75] Although the anti-*xiejiao* discourse took pains to emphasize that *qigong* was a gem of Chinese culture and that only Falungong was being targeted, in reality, the authorities feared that other *qigong* groups could potentially become like Falungong, and all of them were disbanded. From then on, the organized *qigong* sector ceased to exist, even if individuals were free to continue practicing the exercises.

The discursive network on "evil cults" was made up of the Ministry of

71. Ibid., 262–63; Chen Xingqiao, *Fojiao "qigong" yu falungong*.

72. This was the term used to designate heretical Christian groups before the *xiejiao* label came into usage in the mid- to late 1990s (Kupfer, "Christian-Inspired Groups," 276).

73. Palmer, *Qigong Fever*, 265.

74. Chen Hongxing & Dai Chenjing, eds., *Falungong yu xiejiao*.

75. National People's Congress, "Decision." See Kupfer, "Christian-Inspired Groups," 278–79, for a table of the types of crimes and punishments for *xiejiao* activity.

Public Security and its specialized anticult units, as well as state-sponsored anticult associations. The identification of *xiejiao* was a responsibility of the provincial-level Public Security Bureau (the national Ministry of Public Security was responsible for identifying cross-provincial *xiejiao*), while local authorities were authorized to implement the suppression of the cults, by confiscating their assets and prosecuting their leaders. A national network of "610 offices," led by a member of the CCP Politburo, was established on June 10, 1999, with the specific duty of implementing the persecution of Falungong,[76] and an office for the "prevention and handling of evil cults" was established under the State Council in September 2000. Two months later the China Anti-Cult Association 中國反邪教協會 was established under the National Association for Science and Technology, followed by a flurry of academic conferences and publications that appeared in the early 2000s, aiming to give further content and academic validity to the *xiejiao* label, drawing heavily on Western anti-cult polemics.[77]

In this literature, the *xiejiao* was defined almost as an antireligion, in sharp contrast to religion, which was depicted in unambiguously positive terms.[78] The new Chinese discourse on *xiejiao* combined traditional notions of heretical doctrines with Western elements derived from Christian apologetics, psychology, and the social sciences. The result was a *xiejiao* category that borrowed from imperial Chinese ideology a concept of heterodoxy/orthodoxy based on notions of order and social harmony, of which the state was the prime protector with the assistance of religion as an instrument of moral education (*jiaohua*). Moreover, it borrowed from Western discourse a universalist approach that defines *social order, religion*, and the like in general and abstract terms, citing examples from the whole world, without giving a special role of arbiter to the Chinese state or to specific religions recognized as orthodox in China. The discourse placed a strong emphasis on the relationship between *xiejiao* and religion, practically defining them as an antireligion. Indeed, many articles stressed how, in contrast to *xiejiao*, religion—even new religious movements—brought positive benefits to society and was conducive to social morality and stability. Significant here was the unambiguously positive evaluation of "religion," of which the "orthodox" nature was understood quite broadly, rarely

---

76. J. Tong, "Anatomy of Regime Repression in China"; World Organization to Investigate the Persecution of Falun Gong, *General Report on the '610 Office,'* 2004.

77. Kupfer, "Christian-Inspired Groups," 276–77.

78. Palmer, "Heretical Doctrines"; see also Wang Zuo'an, *Zhongguo de zongjiao wenti he zongjiao zhengce*, 356–61.

specifically mentioning China's five official religions and even embracing new religions.

There was thus little overlap between the religion and "evil cult" networks: both categories were defined as mutually exclusive, and recognized religious leaders, scholars, and officials who dealt with religion did everything they could to keep the two categories impermeable, in order to protect the legitimacy of their own work and avoid being contaminated by the highly sensitive question of "evil cults."

By the early 2000s, then, a new polarity was taking shape, to a degree—though not completely—replacing the old dichotomy between progressive socialism and feudal religion. At one end was a single, state-supervised religious system of five denominations in which different traditions were organized into almost identical institutional structures under the supreme authority of the CCP, and molded into instruments for implementing the Party's broader goals of creating a "harmonious society." At the other end, the purported enemies of the regime, using religion for their political ends: the Vatican, the "Dalai Lama clique" and Uighur separatists, and, paradigmatically, the demonized evil cults, committed to an eschatological battle against the CCP, and mercilessly suppressed.[79] And in between the two poles, a growing gray area, described in the previous three chapters, in which most of China's religious life occurred.[80]

Other Channels of Institutional Legitimation: Intangible Heritage

In this gray area, religious practices found legitimacy and legality within the discursive networks of categories other than religion. While the Falungong affair had led to the collapse of the qigong sector as one of these alternative realms, several others continued to flourish and expand from the 1990s onward. These included the networks of tourism and economic development,[81] Confucianism, and national studies,[82] as well as culture[83]

---

79. Kindopp, "China's War on 'Cults.'"

80. Yang Fenggang, "The Red, Black and Gray Markets," has used a market analogy, based on the theory of religious economy, to describe and explain the growth of the "gray market" for religion. As mentioned in the introduction, we abstain from using the language of markets here because, while useful in some contexts, it can be misleading in others.

81. Ji Zhe, "Buddhism and the State"; Borchert, "Of Temples and Tourists"; Lang, Chan, & Ragvald, "Temples."

82. Billioud & Thoraval, "Lijiao"; Billioud, "Confucianism."

83. Dutournier & Ji Zhe, "Social Experimentation."

and intangible cultural heritage 非物質文化遺產. This latter category was promoted by UNESCO as a way to do for oral traditions what world heritage sites had done for the protection of monuments and natural sites—in which the Chinese had also enthusiastically participated, successfully registering a number of major religious sites, such as Wudangshan and Taishan. The category was launched by the 2003 Convention for the Safeguarding of Intangible Cultural Heritage, which states that such heritage is manifested, among others, in the following domains: oral traditions and expressions, including language as a vehicle of the intangible cultural heritage; performing arts (such as traditional music, dance, and theatre); social practices, rituals, and festive events; knowledge and practices concerning nature and the universe; and traditional craftsmanship.

The PRC was one of the first states to ratify the convention, in 2004, and set up its own administrative apparatus to list and protect intangible cultural heritage under the aegis of the Ministry of Culture, thus creating a field distinct from the religious field. The nationwide network of cultural affairs bureaus, down to the provincial and county levels, has been mobilized to identify items of traditional culture that are to be officially designated as "intangible heritage," and that are to benefit from special heritage protection and funding. The movement was enthusiastically taken up by communal religion organizers and local officials, who identified it as a powerful way to legitimize their practices and began to send countless applications for recognition at the county, provincial, and national levels. Now not only major local cults to deities such as Mazu and Jigong 濟公, but also village temple festivals 民間社火 have all been registered, along with officially sponsored cults (the Yellow Emperor, Chinggis khan, Confucius).[84] Some of these cults to China's civilizing heroes, such as Yu the Great, in Shaoxing (Zhejiang), were also designated as national sacrifices 國祭 by the Ministry of Culture.[85] Through this process, local ritual traditions and cults to popular deities—none of which are recognized as religion—found a new "canonization," while inscribing themselves into the discursive and institutional norms of cultural heritage protection.

Registration as intangible cultural heritage not only served as one more type of ritual disguise through which Chinese people have been able for centuries to have their local religious tradition appear on the surface as something licit. It has created a whole new category for thinking about

84. Web site of the "The Intangible Cultural Heritage in China," managed by the PRC Ministry of Culture: http://www.ihchina.cn/main.jsp (accessed February 19, 2009).
85. Billioud, "Confucianism."

religious traditions outside the discursive realm of religion, promoting them as living parts of Chinese culture (not as relics to be museified), worthy of preservation for both nationalistic reasons and for tourism development. Thus, in some way the PRC was emulating the Taiwanese and Hong Kong governments, and many other countries such as Korea. In fact, Chinese people were aghast that Koreans had planned to register Confucius and Confucianism as *their* intangible cultural heritage (since UNESCO records a given heritage only once)—an international incident which was a major impetus for the PRC government's strong support for intangible cultural heritage.

The Contested Status of Confucianism

Whereas religion and cultural heritage were distinct and well-defined discursive realms within which certain types of religious practices could be defined as orthodox, the most hotly debated category—Confucianism—remained the most elusive and unstructured. There was no single discursive authority on Confucianism; rather, it straddled different realms, notably primary education, academic research and "national studies," and state ideology.

Confucianism was condemned as an ideological heterodoxy during the Cultural Revolution, as shown during the "anti–Lin Biao and anti-Confucius" campaign of 1973; but it soon reverted to an ambiguous status as intellectuals in the PRC, Taiwan, and the West resumed the early twentieth-century discussions of its "religious" nature and its role in a modern Chinese society. The debate was launched in 1978 by a prominent historian, Ren Jiyu 任继愈 (b. 1916), and has continued unabated ever since.[86] Some, such as Gan Yang 甘陽, advocated a "Confucian socialist republic." Proponents of a vision of Confucianism as a religion gradually grew more numerous, as did the proportion of those who considered this religious nature a positive factor, and a possible resource for building a new Chinese national culture and spiritual identity.[87] Others, notably Kang Xiaoguang 康曉光 (b. 1963) and Jiang Qing 蔣慶 (b. 1953), argued for the establishment of Confucianism as the national religion, or for creating a new political system based on Confucian foundations.[88] The interconnected academic movements of "Confucian studies" (*ruxue*) and "national

86. A. Sun, "The Fate of Confucianism."
87. Ren Jiyu, ed., *Rujiao wenti*; Han Xing, *Rujiao wenti*.
88. Billioud, "Confucianism"; Ownby, "Kang Xiaoguang."

studies" gradually took a culturally nationalist coloration since the 1980s, even though they were not ideologically unified at all; among the forums, journals, and Web sites devoted to them, one finds liberal views as well as cultural conservatives proposing an authoritarian political model enforcing Confucian moral values.[89] The creation of Confucius Institutes abroad since 2004, while taking the form of Chinese-language training centers similar to the German Goethe institutes, has been interpreted by some as an expression of a more assertive policy of exporting China's new cultural nationalism. In 2006, the state-sponsored Confucius Foundation also attempted to fix a standard icon for Confucius, to be erected at numerous places in China and abroad.[90]

At the same time, the PRC state at various levels organized ever more numerous large-scale rituals in the name of Confucian culture, notably for Confucius's birthday in his home temple in Qufu but also in numerous other places.[91] Like the academic discourse on Confucianism, these rituals were highly ambiguous, drawing on tourism and cultural heritage along with a nationalist discourse on a Confucian China. As seen in chapter 7, the increasing practice in the PRC, following earlier attempts during the Republican period and then in Taiwan and Singapore, of recycling Confucian notions into the state moral discourse deprived Confucianism of a place of its own. Confucianism became an orthodox label used by a great variety of different state and other organizations for a wide range of tourism, cultural, and educational projects.

Contrary to the impression of many observers, for whom the resurgence of institutions and practices in the PRC making claims of being Confucian was part of a growing cultural nationalism, many of them were actually grassroots educational movements (discussed in chapter 11), did not have direct links to state policies and academic discussions (grassroots Confucian activists frequently dismissed the academics such as the New Confucians for their lack of practical outlook), and did not necessarily share their culturally nationalist ideas. For many activists who wanted to bring back Confucian education, the issue was less China's identity and place in the world than the moral and intellectual qualities of its future generations.

Meanwhile, the ritual and devotional elements in these various Confucian movements were as a rule very limited, and quite often absent altogether, unlike the spirit-writing and salvationist groups that were the most

---

89. Makeham, *Lost Soul*; Bresciani, *Reinventing Confucianism*; Makeham, ed., *New Confucianism*.
90. Murray, "'Idols' in the Temple."
91. Billioud & Thoraval, "Lijiao."

active of the groups claiming to be Confucian in Taiwan and, to a lesser degree, in Southeast Asia (discussed in chapter 11). These groups, notably Yiguandao, which remained banned in the PRC as *huidaomen*, seemed to have few connections with the academic or educational movements in Mainland China. Confucian salvationist groups, self-confessed Confucian academics, and education activists thus tended to form separate discursive networks.[92]

Opening the Category of Religion

Official policy timidly began to acknowledge the existence and even the legitimacy of this expanding realm of religious life. Chinese scholars of religion, sociology, and anthropology, through their studies of popular religion and new religious movements, and through their adoption of broader definitions of religion, contributed to legitimizing vast realms of activity previously stigmatized or excluded from the category of religion.[93] The increasing intensity of relationships with the outside world also led to a realization that the religious dimension of such exchanges requires coming to terms with the religious diversity of China's international partners. In 2005, a new set of regulations (*zongjiao shiwu tiaoli* 宗教事務條例) was promulgated, which was largely a consolidation of previous regulations and policies.[94] A notable change in these regulations was that the procedure for the registration of religious associations made no mention of the five official religions, making it theoretically possible for other religions to register (but no other religion has succeeded in doing so at the time of writing). Indeed, taking stock of the reality that the religious world extended far beyond the five officially registered religions, in the same year the State Administration of Religious Affairs (SARA, the former national RAB, renamed in 1998) established a fourth division to look into other groups, especially those pertaining to popular faith (*minjian xinyang*) and new religions (*xinxing zongjiao*), as well as to conduct research on religious policy.

By the time of writing, there has been no explicit policy on popular faith and new religions, but there has been a recognition that the phenomena existed and should not be simply banned, and also a willingness to build

92. Jochim, "Carrying Confucianism."

93. Overmyer, "From 'Feudal Superstition' to 'Popular Beliefs.'"

94. Ying Fuk-tsang (Xing Fuzeng), "New Wine in Old Wineskins." See Shuai Feng and Li Jian, eds., *Zongjiao shiwu tiaoli shiyi*, for a detailed official interpretation of the regulations.

direct or indirect relationships with those communities, significantly contributing to removing any stigma associated with them—so long as they were not classified as evil cults or as challenging the CCP's authority or the PRC's territorial integrity. If the category of popular faith (*minjian xinyang*) has emerged in official research documents as a realm of legitimate religious practices, it still has not, at the time of writing, been built into a recognized administrative category.

Most temples to local gods, belonging to and affiliated with none of China's five officially recognized religions, had no natural link with the state bureaucracy, and were technically illegal, their customs and festivals previously stigmatized as "feudal superstitions." The regulations on places of religious worship enacted by the State Council in 1994,[95] which detailed and formalized previous regulations in a context in which officials sensed that the world of temples was underregulated, put the registration of temples under the jurisdiction of provincial Religious Affairs bureaus, and required all places of worship to be affiliated with one of the five official religions. In some areas, such as Fujian, Zhejiang, and Shaanxi, there was thus a trend throughout the 1990s to register temples as Taoist or Buddhist: an arrangement that gave them membership in local state-sponsored religious associations, integrating them into the state's system of religious management. However, the registration procedure was never an easy matter, requiring candidate temples to prove, at least on paper, strong historical links with elite Taoism or Buddhism—links that were most often tenuous at best— and, most important, to cultivate good connections with the local Taoist or Buddhist association.[96] In exchange, temples were required to share a portion of their revenues with the association; attend official political meetings of the association, the Religious Affairs Bureau, and the United Front; acquire training in orthodox Taoism (or Buddhism); and in some cases accept monks or priests assigned to live there by the association.[97] Most of the temples that sought such affiliation were territorial, but a number of shrines of lay salvationist groups (such as Xiantiandao in southern China or Hongyangjiao 弘陽教 in Hebei) also successfully registered with the Taoist association, thus gaining legitimacy.

Different provinces and localities took different approaches, which

95. "Guowuyuan guanyu zongjiao huodong changsuo guanli tiaoli."

96. Chau, "The Politics of Legitimation"; Mayfair Yang, "Fission and Fusion."

97. M. Yang, "Detaching and Re-Incorporating"; Flower, "A Road is Made"; Lang, Chan & Lagvald, "Temples."

were monitored by the fourth division of SARA, and were summarized into three models: (1) no government interference; (2) registering communal temples as Taoist (*minjian xinyang daojiaohua* 民間信仰道教化); or (3) officially registering them as a new category of popular faith. A conference was held by SARA in 2008 to study the three options, but none was chosen, leaving the provinces to continue experimenting. At the same time, there were increasingly explicit indications that communal temples were (along with Buddhism and Taoism) seen as an important resource for slowing the growth of Christianity in the countryside.[98] Other local variations have been observed, such as, exceptionally, temples of the Three-in-One Teachings (*sanyi jiao* 三一教), which registered under that label in some parts of Fujian.[99] According to an official of the Fujian Religious Affairs Bureau,[100] the de facto policy of the provincial bureau toward *minjian xinyang* temples was to delegate such cases to the local authorities, thereby legitimizing the ad hoc arrangements and negotiations made between the latter and specific temples (described in chapter 10). In the context of decentralization, certain areas, notably Fujian, were widely seen as laboratories for experimenting with new religious policies more open to temple cults, which were still unthinkable to many local officials elsewhere. If such experiments were successful and carried out on a larger scale, they would mark a watershed in the long-term state-religion relationship: meaning that the state now stopped giving exclusive recognition to the great world religions.

Meanwhile, friendly exchanges of delegations took place from the early 2000s between the fourth division of SARA and the Confucian Academy of Hong Kong, which was ardently lobbying for establishing Confucianism as the national religion of China,[101] as well as with Yiguandao in Taiwan. The Eastern Orthodox Church, which has believers among the Russian ethnic minority and some Chinese in the far northeast and far northwest, as well as historic properties in Beijing and Shanghai, was registered at the provincial level in Heilongjiang Province; and after long negotiations, Orthodox religious services were authorized (in the premises of the Russian consulate) in Shanghai in the spring of 2008. Foreign Jews living in China—

98. Personal communication, 2009, by a Chinese scholar who attended the 2008 conference; see also Goossaert & Fang Ling, "Temples and Daoists."

99. Ying Fuk-tsang (Xing Fuzeng), "Church-State Relations," 27 n. 42.

100. Personal communication, August 9, 2006.

101. See Ownby, "Kang Xiaoguang," for a discussion of this question.

who had a significant historical presence in Shanghai and Harbin during the early twentieth century—were allowed to associate and worship, but SARA refused to recognize the claims of religious identity by descendants of the Kaifeng Jews, who had settled in China during the Song dynasty.[102]

For "new religions," the main cases being dealt with by SARA were the Bahá'í Faith[103] and the Mormons.[104] Both profess strict obedience to the law as part of their religious teachings and scrupulously avoided establishing religious institutions in Mainland China, earning the trust of the authorities while, through natural friendships and overseas travel, the number of Chinese believers grew. Expatriates from the two religions were allowed to establish associations (limited to foreigners) in major cities, while the authorities generally did not interfere with small-scale, informal gatherings of Chinese believers held in private homes. While the Mormons regularly invited Chinese officials and scholars to Brigham Young University in Utah, USA, which has a strong expertise in religion and law, SARA and the Bahá'í Assemblies of Macau and Hong Kong held regular exchanges of delegations and joint conferences on building harmony and social development, which are important areas of Bahá'í teachings and engagement.[105]

SARA's contacts with these various groups, however, took place in the context of official exchanges with Hong Kong, Macau, Taiwan, or overseas, or with foreigners living in China, and did not necessarily concern policy toward these religions on the mainland. Some of the cases were handled by SARA in the context of managing China's relations with Russia (which aggressively pursued the rights of China's Orthodox Christians), Israel (which, at the diplomatic level, ignored the Kaifeng Jews),[106] and the United States (which pressed for the rights of Mormons under both

102. Wang Zuo'an, *Zhongguo de zongjiao wenti he zongjiao zhengce*, 31. On the Orthodox, Jews, Mormons, and Bahá'ís in China, see Chan Kim-kwong (Chen Jianguang), "Religion in China," 98–100.

103. The Bahá'í Faith's history in China dated to 1902, with small communities in Beijing and Shanghai in the Republican period. Cao Yunxiang 曹雲祥 (1881–1937), the first president of Tsinghua University and one of the earliest Chinese Bahá'ís, had been the first translator of Bahá'í scriptures into Chinese. See Cai Degui, *Dangdai xinxing bahayi jiao*; Hassall, "China in the Bahá'í Writings."

104. Other groups such as Sokka Gakai, the Unification Church, Tiandijiao, Dejiao, and the Red Swastika Society were active on the mainland through cultural, economic, and academic exchanges and philanthropy, but at the time of writing had no known relations with SARA.

105. On these conferences, see www.srdchina.org and http://bahai-academic.hk/collection .php?langu=en-US&collection=Contacts_PRC_Bahai (accessed October 16, 2009).

106. "Fundamentally Freund: Why is Israel Ignoring China's Jews?," *Jerusalem Post*, July 14, 2008; http://www.jpost.com/servlet/Satellite?cid=1215330965901&pagename=JPArticle%2FshowFull (accessed October 31, 2009).

presidents Bush and Obama, who appointed a Mormon as U.S. ambassador to China).[107]

HONG KONG AND MACAU

In Hong Kong, the British colonial authorities ostensibly maintained a laissez-faire attitude toward religion that remained essentially unchanged under the "one country, two systems" regime following the handover to the PRC in 1997: most churches and religious groups were registered as limited companies and as tax-exempt charities, and treated by the government like any other corporation, without regard to whether it was religious or not. This image, however, is belied by the role played by the government, the Hong Kong Chinese elite, and the Christian churches in shaping the religious field. As discussed in chapter 8, since 1928 the management of most local temples had been removed from their local communities and placed under the centralized Chinese Temples Committee, run by leaders of the Chinese merchant elite and the colonial Secretary for Chinese Affairs, which siphoned their revenues to the Tung Hua Hospitals charity and stifled their vitality. On the other hand, the Hong Kong government typically outsourced the provision of education and social services to religious groups, notably the Anglican and Catholic churches. Thus, by 1996, Christian churches operated half of Hong Kong's 1,354 primary and secondary schools. In contrast, the 46 Buddhist-operated schools, 24 Taoist, 3 Confucian, 2 Muslim, and 1 Red Swastika Society schools, *combined*, accounted for only 5 percent of Hong Kong's schools. The numerical dominance of Christianity in education was reinforced by the fact that most of the *best* schools were Christian, clearly shaping the beliefs and attitudes of Hong Kong's elite (even though conversion rates remained rather low, with not more than 10 percent of the population being Christian during the 1990s and 2000s). Through extensive networks—land applications for the establishment of new churches were given special consideration if the premises were also used for hospitals, community centers, nurseries, old age homes, youth camps, and so on—Protestant and Catholic institutions provided 70 percent of Hong Kong's social services.[108]

Another indicator of the special status accorded to Christianity was the

---

107. "Obama Names GOP Gov. Envoy to China," *USA Today*, May 17, 2009; http://www.usatoday .com/news/washington/2009-05-16-china-ambassador_N.htm (accessed October 31, 2009).

108. Kwong, *The Public Role of Religion*, 59–60; Leung & Chan, *Changing Church and State Relations*.

fact that the Anglican and Catholic bishops were listed fifth on the table of colonial protocol, while no other religious leader was included. Catholic and Anglican priests sat as unofficial members of the Legislative Council, and Christian churches were the only religions licensed to hold weddings. The legal New Year was inaugurated at ceremonies held alternately in Anglican and Catholic churches.[109]

Fearing to lose these privileges, and mindful of the situation of Christianity on the mainland, Hong Kong Christian groups reacted with worry and a sense of crisis to the impending reversion of Hong Kong to Chinese sovereignty in 1997—while the Buddhist, Taoist, and Confucian groups celebrated with euphoria. The Basic Law for the first time gave legal protection to religious freedom in Hong Kong, and stipulated that, following the handover, the PRC government would not interfere with religious matters there—it would not establish a Religious Affairs Bureau in Hong Kong, and Hong Kong's religious communities would remain independent of the PRC's official religious associations. Nonetheless, in the years preceding and following the handover, a trend began that gradually reduced the dominance of Christian institutions and at the same time increased the influence of the non-Christian religions. The Anglican and Catholic bishops were dropped from the official protocol, while "religious leaders" in general were placed at the eleventh rank. Unelected Christian clergy were no longer appointed to the Legislative Council. Fewer new schools and social services were contracted to the churches, with nonreligious community organizations playing a greater role. New funding policies were less advantageous to churches managing schools, and a new policy on school governance, introduced in 2004—which handed management of schools to elected boards—caused the Roman Catholic Church to fear losing control over its schools. Non-Christian religious communities, ranging from Taoists and Buddhists to Bahá'ís, were licensed to hold weddings. Buddha's birthday was designated a public holiday in 1997, alongside the four Christian holidays (two days at Easter, two at Christmas) and five traditional festivals (New Year, Grave-Sweeping, Dragon Boat, Mid-Autumn, and Chongyang), and at the time of writing there has been speculation that a Confucian holiday would also be added—a development that spurred the Hong Kong Taoist Association to begin pressing for a public holiday to commemorate Laozi as well. On the other hand, no association pressed for a recognition of the birthday of Tin Hau (天后, known as Mazu in Taiwan), the goddess who had the most temples, the longest history, and the deep-

---

109. Kwong Chunwah, *The Public Role of Religion*, 60.

est popular roots in Hong Kong—but who was not affiliated with a formal religious institution.

Just as before 1997, any religious group could freely incorporate under the companies ordinance. But a new pattern of interactions between the state and religious institutions emerged, which in some ways paralleled the Mainland Chinese configuration of a "religious sector" represented by a single association for each religious tradition. In Hong Kong, this role was taken up by the members of the Colloquium of Six Religious Leaders in Hong Kong, a forum for interreligious dialogue that had been initiated by the Catholic Diocesan Commission for Non-Christian Religions in 1972, and included associations representing the Catholic, Protestant, Buddhist, Taoist, Confucian, and Muslim communities. This group, which held mutual visits and seminars before the handover, was given a more formal role after 1997: its member associations were allotted forty delegates (out of eight hundred) to represent the religious communities as a "functional constituency" in the corporatist election of the Chief Executive of the Hong Kong Special Administrative Region of the PRC, and they were also treated as the chief interlocutors representing Hong Kong's religious sector by the Liaison Office of the PRC government, which followed the United Front approach of nurturing good relationships with cooperative religious leaders. The six member institutions of the colloquium thus acquired a privileged status: the Catholic Diocese, the Hong Kong Christian Council 香港基督教協進會, the Hong Kong Buddhist Association, the Hong Kong Taoist Association, the Confucian Academy 孔教學院, and the Hong Kong Muslim Cultural and Fraternal Association 中華回教博愛會.[110] After the appointment of the outspoken Joseph Zen Zekiun 陳日君 (b. 1936) as cardinal in 2006, the Roman Catholic Church stopped participating.

Communal religion, local temples, and the Zhengyi Taoist priests were not represented, nor were the religions of the non-Christian populations who had come to Hong Kong under British colonial rule: the Hindus, the Zoroastrians, the Jews, and the Bahá'ís, who all had a presence in Hong Kong dating to the late nineteenth century; while the Muslim association represented only Chinese Hui and not the large Muslim communities from India, Pakistan, and East Africa, which had their own organizations.[111] Nor were any redemptive societies represented, although the Taoist association

110. Chan Kim-kwong (Chen Jianguang), "Xiandai shehui zongjiao hexie."
111. Plüss, "Hong Kong's Muslim Organizations"; Ho, "Historical Analysis of Islamic Community Development."

was controlled by large temples that traced their origins to Xiantiandao, Tongshanshe, and spirit-writing shrines. The Confucian Academy was only one of four Confucian associations of Hong Kong, founded by Chen Huanzhang in 1930 after he had failed to have Confucianism recognized as the state religion by the Republican regime in China, and continued to lead a campaign, from its base in Hong Kong, for such recognition by the PRC government.[112] Christianity had clearly lost its privileged status following the handover—but the sheer size, experience, financial clout, and organizational capacity of its institutions continued to dwarf those of the other religions. The Anglican Church, for example, monopolized social services at the new suburb of Tung Chung, adjacent to the new international airport at Chek Lap Kok.[113] However, just as Christians lost their privileged position, some began to advocate taking a more "prophetic" public role, moving from executor to critic of government policy.[114]

A similar situation prevailed in Macau, where the Catholic Church had an even more dominant, virtually monopolistic, official position before the handover in 1999. After that date, a "religious sector" came into being, as the Macau government and PRC Liaison Office now dealt with the leaders of five religious communities: Catholics, Buddhists, Taoists, Protestants, and Bahá'ís. The latter, who had a presence in Macau since 1953, were known for operating the territory's leading international school, and for their active promotion of interreligious dialogue and social development projects within Macau and with the mainland.[115]

In short, then, Hong Kong and Macau maintained their colonial heritage of a subdued (but not inexistent) discourse on religious orthodoxy, with a vast array of religious groups enjoying the right to operate and organize under the shadow of powerful Christian institutions managing much of the territories' publicly funded education and social services—but the influence of the PRC model of officially recognized religious associations was beginning to be felt.

SINGAPORE

In the case of Singapore, the government's overriding concern in dealing with religion was maintaining social harmony in a multiethnic city-state.

---

112. Billioud & Thoraval, "The Contemporary Revival of Confucianism," 110–11.
113. Kwong Chunwah, *The Public Role of Religion*, 160.
114. Nedilsky, "The Anticult Initiative."
115. Li Shaobai, ed., *Zongjiao yu hexie shehui*.

Racial riots in 1951 and especially in 1964, when twenty-two were killed in clashes between Chinese and Muslim Malays, were at the forefront of the concerns of the founding president, Lee Kuan Yew, at independence in 1965. The ethnic divisions and violence in Sri Lanka, which pitted the majority Buddhist Sinhalese against the minority Hindu Tamils, also served as countermodel in Lee's attempt to create a modern cosmopolitan national identity which would be distinct from that of the Chinese, who were by far the dominant ethnic group, numbering 77 percent of the population in 1970, the rest being categorized as Malays (14.8 percent), Indians (7 percent), and "Other" (mostly Eurasians, at 1.2 percent). To each of these ethnic categories was associated one or several religions: the Malays were Muslim, the Indians were Hindu, the Others were Christian, and the Chinese were Buddhist, Taoist, or "Shenist" (a term crafted by scholars to qualify templegoers, based on the Chinese term *shen* 神 for god or spirit). Since religious tensions could provoke or amplify ethnic conflict, the management of religion was a necessary component of policies designed to maintain racial harmony.

The concern for racial and religious harmony dominated the Singapore state's religious policy from the moment of independence until the time of writing this book.[116] This was expressed both in laws and in regulations that prohibited religious groups and leaders from disturbing the interreligious peace, and by bringing religious leaders together through various official or state-sponsored interreligious organizations.[117] This model was similar to the KMT's and CCP's corporatist approach to religious communities, except that instead of each religion having its own, separate monopolistic association as an interface with the state, in Singapore it was interreligious bodies that played this role, building on a long tradition of dialogue first institutionalized in the Inter-Religious Organization (IRO), founded in 1949 by leaders of the Hindu, Jewish, Buddhist, Christian, Muslim, and Sikh communities (Zoroastrians were admitted in 1961, Taoists and Bahá'ís in 1996, and Jains in 2006).[118] In 1992, the Presidential Council for Religious Harmony, composed of representatives of the various religious communities, was established under the Ministry of Home Affairs, with the mandate of advising the government on religious issues and on the implementation

116. On religion in Singapore, see Lai Ah Eng, ed., *Religious Diversity in Singapore*; Tong Chee Kiong, *Rationalizing Religion*; Clammer, *The Sociology of Singapore Religion*; Tham Seong Chee, *Religion and Modernization*.

117. E. Tan, "Keeping God in Place."

118. Lai Ah Eng, "The Inter-Religious Organization of Singapore."

of the Maintenance of Religious Harmony Act passed in the same year. This act, which was passed in response to Muslim concerns about aggressive Christian proselytizing, allowed the authorities to serve restraining orders on religious leaders or followers who threatened religious harmony by their words or actions, as well as those who conducted political or subversive activities under the guise of religion.[119]

Following the 9/11 terrorist attacks, the Ministry of Community Development and Sports initiated a consultation with religious leaders that led to the drafting of a Declaration on Religious Harmony promulgated in 2003, in which the leaders resolved to "Recognize the secular nature of our state, Promote cohesion within our society, Respect each other's freedom of religion, Grow our common space while respecting our diversity, Foster inter-religious communications, and thereby ensure that religion will not be abused to create conflict and disharmony in Singapore."[120] The working group of religious leaders who had drafted the declaration was given a permanent status as the Inter-Religious Harmony Circle, with the role of promoting its principles among the religious communities; its membership included representatives of the Buddhist, Catholic, Hindu, Muslim, Protestant, Sikh, and Taoist associations, as well as the Inter-Religious Organization (represented by Bahá'í and Zoroastrian delegates) and "Others" (represented by delegates of the Dejiao and Red Swastika redemptive societies). The Inter-Religious Harmony Circle was enlisted to support the Community Engagement Programme, a large-scale, grassroots terrorism prevention campaign launched in 2006, which included a variety of projects ranging from interreligious friendship activities to training for post-terrorist social reconstruction operations.

The Singaporean government, then, did not have a list of recognized religions like the PRC or the ROC, and many religious organizations were free to operate there; but several levels of official recognition are in evidence through the organizational setup of the interreligious bodies that worked closely with the government. And all public religious organizations had to subscribe to the orthodoxy of the racial and religious harmony discourse, and could be banned if they did not. The Jehovah's Witnesses were banned from legal incorporation in 1972, and the Unification Church in 1982, although followers of the two churches were free to believe and to associate as individuals. But it was when the state perceived religious networks to be crossing the line of political activity that it intervened most aggressively. For instance, some Catholic priests were arrested when their liberation theology reflection group, which aimed to promote struggles for social justice, was accused of fomenting a Marxist plot against the government. Muslim preachers who called for more radicalism and for Malays to fight back against Chinese influence were banned from their pulpits.[121] And Falungong demonstrations and vigils were dispersed by the police on several occasions.

TAIWAN

The Taiwanese case, following the transition from martial law to democracy during the 1980s, was characterized by a shift from corporatist administration and regulation of religious communities (as discussed in chapter 8) to a situation of virtually unfettered pluralism. The government's religious policies gradually shifted from control to "gentle reform."[122] Ambitious plans from the 1960s to reinvent and impose from above an official vision of "traditional culture" were downscaled, and government cultural agencies began to collaborate with local temples for the organization of festivals, exhibitions, and so on, instead of competing with them. Restrictions on festivals were mostly forgotten, and celebrations became more ostentatious than ever. The lifting of martial law in 1987, the liberalization of social organizations, and the transition to a democratic regime had a strong impact on the religious world. Yiguandao was notably legalized and recognized as a religion in 1987, bringing into the open what had become one of Taiwan's largest organized religious communities. The Mainlander-dominated official Buddhist and Taoist associations lost their monopoly over the affairs of their respective traditions, and struggled to redefine their role as they were ignored by hundreds of new groups, some of which, such as Tzu Chi or Foguangshan, acquired significant national and even international influence.

The Ministry of the Interior also shed most of its supervisory role, merely handling the legal formalities of a growing list of registered religious groups, which included a mix of new religions, spirit-writing cults, and even individual temples that now claimed, and obtained, status as na-

---

121. Kuah-Pearce, *State, Society and Religious Engineering*, 147.
122. Katz, "Religion and the State in Post-War Taiwan."

tional religious associations. Tiandijiao, founded in 1979 by Li Yujie, was registered in 1986; its mother denomination, Tiandejiao, followed suit in 1989; then there was the Yiguandao offshoot Hai Tze Tao, registered in 1990, followed by the China Confucian Society 中國儒教會 (a federation of spirit-writing cults), the Dayijiao 大易教 (which gave itself the English names "Ism" and "The Current Confucian Religion"), and the Japanese group True Light (Mahikari 真光). In the first years of the twenty-first century, two more Yiguandao offshoots were registered, The Great Way of Maitreya (Mile dadao 彌勒大道) and the Yellow Middle (Huangzhong 黃中), as well as the General Association of China's Sagely Teachings 中華聖教總會 (a Confucian group), the Imperial Teachings of Maitreya 彌勒皇教 (a storefront *qigong* school and temple), the Mysterious Gate of the Authentic Transmission 玄門真宗 (a spirit-writing association), the Church of Scientology, and the Daoyuan redemptive society, which registered as the Anterior Heaven Teachings of Salvation 先天救教.[123] The Ministry of the Interior also worked on proposals for a new law on religion, but in the absence of any consensus on the content of such a law, these efforts never came to fruition.[124] There was no policy on religion per se, and various government agencies dealt with issues relating to religion in an ad hoc fashion, such as questions of corporate governance of religious associations, temple registrations (the status of the thousands of unregistered private altars was unclear), management of land use and ownership of temples in the context of urban planning, the registration of religious schools, the regulation of religious forms of therapy, and the role of religious groups in relations with the mainland.[125]

By the end of the twentieth century, the Taiwanese state had effectively abandoned the goal of regulating religion and enforcing any form of orthodoxy. Nor was there, in the realm of Buddhism, Taoism, or temple cults, any single institution capable of internally imposing its norms. The result was a bewilderingly diverse and pluralistic religious field, in which an impressive variety of new forms and combinations of religious traditions emerged, almost completely unfettered by political or religious orthodoxy of any kind.

123. Huang Lixing, *Zongjiao jianjie*. On other new religious movements, primarily from Japan and India, which were active in Taiwan but registered as associations and not as religious groups, see Cui Haiyuan & Zhang Yinghua, "Taiwan wailai xinxing zongjiao."

124. Laliberté, "The Regulation of Religious Affairs." For a complete compilation of all Taiwanese laws and regulations pertaining to religion, see Neizhengbu, *Zongjiao faling huibian*.

125. Wu Huiqiao, *Taiwan zongjiao*, 165–71; Zheng Zhiming, *Zongjiao zuzhi*, 219–42.

THIRTEEN

Global Religions, Ethnic Identities, and Geopolitics

剁 拾·叁 ❧

The forms of religiosity discussed in chapters 10 and 11, though widespread in the contemporary Chinese world, were mainly absent from international discourses on China's religious issues as framed in terms of freedom of religion. They were also, until the very beginning of the twenty-first century, equally absent from most Chinese official and intellectual religious discourse and policy. Much of the discourse on China's religious question, both inside and outside the country, was primarily concerned with traditions that accounted for only a small minority of the nation's people, but were important points of tension in its international relations: Tibetan Buddhism, Islam, and Christianity. In spite of their differences, they had one thing in common: as "foreign" religions, or as the religions of non-Han borderland people, the loyalty of their followers to the CCP regime was suspect—a fact with profound geopolitical implications, in terms of both China's territorial integrity and its international relations. Although numerically marginal, they were the most salient in the CCP's worries about the "religious question" in the post-1966 period. It is to these religions that we now turn, comparing their trajectories during and after the Cultural Revolution, at the articulation between ethnic and grassroots communities, the Chinese nation-state, and international relations.

TIBETAN BUDDHISM

The Cultural Revolution saw all forms of religious culture in Tibet, from monasteries to home altars, banned, destroyed, and struggled against. Any special leniency toward Tibetan religion or exceptions to socialist "class struggle" that had been previously accorded were now discarded. Tibet was targeted just like any other part of China, and the destruction of religion that occurred there was in that sense no different from what occurred in other parts of China. But a crucial difference comes from the fact that the campaigns against tradition, though enthusiastically executed by some Tibetan Red Guards, originated from outside Tibet, and thus could only lead to a sharpening of the ethnic divide between the Han Chinese and Tibetans. Furthermore, the waves of campaigns and countercampaigns that emanated from the center were the products of factional conflicts in Beijing which often had no equivalent in distant Tibet—so that Tibetan traditional culture became a convenient target for attacks, in one campaign after another.[1] The "anti–Lin Biao and anti-Confucius" campaign of 1973, for example, was translated into an anti–Dalai Lama and anti–Panchen Lama movement, leading to further attacks on Tibetan religion. Given the central role of religion and Buddhist institutions in Tibetan social and cultural life and as markers of Tibetan identity, the trauma caused was necessarily greater than in Han China, where religious institutions had already been weak and highly localized, and where, since the May Fourth movement, there existed a strong secular intellectual alternative for the construction of Chinese identity.

As a result, while it was possible after Mao's death for Han China to simply try to write off the Cultural Revolution as a moment of collective folly that could be conveniently blamed on the Gang of Four—and that everyone, for the sake of collective harmony, should put behind themselves and move forward—the Cultural Revolution had led to a far deeper, and perhaps permanent, sense of Tibetan alienation from China. This was already expressed in the Nyemo Revolt of 1968–69, led by a young nun, Thrimley Choedron, who was said to be possessed by a local deity and invulnerable to bullets. The movement quickly attracted hundreds of followers and spread to eighteen counties. Cadres and People's Liberation Army soldiers,

---

1. Tsering Shakya, *The Dragon in the Land of Snows*, 321.

attacked as "enemies of the faith," were mutilated or killed, until the rebels were crushed and their leaders publicly executed in Lhasa.[2] In some ways comparable to the Boxer Rebellion, albeit on a much smaller scale, the Nyemo Revolt was a magico-religious, protonationalist response to the intense pressure and destruction of Tibetan culture caused by the CCP.[3]

After Mao's death, realizing the damage that had been done by the Cultural Revolution in Tibet, the new CCP leadership acted quickly to repair some of the wrongs. Former Tibetan aristocrats, government officials, and leading monks were rehabilitated and given financial compensation. The Panchen Lama (1938–1989), who had been purged in 1964, was released and appointed to the Standing Committee of the Chinese People's Political Consultative Conference; he was able to use his influence in Beijing to secure both the return of several monasteries and government funding for their restoration. Overtures were made to the Tibetan government-in-exile in Dharamsala, India, to negotiate the Dalai Lama's return to Tibet. This led to visits to China of three delegations of exiled Tibetan notables headed by the Dalai Lama's siblings and personal representatives, who visited all the Tibetan areas in China and were greeted by enthusiastic crowds that often turned into anti-Chinese demonstrations. The response showed that the Tibetans' personal loyalty to the Dalai Lama as a religious leader remained intact. In a bid to restore its legitimacy, the CCP adopted a new, two-pronged approach to Tibet: to relax the restrictions on Tibetans' culture and religion, while promoting economic development and alleviating poverty in order to remove the social basis for religion's existence.[4]

The new policy, however, led to an outpouring of religious practice. "Like pent-up air in a balloon whose opening is tied, the religious practices rushed forward when the binds were removed."[5] Much of the religious revival involved the restoration of what had been banned, destroyed, or practiced in secret during the previous two decades. This included the non-institutionalized practices, such as pilgrimages and local festivals, in which Buddhist monasticism played but a small role, and which, like elsewhere in China, resurfaced with different levels of official tolerance, depending on the attitudes of local leaders. The labeling of such practices as *minority nationality culture* could provide better cover and protection for them than popular religious practices in Han areas.

---

2. Ibid., 346; Goldstein et al., *On the Cultural Revolution in Tibet*.
3. Goldstein et al., *On the Cultural Revolution in Tibet*.
4. Tsering Shakya, *The Dragon in the Land of Snows*, 379.
5. Goldstein, introduction to Goldstein & Kapstein, eds., *Buddhism in Contemporary Tibet*, 11.

For Buddhist institutions, the situation was more complex. The institution of reincarnate lamas (*tulku*) acquired critical importance, as the direct reincarnation of ancient masters in a new generation of children made it possible to bridge, at least symbolically, the rupture in transmission caused during the Maoist period, viscerally connecting the present with a more distant past. Similarly, the *ter* tradition, in which unusually gifted masters discover texts or ritual objects buried in the earth or in the spiritual realm, flourished as it facilitated the recovery of a memory of Buddhist presence in a sacred geography fractured by the Red Army's invasion.[6]

As in some parts of Han China, a wave of temple building occurred in the early 1980s, in part thanks to the sudden rise in prosperity following de-collectivization, and to the cultural tendency of Tibetans to invest much of their surplus into temple donations. In some places, the number and size of temples even surpassed pre-1959 levels. However, as was the case with many temples in Han areas, the monasteries could no longer count on the huge landholdings as a source of revenue and political influence (in the early twentieth century, monasteries had held almost half the arable land in Tibet[7]). Nor could they count on large populations of serfs, a condition that was abolished in 1959, bolstering the CCP's claims that it had actually liberated Tibetan peasantry.

Lack of economic means to sustain large numbers of monks thus contributed to political restrictions as a factor in preventing the revival of the institution of mass monasticism. For instance, Tibet's largest monastery, Drepung, had 10,000 monks in 1959; only 715 remained six years later. After the monastery was reopened after the Cultural Revolution, it was forced by economic and political constraints to accept a ceiling of around 600 monks, who were required either to devote themselves to full-time religious study with their living expenses covered by the monastery, or to engage full time in sideline businesses to provide income for the monastery. It also established a modern-style primary school teaching both secular and religious subjects for the many novices living with older monks. Overall, tension continued between the traditional custom of admitting to the monastery anyone who wished, and the strong political and economic restraints to such a practice, so that there were always a few hundred more monks unofficially residing in the temple above the official ceiling.[8] Low enrollments led to the abolition of the independent colleges (*dratsang*)

6. Germano, "Re-membering the Disembodied Body of Tibet," 91.

7. Goldstein, "The Revival of Monastic Life," 19.

8. Ibid., 45.

within each of the elite monasteries; these had maintained distinctive philosophical, textual, and ritual traditions and stimulated intellectual life through their competition. Furthermore, monastic life often had to be adjusted to suit the needs of the tourist industry, such as convening the daily debate sessions so that they would coincide with the arrival of tour buses.[9] Indeed, the numbers of monks permitted were just high enough to keep the monastery running as a cultural relic and tourist destination. Although the Drepung monks' response to these constraints was far from uniform, it is clear that resentment was high.

But at least until the early 2000s, when the escape into exile of leading reincarnations radicalized the situation, there appeared to be more room for growth in the monasteries of the Tibetan areas outside the Tibetan Autonomous Region—notably the regions of Amdo and Kham, in the Chinese provinces of Qinghai, Gansu, Sichuan, and Yunnan—which historically had not been under the rule of Lhasa and had more extensive and historically deep relations with their Han neighbors.[10] For instance, Labrang, in southern Gansu, which was one of the six main centers of the Gelugpa sect, managed to admit 2,300 monks compared with 3,800 before 1958, and to recreate the scholarly life of its colleges, which followed essentially the same program of instruction as in pre-Communist times.[11]

Elsewhere, some movements emerged that tried to renew Tibetan Buddhism within the existing political constraints but outside the overcontrolled monastic institutions. This was the case, for example, of camplike training sites organized around charismatic masters. Most notable was the Serta Institute established in the Golok region of northwest Sichuan Province by Khenpo Jikphun (1932–2004). Viewed as the reincarnation of Sogyal Rinpoche, a tutor of the Thirteenth Dalai Lama, Khenpo Jikphun maintained good relations with both the Dalai Lama and with Beijing, mostly by stressing ethics over political activism. Seen as possessing miraculous powers and renowned as the most accomplished contemporary master of the *ter* tradition for uncovering lost scriptures and sacred objects, he advocated a return to the strict observance by monks of monastic precepts, particularly celibacy, simplicity, and serious textual study, which were widely seen as being flouted by many Tibetan monks, especially those of the Tantric tradition to which he belonged. In 1980, Khenpo Jikphun

9. Cabezon, "State Control of Tibetan Buddhist Monasticism," 279–80.
10. Kolås & Thowsen, *On the Margins of Tibet.*
11. Slobodnik, "Destruction and Revival." For a book-length ethnography of Labrang, see also Makley, *The Violence of Liberation.*

built a small home in the barren grasslands of Serta, and lived with a handful of disciples. Gradually, through word of mouth, growing numbers of monks settled around his hermitage, until by the late 1990s the number of inhabitants was said to have reached eight thousand.

The quality and size of the academy made it into one of the foremost centers of Tibetan learning in the world, going against the trend that had seen most accomplished Tibetan scholar-monks scattered in exile. Since the academy was not a formal monastery, it was not subject to state regulation, and for a time even benefited from assistance from the prefectural government, in which Khenpo held an official post. Contrary to traditional Tibetan Buddhist practice, women were accepted to the encampment on an equal basis with men, and a nunnery was established for them. Hundreds of Han Chinese also moved to Serta, including both monks and laypersons, who were taught in Mandarin by one of Khenpo's early disciples, Khenpo Suodaji, who himself became a widely known author among Chinese Buddhists.[12] In 2001, however, a work team descended on the academy and expelled most of the inhabitants and pilgrims, especially the Han, limiting the number of residents to 1,400. In a very volatile political situation, it is not clear at the time of writing whether such new venues for transmitting Tibetan Buddhism will succeed in overcoming the constraints set by the Chinese authorities, which had led to the decline in monasticism.

Meanwhile, attempts at rapprochement between the exiled Fourteenth Dalai Lama and the Chinese government failed. The Chinese had been willing to negotiate the personal return of the Dalai Lama to China as vice-chairman of the National People's Congress—on the condition that he refrain from advocating Tibetan independence and from taking up residence in Tibet—but he and the government-in-exile in Dharamsala insisted on negotiating the status of the entire Tibetan people: that all Tibetan-speaking areas be unified under a single jurisdiction and enjoy the same degree of autonomy as was proposed to Hong Kong and Taiwan under the "one country, two systems" framework. By the second half of the 1980s, both sides hardened their position: Beijing judged that the reformist policy in Tibet was working and that the Dalai Lama's legitimation was no longer essential for securing CCP domination over Tibet, while Dharamsala, bolstered by growing sympathy and support in the West, sought to exert pressure on China by internationalizing the issue.

Encouraged by the warm reception given the Dalai Lama when he addressed the United States Congress on September 19, 1987, a week later

12. D. Yu, "Religion in a Panoptic Modernity."

twenty-one monks from Drepung Monastery staged a demonstration in central Lhasa, waving the Tibetan national flag and shouting demands for independence. The beating and arrest of the monks by the Chinese police triggered a series of further protests, which continued intermittently until, on March 5, 1989, between 75 and 150 Tibetans were killed by the police at the largest anti-Chinese demonstration since 1959. After three days of fighting, martial law was imposed.[13]

Only months later, the Tian'anmen crackdown led to a general political hardening throughout China, one that would continue in Tibet even after the atmosphere began to relax again in most parts of the country about 1992–93. For Tibet, the relatively lenient policy advocated in the early 1980s by Premier Hu Yaobang, which recognized Tibet's specific conditions and, to a degree, tried to bend backward to make amends for the wrongs committed during the Cultural Revolution, was replaced by a strategy to fully integrate it into Chinese society, notably through the massive construction of infrastructures linking the territory to the rest of China, promoting accelerated economic growth, and dealing harshly with all forms of dissidence. The rule banning religious education for children, which had not been strictly enforced in Tibet in the 1980s, when many underage novices, following tradition, had entered the monkhood, was now more strictly enforced.

In the 1980s, the Dalai Lama had been condemned for his political stance, but his veneration by Tibetans as a supreme spiritual leader had been tolerated, and his portrait was everywhere. This was in itself a new phenomenon, in which he acquired a stature transcending his sectarian affiliation as head of the Gelugpa order and became the object of a personal cult through laminated photographs displayed in homes and in vehicles — the same material props as the Mao cult in the Han areas. From the 1990s, however, the Dalai Lama's stature as a religious leader was also condemned and his photographs banned. The issue took full salience in the controversy over the selection of the successor to the Tenth Panchen Lama, who had suddenly died in early 1989, shortly after giving a speech critical of the Chinese policies in Tibet.

In 1991, a State Council directive stated that "reincarnation is allowed, but not all can be reincarnated" 可以轉世, 不可全轉. This was to "avoid increasing the burden of the masses"; numbers were to be limited to one reincarnate lama per ordinary monastery, one to three for influential monasteries at the prefectural level, and 10 to 15% at highly influential monas-

13. Tsering Shakya, *The Dragon in the Land of Snows*, 430.

teries at the provincial or autonomous region level. The selection process combined religious and political criteria: reincarnate lamas were to be selected following religious ritual and historical tradition under the guidance of the Buddhist association, and then approved by the Religious Affairs Bureau (RAB) at the municipal level or higher. Following these procedures, the Sixteenth Karmapa, recognized on June 25, 1992, was the first officially recognized reincarnate lama since 1959.[14] Historical precedents for Chinese state involvement in the selection of reincarnate lamas, going back to the Ming and Qing dynasties, were regularly invoked when the procedures were questioned, such as in the disputed selection of the Panchen Lama.

Although the Dalai Lama had traditionally played a role in the recognition of the Panchen Lama, the Chinese authorities quickly moved to impose a ritual procedure for the search of the new incarnation, which combined current Tibetan tradition with a system of drawing by lots from a golden urn, previously used in the eighteenth century by the Qing emperor. The RAB in Beijing would have the final say in the selection. By eliminating the Dalai Lama from the search process, however, the legitimacy of the choice was undermined, and it was rumored that the search team secretly consulted with the Dalai Lama. But in any case, the latter trumped the Chinese by announcing, in May 1995, his recognition of Gedhun Choekyi Nyima, a young boy from Nagchu in northwestern Tibet, as the eleventh reincarnation of the Panchen Lama. The boy disappeared shortly thereafter and is still being held in confinement by the authorities at the time of writing. On November 11 of the same year, in a secret ceremony in Lhasa, based on a list of candidates that did not include the Dalai Lama's choice, the name of Gyaincain Norbu was drawn from the golden urn and consecrated as the Eleventh Panchen Lama by the RAB. In the wake of this controversy, regulations were promulgated for the selection of all reincarnate lamas, emphasizing that the search be supervised by the secular authorities, that only lamas living on PRC territory be involved in the search process, and that such a process could only designate children residing on PRC territory as reincarnate lamas.[15] Moreover, only a fraction of the numerous reincarnate lines were allowed to continue, and most reincarnate lamas who died during and after the Cultural Revolution were not "reborn."

In 1996, in a campaign reminiscent of the Cultural Revolution, work

14. Chen Jinlong, *Zhongguo gongchandang*, 315–16.
15. Cabezon, "State Control of Tibetan Buddhist Monasticism," 276.

teams of CCP cadres were sent to the major monasteries for weeks or even months at a time to train the monks in "patriotic education," with the aim of purging the monasteries of separatist elements. Over one hundred officials descended on Drepung in the summer of 1996 and stayed for half a year, giving endless political lectures, interviewing each monk individually, and requiring each one to denounce the Dalai Lama as a "splittist." Four monks openly challenged the work team and were sent to labor camps, one committed suicide, and some sixty voluntarily quit the monastery rather than denounce their spiritual leader. Some of the latter group later fled to India. Resistance to the official denunciation of the Dalai Lama was so strong, however, that the work team was forced to back down, and removed the requirement.[16] In 2006, however, another work team returned to Drepung, and this time would not compromise. The abbot and four other monks, who refused to sign the denunciation of the Dalai Lama, were arrested—a move that triggered a sit-in protest by four hundred of the Drepung monks, as one of them was reported to have said, "Why don't you try and make the Hui people eat pork? If you succeed, then we'll denounce the Dalai Lama."[17]

At issue for the Tibetan monks was the political orientation of their religious life: either to accept the framework and restrictions imposed by the socialist regime, and attempt to rebuild their institutions and religious life within it, or, in a high-stakes gamble, to tie the future of Tibetan Buddhism to that of the political status of the Tibetan nation, and participate in a nationalist struggle for Tibetan independence from China.[18] In the major monasteries around Lhasa, a large proportion of the monks seemed ever since the 1980s to have opted for the nationalist option, creating a highly volatile and politicized atmosphere. The increasing frequency and intensity of "patriotic education" campaigns by the Communist regime in the late 1990s and early 2000s only exacerbated tensions and resentment.

Meanwhile, in the exile community, the Dalai Lama's moderate stance was increasingly questioned by the younger generation of Tibetans. Secular organizations like the Tibetan Youth Congress and Students for a Free Tibet, using media-savvy activist techniques pioneered by Greenpeace and other global civil society groups, devised a strategy to use the 2008 Beijing

16. Goldstein, "The Revival of Monastic Life," 49.
17. Cabezon, "State Control of Tibetan Buddhist Monasticism," 285; "La semaine qui ébranla le Tibet," *Le Monde*, April 4, 2008.
18. Goldstein, "The Revival of Monastic Life."

Olympics to mobilize world public opinion to pressure the CCP into liberating Tibet.[19] Encouraged by the award by U.S. president George Bush of a Congressional Gold Medal to the Dalai Lama, in addition to his welcome by several Western heads of state who had previously shunned him to avoid offending Beijing, three hundred monks marched out of Drepung and into Lhasa in October of 2007. On the anniversary of the 1959 Tibetan revolt on March 10, 2008, hundreds of monks marched from Dharamsala toward the Chinese border, aiming to reach Lhasa. Although they were stopped by the Indian and Nepalese military, on the same day a few hundred monks had again marched out of Drepung toward downtown Lhasa, where they staged a quiet sit-in. In the following days, they were joined by monks from Sera and Ramoche, the other main monasteries in the Lhasa area. Clashes with police and paramilitary forces ensued, and by March 14 the monks were joined by lay onlookers, who erupted into riots, mobbing Han and Hui onlookers and setting fire to government vehicles and buildings, shopping centers, and a mosque. Over the next few days, between 22 and 140 persons were killed in the riots and the ensuing military crackdown, while state propaganda moved into full gear to denounce the Dalai Lama for instigating anti-Chinese violence. Over the next month, the disturbances spread to the entire Tibetan areas, including in Gansu and in western Sichuan, in what represented the longest and most determined campaign of resistance to Chinese occupation since 1959—one in which the majority of participants were now laypeople, a change from the demonstrations of the 1980s and 1990s.[20] The Chinese authorities responded by deciding to further intensify "patriotic education," while overseas, the Tibetan activist groups continued their media campaign to systematically disrupt the Olympic torch relay in each city it passed through.

In this context of increasing polarization, in which his authority over the more radical younger generation was under question and the PRC authorities appeared intent on waiting for his death in order to appoint a subservient successor, the Dalai Lama put both his political and religious functions into question. After the Lhasa riots, he threatened to resign from his political position as head of the Tibetan government-in-exile (while remaining Dalai Lama) if Tibetans acted violently.[21] Only a few months ear-

---

19. Doug Saunders, "How Three Canadians Upstaged Beijing," *Globe and Mail* (Toronto), March 29, 2008.

20. "La semaine qui ébranla le Tibet," *Le Monde*, April 4, 2008; Barnett, "The Tibet Protests of Spring, 2008."

21. "Dala Lama 'to resign' if violence worsens," CNN, March 18, 2008; available online at www.wwrn.org/article.php?idd=28029&sec=52&cont=4 (accessed April 6, 2008).

lier, however, concerned that the PRC would attempt to control the nomi-
nation of his own future successor as spiritual head of the Tibetan people,
he had floated several ideas which put into question the very perpetuity of
the institution of the Dalai Lama, including holding a referendum among
Tibetans to decide whether or not the institution should be abolished, or
naming a new Dalai Lama before his own death. Ironically, the (atheist)
Chinese government blasted the proposals for "violating established religious rituals and historical conventions" and insisted on continuing to
reincarnate Dalai Lamas—a selection which, stressed one Chinese Tibet-
ologist, had been conducted under the approval of the Chinese central
government since the Fifth Dalai Lama in the sixteenth century.[22]

The Mongols of Inner Mongolia, who shared with Tibetans the same
Buddhist traditions, found themselves in a very different political situation
in the post-Mao period. With no charismatic reincarnate lama and with
links to the major training centers in Tibet severely restrained, Mongol
Buddhism was left in a weak state. The Mongols having long been a minority in the Inner Mongolia Autonomous Region, political nationalism
was by and large a thing of the past there by the 1970s, even though Mongols strove to maintain some cultural identity, notably through Buddhism
and the Chinggis khan cult.[23] Both Buddhism and the Chinggis khan cult
were also manipulated by the government, however, with monasteries and
shrines reopened but reorganized in a Chinese style, and massively used
by the local Han. As a result, Tibetan Buddhism in Inner Mongolia was in
many ways less constrained than in Tibet, but also less vibrant; the situation there also paled with that in the Republic of Mongolia, where after
1990 Buddhism became an important element of a self-conscious national
spiritual renewal.[24]

Meanwhile, outside Tibet and Mongolia, Tibetan Buddhism continued
to spread among the Han Chinese, as discussed in chapter 11—a phenomenon facilitated by the fluency in Chinese of a large number of Tibetan
lamas, who had, ironically, either learned the language in the prisons

    22. "Vote to Be Held on Tibetan Leadership," Associated Press, November 27, 2007; online
at http://wwrn.org/article.php?idd=26991 (accessed April 6, 2008); "China Condemns Dalai
Lama for Ideas on Succession," Reuters, November 29, 2007; online at www.wwrn.org/sparse
.php?idd=27024 (accessed April 6, 2008); "Traditions of Living Buddha Reincarnation Should
Be Followed, Expert Says," *Xinhua* (Beijing), April 2, 2008; online at www.wwrn.org/article
.php?idd=28189&sec=52&cont=4 (accessed April 6, 2008).
    23. Khan, "Chinggis Khan"; Aubin & Hamayon, "Alexandre, César et Gengis Khan."
    24. Charleux, "The Reconstruction of Buddhist Monasteries"; Erhimbayar, "Mongolian Buddhist
Monasteries."

and work camps during the Cultural Revolution or held political or academic appointments at the universities for the training of minority nationality cadres. Several of the latter wrote popular books on Buddhism in Chinese.[25]

The popularity of Tibetan Buddhism was even more evident among the Chinese of Taiwan. This interest had been stimulated by the visits of exiled Tibetan masters beginning in the 1980s, as the KMT government's Mongolian and Tibetan Affairs Commission—which, until then, had basically agreed with the CCP line on Tibet being an inalienable part of China—began to build relations with the Dharamsala government-in-exile. A Tibetan Temples Committee was established, with the goal of rebuilding the Potala Palace in Taiwan. While that goal was never realized, the committee did stimulate the construction of numerous Tibetan Buddhist monasteries, hermitages, and associations on the island.[26] This growth was given a big boost by the Dalai Lama's visit to Taiwan in 1997, after President Lee Teng-hui publicly accepted the Dalai Lama's peace plan. This was followed by teaching tours by several respected exiled reincarnate lamas. During these visits, meetings and exchanges took place between Tibetan lamas and Han Buddhist monks, bringing Tibetan Buddhism into the mainstream of Taiwanese Buddhist circles. A wave of interest in Tibetan religion and culture was stimulated in Taiwan, and a handful of Chinese children on the island were identified as reincarnate lamas.

Tibetan Buddhist practices blended well with the popular religious culture of Taiwan: Tibetan temples offered, on a regular basis and on demand, rituals for prosperity, for dispelling illnesses, and for funerals, as well as divination services, amulets for sale, and meditation courses. Major rituals were often staged on festivals from the Chinese calendar, such as Grave-Sweeping and Ghost Festival. At the same time, the organization of Tibetan Buddhism in Taiwan completely followed the model of Chinese temple religion: the temples were run by boards of laypeople, who hired Tibetan monks from abroad on fixed-term contracts; the monks' role was limited to giving ritual and spiritual services, with little say in temple management.[27]

Outside the Chinese world, the exile of the Dalai Lama and of several thousand monks had the effect of disseminating Tibetan Buddhism to distant lands. In India, the construction of exile Tibetan monasteries had the

---

25. D. Yu, "Religion in a Panoptic Modernity."
26. Huang Huili, *Zangchuan fojiao zaitai fazhan chutan*, 35.
27. Ibid., 101–3; Yao Lixiang, "Zangchuan fojiao zai Taiwan."

effect of decentering Tibetan Buddhism, with many of the famous mon-asteries, such as Sera and Drepung, reestablished by exile monks in India and claiming to hold the authentic traditions. It is unclear to what extent, if any, the Tibetan exiles engaged in a process of mutual influence with the contemporary Indian religious culture.

Of great significance, however, was the expansion of Tibetan Buddhism in the West. Although, until the 1970s, knowledge of Tibetan Buddhism was limited to the esoteric milieu of Theosophists and readers of early spiritual adventurers such as Alexandra David-Neel, by the 1980s, stimulated by the Dalai Lama's trips to the West and his receiving the Nobel Peace Prize in 1989, hundreds of Tibetan Dharma centers were established, several lamas settled in Western countries and acquired a measure of fame, and Tibetan Buddhism surpassed Zen as the most popular Buddhist tradition in the West.[28]

But it underwent significant modifications in form and content in the new cultural context. Instead of monasteries with a large resident population of monks, some of whom would pursue several years of intensive and systematic study, the Western model was that of the Dharma center, which typically offered weeklong or weekend courses and retreats given by lamas on tour from Asia. In a commercialized spiritual market, and given the short-term expectations of practitioners, there was pressure to constantly teach different and higher-level spiritual techniques, instead of providing a strong foundation in fundamental Buddhist doctrine and faith.[29] Meanwhile, the Dalai Lama became one of the most respected religious figures in the West, his fame comparable to that of the pope. His numerous popular books became best sellers in the religion and spirituality category, while "Tibetan chic" gripped Hollywood.

By the end of the twentieth century, then, Tibetan Buddhism, in the space of a few short decades and largely as a result of the CCP-led repression, had become a truly globalized religious movement. The restrictions in the Tibetan heartland could only slow down, but not stop, its revival there, as it was experiencing perhaps the greatest expansion in its sphere of influence since the conversion of Mongolia in the sixteenth and seventeenth centuries. Whereas Tibetan Buddhism had always enjoyed a certain prestige among elements of the Chinese elite since the Qing, it was now, in Han China and Taiwan, planting deeper popular roots than perhaps ever

28. Paine, *Re-Enchantment.*

29. Alan Wallace, "Tibetan Buddhism in the West: Is It working?," interview in *The Snow Lion* newsletter; online at www.snowlion.com/pages/N52.4.php (accessed December 2, 2006).

before. At the same time, it returned to the birthplace of Buddhism in India and became a visible component of the new religious culture of the West. Political restrictions in the heartland and widely divergent social conditions elsewhere, however, meant that the traditional Tibetan institution of mass monasticism and intimate state-monastic ties were, with the exception of Bhutan, permanently shattered. While the lamas retained their institutional charisma, how the sangha (monastic community) would evolve as an institution remained an open question.

ISLAM

Like all other religions, Islam was severely persecuted during the Cultural Revolution. The China Islamic Association was disbanded, the mosques were closed, and the imams were struggled against and branded as feudal counterrevolutionaries. In a frontal attack on Islamic sensitivities, many Muslims were forced to raise pigs and eat pork. However, many families continued to say prayers at home, while imams continued giving religious instruction under the cover of social home visits. Then in July 1975, in what may have been the single bloodiest incident of the entire Cultural Revolution, over sixteen hundred Hui Muslims were massacred in the town of Shadian in Yunnan Province, a key center for Islamic culture in the southwest, as pent-up resentments violently exploded after pork bones were thrown into the town wells in a deliberate scheme to contaminate the Muslims' water. The army, called in to quash the disturbance, indiscriminately fired on the inhabitants, while air bombing flattened the entire agglomeration.[30] In 1979, the Yunnan provincial Party committee admitted its error, offered compensation to the victims' families, and rebuilt the town, which once again became an important hub of Hui culture in the province, developing links with Middle-Eastern organizations and sending imams to remote villages to rebuild mosques and revive the practice of Muslim laws.[31]

The 1980s were indeed a period marked by the reestablishment of official Islamic institutions and the revival and expansion of infrastructures. Mosques were restored and rebuilt until, by some accounts, there were now more mosques than before 1949. Pilgrimages to Mecca were resumed, with believers traveling to Saudi Arabia through both official and unofficial channels in rapidly increasing numbers. Publishing operations, both offi-

---

30. Gladney, *Muslim Chinese*, 137–46.
31. Hillman, "The Rise of the Community."

cial and informal, were reactivated as scores of books and periodicals in Chinese, Arabic, and minority languages were released, including reprints of classical Chinese works of exegesis and of expositions of Islamic teachings, as well as contemporary debates stimulated by current events and trends in other Muslim countries. Both the state-sponsored Islamic training institutes and the smaller mosque schools were revived; they continued some of the trends in the reform of Islamic education which had begun earlier in the century. These schools, which offered a secular curriculum in addition to religious courses for very low tuition, became for Muslims an increasingly popular alternative to the neglected state schools in the poorer areas. They were seen as offering good prospects for employment as imams or Arabic-language interpreters. Remarkably, women's Islamic schools also underwent a rapid growth.[32]

The official China Islamic Association, reestablished in 1980, expanded its presence to a far greater degree than in the 1950s and 1960s, when its presence was essentially limited to the major cities of the western provinces with high Muslim populations. Now hundreds of cities and counties also had their branches, increasing the ability of the association to play a role in local Muslim affairs, including the endorsement of imams, the distribution of funds, and the selection of pilgrims. And yet, while the association was theoretically responsible for the training of clergy, by 1995 its academy had only 444 graduates, only half of whom returned home to become imams—compared with the total number of 42,000 imams and their 26,000 disciples in all of China.[33] The rest of the graduates found more lucrative jobs as interpreters for businesses conducting trade with the Middle East.

As in the 1950s, the China Islamic Association was dominated by members of the Ikhwan movement, the anti-Sufi reformist group of Wahhabi origins that had been so active as Chinese nationalists in the Republican period. Most of the mosques rebuilt with state funds after the Cultural Revolution were affiliated with the Ikhwan, while the Sufi and traditional Islam (known as "old teachings," or *gedimu*, from the Arabic *qadim*) continued to predominate in rural Hui villages. Having been so effectively co-opted by the state, however, the Ikhwan lost some of its legitimacy in the eyes of many Muslims, who did not appreciate the bureaucratism and even corruption of many association officials. In a telling incident, when the state sponsored the rebuilding of the South Gate mosque of Yinchuan, the

---

32. Allès, "Muslim Religious Education in China"; see also Jaschok, *the History of Womens' Mosques.*
33. Allès et al., "Chinese Islam," 11.

capital of the Ningxia Hui Autonomous Region, and staffed it with Ikhwan imams, the local Muslims continued to frequent other, smaller mosques, forcing the managers to turn it into a tourist attraction charging admission fees.[34]

Disaffection with the Ikhwan seems to have stimulated the growth of the Salafiyya movement, introduced to China in the 1930s, which advocated political quietism and an uncompromising adherence to scripture, rejecting the Ikhwan drift toward secularism, Marxism, and political co-optation. The Salafiyya may have been the fastest-growing movement within Hui Islam in the post-Mao period. Unlike the common image of Salafis in the Middle East as engaged in radical political Islamism, however, Chinese Salafiyya remained obstinately nonpolitical and were radical only in their refusal to collaborate with the state; and like the Ikhwan, they defined themselves less against the West than against *Chinese* cultural influence on Islam. In the late 1990s, wrote Dru Gladney, "the movement offer[ed] more of an orthodox withdrawal from the issues of modern China, rather than a commitment to transform it."[35] At the time of writing the present text, however, it is unclear to what extent the Salafiyya are organizing as networks and linked to other movements outside China, and possibly influencing the overall landscape of Islam and its relations with the broader Chinese society.

What has been sure, however, is that the classification of Chinese Muslims as minority nationalities, coupled with the geopolitical context and Chinese diplomatic strategies, has had a profound but highly differentiated impact on the evolution of China's Muslim communities—most favorably for the Hui, historically closest to the Han, and with devastating consequences for the Turkic-speaking groups (and small numbers of speakers of Persian-related languages), especially the Uighurs, of the far western province of Xinjiang. The designation of the Hui as one of China's fifty-five officially recognized minority nationalities—and as the only nationality whose sole defining characteristic was religion—allowed the Hui to benefit from privileges in religious practice, defined as nationality customs to be protected, which were denied to practitioners of any other religion, as well as to the members of "sensitive" minority nationalities such as the Tibetans and Uighurs. Their separation from the culturally and geographically more distant Uighurs and other Turkic-speaking peoples, who had all been grouped together as Hui before 1949, left them as the geographically dispersed and more culturally assimilated, and thus less threatening, "Chi-

34. Gladney, "The Salafiyya Movement," 129–30.
35. Ibid., 144.

nese Muslims."[36] Affirmative action programs such as a more relaxed birth control policy and lower entrance standards for university, enjoyed by all minority nationalities, encouraged Han people to marry into or otherwise seek to join these nationalities, so that between 1982 and 1990, the Hui population grew by 19 percent in eight years. While some Chinese scholars and ideologues had attempted to stress the distinction between the Hui as a *nationality* and Islam as a *religion*, and many Hui were not religiously observant and some were even atheists, Muslim practice and ritual were such salient markers of Hui ethnic identity that it was impossible to completely dissociate the two.

In one study, for instance, the head of an impoverished small Hui village in northwestern Yunnan, whose inhabitants had long abandoned most Muslim customs and frequently intermarried with neighboring ethnic groups, campaigned to have a new mosque built to draw the tourists flocking to the nearby Tibetan monasteries. Although the original motive was to instrumentalize "Hui nationality customs" for economic gain, the fund-raising efforts of the project's initiator led him to the regional Islamic hub of Shadian, where a Muslim leader offered not only to finance the building of the mosque but also to send imams to teach the Islamic faith. After a few years, the imams had successfully converted the village to a rigorous practice of shunning pork, alcohol, and cigarettes, had stopped intermarriage with non-Hui, turned the mosque into the center of village affairs, and marginalized the nonpracticing village head who had initiated the project.[37]

A comparable case is reported near Quanzhou, Fujian, of a lineage whose genealogies indicated ancestry among Arab traders of the Song dynasty, but who practiced Chinese religion, ate pork, and knew virtually nothing of Islam. After successfully applying for legal recognition as Hui, the lineage not only received generous government subsidies for the education and economic development of national minorities but also built a new mosque staffed by an imam from Inner Mongolia, and sent eighteen youth to train as imams in northwestern China.[38] In both cases, nonreligious motivations for asserting Hui identity led to ties with distant Muslim communities and the importation of Islamic religious practice.

The situation of the Hui in the PRC contrasted with that of Taiwan, where the state considered its twenty thousand Hui to be members of a

36. Allès, *Musulmans de Chine*.
37. Hillman, "The Rise of the Community."
38. Gladney, *Ethnic Identity*, 153; Fan Ke, "Traditionalism and Identity Politics."

religion, not of a nationality, so that when they ceased to practice Islam, they no longer identified as Hui or as Muslims, and assimilation into the Han majority was more rapid.[39] Similarly, the Hui had no special status in Hong Kong, where, though they were numerically dominant among the seventy thousand Muslims at the end of the 1990s, Muslim organizations were historically dominated by the Indian, Pakistani, and Ismaili communities.[40] It was only after the 1997 retrocession that the Hong Kong Chinese Muslim Association (which excluded non-Chinese Muslims) became visible as the sole Islamic organization among the "group of six"—the representatives of the Roman Catholic, Protestant, Taoist, Buddhist, Muslim, and Confucian communities which attempted to informally monopolize political representation of religious communities and act as an interface with the PRC government (discussed in chapter 12).

In Malaysia, where Islam was associated with the ethnic Malay majority, there was no room at all for expressing a Hui or Chinese Muslim identity— early Hui members of the diaspora had mostly assimilated with either the Malays or the non-Muslim Chinese. But when, in the 1960s, some did become Muslims in response to a government campaign to convert the Chinese to Islam, they were rejected by both the Chinese for reneging on their ancestors, and the Malays as insincere and not "true" Muslims. It was only after the 1980s and 1990s, with greater communication and knowledge among both Chinese and Malays about Islam in other countries—including, not least, China itself—that ethnicity and Islamic religion came to be seen as distinct, leading to more acceptance of Chinese Muslims. By the late 1990s, there were thus almost one hundred thousand Chinese Muslims, a little more than 1 percent of Malaysia's Chinese population.[41]

Just as, in the 1950s, the CCP had adroitly played its Muslim card as part of its diplomatic strategy, the same approach was used in the post-Mao period, as trade and economic links boomed between China and Muslim countries in Southeast Asia and the Middle East—the latter being crucial suppliers of oil and important clients for Chinese-sponsored infrastructure development projects. Many of these collaborations involved Hui as leaders, interpreters, or cultural consultants, while the increased links also facilitated religious exchanges: hundreds of Chinese Muslims obtained scholarships to pursue Islamic studies in Egypt, Saudi Arabia, Syria, Iran,

39. Gladney, *Ethnic Identity*, 150–52.

40. Plüss, "Hong Kong's Muslim Organizations."

41. Giap, "Islam and Chinese Assimilation." On Chinese Muslims in Singapore, see Mak Lau-Fong, *The Role of Saudara Baru in Ethic Relations*.

Pakistan, and Malaysia, and foreign Islamic foundations funded the construction of mosques and Islamic schools in China, largely through the China Islamic Association.

Geopolitical influences and sensitivities may have been behind the "Chinese Salman Rushdie" affair of 1989, when three thousand Chinese Muslims held a march in Beijing on May 12, 1989—in the midst of the Tian'anmen student demonstrations—protesting the publication of material offensive to Islam in a Chinese book on sexual customs in foreign lands; this demonstration was followed by large marches in several cities in northwestern China. All this occurred a few days after a state visit by Iranian president Ali Khamenei, who had openly expressed his support for the Hui grievances and reiterated the condemnation of Salman Rushdie.[42] In stark contrast to the brutal suppression of the Tibetan riots a few months earlier and of the student movement three weeks later, the Muslim protests were given logistical support by the authorities, all their demands were acceded to, and most of those who behaved violently were only lightly punished. This "special" treatment illustrated the leverage acquired by the Chinese Muslims, especially the Hui, as both a recognized religion and a nationality that played an important role as a symbolic and practical conduit for Chinese relationships with Muslim nations. On the other hand, however, when Chinese Muslim leaders repeatedly expressed their opposition to the U.S. invasion of Iraq in 2003 and planned to hold anti-American protests, permission was consistently denied.

China's increased links with other Muslim countries, especially of the Middle East, had a certain impact on the practice and values of the Hui. Arabia, as the root of Islam, was seen as the standard for Islamic authenticity, and as the source of an alternative civilizing discourse to the Han-centered hegemony emanating from the Chinese state. Countering Han-centered stereotypes of Hui backwardness, many stressed the higher principles of purity, truth, and hygiene contained in Islamic civilization, and identified with the prosperity and material advancement of the Arabian states—producing a trend of "Arabization" among the Hui, including the adoption of Arabic domes for mosques (replacing the Chinese temple style of older mosques) and also for hotels and shopping malls, enrolling in Arabic language lessons, watching Middle-Eastern videos, and adopting Arabic "Muslim" dress codes (such as blandly colored women's headdresses and *hijab*).[43] The government also granted Muslims a special dispensation from

42. Gladney, "Salman Rushdie in China."
43. Gillette, *Between Mecca and Beijing*, chap. 8; see also Zang, *Ethnicity and Urban Life*.

the laws imposing cremation, allowing them to practice Islamic burial—a privilege extended to no other part of the population.[44]

If geopolitical considerations were a factor in an exceptionally lenient treatment of the religious practices of the Hui, it was just the opposite for the Uighurs and other Muslim peoples of the far west. Here, in the face of violent acts of resistance by Uighurs, the Chinese state successfully lobbied both the neighboring Central Asian states, which were ethnically and historically close to the Uighurs, and the United States, otherwise keen to take up the cause of human rights in China, to give it carte blanche to brutally suppress any expression of perceived Uighur nationalism, in a campaign whose targets included any expressions of Islam outside narrow, officially sanctioned confines.

Assimilation of the Uighurs and other Turkic-speaking Muslim peoples presented an even greater challenge to the Chinese state than Tibet, owing to a wider cultural distance and a shorter and more tenuous history of Chinese penetration, especially in the Uighur heartland of the Kashgar plain, near the borders with India, Pakistan, Afghanistan, and Kirgyzstan. Two short-lived independent republics of East Turkestan had existed during the 1930s and 1940s (see chapter 2), and the imposition of Communist rule had not been easy. As early as 1954, an uprising, led by the Sufi *shaykh* Abdimit in Khotan, had aimed to establish an independent Islamic republic.[45] For a period during the 1960s and 1970s, nationalist resistance was largely channeled by the secular Marxist East Turkestan People's Revolutionary Party, which received aid from the Soviet Union; but with the post-Mao reforms and the demise of the USSR, Islam once again became an important ingredient of Uighur resistance to Han domination. Religious leaders returned to the core of community life; the mosque remained the central institution in rural Turkic areas, and there were mosques in practically every lane in Kashgar and in the Uighur sections of the Han-dominated provincial capital, Urumqi.[46]

Sporadic anti-Han protests and incidents occurred throughout the 1980s, and in Xinjiang, the protests against the "Chinese Salman Rushdie," which had been supported by the government elsewhere, were denounced and the leaders sentenced to life imprisonment. Some Uighur resistance groups took inspiration from the Mujahideen victory against the Soviets

44. On Hui memories of past conflicts with the Han, see Gillette, "Violence, the State."
45. Dillon, *Xinjiang*, 53.
46. On the Uighurs, see also Bellér-Hann, *Community Matters*; Bellér-Hann et al., eds., *Situating the Uyghurs*; Wang Jianxin, *Uighur Education*; McKerras & Clarke, *China, Xinjiang and Central Asia*; Starr, ed., *Xinjiang*; Bovingdon, "The Not-So-Silent Majority."

in Afghanistan in 1989. It was the Baren rebellion, launched near Kashgar with calls to *jihad* in April 1990—in which dozens of rioters were killed by the army—that marked a turning point in the state's approach to the Uighurs and Islam in Xinjiang. From then on, the CCP resolved to crush any signs of dissent and to strictly control religious life. This occurred only months after the Tian'anmen student movement, and just as the Soviet bloc was collapsing, with several new Muslim-majority republics attaining independence on the western borders of Xinjiang. China's leaders feared the breaking away of Xinjiang, leading by domino effect to the disintegration of China and the end of the CCP regime. Tensions were aggravated by a series of bomb blasts in Urumqi and even in Beijing in the mid-1990s. The "strike hard" campaign launched in 1996 to fight crime throughout China was, in Xinjiang, primarily directed at any suspected "separatist" activity, including much of the religious life. New regulations on the management of religious affairs in Xinjiang, enacted in 2001, were, contrary to the general trend in China, more restrictive than the previous rules issued in 1994.[47] Unregistered mosques were closed, loudspeakers for the call to prayer were removed from minarets, in some instances certain prayers were banned, children were punished at school for showing signs of Islamic practice, and teachers and employees at state-run units were deliberately offered meals during the fast of Ramadan. Religious regulations that were only loosely enforced among the Hui elsewhere in China, such as limiting to two the number of students under each imam, were strictly applied.

Capitalizing on the fear of political Islam in the neighboring Central Asian republics, China, together with those countries' leaders, established an international body in 1996, later called the Shanghai Cooperation Organization, to secure its western borders and influence in Central Asia. These alliances lessened the possibility of support for Uighur nationalism and/or Islamic radicalism in those countries. After the 9/11 terrorist attacks, China's swift support for the U.S.-led war on terror aimed to garner international support for its suppression of Uighur separatism, justified by the arrest of a handful of them in the Al Qaeda camps in Afghanistan. In 2002, a U.S. State Department report, apparently accepting Chinese accusations at face value, labeled a hitherto-unknown group, the East Turkestan Independence Movement, as a terrorist organization with links to Al Qaeda leader Osama Bin Laden, reinforcing by association, and with American legitimation, the depiction of all Uighur nationalists as "terrorists."[48]

47. Kung, "National Identity and Ethno-Religious Identity," 385.
48. Castets, "The Uyghurs in Xinjiang"; Gladney, "Islam in China."

Due to the dearth of in-depth research, it was impossible to accurately gauge how deeply Islam was associated with Uighur nationalism, with some scholars stressing that the Islamic dimension was but a minor element.[49] Clearly, however, Islam was being driven underground, and it seemed likely that in the absence of any other source of international support, and with possibilities for employment and material advancement increasingly blocked by Han immigrants, coupled with the increasing pressure on traditional Uighur culture, Islam was possibly the only remaining cultural and spiritual resource to which the Uighurs could turn.[50]

CHRISTIANITY

Our discussion of Christianity will focus on both the Catholic and the Protestant churches, whose trajectories in the post-Mao period were parallel in some aspects but quite divergent in others. Perhaps more than for any other religious tradition, the Cultural Revolution had a defining impact on the evolution of Chinese Christianity. Owing to their direct association with foreign imperialists and a sometimes explicitly and actively anti-Communist orientation, the persecution of Christians was intense and systematic throughout the Mao years. And yet the Christian community survived, and even expanded, through the worst years of oppression. Already, the failure of the state-controlled patriotic Catholic and Protestant associations to rally most of the faithful in the 1950s had driven many to meet in small groups in their homes—the beginning of the "house church" movement—and led to the emergence of underground Protestant and Catholic networks.[51] The imprisonment, torture, and execution of many priests, ministers, and lay leaders only steeled the resolve of communities, which developed narratives of martyrdom and of bearing the cross for their faith. While public humiliations and stints in "cowsheds," prisons, and work camps were the lot of a large proportion of the Chinese population at some point during the Mao years, Christians gave a spiritual meaning to their sufferings, endowing them with a force with which they could bear the abuse and emerge with an even stronger faith. It was such people who, once released, returned to minister to their flocks in caves, in fields, and in private homes at night, or even to missionize to other villages. These underground churches were definitively cut off from Western influence,

49. Ibid.
50. Fuller & Lipman, "Islam in Xinjiang."
51. See, e.g., Joseph Lee, "Politics of Faith."

8

were strongly rooted in the local contexts of believers' lives, and became far more "self-governing, self-financing, and self-expanding" than the official "Three-Self" churches could ever have hoped to become. These were communities in which the frequent absence of the clergy due to repeated arrests and imprisonment led to the laity's coming to play a strong role in the organization of liturgical and community life—a situation that continued into the twenty-first century, when all churches faced an acute shortage of clergy that could not keep up with the growing numbers of believers.[52]

The dynamics of Protestant expansion during the Cultural Revolution are illustrated by the case of Li Tian'en 李天恩 (b. 1928), a house church evangelist who had operated in rural Pudong, Shanghai, during the 1950s, and who returned to his home province of Henan in 1971 after spending ten years in a labor camp. Traveling from county to county, he established hundreds of local churches until he was rearrested in 1975 after holding an underground training camp for no less than four thousand local Christian leaders in Fangcheng County, Henan—laying the foundations for what would later become the largest house church network in China.[53] This growth occurred in villages that initially had few or no Christians, and in which many of the conversions occurred due to miraculous healing experiences.

By contrast, Catholics, who were concentrated in specific villages and counties where they often made up the majority of the population—the result of previous mission policy to create entire Catholic communities rather making unrelated individual conversions—were often singled out for harsher treatment during political campaigns than neighboring non-Christian villages. This reinforced the Catholic community as an ascriptive "ethnic" group that shares the same community rituals, rites of passage, and Catholic identity, whether or not individual members believed in God or Roman Catholic dogma.[54] As a consequence, Catholics were much less active at proselytizing and creating new networks of practice; like Muslims, their numbers grew essentially through marriage rather than conversion.

By the late 1970s and early 1980s, the seeds that had been planted during the Cultural Revolution began to come to fruition, as both Catholic and Protestant religious activity came back into the open. On the one hand, religious activity was more tolerated, many churches and cathedrals were reopened or rebuilt, some church property was returned, and it was no

52. Hunter & Chan, *Protestantism*; Vala, "Pathways to the Pulpit."
53. Aikman, *Jesus in Beijing*, 69, 76–77.
54. Madsen, *China's Catholics*, 53–56.

longer necessary to meet secretly to worship. On the other hand, the RAB and the state-sponsored Patriotic Associations were reestablished; these once again attempted to exert their power over the believers, leading to renewed conflicts over legitimacy and authority, and to the division of Christian communities into the state-sponsored churches and unofficial, autonomous groups that did not come under state control.

For the Catholics, the issue was the existence of two parallel hierarchies, one loyal to Rome and the pope, the other to Beijing and the CCP. Unilateral consecrations of bishops by either side led to periodic flashes of tension, although the reality on the ground was quite complex. While in some places, members of the official and unofficial Catholic churches boycotted each other, leading some to speak of a "schism," in other places official and unofficial clergy informally divided territories between themselves to avoid conflict, or even jointly ministered to the same community. Up to two-thirds of the bishops were recognized by both Rome and Beijing, showing that a pragmatic modus vivendi was coming to function in the day-to-day operations of church activities. Many rural Catholic communities were too remote and isolated to be much affected by the politics of the CCPA.[55]

For Protestants, the issue was not one of two parallel hierarchies but an asymmetrical relationship between a centralized, state-sponsored institution and a diffused galaxy of thousands of independent congregations ranging in size from prayer groups in homes to national networks of hundreds of thousands of believers, which had their own printing presses, retreats, and training systems. Some were nominally registered with the TSPM, receiving occasional visits from official pastors, while others were clearly antagonistic to it and others ignored the official associations altogether.[56] Although the official churches controlled most buildings and assets in the large cities, this did not stop the growth of house churches among urban residents, while in the rural areas and in the hinterland some unofficial groups became so large that they often moved out of the "houses" and built large church structures seating thousands. According to an explicitly ambiguous official policy, the house churches were illegal but to be tolerated to a degree left to the discretion of local officials: Document 19 of 1982 stipulated on the one hand that "as for Protestants gathering in homes for

---

55. Lozada, *God Aboveground*; Liu & Leung, "Organizational Revivalism"; Chan Kim-kwong, "Tension"; Chan Kim-kwong, *Religion, State and Society.*

56. For a typology of Chinese Protestant churches, see Yip Ching-wah, "Protestant Christianity in Contemporary China."

worship services, this should not be allowed," but on the other hand that "this prohibition should not be too rigidly enforced."[57]

In consequence of this policy, violent repression of house churches was rare and sporadic, though not absent; destructions of churches by local authorities did occur, often followed, as in the cases of Chinese temples, by the believers rebuilding the structure shortly thereafter, once the overzealous local officials were out of the picture. The tension increased, however, beginning in the late 1990s, especially in areas of very strong Protestant presence, such as Wenzhou in southern Zhejiang, widely dubbed "China's Jerusalem." As a result, RAB officials said in informal conversations that their local branches were now staffed in proportion to the number of local Protestant converts.

The Fangcheng Fellowship mentioned above sent pairs of young evangelists to thirty provinces and municipal regions, reaching a claimed following of 5 million.[58] The China Gospel Fellowship, with its roots in another county in Henan, also spread to all corners of China, converting hundreds of thousands in Inner Mongolia and even sending missionaries among Chinese workers in Russian Siberia.[59] The Born-Again movement (Chongsheng pai 重生派) also spread out of Henan; it became known as the "Weepers," as it emphasized tearful repentance as evidence of the work of the Holy Spirit. Another network, descended from the Little Flock founded by Watchman Nee earlier in the century, was known as the "Shouters" (Huhan pai 呼唤派) for their habit of shouting "Jesus is Lord!" at times of worship or when threatened.

These networks, and many others, practiced charismatic and Pentecostal forms of worship. Healing, speaking in tongues, and prophecy were integral to their practices of worship; morality and repentance were central to their spirituality. In the words of Alan Hunter and Kim-Kwong Chan, the unofficial churches were typically "vibrant in faith, evangelistic in outreach, fundamentalist in doctrine, pious in devotion, informal in liturgy, spontaneous in development, and flexible in structure."[60]

---

57. Document 19 (translated in toto in MacInnis, *Religion in China Today*, 8–25); quoted in Hunter & Chan, *Protestantism*, 88; M. Cheng, "House Church Movements"; Huang Jianbo & Yang Fenggang, "The Cross Faces the Loudspeakers."

58. Aikman, *Jesus in Beijing*, 78. On the regional distribution of Christian populations, see Ying Fuk-tsang (Ying Fuzeng), "The Regional Development of Protestant Christianity."

59. Aikman, *Jesus in Beijing*, 86.

60. Hunter & Chan, *Protestantism*, 178; see also Yip Ching-wah, "Protestant Christianity and Popular Religion in China."

For both Catholics and Protestants, the weak legitimacy of the official church resulted in the undermining of all forms of institutional authority. Although most Catholics remained loyal to Rome, lines of communication with the Holy See were virtually cut off, and they were largely left to their own devices. There was no system of formal training for clerics in the unofficial church; instead, most were ordained after a period of apprenticeship under a more experienced priest—a practice that led to patron-client relations and factionalism within the unofficial hierarchy, while uncontrolled appointments of priests and bishops were so numerous that their qualifications were cast in doubt by some in the Roman church hierarchy.[61]

Among Protestants, the cell structure and loose network organization of the unofficial congregations was ideally adapted for resistance and even growth during periods of repression, but also led to constant fissuring, which undermined the unity of the Christian community.[62] Many churches became so colored with local culture that they increasingly resembled the salvationist movements of Chinese religion, with charismatic preachers leading their followers to Christ for healing and exorcism.[63] Some groups, such as the Oriental Lightning (Dongfang shandian 東方閃電), created in the early 1990s, which claimed that Jesus had returned as a young girl in Henan Province, were accused of engaging in violent clashes, kidnappings, and murders of members of other Christian groups on which they focused their proselytizing.[64]

Attempts by the unofficial churches to create some form of national structure met with mixed results, owing to both their own internal divisions and political restrictions. In November 1989, several underground Roman Catholic bishops established a pro-Roman bishops' conference at a secret meeting in Shanxi Province; however, the gathering was discovered and several of the bishops arrested.[65] The major Protestant house church leaders began to meet frequently starting in the mid-1990s, with the objective of finding common ground in reaction to the TSPM on the one hand and groups they considered "heretical" (*xiejiao* 邪教), such as Oriental Lightning, on the other. In August 1998, these leaders, coming mostly from Henan and Anhui but excluding the Shouters, issued a "United Appeal of the Various Branches of the Chinese House Church," which called on the

61. Hunter & Chan, *Protestantism*, 248–49; Madsen, *China's Catholics*, 42–44; Leung, "Communist Party–Vatican Interplay."

62. Hunter & Chan, *Protestantism*; Kindopp, "Fragmented yet Defiant."

63. Bays, "Chinese Protestant Christianity," 496–78.

64. Dunn, "'Cult,' Church, and the CCP."

65. Madsen, *China's Catholics*, 43.

government to "admit God's power," recognize the house churches as the representatives of Chinese Christianity, release all detained Christians, and change the definition of "heretical teachings" to conform to "international standards" rather than label as heretical and illegal all non-TSPM churches. A few months later, these leaders issued a "Confession of Faith," which formalized the common points of Christian doctrine as understood by the majority of house churches, explicitly stated their affiliation with the fundamentalist and evangelical tradition, affirmed the inerrancy of the Bible as the literal word of God, and outlined the reasons for the house churches not registering with the TSPM. These reasons included, in addition to their rejection of state authority over religion, their objections to official policy requiring registered churches to limit their activities to a designated location with designated personnel and covering a designated geographic area: for the unofficial communities, any place was suitable for worshipping the Lord, anyone with a calling from the Lord could preach, and the whole earth was mission territory.[66] In spite of these statements, the house church leaders had difficulty in maintaining their unity: the Shouters were definitely excluded in 2002, followed by the Born-Again movement, while the TSPM continued to be condemned for its "deviant" liberal theology.[67]

Though now deeply rooted in Chinese soil, the churches were increasingly linked to global networks. The first recipients of the "Appeal" were two American journalists, who were asked to disseminate it into China from abroad, while the "Confession of Faith" was drafted with the guidance of a Chinese-American theologian, Jonathan Chao. The movement toward Pentecostalism was promoted by an American evangelist, Rev. Dennis Balcombe, who had cultivated good relations with major house church leaders. Material support from churches in Hong Kong and Taiwan was an important boost for several congregations in Mainland China.

Here again, the contrast between the Catholic and Protestant cases was linked to their different visions of church hierarchy and patterns of organization, as well as to geopolitical factors. For the Catholics, the issue of authority within the church—the CCP's willingness to grant the pope spiritual authority, but no institutional power—was compounded by the question of diplomatic recognition, the Vatican remaining as one of the few states in the world to recognize the Republic of China on Taiwan rather than the PRC. While the Vatican had succeeded in making "Concordat"-style arrangements, such as joint appointment of bishops, with other com-

---

66. These documents are reproduced in Aikman, *Jesus in Beijing*, 293–307.
67. Ibid., 94.

munist regimes such as the USSR and Vietnam, the will seemed to be lacking in both Rome and Beijing to do the same for China. Both governments were divided between hard-line and accommodationist factions, and overtures were consistently torpedoed by provocative actions. Typically, these actions included unilateral appointment of bishops by either side; another example, from October 1, 2000, was the National Day canonization as saints of 120 Chinese Catholic martyrs and missionaries to China—most of them victims of the Boxers, toward which the CCP has an ambiguous stance—an action the PRC government harshly condemned as an insult to the Chinese victims of the imperialist forces with whom the missionaries were allied.

On the Vatican side, Pope John Paul II (1920–2005), who had encouraged the role of the Roman Catholic Church in his native Poland as a key force for anti-Communist resistance, was not strongly inclined to compose with a socialist regime. And it was precisely because of the church's role in the breakdown of the USSR's grip on Eastern Europe that, after 1989, Beijing took an even harsher stance toward a church still seen as viscerally anti-Communist. In addition, CCPA leaders feared for their positions in the event of a Sino-Vatican rapprochement. At the same time, Catholicism was clearly not seen by Beijing as presenting any potential geopolitical strategic interest that could be exploited to its advantage, in contrast to Islam or Han Buddhism. By the early twenty-first century, there appeared to be a stronger desire for breaking the impasse on the part of both the Chinese authorities and the new pope, Benedict XVI, but it is unclear at the time of writing if any mutual accommodation could be found.[68]

For the Protestants, the geopolitical issue was also sensitive due to the strong support for house churches in the United States, where the politically influential evangelical circles openly looked forward to the day when Christianity would become China's dominant religion, turning China into an American ally on the world stage against radical Islam. Such visions reinforced CCP fears of Protestantism as a dangerous imperialist force. At the same time, the sheer importance of the Sino-American relationship for both sides on questions of trade, investment, and regional security had a moderating influence on Chinese repression of house churches and American criticism of it. And the diffused, nonhierarchical links between Chinese and foreign Protestant networks made these contacts almost impossible to control. Thousands of missionaries from South Korea, Scandinavia, Taiwan, and North America operated in China as students, language teach-

---

68. On Sino-Vatican relations, see Leung, *Sino-Vatican Relations*, "The Sino-Vatican Negotiations."

ers, and businessmen, usually with the tacit tolerance of local authorities;[69] channels were established for the importation and distribution of Bibles and other religious literature and training materials; foreign-based Christian radio stations beamed programs into China in several regional dialects; and thousands of Web sites made it relatively easy for Chinese in any part of the country to gain access to the Gospel.

While Catholicism continued to grow at the same rate as China's population, Protestantism witnessed a phenomenal expansion—from 1 million in 1949 to at least 30 million by the end of the century, a thirtyfold increase. While such a figure still represented only 2 percent of the population, the rate of growth was so rapid that, if sustained over several decades in the twenty-first century, Christians could hope to bring into their faith, if not the majority of China's people, at least a significant minority.[70] Already, some ethnic groups in the southwest had converted to Christianity—with the support of local authorities delighted at their accomplishments in curbing drug trafficking and crime[71]—and several house churches dreamed of, and began preparations for, sending one hundred thousand Chinese missionaries to convert the Muslims of the Middle East, the last stage in a movement "back to Jerusalem" in expectation of the Second Coming.[72]

CONCLUSION

The long-term result of the Maoist era and especially the Cultural Revolution was clearly opposite to the CCP's aim of weakening the hold of religion on the Chinese masses. The religious identity of all communities discussed in this chapter was strengthened by the repression and abuses of the Cultural Revolution; for some, such as Tibetans and Turkic Muslims, religion was reinforced as the prime marker of ethnic identity and vehicle of anti-Han nationalist sentiment. For others, such as the Protestants, repression led to the emergence of a foundational mythology of resistance and martyrdom, which strengthened visions of redeeming the Chinese nation through Christ.

69. For the case of evangelical missionaries active in Tibet, see Pommaret, "La dernière frontière himalayenne."

70. See Liu Zhijun, *Xiangcun dushihua*, on how Christianity is expanding faster than the revival of communal religion in a suburban area of Shanxi. On the patterns of Christian recruitment, see Vala & O'Brien, "Recruitment to Protestant House Churches."

71. Qian Ning, ed., *Jidujiao yu shaoshu minzu*.

72. Aikman, *Jesus in Beijing*, 193–205; see the Web site www.backtojerusalem.com (accessed June 25, 2010).

Aware of the damage done during the Cultural Revolution, the CCP had adopted a relatively lenient attitude in the early 1980s, which allowed the religious communities to resurface and flourish, and take advantage of the state's promotion of international trade and exchanges, to strengthen their foreign and global ties. Tibetan Buddhism became a global religious movement; the Muslims became intensely tied to global Islamic networks in Central Asia, the Middle East, and Southeast Asia; and Catholics could more easily communicate with their counterparts in other parts of the world, while Protestants became a growing force in the global shift of Christianity toward the south, with an emphasis on Pentecostal, charismatic, and fundamentalist religiosity. There were possibly more churchgoing Christians in China than in western Europe,[73] and more Muslims in China than in many Arab countries. China could already be considered one of the world's major Christian *and* Muslim nations.

These religions' fortunes in China were strongly affected by geopolitical factors and the nation's diplomatic strategies, with differential impacts on each of the religions in question. A turning point for all communities occurred after 1989, when the Tian'anmen protests, coupled with the role of religion in the downfall of the Soviet empire and the independence of its European and Central Asian satellites, led to a generally more restrictive state policy, which varied in function of international power relations.

At the same time, the international discourse on freedom of religion in China grew in impact and complexity, and managed to influence diplomacy to a limited but not negligible extent. This discourse was developed by the media, academics, religious institutions, NGOs, and public bodies such as the United Nations Commission on Human Rights or the U.S. Commission on International Religious Freedom. The latter, which publishes annual reports and advises the government on religious issues, classified China as a country of special concern in 1999. Many of these organizations and bodies were affiliated with, or obtained much of their information from, Protestant movements, and thus tended to emphasize constraints on Christianity over other issues, whether they sought engagement and dialogue with the Chinese government or focused on denouncing China and lobbying Western governments.[74] In all cases, these various discourses influenced one another, and tended to focus on those forms of religious restrictions or persecution that were internationalized, such

73. Bays, "Chinese Protestant Christianity."
74. Bays, "American Public Discourse."

as those discussed in this chapter, rather than on communal religion or indigenous new religious groups, which Western public policy specialists had difficulty conceptualizing.

With no supporters abroad and tainted by the stigma of terrorism, the Uighurs bore the harshest repression, which could only radicalize their Islamic identity. Aided by the Dalai Lama's image abroad and his moderate stance toward the Chinese, the Tibetans fared somewhat better. But they lacked substantial *political* support, and in the absence of progress for their cause, the possibility of radicalization leading to harsher treatment, especially after the Dalai Lama's death, could not be discounted. Although the riots of March 2008 succeeded in embarrassing the CCP in the run-up to the 2008 Olympics, the immediate effect for Tibetans was harsher controls and an intensification of restrictions on Tibetan Buddhism. For the Catholics, improved conditions hinged on the establishment of diplomatic relations between Beijing and the Vatican, a prospect that was clearly within reach if the will existed on both sides. The CCP response to the "threat" posed by a booming Protestantism was attenuated by American influence and by the cautious behavior of the Protestants themselves, who did their best to keep a low profile and avoided any action that could be interpreted as politically oppositional.

It was the Hui, however, who enjoyed the best conjunction of domestic and international conditions: perceived as almost assimilated and loyal to China, protected by their status as a minority nationality, playing a pivotal role in developing links with the energy-rich Muslim countries, they suffered the least repression at home and were able (to a limited degree) to impose their concerns on the nation, successfully protesting for the banning of offensive books and even, during the Spring Festival of the Year of the Pig in 2007, obtaining the banning of representations of pigs in the Chinese mass media.

These cases can be contrasted with the other internationally sensitive religious case for China, that of Falungong. In 1998 and 1999, Falungong practitioners, whose numbers were booming, did not follow the Protestant strategy of trying to stay below the radar by understating their numbers and avoiding large public confrontations; rather, they chose to seek maximum visibility, practicing in parks and streets, exaggerating their numbers (claiming 100 million followers), holding large public rallies of thousands of practitioners, and, like the Muslims, staging sit-ins and demonstrations to protest newspaper articles and television reports that "hurt their feelings," letting it be understood that offending such large masses of people could have adverse consequences for social order.[75] They went even further than the Muslims by staging a ten-thousand-strong demonstration at Zhongnanhai, the nerve center of the CCP, on April 25, 1999. But Falungong leader Li Hongzhi overplayed his hand: if the Hui could effectively leverage their international support and their influence on social stability in some parts of China, such was not the case for Falungong, which came to be seen by the CCP as a dangerous cult that, unlike a historical religion, could be completely and rapidly eradicated through a ruthless campaign initially aimed at eliminating all the leaders and leaving the mass of practitioners alone. But the CCP, too, overplayed its hand—a propaganda and repression campaign begun in July 1999, which, harking back to the methods of the Mao era, produced predictable effects: whereas most followers abandoned the practice, the most devoted persisted, developing a mythology of resistance and martyrdom, and the case became internationalized. With Li Hongzhi and many key disciples based in the United States since 1996, there was little the CCP could do to stop Falungong's operations on the world stage.

Indeed, by the late 1990s Falungong had become a global network, with practice groups established in all Western and Southeast Asian countries as well as countries as varied as Pakistan, Bolivia, and Israel. The overwhelming majority of practitioners in these countries remained first-generation immigrants from Mainland China, and the exclusive concern of Falungong in its relations with the broader community was campaigning for an end to its repression and, increasingly, for the downfall of the CCP. Practitioners established several organizations dedicated to publicizing the repression and launching lawsuits around the world against visiting Chinese officials implicated in the repression. One of these agencies, Friends of Falun Gong, included as its advisors leaders of the U.S. Congressional Human Rights Caucus and of Freedom House, a high-powered Washington organization devoted to toppling the world's dictatorships.

Overseas Chinese media founded and staffed by Falungong activists—the *Epoch Times* newspaper and the NTD cable TV network, which aimed to be and succeeded in becoming one of the largest overseas Chinese media organizations, and an alternative voice to pro-CCP overseas Chinese media—focused on two fronts. First, they sponsored cultural shows in major Western theaters and Chinese New Year extravaganzas on television designed to rival those of the China Central Television, to spearhead a movement to restore and revitalize Chinese culture, as symbolized by the name

75. Palmer, *Qigong Fever*, 256, 272–73.

of the cable TV station: New Tang Dynasty. Second, they directly attacked the CCP by distributing anti-Communist tracts labeling the Party as an "evil party," and spearheading an Internet campaign to destroy the Party by inciting its members to renounce their membership—a campaign which claimed to have led over 67 million CCP members to have quit by the beginning of 2010[76] (a figure roughly equivalent to the total membership of the CCP, although the Party showed no signs of shrinking or weakening). The *Epoch Times* and its Web sites also endorsed a "China Interim Government," founded on January 1, 2008, which aimed to destroy the CCP.[77]

Although by the early 2000s Falungong had become a largely foreign-based movement, its concerns—like those of the *qigong* movement before it, albeit in a radically different manner—continued to revolve around the CCP and its relationship to Chinese culture and nationhood. Meanwhile, Zhang Hongbao, the founder of Zhonggong, one of China's largest *qigong* organizations (see chapter 11), had sought asylum in the United States in 2000, and proclaimed himself "President of the China Shadow Government" and "His Holiness Hongbao of World Religion the Vatican," causing many controversies in Chinese dissident circles until his death in a car accident in 2006.[78]

Powerless to stop the Falungong activism abroad—except by hiring thugs to intimidate protesters—the only thing the Chinese authorities could do was to attempt to hermetically seal China's borders against information on these actions. But Falungong hackers were nonetheless able to break through Internet firewalls to send mass e-mails, faxes, and automated phone calls to Chinese residents, and even, in some localities, to intercept television transmissions and beam Falungong documentaries in the place of the evening news. At the same time, media fatigue and increasing doubts about the credibility of Falungong's claims seriously reduced its impact on international public opinion.

The line of defense the CCP hoped to establish against the global reach of its dissident and underground religious groups was further weakened by the retrocession of Hong Kong in 1997. Under the "one country, two systems" formula, Hong Kong's religious freedom was to be preserved, giving groups like Falungong a space on Chinese soil where they could

76. Online at http://quitccp.org/cms/ (accessed January 17, 2010).

77. Online at http://chinainterimgov.org/en/index.php; http://www.theepochtimes.com/n2/component/option,com_ettopic/topicid,13/ (accessed January 17, 2010).

78. Thornton, "Manufacturing Dissent," 192–95; http://www.tianhuaculture.net/eng/a0_2_060831.html (accessed January 17, 2010).

freely operate, hold demonstrations, and distribute tracts to delegations of officials and tourists from the mainland. Pressure from the PRC government in response to this activity was a factor in the Hong Kong government's proposal to amend the Special Administrative Region's (SAR's) Basic Law (which became the SAR primary source of law after the retrocession) in 2003, adding an antisubversion clause (Article 23) that would have prohibited "any act of treason, secession, sedition, subversion against the Central People's Government."[79] Other religious groups, and notably the Roman Catholic Church, which in Hong Kong was not related to the pro-Beijing Catholic Patriotic Association on the mainland, were concerned that such a clause could one day be used to ban them in the SAR. Hong Kong's bishop, Cardinal Joseph Zen Zekiun, became the most vocal spokesman of a surge in popular opposition to Article 23; his call for a mass protest on July 1, 2003, was heeded by over 500,000 people, an unprecedented turnout for the typically apolitical Hong Kong residents. The protest caused the withdrawal of the government's proposal and was a factor in the eventual sacking of the SAR's Beijing-appointed chief executive, Tung Chee-hwa 董建華 (b. 1937), in 2005. Significantly, it was two of the organizations with the most conflictual relationships with Beijing—Falungong and the Roman Catholic Church—that were most acutely implicated in what was the greatest test to Hong Kong's "one country, two systems" regime.[80]

In cases where religious issues were institutionally combined with political interests—as with the pope as head of state of the Vatican, which accorded diplomatic recognition to the ROC on Taiwan, or the Dalai Lama as head of the Tibetan government-in-exile, associated with the Tibetan autonomy movement—the CCP was ultimately inflexible. Together with the fear of Uighur separatism and of Falungong's direct challenge to the CCP's authority, these issues struck at the heart of the Party's existential claims of moral and political legitimacy within the People's Republic of China. But where the issue for the Christians, Tibetan Buddhists, or Uighur Muslims concerned the *degree* of freedom and restriction, which could be adjusted and negotiated, for Falungong the ban remained total and uncompromising. In a globalized world, however, the Chinese state could no longer unilaterally control the agenda in relation to the religious question within its borders.

79. Article 23 is available online at http://www.basiclaw23.gov.hk/english/ (accessed June 25, 2010).

80. Kung Lap Yan, "Politics and Religions in Hong Kong"; Leung, "The Hong Kong Catholic Church."

Conclusion

In this volume, we have mapped the Chinese world's religious landscape and its changes, from the late nineteenth to the early twenty-first century. We have narrated the invention of categories of religion, superstition, science, "evil cults," and others, while highlighting the permutations between them: local cults, once part of orthodoxy, became superstition, then "cultural heritage," and sometimes were reintegrated into Buddhism or Taoism, all the while playing a role in local politics and social services. Moral discourses and self-cultivation practices were, often simultaneously, reinvented by the Nationalist and Communist parties, redemptive societies, and reformist Buddhist, Christian, or Muslim leaders. A host of marginal or powerful figures promised to fulfill utopian expectations of a new Chinese spiritual civilization by reconfiguring preexisting texts, ideas, and practices. Such intense reinventions, borrowings, and "traffic," to use Prasenjit Duara's term,[1] undermine any idea of an inexorable trend toward secularization—while top-down secularist projects have been aggressively at work for over a century, Chinese societies, in all their diversity, have never been truly secularized.

1. Duara, "Religion and Citizenship."

For all its cultural specificities, the Chinese world's religious trajectory bears comparisons with that of other parts of the world, and such comparisons may help bring out some general lessons. The brutal top-down imposition of a secularist-cum-corporatist model during the Republican and Communist periods parallels similar experiences, not only in the Soviet empire, but also in those parts of the Muslim world (notably Kemalist Turkey, but also 1920s and 1930s Iran, postindependence Baathist Iraq, Syria, and Tunisia, and so on) that implemented various forms of "authoritarian secularism."[2] In all these countries, public expression of religious beliefs was banned, reforming the use of public space and body behavior in ways reminiscent of New Life and Communist campaigns; religious places and specialists were brought under direct control and surveillance of specialized state agencies; campaigns to rationalize, modernize, and ethicize religion were launched by reformers; and state ideologies of nationalism and progress came to recycle religious discourses and mobilization practices. And, all the while, religious freedom was maintained—as a purely individual matter.

Although direct influence between these models was significant (Turkish and Soviet models of managing religion were often mentioned by Chinese politicians and intellectuals), they also shared common origins in the modern expansion of the Western powers that exported their categories of religion and modernity. As a result, the experience of these countries also shares common features with that of China. First, the reformist, antisuperstition projects (by both state agents and reformers) never fully attained their objectives. Whether traditional orthodox devotionalism in Russia, Sufi brotherhoods and cults of the saints in the Muslim world, or local cults and ritual traditions, geomancy, and spirit mediums in China—religious beliefs and practices not only have survived a century of repression, denigration, and systematic demonization but have actually adapted and thrived in countless unforeseen ways. Second, religion could never fit in the constrained corporatist space left for it by authoritarian secular regimes, and spilled over to create new forms of associations and networks that played a major role in the emerging civil society of these various countries, including charities, grassroots educational movements, and NGOs.

While in some cases this religious sector of the civil society was influential enough to eventually reach political power, such as in Turkey, in most other cases it was doomed to an ambiguous gray area or an oppositional stance to the state. There have been moves in both directions in

---

2. Luizard, *Laïcités autoritaires*.

the Chinese world, notably in Taiwan, where religious groups that developed outside the state-controlled corporatist framework have also played an important role in the formation of civil society and the transition to democracy. What needs to be stressed is that it is not an inherent political nature of the religious traditions in question (Buddhism, Islam, Christianity, and so on) that caused the emergence of religious groups active in civil society, but the authoritarian management of religion by secular regimes that forced the development of religions in places other than their "traditional" realms of neighborhood temples, mosques, or churches that were excessively constrained by state-led hierarchical systems of control. In that sense, as in many others, secularizing political regimes have been constitutive of modern forms of religion.

But the modern history of religion in China as in other parts of the world is not only about state control and religious resistance/adaptation. What comes out of our narrative of one long century of Chinese religion is tremendous creativity and invention, and not only during the last few decades of presumed "religious revival." This is also paralleled in other parts of the world where, even though the political regimes might not be authoritarian and may have a more liberal approach to secularism, the state and religion have nonetheless, like in the Chinese world, been inventing themselves in constant cross-reflection. Maybe the most fascinating parallel to be made is with India: according to Peter van der Veer, it is in the colonial encounter, continuing in the post-1947 postcolonial trajectory, that the Indian nation-state and the Indian "religions" were invented.[3] He evidences a simultaneous production of "religion," secularism, and modernity: the separation of religions from the state creates religion under new, national forms, and actually provokes their expansion into the public sphere.[4] Indeed, the religious productions of twentieth-century India offer some parallels to their Chinese equivalents: some are global networks based on body cultivation and individual fulfillment; some, more akin to Chinese redemptive societies, attempt to recycle body techniques (including martial arts), the classic scriptural tradition (which they print, teach, and disseminate), and universalist ideals to mobilize people nationwide in revivalist movements. While these movements criticize the Indian state's secular ideology (especially in the case of movements affiliated one way or another to political Hinduism), they are by the same token the very product of modern secularism, just like the wave of Chinese redemptive

3. Van der Veer, *Imperial Encounters*, "Global Breathing."
4. Ashiwa & Wank, "Making Religion, Making the State," make a similar point for China.

societies during the 1910s to 1930s, and the wave of *qigong*, Confucian movements, and Taiwan-based new religious groups since the 1970s, are also products of Chinese secularisms.

These comparisons, illuminating as they may be for understanding the past century of Chinese religious and political history, do not have very strong predictive value, except for suggesting that religious groups will surely play a role in any future social and political change. Indeed, in the minds of many the most important aspect of the Chinese religious question is what lies in store for the future, most crucially in the PRC. While other Chinese polities play a role in providing models and interacting with Mainland Chinese society, the People's Republic itself is our focus here. We begin by addressing the question of the future of religion in China, in the form of three parallel scenarios—all of which further amplify the complexity of the religious field and the "question" of religion in Chinese society. In light of this complexity, we then unpack the religious question into five overlapping issues that have appeared since the mid-nineteenth century, have remained unsolved, and, with China's growing influence and integration into the world system, are being carried into the global arena.

All three scenarios assume that, based on the trends observed in China among all traditions, and likewise confirmed in most parts of the world accompanying the loss of faith in secular ideologies and institutions, religiosity will continue to increase. Rodney Stark and William Sims Bainbridge have argued that, historically, where there has been a mutually reinforcing alliance between the state and a dominant religion, such as in pre-Enlightenment Europe (or, we would add, in China, where the Qing state was itself the dominant religious institution), political dissidence became a religious sin. In such a context, political opposition typically sought legitimacy through merging with or seeking alliance with religious heterodoxy, expressed as heretical rebellions. The only other option was to reject the sacred foundations of the state by attacking the very idea of religious legitimacy.[5] This radical solution first occurred with the French Revolution, evolved into Marxism, penetrated the Chinese intellectual field following the May Fourth movement, and became the dominant ideology after 1949. In this solution, the radical political movement, in attempting to eradicate religion, substitutes the otherworldly rewards promised by religion with the promise of future, this-worldly rewards—and, against the promise of

5. Stark & Bainbridge, *The Future of Religion*, 524–26; also, on a similar theme, Li Xiangping, *Xinyang, geming yu quanli*.

these rewards, demands a commitment, a fervor, and an ascetic self-denial comparable to the most high-tension religious sects.

But, come the revolution, the utopian promise is not fulfilled. Inequalities and suffering continue to exist, people continue to have unsatisfied desires and hopes. Faced with revolutionary disillusionment, the Chinese regime, through the post-Mao reforms, was able to continue promising future rewards and, for hundreds of millions, to begin to deliver the long-awaited material prosperity. But even when prosperity is attained, the money, the TV sets, the air conditioners, the decorated homes and the private cars, the lavish banquets and the karaoke clubs cannot supply the ultimate meaning and the eternal life promised by religion. As they lose their faith that all desires can be satisfied in this world, rich and poor alike become more receptive to the general, otherworldly benefits promised by religion. And as the utopian enthusiasm that sustained the building of a new social order gives way to disappointment, cynicism, apathy, and corruption, the this-worldly social benefits—the moral guidance, the communal ties, and the sense of meaning and purpose offered by religion— become, in contrast, all the more attractive.

Assuming that the future will see a rise in popular religiosity, the trends in the evolution of China's religious landscape allow us to sketch three possible scenarios for the future—each of which seems to follow a different logic leading to different results, but which, in fact, are unfolding simultaneously, leading to continued complexification.[6] They assume that the tendency observed since the late 1970s will continue, in which the evolution of Chinese state governmentality gradually opens more space for spiritual and religious seeking and expression. The question, then, is not so much whether Chinese people will on the whole become more religious and whether or not it will be easier for them to do so, but rather, how the social and institutional configuration of this growing religiosity will evolve.

The first scenario is the one called for and eagerly awaited by most Western observers, leading to the expansion of religious freedom and an increased space for the autonomy of religious communities. China would follow the path of Hong Kong and Taiwan, leading to a Western model of a secular state with a generally laissez-faire approach to the religious sector. And, to be sure, the trend in Mainland China has been timidly in that direction—communal religion and religions other than the five state-sponsored

6. For other scenarios, see Yang Fenggang, "Cultural Dynamics in China"; Chan Kim-Kwong, "Religion in China in the Twenty-First Century."

associations are often tolerated; the authorities seek to "normalize" unregistered house churches and temples, which are increasingly accepted by the authorities as posing no particular problem; and some scholars in China are vocal in openly advocating greater liberalization of religion—often under the rationale of applying "market" principles to religious groups: just as businesses have been allowed to freely operate and compete within a fair regulatory framework, the state should stop managing, restricting, or subsidizing religious groups and simply let them be, intervening through the judicial system only when they break the law or put society in danger.

But while there were incremental steps in this direction, at the time of writing there are no signs that the state will simply give up a model of religious administration that, in its fundamental features, had come into being in the 1950s. Even as they tolerate nonofficial forms of religion, state agents at all levels as a rule observe, keep files, and let it be known that they might intervene whenever they see fit. From their point of view, the risks are too great of an unfettered proliferation of hundreds of thousands of religious groups, some of which would likely aggravate interethnic or interreligious tensions, seek to undermine the sociopolitical system, or break up the territorial integrity of the PRC, and which would undoubtedly include thousands of new sects led by self-proclaimed Buddhas, messiahs, and emperors. The state prefers to be more tolerant in local practice without expanding the legal space for religion, so that it will retain the freedom to stamp out or restrict any groups it deems harmful for social and political stability. The most likely result of this first scenario is thus a growing gray area of uncertain legality for groups, temples, and churches that are allowed to multiply and are tolerated, but are neither integrated into the state system nor given legal status.[7]

The second scenario sees China reverting to a configuration approaching the Qing model, in which the state acts as the ultimate arbiter of religious orthodoxy, differentially favoring and even promoting some religious symbols and traditions over others. This occurs through a process of mutual co-optation and interpenetration between religious groups and state agents. This process is already at work: it is especially widespread in rural areas, through relationships between temples and local authorities. It also occurs at many levels, up to the central state itself, through the "canonization" of rituals and even divinities as intangible cultural heritage. State-sponsored cults to Confucius, the Yellow Emperor, and other civiliz-

---

7. This scenario is similar to the "gray market" of religion described by Yang Fenggang ("The Red, Black and Gray Markets").

ing heroes and ancestors partake of this logic as well, as do the varying degrees of covert or official encouragement of Buddhism, Confucianism, Taoism, and even communal religion by some government agents. Interventions, such as designating some groups as "evil cults," and in the choice of Tibetan reincarnations, are examples of the state claiming the mantle of religious orthodoxy to exclude and include groups and individuals from the religious field. However, since the state remains resolutely atheist and secularist, it cannot claim religious authority; the legitimacy of its interventions remains suspect for many believers. The common ground for mutual co-optation with the state is always something *other* than religion, such as economic development, tourism, cultural heritage, nationalism, social stability, health, and so on—defeating the state's own purpose of strictly circumscribing the religious sector. The result is a growing gray area of religious activity going on under the cover of other labels, sometimes changed or distorted by the logic of these other sectors, and blurring the line between these activities and the narrowly defined category of religion. Qing-style direct accommodations (on a cosmological as well as political level) between the state, deities, and religious communities remain unconceivable unless official atheism is dropped in favor of something else, a possibility that is only dreamt of aloud by a few.

The third scenario sees the state reviving its civilizing mission and adopting certain functional characteristics of religion, in a manner analogous to other countries' "civil" or "political" religions—a tendency we have seen under different guises in imperial, Republican, and socialist regimes.[8] Using enhanced and more sophisticated means of propaganda and the cooptation of leading cultural creators such as the film director Zhang Yimou 張藝謀,[9] drawing, depending on circumstance, on either ancient Chinese civilization, notably Confucianism, or revolutionary mythology, the civilizing project is used to raise a population of patriotic citizens and to project soft power onto the world stage—and at times considers recruiting religion to assist in this purpose. Since this scenario relies on the cultural resources of traditional Chinese civilization and aims to train moral citizens, it opens up and promotes a discursive space for concepts of morality, spirituality, and tradition that find their source in religion. But since the state remains resolutely atheist, it cannot fully substitute itself for religion (nor,

8. On explicit proposals to adopt Confucianism as a state religion or civil religion, see Ownby, "Kang Xiaoguang"; Yang Fenggang, "Confucianism as Religion?"

9. Zhang Yimou was the choreographer of the pharaonic opening ceremony of the 2008 Olympics, which drew heavily on traditional and Confucian symbolism.

since the end of the Cultural Revolution, does it have the desire to do so), nor can it seriously engage with theological and cosmological worldviews. The result—again—is a growing gray area of discourse on spirituality, morality, tradition, and religion, in which it is legitimate to evoke materials from religious sources but not to seriously engage with the theology or cosmology at their core.

These three scenarios are unfolding simultaneously, and all lead to a greater space for and influence of religiosity within Chinese society, in a context of "distended communism"[10] that allows a greater space, but neither full recognition nor autonomy, to social groups. But for different reasons which boil down to the fact that the state is not secular and religiously neutral but committed to a civilizing project that is ideologically atheist and materialist, and competing against religion, it cannot fully and directly engage with the religious space it has accepted and allowed to expand. None of the scenarios can thus come to a full fruition. All three scenarios lead to a growing gray area of noninstitutionalized groups, practices, and discourses in an unclear and ambiguous relationship with the norms and institutions of the state. As a consequence, popular religiosity proliferates, not only beyond the regulatory reach of the state, but beyond the normative reach of official religious institutions, which have little room to strengthen and expand, and little influence on the religious life of the masses. Chinese religious institutions, to begin with, were historically already highly localized; they were decimated during the Maoist period, and still highly restricted in their action when they revived in the reform period. Furthermore, to the extent that they conform with the state's secular ideology and offer a tepid religiosity, they are less attractive than the more vigorous, less institutionalized groups, which expand the most and meet the popular thirst—those which offer more intense connections to tradition, more fulfilling spiritual disciplines, or more innovative responses to the challenges of modern life. Meanwhile, escalating ethnic tensions between Han and minority ethnic groups may sharpen the latter's religious identity, especially in the case of Tibetan Buddhists and Uighur Muslims. China has thus become a huge religious laboratory, in which all kinds of spirituality and religiosity—traditional, modern, and postmodern, old and invented, indigenous and imported, and all combinations between them—have become possible in a massive cauldron, an expanding gray area that largely falls beyond direct legal and institutional control.

10. Chevrier, "De la révolution à l'Etat," 109–10.

By the second decade of the twenty-first century, however, a sea change has been under way in how Chinese elites perceive this growing and multiform religiosity. The ideological commitment to radical secularism is weaker than ever. With China's growing power, prosperity, and self-confidence on the world stage, there is less self-denigration and rejection of China's traditional heritage, religious customs, and ethical concerns, and even a more positive identification with them. A single-minded obsession with economic growth is giving way to broader concerns about the spiritual quality of life and about the moral consequences of unfettered materialism, provoking earnest consideration of religious teachings, whether of Chinese or overseas origin. A century of ideological warfare against, at various times, many or all forms of religiosity, and supported by much of China's intellectual and political elite, is subsiding. And after a century of surviving, resisting, adapting, reinventing, and reviving, the many forms of religion that exist in China today, while transformed, are growing and gaining in strength. China's relationship with herself, with the world, and with religion is undergoing a profound change. The master narrative of modernization, secularization, and the responses to it, resulting in the countless permutations that have been the subject of this book, will be less operative as the new century advances. But to be followed by what?

China's "religious question" thus remains as intractable as ever. The "question" itself can be seen as five distinct issues that pose themselves as acutely today as a century ago. The first is the question of religion, modernity, and secularization—the question that Europeans had begun to ask themselves at the time of the Enlightenment: the problem of how to scale back religion's domination of culture and society in order to free the human mind and carry forward the march of modernization. By the early twentieth century, this question seemed to have been solved in the West—religion had been put in its place, restricted to the private sphere of the family and individual subjectivity and, through education, philanthropy, and missionizing, to the socializing of the young, the sick, the poor, and the colonized. Categories such as religion, science, and superstition, as well as the theoretical and disciplinary foundations of social science itself, were rooted in this first question and its presumed resolution through modernization and secularization. Authority over elements of social and cultural life—cosmology, theology, knowledge, education, ritual, morality, self-cultivation, sacred times and places, political legitimacy, health, charity, and so on—were fought over and distributed between the increasingly differentiated institutions of government, religion, and science.

Such was the question, and the categories that framed it, which was posed by Chinese reformers in the early twentieth century, who asked how China could also follow the path of modernization and overcome the yoke of its traditions and superstitions. But they were then confronted with the second religious question: the Chinese cultural and social landscape was organized very differently than in Europe. The modern set of concepts cut up reality in a vastly different way, and its imposition proved to be a vexing issue indeed, as we have recounted in detail in this volume: concepts and practices excluded from the realm of religion did not disappear at all but mutated quickly and unpredictably as redemptive societies, political utopianism, *qigong* movements, and more. The modern political regimes of Chinese societies, be they Republican, colonial, or Communist, as a result of their histories of negotiations between traditional and Western ideologies and social formations, constructed different institutional distributions of the various elements of culture. And since this second question—that of the mismatch between Western and Chinese categories—always raised its head, the first question remained unsettled as well.

In the People's Republic, a third, more acute and precise question posed itself: the "religious question," which was explicitly dealt with by CCP policy, referred not merely to the broad problem of modernization but to the specific issue of loyalty to the regime and to the socialist system. Religion often implied social formations repulsive to the CCP, be they "feudal" landholding systems or institutions centered on otherworldly aims, and which were often openly hostile to socialism and the Party, or culturally dominant in borderland ethnic groups. The question for the CCP was: how to wean the members of such social formations away from religion without alienating them from Party rule? And, for the intermediate period in which religion would continue to exist, how to create religious institutions that could be compatible with the socialist system?

By the 1990s, it was clear that modernization was not leading to the decline of religiosity, which was booming. The original question of secularization was reopened; the second question of categories posed itself anew with the effervescence of communal religion, *qigong*, Confucian movements, and so on, all of them redeployed in the realms of health, science, education, charity, or cultural heritage; and the third question—that of religion's political loyalty to the nation-state—had not gone away with the reforms and opening up, especially since the campaigns of the Mao era, notably during the Cultural Revolution, *had* effectively alienated many religionists from the CCP. Furthermore, with China's opening up and the rapid pace of globalization, Chinese religious communities were increasingly connected to international networks, undermining the regime's control over information and opening spaces for transnational loyalties.

These global connections linked Chinese people to a world in which religion had suddenly become a prominent issue. The "religious question" was now not a uniquely Chinese problem but a global one, and this global dimension is the fourth issue subsumed under the term *religious question*. In a postmodern world, the question of religion and modernization was no longer obviously solved—secularization theories were challenged by a growing and assertive religiosity in most parts of the world. The question of the category of the religious had opened up in the West as well, with the decline of the established churches, the growth of noninstitutionalized forms of spirituality and religiosity, and the growing sensitivity to non-Western histories and experiences. And with transnational religious networks and organizations becoming important actors on the geopolitical arena, but not fitting neatly within national or even cultural boundaries—thus undermining Huntington's "clash of civilizations" hypothesis—the question of the fit between religion and the nation-state posed itself everywhere.

And finally, the fifth question was the one that posed itself to religious individuals, communities, and institutions in a radically changed social context: after over a century of tumult around the world, religion was no longer the primary foundation of social integration, replaced by secularized political, bureaucratic, and economic structures.[11] Would religion become a trove of commodified fantasies and practices for sale in the markets for culture, leisure, health, and psychotherapy? Would it lend itself as a source of symbols and rituals for projects of local, ethnic, or national identity construction? Would it act as an auxiliary to the state in its provision of social services, or strive to reinvest the public sphere?[12] Would it propose radical critiques of secular values, leading to utopian social movements? Would it build alternative forms of social relations, embedded within but still distinct from the logics of the market and of the state? Or even, where secular authority weakened, attempt to rebuild society on a sacred foundation?

The question is no longer simply the place of religion in the increasingly contested and changing institutional configuration of states and national cultures, but indeed the role of religion itself in the social construction, and in the institutional integration, of an intensely interconnected but highly unstable global society—a global society that is now the defining context within which national religious issues play themselves out. It is in

11. Vermander, "Religious Revival and Exit from Religion"; Dobbelaere, *Secularization*.
12. Casanova, *Public Religions in the Modern World*.

such a context that China is playing a growing role in world affairs. By its sheer size, expanding economic clout, and emerging cultural influence, China will inevitably have a major impact on the religious configuration of global society—but one about which we can only say with certainty that it will bring to the world all of its unresolved religious questions.

Bibliography

ABLAHIN, Andrew J. "A Sixth Religion? Confucianism and the Negotiation of Indonesian-Chinese Identity under the Pancasila State." In WILLFORD & GEORGE, *Spirited Politics*, 119–42.

ABRAMSON, Daniel Benjamin. "Places for the Gods: Urban Planning as Orthopraxy and Heteropraxy in China." In *The Transforming Asian City: Innovative Urban Planning Practices*, edited by Nihal PERERA & TANG Wing-Shing, 7–27. Online at http://geog.hkbu.edu.hk/tacconf/ PROCEEDING%20BOOK%20OF%20TRANSFORMING%20ASIAN%20CITIES.pdf (accessed August 5, 2009).

AGREN, Hans. "Patterns of Tradition and Modernization in Contemporary Chinese Medicine." In KLEINMAN, *Medicine in Chinese Cultures*, 37–51.

AHERN, Emily Martin. *Chinese Ritual and Politics*. Cambridge: Cambridge University Press, 1981.

———. "The Thai Ti Kong Festival." In *The Anthropology of Taiwanese Society*, edited by Emily Martin AHERN & Hill GATES, 397–425. Stanford CA: Stanford University Press, 1981.

AIJMER, Göran. "Political Ritual: Aspects of the Mao Cult during the Cultural Revolution." *China Information* 11 (1996): 215–31.

AIJMER, Göran, & Virgil K. Y. Ho. *Cantonese Society in a Time of Change*. Hong Kong: Chinese University Press, 2000.

AIKMAN, David. *Jesus in Beijing: How Christianity Is Transforming China and Changing the Global Balance of Power*. Washington, DC: Regnery Publishing, 2003.

ALITTO, Guy S. *The Last Confucian: Liang Shu-Ming and the Chinese Dilemma of Modernity*. Berkeley and Los Angeles: University of California Press, 1979.

ALLÈS, Elisabeth. *Musulmans de Chine: Une anthropologie des Hui du Henan*. Paris: Editions de l'EHESS, 2000.

———. "A propos de l'Islam en Chine: Provocations antireligieuses et attitudes anticléricales du xixe siècle à nos jours." *Extrême-Orient Extrême-Occident* 24 (2002): 65–76.

——. "Muslim Religious Education in China." *China Perspectives* 45 (2003): 21–33.

ALLÈS, Elisabeth, Leila CHÉRIF-CHEBBI, & Constance-Hélène HALFON. "Chinese Islam: Unity and Fragmentation." *Religion, State and Society* 31, no. 1 (2003): 7–36.

ANAGNOST, Ann S. "The Politics of Ritual Displacement." In KEYES, KENDALL & HARDACRE, *Asian Visions of Authority*, 221–54.

——. *National Past-Times: Narrative, Representation, and Power in Modern China*. Durham, NC: Duke University Press, 1997.

——. "The Corporeal Politics of Quality (Suzhi)." *Public Culture* 16, no. 2 (2004): 189–208.

ASAD, Talal. *Genealogies of Religion: Discipline and Reasons of Power in Christianity and Islam*. Baltimore: Johns Hopkins University Press, 1993.

——. *Formations of the Secular*. Stanford, CA: Stanford University Press, 2003.

ASHIWA Yoshiko & David L. WANK. "The Globalization of Chinese Buddhism: Clergy and Devotee Networks in the Twentieth Century." *International Journal of Asian Studies* 2, no. 2 (2005): 217–37.

——. "The Politics of a Reviving Buddhist Temple: State, Association, and Religion in Southeast China." *Journal of Asian Studies* 65, no. 2 (2006): 337–59.

——, eds. *Making Religion, Making the State: The Politics of Religion in Contemporary China*. Stanford: Stanford University Press, 2009.

——. "Making Religion, Making the State in Modern China: An Introductory Essay." In ASHIWA & WANK, *Making Religion, Making the State*, 1–21.

Asia Watch Committee. *Freedom of Religion in China*. Washington, DC: Human Rights Watch, 1992.

AUBIN, Françoise. "Islam on the Wings of Nationalism: The Case of Muslim Intellectuals in Republican China." In *Intellectuals in the Modern Islamic World: Transmission, Transformation, Communication*, edited by Stéphane DUDOIGNON, KOMATSU Hisao, & KOSUGI Yasushi, 241–72. London: Routledge, 2006.

AUBIN, Françoise, & Roberte HAMAYON. "Alexandre, César et Gengis Khan dans les steppes d'Asie Centrale." In *Les civilisations dans le regard de l'autre, actes du colloque international (Paris, 13 et 14 Décembre 2001, Unesco–Ephe)*, edited by Olga WEBER et al., 73–106, 262–69. Paris: UNESCO, 2002.

BAKER, Hugh D. R. *A Chinese Lineage Village: Sheung Shui*. Stanford, CA: Stanford University Press, 1968.

——. *Chinese Family and Kinship*. New York: Columbia University Press, 1979.

BAKKEN, Børge. *The Exemplary Society: Human Improvement, Social Control, and the Dangers of Modernity in China*. Oxford: Oxford University Press, 2000.

BARMÉ, Geremie. *Shades of Mao: The Posthumous Cult of the Great Leader*. Armonk, NY: Sharpe, 1996.

BARNETT, Robert. "The Tibet Protests of Spring, 2008: Conflict between the Nation and the State." *China Perspectives* (2009): 3, 6–23.

BASTID-BRUGUIÈRE, Marianne. "Sacrifices d'etat et légitimité à la fin des Qing." *T'oung-pao* 83 (1997): 162–73.

——. "Liang Qichao yu zongjiao wenti 梁啟超與宗教問題." *Tôhô gakuhô* 東方學報 70 (1998): 329–73.

——. "La campagne antireligieuse de 1922." *Extrême-Orient Extrême-Occident* 24 (2002): 77–93.

BAUM, Richard, & Frederic C. TEIWES. *Ssu-Ch'ing: The Socialist Education Movement of 1962–1966*. China Research Monographs, no. 2. Berkeley and Los Angeles: University of California Press, 1968.

BAYS, Daniel H., ed. *Christianity in China: From the Eighteenth Century to the Present*. Stanford, CA: Stanford University Press, 1996.

——. "The Growth of Independent Christianity in China, 1900–1937." In BAYS, *Christianity in China*, 307–16.

———. "Chinese Protestant Christianity Today." In Overmyer, *Religion in China Today*, 488–504.

———. "American Public Discourse on the Church in China." *China Review* 9, no. 2 (2009): 1–16.

Bays, Daniel H., & Ellen Widmer, eds. *China's Christian Colleges: Cross-Cultural Connections, 1900–1950.* Stanford, CA: Stanford University Press, 2009.

Béja, Jean-Philippe. "The Rise of National-Confucianism?" *China Perspectives* 2 (1995): 6–11.

———. "Nationalisme: Les intellectuels sont partagés." *Perspectives Chinoises* 34 (1996): 6–9.

Bellah, Robert N., Richard Madsen, William M. Sullivan, Ann Swidler, and Steven M. Tipton. *Habits of the Heart: Individualism and Commitment in American Life.* New York: Harper & Row, 1986.

Bellér-Hann, Ildikó. *Community Matters in Xinjiang 1880–1949: Towards a Historical Anthropology of the Uyghur.* Leiden: Brill, 2008.

Bellér-Hann, Ildikó, Cristina M. Cesàro, Rachel Harris, & Joanne Smith Finley, eds. *Situating the Uyghurs between China and Central Asia.* Aldershot, UK: Ashgate, 2007.

Bergère, Marie-Claire. *Sun Yat-Sen.* Paris: Fayard, 1994.

Billeter, Térence. *L'empereur Jaune: Une tradition politique chinoise.* Paris: Les Indes Savantes, 2007.

Billioud, Sébastien. "Confucianism, 'Cultural Tradition' and Official Discourses in China at the Start of the New Century." *China Perspectives* 3 (2007): 50–65.

Billioud, Sébastien, & David A. Palmer, eds. "Religious Reconfigurations in the People's Republic of China." Special issue, *China Perspectives* 4 (2009).

Billioud, Sébastien, & Joël Thoraval. "The Contemporary Revival of Confucianism: *Anshen liming* or the Religious Dimension of Confucianism." *China Perspectives* 3 (2008): 88–106.

———. "Jiaohua: The Confucian Revival in China as an Educative Project." *China Perspectives* 4 (2007): 4–21.

———. "Lijiao: The Return of Ceremonies Honouring Confucius in Mainland China." *China Perspectives* 4 (2009): 82–100.

bin Ismail, Mohamed Yusoff. "Two Faces of Buddhism: Chinese Participation in the Thai Temples in Kelantan." In Tong, *Chinese Beliefs*, 165–86.

Birnbaum, Raoul. "The Deathbed Image of Master Hongyi." In *The Buddhist Dead: Practices, Discourses, Representations*, edited by Jacqueline I. Stone & Bryan J. Cuevas, 175–207. Honolulu: University of Hawai'i Press, 2007.

Bonnin, Michel. *Génération perdue: Le mouvement d'envoi des jeunes instruits à la campagne en Chine, 1968–1980.* Paris: Editions de l'Ecole des hautes etudes en sciences sociales, 2004.

Borchert, Thomas. "Of Temples and Tourists: The Effects of the Tourist Political Economy on a Minority Buddhist Community in Southwest China." In Yang & Tamney, *State, Market, and Religions*, 87–111.

———. "Worry for the Dai Nation: Sipsongpanna, Chinese Modernity, and the Problems of Buddhist Modernism." *Journal of Asian Studies* 67, no. 1 (2008): 107–42.

Bosco, Joseph 林舟. "Yiguan Dao: 'Heterodoxy' and Popular Religion in Taiwan." In *The Other Taiwan: 1945 to the Present*, edited by Murray A. Rubinstein, 423–44. Armonk, NY: Sharpe, 1994.

———. "Tianhou gong zhi chongjian yu huoli: taiwan yu xianggang bijiao yanjiu 天后宮之重建與活力: 台灣與香港比較研究." In *Mazu xinyang de fazhan yu bianqian* 媽祖信仰的發展與變遷, edited by Lin Meirong 林美容, Chang Hsun 張珣, & Tsai Hsiang-hui 蔡相煇, 95–116. Taipei: Taiwan Association for Religious Studies and Beigang Chaotian Gong, 2003.

Bourdieu, Pierre. "Genèse et structure du champ religieux." *Revue française de sociologie* 12 (1971): 295–334.

Bovingdon, Gardner. "The Not-So-Silent Majority: Uyghur Resistance to Han Rule in Xinjiang." *Modern China* 28, no. 1 (2002): 39–78.

Bresciani, Umberto. *Reinventing Confucianism: The New Confucian Movement*. Taipei: Taipei Ricci Institute, 2001.

Brokaw, Cynthia J. *The Ledgers of Merit and Demerit: Social Change and Moral Order in Late Imperial China*. Princeton, NJ: Princeton University Press, 1991.

Brook, Timothy. "The Politics of Religion: Late-Imperial Origins of the Regulatory State." In Ashiwa & Wank, *Making Religion, Making the State*, 22–42.

Brownell, Susan. *Training the Body for China: Sports in the Moral Order of the People's Republic*. Chicago: University of Chicago Press, 1995.

———. "Beijing's Olympic Education Programme: Re-Thinking Suzhi Education, Re-Imagining an International China." *China Quarterly* 197 (2009): 44–64.

Bruun, Ole. *Fengshui in China: Geomantic Divination between State Orthodoxy and Popular Religion*. Copenhagen: NIAS Press, 2003.

Burgess, John S. *The Guilds of Peking*. New York: Columbia University Press, 1928.

Bush, Richard C., Jr. *Religion in Communist China*. New York: Abingdon Press, 1970.

Busto, Rudy V. "The Gospel according to the Model Minority? Hazarding an Interpretation of Asian American Evangelical College Students." In Yoo, *New Spiritual Homes*, 169–87.

Cabezon, José Ignacio. "State Control of Tibetan Buddhist Monasticism in the People's Republic of China." In Yang, *Chinese Religiosities*, 261–91.

Cai Degui 蔡德贵. *Dangdai xinxing bahayi jiao yanjiu* 当代新兴巴哈伊教研究. Beijing: Zhongguo renmin chubanshe, 2007.

Cao Nanlai. "The Church as a Surrogate Family for Working Class Immigrant Chinese Youth: An Ethnography of Segmented Assimilation." *Sociology of Religion* 66, no. 2 (Summer 2005): 183–200.

———. "Christian Entrepreneurs and the Post-Mao State: An Ethnographic Account of Church-State Relations in China's Economic Transition." *Sociology of Religion* 68, no. 1 (Spring 2007): 45–66.

———. "Raising the Quality of Belief: Suzhi and the Production of an Elite Protestantism." *China Perspectives* 4 (2009): 54–66.

Carnes, Tony, & Yang Fenggang, eds. *Asian American Religions: The Making and Remaking of Borders and Boundaries*. New York: New York University Press, 2004.

Casanova, José. *Public Religions in the Modern World*. Chicago: University of Chicago Press, 1994.

Castets, Rémi. "The Uyghurs in Xinjiang—the Malaise Grows." *China Perspectives* 49 (2003): 34–49.

Center for Religious Freedom. *Report Analyzing Seven Secret Chinese Government Documents*. Washington, DC: Freedom House, 2002.

Chan, Anita, Richard Madsen, & Jonathan Unger. *Chen Village under Mao and Deng*. Berkeley and Los Angeles: University of California Press, 1992.

Chan Kim-kwong (Chen Jianguang) 陳劍光. *Towards a Contextual Ecclesiology: The Catholic Church in the People's Republic of China (1979–1983); Its Life and Theological Implications*. Hong Kong: Phototech System, 1987.

———. "Tension in the Chinese Catholic Church (1979–1983)." *Ching Feng* 34, no. 3 (1991): 168–99.

———. "Religion in China in the Twenty-First Century: Some Scenarios." *Religion, State and Society* 33, no. 2 (2005): 98–100.

———. "Xiandai shehui zongjiao hexie moshi de gean: xianggang zongjiao zhi dongtaiyu guanxi 现代社会宗教和谐模式的个案：香港宗教界之动态与关系." In *Wenming hexie yu chuangxin* 文明和谐与创新, edited by Pang Xuequan 庞学铨 & Chen Cunfu 陈村富, 308–15. Hangzhou: Zhejiang daxue chubanshe, 2009.

Chan Kim-kwong & Carlson, Eric C. *Religious Freedom in China: Policy, Administration and Regulation; A Research Handbook*. Santa Barbara, CA / Hong Kong: Institute for the Study of American Religion / Hong Kong Institute for Culture, Commerce and Religion, 2005.

CHAN, Selina Ching. "Selling the Ancestors' Land: A Hong Kong Lineage Adapts." *Modern China* 27, no. 2 (2001): 262–84.

CHAN, Selina Ching, & LANG, Graeme S. "Temple Construction and the Revival of Popular Religion in Jinhua." *China Information* 21 (2007): 43–69.

CHAN Wing-Tsit. *Religious Trends in Modern China.* New York: Columbia University Press, 1953.

CHAN Yuk Wah. "Packaging Tradition: Chinese Death Management in Urban Hong Kong." *Asian Anthropology* 2 (2003): 139–60.

CHANG Hao. *Chinese Intellectuals in Crisis: Search for Order and Meaning, 1890–1911.* Berkeley and Los Angeles: University of California Press, 1987.

Changli xianzhi 昌黎縣志. Jin Liangji 金良驥 et al., comps. 1933.

CHAO Shin-yi. "A Danggi Temple in Taipei: Spirit-Mediums in Modern Urban Taiwan." *Asia Major*, 3rd ser., 15, no. 2 (2002): 129–56.

CHAPMAN, Elana. "The De-Territorialization of Ritual Spheres in Contemporary Taiwan." *Asian Anthropology* 8 (2009): 31–64.

CHARBONNIER, Jean. "World Religions and Asian Culture: The Singapore Experience." In *Religion and Culture: Past Approaches, Present Globalisation, Future Challenges*, edited by Macau Ricci Institute, 213–26. Macau, 2004.

CHARLEUX, Isabelle. "The Reconstruction of Buddhist Monasteries in the Chinese Autonomous Region of Inner Mongolia: Between Sanctuary and Museum." In *Revival of Buddhism in Mongolia after 1990*, edited by Agata BAREJA-STARZYNSKA & Hanna HAVNEVIK. Warsaw, 2009.

CHAU, Adam Yuet. "Popular Religion in Shaanbei, North-Central China." *Journal of Chinese Religions* 31 (2003): 39–79.

———. *Miraculous Response: Doing Popular Religion in Contemporary China.* Stanford, CA: Stanford University Press, 2005.

———. "The Politics of Legitimation and the Revival of Popular Religion in Shaanbei, North-Central China." *Modern China* 31, no. 2 (2005): 236–78.

———. "Superstition Specialist Households? The Household Idiom in Chinese Religious Practices." *Minsu quyi* 153 (2006): 157–202.

———. "Mao's Traveling Mangos: Food as Relic in Revolutionary China." *Past and Present* (2010), Suppl. 5, pp. 256–75.

CHEN Bing 陈兵 & DENG Zimei 邓子美. *Ershi shiji Zhongguo fojiao* 二十世纪中国佛教. Beijing: Minzu chubanshe, 2000.

CHEN, Carolyn. "The Religious Varieties of Ethnic Presence: A Comparison between a Taiwanese Immigrant Buddhist Temple and an Evangelical Christian Church." *Sociology of Religion* 63, no. 2 (2002): 215–38.

CHEN Cunfu 陈村富. *Zhuanxing qi de Zhongguo jidujiao—zhejiang jidujiao de ge'an yanjiu* 转型期的中国基督教—浙江基督教个案研究. Beijing: Dongfang chubanshe, 2005.

CHEN Gang. "Death Rituals in a Chinese Village: An Old Tradition in a Contemporary Social Context." Ph.D. diss., Ohio State University, 2000.

CHEN Hongxing 陈红星 & DAI Chenjing 戴晨京, eds. *Falungong yu xiejiao* 法轮功与邪教. Beijing: Zongjiao wenhua chubanshe, 1999.

CHEN Hsi-yuan 陳熙遠. "Confucianism Encounters Religion: The Formation of Religious Discourse and the Confucian Movement in Modern China." Ph.D. diss., Harvard University, 1999.

———. "'Zongjiao'-yige Zhongguo jindai wenhua shi shang de guanjian ci 宗教一個中國近代文化史上的關鍵詞." *Xin shixue* 新史學 13, no. 4 (2002): 37–66.

CHEN Jialun 陳家倫. "Xin shidai yundong zai taiwan de fazhan 新時代運動在台灣的發展. Xinxing zongjiao xianxiang yantaohui 新興宗教現象研討會." *Academia Sinica* (March 29, 2002); online at www.ios.sinica.edu.tw/pages/seminar/twnrp2002/twnrp.htm (accessed September 27, 2007).

CHEN Jinlong 陈金龙. *Zhongguo gongchandang yu Zhongguo de zongjiao wenti—guanyu dang de zongjiao zhengce de lishi kaocha* 中国共产党与中国的宗教问题: 关于党的宗教政策的历史考察. Guangzhou: Guangdong renmin chubanshe, 2006.

CHEN Qizhang. *Dalu zongjiao zhengce yu fagui zhi tantao* 大陸宗教政策與法規之探討. Taipei: Xingzhengyuan dalu weiyuanhui, 1993.

CHEN Xiaoyi 陳曉毅. *Zhongguo shi zongjiao shengtai* 中國式宗教生態：青岩宗教多樣性個案研究. Beijing: Shehui kexue wenxian chubanshe, 2008.

CHEN Xingqiao 陈星桥, ed. *Fojiao "qigong" yu falungong* 佛教 '气功' 与法轮功. Beijing: Zongjiao wenhua chubanshe, 1998.

CHEN Yaoting 陈耀庭. "Shanghai daojiao shi 上海道教史." In *Shanghai Zongjiao Shi* 上海宗教史, edited by RUAN Renze 阮仁泽 & GAO Zhennong 高振农, 353–438. Shanghai: Shanghai renmin chubanshe, 1992.

CHEN Yingning 陳櫻寧. *Daojiao yu yangsheng* 道教与养生. Beijing: Huawen chubanshe, 2000.

CHEN Yung-fa. *Making Revolution: The Communist Movement in Eastern and Central China, 1937–1945*. Berkeley and Los Angeles: University of California Press, 1986.

CHENG, May M. C. "House Church Movements and Religious Freedom in China." *China: An International Journal* 1, no. 1 (2003): 16–45.

CHENG Yinghong. *Creating the "New Man": From Enlightenment Ideals to Socialist Realities*. Honolulu: University of Hawai'i Press, 2009.

CHEVRIER, Yves. "De la révolution à l'Etat par le communisme." *Le débat*, no. 117 (2001): 92–113.

CHIANG Kai-shek 蔣介石. "Xin shenghuo yundong zhi yaoyi 新生活運動之要義." In *Xian zongtong—jianggong sixiang yanlun zongji* 先總統—蔣公思想言論總集, compiled by QIN Xiaoyi 秦孝儀. Taipei: Zhongguo guomin dang zhongyang weiyuan hui shiwei yuanhui, zhongyang wenwu gongying she, 1983.

Chizhai de zhenyi 持齋的真義. Taipei: Guanghui, 2004.

Chongjian Jinling Yuxuguan jishi zhengxin lu 重建金陵玉虛觀紀事徵信錄. WANG Lianyou 王蓮友. 1936 edition in *Zhongguo daoguan zhi congkan* 中國道觀志叢. Nanjing: Jiangsu guji chubanshe, 2000 (vol. 11).

CHOW Kai-wing. *The Rise of Confucian Ritualism in Late Imperial China: Ethics, Classics, and Lineage Discourse*. Stanford, CA: Stanford University Press, 1994.

CHOW Tse-tsung. *The May Fourth Movement: Intellectual Revolution in Modern China*. Stanford, CA: Stanford University Press, 1960.

CHUNG, Sue Fawn & WEGERS, Priscilla, eds. *Chinese American Death Rituals*. Lanham, MD: AltaMira Press, 2005.

CI Jiwei. *Dialectic of the Chinese Revolution: From Utopianism to Hedonism*. Stanford, CA: Stanford University Press, 1994.

CLAMMER, John. *The Sociology of Singapore Religion: Studies in Christianity and Chinese Culture*. Singapore: Chopmen Publishers, 1991.

———. "Religious Pluralism and Chinese Beliefs in Singapore." In TONG, *Chinese Beliefs*, 199–224.

CLANCEY, Gregory K., Hui-chieh LOY, & Alan K. L. CHAN, eds. *Historical Perspectives on East Asian Science, Technology and Medicine*. Singapore: Singapore University Press; World Scientific, 2001.

CLARKE, Ian. "Ancestor Worship and Identity: Ritual, Interpretation, and Social Normalization in the Malaysian Chinese Community." *Sojourn: Social Issues in Southeast Asia* 15, no. 2 (2000): 273–95.

CLART, Philip. "The Phoenix and the Mother: The Interaction of Spirit-Writing Cults and Popular Sects in Taiwan." *Journal of Chinese Religions* 25 (1997): 1–32.

———. "The Ritual Context of Morality Books: A Case-Study of a Taiwanese Spirit-Writing Cult." Ph.D. diss., University of British Columbia, 1997.

———. "Opening the Wilderness for the Way of Heaven: A Chinese New Religion in the Greater Vancouver Area." *Journal of Chinese Religions* 28 (2000): 127–44.

———. "Chinese Tradition and Taiwanese Modernity." In CLART & JONES, *Religion in Modern Taiwan*, 84–97.

———. "Confucius and the Mediums: Is There a 'Popular Confucianism'?" *T'oung Pao* 89, nos. 1–3 (2003): 1–38.

———. "Moral Mediums: Spirit-Writing and the Cultural Construction of Chinese Spirit-Mediumship." *Ethnologies* 25, no. 1 (2003): 153–90.

———. "The Concept of 'Popular Religion' in the Study of Chinese Religions: Retrospects and Prospects." In *The Fourth Fu Jen University Sinological Symposium: Research on Religions in China; Status Quo and Perspectives*, edited by Zbigniew WESOLOWSKI, 166–204. Xinzhuang: Furen Daxue chubanshe, 2007.

CLART, Philip, & Charles B. JONES, eds. *Religion in Modern Taiwan: Tradition and Innovation in a Changing Society.* Honolulu: University of Hawai'i Press, 2003.

COHEN, Erik. *The Chinese Vegetarian Festival in Phuket: Religion, Ethnicity, and Tourism on a Southern Thai Island.* Bangkok: White Lotus Press, 2001.

COHEN, Myron L. "Souls and Salvation: Conflicting Themes in Chinese Popular Religion." In WATSON & RAWSKI, *Death Ritual in Late Imperial and Modern China*, 180–202.

———. "Lineage Organization in North China." *Journal of Asian Studies* 49, no. 3 (1990): 509–34.

———. "Being Chinese: The Peripheralization of Traditional Identity." In *Kinship, Contract, Community, and State: Anthropological Perspectives on China*, edited by Myron L. COHEN, 39–59. Stanford, CA: Stanford University Press, 2005.

COHEN, Paul A. *China and Christianity: The Missionary Movement and the Growth of Chinese Antiforeignism, 1860–1870.* Cambridge, MA: Harvard University Press, 1963.

———. *History in Three Keys: The Boxers as Event, Experience, and Myth.* New York: Columbia University Press, 1997.

———. "Boxers, Christians, and the Gods: The Boxer Conflict of 1900 as a Religious War." In *China Unbound: Evolving Perspectives on the Chinese Past*, edited by Paul A. COHEN, 105–30. London: RoutledgeCurzon, 2003.

COMPTOM, Boyd. *Mao's China: Party Reform Documents, 1942–44.* Seattle: University of Washington Press, 1952.

COPPEL, Charles. "The Origins of Confucianism as Organized Religion in Java, 1900–1930." *Journal of Southeast Asian Studies* 12, no. 1 (1981): 179–96.

CROIZIER, Ralph C. *Traditional Medicine in Modern China: Science, Nationalism, and the Tensions of Cultural Change.* Cambridge, MA: Harvard University Press, 1968.

———. "Traditional Medicine as a Basis for Chinese Medical Practise." In *Medicine and Public Health in the People's Republic of China*, edited by Joseph QUINN, 3–21. Washington, DC: Department of Health, Education, and Welfare, 1973.

———. "Medicine and Modernization in China: An Historical Overview." In KLEINMAN, *Medicine in Chinese Cultures*, 21–35.

CUI Haiyuan 瞿海源 & ZHANG Yinghua 章英華. "Taiwan wailai xinxing zongjiao fazhan de bijiao yanjiu 臺灣外來新興宗教發展的比較研究. Xinxing zongjiao xianxiang yantaohui 新興宗教現象研討會." *Academia Sinica* (March 29, 2002); online at www.ios.sinica.edu.tw/pages/seminar/twnrp2002/twnrp.htm (accessed September 27, 2007).

CULP, Robert. "Rethinking Governmentality: Training, Cultivation, and Cultural Citizenship in Nationalist China." *Journal of Asian Studies* 65, no. 3 (2006): 529–54.

DAI Liyong 戴立勇. *Xiandaixing yu Zhongguo zongjiao* 现代性与中国宗教. Beijing: Zhongguo shehui kexue chubanshe, 2008.

DAIBER, Karl-Fritz. "Les associations des cinq religions officiellement reconnues en république populaire de Chine." *Social Compass* 51, no. 2 (2004): 255–71.

Daojiaohui bugao 道教會布告 (1912). In *Zangwai daoshu* 藏外道書. Chengdu: Bashu shushe, 1992–1994 (vol. 24).

DAVID, Beatrice. "The Evacuation of Village Funerary Sites." *China Perspectives* 5 (1996): 20–27.

DAVIS, Edward. *Society and the Supernatural in Song China.* Honolulu: University of Hawaiʻi Press, 2001.

DAY, Clarence Burton. *Chinese Peasant Cults, Being a Study of Chinese Paper Gods.* Shanghai: Kelly and Walsh, 1940.

DE GROOT, Jan Jakob Maria. *Sectarianism and Religious Persecution in China.* Amsterdam: Johannes Müller, 1903.

———. *The Religious System of China.* 6 vols. Taipei: Literature House, 1964.

DEAN, Kenneth. *Taoist Ritual and Popular Cults of South-East China.* Princeton, NJ: Princeton University Press, 1993.

———. "Ritual and Space: Civil Society or Popular Religion?" In *Civil Society in China*, edited by Timothy BROOK & Michael FROLIC, 172–92. Armonk, NY: Sharpe, 1997.

———. *Lord of the Three in One: The Spread of a Cult in Southeast China.* Princeton, NJ: Princeton University Press, 1998.

———. "China's Second Government: Regional Ritual Systems in Southeast China." In *Shehui, minzu yu wenhua zhanyan guoji yantaohui lunwenji* 社會民族與文化展演國際研討會論文集, edited by WANG Ch'iu-kui 王秋桂, ZHUANG Yingzhang 莊英章, & CHEN Zhongmin 陳中民, 77–109. Taipei: Hanxue yanjiu zhongxin, 2001.

———. "Local Communal Religion in Contemporary South-East China." In OVERMYER, *Religion in China Today*, 338–58.

———. "Further Partings of the Way." In ASHIWA & WANK, *Making Religion, Making the State*, 179–210.

———. "Daoists and Transnational Chinese Society: The Circulation of Daoist Priests, Three in One Self-Cultivators, and Spirit Mediums between Fujian and South-East Asia." In PALMER & LIU, *Daoism in the Twentieth Century.*

DEBERNARDI, Jean E. "Malaysian Chinese Religious Culture: Past and Present." In SURYADINATA, *Ethnic Chinese in Singapore and Malaysia*, 301–23.

———. *Rites of Belonging: Memory, Modernity, and Identity in a Malaysian Chinese Community.* Stanford, CA: Stanford University Press, 2004.

———. *The Way That Lives in the Heart: Chinese Popular Religion and Spirit Mediums in Penang, Malaysia.* Stanford, CA: Stanford University Press, 2006.

DELIUSIN, Lev. "The I-Kuan Tao Society." In *Popular Movements and Secret Societies in China, 1840–1950*, edited by Jean CHESNEAUX, 225–33. Stanford, CA: Stanford University Press, 1972.

DILLON, Michael. *Xinjiang, China's Muslim Far Northwest.* London: RoutledgeCurzon, 2004.

DING Hong 丁宏 & ZHANG Guojie 张国杰, eds. *Bai nian Zhongguo musilin* 百年中国穆斯林. Yinchuan: Ningxia renmin chubanshe, 2002.

DING Renjie (TING Jen-chieh) 丁仁傑. *Shehui fenhua yu zongjiao zhidu bianqian: Dangdai taiwan xinxing zongjiao xianxiang de shehuixue kaocha* 社會分化與宗教制度變遷: 當代台灣新興宗教現象的社會學考察. Taipei: Lianjing chuban shiye, 2004.

DING Shu 丁抒. *Yangmou: "Fanyou" qianhou* 陽謀: '反右' 前後. Hong Kong: Jiushi niandai zazhishe, 1993.

DIRLIK, Arif. "The Ideological Foundations of the New Life Movement: A Study in Counterrevolution." *Journal of Asian Studies* 34, no. 4 (1975): 945–80.

———. "Confucius in the Borderlands: Global Capitalism and the Reinvention of Confucianism." *Boundary* 2 (1995): 229–73.

DOBBELAERE, Karel. *Secularization: An Analysis at Three Levels.* Brussels: P.I.E.-Peter Lang, 2002.

———. "China Challenges Secularization Theory." *Social Compass* 56 (2009): 362–70.

Doleželová-Velingerová, Milena, & Oldřich Král, eds. *The Appropriation of Cultural Capital: China's May Fourth Project*. Cambridge, MA: Asia Center, Harvard University, 2001.

Dorfman, Diane. "The Spirits of Reform: The Power of Belief in Northern China." *Positions* 4 (1996): 253–89.

Du Jingzhen 杜景珍. "Lüelun Daoyuan zaojin (1928) hou de dongxiang 略論道院遭禁 (1928) 後的動向." *Minjian zongjiao* 民間宗教 3 (1997): 227–33.

Duara, Prasenjit. *Culture, Power, and the State: Rural North China, 1900–1942*. Stanford, CA: Stanford University Press, 1988.

———. "Superscribing Symbols: The Myth of Guandi, Chinese God of War." *Journal of Asian Studies* 47, no. 4 (1988): 778–95.

———. "Knowledge and Power in the Discourse of Modernity: The Campaigns against Popular Religion in Early Twentieth-Century China." *Journal of Asian Studies* 50, no. 1 (1991): 67–83.

———. *Rescuing History from the Nation: Questioning Narratives of Modern China*. Chicago: University of Chicago Press, 1995.

———. *Sovereignty and Authenticity: Manchukuo and the East Asian Modern*. Lanham, MD: Rowman and Littlefield, 2003.

———. "Religion and Citizenship in China and the Diaspora." In Yang, *Chinese Religiosities*, 43–64.

DuBois, Thomas D. *The Sacred Village: Social Change and Religious Life in Rural North China*. Honolulu: University of Hawai'i Press, 2005.

———. "Local Religion and the Imperial Imaginary: The Development of Japanese Ethnography in Occupied Manchuria." *The American Historical Review* 111, no. 1 (2006): 52–74.

———, ed. *Casting Faiths: Imperialism and the Transformation of Religion in East and Southeast Asia*. London: Palgrave Macmillan, 2009.

———. "Introduction: The Transformation of Religion in East and Southeast Asia—paradigmatic Change in Regional Perspective." In DuBois, *Casting Faiths*, 1–22.

———. "The Salvation of Religion? Public Charity and the New Religions of the Early Republic." *Minsu quyi* 民俗曲藝 172 (2011).

Dunch, Ryan. *Fuzhou Protestants and the Making of a Modern China 1857–1927*. New Haven, CT: Yale University Press, 2001.

———. "Christianity and 'Adaptation to Socialism.'" In Yang, *Chinese Religiosities*, 155–79.

Dunn, Emily C. "'Cult,' Church, and the CCP: Introducing Eastern Lightning." *Modern China* 35, no. 1 (2009): 96–119.

Dutournier, Guillaume, & Ji Zhe. "Social Experimentation and 'Popular Confucianism': The Case of the Lujiang Cultural Education Centre." *China Perspectives* 4 (2009): 67–81.

Dutton, Michael. "Mango Mao: Infections of the Sacred." *Public Culture* 16, no. 2 (2004): 161–187.

Eastman, Lloyd E. "Fascism in Kuomintang China: The Blue Shirts." *China Quarterly* 49 (1972): 1–31.

Eng, Irene, & Yi-Min Lin. "Religious Festivities, Communal Rivalry, and Restructuring of Authority Relations in Rural Chaozhou, Southeast China." *Journal of Asian Studies* 61, no. 4 (2002): 1259–85.

Erhimbayar. "Mongolian Buddhist Monasteries in Present-Day Northern China: A Comparative Study of Monasteries in Liaoning and Inner Mongolia." *Inner Asia* 8, no. 2 (2006): 183–203.

Esenbel, Selçuk. "Japan's Global Claim to Asia and the World of Islam: Transnational Nationalism and World Power, 1900–1945." *American Historical Review* 109, no. 4 (2004): 1140–70.

Esherick, Joseph W. *The Origins of the Boxer Uprising*. Berkeley and Los Angeles: University of California Press, 1987.

Faèllman, Fredrik. *Salvation and Modernity: Intellectuals and Faith in Contemporary China*. Stockholm: Department of Oriental Languages, Stockholm University, 2004.

Fan Guangchun. "Urban Daoism, Commodity Markets and Tourism: The Restoration of the Xi'an City God Temple." In Palmer & Liu, *Daoism in the Twentieth Century*.

Fan Hua 范華 [Patrice Fava]. "Miaofeng shan xingxiang zouhui 妙峰山行香走會." *Faguo hanxue* 法国汉学 7 (2002): 271–321.

Fan Ke. "Traditionalism and Identity Politics among the Ding Hui Community in Southern Fujian." In Tan, *Southern Fujian*, 35–68.

Fan Lizhu 范丽珠. *Dangdai Zhongguoren zongjiao xinyang de bianqian* 當代中國人宗教信仰的變遷: 深圳民間宗教信徒的田野研究. Taipei: Wenbo wenhua, 2005.

Fan Lizhu 范丽珠, Evelyn Eaton Whitehead, & James D. Whitehead. "The Spiritual Search in Shenzhen: Adopting and Adapting China's Common Spiritual Heritage." *Nova Religio* 9, no. 2 (2005): 50–61.

Fang Ling. "Les médecins laïques contre l'exorcisme sous les Ming: La disparition de l'enseignement de la thérapeutique rituelle dans le cursus de l'institut impérial de médecine." *Extrême-Orient Extrême-Occident* 24 (2002): 31–45.

Fang Ling & Vincent Goossaert. "Les réformes funéraires et la politique religieuse de l'État chinois, 1900–2008." *Archives de Sciences Sociales des Religions* 144 (2008): 51–73.

Faure, David. *The Structure of Chinese Rural Society: Lineage and Village in the Eastern New Territories, Hong Kong*. Oxford: Oxford University Press, 1986.

———. *Emperor and Ancestor: State and Lineage in South China*. Stanford, CA: Stanford University Press, 2007.

Faure, David, & Tao Tao Liu, eds. *Town and Country in China: Identity and Perception*. Basingtoke, UK: Palgrave, 2002.

Feng Erkang 冯尔康. *Shiba shiji yilai Zhongguo jiazu de xiandai zhuanxiang* 18 世纪以来中国家族的现代转向. Shanghai: Shanghai renmin chubanshe, 2005.

Fer, Yannick. "The Growth of Pentecostalism in French Polynesia: A Hakka history; Migration, cultural identity and Christianity." *China Perspectives* 57 (2005): 50–57.

Feuchtwang, Stephan. "City Temples in Taipei under Three Regimes." In *The Chinese City between Two Worlds*, edited by Mark Elvin & G. William Skinner, 263–301. Stanford, CA: Stanford University Press, 1974.

———. "A Chinese Religion Exists." In *Old State in New Settings: Studies in the Social Anthropology of China*, edited by Hugh D. R. Baker & Stephan Feuchtwang, 139–60. Oxford: JASO, 1991.

———. "Local Religion and Village Identity." In *Unity and Diversity: Local Cultures and Identities in China*, edited by Taotao Liu & David Faure, 161–76. Hong Kong: University of Hong Kong, 1998.

———. "Religion as Resistance." In Perry & Selden, *Chinese Society*, 161–77.

———. *The Imperial Metaphor: Popular Religion in China*. Surrey: Curzon, 2001.

Feuchtwang, Stephan, & Wang Mingming. *Grassroots Charisma: Four Local Leaders in China*. London: Routledge, 2001.

Fisher, Gareth. "The Spiritual Land Rush: Merit and Morality in New Chinese Buddhist Temple Construction." *Journal of Asian Studies* 67, no. 1 (2008): 143–70.

Flath, James A. *The Cult of Happiness: Nianhua, Art and History in Rural North China*. Vancouver: University of British Columbia Press, 2004.

———. "Temple Fairs and the Republican State in North China." *Twentieth-Century China* 30, no. 1 (2004): 39–63.

Flower, John Myers. "Portraits of Belief: Constructions of Chinese Cultural Identity in the Two Worlds of City and Countryside in Modern Sichuan Province." Ph.D. diss., University of Virginia, 1997.

———. "A Road Is Made: Roads, Temples, and Historical Memory in Ya'an County, Sichuan." *Journal of Asian Studies* 63, no. 3 (2004): 649–85.

Flower, John Myers, & Pamela Leonard. "Defining Cultural Life in the Chinese Countryside: The Case of the Chuan Zhu Temple." In *Cooperative and Collective in China's Rural Develop-*

ment: Between State and Private Interests, edited by Eduard B. VERMEER, Frank PIEKE, & WOEI Lien Chong, 273–90. Armonk, NY: Sharpe, 1998.

FORBES, Andrew D. *Warlords and Muslims in Chinese Central Asia: A Political History of Republican Sinkiang 1911–1949.* Cambridge: Cambridge University Press, 1986.

FORMOSO, Bernard. "Chinese Temples and Philanthropic Associations in Thailand." *Journal of Southeast Asian Studies* 27, no. 2 (1996): 245–60.

———. *Identités en regard: Destins chinois en milieu bouddhiste thaï.* Paris: Éditions de la Maison des Sciences de l'Homme, 2000.

———. "Marchands et philanthropes: Les associations de bienfaisance chinoises en Thaïlande." *Annales: Histoire, Sciences sociales* 58, no. 4 (2003): 833–56.

Foxue congbao 佛學叢報. Shanghai 1912–, monthly.

FREEDMAN, Maurice. "Colonial Law and Chinese Society." *Journal of the Royal Anthropological Institute* 80 (1950): 97–126.

———. "Immigrants and Associations: Chinese in Nineteenth-Century Singapore." *Comparative Studies in Society and History* 3, no. 1 (1960): 25–48.

———. *Chinese Lineage and Society.* London: Athlone Press, 1971.

FRESNAIS, Jocelyne. *La protection du patrimoine en république populaire de Chine (1949–1999).* Paris: CTHS, 2001.

FRIEDMAN, Edward. "Einstein and Mao: Metaphors of Revolution." *China Quarterly* 93 (1983): 51–75.

FRIEDMAN, Edward, Paul G. PICKOWICZ, and Mark SELDEN, with Kay Ann JOHNSON. *Chinese Village, Socialist State.* New Haven, CT: Yale University Press, 1991.

FRIEDMAN, Sara L. "Civilizing the Masses: The Productive Power of Cultural Reform Efforts in Late Republican-Era Fujian." In *Defining Modernity: Guomindang Rhetorics of a New China, 1920–1970,* edited by Terry BODENHORN, 151–94. Ann Arbor: Center for Chinese Studies, University of Michigan Press, 2002.

———. "Embodying Civility: Civilizing Processes and Symbolic Citizenship in Southeastern China." *Journal of Asian Studies* 63, no. 3 (2004): 687–718.

FU Zhong 孚中. *Yiguandao fazhan shi* 一貫道發展史. Taipei: Zhengyi shanshu chubanshe, 1999.

FULLER, Graham, & Jonathan LIPMAN. "Islam in Xinjiang." In STARR, *Xinjiang,* chap. 13.

GAMBLE, Sidney D. *Ting Hsien, a North China Rural Community.* Stanford, CA: Stanford University Press, 1954.

GAN Chunsong 干春松. *Zhiduhua rujia jiqi jieti* 制度化儒家及其解体. Beijing: Zhongguo renmin daxue chubanshe, 2003.

GAO Shining 高師寧. *Dangdai Beijing de jidujiao yu jidutu—zongjiao shehuixue ge'an yanjiu* 當代北京的基督教與基督徒—宗教社會學個案研究. Hong Kong: Institute of Sino-Christian Studies, 2005.

GARON, Sheldon M. "State and Religion in Imperial Japan, 1912–1945." *Journal of Japanese Studies* 12, no. 2 (1986): 273–302.

GATES, Hill. *China's Motor: A Thousand Years of Petty Capitalism.* Ithaca, NY: Cornell University Press, 1996.

GAUSTAD, Blaine. "Prophets and Pretenders: Inter-Sect Competition in Qianlong China." *Late Imperial China* 21, no. 1 (2000): 1–40.

GERMANO, David. "Re-Membering the Dismembered Body of Tibet: Contemporary Tibetan Visionary Movements in the People's Republic of China." In GOLDSTEIN & KAPSTEIN, *Buddhism in Contemporary Tibet,* 53–94.

GIAP, The Siauw. "Islam and Chinese Assimilation in Indonesia and Malaysia." In TONG, *Chinese Beliefs,* 59–102.

GIDDENS, Anthony. *Central Problems in Social Theory: Action, Structure and Contradiction in Social Analysis.* London: Macmillan, 1979.

———. *The Constitution of Society.* Cambridge: Polity Press, 1984.

GILLETTE, Maris Boyd. *Between Mecca and Beijing: Modernization and Consumption among Urban Chinese Muslims*. Stanford, CA: Stanford University Press, 2000.

———. "Violence, the State, and a Chinese Muslim Ritual Remembrance." *Journal of Asian Studies* 67, no. 1 (2008): 1011.

GLADNEY, Dru C. "Salman Rushdie in China: Religion, Ethnicity, and State Definition in the People's Republic." In KEYES, KENDALL & HARDACRE, *Asian Visions of Authority*, 254–78.

———. *Muslim Chinese: Ethnic Nationalism in the People's Republic*. Cambridge, MA: Council on East Asian Studies, Harvard University, 1996.

———. *Ethnic Identity: The Making of a Muslim Minority Nationality*. Fort Worth, TX: Harcourt Brace College Publishers, 1998.

———. "The Salafiyya Movement in Northwest China: Islamic Fundamentalism among the Muslim Chinese?" In *Muslim Diversity: Local Islam in Global Contexts*, edited by Leif MANGER, 102–49. Surrey: Curzon Press, 1999.

———. "Islam in China: State Policing and Identity Politics." In ASHIWA & WANK, *Making Religion, Making the State*, 151–78.

GLOSSER, Susan L. *Chinese Visions of Family and State, 1915–1953*. Berkeley and Los Angeles: University of California Press, 2003.

GOLDFUSS, Gabriele. *Vers un bouddhisme du xxe siècle: Yang Wenhui (1837–1911), réformateur laïque et imprimeur*. Paris: Collège de France, Institut des Hautes Études Chinoises, 2001.

GOLDSTEIN, Melvyn C. *A History of Modern Tibet, 1913–1951: The Demise of the Lamaist State*. Berkeley and Los Angeles: University of California Press, 1989.

———. Introduction. In GOLDSTEIN & KAPSTEIN, *Buddhism in Contemporary Tibet*, 1–14.

———. "The Revival of Monastic Life in Drepung Monastery." In GOLDSTEIN & KAPSTEIN, *Buddhism in Contemporary Tibet*, 15–52.

———. "The United States, Tibet, and the Cold War." *Journal of Cold War Studies* 8, no. 3 (2006): 145–64.

GOLDSTEIN, Melvyn C., BEN Jiao, & TANZEN Lhundrup. *On the Cultural Revolution in Tibet: The Nyemo Incident of 1969*. Berkeley and Los Angeles: University of California Press, 2009.

GOLDSTEIN, Melvyn C., & Matthew T. KAPSTEIN, eds. *Buddhism in Contemporary Tibet: Religious Revival and Cultural Identity*. Berkeley and Los Angeles: University of California Press, 1998.

GONG Xuezeng 龚学增. *Shehui zhuyi yu zongjiao* 社会主义与宗教. Beijing: Zongjiao wenhua chubanshe, 2003.

GOOSSAERT, Vincent. "Counting the Monks: The 1736–1739 Census of the Chinese Clergy." *Late Imperial China* 21, no. 2 (2000): 40–85.

———, ed. "Anticléricalisme en Chine." Special issue, *Extrême-Orient Extrême-Occident* 24 (2002).

———. "Starved of Resources: Clerical Hunger and Enclosures in Nineteenth-Century China." *Harvard Journal of Asiatic Studies* 62, no. 1 (2002): 77–133.

———. "Bureaucratic Charisma: The Zhang Heavenly Master Institution and Court Taoists in Late-Qing China." *Asia Major*. 3rd ser. 17, no. 2 (2004): 121–59.

———. "Chinese Popular Religion." In *Encyclopedia of Religion*, 2nd ed., edited by Lindsay JONES, 3:1613–21. Farmington Hills, MI: MacMillan, 2004.

———. *L'interdit du bœuf en Chine: Agriculture, éthique et sacrifice*. Paris: Collège de France, Institut des Hautes Études Chinoises, 2005.

———. "1898: The Beginning of the End for Chinese Religion?" *Journal of Asian Studies* 65, no. 2 (2006): 307–36.

———. "Jindai Zhongguo de guojia yu zongjiao: Zongjiao zhengce yu xueshu dianfan 近代中國的國家與宗教：宗教政策與學術典範." *Zhongyang yanjiuyuan jindai shi yanjiusuo jikan* 中央研究院近代史研究所集刊 54 (2006): 169–209.

———. "Les sens multiples du végétarisme en Chine." In *A croire et à manger: Religions et alimentation*, edited by Aïda KANAFANI-ZAHAR, Séverine MATHIEU, & Sophie NIZARD, 65–93. Paris: L'Harmattan, 2007.

———. *The Taoists of Peking, 1800–1949: A Social History of Urban Clerics*. Cambridge, MA: Asia Center, Harvard University, 2007.

———. "Irrepressible Female Piety: Late Imperial Bans on Women Visiting Temples." In "Women, Gender and Religion in Premodern China," special issue, *Nan Nü: Men, Women and Gender in China* 10, no. 2 (2008): 212–41.

———. "Republican Church Engineering: The National Religious Associations in 1912 China." In Yang, *Chinese Religiosities*, 209–32.

———. "The Destruction of Immoral Temples in Qing China." In *ICS Visiting Professor Lectures Series*, 2:131–53. Hong Kong: Chinese University Press, 2009.

———. "Daoists in the Modern Chinese Self-Cultivation Market: The Case of Beijing, 1850–1949." In Palmer & Liu, *Daoism in the Twentieth Century*.

———. "Managing Chinese Religious Pluralism in the Nineteenth-Century City Gods Temple." In *Chinese Religions in the Age of Globalization, 1800 to Present*, edited by Thoralf Klein, Christian Meyer, & Thomas Jansen. Boston: Brill, forthcoming.

———. "Taoism, 1644–1850," In *Cambridge History of China*, vol. 9, part 2. Cambridge: Cambridge University Press, forthcoming.

Goossaert, Vincent, & Fang Ling. "Temples and Daoists in Urban China since 1980." *China Perspectives* 4 (2009): 32–40.

Goossaert, Vincent, & David Ownby, eds. "Mapping Charisma in Chinese Religion." Special issue, *Nova Religio* 12, no. 2 (2008).

Goossaert, Vincent, & David A. Palmer, eds. "Catégories et politiques du religieux en Chine." Special issue, *Archives de sciences sociales des religions* 144 (2008).

Granet, Marcel. *La religion des chinois*. Paris: Payot, 1979.

Gray, Jack. *Rebellions and Revolutions: China from the 1800s to 2000*. Oxford: Oxford University Press, 2002.

Grootaers, Willem A. *The Sanctuaries in a North-China City: A Complete Survey of the Cultic Buildings in the City of Hsüan-Hua (Chahar)*. Bruxelles: Institut Belge des Hautes Etudes Chinoises, 1995.

Guangxu chao donghua lu 光緒朝東華錄. Beijing: Zhonghua shuju, 1958.

Guest, Kenneth. "Liminal Youth among Fuzhou Chinese Undocumented Workers." In Carnes & Yang, *Asian American Religions*, 55–75.

Guiheux, Gilles, & Kuah-Pearce, K. E., eds. *Social Movements in China and Hong Kong: The Expansion of Protest Space*. Amsterdam: ICAS / Amsterdam University Press, 2009.

Guo Qitao. *Exorcism and Money. The Symbolic World of the Five-Fury Spirits in Late Imperial China*. Berkeley, CA: Institute of East Asian Studies, University of California, Berkeley, 2003.

Guojia zongjiao shiwuju zhengce faguisi 国家宗教事务局政策法规司. *Quanguo zongjiao xingzheng fagui guizhang huibian* 全国宗教行政法规规章汇编. Beijing: Zongjiao wenhua chubanshe, 2000.

"Guowuyuan guanyu zongjiao huodong changsuo guanli tiaoli 國務院關於宗教活動場所管理條例." In *Xin shiqi zongjiao gongzuo*, edited by Zhonggong Zhongyang et al., 1995, 275–77.

Guowuyuan zongjiao shiwuju zhengce faguisi 国务院宗教事物局政策法规司. *Zhongguo zongjiao tuanti ziliao* 中国宗教团体资料. Beijing: Zhongguo shehui chubanshe, 1993.

Hamm, John Christopher. *Paper Swordsmen: Jin Yong and the Modern Chinese Martial Arts Novel*. Honolulu: University of Hawai'i Press, 2005.

Han Xing 韩星. *Rujiao wenti-zhengming yu fansi* 儒教问题—争鸣与反思. Xi'an: Shaanxi renmin chubanshe, 2004.

Handlin Smith, Joanna F. "Benevolent Societies: The Reshaping of Charity during the Late Ming and Early Ch'ing." *Journal of Asian Studies* 2 (1987): 309–37.

Hardacre, Helen. *Shintô and the State, 1868–1988*. Princeton, NJ: Princeton University Press, 1989.

Harrison, Henrietta. *The Making of the Republican Citizen: Political Ceremonies and Symbols in China, 1911–1929*. Oxford: Oxford University Press, 2000.

———. *The Man Awakened from Dreams: One Man's Life in a North China Village 1857–1942*. Stanford, CA: Stanford University Press, 2005.

Hassall, Graham. "China in the Bahá'í Writings." Online at http://bahai-library.com/file .php?file=hassall_china_bahai_history 2003 (accessed November 20, 2009).

He Fengjiao 何鳳嬌, ed. *Taiwan sheng jingwu dang'an huibian-minsu zongjiao bian* 臺灣省警務檔案彙編. 民俗宗教篇. Taipei: Guoshiguan, 1996.

He Guanghu 何光沪, ed. *Zongjiao yu dangdai Zhongguo shehui* 宗教与当代中国社会. Beijing: Zhongguo renmin daxue chubanshe, 2006.

Hillman, Ben. "The Rise of the Community in Rural China: Village Politics, Cultural Identity and Religious Revival in a Hui Hamlet." *China Journal* 51 (2004): 53–74.

Hiniker, Paul J. *Revolutionary Ideology and Chinese Reality—dissonance under Mao*. Beverly Hills, CA: Sage, 1977.

Hirotaka Nanbu. "Religion in Chinese Education: From Denial to Cooperation." *British Journal of Religious Education* 30, no. 3 (2008): 223–34.

Ho, Wai Yip. "Historical Analysis of Islamic Community Development in Hong Kong: Struggle for Recognition in the Post-Colonial Era." *Journal of Muslim Minority Affairs* 21, no. 1 (2001): 63–77.

Holm, David L. *Art and Ideology in Revolutionary China*. Oxford: Clarendon Press, 1991.

Hoskins, Janet. "From Kuan Yin to Joan of Arc: Iconography and Gender in Cao Dai Temples." Paper presented at the conference "Asian Studies on the Pacific Coast," Claremont Graduate University, July 17–19, 2005.

Hsiao, Hsin-Huang Michael, & David Schak. "Taiwan's Socially Engaged Buddhist Groups." *China Perspectives* 59 (2005): 43–55.

Hsu, Francis L. K. *Under the Ancestors' Shadow: Chinese Culture and Personality*. London: Routledge & Kegan Paul, 1949.

Hu Fuchen 胡浮琛. "21 shiji de xin daoxue wenhua zhanlue. 21 世纪的新道学文化战略." In *Daoxue tonglun* 道学通论, edited by Hu Fuchen 胡浮琛 & Lü Xichen 吕锡琛, 716–44. Beijing: Shehui kexue wenxian chubanshe, 2004.

Hu Shi 胡適. *Hu shi zaonian wencun* 胡適早年文存. Taipei: Yuanliu chuban shiye gongsi, 1995.

Hua Shiping. *Chinese Utopianism: A Comparative Study of Reformist Thought with Japan and Russia, 1898–1997*. Washington, DC: Woodrow Wilson Center Press; Stanford, CA: Stanford University Press, 2009.

Huai Bing. "La Chine en quête d'une nouvelle morale." Original publication in *Zhengming* 214 [1995]: 81–82, translated by Xavier Gange. *Perspectives Chinoises* 30 (1995): 12–15.

Huang, C. Julia, ed. "Wings of Belief: Modern Chinese Religious Transnationalism." Special issue, *European Journal of East Asian Studies* 2, no. 2 (2003).

———. *Charisma and Compassion: Cheng Yen and the Buddhist Tzu Chi Movement*. Cambridge, MA: Harvard University Press, 2008.

Huang, C. Julia, & Robert P. Weller. "Merit and Mothering: Women and Social Welfare in Taiwanese Buddhism." *Journal of Asian Studies* 57, no. 2 (1998): 379–96.

Huang Huili 黃慧琍. *Zangchuan fojiao zaitai fazhan chutan* 藏傳佛教在台發展初探. Tainan: Guoli Tainan shifan xueyuan xiangtu wenhua yanjiusuo, 2000.

Huang Jianbo & Yang Fenggang. "The Cross Faces the Loudspeakers: A Village Church Perseveres under State Power." In Yang & Tamney, *State, Market, and Religions*, 41–62.

Huang Kewu 黃克武. "Minguo chunian Shanghai de lingxue yanjiu: Yi 'Shanghai lingxuehui' wei li 民國初年上海的靈學研究：以'上海靈學會'為例." *Zhongyang yanjiuyuan jindai shi yanjiusuo jikan* 中央研究院近代史研究所集刊 55 (2007): 99–136.

Huang Lixing 黃麗馨, ed. *Zongjiao jianjie* 宗教簡介. Taipei: Neizhengbu, 2005.

Huang, Philip C. C. *Code, Custom, and Legal Practice in China: The Qing and the Republic Compared*. Stanford, CA: Stanford University Press, 2001.

HUANG Zhangjian 黃彰健. *Kang Youwei wuxu zhen zouyi (fu Kang Youwei wei wuxu zougao)* 康有為戊戌真奏議 (附康有為偽戊戌奏稿). Taipei: Zhongyang yanjiuyuan Lishi yuyan yanjiusuo, Shiliao congshu, 1974.

HUBBERT, Jennifer. "(Re)Collecting Mao: Memory and Fetish in Contemporary China." *American Ethnologist* 33, no. 2 (2006): 145–61.

HUNG Chang-tai. "Mao's Parades: State Spectacles in China in the 1950s." *China Quarterly* 190 (2007): 411–31.

HUNTER, Alan, & Kim-Kwong CHAN. *Protestantism in Contemporary China*. Cambridge: Cambridge University Press, 1993.

IKELS, Charlotte, ed. *Filial Piety: Practice and Discourse in Contemporary East Asia*. Stanford, CA: Stanford University Press, 2004.

IMAHORI Seiji. *Peipin shimin no jiji kôsei* 北平市民の自治構成. Tokyo: Bunkyûdo, 1947.

JAGOU, Fabienne. *Le 9e Panchen Lama (1883–1937): Enjeu des relations Sino-Tibétaines*. Paris: Ecole française d'Extrême-Orient, 2004.

JAMMES, Jeremy. "Le caodaïsme: Rituels médiumniques, oracles et exégèses; Approche ethnologique d'un mouvement religieux vietnamien et de ses réseaux." Ph.D. diss., Université Paris 10, 2006.

JANKOWIAK, William R. *Sex, Death, and Hierarchy in a Chinese City: An Anthropological Account*. New York: Columbia University Press, 1993.

JASCHOK, Maria. *The History of Women's Mosques in Chinese Islam: A Mosque of Their Own*. London: Curzon, 2000.

JEUNG, Russell. "Creating an Asian American Christian Subculture: Grace Community Covenant Church." In CARNES & YANG, *Asian American Religions*, 287–312.

JI Zhe. "The Establishment of a Lay Clergy by the Modern Chan Society: The Practice of Modern Chinese Buddhism." *China Perspectives* 59 (2005): 56–65.

———. "Traditional Education in Contemporary China: Conservative and/or Liberal?" *Chinese Cross Currents* 2, no. 3 (2005): 32–41.

———. "Non-Institutional Religious Re-Composition among the Chinese Youth." *Social Compass* 53, no. 4 (2006): 535–49.

———. "Buddhism and the State: The New Relationship." *China Perspectives*, no. 55 (2004): 2–10.

———. "Educating through Music: From an 'Initiation into Classical Music' for Children to Confucian 'Self-Cultivation' for University Students." *China Perspectives* 3 (2008): 107–17.

———. "Secularization as Religious Restructuring: Statist Institutionalization of Chinese Buddhism and Its Paradoxes." In YANG, *Chinese Religiosities*, 233–60.

———. "Territoires migratoires et lieux religieux: Cartes des religions des Chinois en Île-de-France." In *Dieu change en ville: Religion, espace et immigration*, edited by Lucine ENDELSTEIN, Sébastien FATH, and Séverine MATHIEU. Paris: L'Harmattan/AFSR, forthcoming.

———. "Religion, Youth and Modernity: Summer Camp as a New Ritual Practice of Chinese Buddhism." *Social Compass* (forthcoming).

JIANG Canteng 江燦騰. *Taiwan fojiao yu xiandai shehui* 臺灣佛教與現代社會. Taipei: Dongda tushu gongsi, 1993.

———. *Riju shiqi taiwan fojiao wenhua fazhan shi* 日據時期臺灣佛教文化發展史. Taipei: Nantian shuju, 2001.

———. *Taiwan jindai fojiao de biange yu fansi—quzhiminhua yu taiwan fojiao zhutixing queli de xin tansuo* 臺灣近代佛教的變革與反思—去殖民化與臺灣佛教主題性確立的新探索. Taipei: Dongda tushu gongsi, 2003.

JIANG Zemin 江泽民. *Lun "sange daibiao"* 论三个代表. Beijing: Zhongyang wenxian chubanshe, 2001.

JIANG Zhushan 蔣竹山. "Tang Bin jinhui wutong shen-qingchu zhengzhi jingying daji tongsu wenhua de gean 湯斌禁毀五通神—清初政治菁英打擊通俗文化的個案." *Xin shixue* 新史學 6, no. 2 (1995): 67–110.

————. "1930 niandai Tianjin Duliu zhen shangren de zongjiao yu shehui huodong canyu—yi 'Zailijiao' weili 1930. 年代天津獨流鎮商人的宗教與社會活動參與—以在理教為例." In *Ming qing yilai minjian zongjiao de tansuo—Jinian Dai xuanzhi jiaoshou lunwen ji* 明清以來民間宗教的探索—紀念戴玄之教授論文集, edited by WANG Jianchuan & JIANG Zhushan, 266–91. Taipei: Shangding wenhua chubanshe, 1996.

JIN Guantao 金觀涛. "Dangdai Zhongguo makesi zhuyi de rujiahua 當代中國馬克思主義的儒家化." In *Rujia fazhan de hongguan toushi* 儒家發展的宏觀透視, edited by TU Weiming 杜維明, 152–83. Taipei: Zhengzhong shuju, 1988.

JING Jun. *The Temple of Memories: History, Power, and Morality in a Chinese Village*. Stanford, CA: Stanford University Press, 1996.

JOCHIM, Christian. "Flowers, Fruit, and Incense Only: Elite Versus Popular in Taiwan's Religion of the Yellow Emperor." *Modern China* 16, no. 1 (1990): 3–38.

————. "Carrying Confucianism into the Modern World." In CLART & JONES, *Religion in Modern Taiwan*, 48–83.

JOHNSON, David. "Communication, Class, and Consciousness in Late Imperial China." In JOHNSON, NATHAN, & RAWSKI, *Popular Culture in Late Imperial China*, 34–72.

JOHNSON, David, Andrew J. NATHAN, & Evelyn S. RAWSKI, eds. *Popular Culture in Late Imperial China*. Berkeley and Los Angeles: University of California Press, 1985.

JONES, Charles Brewer. *Buddhism in Taiwan: Religion and the State 1660–1990*. Honolulu: University of Hawai'i Press, 1999.

————. "Religion in Taiwan at the End of the Japanese Colonial Period." In CLART & JONES, *Religion in Modern Taiwan*, 10–35.

JONES, Stephen. *Plucking the Winds—lives of Village Musicians in Old and New China*. Leiden: CHIME, 2004.

————. *In Search of the Folk Daoists*. Aldershot, UK: Ashgate, forthcoming.

JORDAN, David K. "The Recent History of the Celestial Way: A Chinese Pietist Association." *Modern China* 8, no. 4 (1982): 435–62.

————. "Changes in Postwar Taiwan and Their Impact on the Popular Practice of Religion." In *Cultural Change in Postwar Taiwan*, edited by Stevan HARRELL & C.-C. HUANG, 137–60. Boulder, CO: Westview Press, 1994.

JORDAN, David K., & Daniel OVERMYER. *The Flying Phoenix: Aspects of Chinese Sectarianism in Taiwan*. Princeton, NJ: Princeton University Press, 1986.

KALIR, Barak. "Finding Jesus in the Holy Land and Taking Him to China: Chinese Temporary Migrant Workers in Israel Converting to Evangelical Christianity." *Sociology of Religion* 70, no. 2 (Summer 2009): 130–58.

KANG Xiaofei. "Rural Women, Old Age, and Temple Work: A Case from Northwestern Sichuan." *China Perspectives* 4 (2009): 42–53.

————. "Two Temples, Three Religions, and a Tourist Attraction. Contesting Sacred Space on China's Ethnic Frontier." *Modern China* 35, no. 3 (2009): 227–55.

KANG Youwei 康有為. *Datongshu* 大同書. Shanghai: Shanghai guji chubanshe, 1995.

Kang Youwei quanji 康有為全集. Edited by JIANG Yihua 姜義華 and WU Genliang 吳根樑. Shanghai: Shanghai guji chubanshe, 1990.

KARL, Rebecca E., & Peter ZARROW, eds. *Rethinking the 1898 Reform Period: Political and Cultural Change in Late Qing China*. Cambridge, MA: Asia Center, Harvard University, 2002.

KATZ, Paul R. "Religion and the State in Post-War Taiwan." In OVERMYER, *Religion in China Today*, 395–412.

————. *When Valleys Turned Blood Red: The Ta-Pa-Ni Incident in Colonial Taiwan*. Honolulu: University of Hawai'i Press, 2005.

————. "'It Is Difficult to Be Indifferent to One's Roots': Taizhou Sojourners and Flood Relief During the 1920s." *Bulletin of the Institute of Modern History, Academia Sinica* 54 (2006): 1–58.

———. *Divine Justice: Religion and the Development of Chinese Legal Culture*. London: Routledge, 2008.

KATZ, Paul R., & Murray A. RUBINSTEIN, eds. *Religion and the Formation of Taiwanese Identities*. New York: Palgrave Macmillan, 2003.

KENDALL, Laurel. "The Cultural Politics of 'Superstition' in the Korean Shaman World: Modernity Constructs Its Other." In *Healing Powers and Modernity: Traditional Medicine, Shamanism, and Science in Asian Societies*, edited by Linda H. CONNOR & Geoffrey SAMUEL, 25–41. Westport, CT: Bergin and Garvey, 2001.

KEYES, Charles F., Laurel KENDALL, & Helen HARDACRE, eds. *Asian Visions of Authority: Religions and the Modern States of East and Southeast Asia*. Honolulu: University of Hawai'i Press, 1994.

KHAN, Almaz. "Chinggis Khan, from Imperial Ancestor to Ethnic Hero." In *Cultural Encounters on China's Ethnic Frontiers*, edited by Stevan HARRELL, 248–77. Seattle: University of Washington Press, 1995.

KIESCHNICK, John. "Buddhist Vegetarianism in China." In *Of Tripod and Palate: Food, Politics and Religion in Traditional China*, edited by Roel STERCKX, 186–212. New York: Palgrave, 2005.

KIM, Hodong. *Holy War in China: The Muslim Rebellion and State in Chinese Central Asia, 1864–1877*. Stanford, CA: Stanford University Press, 2004.

KINDOPP, Jason. "China's War on 'Cults.'" *Current History* 100, no. 651 (2002): 259–66.

———. "Fragmented yet Defiant." In KINDOPP & HAMRIN, *God and Caesar in China*, 122–48.

KINDOPP, Jason, & Carol Lee HAMRIN, eds. *God and Caesar in China: Policy Implications of Church-State Tensions*. Washington, DC: Brookings Institution Press, 2004.

KIPNIS, Andrew B. *Producing Guanxi: Sentiment, Self, and Subculture in a North China Village*. Durham, NC: Duke University Press, 1997.

———. "The Flourishing of Religion in Post-Mao China and the Anthropological Category of Religion." *Australian Journal of Anthropology* 12, no. 1 (2001): 32–46.

KLEINMAN, Arthur. *Medicine in Chinese Cultures: Comparative Studies of Health Care in Chinese and Other Societies*. Washington, DC: Department of Health, Education, and Welfare; Public Health Service; National Institutes of Health, 1975.

KNAUS, John Kenneth. "Official Policies and Covert Programs: The U.S. State Department, the CIA, and the Tibetan Resistance." *Journal of Cold War Studies* 5, no. 3 (2003): 54–79.

KNIGHT, Nick. "From Harmony to Struggle, from Perpetual Peace to Cultural Revolution: Changing Futures in Mao Zedong's Thought." *China Information* 11 (1996): 176–95.

KOHN, Livia. "Quiet Sitting with Master Yinshi: The Beginnings of Qigong in Modern China." In *Living with the Dao: Conceptual Issues in Daoist Practice*, edited by Livia KOHN. E-Dao series. Cambridge, MA: Three Pines Press, 2002.

KOLÅS, Åshild. *Tourism and Tibetan Culture in Transition: A Place Called Shangrila*. New York: Routledge, 2008.

KOLÅS, Åshild, & Monika P. THOWSEN. *On the Margins of Tibet: Cultural Survival on the Sino-Tibetan Frontier*. Seattle: University of Washington Press, 2005.

KOMJATHY, Louis. "Qigong in America." In *Daoist Body Cultivation: Traditional Models and Contemporary Practices*, edited by Livia KOHN, 203–36. Magdalena, NM: Three Pines Press, 2006.

KUAH-PEARCE, Khun Eng. *Rebuilding the Ancestral Village: Singaporeans in China*. London: Ashgate, 2000.

———. *State, Society and Religious Engineering: Towards a Reformist Buddhism in Singapore*. Singapore: Eastern Universities Press, 2003.

———. "The Worship of Qingshui Zushi and Religious Revivalism in South China." In TAN, *Southern Fujian*, 121–44.

KUNG Lap Yan. "Politics and Religion in Hong Kong After 1997. Paper presented at "Workshop on Chinese Religion and Traditional Culture," University of Hong Kong, March 17–19, 2003.

———. "National Identity and Ethno-Religious Identity: A Critical Inquiry into Chinese Religious Policy, with Reference to the Uighurs in Xinjiang." *Religion, State and Society* 34, no. 4 (2006): 375–91.

Kuo Cheng-Tian. *Religion and Democracy in Taiwan*. Albany: SUNY Press, 2008.

Kuo Ya-pei. "Redeploying Confucius: The Imperial State Dreams of the Nation, 1902–1911." In Yang, *Chinese Religiosities*, 65–84.

———. "The Emperor and the People in One Body: The Worship of Confucius and Ritual Planning in the Xinzheng Reforms, 1902–1911." *Modern China* 35, no. 2 (2009): 123–54.

Kupfer, Kristin. "Christian-Inspired Groups in the People's Republic of China after 1978: Reaction of State and Party Authorities." *Social Compass* 51, no. 2 (2004): 273–86.

Kwok Pui-lan. *Chinese Women and Christianity, 1860–1927*. Atlanta: Scholars Press, 1992.

Kwong Chunwah. *The Public Role of Religion in Post-Colonial Hong Kong: An Historical Overview of Confucianism, Taoism, Buddhism, and Christianity*. New York: Peter Lang, 2002.

Lagerwey, John. *Taoist Ritual in Chinese Society and History*. New York: Macmillan, 1987.

———, ed. *Traditional Hakka Society Series* 客家傳統社會叢書. Hong Kong: Traditional Hakka Studies Association / EFEO, 1996–2008.

———. "A propos de la situation actuelle des pratiques religieuses traditionnelles en Chine." In *Renouveau religieux en Asie*, edited by Catherine Clémentin-Ojha, 3–16. Paris: EFEO, 1997.

———, ed. *Religion et politique en Asie: Histoire et actualité*. Paris: Les Indes Savantes, 2006.

Lai Ah Eng. "The Inter-Religious Organization of Singapore." In *Religious Diversity in Singapore*, edited by Lai, 2008, 605–31.

———, ed. *Religious Diversity in Singapore*. Singapore: Institute of Southeast Asian Studies / Institute of Policy Studies, 2008.

Lai Chi-tim 黎志添. "Minguo shiqi Guangzhou shi 'namo daoguan' de lishi kaojiu 民國時期廣州市南嘸道館的歷史考究." *Zhongyang yanjiuyuan jindai shi yanjiusuo jikan* 中央研究院近代史研究所集刊 37 (2002): 1–40.

———. "Daoism in China Today, 1980–2002." In Overmyer, *Religion in China Today*, 413–27.

———. *Guangdong difang daojiao yanjiu: Daoguan, daoshi ji keyi* 廣東地方道教研究: 道觀、道士及科儀. Hong Kong: Chinese University Press, 2007.

Laliberté, André. "Tzu Chi and the Buddhist Revival in Taiwan: Rise of a New Conservatism?" *China Perspectives* 19 (1998): 44–50.

———. *The Politics of Buddhist Organizations in Taiwan: 1989–2003*. London: RoutledgeCurzon, 2004.

———. "'Harmonious Society,' 'Peaceful Re-Unification,' and the Dilemmas Raised by Taiwanese Charity." In *The Chinese Party-State at the Turn of the Millennium: Legitimacy and Adaptation*, edited by André Laliberté & Marc Lanteigne, 78–105. London: Routledge Curzon, 2008.

———. "Entre désécularisation et resacralisation: Bouddhistes laïcs, temples et organisations philanthropiques en Chine." *Social Compass* 56, no. 3 (2009): 345–61.

———. "Introduction." *Social Compass* 56 (2009): 307–11.

———, ed. "A New Take on Secularization Theory through Contemporary China." Special issue, *Social Compass* 56, no. 3 (2009).

———. "The Regulation of Religious Affairs in Taiwan: From State Control to Laisserfaire?" *Journal of Current Chinese Affairs* 38, no. 2 (2009): 53–83.

Lambert, Tony. "The Present Religious Policy of the Chinese Communist Party." *Religion, State and Society* 29, no. 2 (2001): 121–29.

Landsberger, Stefan R. *Chinese Propaganda Posters—from Revolution to Modernization*. Amsterdam / Singapore / Armonk, NY: Pepin Press / Sharpe, 1995.

———. "Mao as the Kitchen God: Religious Aspects of the Mao Cult during the Cultural Revolution." *China Information* 11 (1996): 196–214.

Lang, Graeme, Selina Chan, & Lars Ragvald. "Temples and the Religious Economy." In Yang & Tamney, *State, Market, and Religions*, 149–80.

LANG, Graeme, & Lars RAGVALD. *The Rise of a Refugee God: Hong Kong's Wong Tai Sin*. Hong Kong: Oxford University Press, 1993.

———. "Spirit-Writing and the Development of Chinese Cults." *Sociology of Religion* 59, no. 4 (Winter 1998): 309–28.

LEARMAN, Linda. "Modernity, Marriage, and Religion: Buddhist Marriages in Taiwan (China)." Ph.D. diss., Boston University, 2005.

LEE, Jonathan H. X. "Contemporary Chinese American Religious Life." In MILLER, *Chinese Religions in Contemporary Societies*, 235–56.

LEE, Joseph Tse-Hei. "Politics of Faith: Christian Activism and the Maoist State in Chaozhou, Guangdong Province." *China Review* 9, no. 2 (2009): 17–39.

LEI, Sean Hsiang-lin. "When Chinese Medicine Encountered the State: 1910–1949." Ph.D. diss., University of Chicago, 1999.

LEUNG, Beatrice. *Sino-Vatican Relations: Problems in Conflicting Authority, 1976–1986*. Cambridge: Cambridge University Press, 1992.

———. "Religious Freedom and the Constitution in the People's Republic of China: Interpretation and Implementation." *Diskus* 3, no. 1 (1995): 1–18.

———. "The Sino-Vatican Negotiations: Old Problems in a New Context." *China Quarterly* 153 (1998): 128–40.

———. "Communist Party–Vatican Interplay over the Training of Church Leaders in China." *Journal for the Scientific Study of Religion* 40, no. 4 (2001): 657–73.

———. "China's Religious Policy: The Art of Managing Religious Activity." *China Quarterly* 184 (2005): 894–913.

———. "The Hong Kong Catholic Church: A Framing Role in Social Movements." In GUIHEUX & KUAH-PEARCE, *Social Movements in China and Hong Kong*, 243–56.

LEUNG, Beatrice, & Shun-Hing CHAN. *Changing Church and State Relations in Hong Kong, 1950–2000*. Hong Kong: Hong Kong University Press, 2003.

LEUNG, Beatrice, & William T. LIU. *The Chinese Catholic Church in Conflict, 1949–2001*. Boca Raton, FL: Universal Publishers, 2004.

LI Jinghan 李景漢. *Dingxian shehui gaikuang diaocha* 定縣社會概況調查. Beiping: Zhonghua pingmin jiaoyu cujinhui, 1933.

LI Shaobai 李紹白, ed. *Zongjiao yu hexie shehui* 宗教與和諧社會. Macau: New Millennium Publications, 2007.

LI Shiwei 李世偉. *Zhonggong yu Zhongguo minjian wenhua* 中共與中國民間文化. Taipei: Zhishu fang chuban, 1996.

LI Shiyu 李世瑜. *Xiandai huabei mimi zongjiao* 現代華北秘密宗教. Shanghai: Shanghai wenyi chubanshe, 1990 [1948].

———. "Tianjin Zailijiao diaocha yanjiu 天津在理教調查研究." *Minjian zongjiao* 民間宗教 2 (1996): 169–210.

LI Suju 李素菊 & LIU Qifei 刘绮菲. *Qingnian yu "zongjiao re"* 青年与"宗教热." Beijing: Zhongguo qingnian chubanshe, 2000.

LI Xiangping 李向平. *Xinyang, geming yu quanli zhixu: Zhongguo zongjiao shehuixue yanjiu* 信仰、革命与权利秩序：中国宗教社会学研究. Shanghai: Shanghai renmin chubanshe, 2006.

———. *Zhongguo dangdai zongjiao de shehuixue quanshi* 中国当代宗教的社会学诠释. Shanghai: Shanghai renmin chubanshe, 2006.

LI Xiaoti 李孝悌. *Qingmo de xiaceng shehui qimeng yundong: 1901–1911* 清末的下層社會啟蒙運動. Taipei: Zhongyang yanjiuyuan jindaishi yanjiusuo, 1992.

LI Yangzheng 李养正. *Dangdai Zhongguo daojiao* 当代中国道教. Beijing: Zhongguo shehui kexue chubanshe, 1993.

LI Zehou 李澤厚. *Makesi zhuyi zai Zhongguo* 馬克斯主意在中國. Hong Kong: Mingbao chubanshe, 2006.

LIAN, Xi. "The Search for Chinese Christianity in the Republican Period (1912–1949)." *Modern Asian Studies* 38, no. 4 (2004): 851–98.

———. "Western Protestant Missions and Modern Chinese Nationalist Dreams." *East Asian History* 32/33 (2006–7): 199–216.

———. "A Messianic Deliverance for Post-Dynastic China: The Launch of the True Jesus Church in the Early Twentieth Century." *Modern China* 34, no. 4 (October 2008): 407–41.

LIANG Jinghe 梁景和. "Wusi shiqi sanzang lisu de gaige 五四时期丧葬礼俗的变革." *Shoudu shifan daxue xuebao (Shehui kexue ban)* 首都师范大学学报(社会科学版) 4 (1997): 52–58.

LIANG Yong 梁勇. "Qingmo 'miaochan xingxue' yu xiangcun quanshi de zhuanyi—yi baxian wei zhongxin 清末'庙产兴学'与乡村权势的转移—以巴县为中心." *Shehuixue yanjiu* 社會學研究 1 (2008): 102–19.

Liangxiang xianzhi 良鄉縣志. Lü Zhi 呂植 et al., comps. 1924.

LIFTON, Robert J. "Thought Reform of Chinese Intellectuals: A Psychiatric Evaluation." *Journal of Asian Studies* 16, no. 1 (1956): 75–88.

———. *Thought Reform and the Psychology of Totalism: A Study of "Brainwashing" in China*. New York: Norton, 1961.

Lilun redian mianduimian 2008 理论热点面对面. Zhonggong zhongyang xuanchuanbu lilunju 中共中央宣传部理论局, comp. Beijing: Xuexi chubanshe/Renmin chubanshe, 2008.

LIM Chee-Han. "Purging the Ghost of Descartes: Conducting Zhineng Qigong in Singapore." Ph.D. diss., Australian National University, 2009.

LIN Benxuan 林本炫. *Taiwan de zhengjiao chongtu* 臺灣的政敎衝突. Taipei: Daoxiang chubanshe, 1990.

LIN Boyuan 林伯原. *Zhongguo wushu shi* 中國武術史. Taipei: Wuzhuou chubanshe, 1996.

LIN Guoping 林国平. *Dangdai Taiwan zongjiao xinyang yu zhengzhi guanxi* 当代台湾宗教信仰与政治关系. Fuzhou: Fujian renmin chubanshe, 2006.

LIN, Irene. "Journey to the Far West: Chinese Buddhism in America." In Yoo, *New Spiritual Homes*, 134–65.

LIN Meirong 林美容. "You jisi quan dao xinyang quan 由祭祀圈到信仰圈." In *Taiwan shi lunwen jingxuan (shang)* 台灣史論文精選（上）, edited by ZHANG Yanxian 張炎憲, LI Xiaofeng 李筱峰, & DAI Baocun 戴寶村. Taipei: Yushan she chuban, 1985.

———, ed. *Taiwan minjian xinyang yanjiu shumu* 臺灣民間信仰研究書目. Taipei: Zhongyang yanjiuyuan minzuxue yanjiusuo, 1998.

———. *Jisiquan yu difang shehui* 祭祀圈與地方社會. Taipei: Boyang wenhua, 2008.

LIN Rongze 林榮澤. *Yiguandao lishi, dalu zhi bu* 一貫道歷史大陸之部. Taipei: Mingde chubanshe, 2007.

LING Chi-Shiang. "Morality Books and the Moral Order: A Study of the Moral Sustaining Function of Morality Books in Taiwan." In YANG & TAMNEY, *State, Market, and Religions*, 203–27.

LIPMAN, Jonathan Neaman. *Familiar Strangers: A History of Muslims in Northwest China*. Seattle: University of Washington Press, 1997.

LITZINGER, Charles A. "Rural Religion and Village Organization in Northern China: The Catholic Challenge in the Late Nineteenth Century." In BAYS, *Christianity in China*, 40–52.

LIU Shaoqi 刘少奇. *Lun dangnei douzheng* 論黨內鬥爭. Originally published in *Jiefang ribao* 解放日报, October 9, 1924. Online at http://202.114.90.34/news/news.aspx?id=40606 (accessed January 27, 2010).

———. *How to Be a Good Communist*. Beijing: Foreign Languages Press, 1951.

LIU Tik-sang. "Associating Local Traditions with State Apparatus: A Way of Revitalizing Popular Religion in South China." Paper presented at the conference "'Religion' in China: Rethinking Indigenous and Imported Categories of Thought," Fairbank Center for East Asian Research, Harvard University, May 21–22, 2005.

LIU Wenxing 劉文星. *Li Yujie xiansheng nianpu changbian* 李玉階先生年譜長編. Taipei: Dijiao chubanshe, 2001.

Liu, William T., & Beatrice Leung. "Organizational Revivalism: Explaining Metamorphosis of China's Catholic Church." *Journal for the Scientific Study of Religion* 41, no. 1 (2002): 121–39.

Liu Xin. *In One's Own Shadow: An Ethnographic Account of the Condition of Post-Reform Rural China.* Berkeley and Los Angeles: University of California Press, 2000.

Liu Xun. "In Search of Immortality: Daoist Inner Alchemy in Early Twentieth-Century China." Ph.D. diss., University of Southern California, 2001.

———. *Daoist Modern: Innovation, Lay Practice, and the Community of Inner Alchemy in Republican Shanghai.* Cambridge, MA: Asia Center, Harvard University, 2009.

———. "Scientizing the Body for the Nation: Chen Yingning and the Reinvention of Daoist Inner Alchemy in 1930s Shanghai." In Palmer & Liu, *Daoism in the Twentieth Century.*

———. "Quanzhen Proliferates Learning: The Xuanmiao Monastery and the Modern Reforms in Nanyang, 1880s–1940s." In *Quanzhen Daoism in Modern Chinese Society*, edited by Liu Xun & Vincent Goossaert, forthcoming.

Liu Yongsi 劉泳斯. "Duoyuan yiti de Fushan Chenhou ci jiaohui 多元一體的浮山陳侯祠醮會." Paper presented at the International Conference on the Comparative Study of Ritual in Chinese Local Society, Chinese University of Hong Kong, May 5–7, 2008.

Liu Zhijun 刘志军. *Xiangcun dushihua yu zongjiao xinyang bianqian: Zhangdian zhen ge'an yanjiu.* 乡村都市化与宗教信仰变迁：张店镇个案研究. Beijing: Shehui kexue wenxian chubanshe, 2007.

Lopez, Donald S., Jr. *Curators of the Buddha: The Study of Buddhism under Colonialism.* Chicago: University of Chicago Press, 1995.

Löwenthal, Rudolf. *The Religious Periodical Press in China.* San Francisco: Chinese Materials Center, 1978 [1940].

Lozada, Eriberto P., Jr. *God Aboveground: Catholic Church, Postsocialist State, and Transnational Processes in a Chinese Village.* Stanford, CA: Stanford University Press, 2001.

Lü Xiaobu. *Cadres and Corruption: The Organizational Involution of the Chinese Communist Party.* Stanford, CA: Stanford University Press, 2000.

Lü Xichen. "Yuanjidao: Qigong Science and Prisoner Reform in Post-Mao China." In Palmer & Liu, *Daoism in the Twentieth Century.*

Lu Yunfeng. "Entrepreneurial Logics and the Evolution of Falun Gong." *Journal for the Scientific Study of Religion* 44, no. 2 (2005): 173–85.

———. *The Transformation of Yiguan Dao in Taiwan: Adapting to a Changing Religious Economy.* Lanham, MD: Lexington Books, 2008.

Lu Zhongwei 陆仲伟. *Yiguandao neimu*—贯道内幕. Nanjing: Jiangsu renmin chubanshe, 1998.

———. *Minguo huidaomen* 民国会道门. Vol. 5 of *Zhongguo mimi shehui*, edited by Tan Songlin 谭松林. Fuzhou: Fujian renmin chubanshe, 2002.

Luizard, Pierre-Jean. *Laïcités autoritaires en terres d'Islam.* Paris: Fayard, 2008.

Luo Zhufeng, ed. *Religion under Socialism in China.* Translated by Donald E. MacInnis & Zheng Xi'an. Armonk, NY: Sharpe, 1991.

MacInnis, Donald E., ed. *Religious Policy and Practice in Communist China.* London: Hodder and Stoughton, 1972.

———. *Religion in China Today: Policy and Practice.* Maryknoll, NY: OrbisBooks, 1989.

MacKerras, Colin, & Michael Clarke. *China, Xinjiang and Central Asia: History, Transition and Crossborder Interaction into the 21st Century.* London: Routledge, 2009.

Madancy, Joyce A. "Revolution, Religion and the Poppy: Opium and the Rebellion of the 'Sixteenth Emperor' in Early Republican Fujian." *Republican China* 21, no. 1 (1995): 1–41.

Madsen, Richard. "Religion and Feudal Superstition: Implications of the PRC's Religious Policy for the Christian Encounter with China." *Ching Feng* 22, no. 4 (1979): 190–218.

———. "The Maoist Ethic and the Moral Basis of Political Activism in China." In *Moral Behavior in Chinese Society*, edited by Richard W. Wilson, Sidney L. Greenblatt, & Amy Auerbacher Wilson, 152–75. New York: Praeger, 1981.

———. *Morality and Power in a Chinese Village*. Berkeley and Los Angeles: University of California Press, 1984.

———. *China's Catholics: Tragedy and Hope in an Emerging Civil Society*. Berkeley and Los Angeles: University of California Press, 1998.

———. *Democracy's Dharma: Religious Renaissance and Political Development in Taiwan*. Berkeley and Los Angeles: University of California Press, 2007.

MADSEN, Richard, & James TONG, eds. "Local Religious Policy in China, 1980–1997." Special issue, *Chinese Law and Government* 33, no. 3 (2000): 5–11.

MAK Lau-Fong. *The Role of Saudara Baru in Ethnic Relations: The Chinese Converts in Singapore*. Taipei: Academia Sinica, Program for Southeast Asian Area Studies, 2001.

MAKEHAM, John, ed. *New Confucianism*. New York: Palgrave Macmillan, 2003.

———. *Lost Soul: "Confucianism" in Contemporary Chinese Academic Discourse*. Cambridge, MA: Asia Center, Harvard University, 2008.

MAKITA Tairyô 牧田諦亮. "Seimotsu irai ni okeru byôsan kôgaku 清末以來に於ける廟產興學." In *Chûgoku bukkyôshi kenkyû* 中國佛教史研究, vol. 2, 290–318. Tokyo: Taito shuppansha, 1984. [Originally published in *Chûgoku kinsei bukkyô shi kenkyû* 中國今世佛教史研究 (Kyoto: Heirakuji shoten, 1957)].

MAKLEY, Charlene E. *The Violence of Liberation: Gender and Tibetan Buddhist Revival in Post-Mao China*. Berkeley and Los Angeles: University of California Press, 2007.

MAO Zedong. *Selected Works of Mao Tse-Tung*. Beijing: Foreign Languages Press, 1961–65.

———. *On New Democracy*. Beijing: Foreign Languages Press, 1964.

———. *On Practice: On the Relation between Knowledge and Practice, between Knowing and Doing*. Beijing: Shangwu yinshuguan, 1971.

MARSHALL, Alison R. "Moving the Spirit on Taiwan: New Age Lingji Performance." *Journal of Chinese Religions* 31 (2003): 81–99.

MAUSS, Marcel. *The Gift*. New York: Norton, 1990.

McCARTHY, Susan. "Gods of Wealth, Temples of Prosperity: Party-State Participation in the Minority Cultural Revival." *China: An International Journal* 2, no. 1 (2004): 28–52.

McDOUGALL, Bonnie S. *Mao Zedong's "Talks at the Yan'an Conference on Literature and Art": A Translation of the 1953 Text with Commentary*. Michigan Papers in Chinese Studies, no. 39. Ann Arbor: University of Michigan, 1980.

MEISNER, Maurice. "Utopian Goals and Ascetic Values in Chinese Communist Ideology." *Journal of Asian Studies* 28, no. 1 (1968): 101–10.

MEISSNER, Werner. "Réflexions sur la quête d'une identité nationale et culturelle en Chine." *Perspectives Chinoises*, no. 97 (2006): 45–58.

MENG Guoxiang 孟国祥. "Riben liyong zongjiao qinhua zhi pouxi 日本利用宗教侵华之剖析." *Min'guo dang'an* 民国档案 1 (1996): 99–107.

MEYER, Jeffrey E. "Teaching Morality in Taiwan Schools: The Message of the Textbooks." *China Quarterly* 114 (1988): 267–84.

MILLER, James, ed. *Chinese Religions in Contemporary Societies*. Santa Barbara, CA: ABC-CLIO, 2006.

MITANI Takashi 三谷考. "Nankin seiken to 'meishin daha undô' (1928–1929) 南京政權と迷信打破運動." *Rekishigaku kenkyû* 歷史學研究 455, no. 4 (1978): 1–14.

MOLL-MURATA, Christine. "Chinese Guilds from the Seventeenth to the Twentieth Centuries: An Overview." *IRHS* 53 (2008): 213–47.

MORRIS, Andrew D. *Marrow of the Nation: A History of Sport and Physical Culture in Republican China*. Berkeley and Los Angeles: University of California Press, 2004.

MOU Zongjian 牟種鑒. "Zongjiao wenhua shengtai de Zhongguo moshi 中國文化生態的中國模式." *Zhongguo minzu bao* 中國民族報 536 (2006): 6.

MUEGGLER, Eric. "Spectral Chains: Remembering the Great Leap Forward Famine in a Yi Community." In *Re-Envisioning the Chinese Revolution: The Politics and Poetics of Collective*

Memories in Reform China, edited by Chin Kwan LEE & Guobin YANG, 50–68. Washington, DC: Woodrow Wilson Center Press; Stanford, CA: Stanford University Press, 2007.

MUNRO, Donald J. *The Concept of Man in Contemporary China*. Ann Arbor: University of Michigan Press, 1977.

MUNRO, Robin, ed. "Syncretic Sects and Secret Societies: Revival in the 1980s." Special issue, *Chinese Sociology and Anthropology* 21, no. 4 (1989).

MURPHY, Rachel. "Turning Peasants into Modern Chinese Citizens: 'Population Quality' Discourse, Demographic Transition and Primary Education." *China Quarterly* 177 (2004): 1–20.

MURRAY, Julia K. "'Idols' in the Temple: Icons and the Cult of Confucius." *Journal of Asian Studies* 28, no. 2 (2009): 371–411.

MYERS, James T. "Religious Aspects of the Cult of Mao Tse-Tung." *Current Scene* 20, no. 3 (1972): 1–11.

MYERS, John T. "Traditional Chinese Religious Practices in an Urban-Industrial Setting: The Example of Kwun Tong." In *Social Life and Development in Hong Kong*, edited by Ambrose Y. KING & Rance P. L. LEE, 275–87. Hong Kong: Chinese University Press, 1981.

NAQUIN, Susan. *Millenarian Rebellion in China: The Eight Trigrams Rebellion of 1813*. New Haven, CT: Yale University Press, 1976.

———. *Shantung Rebellion: The Wang Lun Uprising of 1774*. New Haven, CT: Yale University Press, 1981.

———. "The Transmission of White Lotus Sectarianism in Late Imperial China." In JOHNSON, NATHAN, & RAWSKI, *Popular Culture in Late Imperial China*, 255–91.

———. *Peking: Temples and City Life, 1400–1900*. Berkeley and Los Angeles: University of California Press, 2000.

NAQUIN, Susan, & Chün-fang Yü, eds. *Pilgrims and Sacred Sites in China*. Berkeley and Los Angeles: University of California Press, 1992.

NARANGOA, Li. "Japanese Imperialism and Mongolian Buddhism, 1932–1945." *Critical Asian Studies* 35, no. 4 (2003): 491–514.

NATIONAL PEOPLE'S CONGRESS. "Decision of the Standing Committee of the National People's Congress on Banning Heretical Cult Organizations, and Preventing and Punishing Cult Activities." *Beijing Review* 42 (November 8, 1999): 45.

NEDILSKY, Lida V. "The Anticult Initiative and Hong Kong Christianity's Turn from Religious Privilege." *China Information* 22, no. 3 (2008): 423–49.

NEDOSTUP, Rebecca Allyn. "Religion, Superstition, and Governing Society in Nationalist China." Ph.D. diss., Columbia University, 2001.

———. "Ritual Competition and the Modernizing Nation-State." In YANG, *Chinese Religiosities*, 87–112.

Neizhengbu 內政部. *Zongjiao faling huibian* 宗教法令彙編 3rd ed. Taipei: Neizhengbu, 2006.

NG Kwai Hang. "Seeking the Christian Tutelage: Agency and Culture in Chinese Immigrants' Conversion to Christianity." *Sociology of Religion* 63, no. 2 (2002): 195–214.

NG Peter Tze-ming [Wu Ziming] 吳梓明. *Jidu zongjiao yu Zhongguo daxue jiaoyu* 基督宗教与中国大学教育. Beijing: Zhongguo shehui kexue chubanshe, 2003.

———. "The Changing Market Shares of Christianity and Buddhism since the Return of Hong Kong's Sovereignty to China." *Quest* 3, no. 1 (2004): 109–24.

NIVISON, David S. "Communist Ethics and Chinese Tradition." *Journal of Asian Studies* 16, no. 1 (1956): 51–74.

NOGUCHI Tetsurou 野口鐵郎. "Dongnanya liuchuan de liangge Zhongguo ren zongjiao 東南亞流傳的兩個中國人宗教." *Minjian zongjiao* 民間宗教 2 (1996): 51–91.

O'BRIEN, Kevin J., ed. *Popular Protest in China*. Cambridge, MA: Harvard University Press, 2008.

OLDSTONE-MOORE, Jennifer Lee. "The New Life Movement of Nationalist China: Confucianism, State Authority, and Moral Formation." Ph.D. diss., University of Chicago, 2000.

OTS, Thomas. "The Silenced Body—the Expressive Leib: On the Dialectic of Mind and Life in

Chinese Cathartic Healing." In *Embodiment and Experience: The Existential Ground of Culture and Self*, edited by Thomas Csordas, 116–36. Cambridge: Cambridge University Press, 1994.

Overmyer, Daniel L. *Folk Buddhist Religion: Dissenting Sects in Late Traditional China*. Cambridge, MA: Harvard University Press, 1976.

———. *Precious Volumes: An Introduction to Chinese Sectarian Scriptures from the Sixteenth and Seventeenth Centuries*. Cambridge, MA: Asia Center, Harvard University, 1999.

———. "From 'Feudal Superstition' to 'Popular Beliefs': New Directions in Mainland Chinese Studies of Chinese Popular Religion." *Cahiers d'Extrême-Asie* 12 (2001): 103–26.

———, ed. *Religion in China Today*. Issue 174 of *China Quarterly*, 2003 (also published as a book: Cambridge: Cambridge University Press, 2003).

———. "Ritual Leaders in North China Local Communities in the Twentieth Century: A Report on Research in Progress." *Minsu quyi* 民俗曲藝 153 (2006): 203–63.

Overmyer, Daniel L., & Chao Shin-Yi, eds. *Ethnography in China Today: A Critical Assessment of Methods and Results*. Taipei: Yuan-Liou, 2002.

Ownby, David. "Imperial Fantasies: The Chinese Communists and Peasant Rebellions." *Comparative Studies in Society and History* 43, no. 1 (2001): 65–91.

———. *Falun Gong and the Future of China*. Oxford: Oxford University Press, 2008.

———. "Sect and Secularism in Reading the Modern Chinese Religious Experience." *Archives de Sciences Sociales des Religions* 144 (2008): 13–29.

———. "Kang Xiaoguang: Social Science, Civil Society, and Confucian Religion." *China Perspectives* 4 (2009): 101–11.

———, ed. "Recent Chinese Scholarship on the History of 'Redemptive Societies.'" Special double issue, *Chinese Studies in History* 43, no. 4 (forthcoming, 2010).

Oxfeld, Ellen. "'When You Drink Water, Think of Its Source': Morality, Status, and Reinvention in Rural Chinese Funerals." *Journal of Asian Studies* 63, no. 4 (2004): 961–90.

Paine, Jeffrey. *Re-Enchantment: Tibetan Buddhism Comes to the West*. New York: Norton, 2004.

Palmer, David A. "Cyberspace and the Emerging Chinese Religious Landscape—preliminary Observations." In *Cyber China: Reshaping National Identities in the Age of Information*, edited by Françoise Mengin, 37–50. New York: Palgrave MacMillan, 2004.

———. *Qigong Fever: Body, Science, and Utopia in China*. New York: Columbia University Press, 2007.

———. "Heretical Doctrines, Reactionary Secret Societies, Evil Cults: Labeling Heterodoxy in Twentieth-Century China." In Yang, *Chinese Religiosities*, 113–34.

———. "China's Religious Danwei: Institutionalizing Religion in the People's Republic." *China Perspectives* 4 (2009): 17–31.

———. "Religiosity and Social Movements in China: Divisions and Multiplications." In Guiheux & Kuah-Pearce, *Social Movements in China and Hong Kong*, 257–282.

———. "Chinese Redemptive Societies: Historial Phenomenom or Sociological Category? " In Wang & Palmer, *Redemptive Societies*.

———. "Chinese Religious Innovation in the Qigong Movement: The Case of Zhonggong." In *Religious Innovation in China*, edited by Adam Yuet Chau. London: Routledge, 2010.

———. "Tao and Nation. Li Yujie: May Fourth Activist, Daoist Reformer and Redemptive Society Patriarch in Mainland China and Taiwan." In Palmer & Liu, *Daoism in the Twentieth Century*.

Palmer, David A., & Liu Xun, eds. *Daoism in the Twentieth Century: Between Eternity and Modernity*. Berkeley and Los Angeles: University of California Press, 2011.

Palmer, David A., Glenn Shive, & Philip L. Wickeri, eds. *Chinese Religious Life*. New York: Oxford University Press, 2011.

Pan, Hongli. "The Old Folks' Associations and Lineage Revival in Contemporary Villages of Southern Fujian Province." In Tan, *Southern Fujian*, 69–96.

Pang, Choong Chee. "Religious Composition of the Chinese in Singapore: Some Comments on the Census 2000." In Suryadinata, *Ethnic Chinese in Singapore and Malaysia*, 325–36.

PAPER, Jordan D. "Mediums and Modernity: The Institutionalization of Ecstatic Religious Functionaries in Taiwan." *Journal of Chinese Religions* 24 (1996): 105–29.

PARISH, William L., & Martin King WHYTE. *Village and Family in Contemporary China*. Chicago: University of Chicago Press, 1978.

PENNY, Benjamin. "The Body of Master Li." Lecture published online at http://users.senet.com .au/~nhabel/Lectures/penny.pdf (accessed May 19, 2005).

PERRY, Elizabeth J. *Rebels and Revolutionaries in North China, 1845–1945*. Stanford, CA: Stanford University Press, 1980.

———. *Challenging the Mandate of Heaven: Social Protest and State Power in China*. Armonk, NY: Sharpe, 2001.

PERRY, Elizabeth J., & Mark SELDEN, eds. *Chinese Society: Change, Conflict and Resistance*. London: Routledge, 2000.

PICARD, Michel. "What's in a Name? Agama Hindu Bali in the Making." In *Hinduism in Modern Indonesia: A Minority Religion between Local, National and Global Interests*, edited by Martin RAMSTEDT, 56–75. IIAS Asian Studies Series. London: RoutledgeCurzon, 2003.

PITMAN, Don A. *Toward a Modern Chinese Buddhism: Taixu's Reforms*. Honolulu: University of Hawai'i Press, 2001.

PLÜSS, Caroline. "Hong Kong's Muslim Organizations: Creating and Expressing Collective Identities." *China Perspectives* 29 (2000): 19–23.

POLACHEK, James M. "The Moral Economy of the Kiangsi Soviet (1928–1934)." *Journal of Asian Studies* 42, no. 4 (1983): 805–29.

POMMARET, Francoise. "La dernière frontière Himalayenne: Evangélistes et tentative de colonisation des âmes." In LAGERWEY, *Religion et politique en Asie*, 133–56.

POON Shuk Wah. "Refashioning Festivals in Republican Guangzhou." *Modern China* 30, no. 2 (2004): 199–227.

———. "Religion, Modernity, and Urban Space: The City God Temple in Republican Guangzhou." *Modern China* 34, no. 2 (2008): 247–75.

———. *Negotiating Religion in Modern China: State and Common People in Guangzhou, 1900–1937*. Hong Kong: Chinese University Press, forthcoming.

POTTER, Pitman B. "Belief in Control: Regulation of Religion in China." In OVERMYER, *Religion in China Today*, 317–37.

POTTER, Sulamith Heins, & Jack POTTER. *China's Peasants: The Anthropology of a Revolution*. Cambridge: Cambridge University Press, 1990.

PRAZNIAK, Roxann. *Of Camel Kings and Other Things: Rural Rebels against Modernity in Late Imperial China*. Lanham, MD: Rowman and Littlefield, 1999.

PRICE, Don C. "Popular and Elite Heterodoxy toward the End of the Qing." In *Heterodoxy in Late Imperial China*, edited by LIU Kwang-Ching & Richard SHEK, 431–61. Honolulu: University of Hawai'i Press, 2004.

PYE, Lucian W. *The Mandarin and the Cadre: China's Political Cultures*. Ann Arbor: Center for Chinese Studies, University of Michigan, 1988.

———. *The Spirit of Chinese Politics*. Cambridge, MA.: Harvard University Press, 1992.

QIAN Ning 钱宁, ed. *Jidujiao yu shaoshu minzu shehui wenhua bianqian* 基督教与少数民族社会文化变迁. Kunming: Yunnan daxue chubanshe, 1998.

QING Xitai 卿希泰, ed. *Zhongguo daojiao shi* 中国道教史. Vol. 4. Chengdu: Sichuan renmin chubanshe, 1995.

Qiushu 訄書 (Urgency). ZHANG Taiyan 章太炎. In *Zhang taiyan quanji* 章太炎全集. Shanghai: Shanghai renmin chubanshe, 1984 (vol. 3).

QU Haiyuan 瞿海源. "Zhonghua minguo youguan zongjiao 'faling' ji falü caoan huibian 中華民國有關宗教法令及法律草案彙編." *Minzuxue yanjiusuo ziliao huibian* 民族學研究所資料彙編 2 (1990): 113–39.

RAWLINSON, Frank Joseph. *Revolution and Religion in Modern China: A Brief Study of the Effects of*

Modern Revolutionary Movements in China on Its Religious Life. Shanghai: Presbyterian Mission Press, 1929.

RAWSKI, Evelyn S. *The Last Emperors: A Social History of Qing Imperial Institutions*. Berkeley and Los Angeles: University of California Press, 1998.

REILLY, Thomas H. *The Taiping Heavenly Kingdom: Rebellion and the Blasphemy of Empire*. Seattle: University of Washington Press, 2004.

REINDERS, Eric. *Borrowed Gods and Foreign Bodies: Christian Missionaries Imagine Chinese Religion*. Berkeley and Los Angeles: University of California Press, 2005.

REN Jiyu 任继愈, ed. *Rujiao wenti zhenglun ji* 儒教问题争论集. Beijing: Zongjiao wenhua chubanshe, 2000.

RHOADS, Edward. *China's Republican Revolution: The Case of Kwangtung, 1895–1913*. Cambridge, MA: Harvard University Press, 1975.

ROWE, William T. *Saving the World: Chen Hongmou and Elite Consciousness in Eighteenth-Century China*. Stanford, CA: Stanford University Press, 2001.

RUBINSTEIN, Murray A. "Christianity and Democratization in Modern Taiwan: The Presbyterian Church and the Struggle for Minnan/Hakka Selfhood in the Republic of China." In CLART & JONES, *Religion in Modern Taiwan*, 204–56.

SAKAI Tadao 酒井忠夫. "Minguo chuqi zhi xinxing zongjiao yundong yu xin shidai chaoliu 民国初期之新興宗教運動與新時代潮流." Translated by ZHANG Shue 張淑娥, *Minjian zongjiao* 民間宗教 1 (1995): 1–36.

SANGREN, Paul. *History and Magical Power in a Chinese Community*. Stanford, CA: Stanford University Press, 1987.

SAWADA Mizuho 澤田瑞穂. "Seimotsu no shiten mondai 清末の祀典問題." In *Chûgoku no minkan shinkô* 中國の民間信仰, 534–49. Tokyo: Kôsakusha, 1982.

SCHAK, David C. "Community and the New Buddhism in Taiwan." *Minsu quyi* 民俗曲藝 163 (2009): 161–92.

SCHIPPER, Kristofer. *The Taoist Body*. Berkeley and Los Angeles: University of California Press, 1993.

———. "Structures liturgiques et société civile à Pékin." *Matériaux pour l'étude de la religion chinoise—Sanjiao wenxian* 1 (1997): 9–23.

———. *La religion de la Chine: La tradition vivante*. Paris: Fayard, 2008.

SCHRAM, Stuart R. "Mao Tse-tung and Secret Societies." *China Quarterly* 27 (1966): 11–13.

———. "To Utopia and Back: A Cycle in the History of the Chinese Communist Party." *China Quarterly* 87 (1981): 407–39.

SCOTT, James C. *Weapons of the Weak: Everyday Forms of Peasant Resistance*. New Haven, CT: Yale University Press, 1985.

SEIWERT, Hubert Michael. "Religious Response to Modernization in Taiwan: The Case of I-Kuan Tao." *Journal of the Hong Kong Branch of the Royal Asiatic Society* 2 (1981): 43–70.

SEIWERT, Hubert Michael, with MA Xisha. *Popular Religious Movements and Heterodox Sects in Chinese History*. Leiden: Brill, 2003.

SELDEN, Mark. *The Yenan Way in Revolutionary China*. Cambridge, MA: Harvard University Press, 1971.

SHAHAR, Meir. "Vernacular Fiction and the Transmission of Gods' Cults in Late Imperial China." In SHAHAR & WELLER, *Unruly Gods*, 184–211.

———. *Crazy Ji: Chinese Religion and Popular Literature*. Harvard-Yenching Monograph Series 48. Cambridge, MA: Harvard University Press, 1998.

———. *The Shaolin Monastery: History, Religion, and the Chinese Martial Arts*. Honolulu: University of Hawai'i Press, 2008.

SHAHAR, Meir, & Robert P. WELLER, eds. *Unruly Gods: Divinity and Society in China*. Honolulu: University of Hawai'i Press, 1996.

SHAO Yong 邵雍. *Zhongguo huidaomen* 中国会道门. Shanghai: Shanghai renmin chubanshe, 1997.

Shenbao 申報. Shanghai: Shenbaoguan, daily, 1872–1949.

SHIRK, Susan L. *Competitive Comrades: Career Incentives and Student Strategies in China.* Berkeley and Los Angeles: University of California Press, 1982.

SHRYOCK, John K. *The Temples of Anking and Their Cults: A Study of Modern Chinese Religion.* Paris: Librairie orientaliste P. Geuthner, 1931.

SHUAI Feng & LI Jian, eds. *Zongjiao shiwu tiaoli shiyi* 宗教事物条例释义. Beijing: Zongjiao wenhua chubanshe, 2005.

SHUE, Vivienne. "The Quality of Mercy: Confucian Charity and the Mixed Metaphors of Modernity in Tianjin." *Modern China* 32, no. 4 (2006): 411–52.

SIEGLER, Elijah. "Chinese Traditions in Euro-American Society." In MILLER, *Chinese Religions in Contemporary Societies*, 257–80.

———. "Fluid yet Grounded in the Tao: A Sociological Study of the Role of 'American Daoism' in the Identity Formation of Baby Boomers." Paper presented at the conference "Religion and Social Integration in Chinese Societies: Exploring Sociological Approaches to Religion in the Chinese World," Chinese University of Hong Kong, June 28–July 1, 2007.

———. "Daoism beyond Modernity: The 'Healing Tao' as Postmodern Movement." In PALMER & LIU, *Daoism in the Twentieth Century*.

SIEGLER, Elijah, & David A. PALMER. *Dream Trippers: Global Daoism and the Predicament of Modern Spirituality.* Forthcoming.

SINHA, Vineeta. "Theorising 'Talk' About 'Religious Pluralism' and 'Religious Harmony' in Singapore." *Journal of Contemporary Religion* 20, no. 1 (2005): 25–40.

SIU, Helen F. "Recycling Ritual." In *Unofficial China: Popular Culture and Thought in the People's Republic*, edited by Perry LINK, Richard MADSEN, & Paul G. PICKOWICZ, 121–37. Boulder: Westview, 1990.

———. "Recycling Tradition: Culture, History, and Political Economy in the Chrysanthemum Festivals of South China." *Comparative Studies in Society and History* 32, no. 4 (1990): 765–94.

SLOBODNIK, Martin. "Destruction and Revival: The Fate of the Tibetan Buddhist Monastery Labrang in the People's Republic of China." *Religion, State and Society* 32, no. 1 (2004): 7–19.

SMEDLEY, Agnes. *The Great Road: The Life and Times of Chu Teh.* New York: Monthly Review Press, 1956.

SMITH, Richard J. "The Teachings of Ritual and the Rectification of Customs: Echoes of Tradition in the Political Culture of Modern China." In *Jinshi zhongguo zhi chuantong yu tuibian: Liu Guangjing yuanshi qishiwu sui zhushou lunwenji* 近世中國之傳統與蛻變: 劉廣京院士七十五歲祝壽論文集, edited by HAO Yanping 郝延平 & WEI Xiumei 魏秀梅, 1173–216. Taipei: Zhongyang yanjiuyuan jindaishi yanjiusuo, 1998.

SMITH, Steve A. "Local Cadres Confront the Supernatural: The Politics of Holy Water (Shenshui) in the PRC, 1949–1966." *China Quarterly* 188 (2006): 999–1022.

———. "Talking Toads and Chinless Ghosts: The Politics of 'Superstitious' Rumors in the People's Republic of China, 1961–1965." *American Historical Review* 111 (2006): 405–27.

SONG Guangyu 宋光宇. "Cong *Diyu youji* kan dangqian Taiwan shehui wenti 從地獄遊記看當前台灣社會問題." In *Minjian xinyang yu shehui yantaohui* 民間信仰與社會研討會, 116–36. Taipei: Taiwan sheng Minzheng ting; Donghai daxue shehuixue xi, 1982.

———. *Tiandao chuandeng: Yiguandao yu xiandai shehui* 天道傳燈: 一貫道與現代社會. Taipei: Sanyang, 1996.

———. "Zongjiao yu lisu 宗教與禮俗." In *Taiwan jindaishi-wenhuapian* 臺灣近代史–文化篇, edited by LI Guoqi 李國祁, 141–275. Nantou: Taiwansheng wenxian weiyuanhu, 1997.

———. "Ershi shiji Zhongguo yu shijie zongjiao hudong zhi huigu yu zhanwang 二十世紀中國與世界宗教互動之回顧與展望." In *Song Guangyu zongjiao wenhua lunwenji*, 2002, 3–42.

———. *Song Guangyu zongjiao wenhua lunwenji* 宋光宇宗教文化論文集. Yilan: Foguang renwen shehui xueyuan, 2002.

———. "Wang Fengyi de xingli jiangbing 王鳳儀的性理講病." *In Song Guangyu zongjiao wenhua lunwenji*, 2002, 215–44.

Soo Khin Wah 苏庆华. "A Study of the Yiguan Dao (Unity Sect) and Its Development in Peninsular Malaysia." Ph.D. diss., University of British Columbia, 2002.

———. "Malaixiya huaren zongjiaoshi gaishu 马来西亚华人宗教史概述." In *Ma, xin huaren yanjiu—su qinghua lunwen xuanji* 马、新华人研究—苏庆华论文选集, 3–50. Kuala Lumpur: Malaixiya chuangjia xuehui, 2004.

SPENCE, Jonathan D. *God's Chinese Son: The Taiping Heavenly Kingdom of Hong Xiuquan.* New York: Norton, 1996.

STAFFORD, Charles. "Good Sons and Virtuous Mothers: Kinship and Chinese Nationalism in Taiwan." *Man* 27 (1992): 363–78.

STARK, Rodney, & William Sims BAINBRIDGE. *The Future of Religion.* Berkeley and Los Angeles: University of California Press, 1985.

———. *A Theory of Religion.* New Brunswick, NJ: Rutgers University Press, 1996.

STARK, Rodney, & Roger FINKE. *Acts of Faith.* Berkeley and Los Angeles: University of California Press, 2000.

STARR, Frederick, ed. *Xinjiang: China's Muslim Borderland.* New York: Sharpe, 2004.

STRAUSS, Julia. "Morality, Coercion and State Building by Campaign in the Early PRC: Regime Consolidation and After, 1949–1956." *China Quarterly* 188 (2006): 891–912.

SUN, Anna Xiao Dong. "The Fate of Confucianism as a Religion in Socialist China: Controversies and Paradoxes." In YANG & TAMNEY, *State, Market, and Religions,* 229–53.

SUN Yat-sen. *San Min Chu I, the Three Principles of the People.* Translated by Frank W. PRICE. Shanghai: Commercial Press, 1928.

SURYADINATA, Leo. "Confucianism in Indonesia: Past and Present." In TONG, *Chinese Beliefs,* 251–78.

———, ed. *Ethnic Chinese in Singapore and Malaysia: A Dialogue between Tradition and Modernity.* Singapore: Times Academic Press, 2002.

SUTTON, Donald S. "Consuming Counterrevolution: The Ritual and Culture of Cannibalism in Wuxuan, Guangxi, China, May to July 1968." *Comparative Studies in Society and History* 37, no. 1 (1995): 136–72.

———. "From Credulity to Scorn: Confucians Confront the Spirit Mediums in Late Imperial China." *Late Imperial China* 21, no. 2 (2000): 1–39.

———. *Steps of Perfection: Exorcistic Performers and Chinese Religion in Twentieth-Century Taiwan.* Cambridge, MA: Asia Center, Harvard University, 2003.

SUTTON, Donald S., & KANG Xiaofei. "Recasting Religion and Ethnicity: Tourism and Socialism in Northern Sichuan, 1992–2005." In DuBois, *Casting Faiths,* 190–216.

SWEETEN, Alan Richard. *Christianity in Rural China: Conflict and Accommodation in Jiangxi Province, 1860–1900.* Ann Arbor: Center for Chinese Studies, University of Michigan, 2001.

SZONYI, Michael. *Practicing Kinship: Lineage and Descent in Late Imperial China.* Stanford, CA: Stanford University Press, 2002.

———. "Making Claims about Standardization and Orthopraxy in Late Imperial China." *Modern China* 33, no. 1 (2007): 47–71.

———. *Cold War Island: Quemoy on the Front Line.* Cambridge: Cambridge University Press, 2008.

———. "Secularization Theories and the Study of Chinese Religions." *Social Compass* 56 (2009): 312–27.

TAI Hsüan-chih. *The Red Spears, 1916–1949.* Ann Arbor: Center for Chinese Studies, University of Michigan, 1985.

TAM Wai Lun. "The Transformative Power of Chinese Culture as Seen in Buddhism in China and True Buddha School." *Ching Feng* 40, nos. 3–4 (1997): 233–54.

———. "Integration of the Magical and Cultivational Discourses: A Study on a New Religious Movement Called the True Buddha School." *Monumenta Serica* 49 (2001): 141–69.

TAMNEY, Joseph B., & Riaz HASSAN. *Religious Switching in Singapore: A Study of Religious Mobility.* Singapore: Select Books, 1987.

TAMNEY, Joseph B., & YANG Fenggang, eds. *Confucianism and Spiritual Traditions in Modern China and Beyond*. Boston: Brill, forthcoming.

TAN, Charlene. "From Moral Values to Citizenship Education: The Teaching of Religion in Singapore Schools." In LAI, *Religious Diversity in Singapore*, 321–41.

TAN Chee-beng. *The Development and Distribution of Dejiao Associations in Malaysia and Singapore: A Study on a Chinese Religious Organization*. Singapore: Institute of Southeast Asian Studies, 1985.

———. "Chinese Religious Expressions in Post-Mao Yongchun, Fujian." In TAN, *Southern Fujian*, 97–120.

TAN Chee-beng, ed. *Southern Fujian: Reproduction of Traditions in Post-Mao China*. Hong Kong: Chinese University Press, 2006.

TAN, Eugene K. B. "Keeping God in Place: The Management of Religion in Singapore." In LAI, *Religious Diversity in Singapore*, 55–82.

TAN Hwee-San. "Saving the Soul in Red China: Music and Ideology in the 'Gongde' Ritual of Merit in Fujian." *British Journal of Ethnomusicology* 11, no. 1 (2002): 119–40.

TAN Songlin 谭松林 & PENG Bangfu 彭邦富. *Dangdai huidaomen, dangdai hei shehui zushi* 中国秘密社会当代会道门, 当代黑社会组织. In *Zhongguo mimi shehui*, edited by TAN Songlin. Fuzhou: Fujian renmin chubanshe, 2002.

TAROCCO, Francesca. *The Cultural Practices of Modern Chinese Buddhism: Attuning the Dharma*. London: Routledge, 2007.

TAYLOR, Kim. "'Improving' Chinese Medicine: The Role of Traditional Medicine in Newly Communist China, 1949–1953." In CLANCEY, LOY, & CHAN, *Historical Perspectives on East Asian Science, Technology and Medicine*, 251–63.

———. *Chinese Medicine in Early Communist China, 1945–1963*. London: Routledge, 2004.

TEATHER, Elizabeth K. "High-Rise Homes for the Ancestors: Cremation in Hong Kong." *Geographical Review* 89, no. 3 (1999): 409–30.

TEISER, Stephen F. "Popular Religion." *Journal of Asian Studies* 54, no. 2 (1995): 378–95.

TER HAAR, Barend. *The White Lotus Teachings in Chinese Religious History*. Leiden: Brill, 1992.

———. "China's Inner Demons: The Political Impact of the Demonological Paradigm." *China Information* 11, nos. 2–3 (1996): 54–88.

———. *Ritual and Mythology of the Chinese Triads: Creating an Identity*. Leiden: Brill, 1998.

THAM Seong Chee. *Religion and Modernization: A Study of Changing Rituals among Singapore's Chinese, Malays and Indians*. Singapore: Graham Brash, 1985.

THAXTON, Ralph. *China Turned Rightside Up: Revolutionary Legitimacy in the Peasant World*. New Haven, CT: Yale University Press, 1983.

———. "Mao Zedong, Red Misérables, and the Moral Economy of Peasant Rebellion in Modern China." In *Power and Protest in the Countryside: Studies of Rural Unrest in Asia, Europe, and Latin America*, edited by Robert P. WELLER & Scott GUGGENHEIM, 132–56. Durham, NC: Duke University Press, 1989.

THIREAU, Isabelle. "Recent Change in a Guangdong Village." *Australian Journal of Chinese Affairs* 19, no. 20 (1988): 289–310.

THØGERSEN, Stig. "Parasites or Civilisers: The Legitimacy of the Chinese Communist Party in Rural Areas." *China: An International Journal* 1, no. 2 (2003): 200–23.

THOMPSON, Roger R. "Twilight of the Gods in the Chinese Countryside: Christians, Confucians, and the Modernizing State, 1861–1911." In BAYS, *Christianity in China*, 53–72.

THORNTON, Patricia M. "The New Cybersects: Resistance and Repression in the Reform Era." In PERRY & SELDEN, *Chinese Society*, 147–70.

———. *Disciplining the State: Virtue, Violence and State-Making in Modern China*. Cambridge, MA: East Asia Center, Harvard University, 2007.

———. "Manufacturing Dissent in Transnational China." In O'BRIEN, *Popular Protest in China*, 179–204.

Tong Chee Kiong. *Rationalizing Religion: Religious Conversion, Revivalism and Competition in Singapore Society*. Leiden: Brill, 2007.

Tong Cheu Hok. *The Nine Emperor Gods: A Study of Chinese Spirit-Medium Cults*. Singapore: Times Books International, 1988.

———, ed. *Chinese Beliefs and Practices in Southeast Asia: Studies on the Chinese Religion in Malaysia, Singapore and Indonesia*. Petaling Jaya (Selangor Darul Ehsan, Malaysia): Pelanduk Publications, 1993.

———. "The Festival of the Nine Emperor Gods in Peninsular Southeast Asia." In Tong, *Chinese Beliefs*, 17–58.

Tong, James. "Anatomy of Regime Repression in China: Timing, Enforcement Institutions, and Target Selection in Banning the Falungong, July 1999." *Asian Survey* 42, no. 6:795–820.

Topley, Marjorie. "The Emergence and Social Function of Chinese Religious Associations in Singapore." *Comparative Studies in Society and History* 3, no. 3 (1961): 289–314.

———. "The Great Way of Former Heaven: A Group of Chinese Secret Religious Sects." *Bulletin of the School of Oriental and African Studies* 26 (1963): 362–92.

Tremlett, Paul-François. "Death-Scapes in Taipei and Manila: A Postmodern Necrography." *Taiwan in Comparative Perspective* 1 (2007): 23–36.

Ts'ai Chin-t'ang 蔡錦堂. *Nihon teikoku-shugika Taiwan no shūkyō seisaku* 日本帝国主義下台湾の宗教政策. Tokyo: Dōseisha, 1994.

Tsai, Lily L. "Cadres, Temple and Lineage Institutions, and Governance in Rural China." *China Journal* 48 (2002): 1–27.

———. *Accountability without Democracy: Solidary Groups and Public Goods Provision in Rural China*. Cambridge: Cambridge University Press, 2007.

Tsai Yi-jia. "The Writing of History: The Religious Practices of the Mediums' Association in Taiwan." *Taiwan Journal of Anthropology* 2, no. 2 (2004): 43–80.

Tseng, Timothy. "Chinese Protestant Nationalism in the United States, 1880–1927." In Yoo, *New Spiritual Homes*, 19–51.

Tsering Shakya. *The Dragon in the Land of Snows: A History of Modern Tibet since 1947*. London: Pimlico, 1999.

Tsin, Michael Tsang-Woon. *Nation, Governance, and Modernity: Canton, 1900–1927*. Stanford, CA: Stanford University Press, 1999.

Tsou Mingteh. "Christian Missionary as Confucian Intellectual: Gilbert Reid (1857–1927) and the Reform Movement in the Late Qing." In Bays, *Christianity in China*, 73–119.

Tsu, Timothy Y. "Between Superstition and Morality—Japanese Views of Taiwanese Religion in the Colonial Period, 1895–1945." *Zinbun* 33 (1998): 31–56.

Tsui, Bartholomew P. M. "Recent Developments in Buddhism in Hong Kong." In *The Turning of the Tide: Religion in China Today*, edited by Julian F. Pas, 299–311. Hong Kong: Hong Kong Branch of the Royal Asiatic Society, 1989.

Tu Wei-ming. *Confucian Ethics Today: The Singapore Challenge*. Singapore: Federal Publications, 1984.

Tuttle, Gray. *Tibetan Buddhists in the Making of Modern China*. New York: Columbia University Press, 2007.

Tyl, Dominique. "The Formation of New Citizens in China's Secondary Schools." *China Perspectives*, no. 39 (2002).

Urban, George, ed. *The Miracles of Chairman Mao*. London: Tom Stacey, 1981.

Vala, Carsten. "Pathways to the Pulpit: Leadership Training in 'Patriotic' and Unregistered Chinese Protestant Churches." In Ashiwa & Wank, *Making Religion, Making the State*, 96–125.

Vala, Carsten, & Kevin O'Brien. "Recruitment to Protestant House Churches." In O'Brien, *Popular Protest in China*, 108–25.

Van der Veer, Peter. *Imperial Encounters: Religion and Modernity in India and Britain*. Princeton, NJ: Princeton University Press, 2001.

———. "Global Breathing: Religious Utopias in India and China." *Anthropological Theory* 7, no. 3 (2007): 315–28.

VAN DER VEER, Peter, & Hartmut LEHMANN, eds. *Nation and Religion: Perspectives on Europe and Asia.* Princeton, NJ: Princeton University Press, 1999.

VERMANDER, Benoît. "Religious Revival and Exit from Religion." *China Perspectives* 4 (2009): 4–16.

VON GLAHN, Richard. *The Sinister Way: The Divine and the Demonic in Chinese Religious Culture.* Berkeley and Los Angeles: University of California Press, 2004.

WAGNER, Rudolf G. "Reading the Chairman Mao Memorial Hall in Peking: The Tribulations of the Implied Pilgrim." In NAQUIN & YÜ, *Pilgrims and Sacred Sites in China,* 378–423.

WAKEMAN, Frederic, Jr. *History and Will: Philosophical Perspectives of Mao Tse-Tung's Thought.* Berkeley and Los Angeles: University of California Press, 1973.

———. "Revolutionary Rites: The Remains of Chiang Kai-Shek and Mao Tse-Tung." *Representations* 10 (1985): 146–93.

———. "A Revisionist View of the Nanjing Decade: Confucian Fascism." *China Quarterly* 150 (1997): 395–432.

WALDER, Andrew G. *Communist Neo-Traditionalism: Work and Authority in Chinese Industry.* Berkeley and Los Angeles: University of California Press, 1986.

WANG Ch'iu-kuei 王求貴, ed. *Min-su ch' ü-i ts'ung-shu* 民俗曲藝叢書 *Studies in Chinese Ritual, Theatre and Folklore.* 80 vols. Taipei: Shi Ho-cheng Folk Culture Foundation, 1993.

WANG Di. *Street Culture in Chengdu: Public Space, Urban Commoners, and Local Politics, 1870–1930.* Stanford, CA: Stanford University Press, 2003.

WANG Jianchuan [WANG Chien-ch'uan] 王見川. "Lüelun rizhi shiqi zhaijiao de quandao xing lianhe zuzhi: Taiwan fojiao longhua hui 略論日治時期「齋教」的全島性聯合組織：臺灣佛教龍華會." In *Taiwan zhaijiao de lishi guancha yu zhanwang* 臺灣齋教的歷史觀察與展望, edited by JIANG Canteng 江燦騰 & WANG Jianchuan 王見川, 149–90. Taipei: Xin wenfeng chuban gongsi, 1994.

———. "Tongshanshe zaoqi lishi (1912–1945) chutan 同善社早期歷史初探." *Minjian zongjiao* 民間宗教 1 (1995): 57–81.

———. "Cihuitang yu Zhang Tianshi 慈惠堂與張天師." In *Taiwan de minjian zongjiao yu xinyang* 臺灣的民間宗教與信仰, edited by WANG Jianchuan 王見川 & LI Shiwei 李世偉, 261–72. Taipei: Boyang Wenhua, 2000.

———. "Shijie zongjiao datonghui' chutan: jiantan qi yu Jiang Xizhang de guanxi 世界宗教大同會'初探:兼談其與江希張的關係." Paper presented at the conference "Religious Movements and Redemptive Societies in the 20th Century Chinese World," Foguang University, June 12–13, 2007.

———. "Qingmo minchu Zhongguo de Jigong xinyang yu fuji tuanti: jiantan Zhongguo jishenghui de youlai 清末民初中國的濟公信仰與扶乩團體–兼談中國濟生會的由來." *Minsu quyi* 民俗曲藝 162 (2008): 139–67.

WANG Jianchuan (WANG Chien-ch'uan) 王見川 & LI Shiwei 李世偉. *Taiwan de zongjiao yu wenhua* 臺灣的宗教與文化. Taipei: Boyang wenhua, 1999.

———. "Taiwan Xuanyuanjiao de kaocha 臺灣軒轅教的考察." In *Taiwan de minjian zongjiao yu xinyang* 臺灣的民間宗教與信仰, edited by WANG Jianchuan 王見川 & LI Shiwei 李世偉, 147–80. Taipei: Boyang Wenhua, 2000.

WANG Jianchuan [WANG Chien-ch'uan] 王見川 & David A. PALMER, eds. "Redemptive Societies and Religious Movements in Republican China." Special double issue, *Minsu quyi* 民俗曲藝 172 (2010) and 173 (2011).

WANG Jianxin. *Uyghur Education and Social Order: The Role of Islamic Leadership in the Turpan Basin.* Studia Culturae Islamicae, no. 76. Tokyo: Research Institute for Languages and Cultures of Asia and Africa, Tokyo University of Foreign Studies, 2004.

WANG Liqi 王利器. *Yuan Ming Qing sandai jinhui xiaoshuo xiqu shiliao* 元明清三代禁毀小说戏曲史料. Shanghai: Shanghai guji chubanshe, 1981.

Wang Mingming. "'Great Tradition' and Its Enemy." In Tan, *Southern Fujian*, 558–61.

Wang Shuhuai 王樹槐. "Qingmo Jiangsu difang zizhi fengchao 清末江蘇地方自治風潮." *Zhongyang yanjiuyuan jindai shi yanjiusuo jikan* 中央研究院近代史研究所集刊 6 (1977): 313–27.

Wang Zhiyu 王志宇. *Simiao yu cunluo: Taiwan hanren shehui de lishi wenhua guancha* 寺廟與村落—臺灣漢人社會的歷史文化觀察. Taipei: Wenjin chubanshe, 2008.

Wang Zuo'an 王作安. *Zhongguo de zongjiao wenti he zongjiao zhengce* 中國的宗教问题和宗教政策. Beijing: Zongjiao wenhua chubanshe, 2002.

Wank, David L. "Institutionalizing Modern 'Religion' in China's Buddhism: Political Phases of a Local Revival." In Ashiwa & Wank, *Making Religion, Making the State*, 126–50.

Watson, James L. "Standardizing the Gods: The Promotion of T'ien-Hou ("Empress of Heaven") along the South China Coast, 960–1960." In Johnson, Nathan, & Rawski, *Popular Culture in Late Imperial China*, 292–324.

———. "Presidential Address: Virtual Kinship, Real Estate, and Diaspora Formation; The Man Lineage Revisited." *Journal of Asian Studies* 63, no. 4 (2004): 893–910.

Watson, James L., & Evelyn S. Rawski, eds. *Death Ritual in Late Imperial and Modern China*. Berkeley and Los Angeles: University of California Press, 1988.

Watson, James L., & Rubie Watson. *Village Life in Hong Kong*. Hong Kong: Chinese University Press, 2004.

Weber, Max. *The Religion of China: Confucianism and Taoism*. New York: Free Press, 1951.

Welch, Holmes. "The Chang T'ien Shih and Taoism in China." *Journal of Oriental Studies* 4 (1957–58): 188–212.

———. *The Practice of Chinese Buddhism*. Cambridge, MA: Harvard University Press, 1967.

———. *The Buddhist Revival in China*. Cambridge, MA: Harvard University Press, 1968.

———. *Buddhism under Mao*. Cambridge, MA: Harvard University Press, 1972.

Weller, Robert P. "The Politics of Ritual Disguise: Repression and Response in Taiwanese Popular Religion." *Modern China* 13, no. 1 (1987): 17–39.

———. *Resistance, Chaos, and Control in China: Taiping Rebels, Taiwanese Ghosts, and Tiananmen*. Seattle: University of Washington Press, 1994.

———. "Matricidal Magistrates and Gambling Gods: Weak States and Strong Spirits in China." In Shahar & Weller, *Unruly Gods*, 250–68.

———. *Alternate Civilities: Democracy and Culture in China and Taiwan*. Boulder: Westview, 1999.

———. "Living at the Edge: Religion, Capitalism, and the End of the Nation-State in Taiwan." *Public Culture* 12, no. 2 (2000): 477–98.

———. "Worship, Teachings, and State Power in China and Taiwan." In *Realms of Freedom in Modern China*, edited by William C. Kirby, 285–314. Stanford, CA: Stanford University Press, 2004.

———. *Discovering Nature: Globalization and Environmental Culture in China and Taiwan*. Cambridge: Cambridge University Press, 2006.

White, Erick. "Fraudulent and Dangerous Popular Religiosity in the Public Sphere: Moral Campaigns to Prohibit, Reform, and Demystify Thai Spirit Mediums." In Willford & George, *Spirited Politics*, 69–91.

Whyte, Martin King. *Small Groups and Political Rituals in China*. Berkeley and Los Angeles: University of California Press, 1974.

———. "Death in the People's Republic of China." In Watson & Rawski, *Death Ritual in Late Imperial and Modern China*, 289–316.

Whyte, Martin King, & William L. Parish. *Urban Life in Contemporary China*. Chicago: University of Chicago Press, 1984.

Wickeri, Philip L. *Seeking the Common Ground: Protestant Christianity, the Three-Self Movement, and China's United Front*. Maryknoll, NY: Orbis Books, 1988.

———. *Reconstructing Christianity in China: K. H. Ting and the Chinese Church*. Maryknoll, NY: Orbis Books, 2007.

WIELANDER, Gerda. "Protestant and Online: The Case of Aiyan." *China Quarterly* 197 (2009): 165–83.

WIJAYA, Yahya. *Business, Family and Religion: Public Theology in the Context of the Chinese-Indonesian Business Community.* Bern: Peter Lang, 2002.

WILE, Douglas. *Lost T'ai-Chi Classics from the Late Ch'ing Dynasty.* Albany: State University of New York Press, 1996.

WILLFORD, Andrew C., & Kenneth M. GEORGE, eds. *Spirited Politics: Religion and Public Life in Contemporary Southeast Asia.* Ithaca, NY: Southeast Asia Program, Cornell University, 2005.

WILSON, Andrew R. *Ambition and Identity: Chinese Merchant Elites in Colonial Manila, 1880–1916.* Honolulu: University of Hawai'i Press, 2004.

WOEI Lien chong. "Mankind and Nature in Chinese Thought: Li Zehou on the Traditional Roots of Maoist Voluntarism." *China Information* 11 (1996): 138–75.

WOLF, Arthur P. "Gods, Ghosts, and Ancestors." In WOLF, *Religion and Ritual in Chinese Society*, 131–82.

———, ed. *Religion and Ritual in Chinese Society.* Stanford, CA: Stanford University Press, 1974.

World Organization to Investigate the Persecution of Falun Gong. *General Report on the "610 Office," 2004.* Online at http://www.zhuichaguoji.org/en/index2.php?option=content&task=view&id=16&pop=1&page=0 (accessed October 12, 2009).

WU Huiqiao 吳惠巧. *Taiwan zongjiao shehui guancha* 台灣宗教社會觀察. Taipei: Dayuan shuju, 2005.

WU Ka-ming. "The Return of the Folk and the Making of Culture in Yan'an, China." Ph.D. diss., Columbia University, 2007.

WU Xiaoqun 吳效群. *Miaofengshan: Beijing minjian shehui de lishi bianqian* 妙峰山：北京民间社会的历史变迁. Beijing: Renmin chubanshe, 2006.

Wuxu bianfa wenxian ziliao xiri 戊戌變法文獻資料系日. QINGHUA Daxue Lishixi 清華大學歷史系, comp. Shanghai: Shanghai shudian chubanshe, 1998.

XIA Mingyu 夏明玉. "Minguo xinxing zongjiao jieshe: Wanguo daodehui zhi sinei yu biangian 民國新興宗教結社：萬國道德會之思維與變遷 (1921–1949)." Master's thesis, Donghai daxue, 2001.

XIAO Jihong 蕭霽虹 & DONG Yun 董允. *Yunnan daojiao shi* 云南道教史. Kunming: Yunnan daxue chubanshe, 2007.

XIE Sizhong 解思忠. *Guomin suzhi yousi lu* 国民素质忧思录. Beijing: Zuojia chubanshe, 1997.

XIE Wenjie 謝文杰, producer, & YUAN Zhiming 遠志明, director. *China's Confession* 神州. Petaluna, CA: China Soul for Christ (VCD), 2000.

XIE Zhibin. *Religious Diversity and Public Religion in China.* Aldershot, UK: Ashgate, 2006.

XU Xiaoqun. "'National Essence' vs. 'Science': Chinese Native Physicians' Fight for Legitimacy, 1912–37." *Modern Asian Studies* 31, no. 4 (1997): 847–77.

———. *Chinese Professionals and the Republican State: The Rise of Professional Associations in Shanghai 1912–1927.* Cambridge: Cambridge University Press, 2001.

XUE Yu. *Buddhism, War, and Nationalism: Chinese Monks in the Struggle against Japanese Aggressions, 1931–1945.* New York: Routledge, 2005.

YAN Changhong 嚴昌洪. "Minguo shiqi sangzang lisu de gaige yu yanbian 民国时期丧葬礼俗的改革与演变." *Jindaishi yanjiu* 近代史研究 5 (1998): 169–84.

———. *Zhongguo jindai shehui fengsu shi* 中國近代社會風俗史. Taipei: Nantian shuju, 1998.

YANG C. K. *Religion in Chinese Society: A Study of Contemporary Social Functions of Religion and Some of Their Historical Factors.* Berkeley and Los Angeles: University of California Press, 1961.

YANG Der-ruey. "The Education of Taoist Priests in Contemporary Shanghai, China." D.Phil. diss., London School of Economics and Political Science, 2003.

———. "The Changing Economy of Temple Daoism in Shanghai." In YANG & TAMNEY, *State, Market, and Religions*, 113–48.

———. "Revolution of Temporality: The Modern Schooling of Daoist Priests in Shanghai at the Turn of the 21st Century." In PALMER & LIU, *Daoism in the Twentieth Century*.

YANG Fenggang. "Chinese Conversion to Evangelical Christianity: The Importance of Social and Cultural Contexts." *Sociology of Religion* 59, no. 3 (1998): 237–57.

———. "Religious Diversity among the Chinese in America." In *Religions in Asian America: Building Faith Communities*, edited by Pyong Gap MIN & Jung Ha KIM, 71–98. Walnut Creek, CA: AltaMira Press, 2002.

———. "Between Secularist Ideology and Desecularizing Reality: Birth and Growth of Religious Research in Communist China." *Sociology of Religion* 65, no. 2 (2004): 101–19.

———. "Lost in the Market, Saved at McDonald's: Conversion to Christianity in Urban China." *Journal for the Scientific Study of Religion* 44, no. 4 (2005): 423–41.

———. "The Red, Black, and Gray Markets of Religion in China." *Sociological Quarterly* 47 (2006): 93–122.

———. "Cultural Dynamics in China: Today and in 2020." *Asia Policy* 4 (2007): 41–52.

———. "Confucianism as Religion? Sociological Reflections." In *Confucianism and Spiritual Traditions in Modern China and Beyond*, edited by TAMNEY & YANG, forthcoming.

YANG Fenggang & Graeme LANG, eds. *Social Scientific Studies of Religion in China: Methodology, Theories, and Findings.* Boston: Brill, forthcoming.

YANG Fenggang & Joseph B. TAMNEY, eds. *State, Market, and Religions in Chinese Societies.* Leiden: Brill, 2005.

YANG Fenggang & WEI Dedong. "The Bailin Buddhist Temple: Thriving under Communism." In YANG & TAMNEY, *State, Market, and Religions*, 63–86.

YANG, Heriyanto. "The History and Legal Position of Confucianism in Post-Independence Indonesia." *Marburg Journal of Religion*, 10, no. 1 (2005), Web edition. Online at http://archiv.ub.uni_marburg.de/mjr/art_yang_2005.htm (accessed August 2005).

YANG Huilin. "Some Characteristics of the Understanding of the Christian Faith among Contemporary Chinese University Students." *China Study Journal* 17, no. 3 (2002): 5–12.

YANG, Mayfair Mei-hui. *Gifts, Favors, and Banquets: The Art of Social Relationships in China.* Ithaca, NY: Cornell University Press, 1994.

———. "Putting Global Capitalism in Its Place: Economic Hybridity, Bataille, and Ritual Expenditure." *Current Anthropology* 41, no. 4 (2000): 477–509.

———. "Goddess across the Taiwan Strait: Matrifocal Ritual Space, Nation-State, and Satellite Television Footprints." *Public Culture* 16, no. 2 (2004): 209–38.

———. "Spatial Struggles: Postcolonial Complex, State Disenchantment, and Popular Reappropriation of Space in Rural Southeast China." *Journal of Asian Studies* 63, no. 3 (2004): 719–55.

———, ed. *Chinese Religiosities: Afflictions of Modernity and State Formation.* Berkeley and Los Angeles: University of California Press, 2008.

———. "Detaching and Re-Incorporating: Fission and Fusion with the State Body." In *Reenchanting Modernity: Sovereignty, Ritual Economy, and Indigenous Civil Order in Coastal China*, forthcoming.

YANG Tianhong 杨天宏. *Jidujiao yu minguo zhishi fenzi: 1922 nian–1927 nian Zhongguo fei jidujiao yundong yanjiu* 基督教与民国知识分子。1922年–1927年中国非基督教运动研究. Beijing: Renmin chubanshe, 2005.

YANG Yehua 杨业华. *Shehui zhuyi sixiang daode jianshe qianyan wenti yanjiu* 社会主义思想道德建设前沿问题研究. Beijing: Zhongguo shehui kexue chubanshe, 2007.

YAO Lixiang 姚麗香. "Zangchuan fojiao zai Taiwan—zhongxin fuzeren de jingyan fenxi 藏傳佛教在台灣—中心負責人的經驗分析. Xinxing zongjiao xianxiang yantaohui 新興宗教現象研討會." *Academia Sinica* (March 29, 2002); online at www.ios.sinica.edu.tw/pages/seminar/twnrp2002/twnrp.htm (accessed September 27, 2007).

YAO Xinzhong. "Religious Beliefs and Practice in Urban China 1995–2005." *Journal of Contemporary Religion* 22, no. 2 (2007): 169–85.

YAO Xinzhong & Paul BADHAM. *Religious Experience in China Today.* Cardiff: University of Wales Press, 2007.

YAU Chi-on [YOU Zi'an] 游子安. *Shan yu ren tong: Ming Qing yilai de cishan yu jiaohua* 善與人同: 明清以來的慈善與教化. Beijing: Zhonghua shuju, 2005.

———. "Xianggang Xiantiandao bainian lishi gaishu香港先天道百年歷史概述." In *Xianggang ji Huanan Daojiao yanjiu* 香港及華南道教研究, edited by LAI Chi-tim 黎志添, 66–73. Hong Kong: Zhonghua shuju, 2005.

YE Xiaoqing. "Regulating the Medical Profession in China: Health Policies of the Nationalist Government." In CLANCEY, LOY, & CHAN, *Historical Perspectives on East Asian Science, Technology and Medicine*, 198–213.

YEOH, Brenda. "The Body after Death: Place, Tradition and the Nation State in Singapore." In *Embodied Geographies: Spaces, Bodies and Rites of Passage*, edited by Elizabeth K. TEATHER, 240–55. London: Routledge, 1999.

YING Fuk-tsang [XING Fuzeng] 邢福增. "Jiang lunli daode de jidujiao—dangdai Zhongguo shenxue dui shehui zhuyi de tiaozheng yu shiying 講倫理道德的基督教—當代中國神學對社會主意的調整與適應." In *Dangdai Zhongguo zheng—jiao guanxi* 當代中國政教關係, edited by YING Fuk-tsang, 133–85. Hong Kong: Alliance Bible Seminary, 1999.

———. "Church-State Relations in Contemporary China and the Development of Protestant Christianity." *China Study Journal* 18, no. 3 (2003): 19–48.

———. "New Wine in Old Wineskins: An Appraisal of Religious Legislation in China and the Regulations on Religious Affairs of 2005." *Religion, State and Society* 34, no. 4 (2006): 347–73.

———. "The Regional Development of Protestant Christianity in China: 1918, 1949 and 2004." *China Review* 9, no. 2 (2009): 63–97.

YIP Ching-wah, Francis. "Protestant Christianity and Popular Religion in China: A Case of Syncretism?" *Ching Feng* 42, nos. 3–4 (1999): 130–75.

———. "Protestant Christianity in Contemporary China." In MILLER, *Chinese Religions in Contemporary Societies*, 175–205.

YOO, David K., ed. *New Spiritual Homes: Religion and Asian Americans*. Honolulu: University of Hawai'i Press, 1999.

YOUNG, Richard Fox. "Sanctuary of the Tao: The Place of Christianity in a Sino-Japanese Unity Sect." *Journal of Chinese Religions* 17 (1989): 1–26.

YU, Anthony C. *State and Religion in China: Historical and Textual Perspectives*. Chicago: Open Court, 2005.

YU, Dan Smyer. "Religion in a Panoptic Modernity: A Tibetan Buddhist Discourse on Religion and Superstition in Late Socialist China." Paper presented at the International Conference on Religion, Modernity, and the State in China and Taiwan, University of California–Santa Barbara, October 29, 2005.

YU Yingshi 余英时. *Rujia lunli yu shangren jingshen* 儒家伦理与商人精神. Guilin: Guangxi shifan daxue chubanshe, 2004.

YUAN Bingling. *Chinese Democracies: A Study of the Kongsis of West Borneo (1776–1884)*. Leiden: CNWS, 2000.

ZANG, Xiaowei. *Ethnicity and Urban Life in China*. New York: Routledge, 2007.

ZARROW, Peter. *China in War and Revolution 1895–1949*. London: Routledge, 2005.

ZHANG Hua 张华. *Yang Wenhui yu Zhongguo jindai fojiao sixiang zhuanxing* 杨文会与中国近代佛教思想转型. Beijing: Zongjiao wenhua chubanshe, 2004.

Zhang jizi jiulu 張季子九錄. ZHANG Jian 張謇 (1853–1926). Shanghai: Zhonghua shuju, 1931.

ZHANG Juling 张巨龄. "Zhongguo huijiao jujinhui chuchuang jiping 中国回教俱进会初创记评." *Huizu yanjiu* 回族研究 28 (1997/1998): 1–8 (part 1); 29: 10–22 (part 2); and 30: 14–16 (part 3).

Zhang zhidong quanji 張之洞全集. Zhangjiakou: Hebei renmin chubanshe, 1998.

ZHAO Xudong & Duran BELL. "Miaohui, the Temples Meeting Festival in North China." *China Information* 21, no. 3 (2007): 457–79.

ZHENG Guanglu 郑光路. *Qijuan shenzhou* 气卷神州. Chengdu: Chengdu chubanshe, 1991.

ZHENG Guo 郑国. "Jindai geming yundong yu pochu mixin—yi Xuzhou Chenghuangmiao weizhu de kaocha 近代革命运动与破除迷信—以徐州城隍庙为主的考察." *Hefei shifan xueyuan xuebao* 合肥师范学院学报 26, no. 2 (2008): 54–57.

ZHENG Zhiming 鄭志明. *Taiwan dangdai xinxing fojiao—chanjiao pian* 臺灣當代新興佛教—禪教篇. Chia-yi: Nanhua guanli xueyuan, 1998.

———. *Dangdai xinxing zongjiao—xiuxing tuanti pian* 當代新興宗教—修行團體篇. Chia-yi: Zongjiao wenhua yanjiu zhongxin, 2000.

———. "Sangzang wenhua de xiankuang yu zhanwang 喪葬文化的現況與展望." In *Yi renti wei meijie de daojiao* 以人體為媒介的道教, edited by ZHENG Zhiming 鄭志明, 529–57. Chia-yi: Nanhua daxue zongjiao wenhua yanjiu zhongxin, 2001.

———. "Taiwan qigong tuanti de wenhua xianxiang 臺灣氣功團體的文化現象 Xinxing zongjiao xianxiang yantaohui 新興宗教現象研討會." *Academia Sinica* (March 29, 2002); online at www.ios.sinica.edu.tw/pages/seminar/twnrp2002/twnrp.htm (accessed September 27, 2007).

———. *Zongjiao zuzhi de fazhan qushi* 宗教組織的發展趨勢. Taipei: Dayuan shuju, 2005.

Zhonggong zhongyang wenxian yanjiushi zonghe yanjiuzu 中共中央文献研究室综合研究组, Guowuyuan zongjiao shiwuju zhengce faguisi 国务院宗教事物局政策法规司, ed. *Xin shiqi zongjiao gongzuo wenxian xuanbian* 新时期宗教工作文献选编. Beijing: Zongjiao wenhua chubanshe, 1995.

Zhongguo binzang nianjian 中国殡葬年鉴. Beijing: Zhongguo shehui chubanshe, yearly since 2007.

Zhonghua minguo shi dang'an ziliao huibian 中華民國史檔案資料匯編, 3rd ser. Nanjing: Jiangsu guji chubanshe, 1998.

Zhongyang dangxiao keti zu 中央党校课题组. *Xian jieduan woguo minzu yu zongjiao wenti yanjiu* 现阶段我国民族与宗教问题研究. Beijing: Zongjiao wenhua chubanshe, 2002.

ZHUO Xinping. "Research on Religions in the People's Republic of China." *Social Compass* 50, no. 4 (2003): 441–48.

ZHOU Yiqun. "The Hearth and the Temple: Mapping Female Religiosity in Late Imperial China, 1550–1900." *Late Imperial China* 24, no. 2 (2003): 109–55.

Zouding xuetang zhangcheng 奏定學堂章程. ZHANG Zhidong 張之洞 (1837–1909), RONGQING 榮慶 (jinshi 1886), and ZHANG Baixi 張百熙 (1847–1907), January 1904.

ZUFFEREY, Nicolas. "Chen Huanzhang (1881–1933) et l'invention d'une religion confucianiste au début de l'époque républicaine." In *Le nouvel age de Confucius: Modern Confucianism in China and South Korea*, edited by Flora BLANCHON & Rang-Ri PARK-BARJOT, chap. 4. Paris: PUPS, 2007.

ZUO Furong 左芙蓉. *Shehui fuyin, shehui fuwu yu shehui gaizao: Beijing jidujiao qingnianhui lishi yanjiu, 1906–1949.* 社会福音、社会服务与社会改造:北京基督教青年会历史研究 1906–1949. Beijing: Zongjiao wenhua chubanshe, 2005.

ZUO Jiping. "Political Religion: The Case of the Cultural Revolution in China." *Sociological Analysis* 52, no. 1 (Spring 1991): 99–110.

Index